Successful Communication for Business and Management

Successful Communication for Business and Management

EDITION

7

Malra Treece

University of Memphis

Betty A. Kleen

Nicholls State University

Prentice Hall, Upper Saddle River, New Jersey 07458

Acquisitions Editor: Donald J. Hull
Assistant Editor: John Larkin
Editorial Assistant: Jim Campbell
Vice President/Editorial Director: James Boyd
Marketing Manager: Debbie Clare
Associate Managing Editor: Linda DeLorenzo
Production Coordinator: Carol Samet
Permissions Coordinator: Jennifer Rella
Managing Editor: Dee Josephson
Manufacturing Buyer: Kenneth J. Clinton
Manufacturing Supervisor: Arnold Vila
Manufacturing Manager: Vincent Scelta
Design Manager: Patricia Smythe
Interior Design: Amanda Kavanagh
Cover Design: Amanda Kavanagh
Project Management/Composition: University Graphics, Inc.
Cover Art: Gary Eldridge

Copyright © 1998, 1994, 1991, 1989, 1986, 1983 by Prentice-Hall, Inc.
A Simon & Schuster Company
Upper Saddle River, New Jersey 07458

Library of Congress Cataloging-in-Publication Data

Treece, Malra.
    Successful communication for business and management / Malra
Treece, Betty A. Kleen,—7th ed.
        p. cm.
    Rev. ed. of: Successful communication for business and the
professions.
    Includes bibliographical references and index.
    ISBN 0-13-466682-8
    1. Business communication. 2. Business writing. 3. Communication
in management. I. Kleen, Betty A. II. Treece, Malra. Successful
communication for business and the professions. III. Title.
HF5718.T73 1997
658.4′5—dc21   97-27956
                                                                CIP

Prentice-Hall International (UK) Limited, London
Prentice-Hall of Australia Pty. Limited, Sydney
Prentice-Hall Canada, Inc., Toronto
Prentice-Hall Hispanoamericana, S.A., Mexico
Prentice-Hall of India Private Limited, New Delhi
Prentice-Hall of Japan, Inc., Tokyo
Simon & Schuster Asia Pte. Ltd., Singapore
Editora Prentice-Hall do Brasil, Ltda., Rio de Janeiro

Printed in the United States of America

10 9 8 7 6 5 4 3 2 1

Brief Contents

Contents

Preface

Successful Communication for Business and Management, 7th edition, is based on the premise that all elements of communication are interrelated. Principles of effective writing also apply to effective speech. Nonverbal communication enters into both written and oral communication. Ever-changing communication technology affects methods and media of organizational and personal communication, but the basic principles of communication remain the same.

Communication in any form is affected by the many and varied influences that enter into human behavior. Basically, the study of communication, as well as the contents of this book, is the study of meaning and behavior and of how the transmission and reception of meaning affect behavior.

NOTE TO STUDENTS

This seventh edition has been influenced by many classes in business communication made up of students much like yourselves. They had other time-consuming responsibilities, as no doubt you do, including additional classes, outside employment, and, in some cases, care of family members. Yet these students realized that success in any area of learning and growth requires time and effort on a regular and continuing basis. Because of their study and dedication, resulting in their improved communication ability, they have increased their potential for success in their chosen professional fields.

This book is planned to make your study and preparation time as effective and efficient as possible. You will learn the principles of effective communication and how to succeed in your academic, professional, and personal life through successful communication.

Features of this book that are planned to make your out-of-class study and your in-class participation effective and pleasant include the following:

- A readable writing style

- Numerous illustrations and examples

- A summary at the end of each chapter

- Two review exercises at the end of each chapter, including "Test Yourself: Chapter Content" and "Test Yourself: Correct Usage." Solutions to "Test Yourself: Correct Usage" are available in Appendix B.

- Cases following each chapter that are especially appropriate for collaborative writing and working in groups.

NOTE TO TEACHERS

Supplements that accompany *Successful Communication for Business and Management* are these:

Instructor's Manual/Test Item File The Instructor's Manual includes chapter objectives & overviews, as well as answers to all of the questions in the text. Also included are topics of discussion from each chapter. The Test Item File contains multiple choice, true/false, and essay questions that are all new for this edition.

Prentice Hall Custom Test (Windows version) Based on the #1 best-selling, state-of-the-art test generation software program developed by Engineering Software Associates (ESA), *Prentice Hall Custom Test* is not only suitable for your course, but customizable to your personal needs. With *Prentice Hall Custom Test's* user-friendly test creation and powerful algorithmic generation, you can originate tailor-made tests quickly, easily and error-free. You can create an exam, administer it traditionally or on-line, evaluate and track students' results, and analyze the success of the exam— all with a simple click of the mouse.

PowerPoint Slides More than 150 electronic color slides created by co-author Betty Kleen. The slides, which build upon key concepts in the text, can be customized to suit class needs.

Color Transparencies 100 figures that illustrate the major concepts covered in the text.

PH/ABC/WSJ Video Library Our ABC News/Prentice Hall Video Library contains timely and relevant video segments from acclaimed ABC News programs, such as Nightline, World News Tonight, Prime Time Live, 20/20, and *The Wall Street Journal* available for the college market exclusively through Prentice Hall.

APPROACH

Harmonious personal relationships, ethical and legal considerations, intercultural communication, and changing technology are emphasized throughout the book in relation to the specified content of each chapter. Also included is the correct and effective use of language and knowledge about nonverbal communication.

If communication is sincere, it is likely to build harmonious personal relationships, provided the sender and the receiver of the message can effectively communicate through words, listening, and actions. Such communication is also likely to be ethical, but at times it may not meet legal standards because communicators are unaware of various laws that apply to written and oral messages.

Special consideration must be given to messages between people from varying cultures, whether these people are from different countries or from different subcultures in the same country. Although basic principles of human communication apply, special problems exist when language and cultural barriers interfere. If communication is to be successful, these barriers must be eliminated or minimized.

Technology continues to affect media and methods of written, oral, and verbal communication, and the changing office environment must be included in the study of all elements of business communication. Nevertheless, language and human actions remain the most important tools for achieving harmonious human relationships and effective communication.

The use of language, including but not limited to correctness, is emphasized throughout. So are pleasant and positive human relationships, especially as they are developed through language.

The study of communication for business and management is by its very nature interdisciplinary. Thus, this book contains instruction in aspects of speech, writing, technology, research sources and methods, individual and organizational behavior, general business management, office management, personnel management, marketing, persuasion, psychology, personal relationships, ethics, etiquette, and intercultural communication. Students also study methods of finding suitable career employment.

Emphasis throughout—in text, illustrations, questions, and problems—is on methods of achieving success in all these areas through effective writing and speech. One method of developing these abilities is through working with others; hence, assignments for collaborative writing and other group work are provided with each chapter.

Although professional in content and organization, all chapters are planned for easy and interesting reading. Readability and interest are considered important from three major standpoints:

- to enable readers to enjoy the book,
- to illustrate techniques of readable and interesting writing, and
- to exemplify by the textbook itself one of the important attributes of human communication, consideration for the receiver of the message.

Successful communicators are much more than skilled technicians; they must have an understanding of the process of communication and of the effect of varying perceptions and emotions upon the reception of meaning. In addition, they are knowledgeable in the subject matter about which they communicate, and their messages are sincere.

ORGANIZATION AND CONTENTS OF THE BOOK

Part I ("An Overview of Communication within Organizations," Chapters 1, 2, and 3) prepares students for the remaining portions of the textbook and the course. Chapter 1, "The Communication Process and Environment," includes a summary of the theory of communication, listening, and nonverbal communication. Chapter 2, "Communication within and from the Organization," describes purposes and methods of organizational and managerial communication. (These topics are continued in Chapter 18.) Chapter 3, "Communicating with the Aid of Technology," includes a comprehensive discussion of present-day communication technology as it applies to almost everyone in a beginning or managerial position.

Collaborative writing and "Think-it-Through Assignments" follow each chapter. Three review sections also follow each chapter: a summary; a quick, short-answer group of questions based on chapter content; and a section that reviews both language usage and chapter content. (These assignments and exercises continue throughout the 18 chapters.)

Part II ("Principles of Effective Writing and Speaking," Chapters 4, 5, and 6) presents communication theory as applied to business and professional writing and speech. Topics include the wise choice of words, correctness, conciseness, completeness, readability, techniques of emphasis, and building goodwill. End-of-chapter exercises provide opportunities for the applications of principles discussed and illustrated in each of the chapters. These principles apply to both written and spoken communication.

Part III ("Frequently Written Business Messages," Chapters 7, 8, and 9) applies principles and techniques discussed in all previous chapters to the composition of letters, memorandums, and sales material.

Part IV ("Communication about Employment," Chapters 10 and 11) includes discussion of preliminary research before looking for a job and research during the employment campaign. The use of databases and the Internet is stressed throughout, as well as computer scanning of resumes by potential employers. Students are urged to prepare their employment applications for their actual use.

Part V ("Communicating through Reports," Chapters 12, 13, 14, and 15) discusses business research, graphics, and the preparation of long and short reports.

Part VI ("Speaking to Groups: Intercultural and Managerial Communication," Chapters 16, 17, and 18) concludes the text with discussion and applications about public speaking; intercultural communication as applied to written, oral, and nonverbal communication; business ethics; etiquette; interviewing for management decisions; meetings and conferences; videoconferencing and television appearances; and cutting the costs of communication.

Appendix A is a guide to the appearance and format of business letters.

Appendix B contains solutions to the "Test Yourself: Correct Usage" exercises at the end of each chapter.

Appendix C is a short guide to dictating business messages.

Appendix D is a brief guide to language usage.

NEW TO THE SEVENTH EDITION

■ Co-author Betty Kleen provides her expertise throughout, but especially on the subject of technology and report writing.

■ The book contains 18 chapters, as compared to 21 in the sixth edition.

■ Added emphasis is given to

  ■ changing communication technology

  ■ diversity and intercultural communication

  ■ collaborative writing

  ■ problem-solving assignments

  ■ ethics

  ■ etiquette

■ The book is updated in all chapters through examples, problems, questions, "Communication Briefs," illustrations, research, and text.

■ Reorganization of chapter content, as follows:

  ■ Format and appearance of letters and memorandums, formerly in Chapter 4, now appears as Appendix A.

  ■ The five chapters that originally appeared in Part III, "Frequently Written Business Messages," have been combined and condensed into three chapters.

  ■ Examples of methods of documentation that originally appeared as Appendix C are now shown in Chapter 13.

  ■ The section on dictating business messages that appeared in Chapter 9 is condensed and shown as Appendix C.

  ■ Discussion of intercultural communication, ethics, technology, word choice, and other important topics is included not only in specified chapters but woven throughout the book in the form of "Communication Briefs," problems, and illustrations.

  ■ A list of objectives has been added to the beginning of each chapter.

ACKNOWLEDGMENTS

Utmost gratitude is expressed to many persons, including teachers and students at the University of Memphis and Nicholls State University, who contributed their ideas and words of encouragement during the preparation of this book and of previous editions.

Special appreciation goes to the following firms and individuals for the use of their material:

Breck's

Land's End

National League of American Pen Women and Wanda Rider

Pacific Crest Outward Bound School

The Royal Bank of Canada

Waterford Crystal

Jamie Amedee

Lance Bland

Brian J. Borne

M. Boudreaux

Mona Casady

Tonya Chauvin

Guy E. Courrege

John Donadieu

Diane C. Dugas

Suzanne B. Durocher

Karen English

Diana Green

Retha H. Kilpatrick

D. Martin

Glynna Morse

Mary Ellen Murray

Binford Peeples

James Calvert Scott

K. Renee Troxler

Iris Varner

Reviewers, users, and other readers have contributed to the development of this Seventh Edition. Their help is greatly appreciated.

James Applewhite
Kutztown University

Judy Baird
CPS, Memphis

Sallye S. Benoit
Nicholls State University

Jean Bush-Bacelis
Eastern Michigan University

Lillian H. Chaney
University of Memphis

Randy Cone
University of New Orleans

Kimihiro Imamura
Itochu Academy, Tokyo

Roberta Krapels
University of Mississippi

Elizabeth Larsen
West Chester University

Jeanette Martin
University of Mississippi

Susan H. Maxwell
Ohio University–Lancaster

Binford Peeples
University of Memphis

Lynette Porter
University of Findlay

Celeste B. Powers,
Nicholls State University

Charles M. Ray,
Ball State University

Special appreciation is expressed to the capable, hard-working and cooperative people at Prentice Hall who contributed their talents toward the development and production of this book:

Don Hull, *Senior Acquisition Editor*

Linda Delorenzo, *Associate Managing Editor*

John Larkin, *Assistant Editor*

Jim Campbell, *Editorial Assistant*

Pat Smythe, *Design Manager*

Additional professional people made valuable contributions:

Nancy Marcello, *Copyeditor*

Melinda Alexander, *Photo Researcher*

Danielle Meckley, *University Graphics, Inc.*

Karyn Morrison, *Permissions Researcher*

ABOUT THE AUTHORS

Betty A. Kleen is a Distinguished Service Professor in the Information Systems Department at Nicholls State University, Thibodaux, Louisiana. She holds an Ed.D. in Business Education from the University of Kentucky and a B.S. and M.S. in Business Education from Western Illinois University.

She is an active member of numerous professional organizations. She has over 75 publications in professional journals, yearbooks, conference proceedings, and curriculum guides. She is a frequent presenter at business communication and information systems conferences. She has over 15 years' experience teaching business communication at the undergraduate level.

Malra Treece is a professor emeritus of the Fogelman College of Business and Economics, University of Memphis. She holds a Doctor of Philosophy degree from the University of Mississippi, a Master of Arts from Memphis State University, and a Bachelor of Science from Arkansas State University.

She is designated as a "Distinguished Member" of the Association for Business Communication. She served on the national Executive Board and as Vice President, Southeastern Region.

She is the author of twelve previously published textbooks on business communication, as well as published articles, short stories, essays, and poems. She is listed in *Who's Who of American Women*.

The Communication Process and Environment

OBJECTIVES

Chapter One will help you:

1 Explain the importance of effective communication to your career and your personal life.

2 Define successful communication.

3 List the various forms of communication and explain how all forms of communication are interrelated.

4 List barriers to communication (including listening) and explain how they may be overcome.

5 Explain the various kinds of nonverbal communication and discuss their relationship to verbal communication.

Welcome to your study of *business communication*. No other ability will be more valuable to you than the ability to relate effectively and harmoniously with other people through communication.

All your life you have communicated almost constantly, and you will continue to do so. Then why should you study communication? Because it *is* such a constant activity is exactly why all of us should strive to increase our knowledge of the subject and to improve our skills and techniques.

Communication is an integral part of daily life. Unless you are a hermit or spend long hours working alone in an occupation that does not include *speaking, writing, reading*, or *listening*, communication with others makes up the major part of your life, both in actual time spent and importance. Even when you are completely alone, you are communicating with yourself and, in a way, with other persons. Your memory and reasoning power are sorting out, organizing, and accepting or rejecting previous bits of conversations, lectures, movies, or written materials. As long as your mind is alive, it will send messages to be received by other minds, and you will receive messages from everyone and everything around you.

Your study of communication will include *reading, writing, speaking, listening*, and *nonverbal* communication. It will also include different kinds of writing, such as letters and reports; different kinds of oral communication, such as public speaking, committee meetings, and interviewing; and the study of communication within organizations, especially as it pertains to management.

It is important to remember, however, that *all aspects of communication are interrelated. Principles of effective writing also apply to effective speech. Nonverbal communication enters into both oral and written communication. Communication in any form is affected by the many and varied influences that enter into human behavior.*

As you increase your understanding of how communication works, you are likely to increase your ability in all areas of the subject. Although techniques differ somewhat, the most important principles are the same.

THE IMPORTANCE OF COMMUNICATION TO YOUR CAREER AND PERSONAL LIFE

Your success in a career, whatever your occupation, position, or organization, will depend greatly on your ability to communicate, perhaps more so than on any other knowledge or skill. You will spend far more time communicating than assuming all other responsibilities of your job. As you are promoted to higher levels, communication will become even more important to you.

According to a survey, *Job Outlook '96*[1] by the National Association of Colleges and Employers, communication skills and the ability to get along with others are rated as the two most important characteristics on the job. Skills were ranked in this order:

Oral communication skills

Interpersonal skills

Teamwork skills

Analytical skills

Flexibility

Leadership skills

Written communication skills

Proficiency in field of study

Computer skills

Notice that although the researcher who completed this study divided communication ability into various categories, in reality *all* categories reflect some aspect of communication, even the seemingly unrelated "computer skills." Computer skills are used to communicate thoughts and ideas and to analyze one's own thinking, a form of intrapersonal communication, as discussed later in this chapter.

In *Survey of College and University Career Center Directors* done by Larry S. Beck in 1994[2], *small* employers look for the following traits in prospective employees:

Characteristic	Percentage of Respondents
Ability to get along with others	99.6%
Communication skills	98.4
Personality/likability	95.3
Generalist skills	92.2
Computer skills	90.7
Interview skills	81.0
Availability	80.2
Loyalty	77.1
Entrepreneurial skills	74.4
Prior experience	50.4
High GPA	7.0
Gender	5.0

In addition to "communication skills," shown by 98.4 percent of the respondents as being important, several of the other characteristics are aspects of communication. Certainly the highest ranked characteristic, "ability to get along with others," is determined almost entirely by communication. (Inclusion of the word *gender* is unexplained.)

In addition to the vocational and professional benefits derived from excellent written and oral communications, your personal and social life is vitally affected, for better or worse, by your relationships with other people. These relationships are built by effective communication.

Like these Hibernia-Bunkie bank merger team members, many employees spend a large portion of their workdays speaking and listening.

DEFINITIONS OF COMMUNICATION

The word *communication* comes from the Latin word *communis*, meaning "common." Thus, for successful communication we are trying to meet on common ground, at least momentarily, with the receivers of our messages. We are trying to establish a commonness or a sharing of information, attitudes, ideas, and understanding.

Dictionary definitions of *communication* include such phrases as "to impart information or knowledge," "to make known," "to impart or to transmit," and "to give or interchange thoughts, feelings, information, or the like by writing, speaking." Other definitions are limited to stimulus-response situations in which messages are deliberately transmitted in order to invoke a response, as when asking a question and expecting an answer, when giving instructions that are expected to be followed, when telling a story to make other persons laugh or cry, or when writing advertising copy to stimulate people to buy.

A simplified definition of communication is "a transfer of meaning." Another definition is that communication is "a process by which one mind influences another mind."

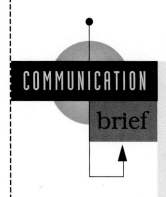

We take language for granted, yet it is one of the most complex things we do. Language allows us to convey our emotions, to share ideas, to create fresh forms of expressions, and to communicate our most intimate thoughts. Without language the very notion of human civilization would be unthinkable. It is not only vivid confirmation of the mind within us; the need to communicate with other humans through language seems as fundamental as the existence of the mind itself.

Richard Restak, *The Mind* (New York: Bantam Books, 1988), 197, 201.

A broader definition of communication includes situations in which there is no intention of transmitting messages, as in much of nonverbal communication, such as an unplanned facial expression, body movement, or a blush. We communicate by our choice of words that carry implied meanings in addition to the actual words spoken or written. Such messages are known as *metacommunications*, explained later in this chapter.

Communication occurs not only between humans but also from machines (particularly computers) to humans and from humans to machines, although perhaps it could be argued that machines are activated only by human thought. Once machines have been set into motion, they can communicate with one another. Animals communicate with one another and with humans, and humans communicate with animals.

Communication can be classified according to the number of persons to whom it is addressed. *Intrapersonal* communication is within the mind of the individual. *Interpersonal* communication is one-to-one contact, as in conversation between two persons (although other persons may be present and also interacting). Interpersonal communication can also occur from writer to reader, as in letters. *Group* communication includes large or small groups, as in an auditorium, classroom, or public meeting place.

Mass communication is sent to large groups of people, especially by radio, television, or newspapers; each person as an individual has little opportunity for identification or feedback.

As you will learn throughout your study, however, *all* communication should be approached as if it were on a one-to-one basis. For example, an effective advertisement sells one person at a time; that is, the wording sounds as if the readers or hearers were being individually addressed. (This is called the *you-approach*.)

Communication is either *verbal* or *nonverbal*. Verbal means *with words*; nonverbal means *without words*. The five processes of verbal communication are *speaking*, *writing*, *reading*, *listening*, and *thinking*. (In the thinking process, which may be in exact words, the sender and the receiver of the message are the same individual.) *Nonverbal communication consists of all methods of communication other than the sending and receiving of words or other verbal symbols.*

HOW WE COMMUNICATE

We communicate by sending meaningful messages. The message transmitted, even though it is meaningful when it leaves the mind of the sender, is often less so when it reaches the mind of the receiver. The process of communication consists of four elements: *(1) the sender, (2) the message, (3) the medium*, or *channel*, and *(4) the receiver.*

Noise hinders the process of communication and prevents or alters the reception of the intended message. Noise is any distraction that interferes with the exact transmission of the intended message; it can occur in the encoding, sending, or receiving process, or in all of these.

Feedback is the return message from the receiver of the original message.

Various models of the communication process have been devised during past decades. C. E. Shannon constructed one of the first. Although his model was planned to apply to mathematical or mechanical communication problems, it also basically applies to all forms of communication. The model was first published in the Bell System Technical Journal and later included in *The Mathematical Theory of Communication*, co-authored with Warren Weaver.[3] It is now known as the Shannon-Weaver model. The general assumption is that the message must move from the source to its destination through a channel, but that its reception may be blocked or altered by noise.

A modified version of the Shannon-Weaver communication model is shown in Figure 1-1. The Shannon-Weaver model does not include feed-

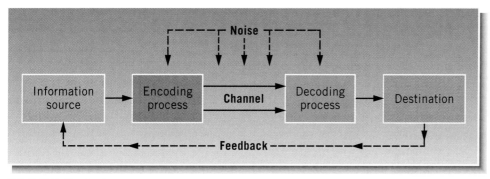

FIGURE 1-1
A communication model

back, which is an essential element of communication, especially of human communication. Perhaps the reason it was omitted is that feedback is actually another act of communication, with the role of the original sender of the message reversed to that of the receiver of the return message.

The most important idea illustrated by the Shannon-Weaver model or similar models is that communication is incomplete until it is received and that ideally the message is received in exactly the same form as that intended by the sender. Realistically, however, we must be satisfied with an inexact reproduction because of the many kinds of noise that interfere in the process. But the received message must be reasonably similar to the transmitted one or communication cannot occur.

Verbal encoding processes are speaking and writing; *nonverbal encoding processes* include touching, smiling, gesturing, and many others. Verbal decoding processes are the receiving processes of reading and listening. Other decoding processes include seeing, tasting, smelling, and touching. *Intrapersonal communication* (communication with self) includes both verbal and nonverbal communication. We think with words, but we also think without words; for example, we can see pictures or hear music in our minds.

The minds of the sender and the receiver vitally affect the content and delivery of the message. Because the perception of the sender is different from that of the receiver, the message in the mind of the receiver is almost certain to be different from that intended by the sender of the message. In addition, various changes in even the most simple message—written, oral, or nonverbal—can occur between the encoding and decoding stages, resulting in inexactness.

WHY WE COMMUNICATE

Three often-stated purposes of communication are *to inform* (or *to inquire*), *to persuade*, and *to entertain*. A message may be planned to accomplish one of these purposes, two of them, or all three. For example, a speaker whose most important purpose is to convince an audience to take certain actions or to accept a point of view can do so by providing information on the subject in such a persuasive way that the mission is accomplished. Entertainment, especially in the form of relevant, inoffensive humor, can be added to all presentations except on extremely serious occasions.

All intentional communication is persuasive in the sense that the sender wishes the receiver to understand the message and to accept or be influenced by the message. David Berlo states: "In short, we communicate to influence-to affect with intent."[4]

CRITERIA FOR SUCCESSFUL COMMUNICATION

In simple terms, successful communication has occurred when

1   The message is understood.

2   The message accomplishes its purpose.

3   The sender and the receiver of the message maintain favorable relationships.

These three attributes of successful communication apply to intentional messages. For example, a memorandum addressed to employees must be understood in approximately the same way as the writer intended; it must result in the expected outcomes, such as a change in procedure; and it must build or maintain goodwill. An advertisement must present the product or service in words that the listener or reader will understand; it must sell the product; and it must build and maintain goodwill in order to provide continuing customer satisfaction and pleasant relationships.

Much communication is unintentional. Tone of voice, facial expressions, and "body language" may convey meaning entirely different from accompanying words, as discussed later in this chapter.

In addition, much conversation is casual, with no definite purpose of being informative, persuasive, or entertaining. We communicate simply because we must. We have a normal, demanding urge to smile when we are happy, to laugh when we are amused, to shout when we are angry, to weep when we are sad. We want to express our emotions and opinions and to have them received, understood, and accepted by other persons. This urge is one reason, perhaps the most important one, that people write poetry or novels, compose music, paint, or communicate through photography. It is why we want to talk with those we love, as well as to converse with strangers we meet on the bus or in a waiting room.

To inform, to persuade, to entertain, or a combination of these purposes, describe purposeful communication and much of casual communication, but not all. The remark, "Isn't it a lovely day?" does not actually present unknown information about the weather. It does impart information about the speaker. It tells the listener: "I accept you, at least to a limited extent. You and I share together this lovely day." At least this is the usual message sent to psychologically mature, secure individuals. Like all other messages, though, even this simple one can become distorted by the time it reaches the mind of the receiver, as will be illustrated in following sections of this chapter.

WHY THE MESSAGE GOES ASTRAY

As speakers and writers we strive to convey exact meanings through word choice and method of delivery. No matter how hard we try, the message as interpreted (decoded) by the receiver is often different from the intended one. This lack of preciseness is due to various kinds of noise.

▶ NOISE

The word *noise* is used to mean any interference with the reception of the intended message. Noise may be *physical*, such as the sound of automobile traffic that drowns out a speaker's words. Physical noise in the workplace is likely to cause both *physiological* and *psychological* noise because of the adverse effect on senders and receivers of spoken and written words. *Semantic* noise occurs because words are misinterpreted; the sender may have chosen them unwisely or the receiver may resist the words for various reasons or fail to understand their meaning. Some words have *connotations* that are unpleasant or offensive to a listener or reader; when such words are used, they cause psychological as well as semantic noise.

A speaker may inject noise into a presentation by confusing gestures, an unpleasant voice, inappropriate choice of clothing, or visible lack of confidence. A writer creates noise by poor word choice, an unattractive arrangement or dim print, and numerous other undesirable factors, as discussed throughout this book.

Even conditions that are usually considered desirable can create noise. For example, a student stated that his French teacher was so beautiful and charming that he couldn't concentrate on learning French. (Could this have been a rationalization?)

Much noise in both written and oral messages consists of psychological barriers. The sender of communication cannot predict accurately the mindset of the intended receiver. As communicators, however, we *can* predict to a certain extent the reception of our message, or at least what the reaction of an average person would be. (An important reminder is that no person is *truly* average, and that no one wishes to be thought of as average—but as above average.)

We can be sure that our listeners will react negatively to condescending, negative, accusing words and to threatening mannerisms. Pointing a finger or shaking a fist will be understood and perhaps never forgotten.

To return to the "Isn't it a lovely day?" comment, suppose that the person who makes the comment is the president of the company and the listener is a new employee. The listener may attach far more significance to the casual, routine remark than the speaker intended. "Ah, she's noticing me already." Or if an employee has a weak self-concept or a suspicious nature, or if he has not been having a good day, he may feel that the president is testing him to determine whether he can converse with important persons. As a result, a stammering reply indicates that he is not able to converse with anyone.

An unhappy person has not noticed the lovely day. She agrees that it is nice, since that is the expected answer, but she is not really convinced because her own world is less than fair.

An unfavorable reception can occur for many reasons: because the listener does not like the speaker's appearance, voice, foreign or regional accent, or the magazine he is holding in his hand; because the speaker resembles someone whom the listener dislikes; because he distrusts all strangers who speak to him.

Some persons will not even hear the remark because of being engrossed in their own thoughts. Some will not hear because the speaker mumbles. Some will not hear because the roar of an airplane or another sound is louder than the speaker's words.

A listener may not agree (although she may not say so) because she has already made up her mind that she doesn't like the climate of the particular city, so there can be no such thing as a lovely day.

If a speaker and a listener meet each day and the speaker usually comments on the foulness of the weather, he will be expected to do so again, and the listener may actually believe that he said, "Isn't it a rotten day?" We often receive the meaning that we expect to receive.

If a listener has no understanding of the English language, he will not understand the meaning of the words in the remark; but a pleasant look on the face of the speaker may make him nod and smile. He has not understood the code system of the language, but rather the nonverbal symbols.

If so many things can go wrong in the reception of the simple comment, "Isn't it a lovely day?" is it any surprise that an intended message does not always reach the mind of the reader or listener, or, if it does, that it does not achieve its intended purpose? Even less surprising, written messages are often unread, misunderstood, and unaccepted; sales messages do not always sell; newspaper stories do not convey to all readers the same understanding of the printed word; instructions are not always understood or followed.

These varying reactions (although perhaps exaggerated) to a simple comment about the weather show how the preconceived opinions, attitudes, and beliefs of the receiver affect the reception of the intended message.

LANGUAGE AS A CAUSE OF MISCOMMUNICATION

Verbal communication errors are related to the basic premise of *general semantics*, that language affects thought and behavior. Some principles of general semantics are these:

1   A statement is never the whole story. We can never say everything about anything. Every instance of speaking or writing results from choosing what to include and what to omit.

2   Abstract words are less forceful than more specific ones. What do superlatives like *finest, best,* and *awful* indicate if they have no more specific terms to substantiate them? Or *good, bad; big, little; rich, poor; success, failure?* All such words are relative and abstract, as are many other words. We will continue to use and to receive abstract words, as we should. The danger lies in interpreting them as specific ones and in using them when we should be more exact and objective. (When conveying unpleasant news, general words are usually a better choice than specific words, as discussed in Chapter 8.)

3   Even words that are usually regarded as specific are not completely so, because no two things—or people or events—are exactly alike. Because words have no meaning within themselves but as human minds give them meaning, communication at its best is far from exact. Nevertheless, by realizing that communication is always imperfect, we can make it more nearly perfect.

4   Words have various *connotative* meanings in addition to their *denotative,* or "dictionary," meanings. These connotative meanings are based in part on emotions and various experiences of the sender and the receiver of the intended message.

► STEREOTYPING

Stereotyping is categorizing people or events according to what we expect these people or events to be. Stereotypes are based not only on our personal experiences with one or more individuals of a group but also on images or characters portrayed in printed material, movies, plays, and television programs.

Stereotyping enters into our judgment of people and events every day of our lives, either consciously or subconsciously. It is especially frequent and harmful as it affects communication and relationships with individuals from other nations or cultures.

For example, stereotypes of women (at least in the minds of a few people) portray them as being emotional and indecisive. Southerners were once perceived as being slow of speech and perhaps a bit dim-witted, but gracious and kind. Truck drivers are assumed to be hardworking, but uneducated and uncouth. For centuries, professors have been categorized as absent-minded. Business students are believed to be interested only in employment opportunities, not in obtaining a liberal education.

All of these examples apply to groups of people, not to individuals. Even when applied only to groups, they are still stereotypes that are often completely untrue. Nevertheless, much of our communication is influenced by stereotypes of one kind or another. They prevent open and objective speech, writing, listening, reading, and thinking. As we view others through our stereotypes, we are also stereotyped in the minds of those with whom we communicate. Is it any surprise that communication is often poorly under-stood or accepted? Recognizing that stereotypes exist, however, will improve personal relationships and all forms of communication.

INCORRECT OR INCOMPLETE FEEDBACK

Feedback occurs after a communication is received. Feedback is an indica-tion to the sender of acceptance and understanding, or the lack of it. Most people will pleasantly agree that it is a lovely day. Others will ignore the comment and turn away, not wanting to get involved in a conversation or a possible friendship. A person from another country may smile and nod pleasantly; although he or she does not understand the words, meaning is conveyed through a smile and a pleasant voice.

One listener will state emphatically that it is a miserable day, for no weather is like that in San Diego and he has already made up his mind that he wants to return there. Another person will say that the day would be all right if she didn't have this horrible cold. (Personal problems have interfered with the perception of reality.) Some persons will suddenly realize that it is a lovely day; they hadn't thought of the weather until it was mentioned.

Feedback is received by letter writers when they learn that their letters have accomplished their purpose or that they have not. It is obtained by a speaker when listeners react, if only by going to sleep. The effectiveness of sales campaigns is measured by the number and amount of sales. The bas-ketball coach receives feedback from the results of the team's performance. The teacher receives feedback, positive or negative, through students' exam-ination scores, their comments, the expressions on their faces, and many other reactions.

The results of communication are obtainable only through feedback, which in turn exerts influence over future messages. In successful commu-nication there is an interdependence between the original source and the receiver, with the receiver becoming the source of a subsequent mes-sage.

To summarize, less than perfect communication occurs because of weak-ness on the part of the sender or of the receiver of the message, or of both, and also because of influences exerted along the way.

EFFECTIVE AND EFFICIENT LISTENING

Listening, like reading, involves receiving the verbal messages of other per-sons. However excellent the spoken or written message sent to us, we can-not rely solely on the knowledge and skills of the speaker or the writer. We must exert an active effort to receive these messages.

▶ THE IMPORTANCE OF LISTENING

Various studies have indicated that most businesspersons spend from 40 to 60 percent of their working day listening. The business manager usually spends even more time. A manager is paid to listen. Management is basically decision making, and decisions are based on information about problems and possible solutions. Much of this information is presented orally. In order to make intelligent decisions, the manager must listen, completely, exactly, and critically.

In addition to the obvious purpose of receiving information, our listening is essential to the persons we supervise. "Oh, if someone would only listen!" is a cry heard on occasion in occupations of all kinds, a cry that sometimes disappears in despair because individuals have given up the hope that anyone will ever listen. Employees want to feel that they count, that they are a part of the organization, that their words are worth hearing or reading.

Some managers and company presidents may proclaim their open-door policies and go so far as to admit everyone who comes in the office. Then they interrupt by anticipating the speaker's words, looking at the clock, or indicating that they are impatient in some way. They are likely to do too much of the talking themselves.

A research study published in 1989 by Sypher, Bostrom, and Seibert was designed to determine the relationship between listening and other communication abilities, between one's listening abilities and one's job levels in the organization, between listening abilities and upward mobility, and the listening differences between supervisors and nonsupervisors. Participants in the study included 36 employees of a large insurance corporate headquarters located in the northeastern United States.

The authors state: "What we can conclude from this study is that listening is related to other communication abilities and to success at work. Better listeners held higher level positions and were promoted more often than those with less developed listening abilities. Short-term listening with rehearsal appeared to have the greatest effect on level and mobility. . . . It [listening] can enhance one's job performance, and perhaps promotions, raises, status, and power are more attainable for the better listener.[5]

A research study published by Haas and Arnold in 1995 was undertaken to determine the attributes that contribute to competent communicators. Participants included 48 employees, 92% of the total number in the organization, a daily city newspaper. Of the 493 attributes listed in the survey, "Listens Well/Effectively" was the most frequently chosen one.[6]

▶ BARRIERS TO LISTENING

Why do we not listen? Think of the reasons you have not listened to others. Why have you not received these messages? Why do persons not listen to you as you engage in conversation or speak to groups? Or why do they not understand you or remember what you said?

Check your listening habits. Could the quality of your listening have any relationship to:

1 Your actual physical ability to hear?

2 Attention to the speaker's voice, appearance, pronunciation, accent, use of grammar, or mannerisms to the exclusion of what the speaker is trying to say to you?

3 Discounting and disregarding what the speaker is saying because you do not like his or her physical appearance, voice, pronunciation, accent, use of grammar, or mannerisms?

4 Listening to words only, not to the underlying feeling behind the words, much of which is communicated by nonverbal methods?

5 Listening for details to the exclusion of the overall meaning, or to the exclusion of the ideas and principles on which the details are based?

6 Allowing preconceived beliefs about the particular subject being discussed to prevent you from receiving the speaker's ideas?

7 Allowing emotional feelings about the subject to "turn you off," especially if the speaker uses emotional words?

8 Concentrating on notetaking to the extent that you lose the train of thought?

9 Interrupting?

10 Being sure that you already know all there is to know about the subject?

11 Inattention because you do not like to consider unpleasant, complicated, or difficult subjects?

12 Inattention because you are tired, sleepy, hungry, and want to go home?

13 Inattention because you know that whatever is said, you could say it better?

14 Inattention because you have more important things to think about?

15 Boredom because you have already heard too many speeches, lectures, discussions, conversations, and people "talking at you"?

16 Inability to keep your mind on the subject?

17 Inattention to the speaker's words because you are trying to think of a reply, or of a question to ask during the discussion period?

18 Confusion because you don't have the faintest idea of what the speaker is talking about and have never heard the words before?

19 Lack of understanding because you do not look at the speaker to grasp the full effect of what is being said, as well as to notice gestures, facial expressions, and other nonverbal signals?

20 Lack of concentration because your mind moves faster than the speaker's voice and wanders into side paths so that you lose the train of thought?

What other considerations enter into your reception of spoken words? As listeners, we cannot control all the sources of noise that prevent our receiving the message exactly as the sender intended. We cannot control the actual physical noise in the room, nor can we control miscommunication caused by the speaker, such as using inexact or incorrect words. By our careful attention and thought, however, we can recognize these inconsistencies and adjust our thinking to them.

Perception affects our reception of the message in any form of communication, especially in the listening process. We cannot immediately remove all the barriers to the accurate and complete perception of the intended message. For example, we cannot simply resolve that we will dispense with all our own preconceived notions and prejudices (we all have them) and find them gone. But our recognition of these particular biases, probably even our acceptance of them (if it is reasonable to accept a prejudice), can serve as a warning that they interfere with our reception of the spoken message as well as of the written one.

Listening, like reading, requires attention and energy. The better you listen, however, the less demanding it seems to be. Six bad habits that prevent effective listening, as stated by Nichols and Stevens, are listed below. (Nichols and Stevens are well-known pioneers in the field of listening research.) The following comments are concerned mostly with listening to a lecturer or a discussion leader, but they also apply to direct, face-to-face discussion.

1 *Faking attention.* You are deceiving only yourself, for you will not deceive other persons for very long. Besides, you are cheating yourself out of the opportunity to learn whatever it is that is being said.

2 *"I get the facts" listening.* Although Nichols does not say that facts are unimportant, he says that memorizing facts is not the way to listen. When persons talk with you, they usually want you to understand their ideas. We should remember facts only long enough to understand the ideas that are built from these facts. Then the understanding of the ideas will help the listener to remember the supporting facts more effectively than does focusing on facts alone.

3 *Avoiding difficult listening.* Concentration is necessary in order to understand a lecture or a discussion. We should be willing to devote the effort needed to grasp the meaning. If we are affected with this listening habit, we should make a planned and periodic effort to listen to difficult material, lectures, and discussion topics that require mental effort, such as radio commentaries, panel discussions, and lectures.

4 *Premature dismissal of a subject as uninteresting.* G. K. Chesterton once said that there is no such thing as an uninteresting subject; there are only uninterested people.

5 *Criticizing delivery and physical appearance to the extent that we do not listen to the spoken words.* Although listeners are affected by appearance and delivery, the content of the message is more important than the form of the delivery.

6 *Yielding easily to distractions.*[7]

Another reason we have difficulty in listening is that our thought processes move much faster than the speed of the spoken word. The average lecturer speaks at an estimated rate of 125 words a minute with a range of 80 to 160. Our minds, even on a slow day, move faster. Because of this difference, our minds wander, and we anticipate what is coming next, which may or may not be what actually does come next. Or we mentally take a little rest because we think we know what the speaker is going to say. If our thought processes were slower than the spoken word, we would be even worse listeners. We would not have time to notice the speaker's nonverbal clues, to determine the feeling behind the words, or to notice the speaker's particular use of words and word meanings.

All these functions enter into effective listening, as well as actually hearing the words themselves. But as we do all these things, we should not fail to concentrate on what the speaker is saying at the moment—and often this is exactly what happens. We get so tangled up in our own thoughts, which have perhaps started in relation to something the speaker has said, that we lose the train of thought or miss a great deal of what has been said. This is especially true when we are listening to lectures, but it can be true when we are in a group or listening to one individual.

Information received from oral words is likely to be far less permanent in the mind of the receiver than are written words. Studies show that people usually forget from one third to one half of what they hear within eight hours after hearing it. Some loss will always occur, regardless of improvements in listening ability. Make notes about oral instructions as an aid to remembering, but do not let notetaking prevent you from actually listening to the speaker's words.

▶ SYMPATHETIC VERSUS CRITICAL LISTENING

You engage in *sympathetic listening* when you observe the 20 considerations previously mentioned—for example, listening mainly for content and not to the speaker's accent, pronunciation, or grammar; recognizing your own particular bias; and giving the speaker your undivided, conscientious attention.

Sympathetic factors that make for good listening include all the aspects of actively being willing to receive the message insofar as it agrees with your own intelligent observation. *Critical listening* involves evaluation. Listen critically, for you cannot and should not accept completely everything you hear, just as you cannot accept or believe everything you read.

The world is full of propaganda, high-pressure advertising, and public relations experts and speechwriters who distort facts to suit their own particular purposes. Even if the message is not planned to be deceitful, the speaker may be misinformed. Individuals may be absolutely and completely sincere and also absolutely and completely mistaken.

Just as you evaluate what you read, you should evaluate what you hear; but do not evaluate too soon. Give the lecturer or the conversationalist an opportunity to present the complete story or to express opinions. Avoid interrupting the flow of thought directed toward your mind (either interrupting with your own thoughts or interrupting with spoken words). No one can honestly and completely evaluate another's words until actually listening to those words.

Consider the reliability of the speaker's words. Are they based on facts or on inferences or value judgments? Also ask yourself:

► Is the speaker up to date? Has the speaker taken into consideration that what was true yesterday is not necessarily true today?

► Is the speaker competent, as well as nonbiased? Does the speaker have a broad background of knowledge and experience?

► Is the speaker giving complete information? Although "the statement is never the whole story," has the speaker abstracted the most important information?

► If points are omitted, do you believe that these omissions were intentional?

► Does the speaker express ideas in abstractions and generalities instead of using specific, concrete language?

► Does the speaker attempt to persuade by relying on emotional words and phrases instead of on rational, objective language?

To summarize, a good listener actively participates with the speaker. Listening requires patience and cooperation. Becoming an efficient listener is not easy, but we should determine to do so for our own benefit as well as a courtesy to senders of the spoken word.

NONVERBAL COMMUNICATION

Think of the importance of the handshake. What does this important nonverbal message mean? It should convey confidence, friendliness, trust, and acceptance. How can such a universal action do so much? (Initiate the handshake. Use a firm handshake, not limp or timid. Do not use a bear grip or squeeze too hard. Do not remove your hand hurriedly; also do not hold the other's hand too long. Maintain eye contact.)

As you read this section on nonverbal communication, notice the kinds of nonverbal communication that enter into a simple handshake. Also think of the ways you are communicating nonverbally (provided someone else is in the room) as you read these passages.

You have been sending and receiving wordless messages all your life. It is impossible not to communicate, even when you remain completely silent and motionless.

Nonverbal communication permeates all speech and much, if not all, of written communication. Estimates from authorities in the field indicate that nonverbal messages make up as much as 70 to 90 percent of the transfer of meaning and emotion in face-to-face interaction.

A business letter communicates nonverbally by its attractive appearance, or the lack of it, as well as by the time it is sent. Your written application letter and resume are judged by their appearance and correctness, perhaps beyond your other qualifications for employment. Your appearance and actions during an employment interview are likely to be far more important than your words.

Because much nonverbal communication is unconscious, it is likely to be sincere. You can improve interpersonal relationships by learning to receive

Face-to-face communication allows both senders and receivers to observe nonverbal communication facets such as facial expressions and gestures.

the unspoken and often unplanned messages of other people and by becoming aware of your own unspoken language.

It is important to remember, however, that the methods of nonverbal communication should not be considered as tools for manipulation of other people, for looking into their minds and determining their innermost thoughts. You could not do so even if you wanted to, regardless of how much you know about nonverbal communication. Psychologists and others who study nonverbal communication base their decisions about individuals on long-term study, and even then some of their judgments are incorrect. Isolated movements, postures, actions, facial expressions, and other bits of nonverbal communication should not be considered alone.

Like words, sentences, and paragraphs, nonverbal communication should not be taken out of its context. It should be interpreted according to the environment, the particular situation or circumstances, and previously established personal relationships.

Nonverbal communication is inseparable from the total communication process. Ray Birdwhistell, a pioneer in the field of *kinesics* (popularly referred to as body language), remarked that studying communication apart from its nonverbal aspects is similar to studying noncardiac physiology.

► SIGN LANGUAGE, ACTION LANGUAGE, AND OBJECT LANGUAGE

Human nonverbal communication takes the form of sign language, action language, or object language, according to Ruesch and Kees, researchers and writers in the field. They state:

> In broad terms, nonverbal forms of codification fall into three distinct categories:
>
> *Sign language* includes all those forms of codification in which words, numbers, and punctuation signs have been supplanted by gestures; these vary from the "monosyllabic" gesture of the hitch-hiker to such complete systems as the language of the deaf.
>
> *Action language* embraces all movements that are not used exclusively as signals. Such acts as walking and drinking, for example, have a dual function: on one hand they serve personal needs, and on the other they constitute statements to those who may perceive them.
>
> *Object language* comprises all intentional and non-intentional display of material things, such as implements, machines, art objects, architectural structures, and—last but not least—the human body and whatever clothes or covers it. The embodiment of letters as they occur in books and on signs has a material substance, and this aspect of words also has to be considered as object language.[8]

Others describe the kinds of nonverbal communication differently, but, given a broad interpretation, their descriptions fit into one of the three categories listed by Ruesch and Kees.

We communicate much through personal appearance, which is achieved through both action language, including posture and movements, and object language, as expressed by clothing, jewelry, handbags, and makeup. We express meaning by eye contact, facial expressions, and gestures.

COMMUNICATION BY THE USE OF PERSONAL SPACE (PROXEMICS)

Edward T. Hall is a well-known researcher in the field of communication through space. He coined the word *proxemics*, which comes from *proximity*, to describe his theories and observations about zones of territory and how they are used and defended by persons of different cultures. According to Hall, there are four kinds of interpersonal distance: *intimate distance, personal distance, social distance,* and *public distance.*[9]

The intimate distance, close phase, is the distance of lovemaking and wrestling; the intimate distance, far phase, is 6 to 18 inches. The personal distance, close phase, is $1\frac{1}{2}$ to $2\frac{1}{2}$ feet; far phase, $2\frac{1}{2}$ to 4 feet. The social distance, close phase, is 4 to 7 feet, and the far phase is 7 to 12 feet. The public distance is 12 to 25 feet or more.

Impersonal business occurs at the close social distance, which is also a very common distance for persons at a casual social gathering. Desks in the offices of some people, especially executives, are large enough to hold visitors at the far phase of social distance. Some executives come from behind their desks and sit closer to the person being interviewed, or about the same distance away but without the desk to act as a barrier.

You may have noticed that students often sit in the same place in a classroom day after day, even when seats are not assigned. They also tend to sit in the same general location in all classrooms; that is, if they sit in the front row in one class they often do so in all classes. Some people sit in the same pew in church for a lifetime except when strangers unintentionally take their place. Then the owners of the territory look annoyed and uncomfortable.

In *The Territorial Imperative*, Ardrey discusses human tendencies to identify with an area over time and to defend it against aggressors.[10] We have favorite chairs or favorite spots in a house that we think of as our own. We sometimes resent the intrusion of others.

We carry with us at all times a kind of invisible bubble that we consider to be our own space, wherever we are. We may become uncomfortable when someone intrudes on this space.

Height adds status. One businessman put his desk and chair on a raised platform to increase his feeling of authority. Another not only used an elevated chair but also fastened the visitor's chair to the floor so that the visitor could not move the chair toward the desk, thus intruding on the businessman's space. (No doubt these two men are less than perfectly happy in their jobs.)

We communicate through space by the arrangement of our offices. If you interview persons or frequently talk with visitors, your desk becomes a

barrier. The desk is less a barrier if the visitors can sit beside you. If the visitor is sitting directly in front of you, the wider the desk, the wider the barrier.

Although certain business relationships call for a degree of separation and formality, we are often too much concerned with separation, importance, and dignity, and not enough with real communication. A living-room setting in your office, if you are fortunate enough to have this arrangement, can aid conversation and open communication. Such a setting can also send other messages with object language, or, more bluntly, act as a status symbol.

COMMUNICATION brief

The way we use our bodies to demonstrate our feelings is very important and so is the space around them. In fact, for more than half the world's inhabitants, the space bubble is sacred. The others don't know it exists. Space invaders may be back-slapping Spaniards, arm-gripping Argentinians, or, of course, bone-crushing American handshakes. People from Asian and northern cultures are generally uncomfortable when confronted by the more effusive gestures and behavior of Latins and others.

The feeling of discomfort generally begins at the outset when the "space bubble" is invaded. Orientals, Nordics, Anglo-Saxon, and Germanic people mostly regard space within just over a meter of the self as inviolable territory for strangers, but will allow a smaller personal bubble of half a meter radius for close friends and relatives.

Mexicans, on the other hand, happily come within half a meter of strangers during business discussions. . . . When Mexicans position themselves half a meter away from English people, they're ready to talk business.

The Japanese in particular experience discomfort when their personal space is invaded, while Anglo-Saxons, Nordics, and Germans tolerate close presence with difficulty, and East Asians in general (with the exception of the Indonesians) keep their distance from their interlocutor as a sign of respect. With Latins, Arabs, and Africans, closeness is a sign of confidence and does not indicate a loss of respect.

"Space at a Premium," from *Management Today*, Haymarket Publishing Ltd., September, 1996, 105–106. Reprinted by permission.

► **COMMUNICATION THROUGH "BODY LANGUAGE" (KINESICS)**

The field of *kinesics*, or body language, is still inexact and nonscientific compared to many other areas of knowledge. For example, our judgments of the psychological meaning of the way a person sits in a chair or how one's hands touch the face, hair, or other parts of the body cannot be viewed as an exact interpretation or, in some cases, even an approximation of the meaning. Experienced researchers realize this fact and emphasize it, but many people continue to regard body language as an exact interpretation that they long to read.

This discussion should not be interpreted to mean that body motions are unimportant in nonverbal communication. It is an overstatement, however, to describe body motions as a "language." Avoid hasty inferences and generalizations in your receiving of nonverbal communication; these assumptions are dangerous in all forms of communication.

If you had never heard the terms *body language*, *kinesics*, or *nonverbal communication*, you would interpret, often correctly, the emotions of other persons according to their bodily movements. You are more likely to be able to analyze the movements of persons you know well.

You can recognize in yourself the effect of your emotions on your body. The expression "walking on air" would not apply to your steps when you are discouraged and depressed. You do not clench your fists when you are happy and relaxed. Your hands shake a little when you are anxious or suffering from stage fright. You put your hands on your hips when you are "laying down the law."

Even without books or research studies, we would all realize the importance of kinesics to the transmission of ideas and emotions. You can tell a great deal about the feeling of other persons, particularly those you know well, before they say a word. You learned to do so when you were a child.

To reemphasize: Do not interpret posture and gestures out of context and base conclusions on isolated events. For example, the arms-across-the chest position, which is said to indicate resistance or to be a defensive posture, may mean only that one is cold. If your listeners, however, continually face you with folded arms, they are not receiving with great joy your information or instructions. If you are standing with your hands on your hips while you talk with them, no wonder you are meeting resistance with such a dictatorial pose.

Also notice your own emotions and feelings in relation to these well-known poses and to several others. When you assume these poses, you are likely to be conveying messages to others about your emotions. For example, when you feel insecure, you may give yourself a sense of protection by crossing your arms. You may find that you assume the same position when you resist the suggestions of others. You are not likely to do so when you are relaxed, confident, and in agreement with other people.

Throwing up the hands indicates resignation. Both hands behind one's back indicates deep thought. Drumming of fingers indicates boredom. We scratch our heads when we are puzzled. This gesture is so well known, or at least so widely accepted, that the term *scratching our heads* indicates bewilderment and has become a cliché. Humans, as well as animals, tilt their heads slightly whenever they see or hear something that interests them.

Shaking a fist indicates anger in our culture. Natives of New Guinea pretend to shoot a bow and arrow when they are angry. This action makes sense to them because they use bows and arrows to kill.

For men, the gesture of unbuttoning the coat is a sign of openness, of frankness, of acceptance. A coat can be used in various ways to communicate nonverbally. Men running for political office are often photographed with their coats slung over their shoulders to picture a boyish, hardworking, honest approach. The hero of the play *How to Succeed in Business Without Really Trying* made it a point to be in the process of putting on his coat as he entered his boss's office. This action indicated that he had been working hard and had removed the coat, but that he was now putting it on again in order to show respect.

There are regional differences, as well as differences between nations, in nonverbal communication. These differences are similar to accents in verbal communication. People in the South are said to smile more than those in Maine or New York. People are said to smile more in Atlanta than in any other city in America. Persons in the South also hug one another more often than those in the North, or so it has been reported. This display of affection has been described as hypocrisy, but is not hypocrisy if it is based on sincere emotions.

At times, nonverbal communication differs from messages conveyed verbally; that is, our words say one thing and our bodies say another. The nonverbal message is likely to be the correct one, and it is likely to be interpreted as the correct one.

What does this man's nonverbal communication imply to you?

COMMUNICATION THROUGH TOUCH (HAPTICS)

Touch is a form of kinesics that differs from individual to individual in the same culture and from culture to culture. Hugging is an important and emphatic method of communication through touch. So is a handshake, a touch on the arm, and a slap on the back.

Communication between individuals through touch, like all other forms of communication, can be misunderstood. It can also be offensive to persons who do not wish to be hugged or touched in any other way. On the other hand, to resist a casual and a well-intentioned touch may be interpreted as an insult. A handshake, however, is a form of communication that is likely to be acceptable to all individuals everywhere.

The forms of nonverbal communication, like those of verbal communication, are interrelated. For example, communication through touch can be described not only as a form of kinesics (or action language) but as a form of proxemics. Because we desire our own "bubble of space," the touch of others in crowded elevators or elsewhere causes discomfort because of the invasion of personal space.

COMMUNICATION WITH THE EYES (OCULESICS)

Our eyes often communicate involuntarily. Thus, *oculesics* is likely to be sincere even when words are insincere. Research studies have shown that the pupils of the eyes enlarge when they observe pleasant objects or scenes, or when the viewer is pleased, and that the pupils become smaller when the

COMMUNICATION
brief

In the United States, eye contact is extremely important: we don't really trust anyone who won't look us in the eye. The significance of eye contact in determining credibility is acknowledged in the courtroom, where jurors are positioned so that they can look at both the witness and the accused. In one murder trial we heard about, the judge instructed the witness to remove his photogrey glasses, so that the jury could see his eyes.

If possible, you want to be on the same eye level as the person to whom you are speaking. The expressions "look down on someone" and "look up to someone" underscore just how significant height differences can be.

One female manager at a seminar told us it took a long time before she realized why all her family fights occurred in the hallway. Whenever she felt a fight coming on, she'd drag her husband to the hallway and she would stand on the second step. She is 4′9″, her husband is 6′1″. "I didn't know why I did it," she admitted, "but it felt better."

Barbara Pachter and Marjorie Brody, *Complete Business Etiquette Handbook*, (Englewood Cliffs, N.J.: Prentice Hall, 1995), 47.

viewer is displeased in any way. In addition, eyes mirror other emotions, sometimes beyond our control.

Another important factor is the difference between the use or omission of eye contact according to the traditions and customs of various cultures, as discussed further in Chapter 17.

▶ METACOMMUNICATION

Metacommunication includes implied meanings, perhaps through tone of voice, word choice, omissions, or silence. The phrase "reading between the lines" applies to both oral and written communication. Metacommunication may be intentional or unintentional. For example, the words "Good luck" may imply that you will need luck to succeed. The words "You look nice today" may suggest that you looked terrible yesterday.

▶ PARALANGUAGE

Paralanguage is closely tied to metacommunication, and metacommunication may occur because of paralanguage. Paralanguage includes vocal quality, loudness, tempo, and "interrupters," which are such additions to speech as "uh" and "ah," and hesitations. Silence is another aspect of paralanguage.

▶ OLFACTICS

Olfactics is communication through the sense of smell. Remembered fragrances arouse memories and emotions. Fragrances sell baking bread, cosmetics, perfumes, flowers, and many other products. We are positively or negatively influenced by odors of various kinds. At times such influence is not consciously recognized.

▶ COMMUNICATION THROUGH THE USE OF TIME (CHRONEMICS)

Edward T. Hall says:

> Time talks. It speaks more plainly than words. The message it conveys comes through loud and clear. Because it is manipulated less consciously it is subject to less distortion than the spoken language. It can shout the truth where words lie.[11]

Varying attitudes about the use of time are most evident between people of different countries and different cultures. Apart from cultural and national differences, however, individuals differ greatly and tell much about themselves, through their use of time. Promptness in business situations is highly valued in the American culture, as it is in most social situations. (For some parties, arriving too early is worse than arriving late.) Being prompt in attendance at meetings, as in a classroom, is only a matter of courtesy to other participants.

SUMMARY

Your success in business, whatever your specialization or employing organization, will depend to a great extent on your ability to communicate, perhaps more so than on any other ability. You will spend much more time communicating than on any other aspects of your job.

A simplified definition of communication is the transfer of meaning from the sender to the receiver. Communication involves thinking, reading, listening, speaking, and writing, as well as various nonverbal methods.

Although meaningful in the mind of the sender (or information source), the message transmitted is often less meaningful by the time it reaches its destination. The message is not exact or complete until it is understood and accepted in the mind of the receiver.

Noise is any distraction that interferes with the exact transmission of the intended message; it can occur in the encoding, sending, or decoding processes. Feedback is the return message to the sender of the original message.

Various barriers prevent effective listening. Many of these barriers are related to perception, attitudes, and opinions. By recognizing these barriers, you can minimize their effect.

To be a better listener:

► Concentrate. Remain alert.

► Listen sympathetically but also critically.

► Listen for general meaning and for ideas.

► Take notes as necessary and appropriate, but do not let notetaking interfere with the reception of a message.

► Notice the speaker's nonverbal communication.

Three elements of nonverbal communication are sign language, action language, and object language. Space and time are also used as methods of communication. Proxemics refers to the use of personal space. Americans do not view time and space, in relation to communication, in the same way as people in some other countries do.

Kinesics means "body language." Like all areas of nonverbal communication, this field of study is far from an exact science, although many patterns of action have been observed by research studies.

Many factors enter into nonverbal communication: dress and appearance; use of time; facial expressions; posture; eye contact; tone of voice; choice of possessions; arrangement of homes and offices; gestures; and actions of all kinds.

PURPOSES OF END-OF-CHAPTER EXERCISES

A section at the end of each chapter, "Test Yourself: Chapter Content," along with a summary, is planned to help you study and review each chapter. Answers to "Test Yourself: Chapter Content" are expected to be brief and specific.

Additional sections, which also follow each chapter, require more discussion and thought. These sections include "Collaborative Writing and Working in Groups" and "Think-It-Through Assignments"; they apply your knowledge and understanding of chapter content, while "Test Yourself: Chapter Content" primarily reviews it.

Still another section, "Test Yourself: Correct Usage," provides two kinds of review: the principles of English usage and, because of the content of the questions, a further review of the chapter itself.

All questions and problems, however, can be used in various ways as suggested by students or by teachers. For example, as you answer a question that requires merely the answer feedback (in "Test Yourself, Chapter Content"), you may discuss the various kinds of feedback or why it may or may not be understood.

TEST YOURSELF

chapter content

1   Explain how the Latin word *communis* relates to communication.
2   Verbal messages that carry meanings other than those stated in words are known as _____.
3   Communication within the mind of an individual (thinking) is also described as _____ communication.
4   Communication with one or a few persons is known as _____ communication.
5   Communication through such media as television, radio, and newspapers is described as _____ communication.
6   Distinguish between verbal and nonverbal communication.
7   What are five processes of verbal communication?
8   What are three purposes of communication?
9   Any distraction that interferes with the exact transmission of the intended message is known as _____.
10 The return message from the receiver of the message to the sender is known as _____.
11 What are three tests of successful communication?
12 Give examples of sign language, action language, and object language.
13 What is meant by the terms *proxemics* and *kinesics*?
14 What is meant by the term *paralanguage*?

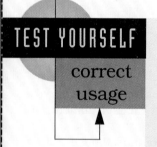

TEST YOURSELF

correct usage

Choose the correctly spelled word in each of the following sentences. Use a dictionary if necessary.

1   We never know the (affect, effect) our words will have on our listeners.
2   Spoken or written communication is (affected, effected) by nonverbal signals.
3   A (principle, principal) reason for poor listening is lack of interest in the subject being discussed.
4   A dog communicates nonverbally by wagging (it's, its) tail.
5   Although nonverbal communication is expressive, we should not consider each gesture to have a (definate, definite) meaning.
6   (Regardless, irregardless) of the communication situation, some nonverbal communication will occur.
7   The study of nonverbal communication is not (altogether, all together) scientific.
8   Effective communication within a (corporation, cooperation) requires the (corporation, cooperation) of all (personel, personnel).

PROBLEMS AND CASES

Note: End-of-chapter questions and problems throughout this book may be used in various ways according to your preference and the instructions of your professor. Although assignments are divided into three sections—"Problems and Cases," "Collaborative Writing and Working in Groups," and "Think-It-Through Assignments"—many from each group may be used as if they were listed in another group. All assignments at the end of chapters throughout the book may be used in this way. For example, almost any problem can be used, with modifications, for group work; and those described as group assignments may be completed individually. In addition, many assignments at the end of Chapters 1 and 2, along with some other chapters, can be appropriately expanded into formal research reports to be prepared with your study of Part V, "Communicating through Reports."

1 Step to the front of the classroom. Introduce yourself to your instructor and to your classmates. Tell them about your major field of study and your career goals. Describe your present employment, if any, especially as it relates to written or oral communication. Tell them anything else about yourself that you wish, provided you keep your remarks to no more than the time limit set by your instructor.

2 "Comments and Bits of Information" Assignment: The purpose of this assignment is to direct your thoughts to the wide field of communication and to give you an opportunity to present a bit of information to the class. To find this comment or bit of any information, look in any printed source. (Do not use this textbook.) Try to find recent sources, and, as much as possible, make the comment understandable to other students who, like you, are probably beginning their first course in business communication.

Your comment or bit of information should be about communication. For example, you might say something like this:

"Time is a factor in nonverbal communication, and not all persons view tardiness in the way we do in the United States. In many countries, time is treated much more casually than it is here." Give your source for your particular bit of information. You may use the exact words of the author, but if you do so, include a statement to that effect. As another example, you might obtain your comment simply by glancing at a newspaper and noting that postage rates are expected to rise soon. Be prepared to present your comment or bit of information orally to the class in the time suggested by your instructor.

3 Prepare your "Comments and Bits of Information" assignment (Problem 2) in written form according to the directions of your instructor.

4 If you are now employed, describe your communication activities in relation to the discussion in this chapter. Examples of topics to be discussed or questions to be answered are these:
   a. Keep track of your communication activities for the next three days. How often are you involved in listening? Speaking? Reading? Writing? Estimate the number of hours spent in each activity and determine what percentage of your workdays was spent in each communication activity.
   b. Do you spend more time in written communication or in oral communication?
   c. What kinds of written messages do you prepare? By which methods (telephone, voice mail, conversation, group discussion, or public speaking) do you communicate orally? What are the purposes of these forms of oral communication?
   d. By which methods (hard copies, fax, or electronic mail) do you communicate in writing? What are the purposes of these forms of written communication?

5   Keep track of your communication activities at work for the next three days. When, how, why, and to whom have you communicated? Has this communication been particularly effective or ineffective? What forms of feedback did you receive? How well have you received the communication of others, and what kind of message did you send in return? What kinds of noise have existed in your communication efforts?

6   Using an example from your experience, write a short description of an instance of miscommunication.

7   Think back to a recent misunderstanding between you and a friend or family member. Using the communication model provided within Chapter 1, identify where the miscommunication originated. Describe the situation and suggest a means of avoiding a similar miscommunication in the future.

8   What kinds of information do you communicate nonverbally to your instructor? To your classmates? To your employer?

9   How can written material communicate nonverbally? What kind of noise can occur?

10 How can an electronic mail message communicate nonverbally?

11 How can the arrangement of a business office communicate nonverbally?

12 How do business managers communicate nonverbally to employees? How do teachers communicate nonverbally to students?

13 What are some of the meanings that silence can communicate?

14 How can you tell the difference between someone who is actively listening versus politely listening?

15 How can too much communication be a barrier to effective listening?

16 Give examples of how nonverbal communication can be a barrier to listening.

17 Give examples of how nonverbal communication can increase effective listening.

18 Explain why the act of copying material a speaker presents via an overhead projector is not an effective listening technique.

19 Why is it important for a teacher to be a good listener to establish good relationships with students? Are the listening skills needed by a teacher different from or similar to those needed by business employees who want to establish good relationships with colleagues and customers?

COLLABORATIVE WRITING AND WORKING IN GROUPS

These problems are the first of a continuing series of assignments planned for collaborative planning, writing, and oral presentations. (Many of the other problems included at the end of each chapter can also be adapted for group work according to the time available and the directions of your instructor.)

20 Form into groups of two. Meet with someone with whom you are not already acquainted, preferably someone you have never seen before entering this class. Spend 10 or 12 minutes (or the time limit set by your instructor) in becoming acquainted with your classmate. Introduce your friend to your instructor and to your classmates, much as you would introduce a speaker at a conference or at another speaking engagement. Tell the class something about this person, perhaps some of the information described in Problem 1.

21 Listening Practice: Meet in groups of four, five, or six. Each person tells his or her name,

including correct spelling, to the others, with several items of personal information, such as major, employment, hobbies or school activities, and goals. After each student has given this information, all members of the group should recall as much as possible about the other members by writing notes about the material they have just heard and then checking their notes for completeness and accuracy. The verified information should be kept for review before the next class meeting, at which time you will greet each one of your group by name.

22 Consider a *handshake* in relation to the discussion of nonverbal communication presented in Chapter 1. Using the terms in the chapter (kinesics, proxemics, and so on), describe how these areas of nonverbal communication enter into a handshake.

23 Form into groups of three or four. Select someone to serve as recorder. Identify as many communication barriers as possible within the time allowed by your instructor. For each barrier identified, provide at least two specific examples that illustrate miscommunication opportunities. As directed by your instructor, either submit your group's list and examples or present specific barriers identified during a class discussion.

24 Meet in a group of three or four students. Individually, list three nonverbal gestures that annoy you. Take turns in the group and share one item on your list, illustrating the particular gesture. Do the other members of the group share the same interpretation of the gesture? Summarize your group's observations for the rest of the class.

THINK-IT-THROUGH ASSIGNMENT [SUMMARIZING]

25 After you have written a short description of an instance of miscommunication, as instructed in Problem 6, meet with two or three class members to compare your descriptions. Decide how each bit of miscommunication relates to a common barrier or barriers to communication, such as differing perceptions, poor listening, inaccurate interpretation of language, or other barriers mentioned in Chapter 1.

   Prepare a summary in oral or written form as directed by your instructor. A suggested arrangement of this particular summary is as follows:
   a. Title
   b. Summarize overall differences; for example, if four of the five instances of miscommunication concern listening, this infor-

mation should be included in Paragraph 1. If most of the instances of miscommunication occurred because of differing meaning of words or interpretations of nonverbal communication, a statement to this effect may be included in the first paragraph, with details listed in following paragraphs.
   c. Devote a short paragraph to the example furnished by each group member.
   d. End with a closing paragraph that relates appropriately to the preceding paragraphs. (This summary may be prepared by the group or individually after meeting with the group.)

26 Adapt Problem 2, "Comments and Bits of Information," to a group assignment, much as the instructions for Problem 25.

ENDNOTES

1 *The Commercial Appeal* (Memphis) May 12, 1996, C3.

2 *The Commercial Appeal* (Memphis) May 12, 1996, C3.

3 Claud Shannon and Warren Weaver, *The Mathematical Theory of Communication* (Urbana: University of Illinois Press, 1949), 7.

4 David Berlo, *The Process of Communication* (New York: Holt, Rinehart and Winston, 1960), 12.

5 Beverly Davenport Sypher, Robert N. Bostrom, and Joy Hart Seibert, "Listening, Communication Abilities, and Success at Work," *The Journal of Business Communication*, 26 (Fall 1989): 293–301.

6 John W. Haas and Christa L. Arnold, "An Examination of the Role of Listening in Judgments of Communication Competence in Co-Workers," *The Journal of Business Communication*, 32 (April 1995): 123–139.

7 Ralph G. Nichols and Leonard A. Stevens, *Are You Listening?* (New York: McGraw-Hill, 1957), 104–111.

8 Jurgen Ruesch and Weldon Kees, *Nonverbal Communication* (Berkeley: University of California Press, 1970), 189.

9 Edward T. Hall, *The Hidden Dimension* (Garden City, NY: Doubleday, 1966).

10 R. Ardrey, *The Territorial Imperative* (New York: Atheneum, 1966).

11 Edward T. Hall, *The Silent Language* (Garden City, NY: Doubleday, 1959), 23.

Communication Within and From the Organization

CHAPTER

2

OBJECTIVES

Chapter Two will help you:

1 Identify and explain the differences between formal and informal communication networks within an organization.

2 Obtain an overview of communication from an organization.

3 Explain the importance of feedback.

4 Discuss the importance of ethics and values within an organization.

5 List and discuss five contemporary issues affecting organizational communication.

COMMUNICATION WITHIN AND FROM THE ORGANIZATION

Communication cannot be considered a separate part of organizational management. In other words, management consists of communication.

Communication affects every decision and almost every activity; it is perhaps the single most vital force within any organization. It includes not only human communication, as the term is ordinarily used, but the management of communications technology—computers, e-mail, voice mail, databases, and all the other technical equipment of the modern electronic office.

Clerical jobs, supervisory work, sales, and advertising are made up almost completely of communication activities. Accountants communicate with figures and graphic presentations as well as with spoken and written words. Advertising writers send messages to the world through television, radio, print media, and the Internet. Public relations specialists try to present their organizations in the best possible way. Receptionists greet visitors and through their words and nonverbal communication reflect the image of the company they represent.

Employees throughout most organizations write at least some letters and memorandums. (Traditional memorandums have been replaced in many instances by e-mail or voice mail.) Researchers write reports and other documents. Managers and other personnel conduct meetings. Writers prepare newsletters, instruction manuals, and promotional material. E-mail, voice mail, and telephone calls flow between workers in all departments and at all levels. Supervisors write instructional material and provide face-to-face guidance. Employees teach each other.

Effective communication will be essential to your career, whatever your chosen field. As illustrated in Chapter 1, studies show that employers and potential employers value communication ability more than any other ability, even more than specialized technical skills.

The principles of general communication discussed in Chapter 1—why and how we communicate, causes of miscommunication, listening, and nonverbal communication—apply to your communication at work, whether you are a beginner or nearing retirement. After all, an organization is made up of *individuals*, and you will communicate to other individuals, not to a corporation. Your writing, speaking, reading, listening, and thinking will greatly affect your entire career and your professional relationships with your supervisors and your co-workers.

COMMUNICATION WITHIN THE ORGANIZATION

Internal communication moves *downward*, *upward*, *horizontally*, or randomly through the *grapevine*. Downward communication is used to coordinate efforts and activities, to instruct, to direct, or to explain company decisions or policies. Upward communication is usually for the purpose of keeping management informed. Horizontal communication flows between employees of approximately the same level of responsibility. A grapevine is an informal communication network.

▶ EFFECTIVE DOWNWARD COMMUNICATION

Written messages that move downward consist of memorandums, instruction sheets, policy statements, newsletters, motivational material, and various other communications that are necessary to keep personnel informed about what is going on and to build or maintain their goodwill. Downward oral communication consists of information presented in departmental or company-wide meetings, and, perhaps most important, in face-to-face conversation.

In order to clarify and classify the kinds of downward communication according to purpose, the following distinctions are made:

1 *Internal downward communication is used to instruct workers.* Information and instructions must flow downward so that employees know exactly what is expected of them and what they can expect from the company. They must know their duties, responsibilities, rights, and opportunities.

According to Roger D'Aprix et al., employees need definitive answers to the following questions:

1 What am I expected to do on this job?

2 Am I performing appropriately?

3 Does anyone care about me in this organization?

4 What are we [the company] up to, and how are we doing?

5 What is our [the company] charter and how does that charter match up to other functions?

D'Aprix goes on to say that only when all of these primary questions have been answered satisfactorily will the employee ask, "How Can I Help?"[1]

For the new employee, extensive training periods, consisting of on-the-job training and perhaps of classroom instruction, are necessary for orientation to company policies and procedures and the responsibilities of a particular position.

The efforts of management toward the new employee are a vital factor in determining the employee's contributions to the organization, as well as to his or her job satisfaction and career development. In addition, effective communication must continue throughout the employee's career, whatever the position or its level.

Perhaps the most important form of communication to employees at any level, or at any time in their career, is the daily face-to-face communication between the employee and the supervisor, as well as with other management personnel. Employees also receive much instruction from co-workers at their own level and even from those below their level; for example, secretaries instruct managers, particularly newly employed ones, about details of company operations. Computer specialists may teach executives how to operate new computers or software.

2 *Downward communication builds and maintains employee morale and goodwill toward the organization and toward management personnel.* Employees have questions about promotions, salary increases, working conditions, and the goals and plans of the organization as a whole. They need to feel that they are a part of a worthwhile, progressive organization to which they are contributing, part of an organization in which their value as individuals is appreciated and paid for.

Some of the media used for instruction and morale building are company magazines and newsletters, bulletin board announcements, annual reports to employees, meetings, family days, and various individual communications, such as interviews, letters, and face-to-face communication between management personnel and workers.

3   *Downward communication keeps the routine and special activities of the organization moving smoothly and efficiently.* This purpose is accomplished through the use of many methods and media, both written and oral. In many instances, this purpose is also an instructional one, although at times the organization is kept moving by seeking information and opinions, not merely by sending messages.

Ann Chadwell Humphries, of the Knight-Ridder News Service, made this statement in an article entitled, "Information Vital to Get Job Done": "Keep people informed. When employees are asked what they need to know to perform well, one of the early things they volunteer is 'Keep us informed.' This isn't new, but we must often relearn lessons."[2]

4   *Downward communication asks for and encourages upward communication, or feedback.* (*Feedback* is discussed in Chapter 1.) Accurate and complete feedback, however, is not always received. Some hesitant workers do not wish to report negative information; if something is going wrong, they fear they will be blamed. Such negative information can be the most valuable of all. Mistakes cannot be corrected if they are unknown and ignored.

On the other hand, employee input is not always encouraged. A survey of 5,000 workers, completed by the Wyatt Company in Boston, reported these results: Only 40 percent said that management seeks their input on important issues, and 25 percent said that they have no freedom to express opinions. On an even more discouraging note, a 1988 survey of 32,000 employees in 26 business organizations revealed that only about half of the employees thought that company communications were candid and accurate, and that company messages were strictly from the top down. Respondents to this survey most often cited their immediate supervisors as their primary source of information, followed by the grapevine.[3]

According to Patrice Johnson, an effective system of downward communication known as *team briefing* is largely ignored in corporate America. In team briefing, information is regularly conveyed to small work groups throughout the organization, from level to level, beginning at the top. Unlike most methods of keeping people informed, team briefing is formal and structured.[4]

Newsletters and employee magazines are widely used through organizations of all kinds. In the late 1800s, National Cash Register (NCR) introduced the NCR Factory News. Now the number of such publications is estimated to be about 25,000 in the United States and Canada.[5]

COMMUNICATION brief

Where does it start, this fear of writing that plagues so many of us? In 12 years as a professional communicator, I've watched countless people wince at the thought of committing their ideas to paper. And while I'm glad to lend a hand, I believe that businesses that take an active role in upgrading their employees' writing skills will, at the same time, improve such important areas as teamwork, attitude, and productivity.

Good communication has a direct impact on your company's bottom line. Effective word choice increases motivation, sales, and success. Communication departments know this. Marketing departments know this. And researchers are confirming this. According to a recent *Wall Street Journal* article, a study by two University of Michigan researchers revealed that well-chosen words in company documents create a positive perception of employers by their employees.

This is no surprise. What's troubling is that so many employees are simply unable to write better.

"Write to the Bottom Line" by Ellen Zimmerman as appeared in *Communication World,* September 1992, p. 42. Reprinted by permission of Ellen Zimmerman, President, The Zimmerman Group (Advertising Agency).

Harmonious professional relationships play a key role in on-the-job communication tasks, especially when the employees are involved in collaborative projects.

Rick Barnhardt, a vice president with U.S. Food Service, said that the company has developed a newsletter that allows us to convey what we value: customer service, safety, employee recognition, and truthfulness. Before the newsletters, company leaders spent much time correcting misinformation conveyed through the grapevine.[6]

Workers at all levels are motivated by communication that assures them of the company's interest in them. They are also motivated by sincere efforts to inform and instruct—about organizational plans, benefits, policies, and newsworthy events. If such an open and nonsecretive policy of communication is to flourish, it must be established by top management and accepted by employees.

A policy of open communication not only strengthens morale but also encourages the flow of vital information, opinions, and criticisms. Good intent, however, is not enough. Poor skills and techniques can lead to poor communication and communication systems. (Your course in business communication and this textbook are planned to help you understand and develop these skills and techniques.)

EFFECTIVE UPWARD COMMUNICATION

As an example of upward communication in a college or university, professors report to department heads, who report to the dean of the college, who reports to a vice president or to the president of the institution. The president reports to a board of regents or to another controlling committee or body.

The upward flow of communication, often in the form of formal and informal reports, furnishes data and recommendations on which intelligent decisions can be made. Upward communication can be complete only in the presence of effective downward communication.

At General Dynamics, the general manager uses "walk-throughs" and small meetings that allow him to converse with assembly line workers in order to receive their suggestions. IBM uses a mail-in system, "Speak up," which allows employees to obtain individual responses to their questions from high-level managers while maintaining their anonymity. Anheuser-Busch and Eastman Kodak have similar programs.[7]

Such meetings and mail-in systems give employees an opportunity to express their concerns and suggestions, which may be extremely valuable. On the other hand, such activities cut heavily into a chief executive's time. If such systems are put into effect, employees should receive prompt responses. If they do not do so, morale may be decreased, not strengthened.

The appropriateness and efficiency of the channels of internal communication are essential to good organizational management. Communication is an important motivating force. Communication is also necessary to enable every person to have the information and instructions that he or she needs in order to perform assigned and related duties.

▶ **HORIZONTAL COMMUNICATION**

Horizontal communication occurs through committee meetings, face-to-face conversations, telephone calls, e-mail, and voice mail. Employees may also communicate with one another through various forms of written messages; for example, members assigned to committees or working together on a group project report to one another.

Sharing of information and ideas strengthens interpersonal relationships and minimizes conflict. Cooperating with workers from various departments promotes understanding and reduces difficulties in solving problems.

▶ **THE GRAPEVINE**

The grapevine (also called grapevine telegraph) is defined in dictionaries by such words as "a person-to-person method of spreading rumors, gossip, information, by informal or unofficial conversation, letter writing, or the like," or "The grapevine is the informal and unsanctioned information network in any organization."

Keith Davis (a pioneer researcher and writer on the subject) discovered in his studies that the organizational grapevine is an expression of healthy human motivation to communicate. Davis stated that if employees are so uninterested in their work that they do not engage in shop talk about it, they are probably maladjusted.[8]

The grapevine may carry far more information than formal networks do. Although some of the information consists of gossip, rumors, and half truths, much is based on fact. According to a study by CPA Administrative Reports, the grapevine is from 75 to 95 percent accurate and provides managers and staff with better information than formal communication.[9]

Vanessa Arnold writes: "In a normal work situation, upward of 80 percent that comes over the grapevine is accurate. But a communication may be 90 percent correct in details, but that 10 percent is often the most important part of the message." Ms. Arnold goes on to say that managers should use information from the grapevine to improve communication throughout the firm.[10]

An example of accurate information that spread through the grapevine at Upjohn turned out to be true. Massive kickbacks were being given to foreign governments by the company's international division.[11]

The grapevine supplements information supplied through formal channels. Although some of the information from the grapevine is untrue, effective managers realize that they should work with it, not against it, to obtain and provide accurate information throughout the organization.

Rumors are most likely to be spread at times of stress; for example, when a company is downsizing or planning to move to another city. Anxiety is spread from person to person through the grapevine. When the information is incorrect, damage can occur to both morale and productivity.

The best way to eliminate or decrease undesirable effects of the grapevine is for management to maintain an open policy of communication so that

COMMUNICATION
brief

The word *grapevine* appeared in 1863 as meaning a Civil War rumor or unsubstanti-ated bit of news, sometimes being shortened to *grape* by 1864. Such news came by the *grapevine telegraph*, any surreptitious means of transmitting information so it wouldn't be intercepted, as between army units, between a soldier and his family, or between prisoners of war in a military prison, and stems from the construction of makeshift secret telegraph lines like, or perhaps disguised as, vines.

Stuart Berg Fletcher, *Listening to America* (New York: Simon & Schuster, 1982), 77.

employees feel that they are being kept informed. Even better, they should feel that they have a part in making decisions affecting the organizations to which they have devoted part of their lives.

COMMUNICATION FROM THE ORGANIZATION

External communication takes many of the same forms and has some of the same purposes as internal communication. Customers and the public receive directions and instructions about the use of the company's products or services. The organization receives and sends information to customers, stockholders, the public, and government agencies in order to plan and to proceed with manufacturing, selling, and promotional activities.

Customer or potential customer communication includes retail and whole-sale selling by personal contact, telephone conversations, written messages, and various kinds of advertising and public relations releases. Other purposes of customer communication are instructions about credit, collection mes-sages, and the adjustment of claims and complaints. A major part of external communication efforts is directed toward building and maintaining goodwill.

Voice mail, facsimile transmission, and electronic mail are widely used in external communication, as in internal communication. These methods, if wisely planned and used, can be both economical and effective. If they are not wisely planned and used, opposite results occur.

The cost of written correspondence has been increasing each year for a number of years, as have all methods of communication from a business orga-nization. Regardless of cost, wisely planned and well-written business letters remain an important method of communicating to readers outside an organi-zation. For many occasions, individually addressed and personally written let-ters are the only appropriate choice. They are more personal and private, and they imply importance and special consideration. (At times personal letters are sent to employees, as well as to readers outside the company.)

Electronic transmissions, including faxes and e-mail, are quicker and usually less expensive than individually prepared business letters. (Regular mail is often referred to as "snail mail.") Faxes and e-mail, however, are not appropriate for many business and personal occasions.

E-mail messages are conversational and often hastily written. Although a conversational tone is a desirable attribute in both e-mail and business letters, informal wording and an unprofessional approach is carried too far in some e-mail and faxes. Included in a 1995 article by Robert E. Calem are these words:

> Because e-mail tends to be conversational, and used when a person is trying to juggle a lot of tasks, it lends itself to hasty usage. It can turn around and bite you in the same way as an office memo. Therefore, e-mail must be as carefully composed as a letter or it could be misunderstood. If you have strong words to deliver, e-mail is not the best way.[12]

Principles of effective writing and speaking, as presented in Parts II and III, apply to all communication, including forms of electronic transmission.

ETHICS AND VALUES AS THEY RELATE TO COMMUNICATION

Ethics is receiving an ever-increasing emphasis in business, education, and government. (Most people have always given lip service to ethics—after all, who would want to be accused of opposing ethics?)

Codes of ethics have been in existence for centuries, but at this time they are increasing in number or being updated and revised. Some universities encourage the inclusion of ethics in all core courses in order to follow the recommendations of the American Assembly of Collegiate Schools of Business (AACSB).

Kenneth R. Andrews, editor of *Ethics in Practice*, makes this statement:

> Public interest in ethics as a critical aspect of business behavior comes and goes. As the 1990s overtake us, this interest is at an historic high. Stimulated by press attention to blatant derelictions in Wall Street, the defense industry, and the Pentagon, and to questionable activities in the White House, the attorney general's office, and the Congress, many people wonder whether our society is sicker than we suspect.[13]

Business managers and government officials realize that the lack of ethical behavior anywhere in the organization adversely affects the organization and thus all its members. Those who want to improve conditions don't know how to do so, as could be expected. Some believe that adults cannot be taught the ethical principles and behavior that would have been easier learned as a child. (When ethical behavior is mentioned, remember that *behavior* includes *communication*.)

WHAT IS MEANT BY ETHICS?

Ethics is defined by dictionaries as a set of moral principles; rules of conduct recognized in respect to a particular class of human actions or a particular group or culture; or the moral principles of an individual. Dictionaries also mention that ethics is a branch of philosophy dealing with values relating to human conduct.

The trouble with definitions is that *right* and *wrong*, *values* and *ethics*, do not mean the same to all people or to all cultures or groups of people. Our understanding of the meaning of ethics is affected by our backgrounds, by previous experiences, and, especially, by the values that were learned long before we entered a college classroom.

Some actions are considered by many people to be unethical, even though they are not illegal. For example, at one time slavery and Jim Crow laws were established by state law. Throughout history, discrimination against particular groups of people, if not actually established by law, have not been illegal. Conscientious citizens want to obey all laws, but they do not wish to condone actions that in their minds are wrong. What are they to do?

> Charles Garfield defines business ethics in this way: "Ethics is the set of written and unwritten moral principles by which a company operates at a core level. A company's ethics determines how it treats employees, customers, and suppliers; how it develops products and processes; and how it participates in the larger community."[14]

Some companies define ethics by their actions. For example, Levi Strauss spent a great deal of money to reduce below government standards the

formaldehyde levels in the finish of its Sta-Prest pants. The company did so because it had a policy of monitoring all chemicals used by suppliers to discover any potential for harm. Levi Strauss went beyond the legal requirements to ensure that it was "doing what was right."[15]

Other companies especially concerned with ethics are Hewlett-Packard, Digital Equipment, and Silicone Graphics. Each of the three received the sixth annual business ethics award in 1994, sponsored by *Business Ethics Magazine*. The winners were cited for their environmental records, affirmative action records, education awareness programs for AIDS and Alzheimer's, and charitable donations, among other actions and programs.[16]

Winners of the 1995 Business Ethics Award, sponsored by Sears and the *Business Ethics Magazine*, were Home Depot, Odwalla, and Xerox. Home Depot, the Atlanta-based retailer, donated $8 billion in 1995, or about 2 percent of its pretax profit, to community programs. Odwalla received the award for outstanding corporate environmentalism, and Xerox received the award for outstanding workplace diversity.[17]

Winners of the 1996 Business Ethics Award were GM, Reebok, and BankAmerica. GM won for its environmental work. Reebok was cited for human rights work. BankAmerica was honored for "general excellence in ethics."[18]

HOW CAN WE DETERMINE ETHICAL CONDUCT, DECISIONS, AND COMMUNICATION?

Even with the best intentions, we cannot always determine the most ethical course of action. We may feel that we must choose the lesser of two evils.

Numerous if not most professional organizations have written and formally accepted official codes of ethics. Such organizations include, among many others, auditors, professional secretaries, and the American Association of University Professors. Perhaps through your own professional organization you have read a code of ethics planned for your particular occupation. Such a code of ethics, however, will not solve all problems or answer all your questions.

If you work for an organization, you owe loyalty to that organization. You also have an obligation to yourself and to your family; to the public, especially the consumers of your company's product or services; to your co-workers; to shareholders; and to society overall, including the global society. For instance, would you advise your company to ship to overseas markets products that are illegal in the United States because of their harmful effect on users? Would you want to write sales or advertising material for products, regardless of where they are sold, that you believe to be harmful?

Laura L. Nash in "Ethics without the Sermon" lists 12 questions to be answered when trying to make ethical decisions:

1 Have you defined the problem accurately?

2 How would you define the problem if you stood on the other side of the fence?

3 How did this situation occur in the first place?

4 To whom and to what do you give your loyalty as a person and as a member of the corporation?

5 What is your intention in making this decision?

6 How does this decision compare with probable results?

7 Whom could your decision or action injure?

8 Can you discuss the problem with the affected parties before you make your decision?

9 Are you confident that your position will be as valid over a long period of time as it seems now?

10 Could you disclose without qualm your decision or action to your boss, your CEO, the board of directors, your family, society as a whole?

11 What is the symbolic potential of your action if understood? If misunderstood?

12 Under what conditions would you allow exceptions to your stand?[19]

Typical ethical problems are these, as listed in *Public Personnel Management*:

1 Pollution control

2 False advertising

3 "Let George Do It" philosophy

4 Supporting harmful products

5 Cheating by wasting time and money

6 Pilfering—taking home pens, paper, paper clips, and so on, for personal use

7 Not being willing to give of self for company

8 "Nice guys finish last" syndrome

9 "Knocking" the company's products, policies, and the like

10 Using sick leave for vacation breaks

11 Calling in sick in order to care for sick child

12 Taking personal telephone calls or reading magazines on company time

13 Using the company's computer or copying machine for personal projects

14 "Padding" expense accounts[20]

Perhaps taking paper clips for your own use seems too minor to mention, especially as compared to insider trading and embezzlement of millions of dollars. But the cost to American businesses for supplies taken for personal use of employees is estimated to be $120 billion a year.[21]

▶ HOW DOES ETHICS RELATE TO BUSINESS WRITING AND SPEECH?

Whether or not we wish to do so, we influence others through language, and we are influenced by the language of others. The basic principle of general semantics, as taught by Albert Korzybski, S. I. Hayakawa, and others, is that language affects behavior. R. M. Weaver states that all language is "sermonic" and that "we have no sooner uttered words than we have given impulse to other people to look at the world, or some small part of it, in our way."[22]

Skillful writers and speakers can use words honestly and beneficially; they can also use language for their own purposes, not for true communication. This fact has been illustrated over and over again by demagogues who have swayed entire nations by skillful appeal to the emotions and prejudices of their listeners. Some politicians attempt to do so today.

In organizational communication, as in personal interchange of thoughts and ideas between individuals, we must keep in mind that we are socially and morally responsible for the content and effect of our messages. Examples of social responsibility, or lack of it, have been widely discussed in relation to advertising and mass communication, and laws have been passed to prevent deceptive methods of communication.

Another ethical issue concerns *plagiarism*, which is the theft of someone else's words or ideas. Whether or not such material is published or copyrighted, you have an ethical and professional obligation to give credit where credit is due. *When you do not give credit, plagiarism occurs—both when you use the exact words of another and when you paraphrase someone else's words.*

To *paraphrase* is to restate a passage in order to keep the same meaning in different words or sentence structure. An example of paraphrasing is illustrated in the two passages below:

ORIGINAL PASSAGE

Even statements of general knowledge, used without documentation, result in plagiarism when you change a few words and pass the work as your own.

PARAPHRASED PASSAGE

When you read statements in the works of others, even statements of general knowledge, you are plagiarizing when you change only a few words and pass the work as your own.

An exception to the rule of documentation is a statement of general knowledge. For example, if you say that computers have brought many changes to the business world, you have made a statement that everyone except Rip Van Winkle already knows. In such instances you need not credit any *particular* source (although you may wish to do so, either for explanation or credibility). On the other hand, if you use a *particular* passage that you have drawn from another source, complete documentation must be given.

Plagiarism occurs when you use another person's work unfairly. This means work of any kind, including paintings, photographs, songs, television programs, letters, or lectures.

Colleges and universities stipulate severe penalties for plagiarism, ranging from failure in a particular class to permanent expulsion from school.

Although you should read, consider, and perhaps use the work of others, either give credit or use your own words. When in doubt that the information used is general knowledge, give credit.

For further discussion about methods of documentation, fair-use laws, and plagiarism, see Chapter 13, under "Documentating Secondary and Primary Sources: Legal and Ethical Considerations."

CONTEMPORARY AND CONTINUING CONCERNS OF ORGANIZATIONAL COMMUNICATION

The following section is included in this chapter for two purposes: to emphasize and summarize important areas and problems of communication within an organization and to provide an overview of how these areas and problems are presented and discussed throughout this book.

With the exception of innovations in communication technology, these concerns are not new. They have existed throughout the history of organizations; they existed long before business organizations themselves, as we now use the term. All these areas are aspects of human cooperation, understanding, responsibility, honesty, fairness, and harmonious personal and professional relationships. All require knowledge of the subject upon which a particular communication is based. All require the effective use of written and spoken language.

These concerns are described as contemporary because they are now receiving more attention in organizations of all kinds, including government agencies and colleges and universities, than they had in past decades. Students, managers, and workers at all levels realize that true education, including preparation for a vocation, consists of far more than specialized details and technical skills.

ETHICAL AND LEGAL CONSIDERATIONS

Because of their utmost importance, ethical considerations have been discussed earlier in this chapter, along with mention of legal questions. Ethical and legal considerations are discussed further in relevant chapters.

Legal considerations relate to numerous areas of business communication, including employee rights, sales and advertising, credit and collections, equal opportunity for job applicants, the right to privacy, and avoiding defamation. Other laws pertain to plagiarism and copyright ownership. These legal topics and others are included in relevant chapters, interwoven into the text or presented in separate sections.

INTERCULTURAL COMMUNICATION

Intercultural communication is also referred to as *cross-cultural communication*. It is important to remember, however, that intercultural communication is not synonymous with *international* communication; *intercultural* is the broader term. Much intercultural communication occurs between people who have never left the United States (or any other country in which the communication occurs) because differing cultures exist side by side in the same city or on the same block. *Intercultural* describes communication that involves almost everyone at work, at school, and in home communities. It is almost certain to occur when we travel abroad, an event that also involves *international* communication.

However the terms are defined, basic principles are the same. We need to learn as much as possible about different cultures, including their customs and value systems.

Chapter 17, "Intercultural Communication," is devoted entirely to the topic, as are portions of other chapters, both in discussion and in questions and cases. One of many examples of text material is the appearance of letters and expression of dates as they are used in countries outside the United States, as shown in Appendix A. Another topic is the discussion of formality and informality in the United States as compared to other countries; this information is included in Chapter 4, "Choosing Appropriate and Effective Words."

CHANGING COMMUNICATION TECHNOLOGY

Technology, like other major topics previously mentioned, also enters into chapters other than Chapter 3, "Communicating with the Aid of Technology." One example is the use of computerized databases, included with the study of research and report writing. Illustrations of screens from word processing packages are shown in Chapter 5 with the discussion of readability and sentence construction.

Although computers and other equipment speed the preparation, transmission, and reception of messages, human thought expressed through written and spoken words is most important of all. Improving this ability is the primary purpose of all chapters.

▶ COLLABORATIVE WRITING AND WORKING IN GROUPS

In many organizations, important communication projects are planned or written by a group, not by individuals alone. Even if material is individually written, it is often submitted to others for evaluation or editing. Consideration of how to approach problems that will eventually be solved by written or oral communication may be done by committees. Parts of long reports may be written by individuals, then combined for the complete report.

Questions and problems at the end of every chapter in this book can be used for collaborative planning and writing. Some are especially appropriate for group work and are so designated with specific instructions for work in process and the finished product. In addition, students are asked to provide feedback on work previously done by other students, similar to the way that an individual's work would be read in an organization before it is submitted to the final reader. Oral communication, such as a meeting or an important speech, may also be planned by a group.

In addition to the benefits of combining efforts on an assignment or project of some kind, participants practice communication skills while working in groups. (Students, you will enjoy these activities.)

These employees enjoying a break from work may also be contributing to the organization's grapevine.

▶ **HARMONIOUS PERSONAL AND PROFESSIONAL RELATIONSHIPS**

Successful personal and professional relationships, first of all, depend upon the character and the personality of the persons involved. Other factors enter in, however. A person can be filled with good intentions and not "come across" because of a lack of ability to relate to other people—or because of a lack of effective communication.

Textbooks or college courses will not in themselves perfect all human relationships. (Did you ever know anyone who was in perfect harmony with everyone else every hour of the day?) Nevertheless, ideal personal and professional relationships should receive major emphasis in any course about human communication.

SUMMARY

Management techniques and abilities are for the most part communication techniques and abilities.

Formal and informal communication networks exist in all organizations. The informal network is described as the grapevine, which has both desirable and undesirable effects. The best way for managers to eliminate or decrease undesirable effects of the grapevine is to maintain an open policy of communication. When possible, employees should be given an opportunity to have a part in making decisions that affect their company and themselves.

An effective communication system provides for feedback. The effectiveness of upward communication depends on the quality of downward communication, and vice versa.

A sound and workable system of communication is based on openness and honesty. Without trust and confidence, there can be no real communication. Ethical communication practices are essential for an enduring and successful business enterprise.

Other areas of special concern and emphasis, as they pertain to communication, are international and intercultural communication; changing technology; the encouragement of collaborative planning, working, and writing; and harmonious personal and professional relationships.

TEST YOURSELF

chapter content

1 The informal communication network is known as the _____.
2 What are four purposes of downward communication?
3 A response to communication is known as _____.
4 What are five important concerns of organizational communication?
5 Which of the five areas of concern do you consider the most important? Why? Do you consider any one the least important? If so, why?
6 What is your opinion of how harmonious personal and professional relationships are affected by language?
7 According to your text, what is the estimated accuracy rate of material communicated through the grapevine?
8 If you were a manager, would you make an attempt to eliminate the grapevine in your organization or department? Why or why not?

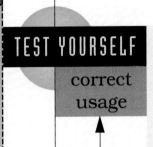

TEST YOURSELF

correct usage

(Related to material in Chapter 2 and principles of correct usage discussed in Appendix D.) Insert all necessary punctuation, including quotation marks, hyphens, and apostrophes. Remove punctuation that has been inserted incorrectly. Choose correct word from each pair or group.

1 Much of a (company's, companies, companies') communication efforts are directed toward building goodwill with (its, it's) customers and increasing (employe, employee) (moral, morale.)
2 Informal oral communication within an organization includes face to face communication telephone calls and voice mail.
3 The United States Postal Service which is the nations largest civilian employer delivers more than 160 billion pieces of mail annually.
4 Within an organization communication flows upward downward or horizontally, these communications are both oral and written.
5 Three important management issues are these intercultural communication changing technology and ethical considerations.
6 Although e-mail is faster than "snail mail" it is less personal and private.
7 The word *grapevine* was used to describe tangled telegraph wires that resembled grapevines. During the Civil War.
8 Written memorandums are used less often than (formally, formerly) because of e-mail.

PROBLEMS AND CASES

Note: End-of-chapter questions and problems throughout this book may be used in various ways according to your preference and the instructions of your professor. Although assignments are divided into three sections—"Problems and Cases," "Collaborative Writing and Working in Groups," and "Think-It-Through Assignments"—many from each group may be used as if they were listed in another group. All assignments at the end of chapters throughout the book may be used in this way. For example, almost any problem can be used, with modifications, for group work; and those described as group assignments may be completed individually. In addition, many assignments at the end of Chapters 1 and 2, along with some other chapters, can be appropriately expanded into formal research reports to be prepared with your study of Part V, "Communicating through Reports."

(*Further Note:* The preceding instructions were first given in Chapter 1; they are repeated here for emphasis and to increase the likelihood that they will not be overlooked. Although they apply to all future chapters, they will not be repeated again.)

1 If you are presently employed or have been in the past, what do (or did) your communication responsibilities include? What do you expect your future responsibilities to be in the career you hope to build?

2 Have you seen harmful or helpful occurrences because of a grapevine? Discuss.

3 Expand on this statement, agreeing or disagreeing according to your beliefs. Justify your position. "As much as possible, employees should be given the opportunity to participate in the decision-making process."

4 "Comments and Bits of Information" Assignment: (See instructions in "Questions and Problems" section of Chapter 1.) Be prepared to step to the front of the classroom and present in one minute a comment or bit of information about any topic discussed in Chapter 2. Your source can be published material, radio or television, an interview with a businessperson, or your own personal experience or observation. Do not use your present textbook except in relation to material obtained from some other source. Prepare a written summary of your presentation according to the directions of your instructor.

5 Write a code of ethics for employees in the kind of organization where you hope to work. (*Note:* A code of ethics is extremely important; it is a document that requires a great deal of thought. The code of ethics you write now, as well as the one for Problem 6, will no doubt be a preliminary one that you will want to revise later. Nevertheless, putting your present ideas into written words will strengthen your understanding of the importance of an ethical code of conduct, including written and spoken words, for your personal and professional life.)

6 Write a code of ethics for the management of the kind of organization for which you hope to work.

7 What are some ethical questions that have arisen because of developments in communication technology? Discuss.

8 Describe the upward and downward communication within your company (or an organization you belong to if you are not employed). What channels are used for different types of communication? How often are the downward and upward channels used? Are the channels being used effectively? What could you suggest to improve the company's communication?

9 As a student, you are involved with both upward and downward communication in the

university setting. In addition to communication between you and your instructor, what channels of upward communication are available to you? For what purposes? How often do you use these upward channels? How effective are they?

10 (Your instructor may wish to use this assignment, or to continue it, with the study of Chapter 3, which is devoted entirely to communication technology.) Interview a computer system manager and determine the most pressing ethics and legality issues in relation to electronic mail, voice mail, Internet usage, and the World Wide Web. Then interview two computer users and ask them the same questions. Compare and contrast answers provided. If available, submit a short summary of your findings via electronic mail to your instructor. If your e-mail system allows, provide a brief cover memo and send a two- to three-paragraph summary of your findings as an e-mail attachment.

11 Talk with someone of a different age group. Ask the individual's opinions about whether business ethics are improving or deteriorating. Share some of your own concerns about business ethics and legality issues. Do the two of you share the same observations? What specific ethics concerns do the two of you have in regard to written and oral communication? Do you share similar or different concerns regarding computer legality and ethics issues? As directed by your instructor, summarize your findings orally in class or in a written report.

12 Complete the assignment described in Problem 11, but talk with someone from a different country.

13 What communication channel would you use to communicate each of the following?
   a. Information about a scheduled renovation of all offices in the building, starting date for the renovation, and actions each employee must take prior to the renovation date.
   b. Information about a company picnic.
   c. An air-conditioning leak that is soaking the carpet in your office.
   d. Changes in procedures for the company's electronic purchase order system.
   e. A weekly progress report to your supervisor; you are currently out of town, but the progress report must be submitted by 8 A.M. tomorrow.

14 Numerous companies are focusing on continuous quality improvement within the organization. In your present or past employment, has the company taken any steps to improve the quality of the organization's communication? Explain.

15 Each semester you must register for courses for the following semester. How can your college or university improve communication during the registration process?

16 Consider your present or past supervisor, a colleague, or some other business or professional person (perhaps a teacher) whom you respect and admire. Does your opinion of this person reflect your belief that he or she is honest and trustworthy? Does he or she have good communication skills? (Discuss or prepare a written reply to this question as your instructor directs. You need not use the individual's name. This problem also adapts well to group discussion or reporting.)

17 Identify major ethical issues that affect communication with employees, stockholders, customers, suppliers, creditors, government, and society.

18 Is it ethical to inflate information on a resume? Explain.

COLLABORATIVE WRITING AND WORKING IN GROUPS

19 In groups of four to six, generate a list of example communication situations where job pressures may result in employees compromising their ethical principles.

20 Are ethical concerns different for accountants, economists, general managers, human resource managers, computer programmers and analysts, and computer end users? Talk with someone you know who is employed in one of these fields about ethical concerns related to key communication activities on the job. Then team with two or three classmates who interviewed people from different fields and compare answers. Share your findings with the entire class or prepare a short written summary as your instructor directs.

21 Write a scenario of a communication action that could have ethical implications for the writer and/or the employing company. Then meet in groups of three or four and share your scenarios. What is the consensus as to the ethics and/or legality of the communication? Share your findings with the class.

22 Meet with four or five other students in your class. Share and compare experiences about some organization with which you are familiar, a business, club, church, or professional group. One member of the group should act as chairperson, another as secretary and recorder. Consider these questions: What are the strengths and weaknesses of the internal communication system? What media are used in internal communication? Compose a short written summary. Consider this arrangement:

Paragraph 1. Begin with a summarizing paragraph that includes the overall gist of the discussion; for example, "The strength of internal communication mentioned most often in Group I was _____; the most often mentioned weakness was _____. The most frequently used media are _____."

Paragraph 2. Include lists of other information; for example, "Other strengths": (followed by a list); "Other weaknesses": (followed by a list).

Paragraph 3. "Other media used in internal communication are these": (followed by a list).

Paragraph 4. "Committee I recommends that internal communication should be strengthened by _____." (This recommendation may include increased or decreased use of certain media.)

23 *Thought Question Only:* Evaluate your own ability as a communicator based on the results of the meeting described in Problem 22. Could you manage the flow of communication within an organization? As a beginning employee, can you contribute effectively to sending and receiving information and ideas? Did you contribute as much or more than any other student to your small group meeting?

24 (Summarizing) Meet in groups to compare your codes of ethics prepared for Problems 5 and 6 with those written by other students. Summarize major similarities and differences.

First paragraph: Start with an opening paragraph that includes the most important conclusions of your comparisons and group discussion. (The paragraph should be short, like opening paragraphs in other business messages. One-sentence paragraphs are correct and often appropriate. Putting the most important information first is known as the "direct arrangement" or "up-front messaging.")

Middle paragraphs: Expand on your statement in the first paragraph or include additional information.

Ending paragraph: Use a strong closing paragraph. What will it be? (*Note:* This written summary may be prepared by the entire group or after discussion by the group, prepared individually, as your instructor directs. All the problems for this chapter and for all others can be adapted in various ways according to the needs of the particular class and the available time.)

THINK-IT-THROUGH ASSIGNMENTS

25 You order a single-station copy of an easy-to-use money management software. When you receive a box in the mail, you find not only the money management software you ordered, but also a copy of a CD-ROM containing lots of really useful clip art. The bill, however, is for the money management software only. Since you recently studied legality and ethics issues in your business communication class, you take a few minutes to assess the situation. Use a framework for analysis as you evaluate the situation. How will you handle the situation? Is your decision legal? Ethical? Write a summary of your analysis that explains how you justified your decision.

26 You note that the class membership in your economics class is approximately half American and half international students. Your instructor wants you to work in groups of three or four for various projects throughout the semester. You are allowed to select your own groups for the first assignment. The resulting groups are either all American or all international students. Before the second group project, the instructor assigns each student to a particular group and provides a mixture of American and international students in each group. Help your instructor justify the assignment of groups. Consider the following questions before providing a response. What are the possible benefits? What are the potential problems? How can the problems be eliminated or minimized? Can a single student help a group with diverse backgrounds work together effectively?

ENDNOTES

1 Roger D. A'prix, quoted by E. Zoe McCathrin, "Beyond Employee Publications: Making the Personal Connection," *Public Relations Journal*, July 1989, 14IA.

2 Ann Chadwell Humphries, "Information Vital to Get Job Done," *The Denver Post*, July 31, 1996, B9.

3 Ibid.

4 Patrice Johnson, "Commitment and Productivity," *Training and Development Journal*, 44, no. 8 (August 1990): 55.

5 E. Zoe McCathrin, "Beyond Employee Publications: Making the Personal Connection," *Public Relations Journal*, July 1989, 14IA.

6 Ibid.

7 McCathrin, "Beyond Employee Publications," 16IA.

8 Jitendra Mishra, "Managing the Grapevine, *United Personnel Management*, 19, no. 2 (June 22, 1990): 213.

9 Carol Hymowits, "Grapevine," *Wall Street Journal*, October 4, 1988, Sec. 2, 1.

10 Vanessa Dean Arnold, "Harvesting Your Employee Grapevine," *Management World*, July 1985, 28.

11 Peter I. Novel, "Cultivating the Office Grapevine, *Modern Office Technology 30* (September 1985): 117.

12 Robert E. Calem, "E-Mail Users Advised: Put Best Foot Forward: Experts Say Messages Should Be Written Like Business Letters," *Crain's New York Business*, July 17, 1995, 1.

13 Kenneth R. Andrews, ed., *Ethics in Practice* (Boston: Harvard Business School Press, 1989), 1.

14 Charles Garfield, "Ethics and Corporate Social Responsibility, *Executive Excellence*, 12, no. 8 (August 1995): 5–6.

15 Ibid.

16 "Do the Right Thing," *Information Week*, November 28, 1994, 92.

17 Ron Trujillo, "Good Ethics Pay Off," *USA Today*, October 23, 1995, 2B.

18 Maggie Jackson, "GM, Reebok, BankAmerica Get Ethics Awards." *The Commercial Appeal* (Memphis), November 19, 1996, 9B.

19 Laura Nash, "Ethics without the Sermon," *Harvard Business Review*, November–December 1981, 79.

20 Donna Holquist, "Ethics, How Important Is It in Today's Office?" *Public Personnel Management*, 22, no. 4, 1993, 537.

21 Marianne Jennings, "Manager's Journal on Business Ethics," *Wall Street Journal*, September 25, 1995, 1.

22 R. M. Weaver, *Language Is Sermonic: Richard M. Weaver on the Nature of Rhetoric*, ed. R. L. Johnnesen, R. Strickland, and R. T. Eubanks (Baton Rouge, La.), as quoted by Martin J. Jacobi, "Using the Enthymeme to Emphasize Ethics in Professional Writing Courses," *Journal of Business Communication*, 27 (Summer 1990): 282.

Communicating with the Aid of Technology

CHAPTER

3

OBJECTIVES

Chapter Three will help you:

1   Identify the basic communication principles that remain unchanged no matter what technological tools are used to prepare or send messages.

2   Describe technological tools available for creating written documents.

3   Describe technological tools available for communicating orally.

4   Discuss uses of electronic databases and the Internet in gathering information.

5   Describe technology typically used by telecommuters when communicating with the office.

6   Apply ethical and legal considerations when communicating with the aid of technology.

Technology affects the sending and receiving of oral and written messages throughout the world. As you work in any business or profession, you will use technological equipment of many kinds. Your knowledge and ability to use this equipment will make your work easier and more effective.

You are likely to have the use of a personal computer at your desk. This computer will allow you to send written messages around the world, or to another office in your building, at the touch of a key. You will send and receive voice mail and e-mail, participate in conferences many miles away, research multiple journals and other reference sources, and prepare reports or other material in collaboration with other individuals or groups. All these tasks, and more, can be accomplished in your own office—without moving from the chair at your desk. In addition, you may not even come to a business office, but telecommute from an office in your home. (Terms used in this paragraph that may not be immediately clear to you are explained later in this chapter.)

As much as possible, prepare yourself for the rapidly changing technological environment. Regardless of your knowledge and skills now or at any time in the future, continuous learning will be essential. In a decade or two, some machines and processes that now seem miraculous will be commonplace or obsolete.

Principles of Communication in Relation to Technology

"The more things change, the more they stay the same" is an adage that applies to effective communication of all kinds. This book and your course in business communication are built around principles of human communication that apply everywhere, regardless of how written or oral messages are prepared, sent, and received. These basic principles apply to casual conversation in the halls and to panel discussions heard by thousands of people via public television or teleconferencing. They apply to written messages sent from one computer to another, or transmitted by satellite, as well as to notes hastily written with pencils on memo pads, and to telephone calls.

Business messages at one time were written with quill pens. In earlier times, words were carved on bark or chipped on stone tablets. In later years, typewriters—to say nothing of word processors—were looked upon as miracles.

"Nothing endures but change" is a quotation of the Greek philosopher Heraclitus, written about 500 B.C. Your workplace, whatever your position or area of specialization, is likely to be different from that of similar workers 20 years ago. You will see many other changes throughout your career, some of which now seem to be impossible. You cannot prepare yourself completely for these changes during your college years, for you will find it necessary to keep on learning, as experienced workers are now doing and will continue to do.

A foundation of basic knowledge and skills, including a study of human behavior (as much as it can be studied) and an expert use of language, will enable you to adapt to ever-changing conditions and responsibilities. Most important of all, you should expect change, welcome it when it is beneficial, and exert the necessary effort to meet new challenges with confidence in your ability to succeed.

Business messages, however they are encoded, transmitted, and decoded, involve the five processes of verbal communication: speaking, writing, listening, reading, and thinking. These skills will not decrease in importance with changing technology; they will become even more important. Harmonious personal relationships, which are built through communication, will increase in importance as well.

Each year the various kinds of equipment used to process information become more comprehensive and amazing; nevertheless, language remains the most useful tool of communication, as it has always been. Automated, sophisticated machines cannot be designed or operated without the use of communication between humans and, especially, the application of human thought.

COMMUNICATION brief

C. B. Bowman, manager of creative services for the Maxwell House division of Kraft Foods, often finds herself multitasking in her office. She often takes phone calls, works on her computer, checks her electronic mail, and uses an adding machine at the same time. She also has a car phone and fax machines and computers at her New York residence and her weekend home.

As in many other organizations, staff reductions have resulted in fewer secretaries; most Kraft managers do numerous clerical chores, including making their own travel arrangements. Bowman notes that the use of speaker phones allows her to complete other tasks such as checking e-mail while she is on the phone with the travel agent. Multitasking has become a necessity in today's office.

"Women's Work is Never Done" by Perri Capell and Virginia Gordon from *Executive Female*, March/April, 1996, 45, 47. Reprinted by permission of National Association of Female Executives.

As computers become "smarter," the question becomes, Who is in charge here, computers or people? Although computers have amazing capacities, they would not exist without the human minds that designed them and utilize them.

Today's business employees, empowered with technology, can communicate from the office, to the office, or virtually anywhere—at any time. (How does this executive communicate nonverbally?)

WRITTEN COMMUNICATION THROUGH TECHNOLOGY

No matter what the size of your document, today's technology can support your written communication tasks. Keep in mind, however, that the greatest portion of the cost of a written communication, regardless of how it is prepared, is the cost of labor. You should learn to use the technology wisely to help reduce overall office costs within your organization.

WORD PROCESSING

Word processing is a computer application that facilitates writing, editing, formatting, and printing text. The ability to keyboard a document, store the document electronically, and edit the electronic version allows you to add, delete, or move text easily. Today's software makes it easy to insert worksheets, charts and graphs, and other visuals into your word processed document, further enhancing the appearance and the clarity of your text. Figure 3-1 shows a word processed document containing text and a chart imported from a spreadsheet program.

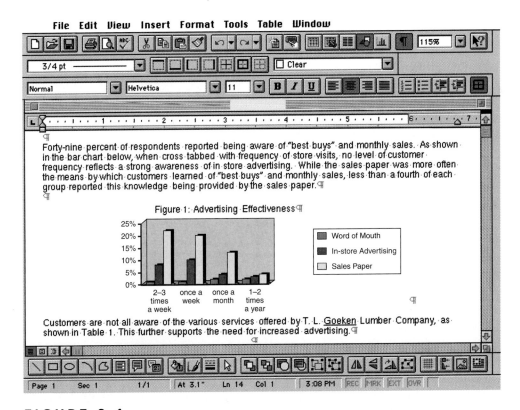

FIGURE 3-1
A word processing document with text and chart

Instant revision contributes to better overall results, whatever you are writing. As writers and teachers have long advocated, revision is almost always desirable in order to produce professional-quality work. A truism is "The only good writing is rewriting."

Word processing packages typically include a spell checker to help you locate keyboarding errors. Grammar checks and thesauruses can also assist you in evaluating sentence construction, determining reading levels, and providing variety in words used.

All these support tools, however, do not eliminate the need for proofreading. Even the smartest computer cannot know what you meant to write. For example, the words *some* and *same* are both correct words; only the writer can determine which one is desired. Likewise, the computer cannot detect omitted words or passages. Carefully proofread your materials to find context errors, content errors, misspelled names and addresses, and so forth. Study the example below. The spell checker of a word processing package would not highlight any of the words in the second sentence as errors.

What the writer intended:
Note that your vacation may be scheduled during July, August, September, or October.

What the writer keyboarded:
Not that our vocation May be scheduled during August, September, or October.

Diagnostics software packages include programs that evaluate grammar, style, usage, and punctuation. Whether you use a stand-alone diagnostics package or the grammar check tool included with your word processor, these tools are not infallible. They have been criticized by many teachers and professional writers because they do not (they cannot) judge the overall quality of writing or its content. For example, Lincoln's Gettysburg Address, when analyzed by a style checker, was described as weak in various ways. The Gettysburg Address has long been considered a masterpiece of literature.

In addition to readability scores, some grammar checks note the number of sentences considered to be too long; the number of adjectives and adverbs, qualifiers that often weaken writing; jargon; construction of sentences; number of verbs in passive voice; and "uncommon words" that may not be understood by the reader.

No computer or formula, however, can accurately and completely evaluate writing of any kind. Although such programs can be an aid to even experienced writers, they cannot replace personal evaluation and revision. Figure 3-2 illustrates a message from a grammar check within a popular word processing package.

Using word processing software, footnotes and endnotes can be prepared quickly and easily. Reference lists can be sorted alphabetically. Envelopes can be printed without rekeying the address on the letter. The software may

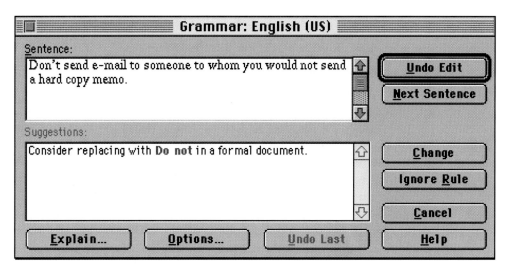

FIGURE 3-2
Grammar check software's feedback to writer

even print bar codes for postal ZIP codes. Many software packages also offer some type of mail merge to place names and addresses on duplicate copies of letters.

Some of the most popular word processing packages provide prepared *templates* for various types of letters, memos, and other typical documents. Templates are patterns or blueprints for a document. Some templates provide a format only; other templates include formats and actual text a writer can use. Take care when tempted to use the text provided within these templates. Each situation requiring a letter or memorandum is unique. As a writer, you have your own tone and style; the content you must include in your memo or letter may also differ from the template materials.

Although you are likely to keyboard your own documents, you may have an opportunity to dictate your messages for transcription into mailable copy by a personal secretary or by a worker in a word processing center. The principles of effective dictation described in Appendix C, "Dictating Business Messages," apply to origination of messages to be transcribed by someone else.

DESKTOP PUBLISHING

Desktop publishing is a term that commonly describes professional-quality publishing using a personal computer or microcomputer. Desktop publishing software such as Adobe's PageMaker, Quark, Inc.'s QuarkXPress, and Ventura Software's Ventura integrates text and graphics to produce high-quality print publications using laser printers. Both word processing files and graphics files can be placed and manipulated on the same page, using page composition capabilities of the desktop publishing software. When you use a desktop publishing package, you can add boxes, borders, illustrations, clip art, multicolumns, various size type fonts, and other features associated with professional printing. Common applications of desktop publishing include newsletters, brochures, flyers, pamphlets, posters, and sales messages.

High-end desktop publishing has the ability to use any image, including scanned photographs, graphs, and drawn artwork. Many packages offer a clip-art library of professionally drawn illustrations and symbols. Image control options include the ability to change the brightness, the contrast, and the size of images used. The more complex desktop publishing software has the ability to import text from popular word processing, spreadsheet, and database software packages. Although the laser printer provides high-quality printing for desktop publishing applications, ink-jet and bubble-jet color printers are also quite popular printing devices.

As software producers add more visual capabilities to word processing software packages, the distinction between desktop publishing and word processing becomes less. Many word processing packages today offer a variety of typefaces, type sizes, and graphic elements of boxes and rulings. In addition, this software can import graphics from other software applications such as spreadsheets and databases. Charts, figures, and graphic aids similar to those in Chapter 14 can be added to word processing documents.

▶ ELECTRONIC MAIL (E-MAIL)

The term *electronic mail* typically refers to messages sent from computer to computer through *local area networks* (used for internal mail), or *wide area networks* and the *Internet*. More than 23 million U.S. workers had e-mail access in 1996, with more than 60 million projected to be connected by the year 2000, according to the Electronic Messaging Association in Washington.[1]

Electronic mail is sent from one computer screen to another. The receiver of the message may be next door or thousands of miles away. Messages are composed on a computer screen, as in word processing, and sent to the "mailbox address" of the receiver until he or she can conveniently pick them up. Many software packages also allow a sender to receive notification when a message has been received.

The receiver of the message reads the message after it appears on a computer screen. It can then be printed out as "hard copy," although a hard copy is often unnecessary. Messages can be stored and filed in electronic folders, much as other computer files are stored on disks. An e-mail message prepared using a popular e-mail software package is illustrated in Figure 3-3.

People in widely separated time zones can send messages back and forth without the inconveniences caused by the time differences. Electronic mail eliminates the frustration and expense of "telephone tag." It allows the receiver of the message to respond at a convenient time instead of answering the telephone when it rings. Electronic mail provides for the "broadcast" of

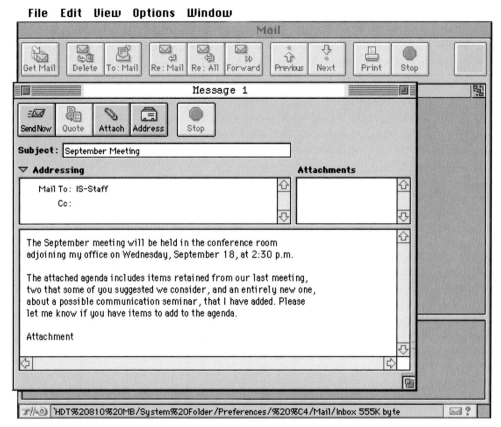

FIGURE 3-3

E-mail message prepared using a popular e-mail software package

messages to many mailboxes, either in the same office or to distant locations. Therefore, instead of the more usual photocopied memorandums, businesspeople receive computer messages.

E-mail is used both *internally* (within the same organization) and *externally* (to receivers outside the organization). Internal e-mail messages are typically sent using the organization's local area network and e-mail software. Ordinarily, external messages are carried by telephone lines; this method requires a computer, modem, and a communication software package. If your business has *Internet* access, sending an e-mail message to someone in another country can be as easy as keying in the person's complete Internet e-mail address and clicking on the "send" button when you have completed the message. (The Internet is discussed in more depth later in this chapter.) As a new employee, you should always check the policies of your company. Some organizations limit electronic mail to internal correspondence and neither send nor receive external e-mail messages.

E-mail allows entire manuscripts to be sent from computers to publishing houses. Newspaper reporters send in stories in this way, even from foreign countries, transmitting messages via satellite. Typical advantages an organization gains by using e-mail are presented in Figure 3-4.

While you may be tempted to word e-mail messages much like conversation rather than a letter, William R. Moroney, president of the Electronic Messaging Association, advises caution. "It is a written record. Think of e-mail as something that can be saved for a long time and shared with a lot of people."[2] Daniel J. Blum, principal of Rapport Communication, a consulting firm specializing in electronic mail and commerce, notes that e-mail isn't in-

---

Electronic Mail Advantages

- Transmission of messages is almost instantaneous.
- Messages are often more personal and informal.
- "Telephone tag" is reduced or eliminated.
- Time necessary for meetings is reduced.
- Hard-copy letters and memos can often be replaced.
- Messages can be sent at any time, day or night, decreasing problems brought about by differences in time zones.
- Messages can be sent to many receivers simultaneously.

Electronic Mail Disadvantages

- Cost. (Depending upon company needs, systems can be cost effective.)
- Senders are more likely to make errors in facts and approach, in addition to errors in logic, grammar, and spelling, because messages are prepared more quickly than most letters and memorandums.
- Incompatibility of electronic mail systems prevents the sending and receiving of messages between these systems.
- E-mail messages may be taken less seriously than traditional business letters.
- Senders of messages have no assurance that the intended receivers will check mailboxes or respond to messages.
- Space available on an e-mail screen is less than that of a single-spaced typewritten page. Multiple screens are likely to be more annoying than a long typewritten letter or memorandum would be.
- Messages are not always delivered because the intended receiver's computer system may be down. E-mail users must observe "undeliverable" messages and attempt to resend.
- E-mail is not guaranteed private.

FIGURE 3-4
Advantages and disadvantages of e-mail

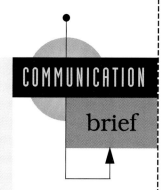

Rob Zee, director of the Internet Marketing Association of Global Enterprises, makes this statement in relation to e-mail:

Use good grammar, spell correctly, and capitalize properly. These may seem like minor suggestions, but remember, talking on the phone is different from sending an e-mail. It will be your e-mail that creates a first impression, not any human contact.

Read through your correspondence carefully before hitting the "send" key. If you don't have time to hit the shift key to capitalize what needs to be capitalized, I don't have the time to take your message seriously.

Tip: Don't use thanx (thanks). Don't use IMHO (in my humble opinion) or BTW (by the way). Don't be cute. Be professional.

"Technology Changes, Rules Stay the Same," *Electronic Commerce News*, 1, no. 39 (October 28, 1996).

teractive. "It hits you all at once, just like a written letter," and it must be as carefully composed as a letter or it could be easily misunderstood.[3]

A major disadvantage of e-mail is the lack of privacy. Anything sent by e-mail can conceivably become public knowledge. You never know who may read it, now or in the future, despite "mailboxes" that are supposedly accessible to only one person. Computer hackers can obtain access to almost all computer information. In addition, a message can become caught in computer backups and remain on tapes for years.

E-mail is not the way to send confidential messages of any kind. One good "rule of thumb" is never to send anything via e-mail that you would not want broadcast on the 6 P.M. news! Although efficient and economical when wisely used, e-mail must be used with discretion. Never use it for personal, nonbusiness communication.

Lack of privacy and other disadvantages of e-mail are listed in Figure 3-4.

If you have access to e-mail at your workstation, you may be tempted to send *all* internal messages of a nonconfidential nature as e-mail messages. Consider who must receive your message. You may find that not all employees within the organization have access to e-mail. In some instances you may still need to send hard-copy memos to some employees even though others receive your message electronically.

How will you as a business writer or speaker be affected by electronic mail? Perhaps the effect on your communication responsibilities and success will be less than you think. Certainly the system should make the sending and receiving of messages more prompt, efficient, and reliable.

Nevertheless, the basic principles of business communication remain the same. You must still know your subject, convey accurate and complete information, express your thoughts in exact words, convince the receiver to accept your ideas or follow your instructions, and strengthen harmonious working relationships. The overall ability to communicate is as important when using electronic mail as when using regular mail, conversing with your business associates, or making a speech. Learning to use the necessary equipment and software is a minor consideration compared to your ability to interact effectively with other people and to use language effectively. You can make friends or enemies using electronic mail just as you can when you use regular mail.

Electronic mail provides many benefits to you as a student or as an employee. However, the technology can be used inappropriately. To be an effective e-mail communicator, observe the following rules.

► Respond to e-mail messages in a timely manner.

► Provide clearly worded subject lines for all messages.

► Use shorter lines and shorter paragraphs than in regular word processing documents.

► Be complete and concise—avoid rambling.

► Use upper- and lower-case letters. This is easier to read; also, all caps is considered "SHOUTING," which should be avoided.

► Use text editors and spell checkers when available.

► Use jargon carefully—consider background of a reader or readers.

► Avoid inappropriate and possibly offensive language.

► Follow the organization's chain of command. Don't send e-mail to someone to whom you would not send a hard-copy memo.

► Avoid trivial responses; they just clutter the e-mail system.

► Avoid firing angry messages back to the sender (flaming).

► Avoid sending "junk" mail.

► Avoid adding too many attachments to your message.

► Avoid use of emoticons (typewritten symbols such as : -) that represent feelings) unless you are absolutely certain your reader will interpret the symbol as you intended.

► Observe the e-mail tone and structure in use in your organization to determine appropriate levels of formality.

► Plan distribution lists carefully. Be sure to include all individuals who have a legitimate need to receive information from you.

► Check distribution lists carefully before forwarding something to another person.

► Get off distribution lists that send you inappropriate or irrelevant materials.

► Use filtering options to weed out messages from certain recipients or messages related to certain subjects.

► Don't expect instant responses to your e-mail messages.

► Avoid gossip or remarks about other individuals, or discussion of proprietary information when using e-mail.

FACSIMILE TRANSMISSION (FAX)

Facsimile (fax) transmission provides an advantage not available through any other form of electronic communication—the transmission to other fax machines, anywhere in the world, of exact copies of written material, drawings, photographs, maps, charts, or other pictorial material. This transmission is completed in only a few seconds, being sent over regular telephone lines or by satellite.

A desktop fax unit links into a telephone and allows the user to feed hard copies of documents through the machine for transmission to another fax machine. Computer fax modems can send an electronic version of a document to another computer or to a stand-alone fax machine. Certain software packages allow users to create a document at a personal computer and automatically fax it to various locations. This material can be sent immediately or delayed to another time, day or night, in consideration of different purposes or time zones. Facsimile transmission is widely used in international communication, supplementing or replacing telex transmission, an older method of transmission.

Today fax machines are so economical that they are practical for even small businesses. Fax machines offer immediate transmission, allowing a company to respond quickly to requests, send orders to suppliers, and so forth.

COMMUNICATION

brief

Miss Manners can hardly wait until the novelty of the fax machine wears off. It is a highly useful gadget in its place, but there are too many people now who can't keep their hands off it.

It's not just wrong numbers, but wasted time. The current standard procedure seems to be to telephone the lucky recipient, either to ask for the fax number or to announce, "I'm going to fax you" and then to get the old machine rattling away on something that could have been said during the call or that doesn't require attention for days or weeks, if ever.

Judith Martin, *Miss Manners Basic Training Communication* (New York: Crown, 1997), 7.

► SCANNERS

Scanners, also called optical scanners or OCR scanners, recognize and interpret typewritten characters, drawings, and photographs. Scanners read materials so that the materials can be put into a computer-readable format without the user having to rekey or redraw materials.

Major advantages of using OCR scanners as an input medium are reduced input time and increased accuracy. Each page of a manuscript can be shown on a display terminal so that a word processor can make desired changes. The corrected page is then printed or stored for future processing.

Today both full-page scanners and hand-held (less than full page at a time) scanners are available. Use of scanners is not limited to business offices; for example, grocery stores and retail stores often use scanners at checkout counters.

► GROUPWARE

Groupware software is typically installed on a computer network and allows many users to communicate in numerous ways. Groupware supports collaborative efforts of work groups. Employees working in offices on different floors of the same building or even thousands of miles apart can be assigned to a project team and communicate easily with other members of their work group.

Groupware software typically includes the capabilities listed below:

► Group writing and commenting

► Electronic mail

► Meeting and appointment scheduling

► Shared time lines

► Electronic meetings

► Shared files and databases

Lee Batdorff notes key benefits for both large and small companies. "The ability to share information easily via groupware carries the benefit at many companies of reducing confusion and the number of meetings. Groupware also allows workers, whether in the same office or around the globe, to work together on projects. Such togetherness cuts down on miscommunication and accelerates work flow."[4]

Groupware allows a user to review ideas of others at any time and to add ideas for others in the group. Documents can be posted; other group members can comment and edit these documents. Even work notes can be stored on groupware so that other group members can see what progress has been made, what activities are planned, what problems have emerged, and so forth.

While Lotus Notes is the most common groupware package, other similar products such as Microsoft Corporation's Microsoft Exchange and ON Technology's Common Knowledge are also available.

ORAL COMMUNICATION THROUGH TECHNOLOGY

Just as today's technology allows you to be more efficient and more effective in your written work, your oral communication tasks can also be supported by technology. As with written communication, all the technological whistles and bells in the world are not a substitute for clear, effective oral communication. Learn to use technology to enhance your productivity, but always remember the needs of your audience and your responsibility to communicate clearly.

VOICE MAIL

Voice mail may also be referred to as voice store-and-forward, voice processing, phone mail, and voice messaging. Spoken messages are recorded for playing back at a later time.

Telephone answering devices are the simplest and least expensive form of voice mail, although voice mail systems have many additional features. A major difference is that with voice mail systems, which include store-and-forward and routing, the user plans to leave a voice message, not to talk directly with a person by telephone. Voice messages are like letters in that they evoke no immediate response.

Like written messages sent by electronic mail, voice messages are placed in "mailboxes." The same message can be "broadcast" to numerous mailboxes simultaneously. Recipients control when the messages are taken, picking them up at their convenience. This feature, however, can result in delayed responses, as with electronic mail or business letters sent by regular mail.

Voice mail can conveniently replace short, rather routine letters, such as requests, replies to requests, notices, or announcements. Voice mail messages are useful in replacing telephone calls for which no immediate response is needed. Some systems even provide a way to tie the system to the employee's pager, a small radio receiver that signals the employee that he or she has a message.

Another feature of voice mail is that it provides information to inquirers who do not use a computer, but only a touch-tone telephone. For example, banks provide information about account balances and whether particular checks have cleared. This information is provided by a computer, although the inquirer has the option of being transferred to a customer service representative.

John Goodman, president of Technical Assistance Research programs, cautions that voice mail technology can be misused. "The minute a customer gets voice mail, you take a 10 percent hit in customer satisfaction because they cannot get their problem solved immediately." Goodman also cautions companies not to let callers get trapped in voice mail without being able to get out. He advises that a company must always limit the number of menu options and always provide the caller the option of speaking to a real person.[5]

Lands' End, a leading direct-mail family clothing company, and Winguth, Donahue & Co., an executive search firm, are two companies that have purposely elected NOT to use voice mail for customer service, although both companies use it within the corporate office. Both companies cited the need to avoid wasting customer time and getting customers directly to a real person for fast and considerate service as reasons they eliminated customer service lines from their voice mail systems.[6]

COMMUNICATION brief

VOICE MAIL TIPS

Richard Gordon, president of R. J. Gordon & Co., a Los Angeles–based consulting firm, has used voice mail for 11 years. Gordon checks his voice mail every 10 minutes; he also forwards and creates messages for employees, customers, and vendors who are on his voice mail system. He says, "You can use it anywhere. I couldn't manage without voice mail." To get the most from voice mail systems, Gordon recommends the following:

► Use the "remote" notify feature to set up voice-mail boxes for important clients and vendors.
► Use the system to reach key personnel in an emergency.
► Use the system to remind people exactly what the system can do for them.
► Use the system to save on long-distance calls.
► Use preprogrammed voice-mail lists sparingly.

"Managing Technology: Getting the Most Out of Voice Mail," by Phaedra Hise. Reprinted with permission, *INC. Magazine* (August, 1996). Copyright (c) 1996 by Goldhirsh Group, Inc., 38 Commercial Wharf, Boston, MA 02110.

Voice Mail Advantages	Voice Mail Disadvantages
• Twenty-four-hour-a-day access to messages • Improved efficiency • Improved flow of messages • Can add comments and send message to another user • Can send message to multiple users • Can easily update message to callers • Lower costs—less receptionist support • Can use as a note taker—call in and leave yourself a message • Marketing tool • Can tie into employee pagers	• Some systems difficult to use • People resist technology • Some systems not economical for small offices • Some people dislike talking to a machine

FIGURE 3-5
Advantages and disadvantages of voice-mail

Many of the advantages and disadvantages that apply to written messages sent by electronic mail also apply to voice mail. When wisely planned and used, however, advantages far outweigh disadvantages.

When using voice mail to transmit messages, be especially careful to plan your communications so that they are complete, clear, and concise. Your words must be clearly enunciated and free of tones, words, or accents that would be confusing to people from other countries or various regions of the United States and Canada. Show callers that you really use the system by personally updating your voice mail daily, providing the date, and telling callers when you will be checking your messages. Then remember to follow through by checking your mail and returning calls.

Key advantages and disadvantages of voice mail are summarized in Figure 3-5.

TELECONFERENCING AND VIDEOCONFERENCING

Teleconferencing is electronic communication between two or more people at two or more locations. In its simplest form, it is the telephone conference call that has been available for many years. With speakerphones in each office, the number of participants can be greatly increased. When using two-way calls, all participants can speak with all other participants. In one-way conference calls, oral messages (for example, statements from a company president) are delivered simultaneously to many locations.

Videoconferencing also occurs over telecommunications links and includes televised pictures of the participants, either as still shots or in full action, like regular television. Videoconferencing can be either one-way or two-way, with several variations of each. A frequently used method, particularly appropriate for large groups, is video presentation of the speaker or speakers, with opportunity for telephone feedback from audiences at widely scattered locations. Your school may participate in videoconferences on important topics; many schools also teach some of their course offerings through videoconferencing.

Many managers and executives spend a large portion of their time in meetings. Because of increasing travel costs, some organizations hold meetings by videoconferencing, either nationwide or in limited geographical areas. An advantage, besides economy, is that more employees are able to participate. A disadvantage is that teleconferencing at its best cannot take the place of face-to-face interaction. As people, we like and need to talk with people, even to reach out and touch them. This fact is not likely to change, regardless of innovations in technological transmission.

▶ CELLULAR PHONES AND PAGERS

Cellular phones, also referred to as mobile phones, use radio waves to communicate with radio towers placed within geographic areas called cells. When you place a call using a cellular phone, your cellular phone transmits the message to the local cell; the message is then handed off from cell to cell until the message reaches the destination cell. The message is then transmitted to the receiving telephone. Cellular phones, coupled with faxes and portable computers, have opened the door for employees to work in "virtual offices." A virtual office can be an employee's automobile, an airplane, a train, a hotel room, or a room in the employee's home. If you use a cellular telephone, use common sense and courtesy, as detailed in the cellular phone etiquette do's and don'ts presented in Figure 3-6.

Use Your Cell Phone . . .	Don't Use Your Cell Phone . . .
• To call for help • To pick up messages • To accept urgent calls • To place urgent calls • To do business from your car when stuck in traffic • To chat in the back of a cab (let the driver know you are going to make a call)	• In subways, elevators, airplanes, or other tiny enclosed spaces • In theaters, churches, and so forth • When you're in motion on foot • While on a city bus • Wherever most people go to relax • When you really don't have to • To say anything you wouldn't want to see repeated in banner headlines in the tabloids.

FIGURE 3-6
Cellular telephone etiquette

Source: " Cell Etiquette" by Blanch Marker from *Executive Female*, March/April 1996, p. 48.
Reprinted by permission of National Association of Female Executives.

Pager technology allows this Motorola executive to be contacted at any time, any place.

Pagers, small radio receivers that signal when the user has a message, are typically used for wireless transmission of brief messages. They provide yet another way for an employee to remain in touch with the office. Voice messaging systems may be linked to an employee's pager to provide immediate notification of any incoming calls.

ELECTRONIC DATABASES

Collecting data for reports and other business purposes has been greatly simplified with the advent of *electronic (computerized) databases*, which will be discussed further in Chapter 13, "Gathering and Reporting Information." Information that once required hours or days to find is now available in a few minutes.

Electronic databases are of two kinds: online and CD-ROM (compact disk; read-only memory). Both types may be available at your school library. Online databases are also widely used by organizations and by individuals, provided they have a computer with a modem and the appropriate software.

Some electronic databases provide abstracts (summaries) of journal articles or other sources; some provide full text of the sources. Still others provide only the bibliographic references, similar to the ones included in printed indexes such as *Business Periodicals Index* and *Reader's Guide to Periodical Literature.*

One of the most valuable computerized databases for business research is ABI/Inform. This database, along with instructions for its use, is likely to be in the reference room of your school library, probably with a number of computer terminals.

Computerized databases are discussed in this chapter on technology, in addition to Chapter 13, because no presentation of communication technology would be complete without the inclusion of this important development. Another reason is that you may wish to use ABI/Inform and other databases for purposes other than report writing throughout your study of business communication.

THE INTERNET

The *Internet* is the world's largest computer information network. It is a network of networks connecting computers around the world. Your school library and various campus computer labs may provide Internet access. You may also have Internet access through a home computer if you have a modem and sign up for an on-line service such as America Online or subscribe to a local Internet access provider.

While a full discussion of the Internet is not possible within this chapter (or within entire books), a brief description of some of the important communication and information retrieval options available is appropriate in this chapter on technology. Business and education use of the Internet is growing immensely each year.

Through Internet access you can send and receive e-mail messages around the world. Many organizations use Internet e-mail to keep in touch with customers and suppliers.

You can use the Internet network tool Telnet to log-in to remote computers and access materials available to the general public. For example, you could use Telnet to electronically access the catalog of the United States Library of Congress.

You can also use File Transfer Protocol (FTP) to move files and data from one computer to another. You can download such items as magazine articles, books, free software, music, videos, and graphics.

▶ WORLD WIDE WEB (WWW)

The *World Wide Web* is a universally accepted set of standards used to store, retrieve, format, and display information available through the Internet. The Web combines text, graphics, sound, and hypermedia, while e-mail, Telnet, FTP, and other methods of locating information through the

Internet are predominantly character based. Web materials are created using hypertext markup language (HTML), which allows designers to plan links to other documents and Web sites.

Using Web browser software, such as Netscape or Internet Explorer, you can point at and click on a highlighted word, phrase, or graphic in a document and be transported to another related document that may be located on that same computer or a computer somewhere else. You can jump from document to document, from place to place, while browsing the Web, following your own interests or your own logic. In addition to reading any materials you access, you can download text, graphics, video, and sound. You can also mark addresses of Web pages of special interest for quick return access with a feature known as a bookmark.

Search directories and search engines such as Yahoo, Infoseek, Alta Vista, Magellan, Savvy, and others are tools for locating specific sites or information on the Internet. They are primarily used to search the World Wide Web. These search engines are valuable tools for a business researcher and are easy to use. When you access a search directory such as Yahoo and enter keywords, the directory searches for matches in the database of regis-

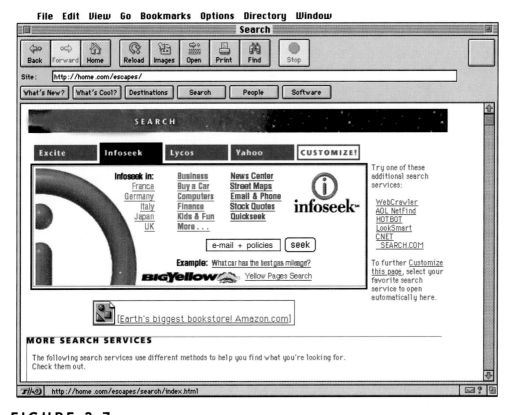

FIGURE 3-7
Keyword search terms to be matched by Infoseek search directory and search engine

tered Web sites. If you access a search engine and search directory such as Infoseek and enter keywords, you can search Web sites, newsgroups, and other Internet resources to find matches. Just as you might search more than one database on CD-ROM or online, you may also benefit by using more than one Internet search engine or directory. Figure 3-7 shows the Infoseek search engine and search directory screen with keywords entered by a researcher.

Using the Internet, you can obtain company and product information, find articles related to a topic you are researching, obtain stock information, travel information, and so forth. The amount and type of information is virtually limitless.

► USENET NEWSGROUPS (DISCUSSION GROUPS)

Usenet newsgroups are worldwide discussion groups available through the Internet. When you sign up for a Usenet newsgroup on a particular topic, you can post messages on an electronic bulletin board for others to read. You can also read the messages posted by others. No e-mail messages clutter your personal e-mail system. You may only post and read the newsgroup's messages when you access the newsgroup's Internet address.

Thousands of newsgroups exist on virtually any topic. You may find a group that focuses on a special interest such as Microsoft Office software, intercultural communication, electronic data interchange, robotics, marketing, and so forth. Carefully selected Usenet newsgroups can be valuable tools for business professionals. Such newsgroups may provide a source for posting questions you have about a certain topic and receiving valuable suggestions from others.

MULTIMEDIA PRESENTATIONS

Presentation software such as Lotus Development's Freelance Graphics, Adobe's Persuasion, Microsoft's PowerPoint, and Corel's Presentations all allow a user to assemble effective presentations incorporating text, graphics, sound, and video. Companies gain several advantages by providing employees with this type of software. For example, American Airlines has equipped sales representatives worldwide with notebook computers and presentation software; at the same time, two positions from its internal graphics department have been cut, because representatives themselves now prepare full-color presentations that include such items as sound effects, personalized graphics with the client's logo, and full-motion video testimonials.[7]

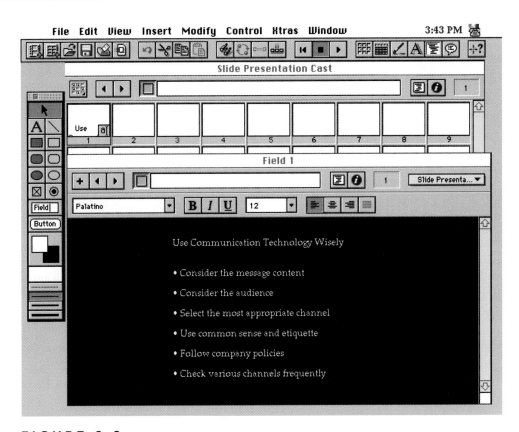

FIGURE 3-8

Slide from a multimedia presentation prepared using a popular presentation software package

Since Lotus, Microsoft, and Corel all bundle presentation software with their respective office suite software, the software is much more readily available than a few years ago. Templates are available to help the user generate a presentation with a professional look.

Figure 3-8 illustrates a slide prepared with a presentation graphics software package.

While presentation software provides you with a tool to prepare full presentations that stand on their own, in other instances you will want to generate a slide show that supplements your own oral presentation. When planning a stand-alone or supplemental multimedia show, use of the right color and text, and other design points are important considerations. Slides must be readable and uncluttered. Any artwork, video clips, and audio clips must be relevant. (Other computerized presentation design tips are discussed in Chapter 16 on public speaking.)

Use caution in selecting photos, diagrams, video clips, and audio clips for use in your slide show. As noted later in the chapter, current copyright laws do not require registration of materials with the Copyright Office in order for a copyright to exist. At minimum, you should acknowledge the source. Check carefully; certain materials may not be used without specific written permission or, in some instances, a fee.

Through careful planning and design, you can prepare a computerized multimedia slide show that enhances, rather than echoes, an oral presentation. Once you learn how to use the software, incorporate computerized slide shows into your oral presentations in other classes or on the job.

TELECOMMUTING

Millions of employees in the United States alone are classified as telecommuters. These employees work outside the physical office location; some telecommute only one or two days a week. Others *never* travel to the organization's physical office. All data and messages to be communicated to and by telecommuters are completed via voice mail, e-mail, and perhaps teleconferencing. While not all jobs are prime candidates for telecommuting, technology makes telecommuting a possibility for millions of employees. Organizations also benefit by meeting clean air standards (because fewer employees commute) and keeping good employees who might otherwise leave the organization for various reasons.

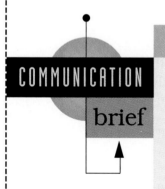

COMMUNICATION
brief

NEW E-MAIL AND INTERNET ACCESS OPTIONS

Wireless Web services are now available in certain areas of the country for executives at their desks; in the near future similar services will be available for business travelers.

AirMedia division of Ex machina provides wireless Web access to small businesses, drawing content from more than two dozen Websites. Using a device called the NewsCatcher, a wireless connection to the Internet is kept open, allowing the user to gather news digests, stock prices, and so forth.

Ricochet, a service from Metricom, is available in selected West Coast cities. Users simply attach wireless modems to the backs of their laptop computers. Approximately 200 executives at the Hewlett-Packard plant in Cornvallis, Oregon, carry Ricochet-equipped laptops and can check their e-mail or log onto a Website from anywhere within the facility without connecting to cables or phones.

While nation-wide wireless computer communication such as the Ricochet service isn't practical yet, smart phones are another option. These cellular units serve as two-way pagers and hand-held Internet browsers.

"Cutting the Cord to the Net," by Alison L. Sprout as appeared in *Fortune Magazine*, November 25, 1996, p. 186. Reprinted by permission.

Ethical and Legal Considerations

Computers and other technological advances have made it possible to access virtually limitless amounts of information. Carefully consider whether you are using the technology and information in both an ethical and a legal manner. Ownership of property, privacy, and access to information should be considered when communicating with the aid of technology.

In a technology-rich environment, we often take such things as computers, fax machines, modems, voice mail systems, and e-mail systems for granted. While it may be quicker to send something by fax or e-mail, there may be some legal issues to consider. Are the contents of the message you are sending contractual in nature? Is an e-mail signature line a legal signature? What happens if the receiver's computer system is down and he or she does not receive your e-mail message? What happens if the e-mail message disappears into a black hole in cyberspace?

Although facsimile machines have been around for over 25 years, a number of years passed before the courts recognized fax signatures as legal. E-mail is a more recent technology, and all related legality issues have not been ruled on by the courts. As you select a method of communication for *any* message, consider your audience, the intent of the message you are sending, and the standard procedures at your school or your employing company.

COPYRIGHT INFRINGEMENT

The Internet provides users virtually limitless access to "free" information on the Net. While the user may access the information at no cost, care must be taken in using the materials to avoid copyright infringement. Today's copyright law does not require an author to register new work with the Copyright Office in order for a copyright to exist. Copyright law protects many materials found on the Internet: audio materials, pictures, videos, and text.

Mark A. Kassel, a practitioner of intellectual property law at Foley & Lardner, states, "A general rule is that a company should ensure that any material being posted to the Net by the company or its employees is not someone else's copyrighted material. . . . Merely viewing copyrighted material posted to the net is unlikely to provide an infringement suit, but reproducing such information in other forms may bring a lawsuit."[8]

Treat materials you find on the Internet as you would materials in printed books, magazines, videotapes, or CD-ROM and online databases. Cite your sources when incorporating another person's words or pictures into your own writing. If you are going to use the materials for commercial purposes, you may need to obtain special permission and may also be required to pay a fee. If your job tasks require you to prepare materials for Web pages that will be posted on the Internet, make certain the materials you post are your own or the copyrighted property of your company.

Another property issue concerns the copying of software. Although some software packages are described as "shareware" and may be copied and used for a brief amount of time without cost or penalty, most software packages are fully copyrighted. Software is sold as books are sold. The person or persons who designed the software (or the employing organization) deserve income from each package. Like plagiarism and like making unauthorized copies of books or musical disks, using copyrighted software without permission is both unethical and illegal.

▶ MONITORING OF E-MAIL AND TELEPHONE CALLS

An organization's computer system administrator or an employee's supervisor may be monitoring e-mail messages. In most cases to date involving e-mail issues, the courts have ruled in favor of businesses having the right to monitor employee e-mail. The courts view the hardware and software as the property of the organization and take the position that e-mail is to be used for business purposes. Results of a recent study by the society for Human Resources Management indicate that while e-mail is used by nearly 80 percent of organizations, it is regulated in only 36 percent of those companies. In those companies without a written e-mail policy, employees don't know the company's position concerning monitoring of e-mail.[9] In other words, even though the company in which you are employed may not have a written policy, someone may be reading your e-mail.

To avoid possible problems concerning your e-mail messages, follow the guidelines concerning e-mail messages presented earlier in this chapter and avoid using the company e-mail system to send personal messages.

In some instances supervisors also monitor telephone calls. While this is most likely to occur in a customer-service or order-entry department, you should take care when communicating via telephone. Like e-mail messages, messages in a computerized voice mail system can be saved for extensive periods of time and can be subpoenaed in court cases. Conduct yourself in a professional manner when placing and receiving phone calls on the job, and avoid placing and receiving personal calls.

▶ PRIVACY LAWS

Users of various communication equipment must be careful not to violate privacy laws. Because the copying and transmission of information are so easily accomplished by e-mail, fax, voice mail, and other methods, communication that should remain confidential may be spread to individuals who have no right to see or hear the message. Another factor that may lead to violation of privacy laws is the ease with which mailing lists can be produced and distributed.

The right of privacy prevents the use of an individual's name, picture, or likeness without the individual's written consent. Other invasions of privacy, similar to libel, include placing a person in a false light and publishing embarrassing private information.

The contents of a letter belong to the writer, not to the receiver. A letter should not be publicized without the writer's permission. To do so results in an invasion of privacy. The same rules apply to e-mail messages; the contents belong to the writer.

Privacy is violated when letters, reports, memorandums, records, and other written materials are read by people not entitled to examine them. Technology has provided various methods of invasion of privacy, including the illegal use of recording equipment. Powerful binoculars and telephoto cameras can be used to look through windows at papers left face-up on desks. Methods exist for photocopying material through a sealed envelope or for reading it without opening the envelope. All such methods are unethical and illegal.

You as a writer should take necessary precautions to guard against confidential materials being read by others. Keep such materials in a secure place, never left lying face-up on your desk. Increase the privacy of mailed letters by using envelopes with a random-pattern lining or by inserting an opaque sheet around the letter. Clear your computer screen when you leave your desk or office.

Eavesdropping or unauthorized interception and written transcription of electronic messages are prohibited by law—the Electronic Communications Privacy Act of 1986—unless permission is obtained from both the sender and the receiver of the electronic message. Such messages include cellular telephone calls, electronic mail, video recordings, and data transmissions.

An earlier law, known as the "Wiretap Act" of 1968, outlawed interception and written transcription of telephone calls and face-to-face conversation.

How Changing Technology Will Impact Communication

Technological changes affect us all. Although computers and related equipment provide opportunities for release from repetitive work so that our time can be spent more creatively, rapid changes are frustrating and frightening to many people. Resisting change of any kind is only human. When technological developments threaten employment status, prestige, and feelings of self-worth, as some people believe computers do, people are understandably reluctant to give up older methods and equipment. They believe that computers are bringing about a nonhuman and inhumane society that is too impersonal and mechanistic. In addition, people see the many errors caused by computers, or at least those attributed to computers, and they prefer traditional human errors.

Communication is becoming faster, easier, and more direct. Mailed letters, as they are now used, are likely to decrease. More messages will be spoken and sent by voice mail or other methods of telecommunications, without being transferred to paper. A completely "paperless office," however, is likely to be rare or nonexistent.

Improved software will provide more help to the writer or other user of word processing equipment.

Although voice recognition hardware and software is now available, the vocabularies are limited and may need to be programmed to accept certain individuals' varying accents and tones of voice. The technology is, therefore, still rather expensive. Applications of voice input technology are growing each year, and sometime in the future you will no longer need to key in the text of your letter or memo.

Effective oral communication, always important, is becoming even more important. None of these changes in methods and equipment, however, mean that effective writing will decrease in value; the opposite is true. Whether words are written on paper, printed on a display screen, or transmitted from computer to computer has little bearing on the choice of words and their arrangement in a convincing message.

Capturing data in a computerized format will allow for rapid retrieval and editing at a later date.

SUMMARY

Today's electronic office provides business communicators with additional channels for sending and receiving messages and gathering data. As a communicator, you have increased responsibilities to communicate clearly and effectively.

A variety of technological tools can assist communicators in creating effective written documents. Today's employee may have access to word processing software and its accompanying tools such as spell checkers, thesauruses, and grammar checkers; desktop publishing software; electronic mail; facsimile transmission; and scanners. When effectively used, these tools can speed the creation, revision, and/or delivery of documents.

The automated electronic office consists of information and communication devices linked together, many of which can be accessed from individual workstations. Employees often have access to electronic databases and the Internet to assist in research tasks.

When the communicator wishes to convey messages orally, voice mail, multimedia presen-

tation software, teleconferencing and videoconferencing, and cellular phones and pagers all provide support for presenting and delivering messages.

The widespread use of these various technological tools has opened the door for millions of employees to become telecommuters. Telecommuters can work in "virtual" offices, whether those offices are in their homes, in hotels, on airplanes, or in automobiles.

Regardless of changing methods and media, the principles of effective communication still apply. Speaking, writing, listening, reading, and thinking skills will increase in importance with changing technology.

Common sense and etiquette should be important considerations when using technology for sending and receiving messages. Additionally, observance of copyright laws, use of technology for business messages only, and respect for privacy should be issues about which all communicators should be concerned.

TEST YOURSELF

chapter content

1   What are the key advantages of using word processing instead of older methods of preparing written communications?

2   In addition to word processing software, software suites often include what other packages?

3   When would it be advantageous to use desktop publishing software in addition to word processing software?

4   What technology provides for exact copies of documents to be transmitted literally anywhere in the world with comparable equipment?

5   What are the major advantages of electronic mail? What are the major disadvantages?

6   What are the major advantages of voice mail? What are the disadvantages?

7   What are the potential advantages of teleconferencing? Are there any disadvantages? If so, what?

8   What key rules should a business communicator observe when using electronic mail? Voice mail?

9   What are some of the popular Internet electronic search directories and search engines?

10   What types of information can an individual gain access to through the Internet? Can any of this information be accessed through other electronic databases?

11 How does U.S. copyright law impact the users of materials found on the Internet?

12 What are some of the most important design tips to keep in mind when designing computerized multimedia presentations?

13 What equipment do today's telecommuters typically have access to in their home or "virtual" offices?

The following sentences contain errors often left after material is run through a spell checker. Find the errors.

14 It is is now true that New York city is the capitol of Massachusetts.

15 Sense you no a individual who prepare manuscripts, perhaps you an pay to have the final copy professionally.

TEST YOURSELF

correct usage

(Related to material in Chapter 3 and principles of correct usage.) Insert punctuation, including quotation marks, hyphens, and apostrophes, according to the guidelines in Appendix D.

1 Since telecommuting offers numerous advantages to both employers and employees the number of telecommuters is expected to increase dramatically in the next few years.

2 Lincoln's Gettysburg Address when analyzed by a computerized writing style checker was described as weak in various ways.

3 Anything sent by e-mail can conceivably become public property employees in all organizations should consider the content of a message carefully before sending it via e-mail.

4 Using Internet search engines and search directories such as Yahoo Infoseek Savvy and Magellan a computer user can search Web sites newsgroups and other Internet sites.

5 When creating a computerized multimedia slide show to accompany a formal presentation, the user must take care to plan a show that will enhance not echo the oral presentation.

6 Successful business writers and speakers must have meaningful messages to send forth that is they must know what they are talking about.

7 The term paperless office refers to an office where everything is recorded by electronic means not on paper.

8 Some people beleive that they receive unnecessary messages through electronic mail and voice mail.

9 Further additions to the office of the future, which could be described as the ultimate office include picture telephones and computers that take dictation.

10 The computer like any other tool can be used unwisely

PROBLEMS AND CASES

1 Interview someone who works in an office where e-mail, voice mail, and facsimile are available and report your findings to the class. Ask the person you interview the following questions:
  a. What types of messages should be sent via e-mail?
  b. What types of messages should *not* be sent via e-mail?
  c. Does the company monitor the employees' e-mail?
  d. What types of messages should be communicated via voice mail?
  e. Does the company have a computer usage policy or a specific e-mail policy? What is included in the policy?
  f. What types of messages should *not* be communicated via voice mail?
  g. What types of messages should be communicated via face-to-face discussions?
  h. What types of materials are sent via facsimile?
  i. Are there any instances where facsimile should not be used?

2 Visit your school library to find answers to the questions presented below. Then send an e-mail message to your teacher and your classmates informing them of your findings. Use the distribution list features of the e-mail system if available. Present the necessary information in a concise, courteous manner. Remember that e-mail messages should be easy to read. Long paragraphs and a jumbled arrangement decrease readability.
  a. What databases are available online? Where are the computer terminals in the library? Do you need to reserve a particular time for their use? Can you access these databases from other locations on campus?
  b. What databases are available on CD-ROM? Where are the computer terminals? Do you need to reserve a particular time for their use?

  c. Is Internet access available in the library? Where are the computer terminals? Do you need to reserve a particular time for their use? Can you access the Internet from other locations on campus?

3 Through ABI/Inform or any other online or CD-ROM database, find three magazine, newspaper, or journal articles on any subject covered in Chapters 1 through 3. Print out the abstracts (summaries) of these three articles. Bring them to class and share them with your classmates or hand in as an assignment, according to the directions of your instructor. (If databases are not available online or on CD-ROM in your library, find three articles in the printed guide, *Business Periodicals Index*, or in a similar printed index.)

4 Use any two of the Internet search engines to find three newspaper, magazine, or journal articles on the same topic you selected for Problem 3. In addition to sharing your findings with classmates, or turning in the articles as directed by your instructor, discuss in class the similarities and/or differences you found in the materials available through online databases such as ABI/Inform versus the Internet.

5 Use the Internet search engines to gather information about a Fortune 500 company of your choice. In addition to accessing any Web site that company may have, investigate other Internet sites that also provide information about the company you selected. Using word processing software, prepare a one-page report in which you list the complete electronic access addresses for five key sites you found; for each, include a brief description of the materials available at that site. Submit your report in one of the following ways, as directed by your instructor.
  a. Send an e-mail message to your instructor and include your report as a separate electronic attachment to your e-mail message.

b. Submit a hard-copy print of your word processed report.

c. Fax a copy of your word processed report directly from a computer to your instructor's computer or fax machine.

6 Use a word processing package to prepare a two- to three-paragraph memo in which you discuss key advantages and possible disadvantages of using voice mail in a business. Run the grammar or style checker. Make note of any items identified by the style checker that you elect not to change. Be prepared to discuss these in class.

7 Prepare a five-minute oral presentation using the materials you gathered in Problem 3 or 4. Prepare a computerized slide show to accompany your oral presentation. At minimum, include a title slide, one or two content slides with some type of clip art or other graphic on one of the slides, and a summary slide.

COLLABORATIVE WRITING AND WORKING IN GROUPS

Note: These problems, like many others specified as group assignments, may also be used for individual work or for class discussion.

8 Work in groups of two to three. Decide which method or methods of communication would be appropriate for the following communication situations. In some situations, depending on the circumstances, more than one form of communication may be used for the same message. You may also have a choice of methods; state the advantages and disadvantages of each. Assume that you and the receivers of your messages have the necessary communication processes and equipment. Consider cost, convenience, accuracy of the message, privacy and security, legality, and all other pertinent factors.

a. You wish to send a copy of your resume to a potential employer in London who has asked to see it within two days, although the decision will not be made for two weeks or more.

b. You wish to send a notice of a meeting to 24 co-workers. The meeting will be held tomorrow.

c. You wish to send copies of a 40-page price list to 120 retailers scattered all over the United States. Changes in prices go into effect in four weeks.

d. As president of a college, you want to express appreciation to a member of the faculty who is retiring.

e. You want to make additional copies of a 210-page instruction manual that was prepared last year. You have a number of changes to make throughout. You prepared the original manual on a personal computer, but the disk has accidentally been erased and you didn't make a backup copy. You have one good copy of the manual. What will you do?

f. You are head of a department in your organization. One of the workers you supervise continues to arrive late, sometimes as much as an hour. How will you communicate with this employee?

g. You are head of enrollment services at a university. You want to make the contents of the university's catalog available to a larger audience in a nonpaper format. How can you do this most effectively?

h. You work in a government agency and supervise writers who prepare materials about preparing income tax returns. Intended readers are taxpayers of all educational levels. One writer constantly uses extremely long sentences and numerous technical words. What will you do?

i. You are a banker who wishes to save the time of employees by updating the bank's equipment. Employees must answer the phone hundreds of times a day to give callers the balance of their accounts, after the callers properly identify themselves. What can you do?

j. You need to hold a meeting with the division managers located at five regional branches in various cities across the country. You do not want to spend travel funds to bring them to the home office for what you anticipate will be a two-hour meeting.

9 Prepare a summary of your conclusions of what to do about the situations described in Problem 8. If directed by your instructor, prepare this summary using word processing software; each group member should write a section of this short report. Revise and edit the report as necessary to reflect a clear, consistent writing style.

10 Work in teams of two or three. Obtain a copy of any computer usage policies your school has in electronic or hard-copy format. Using the Internet, locate computer usage policies at six other schools. Analyze the policies in relation to the following questions:

a. How long are the documents (number of paragraphs, pages, etc.)?

b. How specific are the policies?

c. Do the policies address e-mail specifically?

d. Do the policies address privacy and security issues?

e. Do the policies address issues such as appropriate use of inoffensive materials only?

f. Do the policies indicate actions to be taken when violators of any policies are identified?

g. Are the policies clearly written?

h. Are the policies for students, faculty, and staff alike or different?

i. Which policy is best? Why?

Prepare a short memo report in which you present your findings. Each member of the team should write some of the report, using word processing or collaborative writing software as directed by your instructor. Remember to edit the report for correctness and consistent writing style.

THINK-IT-THROUGH ASSIGNMENT [SUMMARY OF ARTICLE]

11 Find the complete text of one of the articles for which you printed the abstract from the online or CD-ROM database, or the complete text of an article from another magazine, newspaper, or journal. (The article should be on some aspect of communication covered in Chapters 1 through 3.) Write a short report about this article according to the following format and arrangement or according to the method suggested by your instructor. (This outline is suitable for any other article you may read and summarize during this class or for other classes.)

Your name:

Article: Include complete information about the author; title; publication; volume, if given; date; and page number or numbers.

Author's theme: One or two sentences summarizing the gist of the article.

Summary of data: A list of short statements, probably five or six depending on length and complexity of article. Number and list for easy reading.

1. _____

2. _____ (and so on)

Personal agreement or disagreement with author: State your opinions frankly, with supporting evidence.

Overall evaluation: Consider writing style, interest, logic, organization, conciseness, and all the other attributes of good writing.

ENDNOTES

1 Alex Markels, "Managers Aren't Always Able to Get the Right Message Across with E-mail," *Wall Street Journal*, August 6, 1996, Bi(w).

2 Robert E. Calem, "E-mail Users Advised: Put Best Word Forward: Experts Say Messages Should be Written Like Business Letters," *Crain's New York Business*, July 17, 1995, 22.

3 Ibid.

4 Lee Batdorff, "Groupware Offers Paperless Productivity Boost," *Crain's Cleveland Business*, October 2, 1995, T10.

5 Cynthia Scanlon, "Pluses and Pitfalls in Voice Mail," *Nation's Business*, May 1996, 57.

6 John Tschohl, "Voice Mail Found Guilty of Customer Alienation," *Canadian Manager*, Spring 1996, 11–12.

7 Tom Dellacave, Jr. "Now Showing: New Multimedia Tools Put Sound, Video, and Graphics at Your Sales Reps' Fingertips," *Sales and Marketing Management*, February 1996, 68–69.

8 Mark A. Kassel. "Information Found on the Web May Be Protected by Copyright Law. Publishers Have Had Success Suing Those Who Reproduced Wrong Item," *Milwaukee Journal Sentinel*, October 28, 1996.

9 Sara Humphry, ed., "Net Notes: Don't Let Snooping Dogs Lie," *PC Week*, March 11, 1996, (i).

Choosing Appropriate and Effective Words

C H A P T E R

4

OBJECTIVES

Chapter Four will help you:

1   Consider the importance of the choice of words in all forms of written or oral communication.

2   Describe formal and informal writing styles in relation to personal and impersonal writing styles.

3   Explain the need for and demonstrate effective use of nondiscriminatory language.

4   Use positive and pleasant words, objective words, specific words, and grammatically correct words to write effective messages.

5   Recognize ethical and legal considerations that apply to the use of words.

Have you ever thought of the many ways in which words affect our lives?

Do you believe that words have definite, exact meanings, which are given in dictionaries, and that you will become an effective writer and speaker—and achieve harmonious relationships with others—if you can only learn these dictionary definitions?

Do you feel that when you know these definitions, you will be able to handle communication problems logically and sensibly; that is, with the application of common sense? The answers to these questions, with the exception of the first, would be "not necessarily" or "it depends." Many words have emotional effects, and they are far from exact. Our relationships with other people, which are built almost entirely on verbal and nonverbal messages, depend on all our past experiences and our maturity.

THE IMPORTANCE OF WORDS

Our world is filled with words. Unless we shut ourselves off from them, they come to us constantly from television and radio, from newspapers and magazines, from the pulpit, from professors and other lecturers. Sometimes it seems that we are bombarded with words, but we in turn add to the total profusion. An overload of information is one of the reasons we sometimes have difficulty in listening to words we truly wish and need to hear.

People have long been aware of the importance of words in our lives, as shown by many maxims and proverbial sayings. For example, from the Book of Proverbs, "A word fitly spoken is like apples of gold in settings of silver"; from Don Quixote, "An honest man's word is as good as his bond." Mark Twain said, "There is as much difference between the right word and the nearly right word as there is between lightning and the lightning bug." And the common sayings, "I could have bitten off my tongue" and "I really put my foot in my mouth" exemplify our concern with the use and misuse of language.

Words, particularly when arranged into slogans, influence not only our personal and business life but also the history of nations and of the world. Consider the ways that the following words have affected the thought and actions of the American people and the course of American history: "Give me liberty or give me death" (Patrick Henry); "We have nothing to fear but fear itself" (Franklin D. Roosevelt); "We shall overcome" (song and slogan of civil rights movement); "Ask not what your country can do for you, ask what you can do for your country" (John F. Kennedy).

Presidential campaigns have been won or lost because of slogans. Advertising campaigns, tasteful or otherwise, make extensive use of catch phrases. Some become so well known that they can be considered part of the language, at least temporarily.

The maxim "Sticks and stones can break my bones, but words can never harm me" is far from being accurate. In some cases, words can harm more than sticks and stones: They can lead to frowns, misunderstandings, anger, and the use of sticks and stones, to say nothing of the far more devastating weapons of modern warfare.

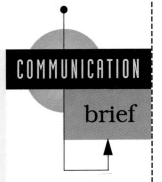

COMMUNICATION

brief

By any standard, English is a remarkable language. It is, to begin with, the native tongue of some 300,000,000 people—the largest speech community in the world except for Mandarin Chinese. Even more remarkable is its geographic spread, in which it is second to none: Its speakers range from Point Barrow, Alaska, to the Falkland Islands near Cape Horn; from the Shetland Islands north of Scotland to Capetown at the southern tip of Africa; from Hong Kong to Australia's island state of Tasmania. It is the predominant language in two of the six inhabited continents (North America and Australia), and possesses a large block of speakers in a third (Europe) and a sizable one in a fourth (Africa).

English is also by far the most important "second language" in the world. It is spoken by tens of millions of educated Europeans and Japanese, is the most widely studied foreign tongue in both the U.S.S.R. and China, and serves as an "official" language in more than a dozen other countries whose populations total more than a billion.

Robert Claiborne, *Our Marvelous Native Tongue* (New York: Times Books, 1983), 3.

FORMAL AND INFORMAL LANGUAGE

Language in the United States is often less formal than it was 100 years ago, in both writing and speaking. Although much writing and speech in professional and business situations cannot be described as formal, neither is it completely informal. In all instances of communication, the appropriate degree of formality depends on the environment, the message, and the audience. When in doubt, use a touch of formality, provided you do not misinterpret the word *formal*. All writing and speech should be natural, simple, and correct. Regardless of the formality of the situation, long words and sentences are less desirable than well-chosen, understandable, and emphatic ones.

Some communication situations are more formal than others. Your letter to a member of Congress or the president of your company will differ in format and wording from a note that you scribble on the back of an envelope to be left on a friend's door or automobile.

You behave and speak more formally at a wedding or a funeral than you do at a neighborhood party. You don't ordinarily wear to church the attire in which you wash your car or take your dog to the vet. (*Vet* is an example of an informal word that is not likely to be stored in your word processor's memory.)

Some people outside the United States believe that we are too informal, sometimes to the point of being disrespectful. They do not like our free and early use of given names, particularly in business offices and with older people. Many Americans consider such use to be appropriately personal and friendly, and the use of "Mr.," "Ms.," or "Mrs." to be overly formal. A touch of formality, however, at least toward new acquaintances, is a better approach than familiarity that could be offensive.

The use of slang should always be avoided in formal writing, although it can sometimes be used effectively in casual conversation. (As with many other words, *formal* and *casual* are relative. How formal is formal and how casual is casual?)

The informal style may occasionally make use of some kinds of slang. Slang, however, should be used with the utmost discretion, for several reasons. First, slang is often not nationwide, so it may not be understood by the reader. Second, even the mildest slang offends some persons; or, if it doesn't offend, it is in questionable taste and unprofessional. Third, slang becomes quickly dated, and what seems fresh and new to the writer may have already been discarded by the reader. Fourth, the use of unusual or startling words or phrases may be distracting and thus delay the reception of the message.

Regardless of how the writing is described or how formal the situation, the writing should not sound unnatural, stilted, or pretentious. A scholarly essay will be more formal than a routine memorandum or an e-mail message, but all written messages should be natural and easy to read. Both should use correct English, and both should be arranged and worded with the reader in mind.

Strictly formal writing will not include contractions, any expression that could be considered slang, or any abbreviated sentences or sentence fragments. It is likely to be written in the impersonal tone, with no first- or second-person pronouns. The informal style will most likely use the personal tone. It may include contractions and casual conversational phrases or modes of expression.

Do not worry a great deal about whether your writing should be formal or informal. Write naturally and correctly, considering the particular circumstances; the reader's preference, if known; and, especially, the purpose of the message.

Your choice of writing style, light or serious, informal or formal, must be influenced by your relationship with the reader and the subject matter of your message. A light, humorous tone, no matter how clever, is inappropriate in some situations. On the other hand, business and professional communications are often concerned with subjects of less than immortal impact, although they are desirable or necessary for whatever purpose they are planned to accomplish.

Some words are designated in dictionaries as informal. Other designations are colloquial, which, according to *Random House Dictionary*, means "characteristic or appropriate to ordinary conversation rather than formal speech or writing." (The word *colloquial* is sometimes thought to mean regional; that is, pertaining to speech in particular regions of the country. Although regional speech is a form of colloquial language, not all colloquial usage is regional.)

To repeat and emphasize, formal words (or at least those that are not definitely informal) are not unnecessarily long. They should not sound pompous or pretentious, nor should they be chosen mainly to impress or to display an extensive vocabulary. Well-chosen words, regardless of the formality of the occasion, are almost always short, familiar, natural words.

Formality is described in this way by an unnamed writer for The Royal Bank of Canada:

> To act formally is to behave according to custom or rule, and we do that more than we realize. Formality serves people well. It signals what is important and makes for order and dignity. As a bonus, it is a source of pleasure from time to time.[1]

The writer goes on to say:

> In the last couple of generations, we in this country have managed to dispense with some formalities that are no longer (and probably never were) necessary. One example is the habit of writing "correct" business letters that are so stilted that the meaning they intend to convey is unclear.[2]

Words and phrases that are inappropriate for most business writing are shown below, with synonyms or near-synonyms that are more appropriate. Terms that are described as too informal include slang, colloquial or regional expressions, and trite words or phrases.

Too informal	More appropriate
hassle	struggle, difficulty
bread, dough, green stuff	money
mix-up, foul-up, snafu	confusion, chaos
kiddies	children
hubby	husband
kibitz	confer, consult
tip, two cents' worth	advice
sweet talk, soft soap	exaggeration, flatter
hang in there, stick it out	persevere
steer clear of	avoid, circumvent
hankering, pining	yearning
wild about	enthusiastic

Regional and other colloquial expressions may be used in conversation as long as they are appropriate for the listener and the situation, but they should ordinarily be omitted from business writing. Examples include *fixing to*, meaning to prepare, to plan, or to get ready, a Southern expression; and *kittycorner*, used in some areas of the North and West to mean "in a diagonal position."

PERSONAL AND IMPERSONAL WRITING STYLES

The impersonal writing style is more formal than the personal writing style. It is ordinarily used when a report or other written material is considered formal in format and wording. Written material can convey formality even with the use of first- and second-person pronouns. Formal writing style and impersonal tone are not synonymous, although they are often used together in the same report or other document.

The impersonal writing style is also referred to as the third-person objective writing style. It includes no *I*'s, *we*'s, *you*'s, or other first- or second-person pronouns.

Most writing for business and the professions is in the personal tone. (The use of *I* and *we* is excessive, even when using the personal tone, if it gives an appearance of expressing the I-attitude, not the you-attitude.) Almost all letters and memorandums and many reports are written in the personal tone.

An advantage of the impersonal tone is that this style of writing seems more objective and nonbiased because the writer is not speaking of himself or herself. The choice of writing style does not affect real objectivity; nevertheless, because it appears to do so, many persons prefer impersonal wording, particularly for reports. The use of *I*'s, *we*'s, and other first- and second-person pronouns may be a form of noise, distracting the reader's mind from whatever it is that you are trying to say.

Examples of passages in the personal and the impersonal writing styles are as follows:

Personal

I recommend that the Marketing Department adopt a flexible time schedule.

Impersonal

The Marketing Department should adopt a flexible time schedule.

Personal

You will notice that prices of some items have decreased about 5 percent.

Personal (implied *you*)

Notice that prices of some items have decreased about 5 percent.

Impersonal

Prices on some items have decreased about 5 percent.

Personal

Please telephone me when I can help.

Impersonal

Employees should telephone their supervisors when they need help.

Do not use the impersonal style unnecessarily. The personal tone is more friendly, natural, and direct. Some kinds of material, however, such as news releases and many reports, should be written in the impersonal style with absolutely no *I*'s, *we*'s, *you*'s, or other first- or second-person pronouns.

NONDISCRIMINATORY LANGUAGE

Speech or writing can be inconsiderate and undiplomatic when it contains discriminatory language. Although the speaker or writer may be absolutely fair and objective in thought and actions, an unwise choice of words can build distrust and decrease acceptance and understanding.

▶ AVOID MASCULINE PRONOUNS EXCEPT WHEN REFERRING SPECIFICALLY TO MALES

The English language has no singular pronoun to represent both sexes. Because of this lack, for centuries masculine pronouns (*he, him, his, himself*) were used with the understanding that they represented either gender.

Although masculine pronouns are still used by some men and women as generic words to indicate either gender, you are wise to avoid such use. It is offensive to many people. Language considered sexist or discriminatory in any other way can destroy goodwill.

In the past, masculine pronouns were used in such sentences as

Obsolete language and equipment; discriminatory *his*

An engineer must know how to use his slide rule.

At the time, the word *his* was more logical than it is today, but it is still likely to occur in such sentences as

Updated equipment; discriminatory word *his*

An engineer must know how to use his computer.

The idea that only men can be engineers is now as outdated as the slide rule. All occupations are open to women, but language is slow to reflect this change.

Neither masculine nor feminine pronouns should be used to describe a person whose sex is unknown. For example, do not refer to a secretary or a nurse as *she* unless you are referring to a particular woman who is a secretary or nurse. To do so is to imply that only women are secretaries or nurses or, worse, that only women should be secretaries or nurses.

In the sentences about the engineer used above, *his* is unnecessary in reference to either the slide rule or the computer. The simple article *a* is sufficient, whether or not the engineer actually owns the slide rule or the computer. Substituting *a* or *the* or reconstructing the sentence in some other way to avoid using pronouns is one of the most appropriate and convenient ways of avoiding *he, his*, or *him*.

Another method of attaining nondiscriminatory writing is to use plural nouns. For example, instead of

An accountant can update his knowledge by attending seminars]- Avoid

change the sentence to

Accountants can update their knowledge . . .]- Prefer

Another method of avoiding generic use of masculine or feminine pronouns is to repeat the noun, although this method should be used with discretion in order to avoid repetition. Also avoid frequent use of *he or she*, although the term may be used when there is no other way to avoid sexist wording and to make your meaning clear. Overuse of *he or she* is distracting and results in awkward writing.

Sometimes the passive voice can be used to avoid pronouns, although this method should also be used sparingly because the active voice is often more direct, concise, and forceful. For example, instead of writing

Each employee should sign and return his approved vacation request form]- Discriminatory language

you could write

Approved vacation request forms should be signed and returned.

In this particular illustration, the sentence with the verb in the passive voice is shorter than the previous one. Apart from the elimination of *his*, the second sentence is preferable because emphasis is upon approved vacation request forms, where the emphasis should ordinarily be placed. If the writer wants to emphasize *each employee* and leave the sentence in the first arrangement, the article *the* can be used to replace the pronoun *his*.

This sentence also could be expressed with a plural noun, as

All employees should sign and return their approved vacation request forms.

Still another method of avoiding masculine pronouns is to use *you;* that is, use the *personal tone instead of impersonal wording.* In the preceding example, if you are writing *to* the employees instead of *about* them, use the word *you* because it is more direct, friendly, and interesting, in addition to being a method of avoiding *his*. To make the preceding sentence more tactful and diplomatic, omit *should* and word the sentence in this way:

Please sign and return your approved vacation request form.

AVOID OTHER FORMS OF DISCRIMINATORY LANGUAGE

In addition to masculine pronouns used to designate either sex, several other terms are viewed as sexist; for example, *woman attorney, male nurse, woman doctor,* or *poetess.* Use *attorney, nurse, doctor,* and *poet.*

Do not say *girl* when referring to an assistant who is a woman. Instead, call her your assistant or, preferably, refer to her by name.

Do not use the term *businessman* unless you are referring to a particular man. Preferably use *executive, business manager,* or *businessperson* for both men and women.

Instead of salesman, unless referring to a specific man, use *sales representative* or *salesperson.*

Instead of *foreman,* use *supervisor.*

The word *chairman* is still used by many men and women, and some women prefer the term, saying that it is the name of a position, not a sexist term. Many others don't like it. Unless you are sure that the woman to whom you are referring chooses to be addressed as *chairman,* use some other word, such as *chairperson, chairwoman, coordinator, department head,* or *department chair.* In all instances, follow known preferences.

From the same standpoint, address women as *Ms., Mrs.,* or *Miss* according to their known preferences. If you do not know preferences, use *Ms.,* which is used more and more to refer to all women. In examples of letters in this book, the use of a title other than *Ms.* is based on the assumption that the writer of the letter knew that the woman to whom the letter was addressed prefers *Mrs.* or *Miss,* probably because she so indicated by her title on a letter. (See Appendix A for examples of how a woman may show her preferred title preceding her typewritten name, NOT before her signature.) If no title is indicated, assume that the preferred title is *Ms.*

Writing in a nondiscriminatory manner means that you also consider other situations where your word choices could be offensive to the reader or listener or possibly convey a negative stereotype. Topics such as national origin, race, religion, appearance, physical abilities and limitations, and age are important areas where you will want to take care to avoid using language that someone views as offensive.

You may find that you can convey the true message you need to send without any reference to one of these potentially sensitive areas. If you wish to make a statement about an employee, for example, focus on the main message.

Ineffective: *Mary, who is crippled, is the office manager.*

Effective: *Mary is the office manager.*

If you must refer to Mary's physical disability for clarity, use more inoffensive terms, such as in the following example.

Mary, who uses a wheelchair, must use the elevator to get to her meeting on the third floor.

Apply the same logic in other situations. Avoid using discriminatory wording. You may be attending classes with students who were born in other countries and are at your school on student visas. You may have no need to refer to a national origin.

Ineffective: *Bill, Sue, and Jon, a French student, must study hard for the exam.*

Effective: *Bill, Sue, and Jon must study hard for the exam.*

If you need to provide a descriptor for clarity, then use an inoffensive one.

Ineffective: *A group of foreign students is sponsoring a luncheon next week in the student union.*

Effective: *A group of international students is sponsoring a luncheon next week in the student union.*

Eliminate all unnecessary references to age, appearance, disabilities, race, or national origin.

SIMPLE, DIRECT, AND NATURAL WORDS

Work for a simple, direct, and natural writing style. A letter or memorandum should sound like informal conversation with your reader.

Short words, provided that they best express the desired meaning, should be preferred to long words. Short words, however, do not always result in easily understood messages. An unusual short word that the reader is not likely to recognize is not as desirable as a more familiar longer word. Also, when we are writing to people who are specialists in a certain field, a longer technical word is preferable to a shorter one that is used mistakenly to make the written material simple.

Short words, appropriately chosen, not only increase readability but also help to form a vivid and forceful writing style. Compare the effectiveness of these words.

Instead of	**Why not use**
approbation	approval
approximately	about
ameliorate	improve
incorporate	include
interrogate	ask
promulgate	publish
peruse	read
utilize	use
engrossment	attention
expectancy	hope
utilizable	useful
salience	importance

Choose words carefully, even when you are trying, as you should, to simplify. Few words have exact synonyms, long or short. Find the word most likely to express your exact meaning to the mind of the reader, but remember that this word is most often a short, familiar one.

DENOTATIVE AND CONNOTATIVE MEANINGS

Words have special characteristics of their own, aside from their dictionary, or *denotative*, meanings. They have *connotative* meanings: either general connotative meanings to most persons who see or hear the word, or special connotative meanings to particular individuals because of their specific experiences with the word.

We cannot rely only on denotative (or "dictionary") meanings. Complete dictionaries, however, give various illustrations of words in the context of how they are used and often give some indication of their connotative meaning.

Although no word is completely specific, regardless of usage and definition, denotative meanings are considered more concrete and tangible than connotative meanings, which are based on experiences, attitudes, beliefs, and emotions. To many minds, the word *home* brings pleasant memories of family, fireside, laughter, good food, friends, comfort, and security. The word *house* has a more neutral meaning. If you sell real estate, do you refer to a piece of property as a residence, a building, a house, or a home?

Effective communicators take care to use nondiscriminatory language in both written and oral communication.

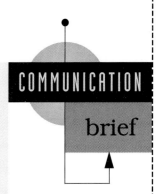

Writing works best when it fits the sounds and rhythms of speaking and listening. Perhaps that is why when we reject one expression for another as we write, we often say: "Oh, the first one didn't sound right."

Write as you speak—when you are speaking very well—because you will then write more clearly and humanly. And people will understand you better.

Arn Tibbetts, *Practical Business Writing* (Boston: Little, Brown & Co., 1987), 135.

If your prospective buyer doesn't like the property, he or she may think of it as a shack, a dump, or a hovel. If one perceives the place as particularly desirable, the neutral house may become a mansion or a dream house. A cottage by the sea may be thought of as a dream come true; a cottage that must accommodate a large family on a year-round basis will be described by some less favorable wording.

Regardless of the words with which it is described, a house is most likely to sell quickly if it is painted a soft yellow, according to real estate experts. Colors as well as words have emotional effects. (Could various reactions to color be described as "nonverbal connotations"?)

Words that usually have unpleasant connotations beyond their actual denotative meanings are *criticize, you claim*, and *cheap*. Although the word *criticize* means to evaluate either positively or negatively, the word almost always connotes an unfavorable evaluation.

We cannot know and control individual connotations based on the experience of the individual reader or listener. Although *criticize, cheap*, and similar words and phrases are likely to convey similar emotions to most people, other words have various connotative meanings to individuals based on their particular experiences.

For example, if a person has had an automobile accident on Perkins Road, the words alone will elicit unpleasant memories and feelings. (He or she may not want the house you are selling on Perkins Road, even if it is painted yellow.) If a young man is in love with a girl named Linda, another girl with the same name will seem more attractive than one named Anna Lou. If a person has been spurred and bitten by a rooster, the word *rooster* arouses in her or his mind a vivid picture, not of an industrious early bird awaking the world, but of a foul fowl that she or he never wants to see or hear of again.

Although a comprehensive and reliable dictionary remains an essential tool for all of us, learning the true nature of words consists of far more than memorizing definitions. Because words have various denotative as well as connotative meanings, humorous misuse sometimes occurs in the translation of passages from one language to another. As an example, the *body* of an automobile has been translated to *corpse*.

Aside from their emotional effect, words have their own particular shades of meaning. Although words are described as synonyms for other words, there are few real synonyms. Words are often similar in meaning to other words; but, because of their particular connotations or the context in which they are ordinarily used, they cannot be substituted for their near-synonyms without some slight change in meaning.

A word is said to have a weak connotation if it has no strong or significant overtones; such a word is also described as being neutral, although in fact no word is completely neutral to all readers and listeners. As mentioned, *house* has more of a neutral tone than does *home*, which has favorable and pleasant implications. The word *student* is more neutral than *scholar* (favorable) or *bookworm* (unfavorable).

Words connote high and low status. Garbage collectors are becoming sanitation engineers; janitors are called maintenance engineers, building engineers, or managers. Salespersons are referred to as representatives, special representatives, or registered representatives. At Wal-Mart, all sales-clerks are referred to as associates, as shown on the badges bearing their names.

In our status-conscious society, titles are important. The mere change of title can be a morale booster and an asset to a person moving to another department or organization. (Some employees mention that a change of title costs less than a raise or promotion.)

In department stores years ago, what is now called the customer service department was called the claims department, which was followed by adjustment department. A credit card may now be referred to as a courtesy card.

Consider the implications of the following words:

► scheme, plan, program of action

► proposition, proposal, presentation

► gamble, speculation, calculated risk

► scrawny, skinny, slim, slender

► stupid, retarded, exceptional, special

► stupid, unsound, unadvised

► favoritism, leaning, undetachment

You could make long lists of similar words. Do you recognize that words have differing and definite personalities of their own?

CHANGING MEANINGS OF WORDS

The English language, like all other living languages, is constantly changing. Could you expect it not to do so? It must change to meet our needs. The change is neither good nor bad, but inevitable.

New words are added and others become obsolete. Many words and phrases are borrowed from other languages, as they always have been. Technology adds to the vocabulary of general usage the words that were first used as specialized terminology, jargon, or slang of a particular field or occupation.

Many words in everyday use that are considered part of the English language are derived from countries other than England, and many of those that came to the United States from England were previously adapted from French, Latin, Spanish, and other languages. The following words, with their country of origin, make up only a tiny portion of the thousands that could be listed.

Greece: arithmetic, cardiac, diet

China: tea, silk, chow

France: mayonnaise, menu, vogue

Germany: diesel, ecology, Fahrenheit

India: bungalow, dungaree, shampoo

Italy: profile, miniature, piano

So-called new words are not necessarily ones that have never been used before. They may be old ones used in a new way. For example, the term *hardware* once meant the varied merchandise in a hardware store, and *software*, if used at all, referred to softer merchandise, such as towels. (Don't go to a linen department to buy programs for your computer.)

Some slang finds its way into dictionaries and becomes acceptable even for standard or formal usage, although much slang fades away and is forgotten. Other slang remains for centuries; *bones* meant *dice* even in Chaucer's day. Although dice are no longer made of bones, but of plastic, this fact probably has little to do with decrease in the use of the term. Words remain in general use long after the original reason for being has disappeared.

Shakespeare used *beat it* to mean *go away*. The word *dough*, meaning *money*, has been in use for more than one hundred years.

Examples of words now in standard usage that were once considered slang are *mob*; *phone* for telephone; *blizzard*; *movie*; and *type* for typewrite. (An earlier use of the word *typewriter* was to name the person who used the machine a *typewriter*, not a *typist*.)

Many thousands of words have changed in meaning during the past two or three centuries. Spelling has also changed, as well as what is considered correct usage. At one time, *you was* was correct; now only *you were* is acceptable. Words change in shades of meaning, as well as completely reversing themselves. At one time, *silly* meant *holy*; *fond* meant *foolish*; *tree* meant *beam*; and *beam* meant *tree*.

The English language, like all others, has always been in a process of change, as it will continue to be. Compared to previous years, written material today includes shorter sentences and wording that is more direct, natural, informal, and conversational. All these changes make a great deal of sense. As in conversation itself, however, writing seems either stimulating, mediocre, or banal, according to the particular writer and the particular reader.

THE LANGUAGE OF BUSINESS

There really is no "language of business," except for some specialized terms that exist in particular organizations, industries, offices, or occupations. Good business writing is like any other good writing.

The business *jargon* that some business writers use is made up of unnecessary, trite, and wordy phrases. This "language," if it can be considered a language, should be discarded or updated. Such usage is not only stereotyped, but also old-fashioned. Some students of 19 or so write as if they were 20 years' past retirement as listed below.

- ► enclosed please find

- ► enclosed herewith

- ► pursuant to your request

- ► we beg to call your kind attention to

- ► please be advised

- ► kindly be advised

- ► thanking you for your kind attention

- ► the same being at hand I wish to state

Yes, these cumbersome phrases are still used in some letters and memorandums, but, fortunately, their use is decreasing. Businesspeople seem to be more likely than other writers to use such unnatural wording. The widespread use of e-mail, however, has resulted in more natural, conversational wording, a welcome change if the informality is not of such an extent that written messages are no longer businesslike and professional.

The wordy phrases and trite business jargon cited in the following list should almost always be omitted or simplified because they are slow, wordy, and nonconversational.

- ► it has come to my attention
- ► in the amount of (for)
- ► to the total amount of (for)
- ► amounting to (for)
- ► totaling the sum of (for)
- ► be advised, be informed, consider yourself informed
- ► this is to inform you, this is for your information
- ► herewith, herein, attached herewith, attached hereto, reference to same, consideration of same
- ► we beg to call your attention to the fact that
- ► thank you in advance, thanking you for your time, thanking you for your consideration
- ► we wish to remain, yours truly
- ► as of this date, as of this writing, as of the present time, due to the fact that, in view of the fact that
- ► at an early date
- ► we beg to remain
- ► pursuant to your request
- ► the undersigned (except in legal papers)
- ► for the purpose of, for the reason that, due to the fact that (*for, to, because*)

Closely related to the wordy and trite phrases listed above are fad words or phrases, which soon become trite and meaningless because of overuse. Some of these overused words and phrases are as follows:

- ► at this point in time
- ► the bottom line
- ► hopefully (although not actually incorrect, it is becoming as frequent as "you know")
- ► back to square one
- ► eyeball to eyeball
- ► interface (used to describe human communication)

Positive and Pleasant Words versus Negative, Unpleasant Words

Positive and pleasant words are more effective than negative, unpleasant ones. Positive and pleasant words build goodwill; negative words destroy it.

Although some written and spoken communication must convey unfavorable information that must be made clear, even unfavorable messages can be expressed in positive words or in neutral, objective words.

Avoid extremely negative words such as *fail, reject, criticize,* and similar words. Express your meaning from the reader's or listener's point of view. Emphasize the positive aspects of a situation, not the negative, as discussed in detail in Chapter 6, "Building Goodwill through Communication."

Judgmental words, especially derogatory ones, should be used with caution, if at all! Objectivity is stressed in the discussion of research and report writing, but it is also important in all business writing.

Some of the many words that should ordinarily be omitted because of their negative connotations are as follows:

unfair	bribery
insane	discrimination
unheard of	high-pressure tactics
lazy	exorbitant
incompetent	senile
unbelievable	suspicious
gullible	unbelievable

Unpleasant words can be replaced with more pleasant words, or at least with neutral, objective ones. For example, *scheme* can be replaced by *plan*; even more favorable is *program of action*. Another example is *bogus* (negative connotation); *artificial* (neutral connotation); and *simulated* (positive connotation). In some instances you will change the meaning slightly. As stated earlier in this chapter, few real synonyms exist. For example, as you try to find another word for *bribe*, you could use *subsidy* or *gratuity*. Although these words are not exactly synonymous, if used in the proper context their meaning would be clear.

At times negative descriptions must be given, as when evaluating employees. When such information is necessary, state specific facts, not your own negative opinions. Examples include the following:

Instead of
Joe Brown is irresponsible. He does not come to work half the time and is always late.

Write or say
Joe Brown has been absent for no stated reason seventeen days during the past year. He has been at least thirty minutes late eleven times.

Although judgmental words that express pleasant and positive ideas can and should be used more freely than those that express negative or accusing thoughts, even these words should be used with discretion. Although so-called emotional wording is often used in sales messages and elsewhere, such usage is not as convincing as positive, concrete, and specific description of favorable attributes or circumstances.

Instead of
This marvelous Ivory soap is wonderful because it is pure.

And instead of
Ivory soap is amazingly pure.

And instead of
You will be astonished at the purity level of Ivory soap.

Prefer

Ivory soap is 99 and 44/100ths percent pure.

Instead of

Our superb president has provided incredible advantages for all of us.

Prefer

President Clifft has increased our profit-sharing income by 20 percent, provided an organized system of recognition and promotion, and encouraged employee participation in decision making.

Be especially careful to avoid nonobjective judgmental words, either positive or negative, in reports or other informational material.

SPECIFIC, CONCRETE WORDS VERSUS VAGUE, GENERAL WORDS

Ordinarily you should use concrete, specific words rather than general, nonspecific words. (For the sake of diplomacy, however, sometimes general, nonspecific words are preferable, as described further in Chapter 6.)

General, abstract	More specific
soon	Thursday, January 8
heavy paper	24-weight paper
computers	IBM personal computers
a good return	10.23 percent annually
contact	telephone
well educated	earned a Ph.D. degree
a well-known company	Exxon
a long table	10-foot conference table
a short speech	a five-minute speech
a long speech	a 90-minute speech

For a number of obvious reasons, you cannot or should not be completely specific in all writing or speech. At times you should express your ideas in general terms to achieve diplomacy or an appropriate psychological approach. At times you may not know exact details; for example, you may not be sure that a conference table is exactly 10 feet long.

In other instances your reader or listener may not expect or want complete descriptions. If you work in an office equipped only with IBM personal computers, you need not describe them as such over and over.

Use specific, concrete, exact wording when it is possible and appropriate. Your writing and speech will be more clear, interesting, exact, and forceful.

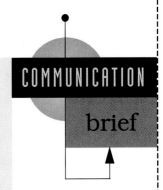

COMMUNICATION

brief

I got a polite, written reprimand the other day from the folks who invented the stuff you pour into your cat's litter box.

In a story, I used the words "Kitty Litter" generically, without capitalizing them or mentioning that Kitty Litter is a brand name. To tell the truth, I didn't know Kitty Litter was a brand name. Well, the people whose job it is to scour all the newspapers and periodicals in America for lower-cased Kitty Litters caught me.

Newspaper people run into this kind of thing every now and then. For instance, you can't use "Kleenex" if you mean just any old tissue. Instead of "STYROFOAM" (capitalize the whole thing), the trademark watchdogs suggest you say "a light polystyrene plastic foam." Right.

"We could lose our trademark if we didn't routinely protest its misuse," said Deborah Kayden, when I called to ask about the fuss over "Kitty Litter."

As a young reporter, I spent a month's salary on a Nikon camera, but my mother brought me back to earth. I proudly strutted through the house, trying to look nonchalant about the gleaming black hardware dangling from my shoulder. "Go snap a picture of my Thanksgiving table with your new Brownie," she said.

Any cleanser is "Bon Ami" to Mother, no matter if the label says "Comet" or "Dutch." All luggage is "Samsonite." To a lot of folks, all refrigerators are "Frigidaires." Which would bother me a lot more if I owned "Whirlpool" or "Norge" or "General Electric" than if I owned "Frigidaire," but then there's no figuring corporate law.

Rheta Grimsley Johnson, *America's Faces* (Memphis: St. Luke's Press, 1987), 327–328.

ETHICAL AND LEGAL CONSIDERATIONS

Business communication, written and oral, is concerned with almost every conceivable topic and situation. Many and various laws apply, as they do to all other business activities.

Ethical approaches to communication, as to other business activities, ordinarily prevent serious legal problems, but not always. Your knowledge of applicable laws can save embarrassing and costly mistakes. If you are ever in doubt about legal matters affecting your communication efforts, do not proceed without investigating further. Many companies have their own legal departments; most organizations provide legal counsel in doubtful situations.

As stated by Lee and colleagues, in *Business Communication,*

The written record that you produce when you write a business communication is, in essence, a legal contract. The partners in this contract are you and your business as the "makers" and your communication partner and the business he or she represents as the "receivers." When you write business messages, consider the following factors:

1 A written communication is acceptable as legal evidence in a court of law. You and your company may be forced to carry out your promises, or you and your company could be sued for breach of contract.
2 Your signature on a letter indicates that you agree with and approve of its contents.
3 You cannot legally change your mind once your written communication reaches the receiver unless you can prove that circumstances have changed enough to legally release you from your previous commitments.
4 If your written statements indicate that a person is unfit to perform his or her job or that a company is unfit to carry on its business, you and your company may be sued for libel.[3]

▶ DEFAMATION (AN ATTACK ON ONE'S REPUTATION)

Written *defamation* is known as *libel*; oral defamation is known as *slander.*

A true defamation must be communicated or "published" (made known to others); it must be based on a malicious intent; and damages must result. Damages are assumed to result from written statements that ridicule others and hold them up for public contempt. If the statements are true and are needed to convey necessary information to the public, libel or slander will not ordinarily be upheld.

Nevertheless, "truth" is often difficult to prove. Even if a court case is won, communicators and their employing organizations are far wiser to avoid the litigation, which is expensive and often damaging to public relations and company goodwill, regardless of who is to blame and the outcome of the case.

Writers of letters about past or present employees and credit applicants must be especially careful to avoid remarks that could be interpreted as libel. Because of such danger, some organizations refuse to release any information about employees other than dates of employment or the title of the employee's position. Writers who provide credit information make sure that the applicant has given the organization as a reference, thus implying that information can be released. All applicants must be made aware that credit information is being requested. Letters or other communications that report an applicant's credit history should include the statement that the information being released is to be considered confidential and is to be used only for the specified purpose for which it is requested.

Writers of collection letters, as well as people who collect in person and by telephone, must be especially careful not to damage the debtor's reputation. Even a letter individually addressed to the debtor can be interpreted as being "published" if the letter is intercepted and read by another person, provided the writer can be assumed to know that such interception was likely to occur. Collection letters should be mailed in sealed envelopes and marked "Personal and Confidential."

A legal right to communicate defamatory information to certain persons is known as *privilege*. For example, dictation to a secretary, testimony in court, and consultation with a lawyer are ordinarily considered privileged

These executives would resent or be amused if referred to as "he," or "salesman."

information, as is information about past employees if provided at their request. Nevertheless, as mentioned earlier, many organizations prefer not to take a chance that a libel suit will result; thus, they release only limited information.

Similar to privileged information is *fair comment*, the right to comment fairly about persons in public life, one of the attributes of free speech. The comments must not overreach fairness or be directed toward an individual's personal life.

WORDS THAT MAY BE CONSIDERED LIBELOUS

Words themselves may be considered libelous. (As emphasized throughout this textbook, negative words should be avoided even if there is not the slightest possibility of a libel suit. They are not conducive to effective and harmonious communication of any kind.) Some of the many words that may be considered libelous are these:

lazy	drug addict	alcoholic	loafer
worthless	inferior	thief	freeloader
inefficient	insolvent	crazy	shiftless
crook	kickbacks	psychotic	deadbeat
dishonest	misconduct	corrupt	fraud
incompetent	quack	incapable	swindle
drunk	bum	bankrupt	racketeer

When you must report negative information in any communication (and make sure that such reporting actually is necessary), do so in specific, neutral words. Report events with dates and objective details. Negative, "name-calling" words are dangerous and usually unfair. They reflect adversely on your own communication abilities. In addition, they may result in a libel accusation.

SUMMARY

Words and slogans influence our professional and business lives and also the history of nations and of the world.

Words have both denotative and connotative meanings. The denotation is the "dictionary" meaning. The connotation is the special meaning of the word based on the individual's experiences and perception. Aside from the emotional effect, words have their own particular shades of meaning. Few words have true synonyms.

Language is constantly changing.

A simple, direct, and natural writing style is desirable for all kinds of material. Short words, provided that they express the desired meaning, should be preferred to longer ones.

The formality of writing and speaking differs depending on the subject, the occasion, the audience, and the content of the message. Most business writing is neither extremely formal nor extremely informal, but semiformal. The impersonal writing style includes no first- and second-person pronouns, which include *I, me, my, us,* and *you* (or implied *you*). The personal writing style may include these pronouns. Business writing should not include stereotyped phrases or business jargon.

Positive and pleasant words are preferable to negative and unpleasant ones, although clarity must never be sacrificed for diplomacy. Objective words are preferable to biased, judgmental ones.

Nondiscriminatory language does not include words and phrases that are often considered sexist. Masculine pronouns should be used only when referring specifically to males.

TEST YOURSELF

chapter content

1   The meaning of a word as it is listed in a dictionary is described as its _____ meaning.

2   A word meaning that includes judgment and may differ from individual to individual is described as its _____ meaning.

3   A writing style that includes the words *I* and *you* is said to be written in the _____ tone.

4   A writing style that includes no first- or second-person pronouns is said to be written in the _____ tone or the _____ writing style.

5   What is meant by objective words?

6   Name three of the many reasons that language changes.

7   What is a disadvantage and a possible advantage of using slang?

8   Name two methods of avoiding the use of the word *he* when referring to either a man or a woman.

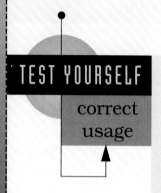

TEST YOURSELF

correct usage

(See a dictionary and "Punctuation as an Aid to Readability" in Appendix D.)

1   Shall we (proceed, precede, procede, preceed) with our discussion about words?
2   How do words (affect, effect) our everyday behavior?
3   Words have emotional (affects, effects).
4   Connotative meanings are based on individual experiences attitudes beliefs and emotions.
5   Words are described as being synonyms for other words but there are few real synonyms.
6   The English language is constantly changing, all other languages also change
7   Well chosen words are likely to be short words.
8   In (past, passed) years this street was rather (quite, quiet).
9   The (stationary, stationery) store is (quite, quiet) profitable although it (formerly, formally) lost money every month.
10   Participants spoke (continually, continuously) throughout the morning without even a short break.
11   An efficient and concerned (personal, personnel, personel) department builds employee (morale, moral).
12   This department was not (apprised, appraised) of the fact that the building must be (apprised, appraised).
13   I (advise, advice) you not to give (advise, advice).
14   I am not (all together, altogether) sure that this (proceedure, procedure) is (alright, all right) for our particular purpose.
15   The City (Council, Counsel) voted to pass the amendment.

PROBLEMS AND CASES

1   Draw up a list of words of high and low status, such as sanitation engineer versus garbage collector, administrators versus clerks, maintenance engineer versus janitor.

2   Look in a dictionary of quotations. Find two quotations about words. Present these in a memorandum addressed to your instructor. Be prepared to read these quotations to the class.

3   Find a word or phrase with a more favorable connotation for each of the following expressions. For some of the words you can think of at least two or more favorable expressions—one or more somewhat neutral and one or more so favorable that it would be considered a *euphemism*.

chore	the old woman
deal	poverty
cheap	racket
affair	blemish
liar	rule with an iron hand
messed up	blunder
stubborn	long-winded

4 Write specific, detailed instructions on how to operate some business machine or equipment with which you are familiar. Be complete and concise.

5 Analyze three or four business letters. Do they include any of the phrases listed under the section "The Language of Business" in this chapter?

6 Using an example from your own experience or imagination, describe an example of miscommunication because of varying interpretations of words.

7 From your travels to different sections of the United States or Canada, give examples of regional words or phrases. Have you witnessed instances when these expressions resulted in miscommunication?

8 Can you think of words, in addition to those mentioned in the chapter, that have been replaced by higher-status words?

9 Ask one or more persons in their seventies or eighties whether they remember examples of slang that were in vogue when they were teenagers. Determine what has happened to these expressions. Have they become almost forgotten or have they become standard language? As your teacher directs, give an oral or written report to the class.

10 Which words in the following sentences would you change or omit because of their connotative meanings?
   a. The new vice-president is the child of the founder of this company.
   b. We have your letter in which you claim your check was mailed three weeks ago.
   c. He was allowed to be president of his fraternity.
   d. I can't say that I blame you. On the other hand . . .
   e. Yes, you got a good buy. But I always feel uncomfortable in cheap clothes.
   f. I'm not as frugal as you are.
   g. You are the only person who has mentioned this problem, if it is a problem.

11 Rewrite the following sentences so that they can be readily understood by people from all parts of the United States and Canada, as well as by people whose first language is one other than English. Also work for more formality.
   a. This comment is just off the top of my head.
   b. The hotel serves good old-time vittles.
   c. I was just fixing to leave for the office.
   d. I reckon that Washington is going to the dogs.
   e. She wears a diamond as big as the Rock of Gibraltar on her little finger.
   f. He acts like a high muckamuck, like a real big shot.
   g. She threw the pencil plumb across the room.
   h. She goes to work wearing ragamuffin clothes and clodhopper shoes.
   i. I've got to hit the books.
   j. She was tickled pink about being transferred to the Big Apple.
   k. Their problems with shipping delays are just the tip of the iceberg.
   l. His efforts didn't cut the mustard.
   m. What does upgrading our computer hardware and software have to do with the price of eggs?

12 Write a description of how to complete one of the tasks you do each day on the job. Assume you are writing the instructions for someone who has just been hired. Select the terms you use carefully; send the written instructions to your instructor via e-mail for feedback.

13 Write specific instructions to tell others how to access the electronic mail system at your school. Write the instructions so that someone unfamiliar with the school's software can successfully access e-mail.

14 Find an article in a trade magazine or professional journal in your field. Make a list of the terms, acronyms, and abbreviations with which you are not familiar. Use a textbook or dictionary to determine the meaning of each of the terms you identified. Rewrite each sentence in which the unfamiliar term appeared, using more understandable words.

COLLABORATIVE WRITING AND WORKING IN GROUPS

15 Prepare a list of a half dozen "red flag" words that you view in a negative manner (or that generate immediate negative reactions from you). Meet in teams of two or three and compare lists. Do your teammates feel as strongly about each of the words on your list as you do? Do you feel as strongly as they do about each word on their lists? If you were all colleagues in a business environment, would there ever be instances when you would use these red flag words you know will annoy another person?

16 Meet in groups of three. Critique the following paragraph contents. Based on your study of Chapter 4, identify any words or phrases that should be changed to provide more effective business communication. Rewrite the entire paragraph to reflect effective wording.

> The employee welfare committee met recently to address some important personal concerns. Pursuant to the request of the human resource manager, the committee addressed such issues as lazy employees, access problems for employees confined to wheelchairs, and the affect of sidestream smoke on nonsmokers. At an early date the committee will report its findings to management.

17 Rewrite: Work for natural, simple wording instead of the extremely old-fashioned and wordy letter shown below. (You are not likely to encounter such writing as this as we near the twenty-first century. This passage is shown to serve as a "horrible example," which can be an excellent teaching tool.)

> In reply to your recent favor we wish to state that shipment of the order you placed approximately a month ago has been delayed. This is to inform you that the order should ship in approximately two weeks, pending our receipt of said merchandise from the manufacturer. Be assured that our staff will process said order in a timely manner.

18 Meet in groups of three or four to discuss one or more of Problems 1 through 14. Work together for the suggested solutions. Report the results of your group work, orally or as a written summary, to the class as a whole.

THINK-IT-THROUGH ASSIGNMENT

19 You have been hired by Brinkman Industries as assistant purchasing agent. Part of your job responsibilities will involve drafting memos and letter for your boss, Brinkman's purchasing agent. Your boss suggests that you study some of the files for examples of memos and letters she has written in the past.

She wants you to write the letters so that they reflect her writing style. After two months you have had adequate time to study documents in the files, and you have identified several communication concerns: (1) Your boss uses a good deal of slang in interoffice memos to other department heads; others in the company do not appear to use slang in their memos. (2) Your boss uses numerous trite and wordy phrases and old-fashioned language. (3) Some messages containing bad news or negative information appear to contain an excessive number of words with negative connotations.

You take extra care to make improvements in these three areas as you draft a two-page short report in memo form for your boss. She returns it to you later in the day, with several notations and also tells you, "This doesn't read like my writing. Please make the changes I've noted." What should you do in relation to the communication going out from the purchasing agent's office?

Should you continue to write in the same style your boss has been using?

Should you discuss this in more detail with your boss? If so, what communication channel will you use? How can you effectively persuade your boss that your changes are good ones she should accept? Write a memo to your instructor in which you describe what actions you would take and why.

After your instructor and your teammates have evaluated the memo to your instructor, write a memo to your boss. Or, if you and your group have decided that the situation should be discussed person-to-person instead of in a memorandum, make detailed notes to guide you in presenting your recommendations.

ENDNOTES

1 "The Functions of Formality," *The Royal Bank Letter*, 68 (May–June 1987): 1.

2 Ibid., 4.

3 Lajuana W. Lee, Sallye S. Benoit, Wilma C. Moore, and Celeste Stanfield Powers, *Business Communication* (Chicago: Rand McNally, 1980), 395–396.

Achieving Correctness, Conciseness, Completeness, Readability, and the Desired Emphasis

CHAPTER

5

OBJECTIVES

Chapter Five will help you:

1   Apply the basic principles of emphasis.

2   Explain readability formulas, including their purpose, strengths, and weaknesses.

3   Write concisely without sacrificing necessary content.

4   Explain and illustrate the use of the active and the passive voice.

5   Use format to increase readability.

A *concise* message is no longer than it needs to be in order to achieve its purpose. *Readability*, as the word implies, means that a written message is easy to read, that it is immediately clear. When written material is planned to achieve the desired *emphasis*, it is likely to be readable as well as arranged in an order that achieves the most desirable psychological approach.

Readability and emphasis are influenced by word choice; by sentence length and paragraph length; by the length of the entire message; by the use or omission of subheads, listings, and other aspects of format; by careful organization, planning, and wording to achieve unity and coherence; and by the way the material is arranged on the sheet.

The shortest message is not necessarily the most clear. If details or explanations necessary for understanding are omitted or vaguely implied in order to keep the communication short, the message will not be understood, and further communication will be required. Material that is not *complete* cannot be *clear* or *readable*. All messages should be *correct* in content and in language usage.

ACCURACY AND KNOWLEDGE: THE VITAL INGREDIENTS

No matter how skillfully we write or speak, this attempt at communication is not effective unless it is based on a sound knowledge of what we are writing about. It has been said that "You can't write writing"; neither can we "communicate communication." We communicate facts, ideas, and opinions. If we are employed in a business organization, we are paid to communicate facts, ideas, and opinions about business subjects through face-to-face and telephone conversations; written memos, letters, and reports; and formal and informal presentations at meetings and conferences.

You will need to find out all you can about your job, your company, and your particular duties and responsibilities. You will need this knowledge and understanding in order to succeed in all functions of your employment.

As you communicate orally, at meetings and conferences or informally with colleagues, your certainty of the correctness of what you are saying will give you confidence and thus improve your communication techniques. Some people, however, even though they possess reliable information and a thorough knowledge of the subject, do not effectively express their thoughts to others. You can learn to communicate, although it is not always easy, if you have something to say. If you don't have anything to say, why bother?

Mark Twain, in one of his cynical moments, did not agree that success is built on real knowledge or ability. He said, "All you need in this life is ignorance and confidence, and then success is sure."

Don't bet on it, Mark Twain.

Every one of us can think back to mistakes we have made because we did not have certain necessary information or because we were misinformed or because we remembered details incorrectly. These errors will continue to occur, regardless of our effort, but at least we can minimize them with sufficient thought and effort.

Because data are reproduced by computers and by other forms of mass reproduction, one error can become thousands of errors. A bit of incorrect information on a letter sent to one individual is bad enough, but a form letter sent to thousands of people greatly multiplies whatever difficulties will be encountered because of the error.

A message can be inaccurate because it is incomplete, and perhaps it is incomplete because the writer or speaker is overly concerned with being brief. A message can have the same effect as being inaccurate if it is misunderstood; that is, the facts may be correct but presented in such a way that the receiver of the message misinterprets them. A message can be inaccurate—actually or in effect—if the chosen words do not mean the same to the receiver as to the sender of the message.

COMMUNICATION

brief

Standard English is defined by scholars as the "prestige dialect" of our language. A Mark Twain or a Will Rogers can achieve humorous effects by deliberate and pointed use of nonstandard idioms. But the radio and television news is always delivered in a formal, generalized Standard English with little or no distinctive regional flavor. Business letters, legal arguments, scientific descriptions, magazine articles, and ceremonial speeches are also written in Standard English. Mastery of this prestige dialect is a key to success in most of the most prestigious activities of the world.

Success with Words (Pleasantville, N.Y.: The Reader's Digest Association, 1983), v.

Conservative, Businesslike Standards of Correctness

Correct writing and speaking, from the standpoint of grammatical correctness and the accuracy of information, is not necessarily effective communication, nor is it necessarily easily understood, interesting, or diplomatic. Correctness is only one of the many components of effective communication. Most business communication, however, cannot be completely effective if it is not basically correct, grammatically as well as in the information it reports.

Some people seem to have the idea that an exact and "correct" use of the English language is somehow unimportant; that they should be concerned about more important matters. To say that we need not be concerned with how we express our thoughts is the same as saying that we are willing to neglect a major aspect of general education and literacy, regardless of our occupation.

We will continue to use language, for we must; therefore, we should exert continued effort in order to use it effectively. Even though you may not become a professional writer or speaker, you will, and do, use the language in your profession, as well as in your personal life.

Aside from its professional and social benefits, your growth in the use of the language will be a source of personal pride and accomplishment—and perhaps this is the most worthwhile motive.

Further discussion of effective and correct English usage is given in Appendix D.

Today's word processors offer various tools to assist a writer. Consider using the grammar check feature offered by your word processor to help identify frequently confused words. The grammar check in Microsoft Word version 7 will identify words often confused, such as *affect* and *effect*, *personal* and *personnel*, and *its* and *it's*. A careful reading of the sentence context can help you identify which word is appropriate. Using your software's thesaurus feature will allow you to check synonyms; this is another tool to

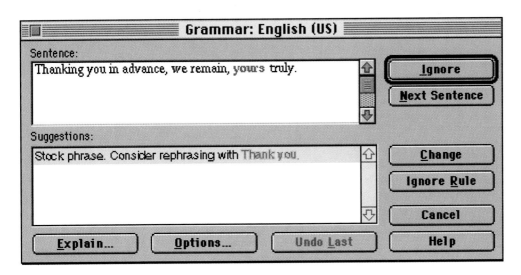

FIGURE 5-1
Screen Capture from grammar check software

help you quickly select the appropriate word from two that are often confused. Or you can choose to access a package such as Random House *Webster's Electronic Dictionary and Thesaurus, College Edition.* Microsoft Bookshelf also contains a dictionary that provides information on parts of speech, pronunciation, definitions, and synonyms.

Figure 5-1 illustrates the way by which certain word processing packages can help you check your written work. Warning about the trite, old-fashioned phrase shown under the heading "Grammar: English(US)" is only one of the many kinds of advice about usage available from grammar checks packaged with word processing software. (In some instances you will need to use your own judgment instead of relying completely on your computer—although certainly the sentence shown in Figure 5-1 should be replaced.)

CONCISENESS AND COMPLETENESS

Conciseness is not a synonym for brevity. Brevity, like short, informal, and other descriptive words, is relative.

Conciseness is always a desirable quality of business communication; brevity is not necessarily desirable. When working for conciseness, remember that the purpose of the message is not merely the imparting of information but also the building and maintaining of goodwill. To build or maintain goodwill—or from the human standpoint of being friendly and courteous—the writer or speaker may be required to include additional words, paragraphs, or pages. *Please* and *thank you* take little time and space. Even if they did, they would be well worth the effort.

A letter or other message that says *no* or relates unpleasant news usually should be longer than one that says yes or relates good news. Suppose, for example, you are refusing a request. You could convey the necessary information in this way:

Dear Mrs. Baker:

NO.

Sincerely,

This letter, although brief, lacks many of the necessary aspects of an effective letter. Although it relates all the necessary information, the message requires some explanation and a goodwill paragraph or two, unless the writer wishes to be particularly emphatic, likely at the expense of future pleasant relationships. (The one-word sentence that makes up the total message dramatically illustrates a method of emphasis: using short, simple sentences standing alone.)

Some writers omit necessary details and explanations because of a concern for brevity, but too much concern for brevity can lead to incompleteness and possibly the lack of courtesy. The shortest letter is not economical if it necessitates another letter or a telephone call to clear up what should have been clearly stated in the original letter.

Your reader or listener does not want needless and irrelevant details or explanations, only sufficient facts and explanations, as well as courtesy and consideration.

A style of writing described as *gobbledygook* is far from concise. Neither is it clear, brief, courteous, or sensible. Gobbledygook is long-winded, multisyllable, complex, pretentious, pompous, ambiguous writing or speech that contains euphemisms, technical words, Latin words and phrases, and a concoction of other words and lengthy phrases that are almost impossible to understand and probably don't mean anything, anyway. (The previous sentence comes close to being gobbledygook.)

Government officials in high positions are likely to write gobbledygook, or at least they have the reputation of doing so. Politicians sometimes speak gobbledygook, perhaps in order to sound scholarly and to prevent their being understood.

Pennsylvania Dutch settlers used the word *gobbledygook* to describe mixed-together leftovers. In 1952, Texas Senator Maury Maverick applied the term to language.

Gobbledygook is also described as *jargon*, although jargon has an additional meaning: The use or overuse of terms peculiar to a particular group, occupation, or field of interest. We speak of business jargon, particularly as it applies to business writing, in such phrases as "Enclosed please find" and "We have your letter of recent date." These phrases are jargon, but they are not considered gobbledygook. Both gobbledygook and jargon violate the principle of direct, simple writing. (Technical terms are useful when people in a specialized field communicate with readers in the same field.)

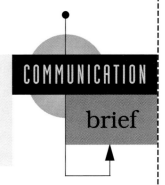

COMMUNICATION
brief

Vigorous writing is concise. A sentence should contain no unnecessary words, a paragraph no unnecessary sentences, for the same reason that a drawing should have no unnecessary lines and a machine no unnecessary parts.

William Strunk, Jr., and E. B. White, *The Elements of Style*, 3d ed. (New York: Macmillan, 1979), xiv.

The following gobbledygook could have been written by a sociologist:

Socially oriented individuals tend to congregate in gregariously homogeneous groupings. (Birds of a feather flock together.)

THE ACTIVE AND THE PASSIVE VOICE

A verb is the strongest and the most vivid part of speech. Verbs are stronger in the active voice than in the passive; they are more direct, forceful, and concise. A good writer chooses the active voice for most sentences unless there is a specific reason for the passive.

The following sentences illustrate the difference between active and passive verbs:

Active
The decorator rearranged the office furniture.

Passive
The office furniture was rearranged by the decorator.

Of the two sentences, the first, with the verb in the active voice, is more direct, forceful, and concise. At times, however, the person who acts is irrelevant or unknown. In such cases, the best sentence construction is as follows:

Passive
The office furniture has been rearranged.

More illustrations of the active-passive dimension are shown below:

Active
We should include more colors in our line of denim slacks.

Passive
More colors should be included in our line of denim slacks.

As the immediately preceding sentence illustrates, the passive voice emphasizes *more colors* by placement in the emphatic first position of the sentence. Perhaps this is the desired emphasis. In the following sentences, however, the active voice is more concise and direct.

Active

Ruth asked many questions.

Passive

Many questions were asked by Ruth.

Active

The committee approved two changes in the constitution.

Passive

Two changes in the constitution were approved by the committee.

The following sentences do not include verbs in the passive voice, but the construction results in the same slow, weak effect.

It is desirable to include more colors in our line of denim slacks.

There should be increased production of our denim slacks.

The words *there* and *it* are function words or "structural fillers" that replace true subjects. They are referred to as expletives. Weaker than specific subjects, they may be used with discretion. *There* and *it* sentence beginnings, provided they are not overused, may be at times the most natural and understandable expressions.

The passive voice is in no way incorrect; neither are sentences beginning with *there* or *it.* They are discussed here because many writers use the passive voice and *there* and *it* as subjects unnecessarily, especially when writing in the impersonal tone. Most sentences can be and should be written with "real" subjects and active verbs.

With the active or passive voice, as with word choice and sentence construction, the most important consideration is to express your meaning exactly.

Although we should usually prefer the active verb, at times the passive construction may be more conducive to goodwill. The following sentence is expressed with the verb in the active voice, but the accusing tone is far from diplomatic.

(Accusing)   ⎡ *You failed to water the plants.*

Expressed in the passive voice, the sentence becomes more neutral because the emphasis is on *plants*, not the culprit who did not water them.

(Neutral)   ⎡ *The plants have not been watered.*

Notice that in the first example *you* is the subject and *failed* is the verb. In the second sentence, *plants*, the subject, receives the action. Because the

This writer knows that providing a variety in sentence structure and using correct grammar and punctuation helps convey the organization's concern for quality.

idea to be expressed is essentially negative, the passive construction is less accusing; emphasis is away from you and toward the plants. The word *failed* adds to the overall accusatory tone.

Rewording of such sentences, however, does not necessarily require the passive construction, as shown by this remedy:

> *The plants seem dry.*   (Active voice, but neutral tone)

Further mention of the active and passive voice, from the standpoint of diplomacy, is included in Chapter 6.

CONSTRUCTION AND LENGTH OF SENTENCES

A knowledge of sentence structure is essential to exact use of punctuation and, more important, to the most effective presentation of your thoughts.

As a general guide, use only complete sentences, although at times sentence fragments are effective in sales and advertising writing and in other informal material. Only complete sentences should be used in formal writing, which includes many reports. Because you do not know the individual preferences of your readers, you are safer always to write in complete sentences. (See "Sentence Construction" in Appendix D.)

Sentences should not be the same length. In order to avoid monotonous reading, both short and fairly long sentences should be used. Most important, sentences should be of the length that best conveys what you wish to express. There can be no exact guide, although *average* sentence length should not exceed 20 words for business writing. A series of short, simple sentences, similar to a first-grade reader, is monotonous, juvenile, and unbusinesslike.

The length of sentence chosen for a particular idea depends on the idea to be expressed. Experienced writers do not consciously think of sentence construction as the material is written or dictated. They often change sentence structure as they revise, particularly to decrease sentence length. All writers should check their work to make sure that only complete sentences are used and that there is a variety of sentence construction. (You can check your average sentence length by using one of the leading word processing packages, including Microsoft Word. Such programs also show the percentage of passive verbs.)

In most business writing, simple sentences should outnumber complex sentences and compound sentences. In almost all writing, compound sentences should be the fewest of the three. Complex sentences are useful for subordinating or emphasizing ideas.

CONSTRUCTION AND LENGTH OF PARAGRAPHS

Short paragraphs are useful in achieving readability in all kinds of writing. A paragraph of many lines is hard to read and discouraging to the reader. At times, paragraphs in a letter, memorandum, or report must be broken arbitrarily to increase readability, especially if the overall work is short.

Overall, paragraphs tend to be shorter in letters and memorandums than in some other types of writing. *Often the first and last paragraphs may correctly consist of only one sentence.* Any paragraph in any kind of material

COMMUNICATION
brief

In general, remember that paragraphing calls for a good eye as well as a logical mind. Enormous blocks of print look formidable to a reader. Therefore, breaking long paragraphs in two, even if it is not necessary to do so for sense, meaning, or logical development, is often a visual help.

William Strunk, Jr., and E. B. White, *The Elements of Style*, 3d ed. (New York: Macmillan, 1979), 17.

may be only one sentence in length if that is all that seems to fit into the particular paragraph, but one-sentence paragraphs should not be overused.

A short, one-sentence paragraph can be used for attention, interest, and emphasis, especially if the sentence is the first one in the communication. A one-sentence paragraph can also be used as a transition from one section of material to another.

Numerous one-sentence paragraphs in a letter or memorandum tend to emphasize a number of things, thus emphasizing nothing at all.

Short paragraphs, if wisely used, aid readability. Long paragraphs discourage the reader and cause confusion. Almost all business writing is read hurriedly. The writer should do everything possible to make messages immediately clear.

READABILITY FORMULAS

Several formulas, or indexes, were developed a number of decades ago, supposedly to measure readability. Two of these are the Flesch Reading Ease Formula and the Gunning Fog Index. The readability score obtained with a formula is expressed in terms of the general educational level of the reader, which may have little relationship to the actual grade completed in school. If, for example, the readability score as determined by the Gunning Fog Index is 17, this number indicates that the material could be read by someone who has completed college. A score of 16 means that a person completing the sixteenth year of schooling, a college senior, could read the material.

Most effective writing of all kinds, however, has a much lower readability score than 16 or 17, even if the material is planned for graduate students. Material may have a readability score lower than high school level and still be suitable for adults.

An important point to remember is that formulas cannot measure the quality of writing, only its complexity, and that to a limited extent. An expert writer can use long words and sentences and make the work more interesting and readable than a writer with less ability, although the expert's work has a higher readability score.

The formulas make no distinction between exact, well-chosen words and vague, confusing words, or between familiar words and rare ones. They measure only word length. They do not distinguish sentences that are constructed wisely in order to express ideas exactly. *Excellent writing cannot be measured by any formula, but an average reader can usually recognize its quality and understand its meaning.*

These cautions about using readability formulas are not given to disparage their worth, for their admittedly limited purposes are valid ones. The formulas can be dangerous, however, if they are misused.

The Gunning Fog Index is as follows:

1   Select a sample of writing of at least 100 words. Divide the total number of words by the number of sentences. This is the average sentence length. [Using several samples will result in a more reliable source. The independent clauses of a compound sentence are counted as separate sentences.]

2   Count the number of words of three syllables or more. Don't count proper names, combinations of short, easy words, such as bookkeeper or teenager; or verb forms made into three syllables by adding *ed* or *es*. This figure is the number of "hard" words in the passage. Divide this figure by the total number of words to find the percentage of "hard" words.

3   Add the average sentence length to the percentage of hard words and multiply by .4. The figure obtained through these calculations is the Gunning Fog Index, or readability score, expressed in grade-reading level.[1]

Let's find the readability score for the following paragraph from *The Mature Mind*, written in 1949 by H. A. Overstreet. This book is easily read because it is well written, but the 12.2 score is higher than an ideal score for short, nontechnical, business communications. (The author Overstreet did not mention television because in 1949 television was only in its infancy.)

> Newspapers, radio, movies, and advertising—these might be called the "big four" of communication. These are the four great money-making enterprises of mind-making. It would be pleasant to report that they make for the fine maturity of human character.
>
> But the report must be otherwise. In spite of what each has contributed to our growth, each has, through its own formula, found it profitable, to keep us from full psychological maturing. Or, to put the best possible face upon the matter, each has found in us some immaturity that waited to be tapped. Engaged in the tapping process, each of these powerful forces has been too busy to think about the long-range consequences of its formula.[2]

The paragraph contains 120 words and 7 sentences. The words of three or more syllables (those not excluded by the formula) total 16.

The readability score of 12.2 was determined in this way

1   120 (total words) divided by 7 (sentences) = 17.1 (average sentence length).

2   16 (number of difficult words) divided by 120 (total words) = 13.3 (percentage of difficult words).

3   Add 17.1 to 13.3 = 30.4.

4   Multiply 30.4 by .4 = 12.16 or 12.2 (readability score).

This reading-level score means that the material could be easily read by someone in the twelfth grade, or approximately so. This is similar to the read-

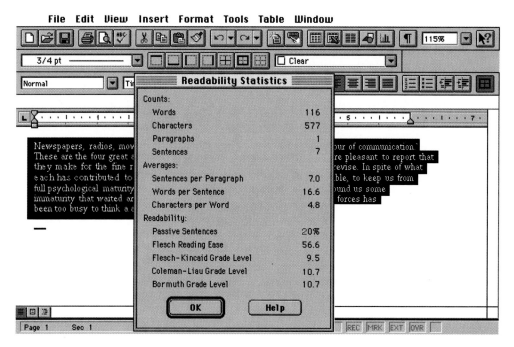

FIGURE 5-2

Readability statistics available in grammar checks packaged with word processing software

ing level of such magazines as *The Atlantic Monthly* and *Harper's*, although articles by different authors vary in difficulty. Other popular magazines, such as *Reader's Digest*, are written at a level below this twelfth-grade score.

To obtain an accurate average score of writing of considerable length, we should use far more material than the paragraph measured here.

Using a computer with the appropriate software is much easier and quicker than the method described above, as shown in Figure 5-2. Grammar and style checkers within word processing packages can determine reading levels according to various scales, as well as check sentence length and percentage of passive sentences. The passage analyzed to obtain statistics shown in Figure 5-2 is the same passage from *The Mature Mind*, by Overstreet, that was used to calculate the Gunning Fog Index. Notice that these formulas result in lower grade levels, but that the reading level differs from formula to formula.

Using Format to Increase Readability

A letter, memorandum, report, or other communication should be arranged attractively, leaving plenty of white space. A minimum of one inch in the side, top, and bottom margins should be left on all work. For short and average-length letters, wider margins are better, as explained in Appendix A.

Subheads are essential to readability if the written message is long, and *long* usually should be considered to apply to any communication of more than one page. Subheads can also be used in material of one page or less. They aid readability in several ways.

Subheads force the writer to organize the material in meaningful units. If the subhead does not include a reference to the information under it, and only to that information, it is not a well-chosen one. Poor subheads are worse than none at all.

Lists and tabulations make ideas stand out and present ideas in a logical order. The arrangement of each statement, question, or idea on a separate line (as illustrated in the following list), with a line space between each line, makes each item easier to understand than if all were crowded together into a paragraph.

To illustrate the use of a listing, as well as to summarize, the following information is repeated.

Readable formats should include

1   Plenty of white space

2   An overall attractive appearance

3   Subheads

4   Lists and tabulation

Basic Principles of Emphasis

When you apply the principles of emphasis, you are also increasing readability and achieving a desirable psychological approach. These and other qualities of excellent communication are interrelated.

▶ EMPHATIC POSITIONS

Position is one of the most important means of achieving emphasis. The beginning position in any kind of writing is the most emphatic one, provided the writer has used this location advantageously. In most communications, the beginning position should be used to present the most important idea. The arrangement is referred to as the direct arrangement.

The first paragraph is the most emphatic section of a memorandum, a letter, or any other short written message. In a long report, the first paragraph is still an emphatic one, but because of the comparative length, the first section, often titled the *Introduction*, becomes especially important because of its position, as well as for other reasons. The first sentence in a paragraph is ordinarily the most emphatic one. The use of a topic sentence

Creating a single readable writing style can be a challenge when the project is a collaborative effort.

as the first sentence therefore increases readability and emphasizes the principal meaning intended for that paragraph.

The first word of a sentence, along with the last one, is in an emphatic position, except for such sentence beginnings as *a*, *an*, and *the*, which are used as introductory words so that the emphasis shifts to the words immediately following. The emphatic first position of the sentence is one reason that it is best not to start several sentences on the same page with the word *I*; the *I* becomes overemphasized and does not convey the desired impression of the you-attitude.

The closing word, sentence, paragraph, or section of a written message is also emphatic, next in importance to the opening word, sentence, paragraph, or section. The last word of a sentence is second in emphasis to the first word of a sentence. Thus, to subordinate an idea or statement, do not place it in the opening or closing position of the written work.

This principle applies throughout business writing: The idea to be subordinated should be somewhere within the body of the letter, not in the opening or the closing paragraph. An idea can be subordinated within a sentence in the same way.

EMPHATIC SENTENCE AND PARAGRAPH CONSTRUCTION

The most emphatic way to present an idea is in a paragraph consisting of only one short, simple sentence. Because the most emphatic position is the first position, you achieve the greatest emphasis by letting this short, one-sentence paragraph be the first paragraph of your message. The short, simple sentence is emphatic because it stands alone, with no distracting or cluttering words or phrases to detract from the meaning.

Suppose that in a sales letter the price is stated in this way:

The cost is $15.98.

If this sentence stands alone as a paragraph, you are probably giving too much emphasis to the cost, for ordinarily the price of an article should be subordinated and stated in connection with the benefits the purchase will bring. An exception is a sales letter in which an unusually low price is a favorable selling point. In such a letter you should emphasize the price.

In a complex sentence, place the idea to be emphasized in the main clause and the subordinated idea in the dependent clause. A phrase can also contain an idea to be de-emphasized. The cost is presented in a prepositional phrase in the following sentence:

You will receive for only $15.98 many hours of listening pleasure.

In addition to the use of the word *only*, the price is de-emphasized by placing it in a phrase and by placing it within the sentence, not at the beginning or the end.

> ## WORD CHOICE TO EMPHASIZE OR TO SUBORDINATE

Specific, concrete language is more emphatic, as well as more descriptive and readable, than vague, abstract wording. Try to emphasize positive, pleasant ideas and to de-emphasize unpleasant ones. (See Chapters 4 and 6.) At times the general word, not the specific, is more diplomatic, although less emphatic and forceful.

An abstract word describes ideas or concepts that cannot be easily visualized, such as *democracy*. Examples of concrete words are *blackbird, plaid, crunch, dawn, rain, saxophone,* and *1968 Mustang*. Concrete words refer to particular objects that can be seen, heard, felt, touched, and smelled. Such words are more emphatic, as well as more vivid and forceful, than abstract ones. (Chapter 4 is devoted completely to word choice.)

Specific words are more emphatic than general words. An example of a general word is *music*; a more specific term is *piano solo*; still more descriptive is *Chopin's "Polonaise in A-Flat" played by Shaun Hagan, a graduate student.*

Fresh, natural words are more emphatic than stale, stereotyped expressions. Avoid trite phrases such as *"spring is just around the corner"* and *"last but not least."* These overused expressions also violate the principles of conciseness.

ATTENTION TO ONE IDEA

Additional time in oral messages, and additional space in written messages, can be a method of emphasis. Giving more time or space to one idea emphasizes it over the remaining parts of the message. Ordinarily the writer does not think, "Well, I will give this more space because it is important," but instead writes the message in detail, which necessarily requires more space.

Use repetition with discretion in order to emphasize. Repetition is often used for sales writing or advertising, especially radio and television commercials, but not always to the best advantage.

The main idea of a message often requires more space in order to be conveyed completely and clearly, which is the reason that using more space is said to be a method of emphasis. You are, however, violating another principle of effective writing if you make the writing longer than necessary to convey the intended message.

MECHANICAL MEANS OF EMPHASIS

Mechanical means are such methods as underlining; the use of all capitals, dashes, and special or unusual means of letter arrangement or indenting; and lists and tabulations. Different colors of ink, especially red, are often used in sales messages. Setting off lines with plenty of white space calls attention to these lines. Mechanical means of emphasis are similar to those used for readability, except that at times the methods used for emphasis are more unusual and extreme.

Subheads emphasize, as well as help to display, the organization of material. A postscript can be used to emphasize an important idea, but this postscript should not be used for something that should have gone into the letter itself.

When overused, mechanical means of emphasis lose any emphatic value that they might otherwise possess. Many points emphasized means that nothing is emphasized. In addition, some persons object to a message filled with underlining, all capitals, or portions typed in red, feeling that such an approach is unbusinesslike or emotional. The overuse of dashes contributes to a scatterbrained appearance of a written message.

SUMMARIZING FOR EMPHASIS

Summarizing is useful for emphasizing important points, especially in longer works. In some reports or books, each section or chapter is summarized and then the entire work is summarized, perhaps through a synopsis attached to the report itself. Summarizing, like the other means of emphasizing, also contributes to readability.

A listing of points, such as those below, makes the items stand out and implies that they are important. They are easy to read and quickly understood.

Emphasis is achieved by

1 Position

2 Sentence and paragraph construction

3 Word choice

4 Space

5 Mechanical means of emphasis

6 Summarizing

REVISING FOR PROFESSIONAL QUALITY

The following letter is another "horrible example." Only the body of the letter is given; all complete letters should contain the opening and closing lines discussed and illustrated in Appendix A.

Dear Ms. Henson:

We are in receipt of your letter and telephone call and e-mail and fax of recent date and in reply wish to state that we shall endeavor to submit to your claim and to send cheaper merchandise than that you previously and heretofore ordered us to send.

Attached please find a new invoice of this cheaper merchandise that you claim should sell better in your neighborhood. (Have you considered changing locations?) We expect payment immediately.

Thanking you in advance for your esteemed favor,

Sincerely,

This letter is not concise because of the many old-fashioned, trite phrases. It also lacks tact and makes no effort to build goodwill. Overall, it is of the quality that we hope never to see in the "real world," although some letters come close to it.

In the first paragraph, everything is unnecessary before *we shall endeavor.* *Heretofore* is redundant, legal jargon, and imprecise. *Attached please find* is trite business jargon, as is *Thanking you in advance. For your esteemed*

Composing a document is only the first step; careful
communicators take the time to revise and edit as necessary to
increase readability and effectiveness.

favor, always unnecessary and overly humble, has been considered old-fashioned for a century or so.

Words with unpleasant connotations are *cheaper* and *endeavor* in the particular way they are used in the sentence. *Claim* is a word that is often accusing, especially in *you claim*, which implies disbelief. In this letter, however, the first use of *claim* is inexact; the writer had made a request. *To submit to* is not only inexact but also inappropriate.

The suggestion that the store be moved to another location is sarcastic, as is the mention of the four ways in which the reader has made the request. (The question arises, however, about the writer's promptness when responding to requests.)

Although this letter includes unnecessary words and phrases, it is also incomplete; for example, the writer states that an invoice is attached but does not mention the merchandise or how it was shipped or will be shipped.

Here is a suggested revision:

Dear Ms. Henson:

(Good news) — *The economical men's clothing you requested is on its way to you. It was sent this morning by UPS. We are glad to make this exchange.*

(Explanation and subtle request for prompt payment) — *Your letter came in time for us to stop your original order. The attached invoice applies to the revised list. By paying the full amount within 15 days, you will receive a 2 percent discount, more than enough to cover the shipping costs. Use the enclosed postage-paid envelope.*

(Compliment; sales promotion) — *You are wise to consider the special needs of your customers. Other budget-priced clothing, both men's and women's, is illustrated in the spring catalog that will soon be sent to you.*

Thank you for your order. We are sure that your customers will like your choice of merchandise.

Sincerely,

Analyze the following letter, which is shown as an example of a message that is extremely weak from several standpoints, including the lack of conciseness, clarity, and diplomacy. It also contains old-fashioned, wordy phrases and negative wording. This is another "horrible example."

Dear Mr. Jones:

We have received your inquiry of November 6. Regarding this inquiry, we would like to state that we are in no position to comply with your request, changing the method of premium payment on your above-numbered policy to the monthly basis, because the monthly premium must amount to at least the sum of $100 per month, inasmuch as the Company has found it impractical to issue policies with a monthly premium of less than this amount.

We might, however, make mention of the fact that your policy contains an Automatic Premium Loan clause and under this clause, unpaid premiums can be taken care of by loan provided there is sufficient cash value in your above policy to warrant doing so, and provided small repayments are made on your loan from time to time.

If it should be your desire to do this, kindly contact us and we shall be pleased to comply with your request.

Faithfully yours,

Analyze the revised letter shown below:

Dear Mr. Jones:

Because your policy contains an Automatic Premium Loan clause, we can arrange to have your premiums paid by loan provided there is enough cash value in your policy. Then you can simply make repayments toward your loan and all will be in order.

(Treated as good news although reader's request is denied)

I'm sorry that we cannot arrange to have you pay premiums on the monthly basis, as you asked, but monthly premiums must amount to at least $100. However, this Automatic Premium Loan arrangement will, in effect, accomplish the same thing.

(Answers reader's question in a positive way)

Let us know if you want us to do this, won't you? It will be a pleasure to take care of it for you.

(Action close and goodwill)

ETHICAL AND LEGAL CONSIDERATIONS

According to Ramsey and Hilton, litigation is increasing because of inaccurate reading. They state:

> America's declining literacy and increasing litigation have driven up the cost of doing business in the U.S. Labels must be worded simply and exactly; a potential complication is the issue of legal bilingualism. There was a time when a company could be sued for inaccurate writing; now the company can be sued because of someone else's inaccurate reading. The liability problems inherent in writing and reading deserve emphasis in business communication courses.[3]

The possibility of limited reading ability, even to the extent that such a weakness could lead to litigation, emphasizes the importance of clear, simple writing. Litigation is expensive regardless of the outcome. A more personal and important concern is that of actual injury to consumers, some of whom may read their native language but not English.

The writer can do nothing about the readers' ability to comprehend or their unwillingness to read. On the other hand, the writer has the responsibility of making sure that there is no reason for the message (label, instruction sheet, or other materials) to be misunderstood by the average reader. Even better, in many instances, is to work to reach the below-average reader.

Writing assignments of such importance should not be left to one person, regardless of his or her capability, but checked by several others, including legal counsel.

SUMMARY OF WRITING TECHNIQUES

1   Write simply. Don't try to impress your readers with an extensive vocabulary of five-syllable words, but also don't give the impression of oversimplification or "writing down." Prefer short words to longer words, provided they are the exact ones to express your intended meaning. Consider the connotative meanings of words as well as dictionary definitions.

2   Express your thoughts exactly. To do so you must have an extensive vocabulary. Be specific. Do not state vague generalities.

3   Write clearly, concisely, coherently, and correctly. Give all necessary information diplomatically and convincingly. Provide answers to Who? What? Where? Why? When? How?

4   Write objectively. Base your interpretations and decisions on facts, not on your personal desires or unsupported beliefs. Although at times you must state what you believe about a situation, or what the data seem to indicate, make sure that the reader understands that this statement is an opinion; give concrete details to support your opinions. On the other hand, avoid an appearance of hedging and timidity. Nobody expects you to have positive and definite answers to everything. If you pretend to do so, nobody will believe you.

5   Use the pronoun *I* as necessary for desired tone and meaning, but avoid using an unnecessary number. Avoid numerous paragraphs and sentences that open with *I*. Some material, such as formal reports, is often written in the "impersonal" tone, or the "third-person objective" writing style.

6   Write in an interesting and vivid style. Keep sentences fairly short, but vary sentence length and construction. Avoid using many sentences that begin with slow expletive openings, such as *there are* and *it is*.

7   Use the active voice to emphasize the actor, the passive voice to emphasize the receiver of the action. Do not use the passive voice when the active voice will more exactly express your idea in vivid terms, as it often will. An exception is the use of the passive voice in order to be tactful and diplomatic.

8   Use strong language and sentence construction. Unnecessary adverbs and adjectives weaken writing. Decrease or eliminate weak modifiers, such as *very, rather, somewhat, little, pretty*. Do not use linking verbs unnecessarily; prefer more active, specific ones.

9   Use short paragraphs, especially beginning and ending ones. One-sentence paragraphs are acceptable and often desirable in business letters and memorandums.

10   Emphasize what you wish to emphasize. Methods of emphasis include position, word choice, sentence structure, and various mechanical means of emphasis, such as underlining. The first and last positions of a letter or memorandum are the most emphatic, as is a beginning topic sentence of a paragraph.

11   Organize! Ordinarily the best method of organization for short communications is the "direct" order, in which the most important part of the message is placed at the beginning. An exception is a message containing bad news or, at times, unexpected information.

12   Omit trite business jargon. If you insert phrases such as "enclosed please find" and "as per your request" because you have seen them in other business letters, don't. Write naturally, informally, and conversationally.

TEST YOURSELF

chapter content

1 Distinguish between the terms *brief* and *concise*.
2 If a writer is overly concerned with brevity, the message may lack _____ or _____.
3 Name six methods of achieving the desired emphasis.
4 According to your textbook, average sentence length for simple letters and memorandums should ordinarily not exceed _____ words.
5 Name two purposes of one-sentence paragraphs.
6 Name two weaknesses of readability formulas.
7 Name three "statistics" that can be obtained by computers and readability formulas.

TEST YOURSELF

correct usage

(Related to material in Chapter 5 and Appendix D.) Insert necessary punctuation, including quotation marks, hyphens, and apostrophes. Choose the correct word from each pair or group.

1 A letter or memorandum should be no longer than necessary to accomplish (its, it's) purposes, but one of these purposes is to build or maintain goodwill.
2 If the writer is overly concerned with brevity the letter or memorandum may lack courtesy or completeness.
3 One purpose of your letter or memorandum is to convince the reader to (accept, except) your instructions or ideas.
4 The successful business writer is (adept, adopt, adapt) in the use of language and (altogether, all together) sure of company policies and (procedures, procee-dures).
5 Business jargon (affects, effects) a letter in several undesirable ways.
6 Short paragraphs increase readability especially short first and last paragraphs.
7 The student (cited, sited) William Faulkner's long sentences when the teacher (recommended, recomended) short sentences.
8 A table or chart (emphasize, emphasizes) specific data.
9 The arrangement of charts and tables (affect, affects) comprehension.
10 The first paragraph as well as the last paragraph of letters and memorandums (is, are) emphatic.

P R O B L E M S   A N D   C A S E S

1 Improve the following sentences from business messages. (Refer to Appendix D if necessary.)

   a. As an outstanding businessman, I request your opinion of the new tax regulations.

   b. The letter, as well as the two reports, were sent to you this morning.

   c. He was asked to remove the clutter, repair the fence, and that he must build a sidewalk.

   d. Taking claims and to analyze them is part of the job's responsibilities.

   e. We hope to receive the check within a week.

   f. We are in receipt of your order of a recent date and in reply wish to state that we thank you for same and for your check in payment that was attached thereto, which was in the amount of $42.50.

   g. Graduates who are the ones with the highest grade point average will be the first ones who will be interviewed.

   h. During the passed year this principal has been in effect.

   i. The reasoning of all our salesmen and supervisors indicate that this product should be discontinued.

   j. Neither the teacher nor the students was concerned about the noise in the hall.

   k. The employer, who we went to Dallas to see, was most courteous to my wife and I.

   l. The secretaries and myself have long been concerned about this matter.

   m. Is it true that Jerry is the one whom is to be considered?

   n. Coming in two different types, I can send you either racquet you prefer.

   o. This letter is in reply to your letter of November 6. In reply to this letter I wish to advise that in reference to your question about the Anderson account, it has now been partially paid $200 of the $350 has been collected.

   p. This policy not only must be read and understood it must be signed and returned.

   q. Meeting at noon, the constitution was completely rewritten by four o'clock by the Board of Directors.

   r. The last game of the season was played in by Bill.

   s. The workers in the department have worked here for three years.

   t. The project was terminated as a result of not being able to bring it to fruition within the annual guidelines.

   u. The aforementioned data was taken under advisement and it was ascertained by management that procedures should be implemented immediately to rectify the situation.

   v. Ms. Boudreaux assigned the financial research to Edward and I.

   w. Kevin Sevin recommended several people whom he thought could do the work.

   x. Lisa Duet is the human resources manager, but Mary Domangue is responsible for hiring people. She has a master's degree in business administration from Nicholls State University.

   y. Cynthia has been recommended as a candidate for president of the organization. She is efficient, dependable, and seems to be able to deal with all members with diplomacy.

   z. Computer spell checkers do not catch all context errors, however, they are useful as a first check before obtaining a hard copy for editing.

2–4 See exercises 1, 2, and 3 in Appendix D, which apply especially to Chapter 5, as well as the discussion and illustrations in Appendix D.

5 Write instructions for using an electrical appliance, such as a tape recorder, clock-radio, or microwave oven, in step-by-step, easily understood language. Speak to the reader directly instead of writing vaguely about the product.

6 Write a letter similar to one of the illustrations described in Chapter 5 as a "horrible example." Fill it with as many weaknesses

as you can (such as trite phrases, wordy sentences, words with negative connotations, poor arrangement of ideas and information). Do NOT, however, intentionally include errors in spelling, grammar, or sentence structure. (Let *something* be right

about it.) In addition, word the letter so that another writer can revise it; in order to do so, the writer must be able to determine the intended meaning.

7 Revise the letter you wrote for Problem 6.

COLLABORATIVE WRITING AND WORKING IN GROUPS

8 (Refer to Appendix D.) Write two paragraphs containing information about yourself. Use simple sentences only; use no compound or complex sentences. Exchange your work with another student and read each other's information. Edit your own composition and assist with the editing of your teammate's work. Revise each to provide a combination of simple, compound, and complex sentences. What benefits will another person gain when reading materials that contain a variety of sentence structures?

9 Use a word processor that contains a grammar check and/or document analysis tool, and create a document that contains the information you edited in Problem 8. Run the grammar check or document analysis tool and determine the readability level of your writing. Compare findings with your teammate. If your software did not contain a Gunning-Fog readability calculation, calculate the score manually. Compare your Gunning-Fog readability score against the other readability scores. What changes could you make to your document to lower the Gunning-Fog score? To raise the score?

THINK-IT-THROUGH ASSIGNMENT

10 Divide into groups according to the directions of your instructor. Discuss the following statements.
  a. Short words can be less readable than longer ones.
  b. Readability formulas can be misleading if used in the wrong way.
  c. Specific words are more emphatic and forceful than general, abstract ones, but at times the more general word is the better choice.
  d. The writer may find it easier to write a

long letter, memorandum, or report than to write a short one.
  e. The use of business jargon can possibly save time, but it may also waste time. In any event, the writer should work for fresh, original expressions.
  f. We can never be "completely complete," as it is impossible to say everything about anything. Thus, all communication is a form of abstraction, choosing exactly what to communicate and what to omit.

ENDNOTES

1 Robert Gunning, *The Technique of Clear Writing* (New York: McGraw-Hill, 1968), 39.

2 H. A. Overstreet, *The Mature Mind* (New York: W. W. Norton, 1949), 225–226.

3 Richard David Ramsey and Chad Hilton, "Illiteracy and the Litigious Society: A Costly Combination" in *ABC Southwest Region 1989 Refereed Proceedings*, ed. Timothy W. Clipson (Nacogdoches, TX: Association for Business Communication, 1989), 55.

Building Goodwill Through Communication

CHAPTER

6

OBJECTIVES

Chapter Six will help you:

1   Explain what is meant by the "you-attitude."

2   Explain what is meant by a positive approach.

3   Illustrate direct and indirect arrangements and identify effective uses of each.

4   Combine the you-attitude, a positive approach, and a direct arrangement in order to achieve diplomacy.

Building *goodwill* should be one of the purposes of all business communications. Goodwill, as the word refers to an organization, is an intangible, salable asset arising from the reputation of a business and its relationship with customers. Each individual in an organization, by his or her words and actions, affects favorably or adversely the image of the organization.

Although many communications of all kinds are directed to readers we have never met, we know that these persons are likely to be similar in many ways, regardless of nationality, race, age, or gender. They respond to fair and courteous treatment. They want to be treated as intelligent adults. They want their ideas and opinions to be taken seriously. They appreciate sincere praise, but they do not enjoy being scolded, bossed, or preached to. They realize that other persons make mistakes, and they are usually willing to overlook honest mistakes. They expect and deserve an apology when one is due, but they do not like excessive apologizing or undue humility.

To reach these readers and listeners, we must try to understand their viewpoint, even when we do not agree with it. Such an approach is referred to as the *you-attitude*, or the *you-approach*. The opposite concept is the *I-attitude* (or *I-approach*).

A SINCERE YOU-ATTITUDE

A letter written entirely in the you-attitude includes positive rather than negative wording, a cheerful rather than a pessimistic outlook, and a pleasant rather than an unpleasant tone. Organization of material and the physical appearance of business letters and memorandums are also aspects of the you-attitude; an attractive presentation is a compliment to the reader.

Ordinarily a writer or speaker who actually feels goodwill can easily express it, but not always. The desire to be pleasant and cooperative does not guarantee proficiency in written or oral business communication, although it is an essential element. In addition, a writer or speaker must acquire certain techniques and skills, as discussed throughout your class and throughout this textbook.

▶ DIRECT YOUR COMMUNICATION TOWARD THE READER

A type of wording that *violates* the you-approach appears in opening sentences such as the following ones:

> *Our company is pleased to announce the opening of our new store.*
>
> *We are very happy that the Smith Sporting Goods Company is now expanding.*
>
> *I am very happy to have your order.*
>
> *The Smith Sporting Goods Company is very happy to have your order.*
>
> *We at Smith Sporting Goods Company thank you for your order.*

(All I-approach (NOT you-approach because of emphasis on writer or company)

All the sentences shown above illustrate an I-approach (NOT you-approach) because of emphasis on the writer or company. Each of the sentences, when read alone, seems only to show pride in the employing company, a worthy attitude but not enough. Letters may be built around the theme that a company is opening a new store or moving to a new neighborhood, but if the reader does not interpret these company changes in the light of personal benefits, the letter has not been written in the complete you-attitude.

In addition, *the sentences are weak because they are used as beginnings of a letter.* As mentioned in Chapter 5, the first sentence, line, or word of a message is particularly emphatic. Such a position should be used to emphasize a pleasant idea that deserves emphasis.

When announcing expansion or other company changes, the writer should show how these changes will benefit the reader, perhaps because of convenience or economy. The sentence

We are now located in your neighborhood

is not nearly as effective as

You are now only five minutes away from the store that can fill all your sporting goods needs.

The sentence

We are shipping your goods today

(Emphatic opening is *we*)

is more effective if written in this way:

Your merchandise is being shipped today.

(Emphatic opening word is *you*)

(In the second example, the emphatic opening word is *your*.)

An even better sentence, because of additional information, is

(*You* opening; also includes specific, positive information)

> *You should receive your complete order within a week. It was shipped today by United Parcel, as you requested.*

Even more effective is a specific, descriptive word rather than *merchandise* or *order*. For example:

(*You*-opening, plus resale)

> *Your beautiful suit is on its way to you [to be followed by specific, positive details].*

The sentence that describes a suit as *beautiful* illustrates the sales approach known as *resale*; it emphasizes the value of a purchase already made. Resale can also be used to reinforce confidence in the company.

Resale is not exactly the same as *sales promotion*, a broader term. Sales promotion includes resale, along with various other kinds of sales messages. The announcement of a forthcoming sale is sales promotion, but not resale. A sales clerk's remark, "You made an excellent choice," is an example of resale.

Avoid unnecessary use of a company name. In the first place, the company name is given in the letterhead. In the second place, unnecessary use of the company name is really the I-attitude. Even though the word *I* is not used, emphasis is away from the reader and back to the company from which the letter comes. Another disadvantage is that the letter sounds stuffy and formal instead of personal, natural, and friendly. The reader knows that the letter comes not from the company (companies can't speak or write letters), but from someone at the company. *I* and *we* should be used when to do otherwise seems stilted or overly formal.

Almost all letters and memorandums, as well as many reports, are written in what is described as the *personal tone*, (see Chapter 5), in which first-person pronouns (*I, we, us, me,* and other pronouns that refer to the writer or speaker) are used when they seem desirable or necessary. The personal writing tone also uses second-person pronouns (*you, yourself*).

Conventional formulas for "I" and "you" abound in many languages. English is the only language that capitalizes "I" in writing, whereas many languages capitalize "you," and this has been interpreted, rightly or wrongly, as a sign of an exaggerated ego on the part of English speakers. A few languages, including Siamese and Hungarian (the latter only in flowery speech), use "slave" for "I."

Mario Pei, *The Story of Language*, rev. ed. (New York: Lippincott, 1965).

The *impersonal tone*, also described as the *third-person writing style*, includes no *I*'s, *we*'s, *you*'s, or other first- or second-person pronouns. The impersonal tone is appropriate for many reports, almost all news stories, and other kinds of written material. A good communicator writes well in both the personal and the impersonal tone and chooses the most appropriate style for the particular material, situation, and readership.

Even when using the personal tone, do not use the words *I* and *we* to excess. Although true consideration consists of far more than the use or omission of first-person pronouns, a letter or memorandum filled with *I*'s, *we*'s, and other words that refer to the writer is not likely to be written with the reader uppermost in mind. *Be careful not to begin all or most paragraphs with I*. The *I*'s (instead of the *you*'s) are given undue emphasis by their emphatic position at the beginning of a sentence.

You may have heard or read that paragraphs should *always* begin with some word other than *I* or *we*. Such advice is too restrictive, although you should avoid starting numerous paragraphs with *I* or *we*.

Within letters or memorandums, two or three paragraphs in sequence beginning with *I* are probably too many. If your letter contains five paragraphs and three of these paragraphs begin with *I* or *we*, revise.

The word *you* can be effectively used to open paragraphs, but even this approach becomes monotonous if it is overused. All writing should be simple, direct, natural, and varied.

TRUE CONSIDERATION CONSISTS OF MORE THAN THE CHOICE OF PRONOUNS

The *you-attitude* may be contrasted with both the *I-attitude* and the *neutral attitude*. The *we-opening* in the following sentence weakens the statement of good news:

We are happy to announce that we are allowing up to 10 percent of base pay to be contributed to each employee's retirement fund.

(Emphasis on *we*; NOT you-approach)

Expressed with *you*, the sentence could read like this:

(Reader benefit)

> *Now you may contribute more each month to your retirement fund, up to 10 percent of your base pay.*

A third way of expressing the same idea does not actually bring the reader into the picture, as the preceding sentence does. An objective and neutral writing reads something like this:

(A neutral approach, neither *I* nor *you*)

> *Employees can now contribute as much as 10 percent of their base pay to the retirement fund.*

Readers will know that their benefits have been increased, but the meaning in the third sentence is not as direct and personal as the one that makes use of the word *you*. Both the first and the second illustrations are written in the *personal tone*. The third example, worded in the *impersonal* tone, refers to neither the writer nor the reader.

At times you may prefer the neutral approach to the you-approach. For example, you might wish to subordinate the cost of a product and thus use a neutral approach, as in the following sentence:

(Neutral wording)
(Not diplomatic; although *you* is used, NOT the you-attitude)

> *This product sells for $22.*

> *This will cost you $22.*

Even worse is this:

(Dictatorial because of words *you must*)

> *You must pay $22 for this product.*

The words *I, we, us, our,* and other first-person pronouns do not in themselves convey the I-attitude instead of the you-attitude. On the other hand, an abundance of *I*'s and other first-person pronouns gives an impression of disregard for the reader, an impression that is likely to be correct; otherwise, numerous references to the writer would not occur.

As shown in the examples below, sentences written in the first person can sometimes be more pleasant and positive than those written in the second person.

(True you-attitude even though *we* is used twice)

> *We are sorry that we cannot grant a further extension of time on the loan.*

(Dictatorial; NOT you-attitude)

> *You must pay the full amount of your loan immediately.*

Notice the wording of the following letter, which definitely does NOT convey the you-attitude:

(Emphasis on writer, NOT reader; egotistical)

> *As newly elected membership director of the Junior Chamber of Commerce, I am in charge of recruiting new members. I would like very much for you to join. I am working for a record-making membership this year.*

(Accusing)

> *I don't know why you are not a member. Most other young businessmen are.*

(Demanding)

> *Fill out the enclosed application blank and return it with your check.*

Analysis: First Paragraph
Definite I-attitude in the emphatic first sentence. Throughout the paragraph, writer benefits are stressed, not those of the reader.

Second Paragraph
Most undiplomatic. Even if readers had been planning to join, this letter is enough to keep them away forever.

Third Paragraph
Dictatorial. Discourteous.

An improved version of this letter could begin with a paragraph like this:

You are wanted—and needed—by the Whitehaven Jaycees. ⎤ (Emphatic you-
 ⎦ opening)

The middle paragraphs could be devoted to describing the advantages of joining the Junior Chamber of Commerce, especially from the standpoint of how the organization helps the community. This letter is essentially a sales letter, as the reader is to be sold on the idea of joining the organization.

A sales message should ordinarily be longer than the first version of this letter. In order to convince the reader to act, it must present sufficient evidence and motivation. An improved closing section could be:

So that you can begin now to enjoy the benefits of membership and to contribute to the welfare of your community, fill out the enclosed membership application and send it in with your check. It will be a small investment that you will remember with pride. ⎤ (Diplomatically ⎥ stated request for ⎦ action)

Our next meeting is Monday, September 8, at 7:30 P.M. at the Quality Inn. We are looking forward to seeing you. ⎤ (Additional information in goodwill ⎦ close)

In summary, the you-attitude expresses a genuine consideration for the reader. Although the word *you* may at times appear to be more considerate than an *I*, the actual content of the message is more important than the choice of words. If the word *I* is used to a great extent, however, it is quite likely that the emphasis is on the writer, not the reader.

In the following example, the closing and opening paragraphs are given in an incorrect, ineffective, or inappropriate way, followed by comments and a suggested revision.

Opening Paragraph
We are happy to inform you that our business has increased to the extent that we, Nationwide Airlines, are now serving Denver with air flights to two cities in Mexico, and we would like to have you take advantage of this added service. We believe that we, Nationwide Airlines, have the best airline in the country, and we are eager to add more cities. ⎤ (Poor opening ⎥ paragraph; I ⎦ approach)

The preceding paragraph is extremely I-oriented, not you-oriented. In addition, it is too long for an opening paragraph. The writer should have been more specific; which two cities in Mexico? The phase to inform you is wordy, unnecessary, and overly formal.

Although the words *we* and *Nationwide Airlines* appear far more often than the word *you*, the actual use of these words alone is less important than the content of the message, which stresses throughout benefits to the airline, not to the reader.

Paragraph Two

(Trite, abbreviated sentence)

Hope to see you soon.

The last abbreviated sentence seems to be a feeble attempt to avoid the use of the word *we* and to express goodwill. The words *I* or *we* should NOT be omitted in sentences such as this one, which is awkward and not grammatically correct because of the omitted subject.

Revised Opening Paragraph

(Improved opening paragraph)

Would you like to spend next weekend in Mexico City or Guadalajara? On our newly scheduled flights, you can leave Denver after a leisurely breakfast and arrive at either of these exciting Mexican cities in time for an early dinner.

The potential vacationer or business traveler is more interested in the exact cities and the time of arrival than in the fact that Nationwide Airlines is prospering, that it is the finest airline company in the country, or that the writer hopes to see the reader soon.

A letter of this kind would require more than the two paragraphs illustrated in this extremely poor letter; at least three or four paragraphs that convincingly describe the cities or the pleasant flights should be included in order to persuade the reader to make reservations. Even if these paragraphs had been included, however, the following ending paragraph would be less than effective.

Weak Closing Paragraph

We are expecting many passengers on our new flights, so hurry to make your reservation. If you don't make it early, you may be left out. We do not offer discount rates, however.

We can't escape a constant interaction with people (unless we choose to live as hermits). We interact all day long with family members, friends, and just plain people—the people at our place of work, the gas station, on the bus, at our house of worship. We react to the toll-road ticket taker, the doctor, barber, manicurist, and to the people who deliver our packages, collect our garbage, and read our utilities meters. They are, each and every one, individuals worthy of respect and consideration; when they behave as if they are not and are beastly to us, we must find a way to control our anger, so that we do not take it out on another human being. . . .

When we graduate from the self-obsessed "I-I-Me-Me" school of philosophy, into a life of caring about other people, we begin to react automatically to those other people, whether they are close friends or not. We react in a uniform, decent, and considerate manner. It's not something we stop to think about. We just do it.

Letetia Baldridge, *The New Manners for the '90s* (New York: Rawson Associates, 1990), 12.

Revised Closing Paragraph

To start planning your trip to Mexico City or Guadalajara, telephone 303-000-0000. Our helpful reservation agents are waiting to answer all your questions and arrange your flight.

A POSITIVE, PLEASANT, AND DIPLOMATIC APPROACH

A *positive approach* and the *you-attitude* are two of the most important elements of effective communication. In effect, we cannot fully achieve one without the other.

The positive approach includes several applications. One is the pleasant approach, which stresses the pleasant and not the unpleasant elements of a situation. Another is stating what can be done instead of what cannot be done. Another is eliminating as much as possible the actual grammatical negatives, such as *no, cannot, will not,* and *can't,* as well as other negative words and phrases, including *criticize, reject, fail, turn down, must,* and *force.* Another application of the positive approach is to avoid a doubtful tone, as discussed later.

▶ EMPHASIZE THE POSITIVE AND SUBORDINATE THE NEGATIVE

An example of the use of the negative approach in an advertisement is given in the first example shown below; the positive approach is shown in the second.

(Negative because of implication)

> *This line of cookware will not become scratched, and food will not stick to it. It won't be ruined in your dishwasher.*

By telling what the cookware does not do, the preceding example suggests to some readers that it may do all these things. Although the following example is not guaranteed to inspire absolute confidence in all readers, it is more likely to do so than the negatively worded statement.

(More positive)

> *Because this sturdy Teflon-coated cookware is highly resistant to heat and pressure, it is completely safe in your dishwasher. It will still be shining and beautiful after many years of non-stick cooking.*

Saying that something is not undesirable is not nearly as effective or positive as stating that it is desirable. Even better is to give specific and definite information as to why it is desirable, in the terms of how it will benefit the reader or listener. The description of the cookware would be more convincing than the sentence given above if it included evidence of why the cookware will remain beautiful. Such evidence might include a descriptive statement of the material or the method of manufacture.

The sentence

(Implies possible regret)

> *You will never regret using our bank.*

is not as positive as saying

(States positive idea)

> *You will benefit from our many banking services.*

Instead of saying

(Implies overcharging)

> *The interest rate on your credit card is not exorbitant*

say something like this:

(More positive and specific)

> *The balance of your account can be carried forward from month to month at an interest rate of 9 percent, up to an agreed-upon credit limit.*

Emphasize the benefits readers or listeners will gain from the product, not difficulties or misfortunes they will avoid. An unpleasant thought tends to make people turn away from the subject and think of something else. Notice the following examples of the negative and positive approach:

Compare the following pairs of statements:

> *The café will close at 11:30 P.M.*
> *The café will remain open until 11:30 P.M.*

> *We cannot ship your sofa until July 1.*
> *Your sofa will be shipped on July 1.*

Notice the first example given above. Let us see how we can make the sentence even more negative or more positive. If we should write:

We close the café every night at 11:30 so that we can go home

we are using not only the negative approach but also the I-attitude because the emphasis is on the store and its employees rather than on the customer. Few writers would use such an extreme sentence, although emphasis on the negative and on *I* rather than *you* is far too common.

Suppose we write:

The café will remain open until 11:30 P.M. for the convenience of our customers.

The preceding sentence tells how long the store will be open, not when it will close. It also brings in the you-attitude, provided the letter is being written to a customer.

This sentence can be improved still further. Suppose we write it this way:

To extend the enjoyment of your dinner hour, the café will remain open until 11:30 P.M.

Do you see why this sentence better conveys the you-attitude than the preceding one? Here the use of the word *your* makes the difference, for the writing is more directly aimed at an individual. To this individual, the word *your* is more direct, more personal, and more friendly than the general and collective words *our customers.*

The word *you* is usually a better choice than *our customers*, even when the message is to be printed and distributed to thousands of customers. Although the same letter is being sent to many persons, each customer reading the message is an individual. Individuals think of themselves alone, not necessarily in relation to thousands of other customers.

Other examples of the positive versus the negative approach include the following:

Negative	**More Positive**
After just one week of our weight-loss program you won't feel fat and miserable.	*After only one week of "Aerobics for Fitness," your clothes will be looser and you will feel strong and trim.*
Red Cross will not be conducting classes any time in September.	*The date of the next Red Cross class is October 6. We invite you to enroll.*
I will not be able to attend the dinner on Friday, March 3, but I will be present for the luncheon.	*On Friday, March 3, I can attend only the luncheon.*
Every resident will have to leave the dormitory over the Christmas holidays, from December 22 through January 13.	*All dormitory residents will live elsewhere during the Christmas holidays, from December 22 through January 13. We wish you all a happy holiday season.*

Negative	Positive
We cannot give you your paycheck until Friday after next.	*You will receive your paycheck on Friday, February 27.*
Your messy laundry won't be half bad after you use Brilliant detergent.	*Your clothes will be fresh and bright after you wash them with Brilliant.*
You will not be allowed to take vacation between January 1 and June 1.	*Please schedule your vacation, at any time you choose, between June 2 and December 31.*
You must pay your bill by the tenth of each month to receive a discount of 2 percent.	*By paying your monthly invoice by the tenth, you will earn a 2 percent discount.*

▶ **AVOID A DOUBTFUL TONE**

Success oriented describes another function of the positive approach. Success-oriented passages imply acceptance or favorable action on the part of the reader. This concept is also referred to as success consciousness. The opposite approach is called the doubtful tone. Words to avoid are *if, hope,* and *trust,* as well as any other words or phrases that suggest doubt.

Notice the doubtful tone in these sentence beginnings:

If you want to follow these instructions

If my qualifications meet your requirements

If you want to order this book

We hope this meets with your approval . . .

We trust this is a satisfactory arrangement

I know that this is less than you expected, but

I know you will be disappointed in us, but

We hope that this unfortunate occurrence will not adversely affect our business relationship, for

All these expressions imply that the reader will not agree to the suggested opinions or actions or will not continue to hold the writer in esteem. More persuasive wordings are these:

You will find these instructions helpful, for . . .

May I come for an interview to discuss my qualifications in detail?

Just sign the enclosed card and Effective Reports *will soon be on its way to you.*

We think you will like this change of procedure because . . .

Perhaps the other doubtfully worded sentences shown above could be omitted entirely. No matter what the situation, a statement such as:

We hope that this unfortunate occurrence will not adversely affect our business relationship

is probably more harmful than the occurrence itself.

Sometimes the positive, diplomatic approach is achieved by what we refrain from stating. For example, you do not need to include the following statement in order to obtain the necessary information:

In your recent order, you failed to include your size. ⎤ (Includes negative
⎦ word *failed*; accusing)

A better wording is:

The sweaters come in these sizes: Small (34–36), Medium (38–40), and Large (42–44). Please check your size on the enclosed card. ⎤ (Asks for action
⎦ without placing blame)

The improved example omits the extremely negative and accusing word *failed* and moves directly to the requested action.

The following statement is another example of a fact that is often best left unexpressed:

Unfortunately, I have no business experience. ⎤ (Stresses a weakness)
⎦

A customer's opinion of the writer and the organization is influenced by the quality of business letters.

This statement from an application letter stresses a supposed weakness. You are not misrepresenting your experience by omitting such references. If no experience is described in your letter or data sheet, the reader should suppose that you have none. Stress strong points, not weaknesses, as:

(Stresses positive factors)

My courses in business administration at Indiana State University have given me an understanding of the fundamentals of management and supervision.

To repeat and emphasize: To achieve the you-attitude and the positive approach, we choose what to emphasize and what to subordinate or to omit. As you learned from Chapter 5, *we emphasize or subordinate by position and arrangement, by sentence construction, and by word choice.* Diplomatic word choice is also discussed in the following section. (Also review Chapter 4.)

► USE SPECIFIC WORDS TO EXPRESS PLEASANT AND NEUTRAL IDEAS

Concrete, specific words should be used to express pleasant or neutral ideas, but more general, abstract terms should be chosen to express unpleasant ideas. For example:

(Overly specific)

I'm sorry you have pneumonia and dermatitis

although more specific and more accurate than

(Improved)

I'm sorry you are ill.

is certainly less diplomatic. Another extreme example is:

(Far too specific. Used here as a "horrible example")

We have learned of the unfortunate circumstances of your accident, illness, and losses in the stock market.

In a situation like this, choose to be less than specific and use some generalized word like *problems*. Although *problems* in most cases is a negative word, here, in comparison with the exact words, it is positively cheerful. Most likely, mention of the unfortunate circumstances should be omitted altogether.

Express pleasant and neutral ideas or statements in specific, forceful words. For example:

Congratulations on being elected president of your senior class!

I am interested in stationery with 25-percent cotton content, 20-pound weight.

For most of your writing, choose specific, concrete words. They are more vivid, direct, and exact. At times, however, choose more general, abstract words in order to express ideas diplomatically.

For the sake of diplomacy and tact, sometimes we communicate best by what we refrain from saying. We do not speak specifically and in detail, at all times, with our friends or family. To be completely, absolutely, and harshly specific about negative facts or assumptions, as we have all witnessed, can be devastating to the ego.

The use of general words instead of overly specific ones can soften an unpleasant message. Unpleasant details that are not necessary for the reception of the intended message are often best omitted. For example, if an applicant was not hired because he scored lower than anyone else had ever scored on a company aptitude test, only a sadistic personnel manager would spell out this unwelcome news.

▶ CHOOSE THE ACTIVE OR THE PASSIVE VOICE

Another principle of forceful, descriptive, concise writing—prefer the active voice—is reversed at times for the sake of tact and diplomacy. (The active and the passive voice are described and illustrated in Chapter 5.)

For example, the following sentence, with the verb in the active voice,

You did not submit your proposed budget on July 19, the date it was due

can be softened by using the passive voice in this way:

The proposed budget was to be submitted on July 19.

This discussion of the positive approach does not mean that you will never use the words *no, not,* or *cannot.* Such words are often necessary in order to express your exact meaning, as in the sentence immediately preceding this one. Your communications can include such words as *cannot* and *no,* provided the overall message is courteous and considerate. Even the word *must* may be necessary in urgent situations, although it should ordinarily be avoided because of its demanding tone.

Clearness should not be sacrificed for the sake of diplomacy, but good writing should be both clear and diplomatic. It can be, although at times there must be a direct statement of necessary information or an unmistakable refusal. For example, instead of *stop,* suppose that the road sign were worded, *Pause, please, if you have time.*

The following letters illustrate the extreme lack of a positive approach because of the choice of words.

You did not submit your report on time. Jack, we cannot hope to complete the project if you are unable to discharge your responsibilities.

Otherwise, meeting our deadline will be impossible. We will regret the delay, for the project is important.

If you want to send in the report within a few days, let me know.

(Extreme example of accusing, negative tone and word choice; sarcastic)

This exaggerated example illustrates various words, phrases, and sentence constructions that result in a negative approach. Seldom would a single letter contain so many negative expressions.

Another important principle is that clarity, importance, and urgency must not be forgotten when working for the positive approach or the you-attitude. For example, in the letter shown above, the reader must under-

COMMUNICATION
brief

TECHNOLOGY AND DIPLOMACY

Miss Manners is alarmed that communication technology (for which she is grateful every day of her life) has inadvertently increased the public danger of being hit by barrages of uncharitable frankness. There are too many people with itchy fingers on the Send key. She shall have to put a restriction on the use of E-mail, even though she thinks it the best means of quick communication since the pony express. (Never did much care for the telephone.) New tools require new rules.

E-mail has the great advantage of not having to be fed, although Miss Manners has to give hers a reassuring pat now and then to get it going. But its speed has done away with the old built-in time lags in which to think the communication through, put it in more diplomatic terms, or decide that expressing it will create more trouble than satisfaction.

Even the imprudent and the friendless used to have the advantage of an enforced waiting period. When it was necessary to dip the quill, powder the paper, and probably set the letter on fire while sealing it, making it necessary to start all over again; and when there was no use rushing off with the results because there would be a wait before the message would be picked up from postbox or out box anyway, there was a natural cooling off period.

. . . But now the message is no sooner thought than sent—and often to more people than intended. You can't burn a letter that's already burning others.

. . . Miss Manners can only intone: Think before you fax.

stand that the report has to be submitted immediately if the project is to be completed on time.

Suggested Revision

Jack, we can complete the project on time only if your report is received in this office within five days.

Everything else is going well. We can meet the scheduled date soon after your report is received. We both realize the importance of this work, and we will both be rewarded for its prompt completion.

Please telephone and let me know when the report will arrive.

In summary, the positive approach is pleasant and diplomatic. It emphasizes what can be done, not what cannot be done; the pleasant, not the unpleasant. It emphasizes the benefits to be gained, not the unpleasant things that could occur, or even those that will not occur. It eliminates words or phrases that are likely to make negative impressions, no matter how the words or phrases are used (words such as *fail*, *reject*, and *criticize*).

USING DIRECT AND INDIRECT ARRANGEMENTS TO ACHIEVE A DIPLOMATIC APPROACH

The difference between direct and indirect arrangements of business communications is this: The *direct* (or the *deductive*) arrangement begins with the main gist of the message and uses the remaining space to expand on the central message by giving details, examples, or pertinent information. The *indirect* (or the *inductive*) builds up to the gist of the message. These arrangements can be used in written works of all lengths. The direct presentation is usually preferable unless there is a definite reason for using the indirect.

The direct arrangement is advantageous in that it is easier to read. The reader immediately knows what the message is about. The emphatic beginning of the message is used as it should be, to emphasize something important. The direct arrangement, however, has a psychological disadvantage in some instances. The reader may not be prepared for the most important part of the message if it is disappointing or something that the reader is not likely to believe or accept.

In such a situation, the indirect arrangement should be used in order to prepare the reader to accept or to believe the conclusions of the letter or report. For example, if reasons are given first or if information is included to show how the final conclusions and recommendations were reached, the reader is more likely to accept these conclusions and recommendations. In addition, some explanation of a situation is often necessary to make the important part of the message clear, even though the reader is willing to accept the message.

News stories and news releases are usually written in the direct order; the main facts of the story are given in the first paragraph, facts of lesser importance are given in the second, and so on. This plan is used in news releases so that any necessary cutting can be done from the bottom. Even when the news article or release appears in its complete and original form, this arrangement of ideas, from the most important to the least, increases reader interest and understanding. Business letters and memorandums, like newspapers, are often read hurriedly. An arrangement that increases quick and easy understanding is ordinarily the best choice, but there are exceptions.

Not all material can be written in the direct order, even when there is no psychological aspect to consider, for to do so would decrease, not increase, reader understanding. The reader must have an idea of the subject to be discussed before understanding the conclusions. There may be need for introductory paragraphs or sections to help the reader comprehend the most important facts.

A letter that is hard to understand does not build goodwill or exemplify either the you-attitude or the positive approach.

The indirect arrangement of letters and memorandums planned for diplomacy or persuasion has been described by the cliché "beating around the bush." This outlook is a misconception. A message arranged in the indirect order definitely should not appear to beat around the bush. If it does, *it is poorly written.*

Communications that misrepresent (or even appear to misrepresent, equivocate, evade, sidestep, hedge, prevaricate, or pussyfoot) are worse than bluntly direct ones. Well-written messages, however, can be diplomatically arranged in an indirect order and also be clear, convincing, and absolutely truthful.

CHOOSING AND PLANNING AN APPROPRIATE ORDER OF ARRANGEMENT

The direct arrangement is the wisest choice for all letters and memorandums unless there is a definite reason for using the indirect or, occasionally, the chronological. The indirect presentation prepares the reader, through reasoning or other explanatory or introductory material, to accept an unpleasant or surprising conclusion or statement. To determine the best arrangement of ideas, consider the nature of the message and the person or persons who will read the communication. Then decide on the reader's probable reaction to the message.

Some communications contain both good news and bad news. Unless the bad news far outweighs the good news, communications can be treated basically as good-news messages. To any message, readers will react in one of the following ways:

1 The reader will be pleased.

2 The reader will be displeased.

3 The reader will be neither pleased nor displeased but will have at least some degree of interest.

4 The reader will have little initial interest.

After considering these reader reactions (sometimes you will guess incorrectly), consider the following kinds of arrangement, classified according to the sequence of ideas, purpose, and probable reader reaction.

1 *Good-news messages, to be arranged in the direct order.* Start with the good news. (A word of greeting sometimes precedes the state of good news.)

2 *Bad-news messages, to be arranged in the indirect order.*

3 *Neutral or informational messages* in which the reader has some initial interest, *to be arranged in the direct order.*

4 *Persuasive messages* in which the reader is assumed to have little initial interest (sales messages, persuasive requests), *to be arranged in a modification of the indirect arrangement*, which is the "sales" arrangement of attention, interest, conviction, and action. The most important difference between this plan and the usual indirect arrangement is the wording of the first paragraph or two of the letter.

The neutral and good-news letters and memorandums discussed in Chapter 7 fall into categories 1 and 3 in the list above. Those discussed in Chapter 8, bad-news messages, fall into category 2. Persuasive messages, as discussed in Chapter 9, apply to categories 3 and 4, most often to category 4.

Further discussion and examples of openings and closings of direct, indirect, and persuasive messages are included in Chapters 7 through 9.

SUMMARY

The positive approach stresses the pleasant elements of a situation. It emphasizes what can be done, not what cannot be done. The positive approach eliminates as much as possible grammatical negatives, such as *no* and *cannot*, as well as other negative words and phrases, such as *fail*, *reject*, *turn down*, *criticize*, and *neglect*.

Messages can be arranged in the direct and the indirect order. The direct arrangement is preferable unless there is a definite reason for using the indirect. Direct arrangements open with the most important part of the message. Indirect arrangements do not open with the most important portion of the message.

Good-news and neutral messages should ordinarily be arranged in the direct order. Bad-news messages, as well as others that need introductory material, should be arranged in the indirect order.

The passive voice is one of several techniques that can make writing or speech more diplomatic.

TEST YOURSELF

chapter content

1 Looking at the situation from the viewpoint of the reader or listener is known as the _____ or the _____.
2 A self-centered approach is known as the _____ or the _____.
3 Words that reemphasize the value of a purchase already made are referred to as _____.
4 What are four applications of the positive approach?
5 A concept that is the opposite of success oriented is described as the _____.
6 A letter or memorandum that begins with the most important item of information is said to be arranged in the _____ order.
7 Name four categories for expected reader response.

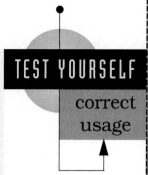

TEST YOURSELF
correct usage

(Related to material in Chapter 6 and principles of usage and appropriate wording discussed in Appendix D.) Insert necessary punctuation, including quotation marks, hyphens, and apostrophes.

1 The you-approach a concept long taught in business communication classes is not always understood.

2 Some writers seem to think that in order to convey a you-approach they must no longer consider themselves this is a mistaken idea.

3 The you-approach and the positive approach are interrelated and often used together but the two techniques are not identical.

4 A well known adage is expressed in these words you can't judge a book by (its, it's) cover.

5 A direct arrangement is the better choice for most letters and memorandums but an indirect arrangement is often more persuasive when conveying bad news.

6 At one time the word *he* was used routinely to refer to either sex this usage was taught in classes in English composition.

7 Although the indirect order of arrangement is widely recommended for bad-news letters the writer must use his or her own judgment depending on the situation.

8 The use of the word you in itself does not guarantee a true you-approach.

9 Although the word *I* is often used unnecessarily and ineffectively the word alone does not prevent a writer from achieving the you-attitude and a positive approach.

10 Correctness alone is not enough many other positive factors are necessary for good writing.

PROBLEMS AND CASES

1 Improve the following passages from business letters in their use of the *you-attitude, diplomacy,* and the *positive approach* and *other aspects of excellent business writing.* Assume any necessary and reasonable details.

a. Our computers are not constructed of cheap components.

b. You claim to have sent a check for $18 for our special two-year subscription renewal offer; we did not receive your check and must cancel your subscription effective next month.

c. We are happy to have your order for The Green Toe Gardener products, which we are sending today by UPS.

d. I regret to inform you that we must deny your request for an extension on your loan.

e. Send your final report of the audit findings immediately.

f. I fail to understand what is taking you so long to write the final document.

g. I would like to call your attention to the fact that our sales were up 43 percent in the Southern Region during the second quarter.

h. We cannot deliver until July 21.

i. The Model 4X printer is not going to break down even when handling the printing needs of an entire office.

j. Items desired should be checked on the enclosed order form.

k. Don't include questions about your bill and a payment in the same envelope.

l. As the owner of Kitty Care, I want to welcome you as a customer. We provide all types of products you need to keep your pet healthy and happy.

m. Sure Shot Development will be unable to complete and test your software by the deadline because of all the changes you requested six weeks ago.

n. Since employees are cluttering up the e-mail system with all types of classified ads, we are having problems getting regular business memos sent in a timely manner.

o. Your department must pay much more attention to producing quality reports; you have let too many errors remain in final documents in the last three months.

p. Failure to install the software in the proper order will result in your not being able to access the Internet.

q. If you do not pay your parking fines before May 1, you will not be allowed to graduate.

r. Smoking will not be allowed in any offices in the building. This order must be obeyed.

s. We have decided to switch insurance carriers since the new carrier offers a system that will greatly reduce our staff's record-keeping activities. (first paragraph of a letter to employees)

t. Your insurance premiums will increase by 7 percent on October 1. (first paragraph of letter to employees; assume reasonable details)

u. Because expenses have skyrocketed the last two years, we have decided to adopt a zero-based budget approach for next year; plan your budget requests accordingly.

v. It's against company policy, so we must reject your request for sample packages for your customers. You must realize that if we give away our merchandise you will have to pay more for what you buy. (from manufacturer's letter to retailer)

w. This letterhead paper is not the thin, flimsy kind that always comes out looking cheap.

x. Do not fail to finish the project by the end of this week.

y. I have not had any experience except for helping my father in his insurance agency.

z. Your memo indicated that you are sadly misinformed about policies in our credit department.

2 As your instructor directs, analyze or rewrite the following sentences. Each violates the you-attitude or a positive approach. (When writing or rewriting, make reasonable assumptions and add necessary details.)

a. We hope that our mistake will not adversely affect our business relationship. (last paragraph)

b. This letter is for the purpose of advising you that your order is being shipped and that credit is being extended, as you requested. (first paragraph)

c. In reference to your letter of October 21, we are advising you that your order is being sent to you on credit. Please make sure that you pay within 30 days. (first paragraph)

d. I am pleased to announce that we have increased our inventory by the addition of a large line of household appliances. (first paragraph)

e. We are sorry that we must reject your request (last paragraph)

3 To improve the goodwill approach, rewrite the following sentences in the passive voice (see Chapter 5). Use any other wording or techniques to increase diplomacy.

a. You delivered the package to the wrong office.

b. All your past employers told me something different about you.

c. You knew the instructions that I distributed to all personnel.

4 For each of the following sentences, all of which violate either the you-attitude or the positive approach or both, *state specifically how the wording needs to be improved, including words that should be omitted because of their negative connotation. Rewrite each.*

a. Since you have failed to complete the loan application properly, your loan request is denied.

b. As editor of the magazine, I am forced to reject the article you submitted for publication.

c. If you do not follow the enclosed instructions, you will not be able to assemble the doll house.

d. In your recent letter you neglected to tell me the date and time of the proposed meeting.

e. As chairman of the fund-raising committee, I would like to request that you make a donation.

f. I hope you won't be dissatisfied with the new procedure.

g. I hope you like this cheaper upholstery material.

h. We cannot guarantee your motorcycle if it is not serviced by an authorized dealer.

i. Failure to complete the enclosed form will result in shipping delays.

j. We can no longer mail a collection report twice a month because of the excessive personnel time that is required.

k. If you are interested in our offer, let us know.

l. You have neglected to reply to my letter of August 11.

m. It will be impossible to open an account for you without copies of your financial statements.

n. We cannot finish your report until after my August vacation.

o. It's against our company policy, so we must reject your suggestions for the improvement of our products. Our engineers have already considered everything that people think are new ideas.

p. I am sorry to take up so much of your valuable time, but I really need this information. (from letter sent with questionnaire)

q. The instructions are plainly stated, as you can see for yourself by turning to page 5 of the instruction manual.

5 Collect several business letters. Compare these letters with all elements of effective communication studied so far. Also compare their style and appearance with the standards shown in Appendix A. Consider the features of business letters listed below and make any additional comments.

a. Appearance, including the choice of letter style and an attractive placement on the sheet.

b. Order of presentation—direct or indirect? Is the order used for this particular letter the most appropriate one for the subject matter presented?

c. Appropriate, concise, and effective beginning and ending.

d. The you-attitude.

e. A positive approach.

f. Fairly short sentences and paragraphs. Notice especially the length of the first and last paragraphs.

g. Mechanical means of emphasis, if any.

h. Natural, conversational wording, with no trite business jargon or stereotype phrasing.

(For the following problems, refer to Appendix A for format.)

6 Write a letter to your instructor explaining why you chose your major field of study.

7 Write a letter to your instructor describing the methods by which you plan to seek career employment when you near graduation.

8 Write a letter to be read by your instructor or your classmates. Describe the kind of reading you do for relaxation, including favorite magazines, favorite writers of novels, and most liked kinds of nonfiction.

9 Write a letter to your instructor or your classmates. State the name of your favorite television program and describe it briefly. Why is this your favorite program?

COLLABORATIVE WRITING AND WORKING IN GROUPS

10 Meet with two or three other students (or with the number suggested by your instructor). Evaluate one of the letters that each of you wrote according to the instructions in Problems 6, 7, 8, and 9. Read each of the letters written by others in your group and make suggestions for improvement. Make corrections on your own letter (if you agree) suggested by other students in your group. As your instructor directs, submit your corrected copy or take it with you to revise and to submit during the next class meeting.

11 Meet in groups of four or five to compare some of the business letters each of you collected for Problem 5, using the criteria shown with the problem. (Before sharing your letters with others, be sure to cut or mark out all identifying names and addresses of the sender or the receiver of the letters.)

12 Summarize the results of the evaluation according to the directions of your instructor. (See guides to summarizing in Think-It-Through assignments in Chapters 1 and 2.)

13 Compare your rewritten sentences from Problems 1, 2, 3, and 4 with the revised versions of other members of your group. With your instructor's permission, revise further any sentences you can now improve because of the advice of your group members.

THINK-IT-THROUGH ASSIGNMENT

14 Analyze the following letter.

> We at Westside Cleaners want to announce our move to a new location. Although our location is not in a brand new building, it is newer than the building we are in currently. The new building also provides our employees with more work area. Beginning next week, we will be located on Canal Street. We will still provide the same services we have in the past. Because our rent in the new building will be more expensive than in our existing location, we must raise both our laundry and cleaning prices. We want to remind all our customers that we do not do inferior work. Your clothes will not come back to you looking like a six-year-old did the pressing. The spots you tell us about are removed carefully, following appropriate treatment. We almost never damage or lose buttons. Bring your clothes to our new location beginning next month. We hope that driving the extra miles will not be too inconvenient.

Based on your study of Chapters 1–6, answer the following questions.

   a. Will the reader's interests be the same as the writer's?
   b. Is the current emphasis on *we, I,* or *you*?
   c. Are reader benefits mentioned?
   d. Is the tone dictatorial?
   e. Are specific details provided for the reader?
   f. Is any request for action phrased in a diplomatic way rather than dictatorially?
   g. Are positive words used instead of those with negative connotation?

h. Has the writer avoided using a doubtful tone?

i. Has the writer used active and/or passive voice appropriately?

j. Rewrite the letter to reflect a sincere you-attitude, and a positive and pleasant approach. Assume any reasonable details. *Remember to divide into appropriate paragraphs.*

k. Compare your letter (or your group's letter) to those of class members or of other groups. How do they differ?

l. Following the directions of your instructor, revise your letter based upon the work and suggestions of your classmates.

Routine and Favorable Letters and Memorandums

OBJECTIVES

Chapter Seven will help you:

1 Describe the pattern of arrangement of messages arranged in the direct order.

2 Apply the principles of emphasis, as discussed in Chapter 5, to messages arranged in the direct order.

3 Write memorandums and e-mail messages.

4 Write special goodwill letters.

5 Write other routine and favorable letters.

6 Explain why the direct arrangement is ordinarily the best arrangement for all written communication unless specific circumstances or content indicate otherwise.

This chapter emphasizes the direct approach as illustrated by various kinds of routine and favorable messages that are usually best arranged in a direct order, which is also referred to as *front messaging. The direct arrangement is the best choice in all written messages unless there is a definite reason for using the indirect or persuasive approach.*

You as a writer will definitely benefit from understanding and being able to apply the most frequently used orders of arrangement, the direct, the indirect, and the persuasive, as illustrated and discussed in Chapters 7, 8, and 9. At times, you may believe that the ordinary use of any one of these three arrangements is not the best choice for a particular message, as discussed later in this chapter and in Chapter 8.

Nevertheless, knowing that the indirect order is most likely to be best for bad-news letters and the direct order is most likely to be best for good-news or routine messages will make you a more efficient and convincing writer.

The suggested arrangements, if well written from other standpoints, are likely to increase reader acceptance and conviction. Another benefit is the saving of time as you compose various kinds of messages. Knowing immediately which arrangement is likely to be the best choice prevents deliberation and indecisiveness in addition to resulting in better letters.

The arrangement and composition of letters and memorandums are similar. At times, however, writers seem to give little thought to memorandums because they are used so routinely and frequently. Nevertheless, the same elements that make letters successful apply to memorandums. The techniques of goodwill building, a you-attitude and positive approach, conciseness, readability, and the proper use of emphasis apply to all kinds of written material and to much oral communication as well.

The plural form of the word *memorandum* is either *memorandums* or *memoranda*. Memorandums is used in this book to conform to the most widely used choice.

PLANNING ROUTINE AND FAVORABLE MEMORANDUMS AND LETTERS

Because the first position of any communication is an emphatic one, use this position advantageously by opening with a statement that tells the good news or sums up the main idea. When you write inquiries or requests, your inquiry itself can often be the opening sentence of the letter.

A *subject line*, which is used in almost all memorandums, is also useful and appropriate in good-news letters, in routine and neutral letters, and in direct inquiries and requests. A well-chosen subject line tells the reader at the beginning what the message is about. It saves explanations or references that would otherwise come in the first paragraph, allowing the first paragraph to be used to move the discussion more quickly into the remainder of the message.

Many writers dictate letters or other material to be transcribed by a secretary before or after the writer returns to the office.

When you request or impart bits of information, arrange and word the questions or statements so that they are easy to read and understand. Lists and tabulations, or statements standing alone as paragraphs, make material much easier to read than if presented in long paragraphs. Subheads, underlining, numbering, and other arrangements in format increase readability, as discussed in Chapter 5.

Communications that present favorable or neutral information are ordinarily conducive to pleasant human relationships, but they can result in an opposite effect. They are less than pleasant and positive if written in a grudging tone. Sometimes they seem to imply that although the writer is doing what the reader requested, the action is inconvenient or unnecessary, or that the reader is not justified in making the request. These approaches can harm pleasant relationships or customer goodwill more than a diplomatic refusal letter.

Ordinarily, favorable letters or memorandums are shorter than unfavorable ones because there is less need for reasons and explanations and for convincing the reader that the action taken is a reasonable one. But even favorable messages can be so short that they seem curt and convey less than complete and necessary information.

▶ PATTERNS OF ARRANGEMENT

In good-news messages, include the good news near the beginning of the communication, usually in the first paragraph and often in the first sentence. The good news may also be included in the subject line of both letters and memorandums. If the message contains both good news and bad news, ordinarily the good news should be given first, although never give the appearance of misrepresentation. (If the bad news outweighs the good news, or if you are not sure how the news will be interpreted, treat the message as a bad-news letter, as discussed in Chapter 8.) In a neutral, routine request or other message, begin with the request or the gist of the information to be conveyed unless introductory statements or explanations are needed for clarity.

In messages that request action from the reader, end with an action close, as described below:

▶ *State the requested action.* Do not assume that the action is implied and will be understood; state it directly, and, if appropriate, in terms of benefits the reader will receive from taking the requested action.

▶ *Make action easy.* Do not ask the reader to write a letter but to check an enclosed card. If you ask for a telephone call, include your telephone number. If you ask the reader to come to your store, include the store address and the hours it is open.

▶ *When appropriate, motivate prompt action.* If there can be no real benefit to the reader, state, without being demanding or dictatorial, the time you will need the information and the reason for the deadline.

To summarize, arrange good-news letters and memorandums in this way:

1 Good news or other pleasant ideas. May open with short greeting or other message of goodwill, followed by good news. (Statement of the good news is usually better.)

2 Details, information, instructions, or other necessary material.

3 Closing thought—a pleasant goodwill close or, if some action is requested of the reader, an appropriate, diplomatic action close. Closing section may include resale or sales promotion.

Arrange neutral letters and memorandums in this way:

1 The most important idea or bit of information, or a brief summary of the entire message; may also open with short expression of goodwill, followed by gist of message.

2 Details, information, instructions, or other needed material.

3 Closing thought—a pleasant goodwill close or, if some action is requested of the reader, an appropriate, diplomatic action close. May include resale or sales promotion.

Open direct requests or inquiries in this way:

1 The request or inquiry, or, if appropriate, an expression of goodwill, followed by the request or inquiry. Request or inquiry can also be stated in subject line.

2 Details, information, instructions, or other needed material.

3 A specific, but diplomatic, action close.

BEGINNINGS IN THE DIRECT ARRANGEMENT

Because the first position of any communication is an emphatic one, use this position advantageously by opening with a statement that tells the good news or sums up the main idea. When you write inquiries or requests, your inquiry itself can often be the opening sentence of the letter or the subject line or both.

Make sure that the important first paragraph of business messages is planned to include material that you want to emphasize, not that which is better subordinated.

Especially important is the first word of the first sentence and of the first paragraph. *Often the first sentence of a business message should make up the entire first paragraph.* A short sentence, standing alone at the beginning of a letter or memorandum, is especially emphatic. (A well-chosen subject line has the same effect as a short opening sentence, but a subject line and a short opening sentence may be used together.)

Here are some examples of opening sentences from good-news letters and memorandums:

The enclosed check for $1,727 is your quarterly bonus. Congratulations, and thanks for a job well done.

Here is the booklet you requested, "Build a Secure Future with Monthly Savings."

Your loan for $52,000 has been approved. Best wishes for the success of your new business.

It is especially important that the first paragraph be short. Nothing is more discouraging to the reader than a long block of type at the beginning of a letter or memorandum. Additional sentences take away from the emphasis that a short paragraph would otherwise express.

Avoid slow, wordy, unnecessary beginnings such as

(Slow, unnecessary)   *We have received your letter of October 1.*

We are writing this letter to advise you.

Just go on and say it. *Advise* used in this way is probably misused; this word means to give advice; it should not be used in any other way.

(A slow, weak, participial beginning)   *Referring to your letter of October 1 . . .*

Replying to your letter of October 1, you will find . . .

Another slow, weak, participial beginning. *Replying* is a dangling participle because it does not modify *you*, although it appears to do so because of the sentence construction. See Appendix D.

(Slow)   *This letter is in reply to your letter of October 1.*

(Terrible!)   *Acknowledging receipt of yours of recent date . . .*

Avoid letter or memorandum beginnings that stress the I-approach instead of the you-approach, as in the following sentences:

Our store has been successful here in Long Beach since 1946.

The reader is likely to think "big deal." Show how your long success record will benefit the customer, if it will. If not, omit.

We are delighted to announce the opening of our new accounting office.

Why? Is there any reader benefit? If so, include. At least invite the reader to come by to visit you.

As chairperson of the fund-raising committee of Central College, I am writing you . . .

Too much emphasis on the writer as chairperson, especially in the emphatic opening words.

In replies to requests for information, the first paragraph may give part of the requested information:

John J. Harris, about whom you inquired in your letter of November 30, was employed in our marketing department as a research assistant from 1994 to 1996.

Yes, 700 copies of <u>The Power of Words</u> can be shipped immediately.

The fabric you requested, Number #2112, is 100 percent cotton. It is definitely appropriate for the shirts you plan to manufacture.

If the information requested is lengthy and complicated, it should be arranged in an orderly, easy-to-understand presentation, perhaps through a tabulation or list. For such a letter, your first paragraph could read:

We are happy to send you the information you requested.

Although this paragraph opens with *we*, it is acceptable because it is written with a courteous, service-oriented attitude. Do not feel that you must eliminate "I" openings entirely. To do so results in unnatural writing, sometimes stiff and seemingly insincere.

Inquiries may begin with a specific question, as:

Do you stock replacement dinner forks for the 1812 pattern of International sterling silver?

Please send information about your cotton material #2112. We would also appreciate color samples. We are considering this material for a new line of dress and sports shirts.

Goodwill messages often open with a greeting, as:

Congratulations!

Best wishes for a happy voyage.

Happy Thanksgiving Day.

▶ ENDINGS IN THE DIRECT ARRANGEMENT

A *doubtful tone*, or a tone reflecting a lack of success consciousness, should not appear in letter endings, although it often does. An example of weak, doubtful phrasing is this:

If you want to look a this set of books, just call our representative . . .

An improved statement is this:

To examine this valuable set of books in your own home, just call . . .

The following expressions

If this plan meets your approval . . .

We hope that you won't disapprove of this suggested plan . . .

are better stated in this way:

I believe you will find this plan to be helpful to both departments.

Some letters and memorandums are not written for the purpose of obtaining immediate action. Examples are letters that give information only and that ask for no further contact, and memorandums telling of changes in methods or procedures.

You are considerate and courteous when you keep channels open for further communication if it is desirable or necessary. You may ask the reader to telephone you or write again for further help or instructions. Such statements should not be used routinely, however, for they may have the negative effect of suggesting trouble or misunderstanding. They may also encourage unnecessary continuing correspondence.

The simple statement

We are glad to be of service

can be an appropriate ending.

This writer is proofreading material before it is mailed. She knows that the spell check and grammar check on her word processing package will not catch all errors.

COURTESY

Why bother with salutations and closings? Why bother saying "Good morning" or "Goodbye" when you can simply start barking at people or turn on your heel and leave them? Because the abruptness is unpleasant, and softening it is a very easy way to demonstrate goodwill.

And now Miss Manners will wish you a good day. Those versed in the conventions will recognize this particular form as the courteous way of saying, "We seem to have nothing more to say to each other."

Judith Martin, "It's Curt to Dispense with Courtesy," Chicago Tribune, February 18, 1996, *WOMANEWS* 4.

Sales promotion material can be used not only to promote sales in a soft-sell way but also to provide a pleasant letter ending. For example:

We have just received a shipment of new spring raincoats. They are especially colorful and attractive this year and are priced lower than last year's models. Come in early so that you will have a wide choice of styles and colors.

In long letters, the final paragraph or paragraphs can serve as a summary.

MEMORANDUMS AND E-MAIL MESSAGES

An example of a simple memorandum (about memorandums) is shown in Figure 7-1.

An e-mail message is shown in Figure 7-2. E-mail messages are the same, except for differences in appearance, as typical typewritten memorandums that have been used for decades. Now most memorandums or any other written communications are far more likely to come from a computer printer.

Many organizations provide printed memorandum forms with the conventional headings, DATE:, TO:, FROM:, and SUBJECT:. If you write memorandums on plain paper, it is not essential to include these headings. By arrangement you can show that your headings are the date, addressee, subject, and sender. A simplified memorandum arrangement is shown in Figure 7-3. This illustration is adapted from one recommended by Dr. Mona J. Casady, a professor at Southwest Missouri State University, and is used here by permission.

A good-news memorandum, arranged in the direct order with the good news stated in the first paragraph, is shown in Figure 7-4.

Memorandums are often sent to more than one person, with the names of all receivers listed at the top or the bottom of the sheet. Knowing the distribution of the message is helpful to each reader.

DATE: November 19, 19——
TO: All correspondence secretaries
FROM: Judith Cox, Supervisor
SUBJECT: ARRANGEMENT OF MEMORANDUMS

(The direct request)
Please single space all memorandums. Remember to double space between paragraphs, as illustrated in this memorandum to you.

(Explanation)
Many of the memorandums you are keying would, if single spaced, fit on one page, instead of the two pages you are using. Although an extra sheet of paper may seem a small economy, numerous two-page memorandums require a great deal of paper. In addition, each extra page increases copying, filing, and handling costs.

(Goodwill)
Your work looks great! Thank you.

Judy

FIGURE 7-1
Example of a simple memorandum

Mail

Get Mail | Delete | To: Mail | Re: Mail | Re: All | Forward | Previous | Next | Print | Stop

Message 1

Message 2

Send Now | Quote | Attach | Address | Stop

Subject: Arrangement of E-Mail Memorandums

▽ Addressing

Mail To: #Everyone
Cc:

Attachments

Please single space all e-mail memorandums. Remember to double space between paragraphs, as illustrated in this memorandum to you. Also, key in text in upper and lower case for easy reading; keying text in all capitals is difficult to read and is often viewed as "shouting" at the recipient.

Keep your messages brief yet clear. Remember that your reader has only a limited number of lines visible at a time. Including your signature at the bottom of the message also assists your reader.

/HDT%20810%20MB/System%20Folder/Preferences/%20%C4/Mail/Inbox

FIGURE 7-2
Example of an e-mail message

9 September 19——
Cassandra DeCrow
VACATION TIME CHANGED

Yes, Cassandra, you are welcome to change your vacation period to January 4–18. Actually, this change is better for us, too. The early part of January is usually a slack time that can easily be covered by temporary help if necessary.   *(Good news, with explanation)*

You are always thoughtful of your associates as well as of our company's goals. Thank you for being such a fine employee!   *(Goodwill)*

Mary Ruprecht
ds

FIGURE 7-3
A modified memorandum arrangement (Courtesy Professor Mona Casady)

■ TRANSCONTINENTAL MOVING COMPANY ■

TO: All Employees
FROM: Samuel Powell, Personnel Manager

SUBJECT: Increase in Take-Home Pay   *(Good news)*
DATE: September 9, 19——

On October 1 your take-home pay will be increased.   *(Good news)*

This increase is due to a 9.09 percent decrease in your insurance premiums. For example, if your present monthly premium is $30, your next paycheck will be increased by $2.73. If your present premium is $40, your take-home pay will be $3.64 more.   *(Explanation)*

Although this amount is relatively small, in these days of ever-increasing costs you are to be especially commended for your efforts that have made this saving possible.   *(Goodwill)*

If your excellent health and safety record continues, perhaps our insurance company (Countrywide) will lower premiums still further. If so, all decreases in premiums will be passed on to you as increases in take-home pay.   *(Explanation and reader benefit)*

I will be glad to discuss your insurance with you should you have questions. Call 5423. *S. P.*   *(Action close)*

FIGURE 7-4
Memorandum that conveys good news, arranged in the direct order

■ **COUNTRYWIDE INSURANCE COMPANY**
SAN FRANCISCO BRANCH ■

DATE: September 9, 19——
TO: Members of Committee IV: Brown, Gray, Roe, Lee, and Blair
FROM: Andrew Williamson, Chairman
SUBJECT: SEPTEMBER MEETING

(Most important information)
    The September meeting will be held in the conference room adjoining my office on Wednesday, September 17, at 2:30 P.M.

(Further information)
    The attached agenda includes items retained from our last meeting, two that some of you suggested we consider, and an entirely new one, about a possible communication seminar, that I have added.

(Action close)
    Please let me know if you have items to add to the agenda.

Attachment
ms

Andrew

FIGURE 7-5
Short memorandum sent to multiple readers

A short memorandum sent to five readers is illustrated in Figure 7-5. Notice the main purpose stated in the first paragraph.

Take advantage of the time-saving features of your e-mail system. Set up and use distribution lists to simplify sending the same message to a group of people. Your system may have a shortcut way to send a message to everyone, but that may be inappropriate for your message content and only serve to "overload" some readers.

Use the help menu to guide you in creating a distribution list and assigning a special name to each distribution list; you can create numerous lists for the various committees and work groups with whom you communicate. Then simply identify the appropriate distribution list in the "To" line when you are ready to compose and send a message.

Always remember to update your distribution lists when people need to be added to or deleted from various lists. To further simplify your e-mail communication tasks, set up a signature line for your messages. A typical business person's signature often includes name, department and/or company, mailing address, business phone number, and e-mail address. Signature lines ensure that your name appears at the end of the message, even if the "From" line has already scrolled off the screen; this provides extra clarity for the reader.

Memorandums and e-mail messages, like all other communications, should not be used unnecessarily. Often oral communication can replace memorandums. In addition, some material of a sensitive nature should not

Composing an e-mail message should be given as much thought as composing a traditional memorandum.

be conveyed in a memorandum or an e-mail message, particularly one that may be seen by someone other than the person addressed.

SPECIAL GOODWILL LETTERS

Special goodwill letters or memorandums are those with the single purpose of building goodwill or of expressing appreciation, congratulations, sympathy, welcome, or good wishes. Promptness in sending goodwill messages is most important. On learning of the occasion for congratulations, sympathy, good wishes, or appreciation, immediately write and mail a letter.

Conciseness is desirable in special goodwill messages. Usually there is not a great deal to say. Say it in a pleasant, natural manner and stop.

Goodwill letters are sent to customers, business associates, friends, and colleagues. Congratulatory letters and notes of greeting are sent on the following occasions, among others:

Promotions

Special accomplishments

Professional appointment or honors

At Christmas and on other holidays

COMMUNICATION brief

To Get Recognition, Give It Away. One way of thinking about the rewards employees receive is in terms of a triad: promotion, remuneration, and recognition. Of the three forms of reward, the first two are relatively unresponsive in the day-to-day operation of an organization. Promotions and wage hikes seldom come oftener than six months apart. On a daily basis, recognition is the reward most noticed and sought after. In the American Management Association survey to which I allude earlier, 40 percent of the respondents indicated that recognition for what they did was their most important reward.

Richard Tanner Pascale, "Zen and the Art of Management," in *Harvard Business Review on Human Relations* (New York: Harper & Row, 1979), 132.

Birthdays

Anniversaries

Special occasions of many kinds

Other letters, harder to write, include condolences and get-well messages.

Because goodwill messages are personal and are applied to many and varying situations, there can be no suggested formula or plan of presentation. These messages may be written by hand or neatly typewritten or printed.

A letter of congratulations is shown in Figure 7-6.

Another letter of congratulations is shown in Figure 7-7.

A letter of appreciation is shown in Figure 7-8.

It's one thing to pass a friend on the street and say, "Hey, that's great about George's promotion!" or, "I hear your daughter and son-in-law had a son. What wonderful news!" or, "I read in today's sports page that you won the tennis tournament. Congratulations!"

It's quite another to sit down with pen and paper (or word processor or typewriter) and write a warm letter of congratulations. Such a communication is read, reread, passed around to family members or at the office or at school, perhaps copied and sent to relatives and friends all over the world. It may end up in a scrapbook and be handed down for posterity. The telephone call or the words in the street are not permanent. The words in the letter are.

Letitia Baldrige, *The New Manners for the '90s* (New York: Rawson Associates, 1990), 574.

■ CENTRAL COLLEGE ■
2289 College Avenue, Kingston, Ontario K7K 7A

January 22, 19——

Ms. Gloria Thomas
Director of Personnel Operations
Regional Medical Center
Toronto, ON M4L 2N4

Dear Gloria:

Congratulations! You have been promoted! Your photograph appears in the "Executive Snapshot" column of the Toronto Business Journal.

I remember you well from several management classes here at Central College during the early nineties. You were a good student. I believed then that you would have a successful career; these predictions came true.

Sincerely,

Robert Jackson

Robert Jackson, Professor

FIGURE 7-6
Example of a letter of congratulations

■ DOROTHY'S HOLIDAY TRAVEL ■

On the Square, Oxford, Mississippi 38677 601-000-0000

January 12, 19——

Mr. and Mrs. Daniel Robinson
Route 3, Box 511
Cleveland, MS 38732

Dear Mr. and Mrs. Robinson:

Congratulations! Fifty years is indeed a significant milestone. Your anniversary party sounds wonderful.

Having all your children and grandchildren together for your party will be another joy, I know. They have scattered to far places.

I read about your anniversary in the Cleveland newspaper, to which I subscribe. Although I have worked with you on your travel plans for twenty years or so, I don't think I ever told you that Cleveland is also my home town. I left there more than 35 years ago, before you moved to Cleveland, but I still feel it is home.

May your special day be happy, as well as all the days to come.

Sincerely,

Dorothy Compton

Dorothy Compton

FIGURE 7-7
Letter of congratulations to customer

2572 Cherry Roadway   ■ **THE SMART SHOPPE** ■   Seattle, Washington 90008

July 5, 19——

Ms. Kyong Kim
The Clarke Company
2345 Hudson Street
Napa, CA 94558

Dear Ms. Kim:

Thank you for your help in making our Fourth of July campaign an outstanding success.

Your coaching of salespeople and the posters and brochures you displayed increased our total sales. Several customers commented on your window arrangements, which were attractive, creative, and colorful.

All of us here at the store enjoyed working with you. We look forward to continued business relationships that will be pleasant and profitable for both your firm and ours.

Sincerely,

Ann Harding

Ann Harding, Owner

FIGURE 7-8
Example of a letter expressing appreciation, written to a wholesaler,
manufacturer's representative, or independent consultant. This letter is arranged in
the semiblock style, as illustrated in Appendix A. This style, once the most widely
used letter style, now is used much less frequently.

ORDERS, INQUIRIES, AND DIRECT REQUESTS

▶ ORDER LETTERS

Order letters are a form of direct requests. They are likely to meet little reader resistance provided that they are easily readable, clear, complete, and courteous.

Orders for merchandise or services are often placed by methods other than by writing and mailing a letter; for example, by telephone, fax, or e-mail, or in person with a sales representative. Order letters are simple to plan, arrange, and write, but many are less than effective because they omit necessary information or expected courtesy.

The example letter in Figure 7-9 is an order sent to Ireland by a shop owner. Such letters are often sent by fax when both the buyer and seller have the necessary equipment.

The letter shown in Figure 7-9 is arranged in the *functional* style, with no salutation or complimentary close. (See Appendix A.)

Analyze the content of the paragraphs in Figure 7-9.

Paragraph 1, including list: Starts with most important information, the desired merchandise.

Paragraphs 2, 3, and 4: Request discounts, with reasons.

Paragraph 5: Action close.

Paragraph 6: Goodwill close.

▶ DIRECT INQUIRIES

Inquiries are, in effect, requests for information. Some inquiries are about products or services being considered for purchase. Replies to these letters are referred to as solicited sales messages. Other requests for information are of various kinds, including information about people being considered for employment or as credit customers. (Because of legal considerations, letters about credit or employment applicants must be carefully worded. Some companies refuse to supply any information beyond their dates of employment.)

The letter shown in Figure 7-10 requests information about convention accommodations. The subject line conveys immediately the basic purpose of the letter. It also is likely to arouse both the attention and the interest of the reader, who is, or should be, interested in promoting sales activities of the hotel.

Notice the parallel arrangement of this inquiry. A great deal of information is needed, and some explanation of each point is necessary in order for the director of the hotel to be able to supply the desired data.

Each paragraph opens with a question; the remaining sentences in each paragraph give the necessary explanations. Also notice the last paragraph, a specific but diplomatic action close.

■ THE SMART SHOPPE ■

2572 Cherry Roadway   Seattle, Washington 90008

June 2, 19——

Shannon Mail Order
Shannon Free Airport
Ireland

Please send the following items by Fastmail.

		Each	Mailing Cost
6 #GB34126	Aran Tam O'Shanter	$ 9.40+	$ 3.50
6 #GB22330	Hand-crocheted vests (medium)	56.50+	6.40
6 #GB22330	Hand-crocheted vests (large)	56.50+	6.40
2 #GB86665	Mohair Capes	296.40+	14.80

Notice that I have listed Fastmail charges by each item, as shown in your catalog, although you have noted that you pay half of the mailing charges when the order is more than $150.

Will you make further discounts because I have ordered more than one of each item and because my order is far more than $150?

In addition, can you offer special prices because I am buying these items to be resold? If so, I may be able to continue making purchases for my shop, which specializes in items from all over the world.

Please charge my gold American Express card (00000) for the lowest amount, including shipping charges, for which you can send the merchandise listed above. I understand that U.S. duty, if levied, will be collected upon delivery.

The items I purchased from you previously were beautiful and of high quality. Thank you for making them available.

Ann Bowling

Ann Bowling, Owner

FIGURE 7-9
Order letter, functional letter style

January 2, 19——

Mr. Phillip Smith, Director
Sandburg Hotel
Las Vegas, NV 89154

Dear Mr. Smith:

(The request) — Subject: REQUEST FOR CONVENTION INFORMATION

(Details of request) — Will you please help the Federal Criminal Investigators' Association to decide whether it can meet at the Sandburg Hotel on July 23, 24, and 25? We need the information requested in the following questions.

(Question: explanation) —
- Can you accommodate a group such as ours on these dates? Approximately 300 members are expected to attend, and they will need about 200 rooms.

(Question, explanation) —
- What are your convention rates? We need assurance of having available a minimum of 225 rooms, and we would be willing to guarantee 200.

(Question, explanation) —
- What are your charges for conference rooms? We shall need five for each of the three days, and each room should have a minimum capacity of 40. Also, during the evening of the 25th, we shall need a large assembly room with a capacity of 350. Can you meet these requirements?

(Question, explanation) —
- Finally, will you please send me your menu selections and prices for group dinners? On the 25th we plan to have our closing election dinner. Approximately 350 are expected for this event.

(Action close) — As convention plans must be announced in the next issue of our monthly bulletin, may we have your responses right away?

Sincerely,

Dave Staplestown

Dave Staplestown
Committee Chairman

FIGURE 7-10
Request for information about convention

2572 Cherry Roadway   ■ **THE SMART SHOPPE** ■   Seattle, WA 90008

June 12, 19——

Mr. Michael O'Daniel, Sales Manager
Shannon Mail Order
Shannon Free Airport
Ireland

Dear Mr. O'Daniel:

REQUEST FOR ADJUSTMENT IN MAILING CHARGES   ]— (The request)

Thank you for the shipment of my order of June 2. Everything is beautiful.]— (Goodwill)

I also appreciate your discount because the merchandise was purchased for resale in The Smart Shoppe, although, frankly, I had expected a larger discount, similar to wholesale prices here in the United
States. Nevertheless, I shall keep all the items because Ireland must be
represented in our international collection.

                                  (Information with
implied request for
further discount)

Please notice, however, that the invoice includes full mailing costs, not
half of this amount, which is advertised in your catalog as being applicable to any order of $150 or more. This overpayment of mailing costs is al-
most as much as the discount because of the quantity purchase for resale.

         (Explanation)

Please credit my American Express account for the amount which is
calculated on the attached copy of your invoice. I appreciate your
prompt service.

         (Action close and
goodwill)

Sincerely,

Ann Bowling

Ann Bowling, Owner

FIGURE 7-11
Request for adjustment of shipping charges

▶ REQUESTS FOR ADJUSTMENTS OR REFUNDS

Requests for adjustments, refunds, replacement of merchandise, modification of terms, or similar requests concerning merchandise or service should be considered as routine. Arrange such letters or memorandums in the direct order unless something about the situation indicates otherwise. Approaching the request directly indicates that you believe there will be no hesitation in settling the matter.

These communications, like all others, should be pleasant, positive, and confident. Anger, sarcasm, or a demanding tone are self-defeating.

Figure 7-11 is a follow-up to the order shown in Figure 7-9.

▶ OTHER DIRECT REQUESTS

An invitation is a direct request that asks for the reader's presence at some function. It is also a good-news message if it can be assumed that the reader is pleased to receive the invitation.

■ PUBLIC RELATIONS DEPARTMENT ■

September 17, 19——

Dear Employees:

(The invitation) — You and your family are cordially invited to attend the Open House at our manufacturing laboratories and administrative and research headquarters on Sunday, September 30, from 1:30 to 4:30 P.M.

(Explanation) — Each family attending the Open House will receive a gift box containing several of the products we make, particularly those that are especially useful in the home. Please bring this letter with you so that you can obtain your gift.

(Explanation) — Refreshments will be served in the cafeteria, and there will be drawings for valuable attendance prizes. All employees and their family members attending the Open House are eligible to win.

(Action close) — The enclosed information sheet contains your numbered ticket for the attendance prizes. Fill it out and drop it in the drawing box when you arrive. Additional tickets may be picked up at the door.

(Goodwill) — We look forward to seeing you and your family. Please take this opportunity to meet other employees and their families.

Sincerely,

Cindy M. Olson

Cindy M. Olson
Enclosure

FIGURE 7-12
Invitation to employees; letter did not contain an inside address.

The letter in Figure 7-12 requires no specific and definite action close because employees are not requested to make reservations. This letter has no inside address because it was photocopied or printed and distributed to all employees. Individual typewritten letters would have been far more expensive and would add little to the goodwill approach.

ACHNOWLEDGMENTS

Acknowledgments are not used after the receipt of all orders, nor do they need to be. For little additional cost, however, photocopied or printed form letters can be included with the shipment of merchandise in order to show appreciation. A penwritten note adds a personal touch.

Figure 7-13 is a simple acknowledgment of merchandise ordered from a company that sells specialty items by direct mail through its catalogs. This letter is a printed form letter, as it must be if cost is to be considered. A courteous tone and an attractive appearance, even though a letter is obviously printed, build goodwill and further sales for the company.

Dear Customer:

Thank you for your order. It is being shipped today by UPS, as you directed.

Welcome to the group of discerning buyers who are our customers. Some have been with us for many years. Perhaps you will be, too.

Look through the new fall catalog that is enclosed. You will find many things that you can buy nowhere else in the world. On the other items that can be purchased elsewhere, you will find no lower prices.

You will be delighted with almost everything you purchase. We are sure of this because of the experience of our many other customers. But if you want to send something back, we'll be glad to take it with no questions asked. See the enclosed sheet that includes instructions for returns.

If you prefer, use your VISA, MasterCard, or American Express account. Just show your card number and the expiration date on the enclosed order blank.

Martha L'Orange

Martha L'Orange, Owner
Enclosures

FIGURE 7-13
An acknowledgment and sales promotion letter prepared as form message

FAVORABLE OR ROUTINE REPLIES AND ANNOUNCEMENTS

▶ GOOD NEWS LETTERS

When the news is good, this good news is the best way to open a letter or memorandum planned to convey the good news. The opposite approach applies when bad news must be conveyed, as discussed in Chapter 8.

The letter shown in Figure 7-14 opens with two words that summarize exactly what the reader wants to know—*You won!*

▶ APPROVED ADJUSTMENTS

An adjustment letter is usually written in response to a claim or complaint. Prompt, cheerful adjustments, made by letter, in person, or by telephone, do much to increase customer goodwill. Adjustments are also approved for employees. Building or maintaining company loyalty is as important as building and maintaining favorable relationships with customers and the general public.

Each claim should be investigated before an adjustment is granted. When you are not sure what should be done, it is usually best to give the claimant the benefit of the doubt. (Refused adjustments are discussed in Chapter 8.)

One purpose of granting adjustments is to maintain goodwill. Another purpose, even more important, is to resolve legitimate complaints. Even when an adjustment is granted, however, a letter will not build or maintain goodwill if it is written in an inconsiderate, hurried, or grudging tone. Your reader may have been inconvenienced by an error made by your organization. You as a company representative must do everything possible to restore faith in your organization and to assure your customer, or your employee, that you are happy to make things right.

Avoid words and phrases like *grant*, *we will allow*, *we want to keep you satisfied*, and *we are willing to*. Such wording sounds condescending and grudging. The person who receives a favorable adjustment should know that you are happy to make it. You should not imply that the adjustment was made merely to satisfy a customer or to avoid controversy.

In approved adjustment messages, the information that the reader's request is being approved should come first in the letter, followed by necessary details, explanations, and a goodwill close. At times, however, when the error is serious and an apology is warranted, the apology should come first in the letter—a reversal of what is ordinarily considered a positive arrangement. In most situations an apology, if necessary, can come after the good news, along with necessary explanations. Do not be overly apologetic.

Do not refer to the error in the emphatic closing paragraph. End with a goodwill paragraph. If appropriate, include resale or sales promotion.

Figure 7-15, a memorandum, is an approved adjustment. Although the error was less serious than some, an apology is warranted.

■ **NEWBURG FABRICS** ■
Newburg, South Carolina 29207

October 25, 19——

Ms. Sally Jones
Sales Representative
Western Region
7070 Smith Grove Road
Anaheim, CA 72043

Dear Sally:

You won!   ⎤– (The good news)

You were the top sales representative in the Western Region. You are ⎤
to be commended for the dedication and hard work that earned you   ⎥ (Good news, con-
this top place—and a cruise through the Canary Islands, along with ⎥ tinued)
your spouse or other family member.   ⎦

The second-place winner in the Western Region, Victor Sims of Salt ⎤
Lake City, has also been awarded a cruise, along with the first- and ⎥ (Explanation)
second-place sales leaders of the other regions. Saundra (my wife) and ⎥
I will also go along. I'm sure we will all have a wonderful time.   ⎦

Winners will be announced at the annual sales meeting next week.   ⎤– (Explanation)
Start making plans. You will receive more details at the meeting.   ⎦

We extend hearty congratulations.   ⎤– (Goodwill)

Sincerely,

Robert Shaw

Robert Shaw
Sales Manager

bt

FIGURE 7-14
Good-news letter

■ CENTRAL COLLEGE ■

HUMAN SERVICES DEPARTMENT

TO: Professor Ellen Blasingame, Management Department

FROM: Richard Ray, Director of Employee Benefits

SUBJECT: Your Accumulated Sick Leave

DATE: January 20, 19——

You are right. You have 271 days of accumulated sick leave instead of the 27 shown on your personalized report of employee benefits.

This error is evidently a typographical one, as your official record here in my office shows 271. Thank you for your courteous telephone call. I am not sure that I could have remained so calm after such a "loss" of accumulated leave.

You can be sure that all of us here in this office will do all we can to make sure that your records and those of all faculty and staff are complete and accurate. The printed report, however, should also be correct. We apologize.

Congratulations for remaining so healthy. Employees like you, who are almost always present, keep the College running smoothly and help to keep down the costs of health insurance for the entire group.

I am sending you another copy of your report, this one showing 271 days. Please keep it on file. Another such report will be issued about a year from now.

Enclosure

FIGURE 7-15
An approved adjustment

▶ **LETTERS ABOUT CREDIT**

Effective letters about credit applicants and credit procedures greatly decrease the number of necessary collection letters. Letters about credit include inquiries and replies about credit applicants; credit approval letters that include a specific statement of terms, due dates, interest rates, and other necessary details; and letters refusing credit.

Requests for information about credit applicants are similar to an inquiry about an applicant for employment, and both are similar to other routine requests. Many credit inquiries are made by telephone.

When written messages are used, form messages with fill-in blanks are chosen for convenience, economy, and prompt response. Many such inquiries by telephone or by form messages go to credit bureaus, not to individual creditors.

Replies to requests for credit information may consist of filling out the form messages mentioned earlier. Regardless of whether the information is presented through fill-ins or check marks on a printed form, in a letter, or by telephone, all information must be completely factual. Confine your remarks only to the requested information. State that your communication is to be considered confidential. Give only data that apply to your own organization; do not report on any investigations that you have made on the applicant. A person who is refused credit has a legal right to know why an application was denied; be prepared to substantiate any facts you report.

Be particularly careful about providing negative information. Determine the policy in your own company. *Some organizations simply refuse to answer or ask the inquirer to consult a credit bureau.*

Credit approvals, like other messages that convey positive information, ordinarily should open with the news that the credit relationship has been established. So that the debtor will be completely sure of the time when payments are due, how payments are to be made, and credit terms, you should include specific statements about these regulations in the credit approval letter. In addition, the customer must be informed in writing, although not necessarily within the letter itself, of the annual interest rate.

A credit approval letter is an appropriate message in which to use sales promotion sentences and paragraphs, as well as other goodwill-building passages.

OTHER MESSAGES ARRANGED IN THE DIRECT ORDER

The direct order is preferable for all letters and memorandums for which there is no evident reason for using the indirect or the persuasive arrangement. The direct order is more concise and it increases readability.

In letters and memorandums of all kinds and in many longer reports, consider the expected reaction of the reader. Arrange your message accordingly, as outlined in the first section of this chapter and in Chapter 6.

All neutral or good-news messages of any kind, whether they are letters or memorandums, are basically the same as all other direct messages. Conversely, each letter or memorandum is different from all others, depending on circumstances, necessary information, and the relationship between the writer and the reader.

Examples of a weak letter and of an improved letter are illustrated in Figures 7-16 and 7-17. Both of these informational letters open with the gist of the information (that is, in the direct order), as they should. The WEAK LETTER shown in Figure 7-16 omits necessary details, which the reader may need. In addition, the WEAK LETTER sounds hurried and abrupt and includes no consideration for the reader. The IMPROVED LETTER shown in Figure 7-17 provides necessary details and effectively uses the you-attitude. The closing sentence makes it easy for the reader to contact Sam Wilson and conveys an attitude of helpfulness. (Short is not always better.)

■ WEAK LETTER ■

July 1, 19——

Mr. Steven Cooper
Information Center Manager
Brinkman Industries, Inc.
P.O. Box 3000
Peoria, IL 61716

Mr. Cooper:

(Subject line not
clearly related)   EVALUATION FORMS

(Emphasis on WE,
not YOU. Incom-
plete details)

I have enclosed a copy of our company's software evaluation forms. As
you should already know, several evaluation criteria are used when selecting software. We have been using this form for a while and our personnel seem to like it.

(Incomplete de-
tails)   If you have any further questions, just give me a call.

Sincerely,

Sam Wilson

Sam Wilson
Manager, Information Systems

enclosure

FIGURE 7-16
Example of a letter that needs improvement

◼ **IMPROVED LETTER** ◼

July 1, 19——

Mr. Steven Cooper
Information Center Manager
Brinkman Industries, Inc.
P.O. Box 3000
Peoria, IL 61716

Mr. Cooper:

SOFTWARE COMPARISON EVALUATION FORMS — (More specific subject line)

A copy of the software comparison evaluation form you requested is enclosed. Please feel free to use it as it appears or modify it to fit your company's specific needs. — (Main idea presented first; you-attitude)

As you review the form, notice that functionality and performance, ease of learning, compatibility, cost, documentation, and vendor support appear as major evaluation points. Less expensive software that doesn't get the job done results in lost productivity and unhappy employees. — (Details and explanation; objective style that does not talk down to reader)

Even when our employees use the evaluation form, there is sometimes no clear-cut first choice. Persons in charge of evaluating software have found that when two or more people complete the evaluation and compare ratings they can reach consensus and make a sound software choice. — (Information)

Please call me at 487-6000 to discuss any of the evaluation points in greater detail. — (More complete ending)

Sincerely,

Sam Wilson

Sam Wilson
Manager, Information Systems

enclosure

FIGURE 7-17
Improved letter, informational and helpful

SUMMARY

Principles for writing effective letters also apply to memorandums and e-mail messages. Writers of communications of any kind must be concerned with goodwill, conciseness, readability, the proper use of emphasis, clarity, and correctness.

Memorandums and e-mail messages are by far the most widely used type of written communication between members of an organization.

When writing memorandums, be especially careful to make your work easily readable. Subheadings, listings, and short paragraphs are elements of format that aid readability. In a memorandum you speak directly to an individual—regardless of the number of readers of any particular message.

Favorable, routine, and neutral letters and memorandums should ordinarily be arranged in the direct order, as should letters and memorandums planned primarily to convey information.

Because the first position in any communication is an emphatic one, it is the best place to tell the good news or to sum up the main idea.

A subject line, which is used in all memorandums and is appropriate for many letters, is particularly useful and appropriate in written communications arranged in the direct order. An action close should be used near the end of direct messages when an action of some kind is requested of the reader.

Suggestions for direct-approach letters and memorandums are these:

1   Use a positive, pleasant tone.

2   Avoid a slow opening, such as *We have received your letter.* Instead, immediately give the good news or state the request.

3   Avoid a dictatorial or demanding action close.

4   Avoid a doubtful, overly humble tone, as *We hope this meets your approval.*

5   Include complete information.

6   State the request or other opening sentence in simple, direct, and specific words.

7   Avoid trite phrasing, such as *please be advised, attached hereto,* and *enclosed please find.*

8   Consider the use of specifically worded subject lines.

9   Use a specifically stated action close. When appropriate, state a date when the action should be completed.

10 Use a goodwill close if no action is requested. This close may include resale or sales promotion.

TEST YOURSELF
chapter content

1   What is the three-step sequence recommended for good-news messages?
2   What is the three-step sequence recommended for neutral messages?
3   What is the three-step sequence recommended for a direct request or inquiry?
4   Give two examples of "slow" letter or memorandum openings.
5   What are three characteristics of an action close?

(Choose the correct phrase or sentence from each pair or group.)

6   (From first paragraph of a good-news letter)
   a. You will receive a $750 bonus on July 1.
   b. We have received your letter asking about a bonus.

7   (Subject line for request for information about prospective employee)
   a. Request for Information
   b. Request for Information about Michael Lee

8   (Subject line of a letter supplying information about a prospective employee who is to be highly recommended)
   a. An Answer to Your Request
   b. Recommendation of Michael Lee

9   (First sentence, letter described in Question 8)
   a. The following information applies to Michael Lee.
   b. Michael Lee, in my opinion, is an excellent choice for your position as assistant credit manager.

10 (First sentence, letter about an applicant whom you cannot completely recommend)
   a. Michael B. Scott is probably not the best choice for your position as assistant credit manager.
   b. I will be glad to talk with you about Michael B. Scott.

11 (From a good-news letter)
   a. Enclosed please find the brochures you requested on October 9.
   b. Here are the brochures you requested on October 9.
   c. We have your letter of October 9 in which you request brochures.

12 (First sentence, request for return of questionnaire)
   a. As Chairman of the Department of Marketing, I am writing you in order to obtain certain information.
   b. Because you were a marketing major, your information and suggestions will be valuable to us as we plan changes in the marketing curriculum.

13 (First sentence)
   a. Referring to your letter of January 9, you will find enclosed a copy of my resume.
   b. The enclosed resume describes my qualifications for Plough's management training program.

14 (Ending, letter requesting information)
   a. Thank you for your time. Please return the questionnaire by January 20 in the enclosed stamped envelope.
   b. Will you please return the questionnaire by January 20, when we plan to tabulate the data. A stamped envelope is enclosed.

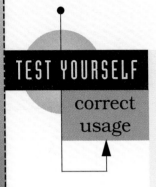

TEST YOURSELF
correct usage

(Related to material in Chapter 7 and principles of correct usage explained in Appendix D.) Insert necessary punctuation, including quotation marks, hyphens, and apostrophes. Choose correct word from each pair or group. Make any other necessary changes.

1 The (principles, principals) of effective letters and memorandums are (similiar, similar).
2 The you-approach is as important in memorandums as in letters perhaps even more so.
3 Increasing readability in many memorandums (is, are) accomplished simply by shortening paragraphs.
4 Some people say that they (receive, recieve) too many memorandums.
5 Although subject lines may be used or omitted in letters they are expected in all memorandums.
6 The secretary asked "Was the invitation meant for my husband and (I, me)?"
7 Make sure that you correctly spell the name of the person (who, whom) you address.
8 When you write a memorandum to members of a committee make sure you know the names of those (who, whom) are expected to attend
9 The ability to write clear memorandums will (affect, effect) your credibility in an organization.
10 In memorandums one sentence paragraphs are acceptable and often desirable.
11 The secretary asked, "(Who, Whom) shall I say called.
12 When some action is desired from the reader the requested action should be specifically stated near the end of the memorandum.
13 When writing letters and memorandums, numerous paragraphs should not start with "I" or "we."
14 A long memorandum was sent to Mr. Harris, Ms. Brown, and (I, me).
15 Slow openings, such as "I have your memorandum of July 7," should be avoided. In memorandums as well as in letters.
16 An action close should specify how when why and where the requested action is to occur.
17 The action close should be (definitely, definately) worded but it should not be dictatorial.
18 A well chosen subject line is useful in routine and favorable letters.
19 Writing is the hardest way of earning a living. With the possible exception of wrestling alligators. [Olin Miller]
20 If people cannot write well they cannot think well, if they cannot think well others will do their thinking for them. [George Orwell]
21 Although the apostrophe has only three basic uses it is frequently omitted or used incorrectly.
22 Apostrophes are used to form possessives to form a few plurals and to indicate omissions.
23 A letter or memorandum in a direct arrangement (state, states) the most important news near the beginning usually in the first paragraph.
24 Short paragraphs especially first ones are desirable in letters and memorandums.
25 (Its, It's) true that a well written paragraph regardless of (its, it's) length is easier to read than an incoherent one.

EVALUATION SHEET: GOOD NEWS AND ROUTINE LETTERS, MEMORANDUMS, AND DIRECT REQUESTS

___ Yes ___ No   **1** Is the good news, the gist of the message, or the direct request given in the first paragraph or very near the beginning of the letter?

___ Yes ___ No   **2** Does the message OMIT slow openings such as *We have received your letter* and *This letter is in reply to your request*, or *The purpose of this memo is to inform you*?

___ Yes ___ No   **3** Does the message OMIT trite business jargon such as *Please find enclosed* and *As per your request*?

___ Yes ___ No   **4** Have you used a subject line? (Although a subject line is not required in letters, it is especially appropriate for good-news and routine letters. It is an expected part of a memorandum.)

___ Yes ___ No   **5** Is the message courteous?

___ Yes ___ No   **6** Does the letter exemplify the you-approach, not the I-approach?

___ Yes ___ No   **7** Does the message exemplify the positive, not the negative, approach?

___ Yes ___ No   **8** Does the message provide all necessary information?

___ Yes ___ No   **9** Are all paragraphs relatively short?

___ Yes ___ No   **10** Does the message end appropriately, either with a diplomatic action close or a goodwill statement?

___ Yes ___ No   **11** Does the message OMIT all doubtful phrases, such as *If this is not what you expected* or similar ones?

___ Yes ___ No   **12** Overall, is the message easy to read?

___ Yes ___ No   **13** Is the letter or memorandum absolutely correct in format, grammar, spelling, and sentence structure?

___ Yes ___ No   **14** After reading this checklist, do you see ways to improve your letter or memorandum?

EVALUATION SHEET: GOODWILL LETTERS

___ Yes ___ No   **1**   Is the message sent promptly?

___ Yes ___ No   **2**   Does the message *OMIT*
obvious flattery?
gushiness?
excess words?
unnecessary, undesirable repetition?
negative or "sad" words (as in
condolences)?
envy (as in letters of congratulations)?

___ Yes ___ No   **3**   If sales promotion is used at
all (applies to business letters
only, not personal ones), are
you absolutely SURE that it is
appropriate for this particular
message and circumstance?

___ Yes ___ No   **4**   Does your metacommunication (implied messages) agree
with your written words?

___ Yes ___ No   **5**   Is the letter or memorandum
written entirely in the you-ap-
proach, without condescen-
sion or undue humility?

___ Yes ___ No   **6**   If you received this letter,
would you feel better than you
did before you received it?

___ Yes ___ No   **7**   Is the message absolutely correct in format, grammar,
spelling, and sentence structure?

PROBLEMS AND CASES

MEMORANDUMS

1 Improve the following sentences to be used to begin memorandums:

a. This memorandum is written for the purpose of asking you to chair Subcommittee IV of the Academic Senate.

b. In response to your memorandum asking me to chair Subcommittee IV of the Academic Senate, I will be happy to do so.

c. After considering your request, which we received yesterday, we have decided that the meeting will be postponed, as you requested.

d. We received your telephone message, which was left on our answering machine, about the possibility of meeting with you in New York during the convention and hope to be able to do so, but we are not sure.

e. The employee you inquired about, Harry E. Boswell, who was one of our former employees in our department, is no longer with us; he left some time ago, January 12 of this year, to be exact.

2 Find the negative and dictatorial words in the following memorandum. (*Note:* Consider this memorandum a "horrible example." We hope that no such memorandum is actually written.)

TO: All Salespeople
FROM: J. X. Taylor, Sales Manager
SUBJECT: Negligence in Turning in Weekly Reports
DATE: January 13, 19——

All weekly sales reports must be received in this office not later than 2:00 P.M. on Wednesday of the week following the week that they cover. You have all been far too careless in submitting the reports on time. Toney and Smith have twice been almost a week late. Don't blame it on your secretaries. Your delay is putting everybody behind here in this office. You may not believe it, but it is actually slowing down the preparation of your paychecks. Maybe you don't need your check, but other people do. Don't forget!

3 Write a memorandum to the students in your class. Give instructions for accessing the e-mail system and sending a short message to your instructor or to another student.

4 Write a memorandum to the students in your class. Give instructions about finding the way from your classroom to the reference room in the library.

5 Write a memo to all employees informing them of a new "Employee of the Year" program that is being implemented. The person recognized as "Employee of the Year" will be recognized at the annual company dinner on June 15. Employees may be nominated by their immediate supervisors or another employee. Nomination forms and selection criteria will be available in all supervisors' offices on April 1. Nomination deadline is May 15. Additional information is available from the human resources office. Provide any additional details you determine necessary.

6 Write a memo to the members of a student organization to which you belong. Include information about an upcoming meeting, including what topics will be addressed. Provide all the necessary details.

7 Send an e-mail memorandum to one of your business communication classmates. In the memo, explain the career for which you are preparing and why you have made that particular choice. Send an electronic copy of your message to your instructor.

8 You are the director of human resources, Countrywide Insurance Company. The president has approved an Education Assistance Program for employees who want to take continuing education or correspondence courses, or courses toward a college degree. The courses or college program must be work-related.

Employees must have worked full-time for

Countrywide for at least six months before enrolling in the Education Assistance Program. They must attend classes regularly and, if grades are awarded for the course or courses in which they are enrolled, earn at least a "C" for each course for which they will be reimbursed.

At the end of the semester or course, the employee must submit proof of attendance and grade(s) earned, and must agree to work for the company for six months from the date the tuition reimbursement check is issued. If the employee resigns or is terminated before the end of the six months, the employee must repay the tuition to the company. No more than two courses, including correspondence courses, may be taken during each term or semester.

Write a memorandum to employees informing them of the new Education Assistance Program. Encourage them to participate. Make sure that your meaning is completely clear, but avoid as much as possible the dictatorial word *must*.

9 Write a memorandum to your instructor informing him or her of the classes in which you are now enrolled, in addition to your course in business communication. Add to this memorandum any other information that could be helpful to your instructor.

GOODWILL LETTERS

10 Write a letter of appreciation to a person toward whom you feel real gratitude—for anything.

11 Write a letter of congratulations to a friend or acquaintance for a recent honor or accomplishment.

12 Write a letter thanking a former employer, teacher, or business associate who has agreed to recommend you when you apply for employment.

13 Assume that 15 years from now you learn that a student who sits next to you in this class has just been elected to Congress, representing your district. Write a letter ex-

pressing your congratulations and support. (Spell the person's name correctly.)

14 Write a letter to one or more of your high school or elementary teachers. Thank the teacher for your school year and state how the instruction has benefited you.

15 You are the credit manager of Goldsmith's Department Store, Midland, Texas. For more than 31 years, Mr. and Mrs. Hector Aquadro have been good customers. Their monthly bills have always been paid within a few days after receipt. Write a letter of appreciation. Their address is 12416 Hideway Cove, Midland, TX 79702.

16 Write a letter of appreciation to the sponsor of a radio or television program that you enjoy.

17 Write a letter of appreciation to the television or radio station (or network) that broadcasts a program that you enjoy.

18 When you receive replies to the letters you wrote for Numbers 16–17, bring the letters to class for discussion and evaluation.

19 As assistant to the director of admissions at your college or university, write a letter of welcome to incoming freshmen. Think back to the time when you entered college. What did you need and want to know? Write a one-page letter.

20 You are a mathematics professor in your thirty-first year at Central College. Five years ago Merrill Berlson came to Central College as the new director of Physical Plant and Planning. Since that time he has made many improvements in landscaping. Flowers are everywhere, and permanent plantings of native shrubs and trees have added much beauty to the campus, which was previously barren. Even within a limited budget, Mr. Berlson has done an outstanding job. Express your appreciation in a letter to Mr. Berlson.

21 Modify Problem 20 to fit a person at your own college or university who, in your opin-

ion, deserves appreciation for a job well done. Write the letter and mail it.

22 Write a letter that you hope will be published in the "Letters to the Editor" section of your local newspaper. Your letter, for example, could support some action of the City Council or a neighborhood group; it could also describe positive aspects of your college or university.

23 As part of a recent team assignment in another business class, you were required to use an electronic spreadsheet package to generate three pie charts and to merge the pie charts within the text of your report. After working for more than an hour, unsuccessfully, you asked a teacher you did not know for help. The instructor spent about 50 minutes with you and taught you how to position the pie charts exactly where you wanted them in the word processing document. Write a letter of appreciation to the faculty member who took time to help you.

ORDER LETTERS

24 You own a computer and a printer. You want to upgrade the memory of your current printer, but you have been unable to find the item in any nearby store. A friend gave you the name and address of a company that sells the 2-megabyte memory upgrade at a very reasonable price of $64.95. This is less expensive than ordering directly from the printer manufacturer. Order the upgrade from the company your friend suggested. You wish to charge the purchase price and any shipping and/or taxes to your credit card. Supply any other necessary information to provide completeness and clarity.

DIRECT INQUIRIES

25 You and your family will be spending two weeks at the beach in North Carolina this summer, and you know that the wind at the beach is great for kite flying. Your old kite was accidentally destroyed when you moved in January, and you need a new one. Write a

letter to Barbara Parkhurst, owner of Tric Kites, 1943 Sandy Drive, Kinnekeat, NC 64943. Tric Kites are sturdy, colorful, and just the thing to fly at the beach or anywhere. Inquire about the kite styles available, colors available, and prices. Since you will be going to the beach in just six weeks, you want her to respond quickly, and you also want to know how quickly your kite can be shipped once you place an order.

REQUESTS FOR ADJUSTMENTS OR REFUNDS

26 Are you now using a product that has been less than satisfactory? Do you feel that you are honestly entitled to a refund or an adjustment? If so, write the required letter to the retailer or manufacturer, as appropriate. Mail the letter.

27 You own Willie's Wood Works and have a steady business of custom work. You also make a number of wooden toys and small furniture items that you sell at craft shows. Over the years you have accumulated a large collection of patterns for a wide variety of items. You recently ordered a number of patterns from a small company you have been ordering from for 7 years. When the patterns arrived, you discovered that you received duplicates of a Williamsburg clock plan, #42-105, for $6.95. A plan for a replica of an 1850s steam engine is missing (#43-601 for $15.95), as is the plan for a floor model quilt rack (#42-501 for $6.95). Since you have an order you must fill very soon, you had to go to a local store and purchase a quilt rack pattern for $7.95 when the one you ordered by mail did not arrive. Write Lloyd's Wood Work Supply, 2200 Oak Drive, Thibodaux, LA 70301, and request an appropriate adjustment. You still want the plan for the replica steam engine. Should you send back the extra copy of the Williamsburg clock plan?

28 On December 1 you had a reservation at the Central Inn in Lynchburg, Virginia, that you had guaranteed with a credit card for late arrival. You are self-employed and your schedule required that you make several calls on clients and drive 250 miles that day. While you were approximately 100 miles from Lynchburg, driving along on a two-lane mountain road at approximately 6:15 P.M., your car overheated and quit running. You have no car phone. Needless to say, it took several hours to get someone to stop and assist you, get a tow truck to the scene, have your car transported to a garage in the nearest town, and make arrangements for repair the next day. When you finally checked into a local motel, you simply forgot about your reservation at Central Inn. On your credit card bill you received today, you find a no-show billing of $82.44. Since you have stayed at Central Inn many times in the past and routinely eat dinner in the dining room and often enjoy breakfast delivered by room service, you decide to write the manager of Central Inn, 1100 Timberlake Drive, Lynchburg, VA 24500, to request that the no-show billing be refunded to you because of the unusual circumstances. You even have copies of the tow truck charges and the repair charges to provide further evidence of the situation. (See Assignment 44.)

APPROVED ADJUSTMENTS

29 You are in charge of mail orders at Benson's Groves, Inc., an Orlando, Florida, company that ships tree-ripened fruit throughout the world. On May 5 you received an order for a bushel of oranges to be sent to Raleigh, North Carolina. The customer sent a check with the order and asked you to enclose a card saying, "Happy Mother's Day, Love, Sue." The customer apparently relied on an old price list, as the cost of the fruit ordered is now $5 more than the customer's remittance. If the fruit is shipped on May 6, it will arrive in time for Mother's Day. If you wait for the customer to send the balance due, the order will be delayed at least a week. Write a letter to the customer to handle this situation. Her name and address are Susan F. Allison, 420 Bay Tree, Farmington, MA 02213.

30 (See Case 28.) You are the manager of Central Inn, Lynchburg, Virginia. Mr. Bauman has stayed in your Inn many times in the past. He has another reservation coming up on January 20 for two nights, so it is in the best interest of the hotel that you adjust this no-show billing. Write a letter to Mr. Bauman acknowledging that he will receive the adjustment he requested.

31 You design woodworking plans and market them through Lloyd's Wood Work Supply. Today you received a letter from a customer concerning some plans you recently shipped. (See Case 27.) After checking your records, you realize that you filled that particular order at the end of a very busy week and must not have double-checked for accuracy as you always strive to do. You should have also included a note that the plan for the replica steam engine would be shipped separately. The plan for the steam engine is now ready to ship, but you notice that your customer requests an adjustment to his bill since he no longer wants the quilt rack plan. The customer also returned the duplicate pattern you did ship in error. Grant the adjustment and assume any other necessary details as you write a letter to your customer, W. F. Parkhurst, 1944 First Avenue, Woodbridge, VA 22191.

32 You are the office manager for City Orthopedics, a medical corporation. In today's mail you receive a letter from Virginia Schmidt, who explains that she was billed for a physical therapy session with Dr. Sarah Maxwell on May 18. Mrs. Schmidt explained that she was not scheduled to see Dr. Maxwell that day and requests that her account be credited for the $75 therapy session. Mrs. Schmidt noted that she was correctly billed for visits on May 17, 19, and 21. After checking your records, you confirm that Mrs. Schmidt's May 18 charge was a mistake. Write an appropriate letter to Mrs. Virginia Schmidt, 2238 165th Street, Chestnut, Illinois 62518.

OTHER MESSAGES ARRANGED IN THE DIRECT ORDER

33 You are the manager of a newly opened resort hotel, the Jamaican Happy Inn, part of an international chain. You are proud of the inn and want to continue the long tradition of friendly, courteous, and honest service established by the founder of the first Happy Inn.

Jamaica's climate is ideal for winter vacationers. Your air-conditioned hotel, located on the beach, provides comfortable surroundings all year round, but many U.S. visitors prefer to come in winter to escape the cold weather of their home states.

The rates of your inn are higher in winter months than in the summer, spring, and fall. You have one set of rates for November, December, January, February, and March; another for April, May, and October; and still another for June, July, August, and September.

It is now April 15. A retired couple from New Jersey spent seven nights at Happy Inn, from April 2 through April 9. A recently employed cashier charged them the March rate, although they were eligible for the lower April rate. The couple paid their bill without protest; you do not know whether they knew they were paying the higher winter rate.

Refund the overpayment of $350, which includes taxes.

In your letter, do not place the blame on the cashier. You want your customers to believe in all Happy Inns. You know that mistakes will happen occasionally, even at a Happy Inn.

Address the letter to Mr. and Mrs. Herbert Moses, 362 Dodd Lane, Princeton, NJ 08540.

34 You are an engineer employed by Maxwell Engineering. Through recent discussions with the client of a project that is currently out for bid, you realize that some changes will have to be made to Drawing 14 of the plan. Write a letter to contractors who may be bidding Job 2281 and explain the changes. Send a new drawing, 14-A, along with your letter. You and the client have es-timated that the changes will increase the cost dramatically. You and the client want any contractor bidding the job to submit bids with two quotes: one quote based on the original drawings, and one quote based on the plans that include drawing 14-A. Also remind the contractors that the bids must be received by 12 noon, November 1.

35 You are an administrative assistant for Reader's Digest Sweepstakes. You have been assigned to write a letter to all winners of a lady's or gentleman's wristwatch, one of the minor prizes, that has a value of about $100. Write the letter. Ask the winner to let you know whether to send the lady's or gentleman's watch. (The letter will be individually addressed by computer, but now your job is to write only the body of the letter.)

36 Assume that you will graduate cum laude at the end of the semester. Write a letter to your older brother (or to another relative). This relative nagged you (in your opinion) all through your school years, from kindergarten through college, saying you were spending too much time with sports and not enough time studying. Tell the relative your good news. Do not gloat. After all, if you had studied a bit more, your average might have been an "A" instead of a "B."

LETTERS ABOUT CREDIT

37 You are Irene Abel, D.D.S. A patient has applied for a six-month payment plan for extensive dental work that you have not yet begun. Although you ordinarily ask patients to finance such work through their banks, this patient, John Chariton, does not wish to do so, saying that he refuses to pay the bank's outrageous interest rate.

If you were firmly established in your practice, you would tell him to go through the bank or to find some other dentist. You would like to do his work, which you have estimated to cost $4,500. He has agreed to this price and, in addition, to a 6 percent interest rate. Because the loan on your new equipment is not yet paid, you need the cash. As references, he lists the local Teachers Credit Union, located at 1326 Luther Lane, St. Louis, MO 63122, and First National Bank, Southeast Branch, 117 East Bodley, St. Louis, MO 63111. He is a professor at George Washington University. Write to one or both of the listed references. (Do you think that you should confirm his employment?)

38 As Irene Abel, D.D.S. (Case 37), write to Professor Chariton (13447 Waterford, Florissant, MO 63033) to tell him that you can begin his dental work immediately. Payments are to be made at the beginning of each month. Each payment is to be one sixth of the total amount (state the exact amount), plus interest of one half of 1 percent on the unpaid balance.

39 You are J. A. Harris, branch manager of First Missouri Bank. Robert Anderson, owner of Computer World of St. Louis, has applied for a $5,000 unsecured line of credit for his business. The company as well as the owner have no previous credit experience with your bank.

Computer World of St. Louis has been in business for 16 years and has an excellent reputation in the community. The credit bureau report on the owner, the Better Business Bureau report on the company, and two of the three suppliers contacted checked out very favorably. One of the suppliers showed the company was 30 days' past due twice during four years of credit experience. This supplier indicated that Computer World

of St. Louis was currently up to date on its account.

Write a credit approval letter to the owner of Computer World of St. Louis approving the $5,000 line of credit. The terms are at an interest rate of prime plus 2 percent with a payment of $150 due the first of each month. When the balance is under $150 the monthly payment will be the same as the balance. There is no initial fee charge to open this account. Should you make any mention of the one supplier's rating? Should you offer the bank's other services?

The address of Computer World of St. Louis is 2230 Lindbergh Avenue, St. Louis, MO 63042.

WRITE YOUR OWN ASSIGNMENTS AND SOLUTIONS

40 *Write your OWN assignments, with solutions, for one or more of the kinds of letters or memorandums described in this chapter.*

This assignment provides practice in describing a situation and giving instructions as well as in writing letters and memorandums. Your problem assignments may be on any subject, preferably about situations likely to occur in a business office. Give all the information another student would need to write a communication as a solution to your problem, including names and addresses and enough details to enable the writer to make appropriate decisions. (By using this assignment, you can write messages that apply to your own organization or to your personal written communication.)

COLLABORATIVE WRITING AND WORKING IN GROUPS

41 Cases 1 through 39 can be used for collaborative writing exercises in various ways, some of which are listed below, according to the suggestions of your instructor.
a. Meet in groups of three or four to discuss the problem assigned or chosen to prepare

outside of class. Discuss any decisions that must be made before the letter or memorandum is written. Prepare a brief outline of the content of each paragraph. Write a preliminary copy of the first and last paragraphs or, if time permits, of the entire letter. Each student then takes the rough draft to revise and refine. *Most important of all: Determine the purpose or purposes of the letter before you begin.* Also estimate the expected reaction of the reader.

b. Modify the instructions in Part a to the extent that each group analyzes and plans three or four cases, a different one for each student.

c. Use a short problem to write in class as a group. Twenty minutes should be enough time.

d. Each member of a group evaluates work completed outside of class by all other members of the group. This outside work may be the revision of the letter discussed in Part a or b.

42 Meet in pairs to complete work with Case 40. Each student is to write a letter or other communication based on the problem prepared by the other student. Then the work written in class is compared with the solution prepared outside of class.

THINK-IT-THROUGH ASSIGNMENTS

Complete this assignment either independently or in groups, as your instructor directs.

43 Your organization, which employs 54 people, has finally installed a voice mail system that will be available to all employees in the organization. The system will be operational next Monday morning; it is operational now on a few phones, including four located in a conference room your company sometimes uses as a training room. One of your job tasks involves training personnel on new technology applications, and you are confident the new voice mail system will work well if everyone receives a short amount (1/2 hour) of structured training. Follow-up questions should then be minimal and easy to answer over the phone. You have already set up a training schedule and grouped employees appropriately. The schedule has already been keyed in and can be sent along with the actual message you write.

a. What channel should you use to notify all personnel about the new system?

b. What is the key message you want to communicate?

c. What will the typical reader reaction be to your message?

d. How should you phrase your message so that all employees, no matter what their educational backgrounds are, will understand it?

e. How can you present your information most concisely?

f. Can you write the message in such a way that the you-attitude and positive approach are evident?

g. Compose an effective message; select an appropriate communication channel for distribution of the message.

44 This assignment is based on Case 28 (request for adjustment—no-show billing by Central Inn). Consider the following questions before writing the letter.

a. Should you open the letter with the statement that unless Central Inn credits your charge card for $82.44 you will no longer stay there when in Lynchburg? Why or why not?

b. Are there certain negative connotation words that you will want to avoid using in your letter?

c. What organizational approach should you use in this letter?

d. Since you have copies of the tow truck and repair charges, should you mention them in the letter and send them along as enclosures? Why or why not?

e. How much detail is necessary to justify your request?

f. What is the advantage of writing a letter instead of calling Central Inn?

g. Write the letter.

45 You work in a human resources department. Write ONE letter to be duplicated and mailed to the home of all employees in your company based on the information listed below. Make any reasonable assumptions.

a. Employees are to receive a Christmas bonus. Employees who have worked for less than six months are not eligible for the bonus.

b. The amount of the bonus is two weeks' base pay. The company does not allow overtime, commissions, or any kind of extra pay to be counted when figuring the amount of the Christmas bonus.

c. The bonus will be added to the check of December 11.

d. Some employees have been working extra hard because of the end-of-year rush.

e. All employees will receive a food basket containing a turkey or ham, fruitcake, and other food and gift items.

This letter is to be prepared on word processing equipment, with individual names and addresses added. For the purpose of this assignment, show the inside address and the employee's name in the usual way. (Letters prepared by this method cannot be distinguished from individually typewritten letters.) Use this inside address:

Mr. James T. Holloway
1967 Luzon Cove
Oklahoma City, OK 73077

Consider the following questions before writing the letter.

a. Notice that the instructions call for one letter to be sent to all employees. What is the advantage of writing one letter to be sent to all, as one group receives a bonus and the other does not? Why not prepare two separate letters?

b. Is this letter a good-news letter to all readers?

c. Should you open the letter with the statement that some employees will receive a Christmas bonus? Why or why not?

d. What are some negative words that you should avoid when writing this letter?

e. Should the statement be included that some employees have been working extra hard during the end-of-year rush? Why or why not?

f. What is the advantage of using word processing to prepare individual letters instead of preparing one copy and making photocopies?

g. What is the advantage of writing a letter instead of a memorandum?

h. What is the advantage of mailing the letters to the home?

i. What do you expect to accomplish by preparing these letters?

Writing About the Unfavorable or the Uncertain

OBJECTIVES

Chapter Eight will help you:

1   Determine whether a direct or indirect arrangement should be used for a particular communication.

2   Outline the pattern for a message arranged in an indirect order.

3   Apply the principles of emphasis discussed in Chapter 5 to the arrangement and wording of a bad news letter, memorandum, or e-mail message.

4   Compose a buffer paragraph or paragraphs that subordinate the refusal without being misleading or irrelevant.

5   Write refusals and unfavorable communications of all kinds that are both clear and diplomatic.

6   Discuss ethical and legal considerations in relation to bad-news messages.

Writing a diplomatic but yet effective bad-news message is one of the most difficult communication challenges you will face. No reader wants to receive such messages, but they must be written. Think back to the times when you have received, in either written or oral form, news that you did not wish to hear. How did you feel? No matter how tactfully the message was worded, you still felt disappointed, or perhaps hurt and rejected. You may have become angry; almost certainly you were if the letter or oral communication was harsh, with no courtesy or consideration. As you write letters to someone else, try to think how you would feel if you received such a letter as the one you are writing.

On the other hand, the reader must understand your decision even though it is negative. A message that will be misunderstood is worse than a specifically worded "no."

Learning to write excellent bad-news letters and memorandums would be beneficial to you even if you never had occasion to write one—an unlikely occurrence. In such letters you apply qualities discussed in previous chapters, particularly the *you-attitude, a positive approach, diplomacy, appropriate word choice, proper use of emphasis and subordination, persuasion,* and *arrangement of ideas and information.*

INTERCULTURAL

The Japanese people seldom use the word *no* for fear of offending the reader or listener. *Maybe* is likely to mean *no*, or a direct answer may be omitted completely. This custom is frustrating to people from the United States who believe in "telling it like it is." Other Pacific Rim cultures share a reluctance to refuse in direct words. This attitude is based on "saving face," not only for themselves but also for the receiver of their message. Even without a direct no, however, they can make their meaning clear to those who understand their method of communication. For example, they may say, "We will see," "Possibly," or "This is difficult." They may simply apologize.

Based on discussion by Gary P. Ferraro in *Business Horizons*, May 1996, 39.

Planning Unfavorable Messages

The first step in planning an unfavorable message is *to determine the purpose.*

An obvious purpose is to convey the information that you want to pass on. To do so, *the reader must understand your message.*

Another purpose, in some instances even more important, *is to retain the goodwill of the receiver of your message*, for yourself and for your organization.

A sincere you-attitude, desirable in all communication, is even more essential for diplomatic bad-news messages. Even when the request must be refused, you can apply the you-attitude by looking at the situation from the other person's point of view and by presenting your message from that standpoint.

CHOOSING A DIRECT OR AN INDIRECT ARRANGEMENT

The kinds of letters and memorandums discussed in this chapter should ordinarily be arranged in the indirect order, not in the direct order discussed in Chapter 7. Communications that convey unpleasant or uncertain news fall into two categories, defined by expected reader reaction:

Messages with which the reader will be displeased or will have little initial interest.

Messages for which reader reaction cannot be predicted.

The indirect order alone does not guarantee a pleasant, diplomatic, and convincing tone. It does not ensure, by any means, that your ideas and suggestions will be accepted. In addition, good writers can arrange bad-news messages in the direct order and, because of word choice and other factors, compose pleasant and convincing messages. Even these skillful writers, however, could often improve their work by using the recommended indirect order of arrangement for the kinds of communications discussed here.

The better choice for disappointing messages is usually (but not always) the indirect order. Such messages should be wisely planned and skillfully worded.

A suggested outline for unpleasant messages is shown below:

1 *Buffer.* Usually one paragraph but can be two. Tells what the letter is about but does not state the obvious. Says neither *yes* nor *no.* Pleasant and relevant. Leads naturally to the following paragraphs.

2 *Explanation and analysis of situation.* Reasons for refusal or other decision. May be one or several paragraphs.

3 *Decision,* stated diplomatically or (preferably) clearly implied. If indicated, an alternative or counterproposal. Decision presented, if possible, in terms of reader benefit. Do not repeat decision.

4 *A friendly, positive close.* A related idea that takes the emphasis away from the refusal or bad news. If appropriate, low-pressure sales promotion, resale, or action close based on the counterproposal.

The preceding outline of steps for unfavorable letters or memorandums—buffer, explanation and analysis, decision, and close—is not necessarily the best choice for all negative messages. Like all other forms of communication, each situation and each reader must be considered individually. No so-called pattern or formula will be successful in every instance.

For example, you may know that your reader is the kind of person who wants the final answer immediately, good or bad. If so, follow his or her wishes.

As another example, your "bad news" may be so minor or the overall letter or memo so short and uninvolved that a direct arrangement is acceptable, and, like all direct messages, quicker and more to the point. The letter shown in Figure 8-2 could have been successful if started directly. The bad news is not really a refusal but a postponement.

Another instance of when the direct arrangement may be appropriate is when the reader refuses to take *no* for an answer, or when the reader may not understand a letter that follows the suggested examples beginning with a buffer. Although you as a writer cannot with complete accuracy estimate your reader's reaction or understanding, do not take a chance that your message will be misunderstood.

Buffers should be omitted when a reader is likely to scan the letter without reading it carefully, as may happen when a letter is sent with a package of other material.

CATHY   by Cathy Guisewite

The indirect arrangement should never be used if there is a possibility of misrepresentation or of giving the impression of misrepresentation. *Bluntness is undesirable in all communication efforts, but it is not as bad as misrepresentation.*

Despite the previously listed exceptions to the use of the indirect arrangement, it is *usually* the better choice for unfavorable messages of all kinds. Learn to use it exactly, clearly, and diplomatically. Then, if you see a definite reason for using another method of approach, do so. (All illustrations in this chapter are arranged in the indirect order, as they should be, with the possible exception of Figure 8-2, which could be arranged in the direct order.) In addition, solutions to all cases following this chapter are best arranged in the indirect arrangement unless your instructor provides different instructions.

THE BUFFER

The buffer paragraph is planned to get in step with the reader. Dangers to avoid are implying that the answer will be *yes*, stating or implying that the answer is to be *no*, beginning too far away from the subject, and seeming to be evasive.

Ordinarily, do not apologize, either in the buffer section or elsewhere, for refusing a request; to do so weakens your explanation of why the request cannot be granted. *Although at all times we should apologize when an apology is due,* a refusal letter usually requires not an apology but courtesy and, for the sake of goodwill, justification.

Consider these ideas for openings for a disappointing communication:

1 *Some pleasant aspect* of the situation.

2 *Agreement or understanding.* If you agree with some point of the reader's letter to you, say so. Show an understanding of the reader's needs or problems.

3   *Appreciation.* Say thank you for information, a check, application, or whatever applies, but make sure that the expression of appreciation makes sense and is sincere. Do not use such phrases as *we were happy to receive your request* if the request is to be denied. (Why are you happy? Because you have an opportunity to refuse?)

4   *Assurance.* Show that careful consideration and investigation occurred before the decision was made.

5   *Cooperation.* Show a sincere desire to be as reasonable and helpful as possible.

6   *Sympathy.* Express sympathy in serious situations and in all other instances if the expression is sincere.

7   *Resale* (emphasis on quality of product or organization). Use only if appropriate, and use this approach subtly and wisely to avoid an I-attitude. A customer is in no mood to believe your product is an excellent one when a request for a refund is being made, a request that you are refusing.

8   *Sales promotion.* Use only if appropriate and, as with resale, with discretion. (As explained earlier, resale techniques reemphasize the value of goods or services already purchased. Sales promotion refers to encouraging future purchases or to building goodwill for a sales organization.)

Although openings of bad-news letters and memorandums are less direct than openings of good-news or routine messages, they should not consist of slow, unnecessary wordings such as *we have received your letter, this letter*

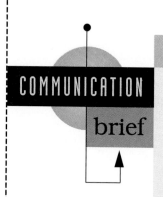

COMMUNICATION brief

"BUFFER" OPENING ESTABLISHING WRITER'S ETHOS:

MY DEAR FELLOW CLERGYMEN,

   While confined here in the Birmingham City Jail, I came across your recent statement calling our present activities "unwise and untimely." Seldom, if ever, do I pause to answer criticism of my work and ideas. If I sought to answer all of the criticisms that cross my desk, my secretaries would be engaged in little else in the course of the day and I would have no time for constructive work. But since I feel that you are men of genuine good will and your criticisms are sincerely set forth, I would like to answer your statement in what I hope will be patient and reasonable terms.

Martin Luther King, Jr., from "Letter From Birmingham Jail" (April 16, 1963) *The Rhetoric of the Civil-Rights Movement*, ed. Haig A. Bosmajian and Hamida Bosmajian. New York: Random House, 1969. Quoted by Gerald J. Alred in presentation at ABC International Convention, New Orleans, November 5, 1992.

is in reply to your request, we have your request, or *we are writing this letter in response to your request.*

A thank-you opening (item 3 in the preceding list) can be used as a buffer if there is any reason for appreciating the letter. If so, *thank you for your letter* is better than the slow openings mentioned in the preceding paragraph. Remember, though, that *thank you for your letter* is so widely used that it has become rather stale, but sincere appreciation will never become trite.

Although an expression of regret can easily violate the principle of the positive approach, it can at times be used appropriately. Suppose that a man has written to you asking that you repair without charge his 11-year-old heating system, although your guarantee expired 8 years ago. You should not open the letter by saying that you are sorry that you cannot repair the equipment without charge, for you would be stating the refusal too early in the letter. In addition, a statement like this one implies that you feel you really should comply with his wishes, but you are not going to do so. You can, however, empathize with the customer to the extent that you can say sincerely, *I'm sorry that your heating system is not working properly.*

Let's look at some opening paragraphs that would be definitely worse:

We will not repair your heating system without charge because your guarantee expired eight years ago.

This opening gives the answer too soon and is also tactless.

We are sorry that we cannot repair your heating system.

Although this is more diplomatic than *we will not,* it is still undesirable, as discussed above.

We will be happy to repair your heating system.

Although you don't say so, the reader will think that the services will be free. A misleading statement is worse than a blunt refusal.

Thank you for your letter . . .

What do you have to thank him for? Nothing, except for the knowledge that your heating systems can break down after 11 years, as you might have guessed. Or you could thank him for the possibility of the amount to be collected for repair, a favor he hasn't meant to grant.

A more satisfactory opening is:

We will be glad to send a service representative to help you determine the cause of your heating problems.

Another refusal letter could open in this way:

Your suggestions for the improvement of our product are greatly appreciated.

A request for photographs used in advertisements could be answered in this way, provided that the request is to be refused:

Thank you for your compliments on our advertising

or

We are glad you like our advertising program.

The following paragraphs can be devoted to reasons why the photographs cannot be released, plus a goodwill closing paragraph.

▶ DETAILS AND REASONS FOR THE UNFAVORABLE DECISION

In correspondence about difficult situations, use a positive, helpful approach and give convincing reasons. In some instances you will be unable or unwise to give exact, specific reasons because of the need for confidentiality or because the explanation would be long and involved. Do not appear evasive, but emphasize that the request has been carefully and sincerely considered.

Do NOT use such phrases as:

1 *It's against company (or departmental) policy.* This is a blanket excuse that is usually meaningless to the reader, as well as somewhat insulting and arbitrary. (The reader may think, "Well, why don't they change the policy?") To the reader, you are the organization, or at least you express the procedures and the outlook of the organization.

   In addition, do not blame someone else in your company, or do not imply that you would comply except for *company policy.* If you think that company policies should be changed, suggest these changes after you have been employed long enough to understand the procedures and to make sure that you are right. But until they are changed, follow them without criticism. To do otherwise is disloyal.

2 *We cannot afford to.* A statement like this reflects the I-attitude, not the you-attitude.

3 *We must reject* (or *turn down, refuse, disappoint you,* or other negative terms). Also avoid, as much as possible, the use of grammatical negatives, such as *no* and *cannot.* In addition, avoid negative words to refer to the problem, such as *failure, defective, inferior,* and *trouble.*

4 *You surely understand, please understand,* or other dictatorial or condescending terms.

5 *We were surprised at your request.* This suggests that the customer is unreasonable. So is the implication that because all other customers are satisfied with the product he or she must just be a complainer.

6 *You claim, you state,* or other phrases suggesting disbelief.

7 *This is the best we can do.* This phrasing implies that what you are doing is very little indeed.

Perhaps you feel that all the *don'ts* given above leave little for you to include in details and reasons. As in all communication situations, however, your sincere and accurate reasoning, stated diplomatically and in terms of the reader's interest, is your best guide to an acceptable psychological approach.

▶ THE DECISION

The reader must understand your decision. This is of first importance. An implied decision, however, can be completely clear, as you will notice in some of the following examples.

At times bad news must be brought to a group. Oral messages can be more persuasive than written ones.

If the decision can be clearly implied, do not use an *I cannot* expression. For example, if you say *we sell only to retailers*, you do not need to add the statement, *therefore, we cannot sell to you, an individual consumer.*

If there is a possibility that the decision will be misunderstood, state it plainly and clearly, even if you must use a *cannot* or similar expressions. But state the decision after most of the explanatory material has been given. Although we wish to subordinate the unpleasant, it is even more important for the reader to understand what we are saying.

Remembering the principles of emphasis, use the reverse procedures to subordinate the refusal or the other unpleasant news. *You make use of a principle of subordination when you move the statement or implication of the decision away from the opening section of the letter, as well as when you refrain from mentioning the unpleasant news in the emphatic position of the last paragraph.* Also remember that exact, vivid, and specific words emphasize, while more general words are softer in expressing unwelcome news.

Because a one-sentence paragraph is emphatic, do *not* express the bad news in a short sentence standing alone.

Include with the expression of the unfavorable news some positive aspect of the situation or offer a counterproposal. For instance, if you cannot approve a requested schedule change, offer an alternative schedule or suggest that the requested change may be possible at a later date. A counterproposal can do much to soften a refusal.

Resale techniques can be used, when appropriate, in the decision section and the remaining sections of the letter to reemphasize the value of a previous purchase or decision. Use resale with care and discretion, however, because such an approach may be interpreted as sarcasm or as a greedy push for sales or the acceptance of the writer's ideas.

▶ A COURTEOUS, POSITIVE ENDING

Do *not* refer to the unfavorable news in the closing paragraph, one of the most emphatic positions in a message.

You may need an *action close*. Perhaps you have suggested an alternative and have asked the reader to make some kind of decision. Such an action will be similar to those used in other kinds of messages, including sales letters. As in all communication, avoid a demanding or "hard-sell" tone. Do not use an action close unnecessarily. In some situations, you do not want to correspond any further. You hope that the reader will drop the whole matter, but you must still be concerned with maintaining goodwill.

Resale or sales promotion material can be effectively used in the closing section of a disappointing message, but make sure that such material is appropriate and diplomatic for the particular situation.

Do *not* close with a suggestion of further trouble, as in

If you have any more trouble, . . .

Also, do *not* express doubt that the decision will be accepted, as in

We hope this meets your approval.

We hope you will not be disappointed.

We hope you will not be angry.

Even worse, don't imply that you fear you will lose a customer or friend, as in

We hope you will keep on doing business with us.

We hope we will remain on good terms.

Do not offer further help if it will give an appearance of insincerity. For example, if you have been able to do absolutely nothing for the reader, don't end with

If we can help further . . .

Call on us again if . . .

The closing paragraph, like the opening one, is particularly emphatic. Use this paragraph to advantage or at the very least as a pleasant close to a disappointing message. Avoid ending all messages too abruptly, and particularly avoid abrupt endings in disappointing messages.

REFUSING REQUESTS AND OTHER BAD-NEWS MESSAGES

Requests are made for many purposes. Some seem completely unwarranted, presumptuous, and absolutely ridiculous to the person receiving the request. In most instances, though, the request seems valid and reasonable to the person making it.

You should assume that people who make requests are sincere and plan the reply from this standpoint. Even if they have in mind "getting something for nothing," a courteous reply will perhaps make them sorry that they tried to hoodwink such a helpful, cooperative organization that had the good sense to refuse their outrageous requests.

The first paragraph in Figure 8-1 is described as a buffer. The decision, the fact that premiums are to be increased, is given within the fourth sentence of the third paragraph.

■ TRANSCONTINENTAL MOVING COMPANY ■

TO: All Employees
FROM: Samuel Powell, Human Resources Manager
SUBJECT: Health and Hospitalization Insurance
DATE: September 9, 19——

[Buffer paragraph] — As you may be aware, comprehensive health and hospitalization insurance benefits are provided to all of you through Countrywide Insurance Company, as they have been for many years.

[Second buffer paragraph] Your policy covers more than 90 percent of all hospital and physicians' charges, with 100 percent coverage for major medical bills over $1,000. This is one of the most comprehensive plans provided for any organization in the nation.

[The bad news combined with reader benefit] — Transcontinental plans to continue this coverage in the most economical way possible and will continue to provide half the cost of your insurance premiums. For every dollar that you pay, your company also pays one dollar. But medical costs have risen rapidly during the past twelve months. In order to meet these costs, Countrywide has been forced to increase monthly premiums by 22.2 percent effective October 1. Your payroll check on that date will reflect this adjustment.

[Reader benefit] — The amount paid by your company will also increase by 22.2 percent. Your comprehensive benefits remain the same.

[Goodwill, reader benefit] — I hope you will remain so healthy that you will have no occasion to use the insurance that you buy. If you ever need to do so, you are well protected.

[Goodwill and action close] — Should you have questions, telephone me at 4523.

FIGURE 8-1
Memorandum arranged in the indirect order because it contains bad news

1172 Broad Avenue Apt. 713
Springfield, MO 65808
April 1, 19——

Miss Ellen Glass
233 Missouri Street
Thayer, MO 64111

Dear Ellen:

Thank you for asking me to speak to the senior class about a career in television. I am honored that you asked.   [Word of appreciation, buffer]

As you probably know, I am a college student in addition to being a newscaster on KWTO-TV. The week of final semester examinations is the same week that you suggested I speak. In addition to the time spent in the examinations themselves, I will need many hours for study.   [Explanation and implied refusal]

Can another date be arranged, either earlier or later? Any time during the morning would be convenient for me, as I am now assigned to the six o'clock news. I sincerely want to come.   [Counterproposal]

Please telephone me at 000-000-0000 after ten at night.   [Action close]

Sincerely,

Ashley Scott

Ashley Scott

FIGURE 8-2
Refused request, with counterproposal

The example in Figure 8.2 is a rejection to an invitation to speak to a senior class. Nowhere in the letter is there a direct refusal such as *I cannot* or *I must refuse*. (Don't ever use the word *refuse*, even when that's what you are doing.) The writer has taken time to explain, diplomatically, why she cannot accept the invitation. The writer of the letter refuses by implication and offers a counterproposal, the offer to speak at another time.

Figure 8-3 is a bad-news memorandum. Memorandums, as much as letters, must be diplomatic and build goodwill.

A letter to an applicant who was not chosen for employment is shown in Figure 8-4. Such letters are often written because applicants so greatly outnumber openings in most organizations. Although even the best-qualified applicants have received or will receive notification that they were not chosen, each refusal is a disappointment. Even though they know that they cannot be the absolutely best choice for all positions, each occurrence is a blow to the ego, often lessening self-confidence, at least temporarily.

■ CENTRAL COLLEGE ■

TO: Ronnie Caruthers, Registration Coordinator
FROM: Harold Evans, Administrative Vice President
SUBJECT: Seminar, Association of American Colleges and Universities
DATE: September 12, 19——

[Buffer; agreement that seminars are beneficial]

Ronnie, seminars like the one you requested have been extremely beneficial to Central College in terms of new and innovative means of improving organization, planning, and job performance. We have been happy to recommend seminars of the type you requested.

[Explanation and decision]

Recent controls on spending and budget cuts have made it necessary for me to review carefully your request to attend the seminar on registration and planning, to be held in Boston in April. In order to meet the revised budget guidelines for our department, such trips must be deferred until next year at the earliest.

[Expression of regret and an apology, appropriate here]

Because of the benefits you would gain from this seminar and in turn pass on to Central College, I regret the necessity of having to make this decision.

[Action close and a forward look]

Please keep me informed about seminars, workshops, and conferences scheduled for the next fiscal year, which begins July 1. As soon as budget restraints are eased, consideration will be given to continuing our participation.

FIGURE 8-3
Refusal of request

■ **QUALITY OFFICE PRODUCTS** ■

4646 Poplar Avenue
Philadelphia, PA 19043
Telephone: 215-000-0000

October 16, 19——

Mr. Jay Richard Palmer
1129 Piping Rock Drive
Fort Lauderdale, FL 33316

Dear Mr. Palmer:

Thank you for the time you spent with us during your recent interviews. I hope that you enjoyed your few days in Philadelphia. — [Goodwill buffer]

We have carefully considered your application for the position of advertising director. As you know, this is a new position that is crucial to our success in a highly competitive market. You are extremely well qualified, as were a number of other finalists. — [Explanation and compliment]

Your resume is being filed with the hope that we will soon have another position that will more nearly fit your particular background and abilities. Another candidate, the one chosen, has extensive experience in another company similar to Quality Office Products. — [Implied decision]

Best wishes for your continued success. — [Goodwill]

Sincerely,

David Rose

David Rose
Sales Manager

es

FIGURE 8-4
Bad-news letter to employment applicant

When it is your turn to write such letters, remember how you felt when you received similar ones—as you are likely to do if you have not already done so.

Writing Unfavorable Messages About a Product or Service

An organization is not always able to provide the merchandise or service that a customer requests. A product may be discontinued, temporarily out of stock, in short supply and reserved for regular customers, or sold to retailers only and not to individuals. Or perhaps the merchandise cannot be shipped because the prospective buyer sent incomplete information. Replies in these situations must be planned with special consideration in order to avoid an implication or accusation.

Whatever the reason for a refused or delayed shipment, the letter of explanation is basically a bad-news message and should be arranged in the sequence of ideas used for other refusals. Avoid such expressions as *you did not state the color* or, even worse, *you failed to state the color.*

Bad-news messages, regardless of a diplomatic approach, will not be gladly received. Nevertheless, the writer should use skill and tact to soften the blow.

REFUSING CLAIMS AND ADJUSTMENTS

According to the outlook of most business establishments, some requests for adjustments must be refused or some compromise must be made.

As a refusal or compromise is explained, the writer must be concerned with maintaining goodwill, as in all communications. Outstanding letters of adjustment keep customers and build sales.

Some companies seem to take the position that the customer is always right, regardless of the particular occurrence. Although some large organizations that follow this policy seem to prosper (no doubt the unconditional guarantee of satisfaction builds public confidence), to accede to all requests for refunds or adjustments, regardless of merit, forces customers who do not make unreasonable demands to subsidize those who do.

In your writing or oral communication about adjustments, you will of necessity follow the set and expected procedures of the organization. If the choice is yours, fairness to all customers seems to indicate that you should determine each adjustment situation on its individual merit.

In adjustment letters, whether they are granted or refused, you should subordinate references to the weaknesses of the product or service. Remember to use specific words to emphasize, general ones to subordinate.

For example, you are being too specific in this sentence: *You say that every time you use your washing machine it runs over and floods your kitchen floor.* This sentence is bad from at least three standpoints. First, the *you say* indicates disbelief. Second, you are wasting both reader and writer time by repeating what the writer told you. Third, you are recalling much too vividly the cause of customer dissatisfaction.

This situation is not one that lends itself to a positive description, regardless of the skill of the writer. (Have you ever mopped a flooded kitchen floor?) Here, though, the words *problem* and *trouble*, although negative in themselves in most instances, are preferable to these exact, descriptive words. An even better approach is to make your answer clear without using negative words of any kind.

Use resale, when appropriate, to reemphasize the value of goods or service, but use discretion. Telling the customer that it is a fine washing machine when the customer is mopping the floor is not exactly convincing. Neither is the fact that the machine was bought at a reduced price.

The letter shown in Figure 8-5 is in reply to a customer's claim for reimbursement for lost plants. The customer had made a special "deal" with the driver of the van that transported her furniture from Florida to California, paying him $100 to water her plants, which she placed in the van, although her moving contract specifically excluded plants, animals, and certain other property.

All 27 plants died, and, because the containers could not be packed like other breakable objects, six large flowerpots were broken.

■ TRANSCONTINENTAL MOVING COMPANY ■

Coral Gables, FL 33134

January 29, 19——

Ms. Roberta Koleas
314 West 17th Street
Costa Mesa, CA 92627

Dear Ms. Koleas:

Your concern about your many plants is understandable. Nothing adds life and vitality to a home quite as much as green plants.

The most sturdy plants, however, are not able to stand a cross-country move in a closed van. Even if our drivers had the knowledge and time to water and tend them daily, the plants would suffer from either heat or cold.

Because your plants must have even more care than your finest furniture, we have always asked owners to move their plants in their automobiles—or to pass them on to friends they leave behind. When people move to California, as you did, they must leave their plants behind because state laws prohibit bringing uninspected plants into California. We would never knowingly break this law.

Your plants are not shown on the contents list; in addition, the contract specifically excludes plants, animals, and other property. Any agreement between you and the driver must not be in violation of the written contract.

The enclosed $60 check is a reimbursement for your broken flowerpots, which are covered by our insurance. We feel sure you will soon have California plants that you prize just as much as you did your previous ones.

The enclosed booklet contains tips on traveling with plants. If you should move again to a state that admits plants, perhaps these suggestions will be helpful.

Sincerely,

W. B. Canestrari

W. B. Canestrari
Customer Service Representative

Enclosure

FIGURE 8-5
Refused request for reimbursement

The letter to the customer is not critical of the driver, although he was reprimanded for his actions. Adverse remarks about any employee weaken confidence in the organization as a whole, although in this instance the customer was not blameless.

Nothing would be gained by pointing out more specifically the unethical actions of either the driver or the customer, although you most certainly do not want a recurrence of a circumstance that resulted in your organization breaking a California law, which prohibits bringing uninspected plants into the state.

Some writers would have perhaps opened the letter with the one bit of good news, that the flowerpots were insured and that the customer was receiving a check for $60. Because the customer had claimed $620 for the plants, however, the news that she was to receive only $60 is far from good.

Another refused adjustment is shown in Figure 8-6.

■ THE SMART SHOPPE ■

232 Main Street
Kenbridge, VA 23944

April 7, 19——

Mrs. R. W. Feller
Route 2, Box 506
Kenbridge, VA 23944

Dear Mrs. Feller:

Thanks for letting us know that you enjoyed our annual spring sale last week. As the city's largest retail sports merchandiser, we take pride in offering you quality as well as the lowest prices in town.   [Buffer, including resale]

Reasonable prices and frequent sales are a major reason you shop with us, we feel sure. At all sales, you are invited to try on the merchandise and thoroughly inspect it before you take it home. These low prices are possible because we accept returns only for regularly priced merchandise.   [Implied refusal]

The first week of May we will have on display a new line of clothes— the Doris May Playwear. Come in to see us. When you buy $25 worth of merchandise, you are eligible for a 10 percent discount.   [Goodwill with sales promotion]

Sincerely,

Mary Vaughn

Mary Vaughn
Customer Service Representative

FIGURE 8-6
Refused adjustment

REFUSING CREDIT

Credit refusals present all the problems inherent in any refusal or bad-news message, plus other ticklish aspects of dealing with the reader's ego and reputation, both of which must be involved when credit is not allowed. In addition, the writer must make sure to abide by all legal stipulations. Some writers give no reasons at all unless readers respond with questions. Then they are given the company's source of information.

The letter in Figure 8-7 is to a college student who had provided no credit information.

Mention of a sale for cash, if it is subtly worded to convey a you-attitude, softens the refusal in that it indicates to the applicant that he or she continues to be a valued customer. Also notice that the customer is allowed to "save face" by the implication that she overlooked the need for credit references. No doubt she has none, but in case the omission is actually an oversight, the application would be reconsidered.

Regardless of the choice of wording, the customer will not be pleased. A curt letter, however, accomplishes nothing except to alienate the applicant.

WRITING OTHER MESSAGES ARRANGED IN AN INDIRECT ORDER

Various other messages, particularly those that convey bad news, are best arranged in an indirect order. The direct and indirect arrangements are as useful and appropriate for memorandums as they are for letters. The same consideration—expected reader reaction—is your guide to the choice of arrangement.

ETHICAL AND LEGAL CONSIDERATIONS

Discreet managers recognize that some material of an extremely sensitive nature should not be put into written form; for example, matters involving such things as employee misconduct or some legal matters that must be kept confidential. Even though you eventually need written documentation for almost any important action, be careful and cautious before putting some kinds of information into memorandums that will be read by a great number of people, or even by a few people other than those directly concerned. For the sake of the privacy of those concerned and for your own

■ **HOLIDAY TRAVEL** ■

On the Square
Oxford, Mississippi 38677

January 14, 19——

Ms. Becky Sue Bird
Box 2400
University, MS 38677

Dear Ms. Bird:

A Holiday Touraway card can indeed make trips convenient and enjoyable. — [Opening in agreement with applicant]

When reviewing your application, we noticed that credit references were omitted, in addition to the amount of your income. Your application is being returned to you so that you may complete this section. — [Tactful implied refusal]

Once you have provided favorable credit information, which is required of all applicants, your application will be thoroughly reconsidered. Until such time, your trips can be arranged on a cash basis. We will do everything possible to make your travel convenient, economical, and enjoyable. — [Further explanation]

May we help you plan your Caribbean cruise during your spring break? The enclosed brochures describe several different ships and ports of call. — [Goodwill and sales promotion]

Sincerely,

Ann Harbison

Ann Harbison
Travel Agent

Enclosures: brochures

FIGURE 8-7
Refusal of credit

protection, do not include such information in routine memorandums. This outlook does not contradict previous references to the importance of openness and keeping employees informed; in fact, such discretion is necessary to the equitable and ethical operation of any organization.

In addition, some matters are of such importance or sensitivity that they should be discussed orally with the person or persons involved, not stated in a more impersonal memorandum. For example, if an employee is to be dismissed, the person who must handle the unpleasant task of informing the individual should at the very least do so in a personal interview, although a written statement may be necessary later.

Memorandums, like letters and other communications, must be free of wording that could be interpreted as defamation or harassment. Writers of memorandums and officials of the organization should be aware of privacy laws by which employees and others are protected from unauthorized publication or distribution of information, photographs, testimonials, or other materials. The Privacy Act of 1974 applies to both governmental and non-governmental files.

Managers and supervisors must be especially careful not to use wording in memorandums or elsewhere that indicates violation of laws that prevent discrimination because of race, color, religion, gender, age, membership in

Bad-news or a reprimand should *never* be given in the presence of another person, as seems to be happening here.

unions or other organizations, marital status, handicaps, pregnancy, and citizenship. These laws apply not only when hiring but also after an employee is hired.

Information kept in governmental files is available for public inspection, according to the Freedom of Information Act of 1966. Another privacy law, the Family Educational Rights and Privacy Act of 1974, permits parents or students over 18 years old to review their files kept in public schools.

Because of possible litigation that can occur years after a memorandum is written, complete files should be kept of material of a sensitive or confidential nature.

Some laws that pertain to credit and collections also relate to libel or slander and to the invasion of privacy. Other laws about credit forbid discrimination and are similar to laws that apply to fair employment practices.

The Truth in Lending Act (1968) requires that credit terms be clearly stated in writing. This provision permits consumers to compare credit costs from different lending institutions.

The Fair Credit Reporting Act (1970) regulates credit bureaus, credit reporting companies, collection agencies, detective agencies, and the use of computerized information about debtors. The act was passed for the purpose of increasing confidentiality, accuracy, and relevancy of information about credit applicants. A person who is refused credit has the right, under certain circumstances, to be informed of the nature and source of the information on which the credit refusal was based.

The Equal Credit Opportunity Act (1974) forbids discrimination because of sex or marital status. Subsequent amendments apply to discrimination because of race, color, religion, national origin, or age. These laws, however, do not prevent lenders from making necessary inquiries and making lending decisions on creditworthiness based on the ability to pay and past credit history.

The Fair Credit Billing Act (1974) was passed to protect consumers against inaccurate and unfair credit card practices. A creditor must acknowledge a written complaint about a bill within 30 days and investigate and resolve the problem within 90 days. Other stipulations prohibit charging interest, closing the account, reporting the debtor to a credit-rating organization, or pushing collection procedures until 10 days after the creditor has answered the inquiry. The act also requires creditors to inform debtors about who has received reports of delinquency.

The Fair Debt Collection Practices Act (1978) prohibits collection efforts that result in oppression, harassment, abuse, or mental distress. Collectors are not permitted to use abusive language, anonymous telephone calls, telephone calls before 8:00 A.M. and after 9:00 P.M., or collection letters that resemble those from credit bureaus, courts, or government agencies. A collector is forbidden to continue to contact debtors (after one legal information call) after being requested in writing to stop.

SUMMARY

Letters and memorandums that convey unpleasant information should ordinarily be arranged in an indirect order consisting of (1) a buffer; (2) explanation and analysis; (3) an implied or diplomatically worded decision; (4) a counterproposal, if appropriate; and (5) a friendly, positive close. A sincere you-attitude, desirable in all communication, is absolutely essential for diplomatic and convincing bad-news messages.

An implied decision is more diplomatic than a specifically worded one. When using an implied decision, you must make sure that your reader will have no reason to misunderstand.

General classifications of bad-news messages include refused requests, unfavorable messages about a product or service, refused adjustments, and credit refusals.

TEST YOURSELF

chapter content

1 What is meant by a buffer as the term is used in planning the arrangement of a letter or other written material?

2 Following a buffer, name three major portions of a disappointing or unfavorable business letter. (These parts of a letter are not necessarily one paragraph each; neither are they completely discrete, or separate, from other parts, which flow together to form logical thought.)

3 Give six suggestions for the content of the buffer paragraph or paragraphs.

4 Give five examples of sentences or phrases that are often included in bad-news messages but should be avoided.

Which is the best choice in each group of sentences of bad-news letters arranged in the indirect order?

5 (from last paragraph)
   a. Best wishes for a happy holiday season.
   b. Again, we are sorry that we cannot do as you asked.
   c. We apologize for any inconvenience.

6 (from last paragraph of a letter to an unsuccessful applicant)
   a. No doubt you can find work elsewhere.
   b. We apologize for taking so much of your time.
   c. We believe that you will be successful in your chosen career.

7 (from third paragraph of a letter wishing to return sale merchandise)
   a. We do not accept returns on sale merchandise.
   b. Our low prices are possible because we accept returns only on regularly priced merchandise.
   c. No, we are sorry, but you cannot return the merchandise.

8 (from first paragraph of answer to a request for use of copyrighted material)
   a. We are sorry that we cannot allow you to use the material you requested.
   b. Your writing project sounds interesting and worthwhile.

(Related to material in Chapter 8 and principles of correct usage.) Insert necessary punctuation, including quotation marks, hyphens, and apostrophes, and remove punctuation that has been inserted incorrectly. Choose the correct word from each pair or group. Make any other necessary changes.

1   One or two paragraphs ordinarily (make, makes) up a buffer.
2   The buffer should let the reader know what the letter is about, it won't if it is completely unrelated.
3   When used in a letter or memorandum that contains bad news the subject line is less specific than the subject line in a good news letter or memorandum.
4   Although a subject line is expected in all memorandums it is not required in most letter styles, in some letters a subject line should be omitted.
5   Resale and sales promotion can be effective when used with discretion but they can sometimes result in an I-approach.
6   Sometimes congratulations should be expressed in a refusal letter. Provided the words are sincere.
7   Words can have a favorable or unfavorable (affect, effect) on the acceptance of a refusal.
8   We can never be sure how our words will (affect, effect) a particular reader.
9   Although an indirect order of arrangement is (recommended, reccommended, re-comended, reccomended) for most bad news messages we must continue to use judgment and discretion at times this arrangement may not be the best possible choice.
10   Because a one-sentence paragraph is emphatic do not express the bad news in a sentence standing alone.

Place the modifier "only" in each of the following sentences so that the intended meaning is exact.

11   The use of the indirect arrangement, beginning with a buffer, should not be considered insincere; it is a technique for achieving diplomacy and persuasion.
12   In order to subordinate a refusal, the writer should include necessary details.
13   A refusal letter should include pleasant or neutral words, not negative ones.
14   Discuss relevant information.

EVALUATION SHEET: BAD-NEWS MESSAGES

___ Yes ___ No   **1** Does the letter or memorandum open with a buffer?

___ Yes ___ No   **3** Does the buffer say neither yes nor no?

___ Yes ___ No   **2** Does the buffer make clear what the message is about?

___ Yes ___ No   **4** Does the buffer build goodwill?

___ Yes ___ No **5** Does the buffer lead naturally to the next paragraph?

___ Yes ___ No **6** Is the refusal preceded by you-oriented and convincing details and explanations?

___ Yes ___ No **7** Is the decision implied (preferably) or diplomatically stated?

___ Yes ___ No **8** Does the letter or memorandum include a counterproposal? (not necessary in all messages)

___ Yes ___ No **9** Does the letter or memorandum end with an action close, if appropriate, or with a goodwill close that takes the emphasis away from the refusal?

___ Yes ___ No **10** Is the letter or memorandum courteous?

___ Yes ___ No **11** Does the letter or memorandum exemplify the you-approach?

___ Yes ___ No **12** Does the letter or memorandum exemplify the positive approach?

___ Yes ___ No **13** Does the letter or memorandum omit all doubtful phrases or unnecessary apologies?

___ Yes ___ No **14** Overall, is the message easy to read?

___ Yes ___ No **15** Is the entire message sincere?

___ Yes ___ No **16** Is the letter or memorandum completely correct in format, grammar, spelling, and sentence structure?

PROBLEMS AND CASES

REFUSED REQUESTS AND OTHER BAD-NEWS MESSAGES

1 You are the public relations manager for Eastern Hospital in Atlanta. As part of your comprehensive benefits package, employees who have worked full time for at least one year are eligible for educational reimbursement if they are pursuing a college degree in their spare time. A waiver for an employee who has worked less than one year can be obtained with a favorable recommendation from his or her immediate supervisor and a favorable one from you. You normally agree with supervisors' recommendations because they are more familiar with applicants' work.

Bill Johnson, a supervisor, has submitted a request for educational reimbursement while pursuing an MBA degree at Georgia Tech. Bob Nelson, Bill's immediate supervisor, has given an unfavorable recommendation, citing Bill's four months' experience with the company and his rather weak performance. This situation is further complicated by the fact that Bill's fellow supervisor, Jim Smith, has recently been granted a waiver for educational reimbursement.

Classes begin in three weeks. Write to Bill, refusing his request for a waiver. Send the letter to his home because he is now on a week's sick leave and will need your answer before he returns to work. His address is 6880 Peachtree, Atlanta, GA 30366.

2 You are the director of administration for Legend Corporation, a company that owns and operates five Happy Inns franchises in four cities in the United States. You have interviewed candidates for an opening as a high-level administrative assistant in Legend's home office in Denver. After a long search you have found a highly qualified, experienced woman for the position, and she has accepted your offer. Your new task is to write letters of rejection to the many other applicants.

Because your company is growing rapidly, you know that you will have similar openings within a year or two. Some of the candidates that you must refuse are very well qualified; some definitely are not, for various reasons. Write two different letters, one to be sent to the applicants whom you would like to interview in the future and one to be sent to the applicants whom you do not wish to encourage.

Letters to both groups should be tactful and diplomatic. Although they will differ slightly in content, they should not differ in tone and courtesy.

3 You recently interviewed three people for a staff accountant position with your firm. There were 47 applicants, and all three people you chose to invite for interviews were bright and capable. The person to whom you offered the position had a stronger knowledge of tax law than the other two, and that particular knowledge will enhance the capabilities of your organization. Ms. Karen Clanin was one of the three people you interviewed. Write a letter to Ms. Clanin, 4852 Forest Lane, Peoria, IL 61734, to let her know that someone else has been offered the position and that you wish her well in her employment search.

4 You are the manager of a large music store (selling compact disks and cassettes) in a shopping mall. You supervise 20 employees who have varying musical tastes. Many promotional compact disks and cassettes are sent to your store from music companies for in-store promotional play. There have been some disagreements among the employees about what kind of music to play in the store.

With this many people working together, you will have some people who prefer heavy metal music, some classical, some country, some easy listening. One wants only Elvis's music, and one would play Willie Nelson's records all day long. Everyone cannot be pleased at the same time. However, the music played in the store is not for the enjoyment of the employees but for the sale and promotion of the music.

Write a memo to all the employees about this situation. What will you say? (You cannot talk with them in a meeting because they work different hours; at no time are all employees in the store together.)

5 You are vice-president of Newburg Fabrics in charge of the Western Region. One of the people you supervise is Joe Reeves, sales manager of the Western Region, a position he has held for 18 years. He has been with the company for 23 years. His goal is to become national sales manager.

A few years ago, Robert Shaw joined Newburg Fabrics. He had just completed his marketing degree from San Francisco State University. This was his first job. Because Reeves was the regional sales manager, he trained Shaw for the job, and it did not take Shaw long to learn.

In a short period of time Shaw began sharing his innovative ideas. Due to his effective marketing strategies and knowledge of present market trends, the company earned handsome profits. In addition, from the beginning the president of the company seemed to like Shaw, as did the president's daughter, who is now married to Shaw. After three years with the company, at age 28, Shaw was promoted to national sales manager.

The president asked you to talk with Reeves before the announcement was made public. Reeves was angry and bitterly disappointed. He said that he would remain with the company only on one condition, that he be transferred to the Eastern Region, with headquarters in Charlotte, North Carolina. He wants to be sales manager of the Eastern Region instead of the Western Region. His parents live in Charlotte. (He is recently divorced.) You do not believe the president will want to move the sales manager of the Eastern Region, but you tell Joe you will talk with the president.

As you expected, the president does not want to disrupt the sales manager of the Eastern Region, although she has been there for less than a year. Write to Joe and tell him the news. Try to convince him to remain in his present position with your assurance that you will do everything you can to move him to Charlotte if the position should become vacant. Urge him to at least take the two months' vacation that he has coming in order to think it over.

6 Each year your company participates in a community fund drive, making contributions based on percentage of sales. This year sales have fallen considerably. The vice-president of your company has received a letter regarding the corporate donation and asking that the company's contribution be increased by 10 percent. The vice-president decides that there will be a decrease in this year's contribution. The public relations manager believes that this decision could prove to be detrimental to a retail firm doing business with the general public.

The two discuss the situation and decide to match last year's contribution instead of either increasing or decreasing the amount. Write a letter to the director of the Loyalty Fund from the vice-president explaining that your company cannot increase the contribution by 10 percent as requested. You will contribute the same amount as last year. How can you explain reasons without presenting a negative image of your company? The vice-president's name is Barbara Barnes. The director's name is Lawrence Cole, 2369 Goodwyn, your city and ZIP code.

7 You are the office manager for a government office. Normal office hours are from 8:00 A.M. until 4:30 P.M. Your office offers employees a flexible hours program with two alternative shifts designed to meet each employee's individual needs. The shifts available are from 7:30 A.M. until 4:00 P.M., and from 8:30 A.M. until 5:00 P.M.

The program is on a trial basis. Employees are allowed to choose their shifts based on seniority as long as sufficient staff continues to work the normal shift.

You have noticed that the employees working the flexible hours are not very productive during the 30-minute periods before 8:00 A.M. and after 4:30 P.M. when the majority of employees are not in.

Write a memorandum to the employees stressing the fact that the flexible shift program is on a trial basis, and that the only way it can continue is if everyone cooperates and puts in his or her fair share of time. This memo can be addressed to all employees or only to the ones working the flexible hours.

8 You are a recent graduate of Central College, having completed a two-year program. You are the only member of the class of business graduates now unemployed. You are now at the University of Toronto.

Graduates have been asked to sponsor installation of central air conditioning in the business building. This installation is needed because of numerous hot days and nights (even in Lake City) and because classes are now held throughout the summer. Because your class is small, each share to be paid is quite large. If 100 percent participation is obtained, a local corporation will match the pledges, which are tax deductible.

Pledges are due one month from today. You wonder why your classmates seem so eager to contribute. They must have far more money than you do. You realize that approximately $250 is not a magnanimous sum, but you are on a meager budget. You pay for your books and other necessities from your income as part-time student helper. You cannot afford to make a contribution of any amount.

You have been subtly informed by two classmates that by not making a pledge you could keep your class from having 100 percent participation, resulting in cancellation of the whole project.

Your savings have been depleted, you have outstanding loans, and your rent is a week overdue. Write to Harry Chang, who is in charge of the fund-raising campaign. His address is 6001 Don Mills Road, Don Mills, Ontario, M3B 2X7 Canada. What will you say?

9   As personnel director of Methodist Hospital (your city), it is your responsibility to write a letter to all employees regarding a new company policy. A new nonsmoking clause has just been added by your company's health insurance carrier. It states that it can no longer cover employees who smoke cigarettes or use smokeless tobacco (snuff). (Because of the importance of this change, you decide to send a letter to the employees' homes instead of communicating through a memorandum that could be overlooked. You will send a letter to all employees because you have no way to identify smokers.)

Your employer is offering therapy in free clinics provided by the company at no cost to the employees. All smokers have six months to quit smoking with or without the free clinics.

Because you feel the new policy is a good idea and a survey of other insurance companies reveals that this policy is soon to be industrywide, any employee who doesn't quit smoking within six months will no longer be covered by the hospital's insurance program.

Because of the 1,240 employees, individually addressing each letter, even with word processing, would be more expensive than omitting each individual name and address. How will you begin the letter? Will you put any kind of special designation on the envelope? You definitely do not want your communication to be considered as just another form letter.

10   You are a librarian at Central College. You have received a telephone call from a former student who now lives in Maryland. You promise to write her after you have had time to investigate her statement that her transfer to the University of Maryland is being prevented by a hold that you have erroneously placed on her transcript.

Your investigation reveals that while she was a student at Central College she checked out eight books that were returned through an outdoor book depository, more than two months late. They were water soaked and mildewed. She did not reply to the two bills mailed to her for the replacement of the books. The amount of the bill was $132.

On the telephone she explained that she had given the books to her father before the due date and that he had assured her they were properly returned. She thinks the books must have been damaged by rain blowing into the outside book depository.

The library assistant who took the books from the outside depository tells you that he found no other water-damaged books in the large number that were in the depository. You know of no other instances of water blowing into the depository, and maintenance personnel reassure you that the container is designed to keep out wind, rain, and snow. It is emptied each weekday morning.

Write to the former student. The $132 must be paid before you will authorize the Records Office to release her transcript. The procedure has been described in the official student handbook for many years. The student's name is Louisa Whitehead, 1416 Bellona Avenue, Lutherville, MD 21093.

11   You are vice-president of your company. The head of the marketing department sent you an e-mail message earlier today and requested an extension on next week's deadline for her department's five-year strategic plan. Each department has known about the deadline for the past six months. You e-mailed all department heads two weeks ago and asked them to give you an update on the status of their strategic plans; the head of the marketing department did not respond. You simply cannot extend the deadline because a committee of top executives must review the various departmental plans to verify their fit with the corporate strategic plan and prepare a report for an

upcoming board meeting in three weeks. Write a memo to the head of the marketing department, Lynn Davis, and refuse her request.

12 You are the head of accounting for your firm. In an effort to cut back on unnecessary expenses, management has decided to make cutbacks in allowable business expenses. In the past, your firm has reimbursed employees for all legitimate business expenses, which basically allowed employees to stay in the hotels of their choice and eat anywhere they wish. Sales representatives were also very generous in inviting clients out for evening meals. However, starting the first of next month, the following new limits will apply. Wherever possible, employees should stay in a Holiday Inn or a hotel of the employee's choice if its rate is less than or equal to the Holiday Inn in that same location. Employees will be allowed $35 a day for meals. Individual meals for clients cannot exceed $20; this should encourage employees to take clients to lunch when appropriate instead of out for more expensive evening meals. Employees must submit receipts for all expenses over $10 if they wish reimbursement. Restaurant receipts must be from a cash register. Write a memo to all employees informing them of the changes in policy.

13 Today you received a request from the human resource specialist in your office for a new computer. The request was in the form of a two-page justification memo and included a purchase price of $2,800. Although you recognize that the new computer and software requested will undoubtedly allow your employee to work more effectively and efficiently, there is no money in this year's budget to pay for the computer requested. Send an e-mail message to Patricia Wysocki telling her that you will not be able to approve her request. When the new fiscal year begins, you will reassess various equipment needs throughout the company and her request will be considered at that time.

14 You are the purchasing agent for your company. On January 2 you converted to an electronic purchase order system for the entire organization. Your staff personally provided training for approximately 150 people involved in the submission of purchase requisitions and orders. During the training sessions and in the reference materials you provided for each user of the system, your staff emphasized that a department could not purchase something and use another account's code. In other words, if a department is out of supply money but still has equipment money, it cannot order printer toner and charge it to the equipment account. The head of the engineering department appears to be ignoring these rules. Your assistant has talked with the engineering department staff and determined that the incorrect account numbers are not being entered because someone does not understand the new system. As purchasing agent, you are not going to allow these purchase orders to go through; they will simply stay in limbo until they are corrected. Three orders in particular have been in limbo for six weeks. Write a memo to the department head in engineering and tell her you will not process the orders until the corrections are made.

UNFAVORABLE MESSAGES ABOUT A SERVICE OR PRODUCT

15 You are manager of the local Quality Office Products store. For many years you have been supplying novelty items to customers and other individuals and groups. Marketing representatives take these items with them on visits to their customers' offices or have the items mailed. These advertising novelties consist of such things as pencils, pens, notepads, paperweights, rain hats, and sewing kits. They have been successfully distributed by the Marketing Department and have become rather well known throughout the city. The company now receives requests from individuals and groups for these free items. They are especially popular for "goody bags" to be given to attendees at conventions.

Over the years the cost of the items has increased. Because the company's profits have fallen considerably, your accountant has advised you to cut expenses wherever possible.

Part A. Write a memorandum to be sent to all sales representatives telling them that only notepads will be distributed once the present supply of other advertising items is depleted. (Notepads can be made from short lengths of your own paper and printed with your company name and advertising message. You will make a special effort to see that these pads are unusually convenient and attractive.) You have on hand what would ordinarily be a three-month supply of assorted items.

Ask representatives to use this remaining supply with discretion. They are not to supply large numbers of anything except the notepads to organizations for "goody bags" or to individuals other than customers. Be sure not to stress negative aspects, including the decline in profits.

Part B. You receive a request from the local president of the alumni chapter of a sorority (Phi Gamma Nu) that is holding its national convention in your city. Ms. Ellen Glass asks for "300 items of everything that you have." Write a letter offering to supply notepads only. Her address is 1278 Macon, your city and ZIP code.

16 You are the sales manager of Quality Office Products. One of your established accounts, Witt Manufacturing Company, has written you with a request for a sizable discount on its purchases.

Witt Manufacturing is located 30 miles out of town. Your free delivery is limited by policy to within the city limits, but to keep the account you have been giving Witt free delivery and quantity discounts on its orders. The vice-president of Witt has been visiting the local plant for the last week, overseeing all operations. He told Mrs. Mary Johnson, the secretary in charge of ordering office supplies, that in California at the company headquarters Witt employees receive a 20 percent discount on all office supplies. It

is now her job to secure this discount. The answer you must give is no.

You did not know that Quality Office Products (your store is one in a national chain) was allowing discounts in California. Anyway, you make the policies in your store (or at least the general manager does), and you know you cannot afford a 20 percent discount plus free delivery. You will increase the quantity discounts to 5 percent on orders of $300 or more. You have now added another 5 percent discount for cash. Write to Mrs. Johnson, 310 Main, Hamlet, PA 19095, to inform her of your decision.

17 One of your part-time jobs while in college is pet sitting for people while they are out of town. You received a note in this morning's mail from Mrs. Celeste Powers, who wants you to pet sit for her while she and her husband are out of town for two weeks beginning June 1. You are unable to reach Mrs. Powers on the phone, so you must write her a letter declining the job. You took care of her Siamese cat during an earlier holiday break, and you simply do not want to do so again. The cat, Spyder, was extremely high-strung and very territorial. Each time you went to the house to tend to him, he jumped from the top of some piece of furniture and dug his claws into your back. You still remember the bad scratches you got all over your hands trying to defend yourself. It is simply not worth the money to put up with being attacked again. Write a letter to Mrs. Powers in which you turn down the job of pet sitting.

18 You are employed in the purchasing office at Western State University. This morning you received notice from Sure Shot Software Development that it will be unable to ship the software ordered by the Accounting Department until about the middle of July. Compose an e-mail message to the head of the Accounting Department, Dr. Benny Zachry, in which you notify him that because of the July shipment date the order must be canceled. According to state rules, all goods and accompanying invoices must be received by June 15

in order to be billed against the current year's budget. Because of tight state finances, all supply budgets will be frozen July 1, the beginning of the new fiscal year. Monies cannot be carried over to the next fiscal year.

REFUSING CLAIMS AND ADJUSTMENTS

19 You are the customer service representative for First National Bank. One of your account holders, Mrs. Jane Irvin, has complained that she has just bounced three checks because of an automated teller error. When she deposited her husband's paycheck, she had mistakenly placed it in their savings account instead of their checking account. Mrs. Irvin claims that the machine made a mistake. Upon further research, you find that the machine was functioning properly, and Mrs. Irvin is in error. The resulting overdraft charges amounted to $60. Write a letter to Mrs. Irvin to explain the reason that you are refusing her request for reimbursement. Use the following address: Mrs. Jane Irvin, 4577 Wynoka Avenue, your city and ZIP code.

20 You are the owner of Green Toe Lawn Care and Landscaping, a successful full-service lawn care and landscaping firm. You and your two employees offer weed and insect treatment, lawn maintenance, shrub and flower care, and basic landscape design and installation. In today's mail you receive a letter from Russ Beaver, in which he informs you that someone from your company sprayed the wrong chemicals on his yard and now his prize shrubs are dying. Mr. Beaver has a total of 20 shrubs, each about 5 feet tall. He demands that your company replace all 20 shrubs with the same type and size of shrub. Shrubs such as those in Mr. Beaver's yard cost $45 each, which does not include the labor cost of planting the shrubs. You wrote up the order for Mr. Beaver yourself; you recall that you told him at the time that the particular chemicals he requested should not be used if he had certain types of shrubs and flowers. He assured

you he did not have any of the identified plants. The office copy of the order form includes a notation making reference to the instances in which the chemicals should not be used on lawns. Mr. Beaver has been your customer for 15 years. Write him a letter refusing his claim. Send your letter to Mr. Russ Beaver, 4728 Wesley Drive, Pekin, IL 61554.

21 You are a financial officer of Northwest Housing Sales. Your company is selling a large block of townhouses. As part of the application, prospective buyers make a $1,000 deposit. They are told at the time they make application that the money will be placed in an escrow account at a local bank. This information is also on the customer's copy of the application. No mention is made that the checks will not be cashed.

For an escrow account, the bank deposits the checks in an account that is closely monitored by the bank and company officials. The money is not available for use by Northwest Housing Sales. If the contract closes, the amount in the escrow account is applied toward the purchase. If the sale is not closed, the money is refunded to the person making the application, subject to certain guidelines set out in the application contract.

Mr. and Mrs. Leon K. Smith have made application to buy a townhouse. He gave a check for $1,000. He had enough money to cover the check but did not think it would be cashed before the contract was closed. He then wrote seven more checks, which the bank returned because of insufficient funds. The Smiths were charged $105 for these returned checks.

Mr. Smith has written you demanding that you reimburse him for the $105 service charges. Reply to his letter. His address is 235 West 16th Avenue, Spokane, WA 99203. You are not refunding the $105.

CREDIT REFUSALS

22 You are a veterinarian in South City. Write to the owners of your patients. Tell them

that after July 1 (it is now May 21) you will no longer carry charge accounts, as you have been doing ever since you came to South City. Now you will ask for cash at the time of each visit or accept Visa or Master-Card cards in payment. Customers will receive a 5 percent discount by paying cash. Write a letter to be included with the statement to be sent out June 1.

23 You are the consumer credit manager for a large Texas bank. (Give it a name.) One of your jobs is to approve applications for individual credit cards. You are young, bright, and ambitious. Important people in the community believe you have an excellent future with the bank and will perhaps be its president someday.

You have received an application from Jeff Blankenship, a college senior at Southern Methodist University in Dallas. He has a long history of poor banking practices, including two delinquent loans and several returned checks. He is now unemployed and is considered an unacceptable risk to the bank.

Just as you are preparing to write a rejection letter, Robert Blankenship, the president of your bank, mentions that his son Jeff, who is a senior at Southern Methodist, will soon be home for the summer and is preparing for a trip to Europe. You have not known until now that Robert Blankenship has a son. Mr. Blankenship says that Jeff is eager for his own credit card.

Due to the credit policies established by the bank, you cannot issue a card to Jeff. Write to him. Do not grant the credit card, but do all you can to stay in the good graces of top management.

His address is 2315 College Drive, Dallas, TX 75501.

24 You are vice-president of First Federal Savings and Loan. Mr. and Mrs. John Wilson have applied for a loan of $75,000 to buy a house.

The Wilsons have recently moved to St. Louis from Sacramento. While living in Sacramento, they were both employed as school teachers. Mrs. Wilson is now unemployed. She wants to stay home and take care of their five children. Mr. Wilson has been self-employed for three months as a building contractor. He stated that he has been working steadily. Their assets consist of household furnishings, a $50,000 life insurance policy, an automobile for which they owe $6,000, a paid-for truck, and a $12,000 savings account, $5,000 of which will be applied to the house, in addition to closing costs. They have an excellent credit rating.

The house at 3020 Estes has an appraised value of $85,000; it is offered for sale at $80,000. You have a policy of not granting credit to self-employed individuals until they have been in business for at least one year.

You regret that you must refuse the loan. Write to the Wilsons. The address is 5127 Blanding, St. Louis, MO 67894.

25 Your best friend wants to borrow $100. He has owed you $400 for a year. Refuse his request.

WRITE YOUR OWN ASSIGNMENTS AND SOLUTIONS

26 *Write your OWN assignments, with solutions, for one or more of the kinds of letters or memorandums described in this chapter:*
   a. *refused requests or other bad-news messages*
   b. *unfavorable messages about a service or product*
   c. *credit refusals*
   OR
   d. *other unfavorable letters, memorandums, or e-mail messages*

   This assignment provides practice in describing a situation and giving instructions as well as in writing letters and memorandums. Your problem assignments may be on any subject, preferably about situations likely to occur in a business office. Give all the information another student would need to write a communication as a solution to your problem, including names and addresses and enough details to enable the writer to make appropriate decisions. (By using this assignment, you can write messages useful in your own organizations, perhaps actual ones.)

A similar assignment is given at the end of Chapters 7 and 9.

COLLABORATIVE WRITING AND WORKING IN GROUPS

Cases 1 through 26 can be used for collaborative writing exercises in various ways, one of which is listed below, according to the suggestions of your instructor.

27 **a.** Meet in groups of three or four to discuss the problem assigned or chosen to prepare outside of class. Discuss any decisions that must be made before the letter or memorandum is written. Prepare a brief outline of the content of each paragraph. Write a preliminary copy of the first and last paragraphs or, if time permits, of the entire letter. Each student then takes the rough draft to revise and refine. *Most important of all: Determine the purpose or purposes of the letter before you begin.* Also estimate the expected reaction of the reader.

b. Modify the instructions in Part a to the extent that each group analyzes and plans three or four cases, a different one for each student.

c. Use a short problem for which you write a solution in class as a group. Twenty minutes should be enough time.

d. Each member of a group evaluates work completed outside of class by all other members of the group. This outside work may be the revision of the letter discussed in Part a or b.

THINK-IT-THROUGH ASSIGNMENTS

28 Part A. You are a division director of a major corporation. The board of directors has decided to close your Indianapolis plant, which employs 450 people, and move the operation to a new plant in Bowling Green, Kentucky. This move will result in considerable long-term savings to the company and greatly increase future profits.

The Board has agreed to relocate Indianapolis employees who wish to move. The company will pay all moving expenses plus a $7,500 bonus to employees who relocate. Employees not wishing to move will receive four months' salary as severance pay. The company will also offer early retirement to employees over 50 (as of July 1 of the current year) with 20 or more years of service (also as of July 1 of the current year). Assistance will be given to employees seeking new employment.

Bowling Green has a population of about 50,000. The cost of living is fairly low, compared to Indianapolis. Outdoor recreation is abundant, and the schools are excellent.

Write a letter to be sent to the home address of each employee. Provide information about the closing of the plant in Indianapolis. Emphasize that the company hopes all employees will go to Bowling Green.

Part B. In addition to writing the letter, discuss other methods of informing employees of this important decision. Should they have been told in some other way? How? Explain. What kinds of messages should precede and follow the letter you wrote for Part A? (THESE QUESTIONS MUST BE ANSWERED BEFORE YOU WRITE THE LETTER). What advantages do you see in sending the letter to the employees' homes? Do you see any possible disadvantages?

Do you know anyone whose company has moved, causing relocation or job loss to the employees? If so, discuss the situation with the employees or with an executive at the company. How was the situation handled there?

29 You are the customer relations manager for a company that produces many consumer products including, among others, laundry detergent. Your company frequently sponsors national contests for consumers to win prizes of various types. In your most recent contest, customers were required to write a 200-word essay telling why they would recommend your laundry detergent, "SUDS PLUS" to their friends and relatives.

However, as explained in your company handbook, your employees and/or their immediate family members are automatically ineligible from entering the contest due to their relationship with the company. In addition, your entry form clearly states this rule.

To protect the integrity of your contest, you always research the background of winners before announcing the results. However, by mistake your assistant wrote to all prizewinners. It has been discovered that one of the winners, Alice Martin, is separated, but not divorced, from her husband, who works for your company. Her essay was outstanding.

Write a letter to Ms. Martin. What will you tell her? Her address is 3284 E. Brooks Rd., Durham, NC 27701. The prize she thinks she won is a Magnavox 32-inch color television set.

30 You are co-owner of a small business and employ 14 employees in your local office. At the request of the employees, you initiated a "casual day" each Friday. Casual day has been in effect for three months, and you are not happy with the result. In fact, one of your good customers arrived in your office this morning and kidded you about not paying your employees enough money to afford to shop at the local discount store. Your assistant and two other employees always dress reasonably on Fridays, but others seem to think that jogging suits, very worn jeans, and tee shirts are acceptable. You can't imagine what they will wear in July and August. Based on this morning's comment by your customer, you worry that other customers are also questioning the dress of your employees. Write a memo to all employees announcing some changes in casual day. You can no longer allow them to wear whatever they want. Unless changes are made, you will rescind casual day.

a. Since three of your employees already dress appropriately on "casual day," should you write your memo to all employees or only to those who are not wearing acceptable apparel on Fridays?

b. What reaction will the majority of employees have to this message?

c. Should you open the memo with a statement about unacceptable dress on Fridays? Why or why not?

d. What are some of the negative words that you should avoid using in this memo?

e. Should you rely on the employees' individual interpretations of what is acceptable or specifically identify what is acceptable casual day clothing?

f. All employees have computers at their workstations, and all are linked to a local area network. Should you write an e-mail message or a hard-copy memo?

g. Write the communication.

Sales Letters and Other Persuasive Messages

CHAPTER

9

OBJECTIVES

Chapter Nine will help you:

1 Apply the concept of a central selling point.

2 Apply the customary arrangement of sales letters—attention, interest, desire, and action.

3 Apply the principles of emphasis discussed in Chapter 5 to the arrangement, format, and wording of sales material.

4 Write effective and also ethical sales material of all kinds.

5 Describe laws pertaining to sales and collection letters and other communications.

Your study of *sales letters* and other *persuasive messages*, like your study of *bad-news letters*, will benefit you even if by some possibility you never compose communications for these two purposes. Principles of persuasion, including the presentation and acceptance of your decisions and ideas, apply to written and spoken messages of all kinds.

Writing a convincing sales letter or *persuasive request*, as discussed in this chapter, applies much of the communication theory you have studied in previous chapters. No other kind of message so vividly illustrates the necessity for the you-approach and for building goodwill, as presented in Chapter 6. Other principles previously discussed include the use of a positive, pleasant tone; readability and the proper use of emphasis; and the importance of word choice. The appearance of sales messages, including envelopes, is related to Appendix A, which includes guidance to achieving an attractive appearance of letters of all kinds.

All effective communication is persuasive if the term is construed in the broadest sense. In this chapter we consider the kinds of business communication that are usually described as persuasive: *sales messages, persuasive requests,* and *collection letters.* Sales messages include *direct-mail solicitations* and *sales promotion letters.* Because principles and approach of advertising by mass media are virtually the same as many sales letters, these messages are also considered throughout.

SELLING BY MAIL

The sales approach, whether used with selling by mail or with any other method, should not be thought of as the "old hard sell," which was never a credible or creditable technique. Sales are made because potential customers are convinced that the purchase will meet their needs and will be more valuable than the cost, as well as better than competing products. To build this conviction, the seller presents the potential purchase in terms of what it will do for the buyer. In addition, the customer must believe that the organization or organizations that manufacture and sell the product, as well as the salespeople, are sincere and dependable. If you do not honestly believe that your product or service is valuable and worthwhile, you probably will not be able to make a convincing sales presentation. Customers are not easily fooled.

Direct mail is usually considered in marketing to mean unsolicited advertising or promotional material sent to an individual or company through the mail. It is also referred to as *response mail*. Other kinds of response mail are telemarketing; TV commercials that give a toll-free 800 number; and magazine and newspaper advertisements that include coupons to be returned by the reader.

Direct mail includes billions (yes, billions) of catalogs that are sent out each year. Customers may respond by filling out an enclosed order blank, but far more often they take advantage of calling a toll-free number. By telephone, expert salespeople take orders, build goodwill, provide additional information, and tell the customers about daily "specials," much as clerks in a department store might do. The catalog often contains a "personal" letter, either on or near the first page of the catalog itself or on a separate sheet.

The direct mail industry provides more than 5 million jobs, accounting for 6 percent of United States employment. According to the Direct Marketing Association (DMA), direct mail is the third most popular advertising medium, exceeded only by television commercials and newspaper advertising.[1]

As an example of exceptional service by a catalog salesperson, a customer phoned Lands' End, toll free, to order a last-minute Christmas present for her brother. She wanted to buy a shirt but did not know his sleeve length. "Perhaps he has ordered from us before," suggested the customer service representative. Without even putting the caller on hold, she checked her computer and found his sleeve length, collar size, and a record of his purchases over the past six months. The shirt the caller wanted was back ordered, but the representative checked her table of substitutions and suggested an alternate. When the caller inquired about a tie to go with the shirt, the representative checked for coordinates. The order for the shirt and tie, shipped by Federal Express the next morning, arrived in time for Christmas.[2]

A CENTRAL SELLING POINT

A good product, even an outstanding one, must be sold. Potential customers "do not beat a path to the door of a person who builds a better mousetrap" if they do not know about it. Customers must be convinced.

In the selling process, even with the best mailing list, the message will go to some people who don't happen to need a mousetrap or who cannot afford to buy one. If the mousetrap maker is to prosper, the sales message must go to buyers who both need and can afford the product. These persons must be convinced that the product will meet their needs and that it is better than competing ones from the buyer's particular standpoint.

A mousetrap ordinarily will not meet their needs because it is beautiful or because it is made of the finest steel or wood (or whatever mousetraps are made of) but because it will catch mice and, more particularly, because it will catch the specific mouse that is now plaguing the potential buyer. (Although some people may be looking for a conversation piece for the coffee table, these buyers will no doubt be limited in number.)

The principles that apply to sales letters also apply to oral communications at trade shows and elsewhere.

The moral of this story is that the product or service must be presented in terms of the reader's most probable interest. To determine this interest, we must know what the product will do and what the buyer is most likely to want. This important principle of selling, regardless of the method, is a further application of the you-approach.

So how is the builder of the better mousetrap to choose a central theme, based on a *central selling point*, that will best market the merchandise? The first step is to analyze the product.

ANALYZING THE PRODUCT OR SERVICE

Is it true that the mousetrap is really better than those of competing companies? If so, why? Is it better from all standpoints, or does it need improvements in certain areas? What are its best features in relation to the customers' expected needs? What are other desirable features? Of all possible selling points, which two are the most likely to be effective? Which *one* particular point is likely to be most effective for the largest group of buyers?

To answer these questions, we must study the particular product or service, and its competition, in every detail. In such an analysis, we may find that even though the product is better overall than all the rest, some competing items have certain features that excel in comparison. For example, a competitor's mousetrap is painted a bright lemon yellow while ours is painted a dull gray (to match the mouse).

Or perhaps another product lasts longer but is not as effective. In this instance, we should not base our sales approach on color, or on our three-year guarantee, if the competing model includes a five-year guarantee. These themes would not be the most effective, anyway, based on the customers' probable needs. To determine these needs, we must analyze as much as possible the potential buyers.

ANALYZING THE POTENTIAL BUYER

The central selling point should be a feature in which the product excels, provided it is also a feature that is likely to make the customer want to buy. This is the real key to choosing a central selling point. *What is it about a particular product that is most likely to make a particular person want to buy?*

The central selling point is chosen to give unity and emphasis to the sales message. We can never be sure that we have chosen the best possible approach or that we have chosen the feature most likely to appeal to the particular reader or group of readers. For example, the prospective buyer who wants a mousetrap to serve as a paperholder on an office desk will not be interested in the fact that the product will also catch mice. If we were attempting to sell through conversation, we could determine individual interests and adjust our presentation accordingly. When we write letters to a large group of readers, we must make an educated guess and choose the approach that seems to be best fitted to the largest group.

How can you study the prospective buyer? Scientifically and objectively, there is no way, in spite of the many specialized books and journal articles about sales psychology. You can find many lists of psychological drives, differing somewhat from book to book. Even without books, we know that we are all interested, at least to a certain extent, in self-preservation, food, bodily comfort, sex, love of beauty, financial security, recognition and our self-respect, affection, pleasure, adventure, and the opportunity to grow and learn. We are also interested in communicating with other individuals so that we do not feel isolated and alone.

We should make use of such information as we have about our potential customers, such as age group, educational background, national origin, occupation, and hobbies. The more we know about our readers or listeners, the more likely we are to be able to adapt our message to their particular interests. A carpenter is more likely to buy a hammer than is a kindergarten teacher, or such is a logical assumption, but the kindergarten teacher might be a more likely customer because the carpenter probably already has a hammer.

Putting persons into categories—or *stereotyping*—is a dangerous practice. Each person is different from every other person. An individual approach, however, is impossible to obtain in sales campaigns in which the same message must be sent to many people because an individual approach would be prohibitive both in time and expense.

Instead, we must generalize, and all generalizations are likely to be less than exact. For this reason, the central selling point is not likely to be the most appropriate one for *all* readers, provided that the contemplated purchase has more than one desirable factor.

Some writers of sales messages do not use a central selling point but try to stress equally all major factors of the product or service. Overall, however, a presentation is likely to be less effective if many points are equally stressed, an approach that in effect emphasizes nothing.

▶ PRESENTING THE CENTRAL SELLING POINT

As a general rule, sales letters are longer than other kinds of business letters. Many sales letters consist of four or more complete pages, plus enclosed leaflets and brochures. (Some marketing experts, however, advocate a one-page letter accompanied with additional sales material presented on enclosures.) Longer sales letters, as well as the complete sales package, are most effective if they are based on a central selling point. In addition to the central selling point, sales letters also present other features of a product or service.

The central selling point is ordinarily the outstanding feature of the product or service offered, chosen in relationship to the needs and desires of potential customers. In some instances, however, the central selling point may be price, or "affordability." *In sales letters that are* not *built around price, it is*

Waterford pours forth memories. It conjures up fantasies, evokes poetic imagery, provokes the creative spirit, celebrates life's mysteries. It is never too early nor too late to assume the title: Waterford Collector. Some begin at birth, others as nonagenarians. To the collector, a piece of Waterford crystal is more than a drinking vessel, more than a vase, a decanter, a lamp, a chandelier, more than a family heirloom, more than an object d'art; it is an incentive to lose weight, to win forgiveness, a way to attract a lover, to distract a patient, to symbolize hope, to crystallize a dream, to bid adieu, to hail the seasons, to raise spirits, to diminish melancholy, to mark events, to start traditions, to end a day; it is a noble rite of passage. Born of the breath of man, Waterford is life's child.

FIGURE 9-1

H. Pesin, from "The Collected Thoughts of Waterford Collectors" (Used by permission.)

subordinated; if price is the central theme, it is discussed throughout the message like any other central selling point. Price as a central theme must be chosen with caution, however, because readers can always decide to save even more money by not buying the product at all. Usually price should *not* be chosen as the central theme.

For example, can you imagine selling Waterford crystal, one of the most expensive brands available, using affordability as the central theme? Do you find any mention of price in the advertisement shown in Figure 9-1? The copy was accompanied by a simple, close-up photograph of the most expensive pattern of Waterford crystal, with the petals of an exotic flower spilling over the top. Another goblet, filled with wine, is in the background. Do the words in the advertising copy shown in Figure 9-1 make you want to buy Waterford crystal? If so, can you determine why the words are so effective? No central theme is put into specific words. Can you put the central theme of the advertisement about Waterford crystal into specific words—or do you prefer to leave it in the poetry in which it is written?

J. Daniel McComas makes the following statements:

People don't buy for rational reasons; they buy for emotional awards. Your goal is to tap into their subconscious yearnings to create or feel a desire. . . . Take a look at how McDonald's markets its products, for example. The company doesn't sell the quality of its burgers. It sells fun, excitement, and shared love. Mercedes sells status. Clairol, youthfulness. Hallmark, quality and love with its slogan, "When you care enough to send the very best."[3]

Characteristics of Sales Letters and Other Sales Material

Most mass-produced sales letters are examples of correct writing and overall effective communication. Because nationally distributed sales messages are written by professionals, they usually consist of clear, correct, and convincing writing and format.

Good sales letters are well designed, using "white space" and other techniques of format. They include short paragraphs, a reader-approach, and vivid, specific descriptions of products and services.

However, not all sales letters, nationally distributed or otherwise, are examples of excellent communication. Some violate the most important principle of all, sincerity. Some statements are gushy, unbelievable, or downright silly.

Some sales letters include exaggerated words and phrases, which are also vague and meaningless; for example: *sensational, perfectly astounding, terrific, amazing, revolutionary, tremendous, the greatest, stupendous, the finest in the world.*

Present a product, service, idea, or yourself in specific ways. If you actually believe that your product is stupendous (or all the other adjectives), prove it with specific, vivid, positive, reader-oriented words.

COMMUNICATION brief

Weasel words. He [Carroll Carroll] defined a weasel word as "a description given by advertising people to that key word in a piece of copy that takes the responsibility out of the most exaggerated claim." As an example, he noted the dishwasher detergent that "leaves glasses virtually spotless." If you think that means without spots, you are wrong. It means practically without spots or with some spots. So, in point of fact, what the ad says is that your glasses will not be completely clean if you use this particular detergent. Another example is the remedy for "simple nervous tension." How do you define "simple"?

"Four out of five dentists surveyed recommend Blah-and-Blah for their patients who chew gum." Surveyed by whom? Perhaps by the manufacturer's 6-year-old daughter gathering material for Show and Tell? How many doctors were surveyed? All five witch doctors in Upper and Lower Slobovia? What was the form of their recommendation? Did they say, "Oh, well, if you must chew gum, we suppose that Blah-and-Blah is the least harmful"? This simply is not using the language to convey truth. It is flimflam.

William Morris and Mary Morris, *Harper Dictionary of Contemporary Usage* (New York: Harper and Row, 1985), 617.

Some of the special characteristics of sales letters are these:

1   An overall informal tone. You have learned that most business messages are rather informal, but that the degree of formality differs according to the purpose of the communication and according to the reader or readers. Sales messages tend to be more informal than other kinds of letters. As in other communication situations, you should plan the degree of formality to best fit the purpose and readership, both of which will be influenced by the product or service you are selling.

2   Use of humor, in addition to other aspects of informality. Humor, however, must be used with caution. It is inappropriate for some products or services; as extreme examples, preplanned funerals and disability insurance. Another less extreme example is banking services, a serious subject to most readers, possibly a subject they do not wish to joke about.

   Another consideration is that humor does not appeal to all readers in the same way. (Some just "don't get it.") An even more important danger is that you could leave the impression that you take neither your product, company, nor reader seriously.

   Even with all these possible disadvantages, humor has been and continues to be used effectively. One advantage is that it may keep your potential customer reading. (Some marketing experts say that you have a seven-second window of opportunity to catch your reader's attention before a sales letter is discarded or put aside.) Another advantage is that the skillful use of humor can present your product or service more vividly and dramatically than straightforward description could do.

   Marjorie Zieff-Finn uses the example of the successful sales and advertising approach of Volkswagen a number of years past:

   . . . the campaign's brochures, billboards, and print ads emphasized its funny little shape and impressive economy aspects, enforcing its homely but lovable image. Dubbed "the Bug" its endearing image generated millions of loyal fans. . . . VW took swipes at conventional manufacturers for changing model designs annually. . . . VW's pledge to keep its amusing beetle shape for years to come won buyers who embraced the concept of owning an "undated looking" car. Later, when the VW bus was introduced, elegance was once again eschewed in favor of droll ads featuring comical, large and bulky items protruding from its revolutionary new sunroof.[4]

3   Special emphasis on descriptive, vivid, forceful words and phrases.

4   Special emphasis on the you-approach by describing the reader enjoying or benefiting from the purchase, perhaps by explaining how the reader can solve problems or increase his or her pleasure by purchasing the item or service.

In the discussion of sales writing in this chapter and in the following questions and problems, we shall refer to this particular application of the *you-approach* as *psychological description*. Psychological description pictures the product or service being sold in terms of reader benefit.

5   More use of the mechanical means of emphasis, such as all capitals, underlining, dashes, special arrangements, and color.

Now let's look at the suggested arrangement of ideas in a sales letter.

ATTENTION, INTEREST, DESIRE, AND ACTION

The arrangement of sales letters in terms of *attention, interest, desire,* and *action (AIDA)* has long been used in the discussion, planning, and writing of sales messages.

Other terms used to describe this pattern are *attention, interest, conviction,* and *action; attention, interest, desire, conviction,* and *action;* and *attention, conviction,* and *action.* All these patterns are basically the same. In the first part of the letter, we must gain the reader's attention. In the middle section of the letter, we present convincing evidence. In the last part of the letter, we ask for action, as we have used the action close in other types of messages.

Principles of effective sales letters also apply to face-to-face selling: using a central selling point, a positive approach, and the you-attitude.

OBTAINING FAVORABLE ATTENTION

The attention section of a *solicited sales letter* differs somewhat from that of an unsolicited one. In responses to inquiries (solicited sales letters), you already have the reader's attention, provided you have replied promptly.

In solicited letters you need only to open with favorable information about the prospective purchase, expressed in terms of the reader's interest. In unsolicited messages, you work harder to gain and keep attention and interest, in order to keep the letter from being thrown into the wastebasket. (A solicited sales letter is shown in Figure 9-2.)

The attention section of *unsolicited sales letters* may consist of a question, a startling statement, mention of an outstanding feature of the product, a proverb, a news announcement, a gadget or gimmick, or other similar approaches. Whatever you use to attract attention, it must make sense and tie in with the following paragraphs. Preferably the message begins with a reference to the chosen theme or leads directly to that theme. It should be reader centered.

The following sentence, used alone as an opening paragraph of a letter planned to sell a barbecue grill, begins with a quotation.

Harry Truman once said, "If you can't stand the heat, you should get out of the kitchen."

This opening paragraph ties in with the central theme of the letter, that the reader will avoid heating the house with the range or oven by cooking outside and will enjoy meal preparation and dining on the patio. Here, as you no doubt recognize, Truman's analogy was reversed to its original and literal meaning.

The opening paragraph of a letter from a manufacturer to a dealer stresses features of the product in terms of reader benefit:

When you show a customer a Gardener, a grass collector that sweeps and combs a lawn in one operation, you have obtained a quick sale, a satisfied customer, and a $40.81 profit.

From a long advertisement from a men's store, accenting quality and traditional, timeless design:

THE KIND OF SPORTSWEAR WE SELL LOOKS BETTER THE OLDER IT LOOKS. ISN'T THAT A DUMB WAY TO RUN A BUSINESS?

The advertisement carried through with the theme that quality and classic design retain their appearance, even when old. The next sentence, after the opening above (which was typed at the top of the advertisement in capital letters), was this:

There are a few things we'd like you to know about our sportswear right from the start: it fades, it tends to wrinkle, and it isn't overly stylish.

Telemarketers are employed by numerous companies, selling hundreds of products and services. People who work for companies that sell from catalogs are not sales representatives. Their main job is to take orders, but through efficiency and courtesy, they "sell" their company.

From a letter from a publisher of textbooks to high school teachers:

Have you ever heard the expression "It's books" to mean that school is now in session—that recess or another free period is over and that it's time to get down to serious business?

The next paragraph explained that "it's books" is an old-fashioned term, once widely used, which expressed the early concern, appreciation, and awe with which students and teachers viewed the few books that were then available. The central theme of the message was that to improve education and our society, books must be reliable, interesting, challenging, and appropriate, and that such books just happen to be the exact kind that the publisher is selling.

Watch for these *weaknesses* in opening paragraphs of sales letters:

1   A too-long first paragraph. Although opening paragraphs should be short in all business letters, overly long ones are particularly bad in sales letters, in which you must gain and hold attention.

2   Questions with obvious answers, such as "Would you like to increase profits?"

3   Obvious statements, such as "To make a profit, you have to move merchandise."

4   A writer-centered opening, such as "We are proud to announce the opening of our new store."

5   Slow openings, such as "We have received your inquiry about our products," "We are writing to give you the information you requested."

6   Openings used only for a surprise or startling effect without regard for relevance or a tie-in with following paragraphs.

7   Obvious flattery, such as "A person with your social position, Mrs. Jones—."

8   Openings that mention a negative aspect of the product or service. These are especially likely to occur when replying to inquiries. The potential customer's questions need not be answered in the order they were asked.

9   A reference to the cost of the purchase, unless price is to be used as the central selling point.

PRESENTING CONVINCING EVIDENCE IN TERMS OF READER INTEREST

Give specific, objective details about the product or service you wish to sell. In addition, present these details in terms of the reader's interest. (This approach is the psychological description mentioned earlier.) Instead of saying simply that a swimming pool is surrounded by a 12-foot-wide redwood sundeck, reword the statement so that the buyer is described using the sundeck. The statement that it is a 12-foot-wide redwood sundeck is good, as far as it goes, and much better than saying that the pool is surrounded by a wide sundeck. (How wide is wide?) But it is even better if you describe the sundeck in specific terms and also imagine the reader enjoying it, as in:

The redwood sundeck (12 feet wide!) that surrounds the pool gives you plenty of room for cookouts and parties for many happy summers to come.

In addition to presenting sales material in emotional terms, give solid, tangible evidence, presented in terms of reader interest. For example:

Look closely and you'll see seams sewn straight and strong, buttons attached to stay, and plenty of reinforcement where it's needed. Small details, perhaps, but important.

The result of all this? Our sportswear won't suddenly fall out of fashion, fall out of your favor, or fall apart. So instead of replacing it every year, you can buy a little more.

A weakness of many sales letters is a lack of attention to conviction by hurrying through from the attention section to the action close. In the middle paragraphs of the letter, give enough time and space to build conviction. You will not convince with vague generalities, such as saying that the product is fine, beautiful, strong, or "absolutely the finest in the world." Give reasons, details, and specifications to convince the reader that the product is absolutely the finest in the world.

Do not speak in generalities. If it's sturdy, why and how? If it's roomy, how big is it? If it's dependable, how do you know? If it's economical to operate, how many miles to a gallon? How do you know that it gets that many miles to a gallon? How do you know that the tests were reliable?

As you describe the product or service, you will often find that you have a great many features to list or describe in addition to your central selling feature. Items are easier to read if they are set up in a listing instead of crowded together in paragraph form. For example, the format below

In sales letters, use

1 *Listings*

2 *Plenty of white space*

3 *Capitals, underlining, special arrangements*

4 *Any other form of mechanical emphasis, as long as it is not used to excess*

is easier to read than if presented in this way:

In sales letters, use listings, plenty of white space, capitals, underlining, special arrangements, and any other form of mechanical emphasis, as long as it is not used to excess.

The cost of an item should be subordinated unless it is used as a major selling factor. If it is not a good price, or only somewhat lower than competing products, it should not be used as a major selling factor.

Remember the principles of emphasis presented in Chapter 5. To subordinate the price, reverse the principles of emphasis. Present the price only after convincing evidence to justify it. But do not leave it for the last paragraph, which is one of the most emphatic ones, unless you wish to emphasize the price.

Do not present the price in a sentence standing alone as a paragraph, one of the methods of emphasis. You achieve more subordination by presenting the price in a minor clause or phrase than by putting it in the more emphatic main clause. You subordinate when you show how the reader will benefit by the purchase, with an emphasis on these benefits, not on the price.

Notice the methods of subordination in this paragraph from a cleaning service using the name "Suzy and Her Menfolks":

Your free week, which Suzy and Her Menfolks by their efforts will make possible, is priced at only $84, including all costs of equipment and cleaning materials.

Although the $84 is presented in the main clause of the sentence, it is tucked into the middle of the sentence and not placed in the emphatic opening or closing position, both of which state definite reader benefits. The *only* and *including all costs of equipment and cleaning materials* suggest that the service is a good buy. The remaining sentences in the paragraph reemphasize reader benefit.

▶ ASKING FOR ACTION

The action close in sales letters is the same as in other types of communications: (1) Specify the action, preferably in terms of reader benefit; (2) make action easy; and, if appropriate, (3) motivate prompt action.

A weakness that often occurs in the action section of sales letters is a pushy and demanding attitude. Even if the reader is prepared to buy, a phrase such as "Get your order to your mailbox this very minute!" is enough to send the letter to the nearest wastebasket this very minute.

Be sure that the reader understands exactly what the necessary action is and how it is to be accomplished. Make this action easy. Don't ask for a letter in return, only a pencil check on a postage-paid card, or perhaps a signature. If you want the reader to telephone, give the telephone number. If you want the reader to come into a store, give the location of the store and the hours it is open.

The closing paragraph shown below is from a publishing house to a high school teacher:

Just return the enclosed card and we will have our sales representative, Andrea Brown, call on you. She will bring a free copy of <u>Practical English for Tomorrow's Leaders</u> *and discuss with you the benefits of using this book in your classroom.*

The following paragraph is from a hotel promoting a bridal suite to a bridegroom-to-be:

Simply fill out the enclosed reservation card, mail it to us, and we will have this beautiful suite waiting for you and your bride—along with fresh flowers and a chilled bottle of champagne.

The following paragraph is from a letter promoting package delivery by a taxicab company:

Give me the opportunity to prove that Yellow Shuttle and Yellow Rush are everything I've said. Paste the enclosed stickers near your telephones and call 536-0000 for your next package delivery.

The men's clothing store (Oak Hall, in Memphis), after devoting a full page to its quality clothing that "tends to wrinkle," used as an action close only the name of the store, OAK HALL, with the phrase "since 1859" and the address of its store locations. If it had been selling by mail instead of in a newspaper advertisement, it would have ended with specific instructions on how to order or would have referred the reader to attachments that included exact instructions.

EXAMPLES OF SALES MESSAGES

A sales letter in response to a request for information is shown in Figure 9-2. This letter meets the description of "favorable information" discussed in Chapter 7, but because of more detailed information and a persuasive approach is a solicited sales message.

Portions of an unsolicited sales letter are shown in Figure 9-3. The entire mailing consists of a long two-page letter and a colorful ten-page folder. Each of eight pages of the folder illustrates a specific variety of perennial tulips, followed by a paragraph of convincing sales material. Two pages of the folder continue the sales approach begun in the letter itself. (Because of the overall length of the letter and the folder, only certain portions are included here. These passages are *adapted* from a 1997 mailing from Breck Holland.)

Because tulip bulbs are available from many other sources, these particular bulbs will be sold because the potential buyer believes that they are unique and better overall than those that can be bought elsewhere for a lower price. A major selling point is the fact that the tulips are perennial, comparable to daffodils. Another feature is the unusually large size of the bulbs, 14 cm or larger, that will produce larger blooms than ordinary tulip bulbs. Another point stressed throughout the letter is the recognition that the reader of the letter is a "preferred customer" who because of previous purchases is assured of the quality and service provided by the company.

Sales messages are distributed in many ways other than through the mail, and each is built around a different approach. The sales letter shown in Figure 9-4 is printed on the program of a live radio production of "A Prairie Home Companion," of which Lands' End is one of the sponsors. The letter differs from the letter about tulips in that the purpose of the letter is not to sell the merchandise directly but to induce readers to send for a catalog.

The letter is built around one theme, that of quality, although the word *quality* is used nowhere in the entire message. Notice the informal approach of this message and the unusual statistics. After the attention-getting opening, "Numbers don't lie," the entire letter before the action close is a form of *CONVICTION*—to convince the reader that the company does things right.

FIGURE 9-2 ▶

A sales letter in response to a request for information (Courtesy of Pacific Crest Outward Bound School)

■ **OUTWARD BOUND** ■

Pacific Crest
Outward Bound School
1010 S.W. Bancroft St.
Portland, Oregon 97201
Telephone 503-243-0000

September 28, 19——

Mr. John A. Delves III
Backpacker Magazine
One Park Avenue
New York, NY 19916

Dear John:

You are right—your readers will be interested in Joshua Tree desert backpacking. I'm delighted you are considering such an article for Backpacker. ⎤ [Attention]

This area provides a perfect respite from winter . . . 68° weather, blue skies, dramatic granite rock formations, and a wide variety of flowering desert plants. Backpackers often hear the call of coyotes at night, and during the day they see wildlife that has also headed south for the winter. Wild donkeys, bighorn sheep, mule deer, and dozens of bird species are common in Joshua Tree. ⎤ [Interest]

You may be interested in sending a writer on one of two courses:

NS-104, October 19–22, four days—current enrollment—three men and three women from New Jersey, Colorado, California, and Missouri.

NS-106, October 28–November 3, seven days—current enrollment—four men and one woman from Mississippi, Hawaii, California, and New York.

The four-day course is full of high-impact teamwork exercises. The seven-day course allows more time for enjoyment of the environment and for more extensive travel. ⎤ [Conviction]

Enrollment for both courses will increase up to the course date with a maximum of twelve people per group. Each group of students has two instructors. A chief instructor will be in charge of the course if there is more than one group of students in the field.

Courses include rock climbing and rappelling as well as backpacking. Our instructors also spend time on route finding and map and compass reading so that students will feel comfortable in an environment without trails. ⎤ [Conviction]

We will have color backpacking and rock climbing slides shot in October, and they will be available for your story. I do hope Joshua Tree fits into your plans for Backpacker. Please give me a call to work out the details. ⎤ [Action]

Cordially,

Darlene Gore

Darlene Gore,
Marketing Director

(ATTENTION, based on two leading features; perennial bulbs and size and vigor of bulbs.)

A delightful surprise is in store for you when your Deluxe Perennial Tulips burst into bloom next spring. You'll be amazed at the size of their huge blooms and by their extra-tall, sturdy stems. And because they are Perennial Tulips, you'll be able to enjoy the same beauty for years to come.

(INTEREST, based on central selling point.)

Recently, Breck's introduced a superior selection of Perennial Tulips to America. Unlike traditional tulips that have a somewhat limited life, these unique varieties have the characteristics of fine daffodils. They grow with vigor and provide increased beauty year after year.

(DESIRE, shows reader enjoying purchase.)

These big, beautiful tulips are not only gorgeous in the garden, they are excellent for cutting. You'll be able to create some of the most spectacular bouquets you've ever seen and display them in every room of your home.

Now, a limited number of jumbo-sized bulbs—all 14 cm or larger—have become available. These huge bulbs grow with greater vigor and produce gorgeous giant flowers.

(CONVICTION, also described as DESIRE.)

Bulbs of this size are normally retained by growers in Holland for their own use and seldom find their way across the Atlantic to America. But through special arrangements with top growers, Breck's has been able to obtain a quantity of these big, plump, healthy bulbs for shipment to the United States in September—October 1997. Because the quantities are so limited, these Deluxe Perennial Tulips are being offered on an exclusive basis to a select group of Breck's Preferred Customers.

(SUBORDINATION OF PRICE, one of several similar paragraphs.)

You might expect to pay a very high premium to obtain rare, jumbo bulbs of these exclusive varieties. Fortunately, because Breck's made an advance commitment for every one of the jumbo-sized bulbs of all five varieties that will be harvested this year, we were able to get special discounts from the growers-savings we can pass along to you.

(REQUEST FOR ACTION)

Because you are one of Breck's Preferred Customers, you don't have to send a single penny when you place your Deluxe Perennial Tulip Collection reservation. We will ship your bulbs direct to your home in September or October, 1997, and you'll have full opportunity to inspect and approve every bulb upon receipt before you pay a cent. Just check the enclosed card.

FIGURE 9-3
Passages from sales material, Breck Holland

NUMBERS DON'T LIE

Take goats, for example.

How many Mongolian goats do you think it takes to get enough fleece to make a single Lands' End Cashmere Sweater? The answer: from 2½ to 4 goats.

And guess how many feet of cotton yarn go into our men's Pinpoint Oxford shirts? 64,306 feet. That's a little over 12 *miles* of cotton in each shirt.

Fact is, we use lots and lots of cotton.

Our Stonewashed Jeans are a tough 14¾ oz. cotton denim; a fine, honest fabric. Know how much denim we used in our jeans last year? Enough to fill 23 railroad boxcars.

Now, we're not just playing with numbers here. Numbers tell a lot about Lands' End.

Like the more than 500 crofters—cottage weavers in Scotland—who hand weave the fabric for our Harris Tweed jackets.

Or the 75 inspectors whose job is trying to make sure that everything that wears a Lands' End label deserves it.

In fact, when you consider what all the numbers say about us—and our *passion* to get things right for our customers—doesn't it make you want to see a copy of our catalog? We'd be happy to send you the latest number.

FIGURE 9-4
Sales message from Lands' End

PLANNING AND WRITING PERSUASIVE REQUESTS

Persuasive requests differ from routine requests (discussed in Chapter 7) in that they do not ordinarily open with the request itself. They are a variation of the indirect letter (discussed in Chapter 8) but are most like regular sales letters discussed previously in this chapter.

At times you may not be sure whether a particular request should be treated as one that the reader will be happy to grant or one that will require persuasion. If you are not sure, it is better to treat the message as a routine one and to open with the request itself or state it early in the letter. As with communications of other kinds, use the direct order unless you see a definite reason to use another arrangement. In some instances, requests that require a great deal of explanation and a sales approach can be effectively arranged in the direct order. Opening with the request, followed with convincing, you-approach details, is far more effective than an arrangement that causes the reader to wonder through several paragraphs what the letter is all about.

In usual practice, however, do not open a persuasive request with a statement of the request itself. Use an attention-getting section, as in sales letters, that states or implies reader benefit. If there is little reader benefit pos-

Effective web pages are arranged so that potential customers can find details of product features, company support, warranties, and how to purchase items they select.

sible, open with convincing and interesting details about the product or service.

A sales-oriented persuasive request is illustrated in Figure 9-5. This request is also an invitation. This is an actual invitation, which was followed by a record attendance.

This letter, like many sales letters, is friendly and informal, a natural approach to a friend. As with all communications, adaptation according to the reader and to the purpose of the message is desirable and necessary.

In persuasive requests, as in sales writing, make the major portion of the letter convincing by describing the suggested action in vivid, specific, positive words that show reader benefit. By presenting features of the product or facets of the idea in terms of reader interest, you convince the reader to buy or to accede to your request or proposal. In order to convince the reader, avoid phrasing or exaggeration that would cause disbelief. Use specific language and vivid description to present favorable aspects.

■ **THE SOUTHEASTERN REGION OF THE ASSOCIATION
FOR BUSINESS COMMUNICATION** ■

and the Management Faculty of Memphis State University
request the pleasure of your company
at the Memphis meeting at the Peabody Hotel
on April 6, 7, and 8, 1989.

In honor of the occasion, dogwoods, redbuds, and azaleas will decorate the entire city, and the Mississippi River will roll on and on, only three blocks from the Peabody.

If you have not seen the Peabody, where the Delta begins in the lobby, you have not yet seen the South.

At eleven each morning (they like to sleep late) the Peabody ducks march over a red carpet, in time to appropriate music, from their reserved elevator to the fountain pool where they spend the day. Then at cocktail time they march back over the red carpet, often to the beat of "When the Saints Go Marching In," to return to their penthouse to spend the night.

Before or after the convention sessions, you may want to visit Graceland, Mud Island, The Orpheum and other theaters, The Dixon Gallery and Gardens, Brooks Museum of Art, the new Oak Court shopping center and other malls, the Rendezvous for ribs, The Pier and other riverside restaurants, Rhodes College, and Memphis State University.

But your most important reason for coming is for professional growth. You have a comprehensive choice of topics relating to many aspects of the broad field of business communication, as listed on the enclosed program. You will meet 84 speakers from 21 states and from Canada.

We cordially invite you to attend. Please RSVP by using the enclosed reservation form.

Glynna Morse

Malra Treece

Glynna Morse and Malra Treece, Directors

Enclosures: Reservation forms for conference and hotel, tentative program, travel information

FIGURE 9-5

An invitation (persuasive request) to a professional meeting (*Note:* Memphis State University is now the University of Memphis.)

THE COLLECTION SERIES

Collection messages are classified here as being in the early, middle, or late stages in the collection series. The *early stage* consists of reminder messages in the form of notes, obvious form letters, or stamped reminders on duplicate bills.

Middle-stage messages are more individualized. They are individually written and dictated or planned to give the appearance of personally directed letters. Middle-stage collection letters are longer than either the early or late messages because they must develop an appeal. *Late-stage* letters are shorter and more direct. They speak firmly of the urgency of the situation and of the importance of immediate payment.

The collection series differs from organization to organization in the number of messages in each stage. It also differs in the length of time from the beginning of the series until the end. It may differ according to the particular group of customers of the same organization.

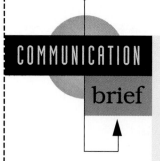

COMMUNICATION
brief

Did you ever think that the Prince of Wales would write a collection letter? He did!

His letter was used to collect debts to the Prince's Youth Business Trust, which supports young people setting up businesses of their own. The letter, which was sent to big businesses by some twenty PYBT firms, resulted in L70,000 of unpaid bills being settled at once. Here is the letter:

Dear _____

I write to explain the difficulty in which your highly reputed firm is unwittingly placing me.

As a successful businessman yourself, you will, no doubt, remember your own early days. I am a very small one-man/woman business set up with help from the Prince's Youth Business Trust and, as you will understand, that organisation only helps those who really need the money to get going.

Before they would consider me, I had to draw up a business plan, but it simply didn't allow for reputable firms like yours taking so long to pay. While my terms are payment within _____ days (of the job being completed/goods being delivered), I have now waited _____ weeks for payment.

Would you, I wonder, look into this matter for me and arrange for my particular circumstances for a cheque to be sent to me immediately—if only to save my business from becoming another statistic. I would be so grateful to you.

I feel sure that it is not the intention of someone like you to stifle entrepreneur enterprise by making it impossible to trade with successful businesses like yours.

Margaret Stone, "Princely Plea to Pay," Associated Newspapers Ltd., *Daily Mail*, July 19, 1993, 34.

As a general rule, the total time of the collection series is longer for good credit risks than for poor ones. More mailings are included, and more time is allowed to elapse between mailings. A typical series may consist of two to four reminders (the early stage of the series), two or three inquiries and appeals (the middle stage), and two or three urgency letters, the final one of which is an ultimatum.

Intervals between mailings vary from 10 to 30 days, with longer intervals at the beginning of the series and shorter ones toward the end.

The series may be lengthened or shortened. It is shortened when readers are considered to be poor credit risks or when conditions indicate that the collection process should be accelerated.

The number of mailings may be reduced and the intervals between the mailings shortened, or some of the steps in the usual series may be omitted altogether. Perhaps there will be no reminders, one appeal, and then an urgency letter, followed by an ultimatum.

Regardless of the length of the series, the tone of the message changes from the beginning to the end.

All collection messages should include a statement of the amount due and the due date.

EARLY-STAGE COLLECTION MESSAGES

The first step in the collection series is the statement, usually a monthly statement, of the amount due.

Reminders may be additional statements with a stamped notation that the bill is past due. Instead of a second or a third statement, the reminder or reminders may be short, simple requests presented as form letters, printed notes, or, occasionally, greeting cards.

Letters, if used in the early part of the collection series, are quite obviously form letters and are based on the assumption that the obligation has been overlooked. These form letters, as well as any other follow-up reminder messages, are purposely impersonal and routine. This approach is the opposite of what is considered the best approach in many other forms of communications. Used in the early stages of collection, they imply something to this effect: *Look, we realize that you have merely overlooked this obligation, as you have been prompt in making past payments. But you understand that of course we must remind you, as we do all other customers, when your check does not arrive on time. Your notice that comes in this form letter (or greeting card, stamped message, note, etc.) is the same one that we send to everyone. We still like you.*

Yes, it is quite a feat to imply all the ideas and attitudes in the preceding paragraph with only the words "just a gentle reminder" or "did you forget?" But, in effect, that is what you are doing in a well-planned reminder message early in the collection series.

In reminder messages we may use humor if we do so with discretion. As in all communication, we must be extremely careful when using a humorous approach because it can very easily appear to be sarcasm.

Resale and sales promotion are also used in reminder messages. You have previously learned that resale and sales promotion can be used to soften a message, as in refusal letters. You are using these passages for the same purpose early in the collection series, as well as for the obvious purpose of promoting sales.

Because of the softening effect, however, we most certainly would not use resale, sales promotion, humor, or any similar approach in the late stage of the collection series. At that time we don't want to soften the approach. We want to emphasize the urgency of the situation and insist that the bill be paid immediately.

A reminder to a customer with a good credit rating, owing a relatively small amount, is shown in Figure 9-6.

▶ MIDDLE-STAGE COLLECTION MESSAGES

The use of humor, resale, and sales promotion may or may not be appropriate for the middle stages of the collection series, depending on the type of merchandise sold, the customer, the particular credit policies of the company, and other considerations.

These approaches soften the urgency of the message. Whether or not they should be included depends on what tone is most appropriate and effective. If you use several messages in the middle stage of the collection series, humor, resale, and sales promotion are more appropriate for earlier letters than for later ones.

In the middle stage, we may begin with an inquiry directed toward the applicant (although the letter may not be individually written), followed by a letter or letters built around an appeal of some kind. In these letters we bring into use a central theme similar to the central selling theme of sales letters. Figure 9-7 illustrates a theme: a good credit rating. Figure 9-8 implies a possible loss of customers.

Messages throughout the series should become increasingly forceful, but "forceful" does not mean that the letters should be rude, sarcastic, demanding, or impolite. We should always refrain from using this tone, regardless of the length of the series. Choose a courteous approach not only from the standpoint of consideration for the reader but also because this approach is more likely to be effective in collecting.

Remember the two main purposes of collection letters: *to get the money and to maintain goodwill.* In addition to maintaining goodwill, a courteous tone is also more likely to result in the collection of the overdue amount. In middle-stage messages, the assumption is no longer that of the reminder stage; that is, that the account has merely been overlooked.

■ NEWBURG HOSPITAL ■

Coastal Highway
Newburg, SC 29209

November 17, 19——

Mrs. Robert Shaw   Patient Name: Saundra Shaw
23 Plantation Estates   Account # 0000000
Newburg, SC 20207   Date of Service: 8/17/——

Dear Mrs. Shaw: Guest Balance Due: $140

Thank you for the opportunity to serve you as a patient. We appreciate the confidence you have shown in us by choosing Newburg Hospital.

While reviewing our accounts, we found that the account referred to above remains unpaid. As this may be an oversight on your part, we have mailed this reminder.

Please send your payment for the amount shown as "Guest Balance Due" within the next ten days. If paying by mail, please write your Guest Account Number on your check or money order. If you prefer, you may pay by credit card by supplying your credit card number and expiration date on the attached form. Please indicate the type of card you are using. We accept MasterCard, VISA, American Express, and Healthline.

If payment has been made since the date of this reminder, please accept our thanks.

Sincerely yours,

Mabra Truee

Your Guest Representative

FIGURE 9-6
Reminder (longer than usual reminders; courteous and sales oriented)

■ QUALITY OFFICE PRODUCTS ■

4646 Poplar Avenue   Philadelphia, PA 19043
215-243-0000

December 7, 19——

Mr. Donald Morgan, C.P.A.
1359 Second Street
Philadelphia, PA 19104

Dear Mr. Morgan:

[Attention and Interest]

When you started your business, a good credit rating made it possible for you to benefit from credit purchases. I'm sure you want to protect your good credit rating so that you can continue to receive equipment and supplies by the convenient credit plans you have enjoyed in the past.

[Conviction]

Quality Office Products has continued to honor this privilege because you have always settled your accounts satisfactorily. At the present time, however, your account is five months' past due. Invoice #97231, which covers a shipment of two printers for a total of $1513.75, remains unpaid.

[Action]

To preserve your good credit rating, send your check for $1513.75. A stamped, addressed envelope is enclosed for your convenience in making immediate payment.

Sincerely,

Margaret Rose

Margaret Rose
Credit Manager
pw

Enclosure

FIGURE 9-7
A letter of appeal for payment, based on retaining credit rating

■ **THEATRE MEMPHIS** ■

630 Perkins Road, Ext.   Memphis, TN 38117
901-682-8323

September 20, 19——

Mr. John Johnson
Johnson's Steak House
4345 Southern Avenue
Memphis, TN 38117

Dear Mr. Johnson:

This copy of the "Kiss Me Kate" program includes your attractive, full-page advertisement on page 3. The program has been passed out to 5,600 theatergoers in the first two weeks of our production. Seven more performances are scheduled.   [Attention]

Many of our members have commented favorably on your new "after-the-theater dinner" promoted in the program copy you furnished us. Your location near the theater makes our audience a select group of prospective customers for your restaurant.   [Interest]

The programs for our next show are being prepared for the printer, and we're sure you will want your advertisement in them and in all programs for our current productions, as we agreed in your contract last June.   [Conviction]

Just send your check for the $200 balance due in the enclosed, addressed envelope, or drop the payment by the theater, and your program copy will be in for the entire season.   [Action]

Sincerely,

THEATRE MEMPHIS

Karen J. English
Advertising Manager

FIGURE 9-8
A letter of appeal. The central theme is the possible loss of customers.

COMMUNICATION brief

"I have a friend who doesn't believe in letting people push her around. So when she placed a $130 order with a catalog company, paid her bill promptly, and then received notice that her payment was overdue, she wasn't happy. And when she had her bank issue a copy of her canceled check (for a fee), sent the copy to the company, and then received notice that the copy could not be located, she was downright annoyed."

Then the company sent a collection letter and, during the next fourteen months, followed it with more than thirty letters and numerous telephone calls. Six years later, the company has not collected a debt it still considers legitimate, and the customer resents the way she was treated, as she has told many friends and neighbors.

The company sent poorly written collection letters and at times resorted to sarcasm. For example, one letter began with these words: "Do you really think that we do not intend to collect the money you owe?"

During the ordeal, the company was investigated by Minnesota Attorney General Hubert Humphrey III, who argued that its 23.94 percent finance charge violated Minnesota's 18 percent limit on revolving charge accounts. Because the company had no stores in the state, it claimed that Minnesota's limit did not apply, but it agreed voluntarily to reduce its interest rate and to offer a refund of "all excess payments" made during the previous two years, plus an extra 10 percent reimbursement premium.

Apparently still mixed up in the bookkeeping and collection departments, the company sent the customer a refund for the interest they had been trying to collect from her (which she did not owe and had not paid) plus 10 percent.

What do you think she did with the check?

Stephen Wilbers, "Writing (and Responding to) Collection Letters," *Star Tribune*, February 17, 1995, Marketplace, 2D.

An inquiry attempts to obtain a response from the reader. Perhaps the customer is dissatisfied with the merchandise, or perhaps because of unexpected financial difficulties the person cannot pay. We should not, however, state these things in our letter to customers or make excuses for the readers.

LATE-STAGE COLLECTION MESSAGES

Late-stage collection efforts are often in the form of telephone calls, telegrams, or even personal visits. They may also consist of letters.

Regardless of the collection methods, attempts at collecting long-overdue accounts state specifically when the amount must be paid and what action will be taken if it is not paid. The writer should not mention a lawsuit if there is actually no possibility of a suit. A late-stage message is illustrated in Figure 9-9.

■ **Quality Office Products** ■

4646 Poplar Avenue   Philadelphia, PA 19043
215-243-0000

June 13, 19——

Mr. Jonathan Wiley, Owner
Wiley Wholesale Foods
3211 Liberty Avenue
Franklin, PA 19019

IMMEDIATE PAYMENT REQUIRED   }— [Attention]

Your account of $4,012 is long overdue. Your office furniture was pur- }—
chased on November 19 of last year.   [Conviction]

Please telephone me immediately at 000-0000 in order to arrange pay- }—
ment and thus protect your credit rating.   [Action]

This is your last notice from this office.   }— [Action]

Harold Bowman

Harold Bowman
Credit Manager

FIGURE 9-9
Late-stage collection letter

Legal Considerations: Laws Pertaining to Sales and Collections

Consumers are protected by law from deceptive sales and advertising practices.

The law of contracts binds both the buyer and the seller to the terms of the contract. Fine print in a contract may be construed under certain circumstances as an attempt to conceal. Technical terms unlikely to be understood by the average consumer may also be interpreted as an attempt to conceal. "Plain language" laws passed by various states provide for clear writing and terminology that is likely to be understood by the "average" reader.

Fraud, according to law, is a deliberate misrepresentation of facts in order to deceive. Such misrepresentation need not consist of written or spoken words but may consist of omission or concealment.

The Fair Debt Collection Practices Act of 1977 prohibits the use of false, misleading, or deceptive information in order to collect a bill. The Federal Trade Commission recently obtained a $10,000 settlement from a collection agency that allegedly told third parties about a consumer's debt and falsely implied that letters and other communications were from an attorney, using letterhead depicting the scales of justice.

A debtor may ask that a collection agency stop making telephone calls or writing letters; the creditor must do so. Laws prohibit actions that could be considered harassment, such as numerous telephone calls in one day or at very early or late hours.

S U M M A R Y

Effective sales messages convince the reader or listener that the suggested purchase will meet the particular need of a specific individual and that the purchase will be more valuable than the necessary cost or effort to acquire the product or service.

The customer must be convinced to believe that the companies manufacturing and selling the product are trustworthy and reliable. The customer must also believe in the salesperson or salespersons who present the product, service, or idea.

The feature most likely to convince the prospective buyer that the product or service best meets the individual's particular needs is called the central selling point.

In order to determine the most effective central selling point, the seller must analyze the product or service and the possible needs of the prospective buyer. Once the central selling point is chosen, the sales letter is built around a theme that presents the central selling point.

Special characteristics of most sales letters are these:

1   An overall informal approach.

2   Use of humor, in addition to other aspects of informality.

3   Special emphasis on descriptive, vivid, forceful words and phrases.

4   Special emphasis on the you-approach, especially from the standpoint of presenting the prospective purchase in terms of reader benefit.

5   Increased use of the mechanical means of emphasis.

A pattern of arrangement long used in planning sales letters is that of attention, interest, desire (or conviction), and action.

The writer must present detailed, specific, convincing evidence in terms of the reader's interests.

Solicited sales messages are planned and written in much the same way as unsolicited ones, except that less emphasis is given to obtaining the attention of the reader. The reader is already interested in the product or service, as shown by a preceding inquiry.

Persuasive requests are treated basically as sales letters.

Collection messages can be divided into those that come in the early, middle, or late stages of the collection series. Although the tone of the message becomes more forceful from the beginning of the series to the end, the writer should never resort to threats, rudeness, or sarcasm.

1 Name one advantage and one disadvantage of buying by mail.
2 What is meant by a central selling point?
3 What is an advantage of a central selling point? A possible disadvantage?
4 What are two important steps that come before the choice of a central selling point?
5 What are four characteristics that distinguish many sales letters from other kinds of business letters?
6 What are the four steps of the long-used "pattern" for a sales letter?

Which of each pair is the better choice for a sales letter?
7 (Paragraph fairly near the end of a sales letter)
  a. The cost is $250, which is not expensive for this quality product that saves electricity.
  b. For $250, a one-time expense, you will reduce electricity costs for as long as you own your house.
8 (Letter to sell a magazine about to be published)
  a. If you want to subscribe to this magazine, just drop us a note.
  b. To reserve your premier issue of *Southpoint*, just place the token into the slot in the red card and mail it in the enclosed reply envelope.
9 (Opening paragraph of a letter that accompanies a catalog that specializes in "down home" products)
  a. We are proud of our new catalog of old-timey products; we look forward to your order.
  b. How long has it been since you've seen a cigar-store Indian, a surrey with a fringe on top, or a hitching post on Main Street?
10 (From a catalog description of a printed velvet jacket)
  a. This velvet jacket is lovely because of the many jewel-like colors and its soft texture.
  b. Where there is music in the air and the anticipation of a happy evening, wear seven sparkling jewel colors in this luscious velvet jacket.
11 **a.** This desk is 60 inches long and 40 inches wide.
  b. This spacious desk, 60 inches long and 40 inches wide, provides plenty of room for you to spread out your work.
12 **a.** This car is economical to operate.
  b. According to tests conducted by *Consumer Reports*, this particular model averages 24 miles to the gallon in city driving. How will you use the extra time and money you save?
13 **a.** This investment plan is profitable and safe.
  b. You will earn 5.5 percent interest, compounded quarterly, by investing in these bonds. The principal and interest are insured until maturity.
14 **a.** Do you want the grass to be greener on your side of the fence?
  b. Are you ashamed that your neighbor's yard always looks better than yours?
15 (From a television commercial for a furniture store)
  a. Hurry, hurry, hurry down to the Smith Store. Save hundreds, thousands, in our going-out-of-business sale! (The same kind of sale the store held last year.)
  b. The fine traditional furniture you have admired all year is now waiting for you at savings up to 40 percent during our August sale.

TEST YOURSELF
correct usage

Insert needed punctuation and correct all misspelled words. Perhaps you will want to review the sections on spelling and on punctuation, especially commas and semi-colons, in Appendix D.

1 You do not convince a reader to buy with vague generalities but with specific facts.

2 Sales letters have many advantages, for example you can present your product to a specific group of individuals.

3 Sales letters have disadvantages one of which is that people call them "junk mail."

4 Because you can mail sales letters to specific groups provided you have accurate mailing lists you can vary the central selling point for each different group.

5 Some sales letters use low price as the central selling point in such letters the price is emphasized not subordinated.

6 A central selling point is a principle characteristic of a letter that will achieve the desired affect.

7 We must give specific objective details about the product we are attempting to sell.

8 In order to receive a reply be sure that the reader or readers understand the requested action and how it is to be accomplished.

9 If an individual's name is inserted into a previously prepared letter the name should be shown in the same type as the letter itself.

10 Buying by mail has several advantages one of which is convenience.

EVALUATION SHEET: SALES LETTERS AND PERSUASIVE REQUESTS

(Use this evaluation sheet to evaluate the letters or other communications you prepare for your study of sales or other persuasive writing.)

___ Yes ___ No 1 Does the letter open with an effective attention-getting paragraph or section?

___ Yes ___ No 2 Is the letter built around an appropriate central selling point?

___ Yes ___ No 3 Is the you-approach used throughout?

___ Yes ___ No 4 Is the positive approach used throughout?

___ Yes ___ No 5 Is the product or service presented in terms of reader benefit?

__ Yes __ No **6** Is the product or service presented specifically, vividly, and correctly?

__ Yes __ No **7** Is format used to aid readability and attract and hold attention?

__ Yes __ No **8** Is all necessary information presented in an easy-to-read form?

__ Yes __ No **9** Is the letter convincing?

__ Yes __ No **10** Is the letter interesting?

__ Yes __ No **11** Is the price subordinated and presented along with reader benefit? (It should

not be subordinated if price is central selling point, but ordinarily it won't be.)

__ Yes __ No **12** Does the action close specify action, make action easy, and, if appropriate, motivate prompt action?

__ Yes __ No **13** Does the letter omit such trite phrases as "Act now" and "Don't delay"?

__ Yes __ No **14** Is the letter completely free of misrepresentation?

__ Yes __ No **15** Is the letter correct in every way?

CASES

1 Choose a product, real or imaginary, that you believe could be sold successfully by direct mail.

  a. Briefly describe this product.

  b. What will you use as your central selling point? Why? (Do not use price as the central selling point in this problem.)

  c. Write an attention-getting beginning for your letter. This beginning should be related to your central selling point.

  d. Write a sentence or longer passage that illustrates the use of psychological description as the term is used in this chapter. This portion of a sales letter, which describes concretely some feature of the product and also shows the reader benefiting from this feature, may or may not be related to your central selling point. (Almost all products or services have features in addition to the central selling point that should be described.)

  e. Write a sentence or longer passage that subordinates the stated price.

  f. Write an action close that refers in some way to the central selling point.

2 Look at several advertisements of approximate full-page length in magazines and newspapers. Analyze these advertisements according to these points:

  a. Is the advertisement built around a central selling point? If so, what is it? Is this theme carried from the beginning of the advertisement to the end? Do you feel that the feature chosen as the central selling point is an appropriate one? Why or why not? Can you think of another feature of the product or service that could be used as a central selling point? Is it also stressed in the advertisement?

  b. Is the product or service described in terms of actual reader benefit? Give examples.

  c. Is humor used in the advertisement?

  d. Would this advertisement make you buy the product, provided it is something you need, want, and can afford?

3 Analyze a number of sales letters as you did the advertisements in the preceding problem. In addition to the factors considered for the advertisement, evaluate the letters from these standpoints:

a. Did the writer make effective use of the mechanical means of emphasis, such as special arrangements, color, unusual spacing, all capitals, or underlining?

b. Is the attention-getting beginning effective? Does it illustrate one of the characteristics of securing attention illustrated in this chapter? Is a theme built around a central selling point used in the attention-getting section of the letter?

c. Does the action close specify action in terms of reader benefit, make action easy, and motivate prompt action? Does the action close include a reference to the central selling point?

d. Does the letter answer all questions that might logically occur to the reader?

e. Would this letter sell the product or service to you? Why or why not?

4 Using the information given in one of the advertisements you analyzed, or in a similar advertisement, construct a direct-sales letter. Choose your advertisement with care; make sure that your product is one that could effectively be sold by mail. If the advertisement does not include all the information that your reader will need, assume reasonable details.

5 Using the information given in an advertisement, construct a sales letter to be sent to retailers. Assume names, addresses, and any needed explanation or details.

6 Look at the advertisements for this year's new cars. Pick the ones you would most like to buy. Assume that you are selling this car. Write a sales letter to persons who are likely to be good prospects. Ask them to come to the showroom for a demonstration. You will need to know a great deal about the automobile in order to make your letter convincing. It should do a great deal more than ask the potential customers to come in to look. You must offer proof in your letter that the automobile is the one they should buy.

7 Follow the instructions given in the preceding problem except that you will choose some product other than an automobile—for example, a motorcycle, camera, sailboat, or any other item you would like to buy. Investigate the features of this product, as well as the features of competing products. Write a sales letter to persons who seem to be good prospects.

8 Write a sales letter, to persons similar to yourself, about one of your favorite possessions that sells for no more than $50. Choose an object that could be effectively sold by mail. Consider the reasons you particularly like this product; its weakness, if any; and the approach that is most likely to sell the same product to other people.

9 You own a taxicab company in your city. You have begun a desk-to-desk scheduled package delivery shuttle between three leading business centers—the airport, downtown, and Easthaven (or use the names of three actual business districts in your city). Your shuttle includes these features:
   - Customer can telephone before 9:30 A.M. for delivery to one or both of the other centers by noon. If customer calls by 2:30 P.M., delivery can be made by 5:00 P.M.
   - Rates are $10 for total deliveries to the same address and up to 25 pounds. For customers who sign up for everyday service, the rate is reduced by 20 percent. (This regular service is known as the "Yellow Shuttle.")
   - The Yellow Rush service, with higher rates, will deliver to any point within the city in no more than an hour, except for unforeseen emergencies.

   You ask the reader to telephone you or, if someone else in the company is in charge of package deliveries, to pass the letter along.

10 You are the general manager of an old hotel, the Arlington, in Hot Springs, Arkansas. Hot Springs is a popular resort town known for its scenery, pottery shops, spas, art galleries, and horse racing. The hotel has been completely refurbished.

   You read announcements of engagements in newspapers of cities in Arkansas and surrounding states. You are to prepare a letter to be sent to each bride and bridegroom asking them to spend their honeymoon in the Arlington. (How will you address the letter?) Write the contents of the letter, which will be duplicated for each individual couple by a microcomputer equipped with word processing software.

Some of the features of the hotel are shown in the following list:

Spacious honeymoon suites (two) with a magnificent view

Lovely dining room. Magnificent breakfast buffet and Sunday brunch.

Lounge located on the rooftop

Fresh flowers and a bottle of chilled champagne for the honeymoon couple

Lovely pool

Horseback riding

Beautiful landscaped grounds

Horse-drawn surrey available for a romantic ride through the winding streets of historic Hot Springs.

Rates for honeymoon suites, $150 to $175 a day. Other rooms from $100 to $110 a day

11 You are the manager of a tax consulting firm in your city. (Give it a name.) Realizing that the recent changes in the tax laws will cause many individual taxpayers who fill out their own returns to make costly mistakes, you write a sales letter to increase your clients in the middle-income group.

The basic philosophy of your tax consulting service is client satisfaction through able assistance by capable, honest, and courteous tax consultants. By knowing the new tax laws and how they affect your clients, you can save them both time and money. You provide the clients with economical help in the preparation of their income tax returns, confidentiality, year-round income tax service, and audit assistance. Fees are based solely on the complexity of the return. The average fee last year was $250 for each tax return. Your fee entitles the client to assistance with tax estimates, audits, and tax questions. Write the letter.

12 Bring a product to class. Give a three-minute sales presentation about this product. As your instructor directs, record this message.

13 Write a 30-second television or radio commercial for any product or service, real or imaginary. Do not modify existing commercials unless your modification is truly original. If you have access to a tape recorder, record your message. (If you prefer, write a one-minute commercial.)

14 As a full-time student paying your own college expenses, you hold a number of part-time jobs to help pay the bills, including some pet sitting for people who are on vacation. Since you like animals, the job is both fun and profitable. You will be attending summer school and will be living in your apartment near the university all summer. You decide to write a letter to faculty and staff to explain about your services and provide some references. (You have already obtained permission to use the names of two professors who have previously used your pet-sitting services.) Write a form letter you could distribute to faculty and staff explaining your services and inviting them to call you when they have need for a pet sitter.

15 You own Goldie's Catering and offer complete mobile catering for dinners, weddings, and parties. In addition to the actual food catering, you are now in a position to provide complete party planning. Your business has grown steadily over the past five years, and you have many satisfied customers. Business is often somewhat slow between Labor Day and Thanksgiving, so you have decided to send out a promotional letter announcing your expanded party planning services. Your goal is to get readers to call you first when they need the services of a caterer, no matter what the occasion or group size. While you want to advise all your previous customers of your expanded services, you also want to attract some new business. Write an effective letter.

PERSUASIVE REQUESTS

16 You are an executive assistant in the president's office of your college. The president is eager to convince the readers of your memorandum to take physical examinations. (Consider this memo a persuasive one as well as an informational one.) Write a memorandum or letter to all permanent, full-time employees. Those employees under age 35 are eligible for a company-paid physical examination every two years. Those age 35 and over are eligible for a physical examination every year. These examinations are recommended but not compulsory.

Examinations will be done by the college physician (Dr. Greer) or by a physician approved in advance by Dr. Greer. One doctor that Dr. Greer has approved (because of the great number of physical examinations to be performed) is Dr. Elaine V. Dowling, 20 South Dudly Street, your city, state, and ZIP code.

This examination is an important fringe benefit to employees.

Personnel are considered permanent if they have been employed continuously for one year. They are eligible for the examination on the anniversary date of their employment but may take it within two months thereafter. For example, employees whose anniversary date is July 1 may take the examination any time during July or August. Tell employees to make appointments with the examining physician early.

17 Write a letter to the television or radio station (or network) that broadcasts a program that you would like very much if certain changes were made. Carefully state your suggested changes, with reasons, in your letter.

18 You are a division manager and have been given the responsibility of overseeing the building of your new plant, which will open this coming Friday, November 23, at 10:00 A.M. Your main office, as well as the new building, is located in a medium-sized town in a farming area. This expansion will be a big boost for the city and should create about 280 new jobs. Besides being very functional, the plant itself will be extremely modern and beautiful.

The president of the company has suggested you write a letter to the local newspaper to request additional publicity. You will want to stress the natural beauty of the building in its wooded surroundings. Write a letter to one of the newspapers inviting reporters to come and help celebrate the grand opening. (Assume a name and address for the newspaper.)

The address of your new plant is 1000 Hilton Drive. Refreshments will be served, and you plan on having as many people as possible there to show community support.

19 You are serving on a student government committee charged with studying the current single eight-week summer school session offered at your school. The committee has researched summer school options at other schools in the state and surveyed students and faculty at your school to find out what summer school configuration they would like. Your committee proposed a summer school plan that would contain two six-week sessions. Committee members believe that two six-week sessions would allow students to take more courses in the summer and provide more course options. At the same time, the school should enjoy increased revenues. The Student Government Association accepted your recommendation and has requested that your committee write a letter to the academic vice-president requesting a change to two six-week sessions beginning next summer. Write a convincing letter.

20 Since you graduated three years ago, you have been working toward establishing an off-campus bookstore that will offer book rentals to students. The university bookstore you would compete with does not offer rental options for textbooks. You and a partner succeeded in obtaining financing and are now ready to open P & W Bookstore, a

full-service bookstore that will offer purchase or rental of textbooks. Your store is located just three short blocks from the northeast corner of campus. The new semester begins in exactly six weeks, and you need to prepare a promotional letter that you will mail to all students registered for the fall semester. You must generate a high amount of sales and/or rentals at the beginning of the semester if your bookstore is to be successful. The local university is a public institution, and you were able to obtain a mailing list from the school. Write an effective letter that will encourage students to visit your store and either rent or buy their books and supplies from you.

21 You graduated a year ago with a major in computer information systems and are currently employed as a computer network administrator for an area business. Within the past six months, you have designed three successful applications for area businesses as an individual consultant. Your employer has no objection to you doing this on your own time, using your own equipment at home in the evenings and on weekends. Since you enjoy the development work and also enjoy the extra money it brings in, you establish Sure Shot Development, a software development firm. Write an effective letter that could be sent to organizations that might be interested in your services.

22 Brinkman Industries is expanding its operations and will be opening a new plant in Delavan, Illinois, within the next six months. As mayor of Delavan, you have worked hard to bring this company to your town of 9,000 residents and are proud of all the new job opportunities that will be opening up for people in the area. You know that the company will be bringing in one of its own people as plant manager for the local operation. Brinkman's vice-president of operations talked with you yesterday and indicated they had found whom they wanted and now just have to convince the individual to make the move. The vice-president asks you, as mayor

of the town, to write a letter to Mr. Dennis LeRoy, Brinkman Industries, 4800 Highway 29, Columbia, IA 50057, to help convince him that Delavan would be a good place to raise his family. Assume any necessary details to write a convincing letter.

23 Modify Case 22 so that your own home town (or suburb) replaces Delavan, Illinois.

24 You have just purchased Apple Farm Inn, a 40-room inn located in a popular tourist area. When you purchased the inn, you realized that you would immediately have to go to work to improve the reputation of the inn by improving the quality of services guests receive. The rooms are being refurbished, but you know that is not the only way guests perceive quality. Guests are judging quality when they are in the lounge, in the restaurant, and whenever they come into contact with any inn employee for any reason. You have decided to institute a continuous quality improvement program in all areas of inn services. Write a letter to all employees announcing the first meeting related to quality improvement and convincing them of the benefits of making a commitment to continuous quality improvement.

25 The alumni association at your high school has asked you to serve as chair of the annual alumni banquet. You still live in your home town and run an insurance agency, so you know a lot of the people who attended your high school are still living in the small community, population 2,000. Attendance at the annual banquet the last five years has been declining steadily, even though special reunion classes are being recognized. In fact, the alumni association has some concern that the annual banquet should be eliminated if attendance does not improve in the next two years. Write a form letter to your high school's alumni convincing them to come to this year's banquet.

26 As dean of the College of Business Administration (your college), you are interested in persuading several of the leading business-

men and businesswomen in your city to give informal speeches at the university. One man in particular, Mr. Sam Smith, Jr., is president of one of the largest cotton brokerage firms in the United States.

You know that Mr. Smith graduated from your college. You also know that he is an extremely busy man. His contribution as an entrepreneur would be especially valuable to the students, as the college does not offer courses in the commodities exchange market. You will not be able to pay him for his time. You want him to share his experiences, problems, and rewards in building his own business. Ask him to speak to your school. Any weeknight during the month of March will be satisfactory.

27 Write a fund-raising letter for your church or for your civic or professional organization.

28 You have been appointed chairperson of a local "Stop Smoking" committee. Write a letter to be published as an advertisement in the local newspaper.

29 Write a letter to secure new members for the Society for the Advancement of Management, or for a similar professional organization. Obtain the information you will need in order to write a convincing letter.

COLLECTION MESSAGES

30 The Raleigh office of Tax Consultants, Inc., has been unable to collect from Mr. Fred Dangerfeld. He operates a hammer-handle manufacturing business in his garage. Every year for the past 10 years, Tax Consultants, Inc., has prepared the income tax return for his small business. This year his return was prepared in January. Since his return was more complex than in prior years, Tax Consultants, Inc., billed Mr. Dangerfeld $285 for tax consulting services. Thirty days later you (the manager) sent a duplicate of the original bill with a reminder.

Since your reminder failed to bring in the money, after another 30 days you sent your first collection letter to him. Mr. Dangerfeld has always paid promptly in the past; you are surprised that your reminder letter did not convince him to pay his bill. Now, 30 days later, you will write a second letter. What should be your approach? Write a convincing letter.

31 Thirty additional days have elapsed, and still no answer from Mr. Dangerfeld. You try to telephone but cannot get an answer. Write a letter. What will you say?

32 Thirty more days go by. You have telephoned twice and someone has said that Mr. Dangerfeld was unable to come to the phone. Write a letter.

33 You are the credit manager for an appliance store. Alice Jones has always been a good customer of yours. She has bought several major appliances from you, as well as small ones occasionally. This is the first time that you have had any difficulty collecting from her. You have already written her once when she missed her first payment because you were sure it was just an oversight on her part. This brought no response. She has missed another payment. You feel you must remind her again and insist on payment. You do not want to lose the goodwill that has built up, but you feel that something is wrong when she misses two payments in succession. Write her a letter attempting to work something out with her and request payment.

34 You are the credit manager of an agricultural chemical company. John Travis, a plantation owner, bought fertilizer for $10,084 in March. He has been buying on open account for more than 20 years. He has always paid in full, but only after one or two collection letters.

At the end of March you mailed him a regular monthly statement but received no reply. At the end of April, you mailed another statement with a past due notation. At the end of May, you wrote a letter asking for the full amount due; you did not receive an answer. You wrote a stronger letter at the end of June but received no reply. You send a representative to the plantation to see him. The representative is told by the farm manager that Mr. Travis has been in Europe but is expected to return on July 15.

It is now July 20. Write to Mr. Travis. What should be your approach at this time?

35 You are the owner-manager of a local dance studio. The three daughters of Dr. and Mrs. Frank Williams have been taking dancing lessons for three years. Write a collection letter to Mrs. Williams, who has always paid for the children's lessons promptly. Now the bill is three months past due. Lessons for the girls cost $240 a month. You are on friendly terms with Mrs. Williams. The girls are excellent students, and you don't want to lose them. A reminder note and a note of inquiry have already gone unheeded. The annual dance recital is coming up next month, with extra expense for yourself and the parents of the young dancers. A newsletter was sent to Mrs. Williams at the beginning of the year explaining that the tuition payments are due at the beginning of each

month. You have tried to telephone but receive only recorded messages; your calls have not been returned. The girls still come to lessons, regularly delivered and picked up by Mrs. Williams' household helper. You last talked with Mrs. Williams in December, more than four months ago, at a meeting of all parents to discuss the annual recital. If this letter obtains no response, what will you do?

WRITE YOUR OWN ASSIGNMENTS AND SOLUTIONS

36 Write your OWN assignment, with a solution, for a *direct-mail sales letter.* Also write your OWN assignment, with a solution, for a *persuasive request* and for a *collection letter, middle stage.* Give all the information that another writer would need to write a letter, memorandum, or other material as a solution to your problem. As with previous assignments for Chapters 7 and 8, this approach provides practice in describing a situation and giving instructions as well as in writing sales material and persuasive requests.

THINK-IT-THROUGH AND COLLABORATIVE WRITING ASSIGNMENTS

37 Form into committees of five or six. Elect a sales manager for each group. Think of a new product or service to be put on the market. Analyze your product or service as to its strengths and weaknesses, especially as to how it compares with similar products or services. Is your product or service one that can be effectively sold or promoted by mail? Should you use direct-sales messages, or should the product be sold through retail outlets? Who will be your most likely prospects? How will you determine your mailing list? What will be the central theme

of your message? As your instructor directs, hold sales meetings to answer the preceding questions and others that occur to you.

38 Write an appropriate sales message for the product or service described in Assignment 37.

39 Write a one-minute (or half-minute) radio ad for your product described in Assignment 37.

40 You are the assistant director of Elite Agency, a firm that specializes in providing assertiveness training for organizations, as well as teaching organizational interpersonal

communication skills and effective public speaking.

Several months ago Gregory Lane, director of Elite, asked you to speak at the annual banquet of "Up and Coming," a non-profit organization that provides job training services and seminars on interview techniques and resume writing to underprivileged adults. Ann Prescott, director of "Up and Coming," specifically requested you to speak. You feel that the publicity from the event will help Elite because some graduates of "Up and Coming" later go to work for your company's clients. Even more important, you believe that the organization contributes worthwhile service to the community.

Part A. Now Mr. Lane insists that you go to an out-of-town conference instead. The conference, which would cost Elite more than $900 for your expenses, is quite similar to one you attended last year; you feel that the "Up and Coming" banquet is more important. How will you convince Mr. Lane that you should speak at the "Up and Coming" banquet instead of attending the conference? Make notes about what you will say.

Part B. Assume that Mr. Lane asks you to put your remarks into a memorandum to him (he has made such requests before) so that he can evaluate your request. Write the memorandum.

Part C. Assume that Mr. Lane still insists that you attend the conference. Write a letter to Ann Prescott offering to prepare a videocassette (of yourself speaking) to be shown as part of the banquet program. You will prepare the cassette in the length she prefers.

ENDNOTES

1 Statistics reported by Robert W. Bly, "Marketing by Mail," *Black Enterprise*, June 1996, 275.

2 Denis Damio, "Romancing Customers in a Recession," *DM News*, January 6, 1992.

3 J. Daniel McComas, "Push Your Prospects' Hot Buttons," *Home Office Computing*, May 1995.

4 Marjorie Zieff-Finn, "It's No Laughing Matter: Using Humor in Direct-Mail Advertising Copy," *Direct Marketing Magazine*, September 1992, 38.

Planning the Search for Career Employment

OBJECTIVES

Chapter Ten will help you:

1   Plan your job search, including an analysis of your qualifications and research into the employment market.

2   Identify and describe methods of obtaining employment by going on-line.

3   Describe chronological, functional, and combination resumes and describe the advantages and disadvantages of each.

4   Prepare resumes that present your qualifications in the most favorable light without misrepresentation of any kind.

Because of the importance of finding the right job, nowhere else will the communication knowledge and skills you have learned in this course and elsewhere be of more benefit to you. You will use your writing skills to prepare your resume and application letter and your oral communication skills in employment interviews, conversations, and group meetings in preparation for the final employment decision. Your knowledge of research methods will enable you to find employing companies that offer opportunities for applicants with your special qualifications.

Research about employing companies has become much easier in the past few years because of technological developments, including computer databases that provide easy and almost instant information about various companies. In addition, employment offerings are displayed on the Internet, as discussed later in this chapter. (Applicants also have the opportunity to "advertise" themselves on the Internet.)

Chapters 10 and 11 are planned to help you communicate effectively through resumes, letters, and interviews. Chapter 10 emphasizes the research phase of the job-seeking process and preparation of a resume. (An alternate spelling is résumé.) Chapter 11 presents the application letter and other letters about employment, plus a discussion of the employment interview.

An outstanding letter of application, submitted with a well-organized, attractive, and convincing resume, can be the deciding factor in securing the kind of employment you are seeking. Although no written presentation alone will get a job for you, it can result in an interview, at which time you continue the process of convincing the interviewer that you are the best possible choice for the position.

BEGINNING THE JOB SEARCH

What matters most in the search for employment is the ability to handle the job. The most creative, attractive, and appropriate letter and resume will not substitute for lack of skill or experience, just as a cleverly worded sales letter will not create sales on a continuing basis unless a truly good product backs up the letter.

Regardless of your outstanding qualifications or of a favorable job market, you should take the initiative in your job search instead of waiting for an employer to offer a position or to advertise one. Taking the initiative has several advantages. You become aware of differing opportunities and are able to compare prospective employers and employment opportunities. You are more likely to find a better job when you actively seek one because you learn about more openings. You are better able to consider your particular strengths in relation to the needs of differing employing organizations.

Another obvious advantage is that your initiative and dedication in looking for a job tell the employer a great deal about you, including the fact that you have enough energy and ambition to plan and conduct a thorough, organized campaign to place yourself. The quality of your work after being hired, with resulting opportunities for advancement to a higher position, is likely to be similar to your efforts in finding and obtaining the job.

In addition, as you survey employing organizations, you will no doubt find one or more in which you are especially interested. Your special interest in a particular organization, which will be apparent in your written application and interview, elicits a positive response from the employer. An applicant who very much wants a job with a particular organization has a definite advantage over an equally qualified applicant who is equally interested in a number of jobs.

VISIT YOUR COLLEGE OR UNIVERSITY PLACEMENT CENTER

Your school placement center is almost certain to be able to help you in finding career employment. Register with your placement office early in your senior year or even before. You will need to know how they will work with you, and, even more important, how you can work with them.

Ordinarily, announcements of interviewers scheduled to come to the campus will be posted on bulletin boards, provided to department heads or professors, or posted on a Web page. These announcements will also be available in the placement center, which you should visit often.

In addition to interviewer information and scheduling, placement offices provide brochures and other information about various companies and government agencies. This information is helpful to job seekers when planning a campaign of unsolicited applications. Such information is absolutely essential when preparing for an interview with a particular organization, as discussed in Chapter 11.

Your placement center may help you develop an employment packet that contains your resume, transcript, letters of recommendation, letters of commendation or lists of awards, and any other material that may be beneficial to you. Placement centers also sponsor seminars and workshops on resume preparation and interviewing.

Placement officers can advise you about the various means of "surfing the net" to find employment opportunities. Some placement centers and university libraries provide these services without cost to students and faculty. For example, The University of Buffalo's Career Planning and Placement Center has an extensive Web site with local, national, and global links for the job seeker.[1]

Regardless of where and how access to the Internet and Web sites is available, you should learn to use these innovative methods. With thousands of databases and dozens of search tools in existence, finding information on the Internet can be time-consuming—and perhaps costly. On the other hand, mailing out dozens of written applications is time-consuming and costly.

COMMUNICATION brief

YOUR CAREER

Here's what recruiters say they want:

Interpersonal skills, public speaking, writing, reasoning, social graces, and computer proficiency

Excellent teamwork skills and strong customer relations expertise

A balanced education: strong on liberal arts, with a technical background and a potent specialization

Multiple talents and a commitment to lifelong learning

Here's where recruiters look for it:

On-campus interviews

Referrals from current employees

Job listings posted with college career services

Internship programs

Referrals from campus organizations or leaders

Borders Book Shop staff research, "Where You Can Go to Find Out More," *The Atlanta Journal and Constitution*, March 27, 1995, 1E.

▶ **FIND A JOB BY GOING ONLINE**

Early in your employment search, if you begin months or a year before your graduation, you may not be able to actively pursue openings that are listed on the Internet. Early research, however, will give you much information about overall opportunities in your field and in various areas of the country.

Thousands of employment ads can be seen on the screen of your personal computer. Gerland and Winer say:

> We've found that the quality of jobs offered are generally high, as companies who have taken the time to post jobs on-line do so in an effort to recruit well-educated potential employees who have a knowledge of computers. Don't worry, though, not all the job listings were found in the computer field.[2]

Many firms are using the Internet for broad-based hiring, storing resumes received through online services. "Gone are the days when most traditional forms of recruiting—stacks of resumes and wall-to-wall interviews—yielded perhaps half a dozen feasible candidates."[3]

The use of online recruiting does *not mean an end to paper resumes*, according to Christine Leonard, a human relations consultant with Lotus. "Employers will still continue to print out resumes that they receive on-line."[4]

Job seekers are automatically matched with appropriate job openings and notified via e-mail using numerous Internet Web sites, including CareerSite. Hundreds of companies—American Express, EDS, Fidelity Investments, Ford Motor Company, Harvard Community Health Plan, Intel, and Lotus—post jobs on this site.[5]

The Web site CareerCity was released on September 16, 1996; it lists 125,000 job openings.[6] Another 1996 release is IntelliMatch, which is used by major employers such as Hewlett-Packard, Oracle, Mitsubishi, Pitney Bowes, Pfizer, Sun Microsystems, and more than 100 others.[7]

Twenty-six percent of the 2,900 executives surveyed by Management Recruiters International say they use the Internet to recruit workers. Boeing started accepting electronic resumes at its site on the World Wide Web on August 8, 1996, and had e-mail responses waiting the next day. Even Hooters of America, the restaurant chain known for scantily dressed waitresses, receives 1 percent of its applications via the Internet.

Stored resumes aren't forgotten. A computer can use key words and phrases to select those applicants that meet the requirements. IBM has 200,000 resumes on file. Texas Instruments, which made 2,000 hires last year, has 100,000 resumes on file. Microsoft keeps the 80,000 resumes it gets each year."[8]

You may also wish to publish your resume on your own Web site. It will cost only a few dollars a month. "The Internet lets workers cast their qualifications to the world, making it easy for companies to find them nestled in their electronic cubbyholes and recruit them away from competitors."[9]

Rebecca Rolwing states:

Dry clean the navy blue suit, get a haircut, brush up the resume, line up references, check the classified advertisements, get online. . . . Those who use the Internet to job-hunt found more than five job leads and secured—on average—more than one job interview each, according to a survey of 525 unemployed job candidates.[10]

Resumix, which was developed in 1988, is a well-known and widely used *computer program* used to scan and process employment resumes. Resumes are placed on a computer scanner, which reads the information and loads it into a computer. An artificial intelligence software program reads the resumes and automatically categorizes prospective employees by skill level, educational background, and job objective. Resumix has tremendous appeal to large companies, including AT&T, General Motors, Bank of America, Digital Equipment Corporation, Walt Disney, General Electric, Advanced Micro Devices, Inc., and Apple Computer, Inc.[11]

Whether you submit your resume by the Internet or by more traditional methods, it is likely to be scanned by a computer using Resumix or a com-

COMMUNICATION brief

GUIDELINES TO SEEKING EMPLOYMENT BY GOING ON-LINE:

► Prepare for your job search as you would do for more traditional methods of contacting employers.

► Seek help from your college placement center, librarians, professors, or technical service personnel if you are inexperienced in using on-line services.

► Recognize that the vast number of openings advertised on Web sites and elsewhere does not guarantee your immediate success in obtaining employment. Although openings are numerous, especially if you are willing to relocate, other applicants are also numerous. Competition is fierce.

► You can find employment opportunities on the Internet, on the part of the Internet described as the World Wide Web, or on commercial on-line services such as America Online, CompuServe, or Prodigy. If you already own a computer and a modem, your cost to link up to the Internet is about $20 a month, a flat fee. (Prices, like everything else, are subject to change.) Some commercial on-line services charge more, based on usage.

► Many companies have set up their own Web sites, which are useful not only for learning of employment opportunities but for seeking information to prepare you for successful interviews.

► Consider, along with others, these sites:
  Career Mosaic
  Careerpath, which combines the classified advertisements of six major newspapers.
  Job Bank USA
  JobWeb, which focuses on entry-level positions
  Onlline Career Center
  The Monster Board
  Online Career Center
  JobTrak

peting service. Thus, as you prepare your resume, consider carefully word choice and format. Your resume will differ little from traditional ones in approach and content. For the most part, an appropriate resume designed for one individual in your hometown will be no different than one in response to listings on the Internet. The overall guide is simplicity, plus the proper use of emphasis. Further discussion and instructions about preparing a resume for electronic scanning are included later in this chapter under "The Resume: A Report on Yourself."

ACCEPT HELP FROM FRIENDS, FAMILY, PROFESSORS, AND PROFESSIONAL ORGANIZATIONS

Many college graduates learn about possible openings by methods other than the Internet or from classified advertisements. Your participation in professional organizations, beneficial to you in many other ways, may provide contact with business leaders in your community through meetings and job fairs. Some professional organizations print annual booklets highlighting graduating seniors in particular fields.

Get to know your professors. (In addition to job leads, you will need references.) Some professors, because of their work as consultants, learn of em-

An employer spends a great deal of time choosing new employees. Although computer-scanned resumes have decreased necessary work, much remains. He or she can consider only outstanding applications.

ployment opportunities in the companies for which they work. In addition, because of their experience with other graduates, they can guide you in various ways, including the names of persons to whom you should address your application. (This information may also be available in printed sources.)

Best of all, talk with present employees of companies you are considering. Find out how they obtained their jobs and whether they are happy with the choice.

▶ READ NEWSPAPERS AND PROFESSIONAL JOURNALS

Read not only classified advertisements but also news items about all business subjects. Companies relocate, expand, plan new services or products, prosper, or decline. Professional journals provide information not only about employment but also about overall predictions for particular industries and organizations.

ANALYZING YOUR QUALIFICATIONS

When you plan a sales campaign, one of your first steps is to make a product analysis. You look at the product, test it, and compare it with competing brands. You then decide on your central theme, or the most important selling feature, also called the *central selling point*.

As you plan a job-seeking campaign, you make this same analysis about yourself. You analyze the "product," compare it with competing ones, and note how the product fits the market for which you are preparing your application. Although this analysis is for your use only, it will be far more beneficial and complete if it is in written form. You will have several features to stress, but the main theme of your presentation will depend on the kind of work for which you are applying, as well as on the type of organization. Because the emphasis will differ according to these considerations, an individually tailored application letter, as well as an individually planned resume, is more likely to be effective than the same two-part application sent to organizations with varying needs.

Because you will not always be sure of the varying needs of each organization, you will not always be correct in your choice of the *central selling point*. Usually the central selling feature will be either your education or your experience. For most persons completing a college degree, especially young college graduates with limited experience, the central selling point is some facet of the educational background, ordinarily the major field. After you have been out of school for several years, your experience is likely to become the most important selling feature if it is similar to the kind of work for which you are making application. If you have diversified experience, emphasize successful experience in a job similar to the one being sought.

In certain instances, extracurricular work or an avocation will be the most convincing central theme. For example, a football star may be hired as a sporting goods sales representative; in this case, the football experience is of more value than is the student's major in, for example, journalism. If the same student were applying for a job as a newspaper reporter, the application should be built around the academic major. The football experience should be mentioned but given only limited coverage.

As when selling a product, do not stress the central selling point so much that you omit or overly subordinate your other selling features. You cannot be completely sure that you are choosing the most logical central selling point. In addition, you are likely to be hired on the basis of overall qualifications, consisting of education, experience, personality, attitude toward work, and the ability to grow and develop in usefulness to the employing organization.

As you analyze yourself, you will no doubt find that you have weak and strong points. As you present yourself to prospective employers, stress strong points. Subordinate or leave unmentioned areas that you consider to be weaknesses, but never misrepresent in any way.

The positive approach, as in other communication situations, "accentuates the positive and eliminates the negative." You can often present in positive terms what you consider to be a weakness. For example, instead of writing "No experience except for part-time work in a grocery store," say "Checker and office employee with Winn-Dixie Grocery Company, 1994–1997. Received Employee of the Month Award three times. Worked average of 20 hours a week yet maintained a grade point average of 3.0 each semester."

Other examples of points to emphasize and subordinate will be given later in this chapter as you learn to prepare the application letter and resume.

EDUCATION

If you are completing college, education to be considered in your self-analysis consists especially of work leading toward a degree. Other educational preparation consists of high school subjects, technical or business courses, and other specialized schooling, as well as educational experience obtained in military service. Consider courses that apply to the job you are seeking, including those within your major field and any others that especially relate.

Consider your scholastic standing overall and in your major field. Whether or not you mention your scholastic standing depends on what it is. According to the principle of the positive approach, you are not obligated to emphasize a negative aspect. If your average is just enough to obtain a degree or very slightly above, emphasize the degree and omit the actual grade-point average.

The degree is a real accomplishment, even if other persons have surpassed you in A's and B's. But if you are asked for your exact standing, be truthful. By being truthful, according to an old adage, you are not forced to remember what you said. Some organizations immediately disqualify any applicant who is discovered to have misrepresented even the slightest bit of information.

You may wish to give your grade-point average only in your major field, not the overall average, as the standing in your major field is likely to be higher. Your performance in your major field should be of most concern to the employer. In some resumes you should mention relevant research projects or papers. After you have completed graduate work, mention of a thesis or dissertation is considered an essential part of your application.

Include specific skills and abilities developed in your education program, such as ability to work with computers or other equipment. (If you have not learned a great deal about computers and widely used software, do so as soon as you possibly can. You will be at a disadvantage without this almost essential knowledge and ability.)

If you have used computers or specialized software in previous employment, mention this ability in the section on experience. If you have not ac-

To find a job, check many sources, including newspapers and professional journals. (At the present time, experienced employees who have been "downsized" may face more difficulties than recent college graduates.)

tually used them but have had training in their use, mention your ability in the educational section of your resume.

As you complete the analysis of your educational preparation, you will probably find that education should be your central selling feature. From the standpoint of emphasis, as you have already learned, this preparation, in terms of how it will benefit the reader, should be described in more detail than other features, and it should be presented before less important information.

► WORK EXPERIENCE

Work experience is ordinarily one of the two most important elements of career preparation, although some college students complete degrees with no work experience whatsoever. If you have no work experience, you should particularly stress your educational preparation. You should also show how participation in professional and social organizations gave you experience in leadership positions and in working with other people. (Try to obtain some kind of work experience before you graduate. Internships count as work experience.)

Some applicants have the idea that only related work experience should be mentioned in the application letter or on the resume. This approach is unwise. Work experience of any kind as long as it is legal and honorable, is better than no experience at all. Any work, even the most menial, indicates that you have the energy and initiative to seek and hold a job. Volunteer work should also be mentioned.

Remember to include experience acquired in military service, which could be your most important and relevant experience and the central theme of your entire application.

► ACTIVITIES, ACHIEVEMENTS, AND PERSONAL CHARACTERISTICS

As you continue with your self-analysis, make a note of all special accomplishments, such as exceeding a sales quota, earning a promotion, or receiving certificates of recognition for unusual achievement. List extracurricular activities; social and professional organizations, including membership and offices held; and any other meaningful activity or accomplishment. Include honors, awards, publications, and other recognitions. (Scholastic awards are usually mentioned with your other educational achievements.) Foreign language abilities, hobbies, personal business ventures, and many other facets of your total experience may have a bearing on your ability to fit into the particular organization to which you are applying.

When you attempt to emphasize a great many things, you succeed in emphasizing nothing. On the other hand, you are not presenting the best possible picture of yourself if you omit favorable data that may show your ability to be a good employee.

Check yourself in these and similar areas:

Ability and willingness to assume responsibility	Self-confidence and poise
Ability to persevere	Emotional and physical health
Ability to think logically and creatively	Appearance
Ability to adapt to changing situations	Maturity
Ability to communicate in oral and written form	Sense of humor
Ability and desire to work with other people	Dependability
Leadership	Neatness
Ability to work alone	Promptness
Judgment	Ability to make decisions
Courtesy and diplomacy	Ambition and enthusiasm

Most important, ask yourself if the field of work being considered is in line with your real interest and ability. What do you want from your career?

After you have made a complete and objective self-analysis, you should have a realistic appraisal of yourself for the job-seeking process. You still have the task of choosing the best method of presenting qualifications and determining which points to stress and which to subordinate. In order to answer these questions, you need to know something of your prospective employer.

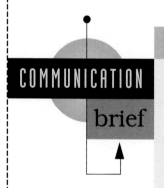

COMMUNICATION brief

YOUR CAREER

We make personal choices all the time, and our lives are shaped by the consequences of them. By thinking them out systematically, we can cut down on the chances of getting them wrong.

Many of us approach the big decisions we face without any great forethought. We make up our minds in the manner of Mark Twain's Huckleberry Finn: "I studied for a minute, sort of holding my breath, and then I says to myself, All right, then I'll *go* to hell." A minute's study is not likely to bring the best results, but our reluctance to undertake a lengthy analysis of the options is only human. "Thinking is the hardest work there is, which is the probable reason so few engage in it," Henry Ford observed. . . . No matter how systematic you have been, there is no guarantee that a decision will turn out successfully. The unforeseen can always happen. Life remains a game of chance, but it is not a game of blind luck; skill and preparation can make a great difference to the outcome.

Royal Bank of Canada, "The Royal Bank Letter," September–October 1987, 1, 4.

Analyzing the Employment Market

A market analysis is the next step in your job-seeking process. You must know your employer and the job requirements in order to show that your qualifications meet the employer's needs. Although many items of information cannot be obtained until the interview, or perhaps not until you actually begin work or have worked for a considerable time, much information will be available if you diligently look for it.

What information will you need? You will need enough to ascertain that the organization will offer you sufficient opportunity, provided you are hired, to justify your accepting this employment. Although this statement may seem obvious, it is the most important answer you are seeking. As you make this investigation, you will also gain enough information for intelligently planning your presentation to the specific organization.

You should not take the attitude that you must accept a job that offers little opportunity for growth or for the kind of work you prefer. You may be forced to accept an offer that is less than ideal, but at least you should aim high. On the other hand, remember that you are not stuck forever in any position or company. Although frequent changes do not look good on your record, most people change jobs several times during their lifetimes. Usually it is easier to find work if you already have a job than if you do not.

Although you may not stay with your first full-time job, you should choose it with care. In one way or another, it will affect your entire career. In addition, the employing organization will spend time and money in hiring and training you, perhaps a great deal of time and money. If you do not enter into an employment contract with the sincere desire to succeed and to remain with the company, you are not being completely fair to the employer or to yourself.

Another purpose of research into employing organizations is to obtain information about how to sell yourself intelligently. If you can determine your possible duties, you will have a better idea of which qualifications to emphasize in order to show how your abilities will be of the most possible benefit to the employer.

Another advantage (as well as an obvious necessity) of doing research into the job market is to know which organizations have openings for applicants like yourself. You can assume that many large organizations will periodically employ persons with widely used specializations, such as engineering, accounting, or sales. For positions such as these, unsolicited letters of application are appropriate and useful. You can, in fact, use unsolicited letters for all possible openings, but you will not always receive a favorable reply.

Even if an unplanned "hit-or-miss" approach seems to succeed, it is still far from being the best method. You are not able in this way to fit your qualifications to the particular employer. You are also likely not to find the organizations for which you would most like to work.

Where will you find all this information? Printed sources, databases (such as NEXIS), and the World Wide Web (see Chapter 3) will provide some of the information you seek. Annual reports of the firms in which you are interested include far more information than the financial statement does. They also tell something of the product or services, as well as the location of the home office or branch offices. They may give information about management policies. You need information about companies to which you send your application; such information is absolutely essential as you prepare for an interview with a particular company.

Various sources of information are available in your college or university reference library and in your placement office. Some printed sources are these:

College Placement Council Annual is especially applicable to persons graduating from college; this four-volume set contains information on the job search and employment opportunities in various fields.

Moody's Manuals of Investments, although intended primarily for potential investors, also provides information essential to the potential employee. Information included in these manuals consists of a summary of the history of each organization, method of operation, location, products or services, and the financial structure. These manuals are available in most libraries.

Standard and Poor's Manuals are also planned primarily for investors. They contain information similar to that contained in *Moody's Manuals*. Another publication of this corporation is *Poor's Register of Directors and Executives, United States and Canada*. The directory may be useful for finding the name and title of the person to whom you should send your application for employment.

A book that has been popular with job seekers for more than 25 years is *What Color Is Your Parachute?* by R. N. Bolles. A new edition of this book is issued annually. It is not a guide to individual companies; instead, it discusses such topics as self-analysis and career choice. The author offers fresh approaches to finding a job.

Sources of information about prospective employers are available in your college library; many are on databases. One full-text database is NEXIS, which provides information on thousands of subjects from hundreds of sources. Some libraries provide this database and others free for student and faculty use. Ask a reference librarian if you need help.

Many government and professional organizations issue publications describing employment opportunities and the necessary qualifications for employees.

Most important, as mentioned earlier, take advantage of the services offered by your college or university placement center.

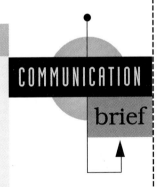

YOUR CAREER

According to the *Detroit News*, within four years more than 1 million people a year will enter the job market with bachelor's degrees.

The number of four-year degrees awarded by American colleges has tripled since the 1960's—when a degree virtually represented a ticket to job and income security. Today, an oversupply of graduates in many fields has eroded the economic value of some diplomas.

"Adding to the uncertainty is a constantly changing job market. By the time students finish college, new and different occupations are out there that weren't when they started," said Vernicka Tyson, director of career and placement services for Michigan State University in East Lansing.

The wrong choice could mean venturing into an occupation already inundated with job-hunters fresh out of college. Experts say that fields that look most promising at this time are these: business, health and medical professions, social services, sciences and engineering, and service industries.

Charles E. Ramirez, *The Detroit News*, September 1, 1996, D1.

SOLICITED APPLICATION LETTERS AND RESUMES

A solicited application is written in reply to advertisements, announcements, or other requests for applicants. Ordinarily, you should use the two-part application, a letter and a resume, for both solicited and unsolicited applications.

You may find advertisements in your local newspaper for career employment in your chosen field. Another place to find announcements of openings in a specialized field is professional journals, although these jobs may require moving to another part of the country. Many advertisements, particularly for executives and engineers, appear in *The Wall Street Journal* and the *National Business Employment Weekly*. And, as discussed previously under "Find a Job by Going Online," thousands of openings are listed nationwide on the Internet. Also watch for posted announcements in libraries, on college or university bulletin boards, or in government agencies.

Writing a solicited application letter differs little from writing a solicited sales letter—that is, an answer to a request for information about a product or service. You must convince the reader that the product you are selling—yourself—is the one that should be selected. As in your sales messages, you convince your reader by specific evidence, not by a high-pressure approach.

Build the opening section and all remaining sections of the application letter and resume around a central selling point. The central theme, based on the central selling point, tells how your most important qualification, or perhaps a group of related qualifications, can benefit the particular employing organization. Emphasize the strength or strengths that you believe will be more applicable to the position for which you are applying, and *include other positive points as well*. The employer looks at your entire background, personality, ability, attitude, and potential value to the organization.

UNSOLICITED APPLICATION LETTERS AND RESUMES

Unsolicited applications can be considered a form of direct-mail advertising, similar to messages planned for direct-mail campaigns to sell a product or service. (Some applications are not "direct mail" from the standpoint that they are posted on the Web by job seekers.)

Prepare a mailing list of organizations for which you would like to work. This list should consist of names of organizations along with names, titles, and addresses of people responsible for receiving and reviewing applications. Instead of sending your application to a personnel department, find the name of the individual, such as a department head or the manager of an office or division, who would be responsible for hiring you.

Make absolutely certain that the addressee's name is spelled correctly and that his or her title is correct. A telephone call to the organization will provide this information. Preparing your mailing list will require that you do a great deal of research in order to select the organizations and individuals to receive your application.

You are not likely to receive favorable replies from all the applications you mail. Depending on current employment conditions in your area of specialization and on your background and qualifications, you may receive a request for an interview or for further information from only a small percentage of your total list. (Yes, a thorough job search requires time and money, but it is far more expensive to be unemployed.)

ADVANTAGES OF A TWO-PART APPLICATION

A two-part application enables you to use the letter to present highlights of the detailed information included on the resume. These important features are presented from the standpoint of what they will do for the reader. As in other sales messages, the letter is more coherent and emphatic when it is built around a central theme.

Prepare the resume; then choose from it important elements to be included in the letter. The letter interprets your most important qualifications (from all those shown on the resume) in terms of reader interest—much as you present important elements of a product when writing a sales letter to be sent with leaflets and brochures. Prepare both parts of the two-part application after you have made a detailed analysis of your qualifications and have researched the companies that interest you.

As much as possible, tailor each application letter and each resume to meet the expectations of the organization and department to which you are applying. Although you cannot always estimate accurately which of your several strong points should be emphasized to the greatest extent, it is unwise to prepare a standard resume or application letter that you consider to be universally acceptable, regardless of the type of job or the individual who will make the final decision about hiring you.

Recent college graduates with limited work experience often use education as their central selling point.

By storing your resume and letter on a word processor, you can make changes in content or order of arrangement without completely rewriting. Although printed resumes are less time-consuming, they are often less effective. Not only are they less personal, but they cannot be "fine-tuned" for each application package.

Find out as much as possible about prospective employers before submitting your application. After completing your research, emphasize your strong points that seem to fit the job—although you can never be sure that what you consider important will be what the employer considers most important. In any event, never emphasize a weakness.

Each letter you send should be individually typewritten or, preferably, prepared on a word processor. Resumes are often printed or reproduced by some process, such as photocopying, that results in attractive copies difficult to distinguish from individually typewritten or word processed material. A better approach, however, is to send originals. Copies can be made from laser printers (thus, they *are* originals), possibly at less expense. If there is a possibility that your resume will be scanned by Resumix or a similar method, do not use photocopies.

THE RESUME: A REPORT ON YOURSELF

The right kind of resume will obtain the interviewer's attention. It will also continue the sales presentation throughout the interview and the negotiation process.

A well-prepared resume should be a truly superior expression of your talents and background. It should be a credit to your creativity and to your ability to put ideas and information into convincing words. The most effective resumes sell ability, talent, and potential as well as education and past experience.

A resume, unlike most kinds of business writing, is appropriately written in less than complete sentences. Specifically worded phrases, as illustrated in all resume examples in this chapter, have several advantages: They eliminate the need for the pronoun *I*, they save words and space, and they place emphasis on important, positive qualifications.

Although you must not misrepresent in any way, you should not understate your qualifications. Two or three hundred applicants may also want the job for which you are applying; now is no time to be modest.

► FORMAT AND APPEARANCE

Be sure that your resume, like the letter that accompanies it, is absolutely perfect in appearance, including quality and color of paper, arrangement on the sheet without crowding, and clear type. If you do not use printed resumes (which may have more disadvantages than advantages because of impersonality), try to prepare your resume using a word processor and a laser printer. Do not use a dot matrix printer.

Work for a professional-looking document. While it may be tempting to use several different fonts and several different type point sizes, too many changes are distracting. You want to provide a format that makes it easy for the reader to find key information about you. Keying your name in 24-point type is not the answer to a successful resume. Pick one font. You may wish to use bolds, italics, underlining, bulleted lists and other techniques for emphasis or readability, but DO NOT use such techniques if your resume is likely to be scanned by Resumix or similar systems.

In order to prevent errors in scanning, follow these procedures:

► Put name and address on separate lines.

► Use fonts of 10 or 12; nothing smaller or larger.

► Choose a simple font, such as Courier. Avoid fancy ones.

► Mail the sheet unfolded; creases may prevent a complete reading.

Do NOT use

► underlining, italics, bolding, other graphics;

► boxed or shaded text;

► multiple columns (scanner reads across the page);

► colored stationery.

Do NOT staple.

Computers are programmed to look for "keywords." Bob Stirling, a national employment authority, recommends putting the phrase "Keyword Summary" on your resume just below your name and address, followed by all the buzz words you think the employer is likely to tell the computer to search for.[12]

Helen Wick-Martin, technology manager for hiring at National Semiconductor, makes this statement:

> Don't use desktop publishing to make it look like some marketing brochure. But that doesn't mean you needn't worry about what your resume looks like. Don't forget that if you get an interview, a copy of your resume will be sent to your interviewer. In expectation of that moment, you certainly need to concern yourself with the overall visual impression of your resume.[13]

Use bond paper of at least 20-pound weight and 20 percent cotton content (also described as "rag" content). If you are sure that your resume will not be scanned by a computer, you may use stationery of cream, buff, light gray, or similar neutral colors. White or off-white, which should be used if resume may be scanned, are the most widely used colors for resumes of all kinds.

Proofread your resume; make sure it is absolutely perfect, with no errors in spelling or keyboarding. Make sure that type is clear and bright and that all material is neatly arranged on the page, without crowding. Leave plenty of white space throughout. Use format and arrangement to achieve readability and emphasis upon your most important qualifications.

ORDER OF ARRANGEMENT

Resumes described as being in the *reverse chronological order* present both education and work experience in reverse chronological order. *Functional* resumes are built around qualifications and abilities rather than on time periods of education or years of work experience. *Combination* resumes combine portions of both the reverse chronological and functional arrangements.

Basic parts of resumes arranged in the chronological order are these:

► The employment objective, which may be included in the heading

► Education

► Work experience

► Skills, publications, activities, other data

► References, or a statement that references will be furnished on request

(A summary sometimes follows or replaces the objective.)

Examine the resumes shown in Figures 10-1 through 10-7 as you consider the usual parts of a resume. Although the following discussion applies primarily to reverse chronological resumes, the kind most frequently used, all resumes require a heading. Most require an objective unless the objective is clear from either the heading or the summary. All resumes should report education and work experience, although functional resumes do not report details of experience and education according to exact time periods.

HEADING

The heading should include your name, address, and telephone number. Sometimes these items of information are used alone to make up the entire heading without some kind of descriptive title as *Resume, Data Sheet, Vita,* or *Qualifications of. . . .* Your objective may be included in the heading instead of being listed in the first section of the resume; for example, *Sherry Clara Aldridge's Qualifications for Accounting Work with Arthur Andersen and Company.* Another method of showing the objective in the heading is to follow your name with a description of your occupation, provided you are applying for similar work; for example, *Joe Lee Cole, Industrial Psychologist.*

To list "accounting work" in the heading or in the separate section of the resume entitled *Objective* is too vague and general if you are aware of a particular opening that can be described in more specific terms. Avoid being overly specific when you are not exactly sure of the kind of work available to you; on the other hand, don't be so general that you say nothing at all. ("I'll do anything, and I can do everything" is not usually a good approach when seeking career employment, although being a generalist is often more advantageous than being able to work only in a narrow specialization.) You are likely to have much competition. Don't eliminate possible opportunities by a too specific description of the job you seek.

Perhaps you should give two addresses and telephone numbers in the heading of the resume, especially if you expect to change your address soon. Students often give their school address and their home or permanent address.

EMPLOYMENT OBJECTIVE

If you do not state the employment objective in the heading of the resume, you should state it in the first section of the resume. Although the objective is sometimes omitted, the resume is much less readable without it. The reader must look through other sections or at the accompanying letter in order to determine your employment goals. This alone could result in your application being discarded when many other more complete and readable resumes are on the reader's desk.

As a truly qualified candidate, you will be able to handle a variety of responsibilities related to your educational background and past experience. Even if you begin in a specialized area, you must be able to assume additional duties to be valuable to the employing organization. Few organizations want an applicant who will be content to remain at an entry-level position. Thus your objective may indicate, without appearing presumptuous or obvious, that you are looking for employment with opportunities for growth. For example, *Objective: Beginning accounting and auditing work with eventual managerial responsibilities.*

Even if the heading of your resume refers to your employment objective, you may include an employment objective section as long as you avoid repeating the objective verbatim. Such an arrangement emphasizes the objective.

INTRODUCTORY SUMMARY

The objective may be included in a section of the resume referred to as an *introductory summary, summary, overview,* or a similar term. The summary includes an abstract of overall capabilities. Such a summary is especially beneficial in a long resume, but it may be used in one of regular length.

An introductory summary of a resume serves the same function as the synopsis or executive summary of a report. The most important and relevant elements are given first, in a very much condensed form, followed by supporting details. As with a synopsis of a report, the reader knows immediately what the entire resume is about and the outstanding qualifications of the applicant. A resume long enough to require an introductory summary is more likely to be one of a person with considerable work experience, not a person with little experience who is about to finish college, although such a summary aids readability in any resume. The introductory summary may be used in addition to, and immediately following, the objective section. Often the two sections may be combined to make the resume more concise.

▶ EDUCATION

An important section of most resumes is entitled *Education, Professional Training and Education, Professional Education, Academic Experiences*, or some similar wording. Choose the most appropriate simple heading that best describes your educational experiences. The section on education often should come after the objective section or after the summary, if included. Place first the section you want to emphasize, which will most likely be either education or experience.

If you are a young graduate with little work experience, education is probably what you should emphasize most; it is your central selling point. If you have had extensive work experience, even if you are just now completing college, related work experience is likely to be as important or more important than your degree. After you have been out of school for a few years, work expe-

Young man studies in order to maintain a high grade point average, which will be useful in his job search.

rience is almost surely the major qualification for work in the same field, although education remains important. In any event, give sufficient attention to both education and experience to convince the reader of your qualifications.

Use care in the wording of the education section of the resume. Ordinarily, if you mean education, say *Education*. When you word headings, use the same simple, direct, straightforward, specific approach that is best for all business and professional communication.

You need not, and should not, work for a cute or clever approach. If you are qualified for the opening, say so in simple, concrete language. If you are not completely qualified, do not apply unless you can convince your reader with specific evidence that your other outstanding abilities compensate for your lack of education or experience in another area.

The content of the section on educational experience is discussed earlier in this chapter under "Analyzing Your Qualifications."

To repeat and emphasize: *Give specific, concrete details (which are of necessity incomplete), interpreted in the light of how your particular educational experiences have prepared you for the job for which you are applying.*

WORK EXPERIENCE

Your present or most recent experience is ordinarily the experience most relevant to your application. From the standpoint of a potential employer, what you are doing now is of far more concern than what you did five years ago. At times, however, a period of employment other than your present or most recent becomes the period you should emphasize. For example, if you worked for seven years in sales, decided to try teaching, then gave up teaching to apply for another sales job, you should stress your sales experience even though it is not the most recent. There are situations, however, in which the teaching experience could be the most important part of your overall experience and the major field to be emphasized. For example, if you are now applying for a job with a publisher that distributes high school textbooks, your high school teaching experience is likely to be more valuable than your previous experience in selling real estate.

Present your qualifications from the standpoint of how the employer will benefit from hiring you. To do so, emphasize your experiences that seem to be the most advantageous to the successful handling of the job. This orientation in a resume is another application of the you-approach.

When using the reverse chronological order, account for all periods of time since you began work. Or, if you have many years of experience, account only for the past ten years if you prefer. When you have had many short-time or part-time jobs, it is not essential to give exact dates of employment, with names and addresses of all employing organizations. You can summarize some work experience; for example, 1992–1993, part-time jobs at service stations, grocery stores, and drugstores while attending college full-time.

A functional resume groups items around four or more key job functions. This arrangement is beneficial to people with wide experience and to those with little experience (see Figure 10-4). A functional resume is particularly appropriate for a "job hopper" whose frequent changes would receive unwanted emphasis if presented in detail in the usual reverse chronological order. The functional resume emphasizes important and impressive capabilities and accomplishments, not years of experience. You can use it to avoid mention of dates, names, and places that might be considered undesirable but would be necessary when using the reverse chronological arrangement, in which you should account for all time periods.

A possible disadvantage of the functional resume is that it is unfamiliar to some employers; it is used far less often than reverse chronological resumes. Because of its difference, some readers may be annoyed not to find expected information in expected places. They may also believe that you have used the functional resume in order to deceive or to be evasive.

▶ OTHER APPROPRIATE SECTIONS OF A RESUME

You are free to choose headings to best describe your qualifications, accomplishments, and abilities that do not fit under headings of experience or education. Some examples of often-used sections are *Professional Affiliations*, *Publications*, *Activities*, *Community Work*, and *Additional Information*.

A section described by such a heading as *Personal Data*, which includes height, weight, marital status, and other such bits of information, is no longer included in most resumes, although a number of years ago such information was considered essential. Now this information is more likely to be omitted because personal characteristics are not relevant to successful performance in most jobs. Employers cannot legally hire applicants on the basis of information that has nothing to do with the ability to succeed in the particular job for which the applicant is being considered. If employers accept such information on resumes of applicants that they hire, they are afraid of being accused of discrimination based on appearance, personal life, or other irrelevant factors.

The question of whether to include age with your application is still debatable. Most people who work in placement or personnel departments agree that you are free to omit completely all such information if you choose to do so. On the other hand, there is nothing to prevent you from giving information that you feel will be to your advantage, although you should not imply that you feel you will be hired because of any personal factors.

Some items of personal data should almost always be omitted, including race, religion, and political party. Even these kinds of sensitive information, however, may belong on some resumes. For example, if you wish to be an assistant to a congresswoman who is a Democrat, you should mention your activities in the Democratic party. (If you worked for her election and don't mention that fact, you don't deserve the job.)

In some instances, experiences in church work, religious organizations on campus, or political organizations may be important to an unrelated job for which you are applying. Such work may show leadership ability and assumption of responsibility. If you have spent a great deal of time in these activities, perhaps you have few other outside interests to report. Use your own judgment whether to show these items in your employment application. Usually you should omit them. If you choose to include them, *make absolutely sure* that you do not intimate that you expect to be hired (for example) because you are a Methodist, because you worship at a temple, or because you are white or African American.

▶ REFERENCES

References are not always listed on a resume. In the references position, which is ordinarily the last one, you may include a statement such as "References will be furnished on request," or you may omit the statement entirely.

Whether or not to include specific references is another debatable question. If you are applying to only a few employers and you have been given permission to use as references people whose names will favorably impress the employers, then list these names. Some employers still expect references, or the mention of references, as an essential part of all resumes. *Do not list people as references until you have their permission to do so.*

When you are mailing a great many unsolicited applications, you are wise to omit the names of people who will recommend you. Offer to send further information and names of references later. Although potential employers are unlikely to contact the persons you name until after an employment interview, they could do so. You then run the risk of having the persons who have agreed to recommend you bothered unnecessarily by inquiries.

If you *do* include references, always state the individual's full name, business organization or occupation, address, and telephone number. Provide a copy of your resume to each person who has agreed to act as a reference. Some employers *do* prefer listed references. According to a 1987 research study, 71.2 percent prefer references on a resume.[14]

You may wish to prepare a separate sheet, to be sent with the resume itself, devoted only to references. This arrangement is preferable to a two-page resume unless you actually need a second page for material other than references. If this is the case, a separate sheet including references may also be sent with the two-page resume as well as with a one-page resume.

Preparing a separate sheet provides added flexibility. With some resumes you may wish to include it while omitting it from others.

MAJOR WEAKNESSES OF RESUMES

The most important weakness of resumes, however it occurs, is one that does not present the applicant in the most favorable way for the particular position sought. Although many factors prevent a resume from being completely effective, some of the more common weaknesses are listed below:

1 Believing that a resume must be no longer than one page. A resume must be concise, but keeping it to one page is not as important as presenting yourself in the most convincing way possible. For most young applicants with little experience, a one-page resume is likely to be sufficient.

2 Writing an unnecessarily long resume, regardless of years of experience.

3 Writing a resume that fills one page with only a few lines on the second page. Work for either a one-page or a two-page resume, but do not crowd.

4 Omitting positive, specific details about work experience and education. Job titles and length of experience are not enough.

5 Submitting an application (letter and resume) that is less than absolutely perfect in appearance.

6 Copying an example from a textbook or elsewhere. You are different in some or many ways from the person described in an example of a resume. Individualize your own resume to present your own particular qualifications.

7 Crowding information together so that it is hard to read.

8 Emphasizing (by choice of format, spacing, content, wording, other methods) unimportant information and omitting emphasis on your most valuable education, experience, or activities.

9 Leaving errors in spelling, capitalization, and word usage.

10 Including inappropriate information, such as race, religion, national origin, or unrelated personal details.

11 Using too many adjectives and adverbs. Use specific, forceful nouns and verbs.

12 Using the word *I*. Subjects can be correctly omitted from statements in a resume, as in *managed mail room, 1995–1996*, instead of *I managed the mail room from 1995 to 1996*. Such abbreviated wording, clear and concise, leaves more room to present your qualifications; in addition, it prevents too much emphasis on *I*—instead of on knowledge, abilities, and capabilities.

ILLUSTRATIONS OF RESUMES

Various types of resumes are shown in Figures 10-1 to 10-7. Letters to accompany these resumes are shown in Chapter 11, Figures 11-1 through 11-6. (No letter is shown to accompany Figure 10-7. See Chapter 11, Assignment 15, under "Think-It-Through Assignments and Working in Groups.")

JAMES LAWRENCE BUTLER

107 Bay Avenue, Seattle, WA 98504
Telephone: 206-000-0000

OBJECTIVE:

Heavy equipment sales representative, with an opportunity to progress to sales management or company management.

EDUCATION:

Bachelor of Business Administration degree, marketing and engineering technology, Washington State University, Pullman, Washington, May 1997.
Special emphasis, computer science and business management.
Grade point average, 3.03 on scale of 4.0.

WORK EXPERIENCE:

Inspector/Surveyor, Washington State Department of Transportation, Pasco, Washington, June–August 1996.
Supervised asphalt surfacing project. Trained employees.
Inspected contractors' projects. Kept precise records.
Managed five-man survey crew. Prepared written reports.

Inspector, Washington State Department of Transportation, Pasco, Washington, June–August 1995.
Inspected $230 million concrete paving project.
Performed concrete tests and analyses.
Ran computerized slope indicator on landslide zones.
Trained and supervised seven new employees.

Technician, Washington State Department of Transportation, Pasco, Washington, May–August 1994.
Performed general ledger work for project engineer.
Calculated estimates for upcoming construction season.
Dispatched asphalt to construction sites.
Surveyed highway at progressing points of operation.

Marketing Agent, Paramount Management Associates, Inc., Richland, Washington, February–August 1993.
Successfully implemented own marketing strategy for area.

OTHER INFORMATION:

Served four years in United States Air Force, 1989–1993.
Willing to relocate and travel.
Recommended by employers and professors. See enclosed sheet.

FIGURE 10-1
Resume of graduating senior with responsible summer employment and relevant degree (suitable for computer scanning)

Tonya Chauvin
510 New Haven Street
Raceland, LA 70394-2515
Tel. (504)000-0000

OBJECTIVE: Marketing internship position with regional health care provider.

SUMMARY: -Pursuing B.S. in marketing from Nicholls State University
-President of NSU American Marketing Association
-Experience in marketing research for a major corporation

EDUCATION: B.S. from Nicholls State University expected May 1998
GPA—3.329   Major—marketing

KEY COURSES: Services Marketing   Business Communication
Technical Writing   Human Resource Management
Computer Applications   Production Management

SKILLS: **Computer Skills**—Proficient typist and word processor, working knowledge of MS-DOS, Lotus 123 for business, dBASE IV, Microsoft Windows, MS Works, MS Money, spreadsheets, CD-ROM, PowerPoint presentation graphics software, and online applications.

Marketing Research—Performed a direct marketing project in coordination with the Nicholls chapter of the American Marketing Association for the company that produces Bell South's Yellow Pages. Conducted the surveys, compiled statistics, and generated in-depth analysis of the results for two separate jobs.

EXPERIENCE: **NSU Financial Aid Office**
June 1996–present
June 1994–February 1995
Part-time student worker—Perform clerical duties and review student files for accuracy and completeness.

Wal-Mart #761
June 1995–June 1996
Organized and maintained a department as an evening sales associate, publicized sales and prices within the store, and regulated inventory using hand-held computer terminals.

REFERENCES: Available upon request.

FIGURE 10-2
Student applicant for internship to local employer

Jamie Amedee
115 Oak Street
Labadieville, LA 70372
(504) 000-0000

Objective: To work as Produce Manager, Winn-Dixie

Education:
Nicholls State University,
Thibodaux, Louisiana 70310

- Candidate for Bachelor of Science degree
- Expected graduation date: December 1997
- Major: Marketing
- Cumulative GPA, 3.0/4.0. Major GPA, 4.0/4.0
- Personally funded 95 percent of college expenses

Key Courses:

Marketing   Business Communication
Business Law   Operations Management
Economics   Technical Writing

Work Experience: 1991–Present

- Winn-Dixie Supermarkets, Thibodaux, LA
- Position: Manager Trainee
- Trained and certified in these departments:

  Dairy/ Frozen Foods   Produce

  Grocery   Seafood

Honors and Awards:

- Three times selected Youth Manager at Winn-Dixie
- Awarded Winn-Dixie Retail Scholarship
- Dean's List—Fall 1992, Fall 1993, Fall 1994, Spring 1995, Fall 1996, Spring 1997
- National Dean's List—Spring 1995 and Spring 1996
- President's List—Fall 1994

FIGURE 10-3
Applicant for higher position in company where he is now employed as a youth manager. He is replying to a posted opening.

WALTER R. WILLIAMS

1982 Punahou Street, Honolulu, HI 96822   808-000-0000

Qualifications for a Career in Public Accounting

DEGREE:
Bachelor of Science in accounting, major in public accounting, minors in computer information systems and management, University of Hawaii, 1998.

COMPUTER SYSTEMS:
Systems Analysis and Design, Information Systems, Computer Program Languages, Decision Mathematics.

COMMUNICATION:
Business communication; fifteen hours of English and journalism; conducted regular meetings of the University of Hawaii Accounting Club; kept minutes of Computer Information Systems Association meetings; prepared various reports on financial conditions of seven companies for accounting courses.

BUSINESS:
Courses include Business Environment, Theory of the Firm, Business Law, Finance. Subscribe to *Business Week* and *The Wall Street Journal*.

MANAGEMENT AND LEADERSHIP:
Office Management; Behavioral Management; Personnel Management; Marketing Management;
Secretary of Computer Information Systems Association, one year;
Vice President of University of Hawaii Accounting Club, one year.

ABILITY TO WORK WITH PEOPLE:
Student tutor in accounting, one year;
Member of Society for Advancement of Management, two years;
Member of Accounting Club, three years;
Member of Computer Information Systems Association, two years;
Member of Tennis Club, four years;
Sold advertising space to businesses for Student Directory.

REFERENCES:
On request, references will be furnished from professors and businesspeople.

FIGURE 10-4

Functional resume of accounting major with little work experience and possibly a less-than-outstanding academic record

ABIGAIL C. DUPRE
8476 Rothschild, Manchester, NH 03106
Telephone: 603-000-0000

EMPLOYMENT OBJECTIVE

To sell commercial real estate with progressive company and to use education, ambition, and energy to increase company's sales.

SUMMARY OF QUALIFICATIONS

University education with strong major in real estate. Experience in real estate and sales experience in another field. Have lived in Manchester since childhood; many business acquaintances.

PROFESSIONAL EDUCATION

Completing Bachelor of Business Administration degree with major in real estate at the University of New Hampshire. Degree to be received in May 1998.
"A's" and "B's" in following real estate courses:

Real Estate Principles	Real Estate Appraisal
Real Estate Law	Housing Determinants
Real Estate Finance	Real Estate Finance
Commercial Developments	

Now enrolled in these courses:
   Internship for Real Estate
   Sales Management

Attended four seminars at Boston Board of Realtors.

WORK EXPERIENCE

Have worked part time in family firm, Dupre-Fisher Real Estate, Manchester, since sophomore year in high school. General clerical work, bookkeeping, correspondence, communication with clients and potential buyers. This company specializes in residential property.

Sales representative, summers, 1995 and 1996, Shopper's News, Nantucket, Massachusetts.

OTHER ACTIVITIES

Enjoy horseback riding, fishing, reading. Active in Neighborhood Association. Friends of the Library volunteer.

FIGURE 10-5
Resume of student whose central selling point is education, combined with experience in family business

ALLISON TUCKER GREEN
218 South Harwood, Anderson, IN 46001   317-000-0000

EMPLOYMENT OBJECTIVE: High school teacher of business subjects, Indianapolis area.

SUMMARY: Recent undergraduate and graduate degrees, Ball State University, Muncie, Indiana. Graduate assistant, two years, including office work and classroom teaching. Spent twenty-two years in various parts of world as Navy wife. One year's experience as secretary and bookkeeper. Twenty-five years' experience as household executive, mother, hostess, financial planner.

EDUCATION: *Master of Education* degree, Ball State University, August 1997, with a 3.5 grade-point average based on a 4-point scale. Graduate work included internship in teaching and a comprehensive thesis. Title of thesis: "Improving Instruction in Word Processing at the Secondary Level."

Bachelor of Business Administration degree, Ball State University, August 1995. Major in *accounting*, minor in *management information systems*. Six other upper division courses in *business management*. Grade point average of 3.68 in major.

WORK EXPERIENCE: *Library Assistant*, Ball State University, October 1997– present. General library duties. Now working at Circulation Desk.

Experience in various areas of unpaid employment while husband served as Naval officer, 1971–1991. More than half the time was spent outside the United States. These experiences abroad will be beneficial in teaching because numerous students now in high school will work outside the United States or with people from other countries.

Secretary-bookkeeper, Best Insurance Agency, Norfolk, Virginia, 1970–1971.

OTHER INTERESTS: Church and community responsibilities; reading; creative writing; music.

REFERENCES: Eight persons who have offered to provide recommendations are listed on the attached sheet, with their positions, addresses, and telephone numbers. This list includes undergraduate and graduate professors, a member of the City Council, two librarians, and a Navy captain.

FIGURE 10-6
Resume of a woman who has been away from job market because of husband's career. She could have chosen functional arrangement.

RHONDA A. BLAKE
1533 Riverdale Road, Germantown, TN 38138 (901) 000-0000

OBJECTIVE: Publishing, public relations, writing, editing.

EDUCATION

Will graduate Magna Cum Laude, University of Memphis, in December 1998, with B.A. and honors in English.

Areas of concentration include technical/professional writing and American literature.

EXPERIENCES AND ABILITIES

Communication: Thirty upper-division semester hours of technical writing, business communications, and literature. Received A's on all research projects, essays, and oral presentations in upper division courses.

Leadership: Planned and supervised projects for handicapped children as volunteer art instructor for Very Special Arts Fair. Frequently appointed as Load/Off-load Captain at Federal Express Corporation. Duties included motivating fellow team members to meet time parameters and assisting in the proper loading and positioning of freight on airplanes. (Worked 20 hours a week, August 1996 through October 1997.)

Graphic Design: Five years formal art training. Chosen Outstanding Brooks Scholar by Memphis Brooks Museum of Art (1995). Attended Governor's School for the Arts (summer 1994). Designed letterhead, business cards and newsletters at Franklin's Printing and Office Supplies (Germantown, TN, 1996).

Computer Systems: Experienced with Windows 95, Word for Windows 7.0, WordPerfect 7.0, and Lotus software.

SCHOLASTIC HONORS AND ACTIVITIES

Phi Kappa Phi National Honor Society
Sigma Tau Delta National English Honor Society
Golden Key National Honor Society
Dean's List, junior and senior years, University of Memphis
British Studies Scholarship—studied five weeks in Great Britain, July–August 1994

FIGURE 10-7

Resume of outstanding student with little work experience. Arranged in combination form; notice that "Experiences and Abilities" replaces usual position of "Work Experience." (No accompanying letter shown in Chapter 11. See Assignment 15, Chapter 11 under "Think-It-Through Assignment and Working in Groups.")

SUMMARY

When looking for employees, most organizations consider these factors: job-related experience, job-related education, dependability, the ability to cooperate with others, and a willingness to work.

When looking for employment, you can use an unsolicited application letter and resume to advantage. This approach shows that you have a special interest in a particular organization and that you have the initiative and ambition to research employing organizations in order to make an intelligent effort to place yourself. Another advantage is that you are more likely to find the kind of work for which you are best suited and that offers the opportunity you are seeking.

In order to plan an effective search for employment, analyze your qualifications and the employment market. After your analyses are completed, plan and write the letter and resume to show how your qualifications meet the needs of the employer.

The application letter is a kind of sales message. The accompanying resume is a report on yourself and is also a form of sales presentation. Like other sales messages, these materials are more effective when they are built around a central selling theme.

For most young college students, education is the most appropriate central selling point. Other central selling themes are work experience and, in special circumstances, extracurricular activities, hobbies, or special interests. Like other business messages, the two-part application should make the most effective use of the you-attitude and the positive approach.

Innovations in technology have changed the approach to job hunting. Openings are posted on the WWW (World Wide Web) and applicants may post their resumes on Web sites. Such resumes, as well as traditional printed ones, can be scanned by a computer using Resumix or a similar service. Special care must be taken when writing resumes that are likely to be scanned.

TEST YOURSELF
chapter content

1   What is meant by a central selling point as it is applied to resumes?
2   Name one advantage of using a central selling point in preparing a resume.
3   One of two factors is usually the central selling point. What are the two?
4   What should be your central selling point? Why?
5   What are two steps that you should take before preparing a resume?
6   What is meant by the two-part application?
7   What is meant by the term *solicited application*?
8   What is an advantage of submitting an unsolicited application?
9   Name two sources that are useful for obtaining information about prospective employers.
10   What is an advantage of including an "objective" section at the beginning of a resume? What is a possible disadvantage?
11   What is the purpose of the introductory summary?
12   What is an advantage of a functional resume? What is a possible disadvantage?
13   What is an advantage of a resume arranged in the reverse chronological order? What is a possible disadvantage?
14   Name one kind of personal information that should ordinarily be omitted from a resume.

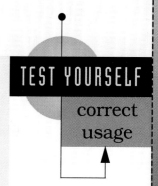

(Related to material in Chapter 10 and principles of correct usage.) Make any other necessary changes. Some of the following items should be omitted. Improve the following passages from resumes.

1 Designed window displays, wrote advertising copy, and advertising copy was written by me and my assistant.

2 Completed courses in English, Accounting, and History.

3 Starting in high school, you will note that I worked in several responsible jobs.

4 One years sales experience in a womens' clothing store.

5 Scholarship recipient.

6 Responsible to three (counselors, councilors).

7 (Principle, Principal) responsibilities were financial ones.

8 Planned (capital, capitol) expenditures.

9 Earned (90 percent, ninety percent, 90%) of college costs.

10 Sold advertising space to business's.

11 Member of Methodist church.

12 Majored in phys ed, Eng., and minored in math.

EVALUATION SHEET: EMPLOYMENT RESUMES

___ Yes ___ No **1** Is the resume presented throughout from the reader's standpoint?

___ Yes ___ No **2** Is the resume built around a central selling point?

___ Yes ___ No **3** Is the factor considered to be the central selling point (usually education or experience) placed before less important information?

___ Yes ___ No **4** Is more space given to the central selling point than to less important factors?

___ Yes ___ No **5** Is the resume worded throughout in phrases with no first- or second-person pronouns?

___ Yes ___ No **6** Is sufficient emphasis given throughout to favorable details, with less favorable details subordinated or omitted?

___ Yes ___ No **7** Is the resume completely factual and truthful?

___ Yes ___ No **8** If arranged in the reverse chronological format, are both education and experience presented in the reverse chronological order?

___ Yes ___ No **9** Is the resume absolutely perfect in appearance?

___ Yes ___ No **10** Is the resume absolutely perfect in spelling, word usage, and all other elements of grammatical correctness?

___ Yes ___ No **11** Are enough positive details given about both education and experience to present yourself in a favorable way?

___ Yes ___ No **12** Does the heading include your name, address, and telephone number?

___ Yes ___ No **13** Does the resume contain an appropriately worded employment objective?

CASES

1 Visit the placement office at your school. Research the following questions and write a memorandum report, addressed to your instructor, detailing your findings.
   a. Does the placement office sponsor any type of job fair that students may attend?
   b. How and where are job openings publicized?
   c. What is the best way to find out about campus interviews?
   d. What type of information is available about companies?
   e. What type of information is available for anyone wanting assistance with writing application letters or resumes?
   f. What type of information is available for anyone wanting assistance with preparing for interviews?
   g. What procedures should be followed to register your credentials with the placement office?
   h. What other services are provided?

2 Make a list of the courses in your studies in which you have
   a. participated in team projects that resulted in a project submitted for a team grade
   b. served as team leader for a group project
   c. worked through group conflicts
   d. produced written assignments in the form of memos, research summaries, formal and informal reports, and the like
   e. made formal oral presentations
   f. made formal oral presentations that included visual aids

   How could you bring this type of information into your interview answers? What would be the benefit of doing so?

3 Prepare a self-analysis similar to that discussed in Chapter 10. Include your education, experience, hobbies, personal characteristics, likes and dislikes, ambitions, and anything else that will affect your success in obtaining employment.

   Make this study complete. Ordinarily it will be more detailed than your resume, but by making a thorough self-analysis you will be better able to decide which items to include and which to emphasize. This analysis is for your use only.

4 Make a list of the kinds of employment for which you are qualified and in which you are interested, based on your self-study. Approach this study from one of two ways:
   a. Assume that you are near graduation and that you are looking for full-time career employment. This assumption is the more valuable one if you expect to graduate within a year or two or if you now have in mind definite career objectives.
   b. Prepare the list of various kinds of work in relation to part-time or summer jobs. Include only the kinds of work that really interest you and that offer opportunities for career employment after graduation.

5 Make a study of employing organizations that seem to offer the opportunities you are seeking. Use the sources described in Chapter 10 and any other useful ones. Write a memorandum to your instructor about how you proceeded in the investigation. List the three organizations toward which you plan to direct your efforts and the reasons for these choices. Give your first choice, with reasons.

6 Prepare a resume from the detailed studies you have made so far. You are to send the letter and a resume to each of the three organizations you have chosen. Depending on the kinds of organizations to which you are submitting your resume, you may be able to use copies of one resume for the three companies.

THINK-IT-THROUGH ASSIGNMENT AND WORKING IN GROUPS

7 Using the resume you prepared in answer to Case 6, meet with two to four other students. Ask for suggestions for your own resume and offer suggestions for the resumes of the other students. Does each resume present the individual effectively? Use the employment resume evaluation sheet to assist you in your evaluations.

8 Obtain a copy of a resume from a friend. Remove the name from the resume prior to meeting in small groups as directed by your instructor. Based on the materials presented in Chapter 10, critique each resume. Refer to the employment resume evaluation sheet at the end of Chapter 10. Be certain to identify strengths as well as any sections that could be improved.

ENDNOTES

1 Jim Gerland and Mark Winer, "Looking for a Job? Let Your Fingers Do the Walking," *The Buffalo News*, August 13, 1996, CLICK, 7E.

2 Ibid.

3 Lakhinder J. S. Vohra, "Online Recruiting Fills Positions," *Denver Business Journal*, August 9, 1996, 27A.

4 Ibid.

5 "Job Seekers Automatically Matched with Openings and Notified by E-Mail Using New Internet Web Site," *PR Newswire*, August 13, 1996.

6 "New Web Site Lists 125,000 Openings," *PR Newswire*, September 16, 1996.

7 "IntelliMatch's Precision Matching Technology," *Business Wire*, September 23, 1996.

8 Gannett News Service, *Sacramento Bee*, September 8, 1996, E1.

9 Gannett News Service.

10 Rebecca Rolwing, "Job Seekers Find Opportunities Online," *Denver Business Journal*, August 9, 1996, 28A.

11 James S. Goldman, "Who Killed Ann Black? Resumix Did—" *The Business Journal*, December 23, 1991, 1.

12 Sherwood Ross, "Does Your Resume Speak Computer?" *The Commercial Appeal [Memphis]*, October 8, 1995.

13 Helen Wick-Martin, as quoted by Lee Gomes, "Casting an Eye on Resumes," *Pittsburgh Post-Gazette*, July 23, 1995, C6.

14 Glynna Morse, "A Study of the Preferences of Executives for the Style, Format, and Content of Resumes." *1987 Proceedings, International Conference*, Association for Business Communication, 100.

Completing the Job-Finding Process

CHAPTER

11

OBJECTIVES

Chapter Eleven will help you:

1   Prepare an application letter to accompany a resume.

2   Write a letter of application that serves as an effective sales letter.

3   Plan and prepare for employment interviews.

4   Write appropriate thank-you letters and other letters about employment.

After you have analyzed your qualifications and the job market and have completed your resume, you are ready to write the *application letter*, which is also referred to as a *cover letter*. Although the term seems to be increasing in use, the word *cover* is incomplete from the standpoint that the letter does far more than "cover" the resume; it is an important part of the application package and may be even more important than the resume itself.

Max Messer, chairman and CEO of Robert Half International (a $630 million placement firm), makes this statement:

> The cover letter will exclude you if it isn't done correctly. Also, it is a chance to work in a sentence or two to catch the reader's attention, not by being cute, but by showing you have an interest in the company's business.
>
> A properly written cover letter and resume can change your life. It is worth some attention. What works is an extremely well-written and well-tailored cover letter. Spend a little time doing homework on your target. The resume, if drafted properly, will list accomplishments. Stay away from the gimmicks.[1]

This chapter includes discussion about application letters, the *employment interview*, and other letters about employment. Illustrations of application letters are designed to accompany six of the seven resumes shown in Chapter 10. Also illustrated are a thank-you letter, a follow-up letter, a letter of acceptance, a letter of refusal, and a letter of resignation.

THE LETTER OF APPLICATION

Prepare the letter of application after you have prepared the resume, but place it in the first-place position in the application package. Do not staple or clip the letter to the resume. Both the letter and the resume should contain your telephone number and complete address.

The application letter should never be longer than one page, even if you have chosen to write a longer resume. Like all other letters, it should be attractively arranged on the page, easy to read, with ample white space. Use the same kind of stationery used for the resume: bond paper, 20-pound weight, some cotton content. (See Appendix A.)

According to L. M. Sixel:

> Most experts advise against being cute in a cover letter. It doesn't usually work.... But for every rule, there's an exception. Jon Hein knew the one-page, anti-cute rule but figured that the only way to get a big-time television producer to notice him was to write a clever cover letter. The recent University of Michigan graduate was looking for a screenwriting job when he penned what has become a famous cover letter:
>
> "A million to one. The Hollywood Reporter. Premier magazine. My skeptical parents. They all agree on my chances of bringing a comedy to television." Hein then went on to list his accomplishments increasing his odds for success. He finally got down to 1,000 to 1. "Not bad, considering where I started, but a brief phone conversation with you would certainly help my numbers." Hein said he mailed the flippant two-page letter to 50 top producers.... To his surprise, 12 producers called, including six on one day, to say they wanted to talk and see more of Hein's writing.[2]

Notice that in the preceding example the applicant wanted a job as a comedy writer. Business students should not attempt such an approach for employment relevant to their majors.

The letter should be looked upon as a soft-sell sales letter; you are selling yourself. The purpose of the letter is to convince your reader to grant you an interview. As when selling a product or service, you convince by showing the reader how he or she, or the employing organization, is likely to benefit by employing you. No matter how much you need or want the job, *emphasize reader benefit, not your own*. This emphasis must be subtle, however, or it will seem insincere.

Achieving the you-approach, at least as far as the use or the omission of the word *I* is concerned, is more difficult in application letters than in letters on other subjects. Because the letter is of necessity about yourself, you must use *I* to refer to yourself; any other method would be unnatural and overly formal. As recommended and illustrated in Chapter 10, you can prevent the overuse of *I* on resumes by writing in sentence fragments, omitting the subject of the sentence. (This resume arrangement has additional advantages: saving room on the sheet and emphasizing strong verbs by placing them first in each item.) Unlike the resume, the application letter, like all other letters, is written in complete sentences. A natural inclination is to make *I* the subject of many sentences, in addition to numerous uses within the sentence. You are likely to find that on the first draft of your application letter your page is covered with numerous and obvious *I*'s.

As discussed in Chapter 6, "Building Goodwill through Communication," *the omission of the pronoun* I *does not in itself result in the you-approach, and the use of* I *does not in itself result in the I-approach;* the key is what is said and the use of other words with their varying connotations. Your letter could include numerous *I*'s and still stress reader benefit, but it is not likely to do so. If you overuse *I*, you are unlikely to have achieved the you-approach by other methods. Even if you have, your letter does not give the impression of doing so because of numerous *I*'s scattered throughout your letter.

Remember (from Chapter 5) that you emphasize what you put first—in a letter, paragraph, or sentence. The first words of paragraphs are especially emphatic; avoid starting all or several paragraphs with *I*. But you need not attempt to avoid all I-beginnings in sentences or paragraphs. Such a rule would result in awkward, unnatural, and nonspecific sentences.

You can decrease the number of *I*'s by reconstructing sentences in various ways and avoiding unnecessary repetition. In addition to decreasing the actual number, try to place *I*'s in less emphatic places than at the beginning of sentences and paragraphs. Nevertheless, do not work so hard to eliminate the word that your writing seems forced or unnatural.

SUMMARY OF GUIDELINES FOR WRITING AN APPLICATION LETTER

As you plan your letter of application to accompany a resume, keep in mind the following guides:

1. Use the positive approach. Emphasize strengths and subordinate weaknesses, but do not misrepresent.

2. Use the you-attitude in that you stress benefits for the reader. Do not use a "hard-sell" method, but state your work experience and educational background in specific and positive terms, especially as they relate to the work for which you are applying.

3. Show that you are definitely interested in the position and the employing company, but don't sound as if this is your last chance.

4. Show that you know something about the company to which you are applying, but be concise.

5. Do NOT copy a letter written by some other person, or one from this book or any other book. This warning applies to all letters and written material of any kind. Even with changed details and paraphrasing, a letter written by or for another applicant is likely to sound stilted and unnatural in your own application. (In addition, such use is unethical.) No one else can express your ideas and your personality as well as you

can. Another consideration is that some personnel managers (as well as teachers) remember the exact book in which the letter originally appeared.

6   Use the words *I*, *me*, and *my* as natural and necessary, but do not use them to excess. Avoid beginning several sentences with *I*.

7   Don't ask for sympathy. This is not the you-approach or the positive approach. You will not be hired because your baby needs diapers but because you can do a good job and earn more for the employer than you are paid. (You must earn more, after training, or you are not a profitable investment.) If a job should be filled because of sympathy, the applicant begins work at a disadvantage, not on a businesslike basis.

8   Don't be unduly humble, and don't apologize for taking the reader's time. Remember that the employer is not doing you a favor by hiring you. If you are qualified and a hard worker, the employing organization will benefit from the employment.

9   Don't complain about past or present employers. Even if you have real grievances, discussing these almost always sounds as if you are to blame. If you find it necessary to explain why you are leaving and this explanation is because of a real dissatisfaction that must be stated, do not mention it in the letter or resume. Save this discussion for the interview.

10   Don't boast or sound aggressive or presumptuous—although it is just as important not to sound unsure of your abilities. A straightforward businesslike approach will let you take the middle road between egotism and a doubtful, overly humble tone. Give concrete examples to prove your abilities; do not merely state that you have these abilities.

11   Don't lecture or waste time stating the obvious.

12   Don't mention salary, fringe benefits, or working conditions in the application. To do so will emphasize the *I-approach*, not the *you-approach*. Such information will be given to you during the interview. If it should not be, ask at that time for information you must have before making a decision. Even better, wait to discuss salary after you have been offered the job or when you feel sure that you are being favorably considered.

13   Don't try to be clever or cute, at least for most jobs. If you are being considered as an advertising copywriter or for similar work, your application letter and resume may be in a more original or unconventional form. Whatever the position, you do have the problem of making your letter stand out from all the others, but you could work so hard for attention that you receive the wrong kind, even to the extent of being eliminated from consideration.

14   Work for original phrasing and eliminate trite, unnecessary, stereotyped wording.

15 Word the first paragraph so that the reader clearly understands that you are applying for a particular job or a particular kind of job.

16 Include in the last paragraph a specific request for an interview. This request is an *action close* discussed in previous chapters: State the action specifically, make action easy, and, if appropriate, motivate prompt action. (Motivating prompt action is usually inappropriate in cover letters; do not be pushy or demanding.) Make action easy by giving your telephone number. Also include your fax number and e-mail address if you have them and if you wish to be contacted by one of these methods.

17 Sign your letter, using a good pen with black ink.

Addressing the Application

Address the letter to an individual, not to an organization. Use a conventional letter arrangement that includes an inside address and a salutation.

Try to find the name of the person who is likely to interview you and address your letter to this person. (You may have been told in an advertisement or position announcement the person to address. If this is the case, follow the instructions exactly.)

Make sure you know the addressee's position in the organization, gender, and, if possible, how the person prefers to be addressed—for example, *Dr.*, *Mrs.*, *Ms.*, *Mr.*, *Professor*.

Be absolutely sure that you spell the addressee's name correctly.

Always use a courtesy title in BOTH the inside address and the salutation. This advice applies to all business letters except the letter styles (simplified, functional) that omit completely the salutation and the complimentary close. These styles should not be used in application letters unless you find it is impossible to obtain an individual's name.

When addressing a letter to a box number, as may be requested in advertisements, use a letter style that omits the salutation and the complimentary close. When writing to a box number, you have no appropriate word to use in a salutation; thus you should omit it. **DO NOT USE** *Gentlemen*, *Dear Sirs*, or *To Whom It May Concern*.

Examples of Letters of Application

Application letters shown in Figures 11-1 through 11-6 accompany resumes shown in Figures 10-1 through 10-6. Figure 10-7 does not have an accompanying letter in Chapter 11 but will be used for discussion of how a letter of application should be composed.

107 Bay Avenue
Seattle, WA 98504
June 15, 1997

Mr. H. B. McDowell, President
Northwest Heavy Equipment Company
1880 SW Broadway
Portland, OR 97201

Dear Mr. McDowell:

May I work for you and increase your heavy equipment sales in the state of Washington?

Mrs. Anita Klein, who works for the Washington State Department of Transportation, said that you will soon have a sales representative to retire. I am acquainted with your representative, Mr. Goodman. I met him several times during the summers of 1995 and 1996 while working on Washington highways. He can tell you of my successful work during those summers, often spending 70 or more hours a week on the job.

I observed much of your equipment in operation during these summers. It is dependable and reasonably priced. Because you sell quality products and operate your organization honestly and efficiently, I want to become a part of your organization.

My college education at Washington State University has prepared me in two areas that should increase my success as a sales representative: marketing and engineering technology. In addition, I worked as a marketing agent for six months before I entered college, preceded by four years in the United States Air Force. This combined experience has proved to be far more beneficial than if I had entered college directly after high school.

Other details of my experience and education are given in the enclosed resume. May I talk with you at your convenience? I can be reached at 206-000-0000.

Sincerely,

James Lawrence Butler

James Lawrence Butler

Enclosure: Resume

FIGURE 11-1

Letter to accompany resume shown in Figure 10-1

510 New Haven Street
Raceland, LA 70394-2515
July 15, 1997

Ms. Kelly Byrd
Director of Marketing
Thibodaux Regional Medical Center
Thibodaux, LA 70301

Dear Ms. Byrd:

Please consider my application for the marketing internship position that was publicized through the College of Business Administration at Nicholls State University. I believe that my education, experience, and career interests qualify me for this position.

Upon receiving a bachelor's degree in marketing next spring, I would like to work in the health care field. Course work at Nicholls has included classes in management, marketing, computer applications, and technical writing that I feel will be extremely useful in my career. One class, in particular, should prove to be valuable to my pursuit of a position in the health care industry. In the Spring 1997 semester I completed a services marketing course which concentrated on managing service-providing businesses. The course work included writing case studies and analyzing organizations to identify problems and opportunities that may arise.

As the President of the NSU chapter of the American Marketing Association, I am responsible for conducting meetings, for creating and distributing information on the group's current activities, and for communicating with other campus organizations. Other duties include publishing the group's periodic newsletter and publicizing upcoming events. This has given me experience in public relations and promotion, which should be useful in a health care marketing position.

My resume is enclosed for your consideration. The education and experience that I possess make me an ideal candidate for this position. Because of my skills and abilities, I feel that I would be an asset to your company, especially in light of the recent marketing campaign the hospital has launched to publicize its improved facilities. Please call me at your earliest convenience to set up an interview to further discuss my qualifications. I can be contacted at (504)000-0000 any evening after 5 p.m.

Sincerely,

Tonya Chauvin

Tonya Chauvin

Enc.: resume

FIGURE 11-2

Letter to accompany resume shown in Figure 10-2

115 Oak Street
Labadieville, LA 70372
July 15, 1997

Mr. Ronnie Bowers
Human Resources Supervisor
Winn-Dixie Louisiana Inc.
600 Edwards Avenue
New Orleans, LA 70123

Dear Mr. Bowers:

Currently, I am employed by Winn-Dixie Supermarkets (Location 1556) in Thibodaux, Louisiana, as a manager trainee. For the past six years, it has been an enjoyable experience to be employed by such a prestigious supermarket chain. In response to the job vacancy posted in our break room, I am pursuing the Produce Manager's position that will be available in our store starting January 1, 1998.

In April 1993, I applied for and received a Winn-Dixie Retail Scholarship, a scholarship designated for those associates who are planning a career with Winn-Dixie after graduation. During the past four years, I have been actively participating in a management training program and am now trained and certified in various departments, including produce. Receiving produce training has enabled me to become familiar with all aspects of managing the department, including ordering and inventory procedures performed by a Produce Manager.

In addition, I will receive a Bachelor of Science degree with a major in marketing from Nicholls State University during the upcoming Fall semester. While at Nicholls, my studies have concentrated on the management and retail aspects of marketing. Maintaining a 3.0 grade point average while working an average of 30 hours per week during semesters displays the hard work ethic and determination set forth when achieving goals.

Please contact me to arrange for an interview at your convenience. Because of my work experience and educational background, I am certain that I can efficiently accomplish all tasks related to managing the produce department. I can be reached at the address shown above or by telephone at 504-000-0000.

Sincerely,

Jamie Amedee

Jamie Amedee

Enclosure: Resume

FIGURE 11-3
Letter to accompany resume shown in Figure 10-3

1982 Punahou Street
Honolulu, HI 96822
June 1, 1998

Mr. John G. Springer, Partner
Pannell Kerr Forster, CPAs
1714 Makaha Towers
Honolulu, HI 96816

Dear Mr. Springer:

A comprehensive educational program in accounting at the University of Hawaii, leading to a Bachelor of Science in Accounting degree, is an important qualification for beginning work with your firm. In addition, I offer competence, dedication, and ambition.

For the sake of my future employer and for my own benefit, I wish to begin and remain with a progressive accounting firm and grow professionally. I realize that years of hard work and outstanding ability are necessary in order to reach the level of partner. I have the necessary ability, stamina, and determination, as shown by my leadership and management positions at the University and as will be reported by the professional people who have offered to provide references.

Please write me at the address shown above or telephone 808-000-0000 to arrange an interview. I will be glad to come at a time convenient for you.

Sincerely,

Walter R. Williams

Walter R. Williams

Enclosure: Resume

FIGURE 11-4
Letter to accompany resume shown in Figure 10-4

8476 Rothschild
Manchester, NH 03106
December 10, 1997

Ms. Elaine Schmitz
Vice President, Real Estate Sales
Schmitz Enterprises
5118 Park Avenue
Manchester, NH 03107

Dear Ms. Schmitz:

Because of a college major in real estate and work experience in a real estate office, I can do a good job for Schmitz Enterprises as a sales representative.

My entire college career has been aimed toward a career in commercial real estate. My years of part-time work in my family's firm, Dupre-Fisher Real Estate, have prepared me for work with your organization. I wish to sell commercial and investment property, not residential. In addition, I plan to leave Dupre-Fisher to prove that I can succeed on my own merits, not because my father is president of the firm.

I have thoroughly researched your organization. You are rebuilding our city and county. Yours is the kind of organization I am seeking, for the benefit of my employer as well as myself.

The enclosed resume provides further information about my abilities, background, and interests. Please write me at the address shown above or telephone me at 603-000-0000.

Sincerely,

Abigail C. Dupre

Abigail C. Dupre

Enclosure: Resume

FIGURE 11-5
Letter to accompany resume shown in Figure 10-5

218 South Harwood
Anderson, IN 46001
February 10, 1998

Dr. Emma Chang
Director of Personnel
Indianapolis Public Schools
79 East Washington Street
Indianapolis, IN 46024

Dear Dr. Chang:

As a high school teacher in Indianapolis, I can offer maturity, ability to work harmoniously with all age groups, energy, and qualifying degrees.

As shown on the enclosed resume and transcript of undergraduate and graduate work, I am prepared to teach most business courses taught in Indianapolis high schools. My particular areas of specialization are accounting and management information systems. My teaching internship consisted of classes in personal finance, accounting, and word processing.

The people listed as references on the attached sheet will speak highly of my ability and dedication. They will also tell you that I am dependable, energetic, and sincerely interested in entering and remaining in the teaching profession.

I have reared five children, seeing them through school from kindergarten to college. Now it is my turn to teach the children of other people.

My experience elsewhere than in the classroom has prepared me for success, I believe, more than a comparable time spent in teaching would have done. I now bring the enthusiasm of a young beginner and the knowledge and maturity gained from travel and various life experiences, in addition to recent undergraduate and graduate degrees. I have nothing to unlearn.

Please write or telephone me at 317-000-0000. I will come for an interview at your convenience.

Sincerely,

Alison Tucker Green

Alison Tucker Green

Enclosures: resume, transcript, and list of references

FIGURE 11-6
Letter to accompany resume shown in Figure 10-6

Only under unusual circumstances is only one person interviewed for a single opening. This necessary and desirable competition requires that the successful applicant continue the sales presentation throughout the interview, presenting superior qualifications and potential for services and development.

THE EMPLOYMENT INTERVIEW

After your resume and application letter accomplish their purpose, you will be asked to come for an interview. As you no doubt realize, a successful interview is crucial to obtaining the employment you wish.

PLANNING AND PREPARING: SELF-ANALYSIS

You have spent much of your life preparing to interview for employment in which you are interested and for which you are qualified, although you may not have been consciously making this preparation. Your educational background, your avocations, your work experience—all these have made you ready for the work for which you are now applying, as well as for a favorable presentation of your qualifications during the interview.

If you have made your detailed self-analysis (as discussed in Chapter 10) and have studied the particular organization to which you are applying, as well as related organizations, you have accomplished a major portion of your preparation for a successful interview. You cannot completely prepare for all aspects of the interview. As in all other communication situations, the outcome will be affected by the personalities of both the applicant and the interviewer and by the circumstances of the environment. If you are truly qualified for the position, however, and if you have learned to communicate effectively in other interpersonal encounters, you are likely to be successful in the employment interview.

Review your self-analysis and a copy of the letter of application and the resume before you go for the interview. Make sure that the details are firmly in your mind. Giving conflicting information will cast doubt either on your integrity or on your memory.

Take with you to the interview two copies of your resume, even if you have previously submitted one to the employing organization. The interviewer is not certain to have a copy, although he or she should have recently reviewed both your letter and resume. In some cases you will go for an interview with organizations to which you have not submitted a resume, especially when the interview has been arranged through college placement offices. For such interviews, bringing along two copies of the resume can save a great deal of time that would otherwise be spent in giving information that can be concisely stated in a well-organized resume. Also take with you a list of references if such a list was not included in your resume.

This applicant is appropriately dressed for an employment interview.

Review the research that led you to apply to the organization. Your knowledge of the organization, as well as your interest in it, can favorably impress the person or persons with whom you talk. This knowledge will be even more beneficial in that it adds to your self-confidence and enables you to ask necessary and intelligent questions.

Add to your self-analysis, if you have not already done so, an examination of what you really want from employment. Remember that not only are you being considered as an employee, you are interviewing a representative of an employing organization to determine whether or not you want the job. (Be extremely careful how you handle this situation, but all experienced interviewers realize that it exists.) If you have no real interest in the work you would be doing or see no opportunity for growth, consider carefully the position, if one is offered, before you make a final decision. (On the other hand, if your lack of enthusiasm shows, you probably won't be offered the job.)

Before Lisa even reached the interviewer's office, she lost her chance for the job. She parked her car in the company lot and arrived at the receptionist's desk on time. When Lisa met the interviewer, she tried some pleasant small talk. "As I parked my car, I noticed the new building section you are putting up. I guess business is going well," Lisa said. The interviewer looked at her. "Don't you know about our product expansion?" asked the interviewer. "No, said Lisa. "Should I?" . . .

The new addition to the building reflected recent major increases in the company's product line. Anyone who did any preliminary research about the company would have learned about the product expansion. As the interviewer saw it, if Lisa didn't bother to research the company, Lisa couldn't be that interested in working there. In turn, the company wasn't interested in Lisa.

Shirley Sloan Fader, "The Big Interview: Start Here," *Working Woman*, August 1984, 49.

Most jobs, however, are better than no job at all, especially if you could use a little money. Having a job also facilitates finding another one, provided you have stayed with the organization long enough to gain experience and to build a favorable reputation.

Working for the same company or even doing the same job for 20 years or more is not likely to happen, although such was the expectation of young applicants a generation or so ago. A large percentage of the jobs we know today will not exist 30 years from now. Nevertheless, choose your beginning job with care. In some way or another, it will affect your entire career.

Speaking of skills and abilities of college graduates, a young man who had been hired by the personnel department of a large supermarket chain reported to work at one of the stores. The manager greeted him with a warm handshake and a smile, handed him a broom and said: "Your first job will be to sweep out the store."

"But," the young man said, "I'm a college graduate."

"Oh, I'm sorry," the manager said. "I didn't know that. Here, give me the broom, and I'll show you how."

Richard L. Weaver II, "Motivating the Motivators," *Executive Speeches*, August–September 1996, 35.

▶ **PLANNING AND PREPARING: CLOTHING AND OVERALL APPEARANCE**

Care with your appearance shows that you have a sincere interest in both the job and the organization; it implies that you will fit in with other employees and project a professional impression that will benefit your organization as well as yourself.

First impressions are extremely important. Substantial judgments are made during the first few minutes of an interview, which is likely to last only 30 minutes. Your positive professional image is enhanced not only through color, style, and quality of your attire, but how you feel in a particular suit or dress. Some clothes make us feel good about ourselves; others do not. Thus, wearing garments you have never worn before is not always a good idea. Your dress or suit should be comfortable; you may be wearing it all day if you are fortunate enough to be asked to other interviews after the first. (One young man went to an interview wearing a new suit; the tag still attached to his coat sleeve was a dead giveaway.)

Plan what you will wear several days before the interview, and try everything on, including shoes and accessories. Have your complete outfit ready to wear the evening before, if not earlier. The morning of the interview is no time to realize that you forgot to take your suit to the cleaners.

Susan Phinney, of the *Seattle Post-Intelligencer*, makes these remarks about dressing for the interview:

> The BA, MBA, 3.96 GPA, gleaming hair, and fancy watch don't count for much if your shirt's wrinkled. . . . A brightly colored suit can land an accounting major a job in Siberia, and an applicant with a nose ring needs an extremely laid back company. Apparel gets scrutinized. A white shirt without a white T-shirt beneath is a no-no. So are shirts that have an "I laundered it myself" look. Skirts ending in the thigh zone, strappy shoes, and big hair also don't work. . . . Employers don't like scruffy shoes, wild masses of hair, excessive fragrance on either sex, gum chewing, or smoking. Students are even told not to smoke in a car en route to an interview so that their clothing won't smell.[3]

Good clothing is not inexpensive, but you have already invested much time and money in your education and other preparation for career employment. Invest a bit more in suitable attire that will be good for months or years on the job. Even if you know that more casual clothing will be acceptable once you are hired, at least on a "casual Friday," do not dress casually for the interview.

Women applicants should prefer a two-piece suit, with the jacket matching the skirt. A conservative dress, dress with jacket, or coordinated jacket and skirt are also appropriate. The skirt should be no shorter than just above the knees; neither should it be too long for the prevailing style at the time. Although a suit should look businesslike, a woman's appearance need not be severe and

An appropriately dressed applicant will make a favorable
first impression.

masculine. An appropriate blouse can soften the suit and still retain a conservative image. Jewelry and makeup should be inconspicuous. Wear closed toe
shoes; do not wear extremely high heels. Do not wear low-cut necklines or
sleeveless blouses or dresses, regardless of the season or the climate. Keep
makeup subdued. (You can still look pretty.) Do not carry a bulky handbag.

Barbara Tannenbaum, a well-known communications consultant and
professor at Brown University, makes this statement: ". . . women shouldn't
wear anything that competes with them. Get rid of flashy jewelry. Wear simple outfits. Pull hair away from the face. Women hide behind their hair."[4]

Get a great haircut, men and women, the best you can afford, and keep it
short and stylish. "Women who have complicated hairstyles, even well-

Six to 12 seconds . . . when you meet a new customer or colleague, that's all the time it takes for that person to form an opinion of you. Make sure it's a positive one.

The impression you create contributes to the general view of the organization you work for. Good products and excellent service are at the heart of commercial success, but each employee's presentation is the gauge by which the public evaluates an organization.

For example, if I meet Susan and initially perceive her to be professional, attractive, and intelligent, I'm also likely to begin to attribute other positive characteristics to her. I might see her as organized, successful, and warm. This is not to suggest that I'll ignore negative characteristics, but it will take me longer to become aware of something negative if my initial perceptions of her are very positive.

If, on the other hand, Susan presents herself to me as sloppily dressed, with bitten fingernails, and a lack of eye contact, I may begin to attribute equally negative characteristics to her—insecurity, lack of knowledge, coldness.

Lee McCoy, "First Impressions; Projecting a Professional Image," *Canadian Banker*, September 19, 1996, 32.

managed ones, can send the wrong signals. And unkempt or badly cut hair can destroy your professional image."[5]

Careful attention to your appearance, including neat and appropriate clothing, favorably impresses most interviewers and adds to your self-confidence. Male applicants are well dressed in a dark business suit with a white shirt, a silk tie, dark socks, and black leather shoes.

Mark Satterfield, director of career services for the Graduate School of Business at Emory University, has this to say to male applicants:

> Men should wear suits unless it is obvious that the position is a "shirt-and-slacks" type of job. In that case, a blue blazer and tie may suffice. For most professional positions, a business suit is the expected attire. A solid gray or navy suit conveys professionalism. . . .
>
> Avoid 100 percent polyester materials because they tend to become shiny. A blend of polyester and wool is ideal. . . . Shirts should be white or light blue. Button-down collars are the most popular choice among male executives. . . . Male business professionals do not wear short-sleeve shirts with their suits. Although it's hot during the summer, the short-sleeve dress shirt is appropriate in only a few industries and should be avoided in the interview.
>
> Good choices in ties include those with stripes or small patterns. Ties should be made of silk.[6]

Take with you a notebook and pen. A good-quality, fairly small briefcase is convenient and impressive for both men and women applicants.

According to Mary Frances Lyons, an executive search consultant, in addition to your clothing, other issues affect appearance:

▶ Stance and posture. Sit and stand before a mirror and pay heed to what you see. Slouching or otherwise using negative body language affects your appearance greatly. Try to lean forward in a sit-down meeting to show your interest.

▶ Check your habits. Do you jingle change in your pockets? Play with a watchband or other jewelry? Clear your throat or peer over your glasses—all the time? . . .

▶ Listen to yourself. What are you saying? Do you make constant use of certain phrases (*basically, in all honesty, as you might know,* etc.)?[7]

Another annoying expression is *you know.* Eliminate it from your vocabulary immediately. Others, plus many more, are *OK?, if you will, frankly, hopefully,* and *at this point in time.*

Another habit that Ms. Lyons does not mention is that of young ladies who twirl a strand of hair around their fingers or continually pat their hair. Another is putting a hand on the face.

PLANNING AND PREPARING: FURTHER RESEARCH

Before the day of the interview, try to learn the name of the person who will interview you, with the correct spelling and pronunciation. Make sure you know how to pronounce the interviewer's name and his or her job title. Learn how to address him or her: for example, *Mr., Mrs., Ms., Dr., Professor.* In many instances you will be interviewed by more than one person; the more you can learn about these people, the better prepared you will be. (If you cannot find all of this information before the interview, ask the receptionist on the day of the interview.)

COMMUNICATION

brief

Think positively. Lastly, get set to think positively. This image will be evident to the interviewer and to other staff with whom you might meet. To help you achieve this mind-set, try a technique called positive mental imagery.

Imagine yourself walking confidently into the interviewer's office, looking directly into his or her eyes, shaking hands, and accomplishing success. People who experience something they've already visualized are most likely to respond as if they've done it before.

Brian D. Spezialetti, "Do's and Don'ts for Winning the Job Interview, *Medical Laboratory Observer,* July 1995, 51.

Learn the exact location of the interview, including the street address, building, and room number. Determine the route to this location and how long the trip will take. The day of the interview is no time to become lost.

Even better, make a trial run, especially if the location is unfamiliar to you. If you are driving, find out where you can park. If you are going by public transportation, leave for the trip earlier than you would ordinarily do in order to allow for unexpected delays.

Regardless of your method of transportation, plan to arrive at the building at least fifteen minutes early so that you will have time to check your appearance without rushing. Arrive in the receptionist's office five to ten minutes before the scheduled time of the interview. Be relaxed and poised, not out of breath and nervous.

▶ PROCEEDING WITH THE INTERVIEW

When you arrive at the office, identify yourself to the receptionist. When you are called into the office, greet the interviewer by name. Shake hands firmly. Be confident. Wait for an invitation before seating yourself. Do not smoke. The first few minutes, probably the first few seconds, are crucial. Fairly or unfairly, decisions are often made based on first impressions.

Allow the interviewer to open the conversation. The interviewer may begin with casual conversation to put you at ease, such as remarks about your trip, your school, or the weather. Or the interviewer may begin by asking direct questions or giving you background information about the organization or about the particular job for which you are applying.

The interviewer perhaps will ask you to expand on the information in the resume, which is of necessity condensed. You may be asked, for example, to give more details about your work experience.

You may be asked to explain why you left a position or positions, to describe the type of work that you liked best and least, to state what you feel you accomplished on each job, and to express your opinions as to whether your supervisor and co-workers were capable and cooperative. Be careful when commenting on this topic; your interviewer is not really asking about your co-workers and supervisors but about yourself. But, as in all other situations, do not be untruthful. Remember, though, that your own competence and spirit of helpfulness and dedication will usually result in your finding the same qualities in other persons.

Principles of communication you have studied previously apply to your attitude toward the interviewer and your conduct in conversation. You have learned, as in written communication, to approach all business interpersonal situations on a straightforward basis of equality. Although you may have much to gain or lose in your search for employment on the outcome of an interview, the representative of the employing organization also has a purpose essential to the welfare of the organization—that of finding the best person for the job.

If you sincerely believe that you are this person and can convince the interviewer of this fact without building resentment because of your egotism or an overly aggressive approach, both you and the employing organization will have benefited from the relatively short time spent in talking about your professional future.

What questions will you ask? Don't be in a hurry to shower the interviewer with questions, many of which will be answered in the course of the conversation. On the other hand, don't merely sit and wait for information to come your way, and do not answer in monosyllables. Although you should not try to take charge of the interview, seize the opportunity to present yourself in the most favorable light. If you cannot communicate well enough to do so, you may leave the impression, probably an accurate one, that your communication skills will be less than ideal for your career. (Perhaps you will wish to ask a friend to help you practice for the interview.)

If you have done adequate research into this organization, along with other organizations, you already know something about the company, including its offices and branches, products, and services. You can also find its recent growth and earnings. By reading company brochures, you will know a great deal about training programs and employee benefits.

In an employment interview, the applicant must continue to emphasize how he or she can benefit the company.

One area of vital concern will be your opportunities for growth and responsibility. Are you likely to become "locked in" regardless of your hard work and ability? You will need to know the company policy on promotions, whether higher positions are filled from the inside or whether you will need to count on moving within a few years to an organization that offers greater opportunity.

Most of all, you will want to know whether the work is the kind for which you are especially well prepared. Is it the kind in which you can excel and maintain a sincere interest? Is this an organization in which you can feel that your work matters and of which you can be proud, not only for the benefit of the employing organization but also for yourself and your family? Without sincere pride in the employing organization, an idealistic person will not be satisfied with a good salary alone. On the other hand, a good income is essential for most persons as a symbol of competence and accomplishment, to say nothing of its being necessary for comfort and security.

▶ RESPONDING TO QUESTIONS

Besides being asked questions about your previous education and work experience, you may also receive surprising questions that are planned to test your ability to think quickly and to react positively and confidently under stress. The following list contains some of the most frequently asked questions, but no list can include all that you may face. A knowledge of yourself and of the employing company will help you to respond well to any kind of question. Be prepared.

1   *Tell me about yourself.* (This is your opportunity to continue the sales presentation that you began with your application letter and resume. Present your qualifications in relation to how they will benefit the company.)

2   *Why do you want this job?* (Show that you have researched the company and know its overall purpose and opportunities. Continue to stress benefits that you can offer to the company.)

3   *Why have you chosen the field of (accounting, sales, management, and so on)?* (This is an opportunity to impress the interviewer, without seeming to be egotistical, with your strengths in your particular field and your interest in professional growth. Do not talk about salary or leisure time. Emphasize your knowledge of, and liking for, the work itself.)

4   *Why should we hire you?* (Be prepared to convince, continuing with your central selling point.)

5 *What salary would you expect?* (Try to let the interviewer state the salary, which you may negotiate later. Prefer to leave discussion of salary until you have convinced the interviewer that you are the best person for the job.)

6 *Why do you want to (did you) leave your job?* (Be as positive as possible by stressing benefits of relocating without dwelling on negative aspects of your present or former job.)

7 *What are your long-range goals?* (Where do you expect to be ten years from now?)

8 *What are your greatest strengths?* (State qualities you possess that will be helpful in the job for which you are applying. Prove that you have these qualities by giving concrete evidence of past accomplishments.)

9 *What are your weaknesses?* (Be extremely careful as you respond to this question. Do not volunteer anything negative unless you can turn the negative into an asset; for example, "I tend to become impatient when I do not meet my goals"; "I tend to become overly involved and committed, but with time management skills and delegation skills I am able to meet my goals"; or "Perhaps I am a workaholic at times." Another possibility is to mention a relatively unimportant area that is not related to the job, or to mention a minor job-related area and show how you are working to improve your ability.)

10 *How do others describe you?* (Show that you work well with other people.)

11 *Can you work well under pressure?* (Give concrete examples.)

12 *Can you work without close supervision?* (Give concrete examples.)

13 *Do you have plans for continued education and study?* (Show that you expect to keep learning all your life. Be specific about any plans for continued formal education.)

14 *What subjects did you like best in school?* (Do not be untruthful, but try to remember something you liked that relates to the position for which you are applying. In addition, mentioning unrelated subjects as well may indicate that you have wide intellectual interests.)

Some other questions you may be asked include these:

15 What do you do in your spare time?

16 Are you willing to relocate?

17 Are you willing to travel?

18 What is the one most important factor you are looking for in a job?

19   What extracurricular activities did you participate in when you were in school?

20   Do you belong to professional organizations? Which ones?

21   Were you in military service?

22   (to full-time employees elsewhere) How many Mondays or Fridays were you absent last year or on leave other than approved vacation leave?

23   How long have you been a resident of this city?

In answer to all the preceding questions, as well as when preparing your resume and application letters, be truthful. Do not exaggerate job duties or change employment dates, educational accomplishments, or even the slightest detail. If your employing organization checks, as should be done when you are being seriously considered, you not only will be embarrassed, but you will most likely lose any hope of being hired.

Kerri Smith, of Scripps Howard News Service, makes this statement:

> Some job seekers fudge employment dates, exaggerate job duties, and claim skills they don't have.
>
> This is stupid. Once you and your snazzy brief case are out the door, the interviewer picks up the telephone and starts verifying everything you've listed on the resume and the application. . . . The interviewer will contact former employers and ask questions. While some companies will only verify dates of employment, most also will verify information that an interviewer reads out loud from a resume. . . . The interviewer likely will check with the records office where you attended college, to see if you actually completed a master's degree or just took a couple of graduate courses. Individuals listed as personal or professional references could be queried, too.[8]

▶ LEGAL CONSIDERATIONS

Certain questions should not be asked in an employment interview. For example, women are sometimes asked questions that would not be asked of male applicants, such as "Who takes care of your children while you work?" or "Do you think your career will interfere with your marriage?" You are not obliged to answer these questions; some applicants state that they prefer not to do so. You are usually wiser to try to determine the intent of the question. For example, if a job requires travel and you are able and willing to do so, assure the interviewer of your understanding that travel is a component of the position and of your willingness to meet your responsibilities and obligations.

Further discussion of the laws that apply to employment, from the employer's standpoint, are included in Chapter 18.

ENDING THE INTERVIEW

You can usually ascertain by the interviewer's remarks and nonverbal signals when the interview is coming to a close. Use these last few minutes to summarize a few important qualifications and to express your continued interest in working for the company. Express appreciation for an informative and interesting interview.

The interviewer will probably tell you when you will be notified or mention the next step in the employment procedure. Offer to supply any additional information or to provide references. Do not linger once it is clear that the interview is over.

SUREFIRE WAYS TO FLUNK YOUR INTERVIEW

- ► Be tardy.
- ► Dress inappropriately.
- ► Reveal poor grooming habits.
- ► Have poor eye contact.
- ► Use negative body language.
- ► Submit sloppy, illegible application form.
- ► Act overconfident and superior; be a "know-it-all."
- ► Be impolite, abrasive.
- ► Display lack of career direction.
- ► Use poor oral communication skills.
- ► Fabricate answers.
- ► Don't listen to interviewer.
- ► Talk negatively about previous supervisors, co-workers, instructors.
- ► Have unrealistic job or salary expectations.
- ► Ask about salary early on in the interview.
- ► Don't thank the interviewer for his or her time.

Brian D. Spezialetti, "Do's and Don'ts for Winning the Job Interview," *Medical Laboratory Observer*, July 1995, 51.

COMMUNICATION
brief

When an applicant is being seriously considered for a position, he or she may be invited to lunch or dinner with executives and other members of the organization.

Following Through in the Employment Search

Your efforts should not end after completing the interview. Continue to indicate your interest in the position and appreciation for the interview, but do not be overly persistent to the point of being thought of as a pest.

▶ **THANK-YOU LETTERS**

Within a day or two after your employment interview, mail a thank-you letter. This letter is a matter of courtesy; you should send it whether or not you feel that you are being favorably considered. The thank-you letter is ordinarily short because you have little to say. It is a goodwill message. Sincerity and a natural, conversational tone are the major requirements.

Many applicants do not send thank-you letters after an interview, perhaps because of a mistaken idea that to do so is "pushy" or, more likely, because of simple procrastination or lack of effort. That few persons send these letters is a point in your favor to make you stand out from other applicants. The letter serves as a reminder of who you are. Even more important, it shows continued interest and initiative.

A thank-you letter is illustrated in Figure 11-7.

4815 Wyandotte Avenue
Mentone, CA 92359
January 11, 19——

Mr. Robert J. Samuels
Sales Manager
Yohanak Corporation
2091 Risser Road South
Madison, WI 53507

Dear Mr. Samuels:

Thank you for a most pleasant and informative interview. I am very much interested in working for the Yohanak Corporation.

The opportunity that you mentioned for possible work outside the United States in a few years appeals to me. As shown on my resume, I speak and write French and Spanish, in addition to English.

I will be glad to supply any more information you may need.

Sincerely,

Carlos Rodriguez

Carlos Rodriguez

FIGURE 11-7
Thank-you letter that includes further mention of an important qualification

At times you will have additional information to convey in the thank-you letter. For example, perhaps you have been asked whether you would move to another city and you have requested time to think it over. If you have made up your mind in the day or two before the thank-you letter should be mailed, you may state your decision in the letter. Or perhaps you have read the brochures provided for you or you have been asked to submit the names of persons to recommend you if these names were not included on the resume.

Additional information is not a requirement. Send a thank-you letter even if you have no new information to convey. Some companies are said to stop considering an applicant who does not show continued interest through a thank-you letter or other follow-ups.

FOLLOW-UP LETTERS

Follow-up letters may be helpful when you have not heard from the employing organization within a reasonable time after the interview. The exact time varies; some college seniors are interviewed near the beginning of their senior year and notified within a month or two of graduation. Usually, however, the applicant is notified within a few weeks or even within a few days.

You may also write a follow-up letter after submitting an application letter and resume if too much time seems to elapse before you are called for an interview.

Do not be surprised if many companies never contact you. As a mere matter of courtesy and perhaps ethics, they should let you know one way or another, but some do not. (When you become a manager, you can change things in your organization.)

Provided they are well written and used at the proper time, follow-up letters accomplish several purposes. They show that you are still interested in the organization and that you are diligent in your efforts to obtain employment. These letters may also report additional information not included in the application letter and resume or reported in interviews—for example, the completion of related courses, additional work experience, or special scholastic honors or other accomplishments.

Avoid a demanding or hurt tone, and don't indicate surprise that you have not been asked for an interview. But don't apologize for writing.

A follow-up letter is shown in Figure 11-8.

1982 Punahou Street
Honolulu, HI 96822
July 7, 19——

Mr. John G. Springer, Partner
Pannell Kerr Forster, CPAs
1714 Makaha Towers
Honolulu, HI 96816

Dear Mr. Springer:

As a follow-up to an application letter and resume mailed to you on June 1, I wish to emphasize to you my continued interest in employment with Pannell Kerr Forster.

My energy and ability can contribute to the progress of your accounting firm. I am willing to work long hours, if necessary, and to travel or relocate.

Since sending you the application, I have begun temporary work in the Hyatt Regency-Waikiki as an accounting clerk. Because your organization specializes in accounting for hotels, my present job may help somewhat in beginning duties with your organization.

You can reach me by telephone (808-000-000) mornings before nine and evenings after six. Or, if you prefer, write me at the address shown above.

Sincerely,

Walter R. Williams

Walter R. Williams

FIGURE 11-8
Follow-up letter

Follow-up letters can be used even when you know that the position for which you applied has been filled by someone else. Fred Berk, president and CEO of Huffman Koos, a New Jersey furniture-store chain, makes this statement:

> Though few applicants do it, sending another follow-up note if the decision proves negative may also pay off. One person I didn't hire as a store manager sent a note saying, "Even though I didn't make the final cut, I enjoyed speaking with you so much that I'd be interested in learning of other opportunities in your organization which you feel might be right for me."
>
> I felt that even though I didn't consider this man experienced enough for store manager, anyone who could write such a classy note should be in this company. I saved it until a sales position in one of our better stores opened up—then called him to make an attractive job offer.[9]

4815 Wyandotte Avenue
Mentone, CA 92359
February 2, 19——

Mr. Robert J. Samuels
Sales Manager
Yohanak Corporation
2091 Risser Road South
Madison, WI 53507

Dear Mr. Samuels:

Yes, I accept your offer of a position as a sales representative for northern California. I look forward to working with you and the other people at Yohanak.

Your letter with the attached handbook is helpful and descriptive. The conditions you mention are satisfactory: a salary of $27,000 a year, plus 10 percent commission over quota; a company car; all expenses; and full employment benefits.

As you requested, I will begin work on March 1 by reporting to your Madison office for orientation. I will be there at 9 A.M.

Please let me know if there is anything else I should do between now and March 1.

Sincerely,

Carlos Rodriguez

Carlos Rodriguez

FIGURE 11-9
Job-acceptance letter

Are you now convinced of the power of the written word as it pertains to seeking employment?

▶ **JOB-ACCEPTANCE AND JOB-REFUSAL LETTERS**

Job-acceptance letters, like other good-news and routine informational letters, are usually best arranged in the direct order, with the acceptance in the first sentence, as in Figure 11-9. Your job-acceptance letter should include any additional information that the employing organization may need and any questions of your own.

In job-refusal letters, remember to express appreciation for the employment offer. As in other negative messages, your letter will be more psychologically convincing and acceptable if reasons are given before the refusal, as in Figure 11-10.

Do everything you can to keep the goodwill of the reader and of the organization.

5012 Jennings Way
Sacramento, CA 95608
September 25, 19——

Dr. Wanda Rider, President
The National League of American Pen Women
The Pen-Arts Building
1300-17th Street, N.W.
Washington, DC 20036

Dear Dr. Rider:

Thank you for offering me the position as your editorial assistant.

After meeting with you in August, I was even more impressed with the importance of the work you are doing with the American Pen Women. As expressed in earlier letters and in the interview, I am very much interested in your organization.

Since I talked with you on August 18, however, changes have occurred in my life. Because of a legacy from my grandmother, I have decided to continue my education, working toward a four-year degree in creative writing and television production at the University of Southern California. Dr. Rider, I regret that timing is such that someone else must be your next editorial assistant.

Best wishes as you continue your work.

Sincerely,

Carol Chen

Carol Chen

FIGURE 11-10
Job-refusal letter

■ **COUNTRYWIDE INSURANCE COMPANY** ■

Home office: New York City
420 Madison, 10577

October 15, 19——

Mr. Martin O'Conner
Communications Supervisor
Countrywide Insurance Company
420 Madison Avenue
New York, NY 10577

Dear Mr. O'Conner:

Working at Countrywide has meant a great deal to me. Thank you, Mr. O'Conner, for hiring me and for being helpful and considerate throughout the fifteen months of employment.

The association with you and the other fine people at Countrywide has taught me many things that will continue to be of benefit. You helped me succeed in my first job and in making the adjustment from my small home town to New York City. You have my deepest appreciation.

In spite of my gratitude and high regard for Countrywide Insurance Company, I plan to leave on November 1 to begin work with Horizon Press here in New York. I have been offered a job as editorial assistant with the possibility of becoming an editor. Because this is the kind of work I have always wanted to do, this letter is my official letter of resignation.

People at Horizon Press have agreed for me to stay a week or two beyond November 1 if you need me to train a replacement, which I will be glad to do.

Best wishes to you and to my other co-workers at Countrywide. You will have my enduring friendship and respect.

Sincerely,

Sally Ann Benson

Sally Ann Benson
Secretary

FIGURE 11-11
Letter of resignation

▶ LETTERS OF RESIGNATION

Even though you are leaving your present position, your letter of resignation can be important to your future career. It may influence recommendations from your present employer. In addition, you could possibly wish to return to your present organization.

A written resignation is often required. It becomes part of your personnel file. The letter should be written at least two weeks before you plan to leave except in rare and justified circumstances. You should discuss your plans with your immediate supervisor before you prepare the written resignation.

Do everything you can to maintain friendly, pleasant relationships. Apart from the fact that you owe your employer for what you have gained from your work—and you have almost certainly gained something in addition to your paycheck—leaving a negative impression with your present employer is a poor start for your new job.

An example of a letter of resignation is shown in Figure 11-11.

SUMMARY

The application letter, sent with a resume, forms a two-part application package. In addition, the letter is a sales message, arranged similarly to a sales letter for a product or service.

You should build your letter around your most outstanding qualification in relation to the position sought. Your central selling point will probably be either education or experience.

The purpose of the application letter and the resume is to obtain an interview. The tone should be straightforward and businesslike; you must show confidence in your ability but refrain from appearing egotistical or overly aggressive. Substantiate positive qualities by concrete evidence of past experiences and accomplishments.

Preparing for the employment interview is necessary for its success. Learn as much as possible about the organization and the interviewer. Wear conservative, attractive, and businesslike clothing and arrive on time.

Questions asked by the interviewer seek knowledge about your background, poise, communication ability, and potential.

Send a thank-you letter after every interview. Follow-up letters may be necessary or desirable. (Follow-up letters may also be helpful after the application is sent and before a response is received.) A letter of resignation should be sent at least two weeks before the effective date.

1 Name seven "don'ts" that apply to letters of application.
2 Briefly describe the first paragraph of an application letter.
3 Briefly describe the ending paragraph of an application letter.
4 Why is it not advisable to begin several paragraphs with *I*?
5 Why should you ordinarily not mention salary?
6 Give five suggestions for preparing for an interview.
7 Name three things that you should take to an interview.
8 Name seven questions that an interviewer is likely to ask.
9 What are two purposes of a thank-you letter?
10 What are two purposes of a follow-up letter?

Improve or omit the following passages from application letters.

1 Enclosed herewith you will find my resume.
2 Thanking you in advance, I am respectfully yours.
3 I want to be interviewed on Tuesday, September 11, sometime in the afternoon.
4 Here is my telephone number. Please do not call before 10 A.M.
5 I am especially interested in your profit sharing plan.
6 I will consider any kind of job you have available.
7 During the passed month I have studied English.
8 It is alright to contact my employer
9 I apologize for using my companys' letterhead stationary, but no other is available.
10 Please do not delay answering my letter.
11 You will never regret hiring me.
12 I am willing to work 40 hours a week, but I don't want to devote my life entirely to work.
13 I have already discovered several problems in your organization by reading *The Wall Street Journal*.
14 Please send me your salary schedule.
15 I can begin work on Monday November 6 1997 in your Los Angeles office.

EVALUATION SHEET: APPLICATION LETTERS

__Yes __ No **1** Is the letter presented throughout in terms of reader benefit?

__Yes __ No **2** Is the positive approach used throughout—a tone of quiet confidence, without egotism or presumption?

__Yes __ No **3** Does the first paragraph make clear that the applicant is applying for a particular job?

__Yes __ No **4** Does the letter omit stereotyped expressions?

__Yes __ No **5** Is the letter written in the words of the applicant, not paraphrased or lifted from examples in textbooks?

__Yes __ No **6** Does the letter omit references to salary or benefits?

__Yes __ No **7** Does the letter omit obvious statements?

__Yes __ No **8** Does the letter include specific and positive details to convince the reader of the applicant's ability and suitability for the opening?

__Yes __ No **9** Are *I*'s, *me*'s, and other first-person pronouns used naturally and as necessary, but not to excess? Do most paragraphs begin with some other word?

__Yes __ No **10** Does the writer specifically request an interview?

__Yes __ No **11** Does the letter indicate that the applicant is familiar with the employing organization because of previous research?

__Yes __ No **12** Is the letter absolutely perfect in appearance and correctness?

CASES

1 Write letters of application to accompany the resumes you prepared for Case 6, Chapter 10. These letters should be individually composed and typewritten for each of the three companies.

2 Mail the letters and resumes you have prepared, or if you are not interested in obtaining or changing employment at this time, save the letters and resumes to be used or modified later. Be sure that the envelopes you use are of good quality and of standard business length so that the letter can be folded in approximate thirds. The envelope should match the paper in weight and quality.

3 Follow through with interviews, thank-you letters, and, if necessary, follow-up letters. (If you did not actually mail the applications, assume that you did so and that three weeks have elapsed. Write a follow-up letter showing your continued interest and asking for an interview.)

4 Assume that you are interviewed by representatives of each of the organizations. Write one or more thank-you letters, as directed by your instructor.

5 Assume that three weeks have elapsed since your interview with each of the organizations. Write one or more follow-up letters, as directed by your instructor.

6 Assume that you are offered the position. Write a letter of acceptance. Assume reasonable details about dates of employment, location, or other necessary material to include in your letter.

7 Assume that you are also offered a position from the organization that was your second choice. Write a letter refusing the position.

8 Assume that two years have passed. You have decided that you would now like to work with the organization that was originally your second choice. Write a letter of inquiry, reminding the company that you were offered a job two years ago. Offer to send a current resume. (In actual use, perhaps you would be wiser to send a current resume with the present letter.)

9 Assume that you are successful in obtaining employment with the organization to which you wrote in Case 8. Write a letter of resignation to your present employer.

THINK-IT-THROUGH ASSIGNMENTS AND WORKING IN GROUPS

10 Analyze the application letter (Case 11) an actual one, which, with a resume, was sent to a small publishing company. You can find many needed improvements, but can you find anything about the letter that is *right?* What?

11 Rewrite the following letter, assuming additional details if necessary. Which details presently used should be omitted? Correct all errors in grammar or usage.

Dear Sir:

I am writing you this letter because I have a full-time job in which my time is limited and because so many establishments are not even accepting applications. So, in order to save both your time and mine, I thought I would send you a brief resume so that, if you have any openings. You can call me for an interview at your convenience. If you have no openings, possibly you could file this until such time that you have.

I have heard that you employ a good many proofreaders. This is something I feel I could do well. I have not done this for another before (I do a little freelancing in my spare time), but I have a feel for the English language that

many seemingly do not. I am willing to take whatever tests might be necessary to establish my ability.

My work record follows, along with a couple of references. Although I prefer that my present employer not be contacted—I might be fired on the spot for considering another job—the one prior to that can vouch for my reliability. I have missed no days in the past two years of 55 to 60 hours of work a week and before that, including a 3 day absence for a bout with pneumonia, I missed a total of 5 days at my previous job in the three years I worked there. Also, I am habitually early.

I would appreciate it enormously if you would consider my application. Thank you for your time.

12 Evaluate the letter as it was originally written according to the evaluation sheet for application letters.

13 Evaluate the revised letter according to the evaluation sheet.

14 Consider the resume of Rhonda A. Blake, shown in Figure 10-7. Discuss. What should Rhonda include in her letter of application?

Should she use a different letter for different jobs? Explain. What do you think her central selling point will be? Can you think of any jobs for which she should consider her central selling point to be something other than her outstanding academic record? What could be considered a weakness in her overall qualifications? How should this weakness be handled in her letter, or should it not be mentioned at all? Should she send a list of references or merely offer to supply them?

Draw up an outline (brief notes) about what should go in each paragraph of her letter. (Before you plan the outline, decide on a specific job or perhaps a specific department of a particular company where she might be advised to apply.) In addition to planning Rhonda's letter or letters, evaluate Rhonda's resume. Revise the resume if you think it should be revised. (*Note:* This assignment, like all others throughout the book, is appropriate for class discussion as well as for group work.)

ENDNOTES

1 Max Messer, quoted by Rosemary Cafasso, "Stupid Resume Tricks," *Computerworld*, July 8, 1996, 97.

2 L. M. Sixel, "Make Job Application Cover Letter Concise, Precise, Unspiced," *The Commercial Appeal [Memphis]*, May 12, 1996, C3.

3 Susan Phinney, "Clothes Make the Job Hunt, and So Do Table Manners, Young Applicants Learn," *The Commercial Appeal [Memphis]*, June 6, 1996, C3.

4 Barbara Tannenbaum, quoted by Elizabeth Rau, *Houston Chronicle*, May 12, 1996, 11G.

5 Mary Frances Lyons, "Career Rx," *Physician Executive*, February 1996, 33.

6 Mark Satterfield, "Dress to Suit Interview, Not Yourself," *The Atlanta Journal and Constitution*, January 6, 1991, 04R.

7 Lyons, "Career Rx," 34.

8 Kerri Smith, "Don't Stretch Truth on Job Application: Employers Verify All Information," *The Patriot Ledger*, September 11, 1996, 19E.

9 Fred Berk, as quoted by Lisa Collier Cool, "Ten Truths You've Never Been Told About the Job Interview," *Cosmopolitan*, May 1991, 94.

An Overview of Reports and Report Planning

CHAPTER

12

OBJECTIVES

Chapter Twelve will help you:

1 Identify and discuss characteristics of effective reports.

2 Explain how reports are used in business.

3 Distinguish between formal and informal reports.

4 Distinguish between informational and analytical reports.

5 Identify and define a report problem.

6 Develop an appropriate outline for a report.

7 Prepare a work plan for a report project.

Your ability to write effective reports can be an outstanding asset to your career in business. Reports of many kinds are vital in the everyday operation of modern business activity. Your ability to gather, organize, analyze, and present needed information may be the determining factor in your success, and the lack of such an ability can keep you in a lower-level position.

CHARACTERISTICS OF REPORTS

A report is a written or oral message planned to convey information or to present a solution. Under this broad and simple definition, many letters, memorandums, telephone calls, and personal conversations are forms of reports. A report may also be a formal written one of hundreds of pages, on which many persons have worked for months or years. Reports may consist of written and spoken words, columns of figures, charts, computer printouts, or a combination of all these and other forms.

In a definition that follows, the word *effective* has been inserted to describe what reports should be, not necessarily what they are. Because even a poor report is called a report, the wording of the exact definition of the term is complicated. Thus:

> An effective business report is an orderly, objective presentation of factual information with or without analysis, interpretation, and recommendations, which is planned to serve some business purpose, usually that of making a decision.

Other descriptions of a report are that it

► is a management tool;

► may vary according to purpose, format, time prepared, subject matter, scope, length, readership, and other factors;

► may vary widely in form, length, and content;

► may merely report information, without analysis, or may report information and, in addition, analyze the information and include recommendations;

► may be planned only to analyze existing information;

► is usually written for one reader or for a small group of readers;

► usually moves up the chain of command;

► tends to be written in a style more formal than that used for other types of business communication;

► is ordinarily assigned;

► may be prepared at specified, regular intervals or only for a special need;

► requires careful planning and organization;

► answers a question or solves a problem.

When planning reports, we must give special attention to organization and to an objective, nonbiased approach. Because reports are often longer than letters or memorandums, they must be especially planned for readability and an orderly progression of thought.

HOW REPORTS ARE USED IN BUSINESS

Every organization, from small to large, has many reasons to generate reports. Whether you are studying accounting, management, marketing, computer information systems, finance, economics, or some other particular aspect of business, the preparation of formal or informal reports will typically be part of your job tasks. The reports you may be asked to prepare can be categorized in several different ways.

INTERNAL AND EXTERNAL REPORTS

Internal reports are prepared for an audience within the organization. Activity and progress reports often move up the organizational ladder. *External reports*, on the other hand, target outside audiences. Reports to governmental agencies such as the Securities and Exchange Commission or the Internal Revenue Service or proposals to a potential client are all examples of external reports.

PERIODIC REPORTS

Periodic reports (or status reports) are submitted at regular intervals, such as weekly, monthly, quarterly, or annually. You may be required to submit periodic reports concerning your activities and progress on the job. Or you may prepare a departmental activity report. Annual employee evaluation narratives can also be considered periodic reports. While periodic reports often have an internal audience, yearly reports to stockholders would be considered external periodic reports.

The departmental quarterly activity report illustrated in Figure 12-1 is prepared as a memorandum and addresses activities, special projects in process or planned, and any problems the writer wishes to share with upper management.

SINGULAR (ONE-TIME) REPORTS

Singular (one-time) reports may be assigned to troubleshoot an existing problem, such as excessive long-distance telephone bills, and recommend solutions to the problem. A department may write a justification or recommendation report to convince those in authority to change particular operations, make specific personnel changes, buy new equipment, and so on. For example, a one-time feasibility report could be written to examine a project such as installation of a voice mail system and identify whether or not to proceed.

The one-time report illustrated in Figure 12-2 was written to justify purchasing new software for a classroom computer laboratory. This internal report is also prepared in memorandum form.

Singular reports may be intended for an internal or external audience, depending on the particular situation. While voice mail feasibility may be targeted for an internal audience, an accountant in a CPA firm who prepares a report for a client detailing accounting treatment of convertible bonds is preparing a one-time report for external distribution.

INVESTIGATIVE REPORTS

Investigative reports focus primarily on facts. For example, as an accountant, you may be asked to prepare a report for a client on disclosure requirements for deferred taxes. A computer analyst may be requested to gather information on security issues related to company usage of the Internet. An investigative report may evolve into an analytical report if it takes a more specific focus on analyzing these findings from the company perspective and making recommendations for changes in security procedures.

Date: April 4, 19——
To: Susan Maxwell, Director of Information Systems
From: Chris Wilson, Manager, Information Center
Subject: Information Center First Quarter Activity Report, 19——

ACTIVITIES COMPLETED

1. Assisted in installation of upgraded local area network for human resources department
2. Completed 23 hardware evaluations for various departments
3. Maintained help desk hotline from 8 a.m. to 5 p.m. daily, providing software problem assistance for all supported software packages: 321 calls logged; all but 43 problems were solved over the phone; remaining 43 solved through visits to workstations
4. Produced Information Center Quarterly Newsletter for distribution to all employees
5. Evaluated 7 new software packages for various departments
6. Completed 15 system prototypes
7. Completed hardware installation and software testing for 19 single-user stations
8. Conducted seven half-day end-user software training seminars: 1 word processing software upgrade; 2 spreadsheet software; 1 project management software; 1 statistics software; 2 multimedia authoring software
9. Maintained Information Center intra-company Web page

SPECIAL PROJECTS SCHEDULED FOR COMPLETION

1. Recommendation report involving reassessment of all software packages officially supported by the Information Center
2. Study of existing security procedures for end-user systems and recommendations to strengthen computer security

PROBLEMS

Increased demand for our prototyping services, coupled with the continuing high use of the help desk hotline and demand for employee training seminars, has put a significant strain on our personnel resources. We are experiencing a three-week backlog on prototyping requests and several weeks' delay in evaluation of software requests. We should be able to reduce some of the backlogs once John Michaels is back to work on a full-time schedule.

FIGURE 12-1
Internal periodic report in traditional memorandum format

April 15, 19——

Dr. Raymond Folse

FORMS DESIGN SOFTWARE UPGRADE FOR ROOM 205 COMPUTER LAB

The existing forms design software available for instructional purposes in the office information systems computer lab in 205 White Hall has not been updated for four years. It is currently the only application software in the curriculum that is not designed to work specifically with the latest version of the Windows operating system installed on the lab computers. Its functionality is also severely limited in comparison to quality form design products on the market today.

Five years ago budget constraints required that we purchase a shareware package in order to hold costs down for installation on 30 computers. The package allowed us to introduce forms design into the curriculum at a time when our competitor schools did not teach forms design competencies. The industry has recognized the value of forms design software, and several full-feature packages are now available that support sophisticated design techniques.

Students quickly recognize that the existing forms design software available in the lab is inadequate; they note that they could do more things with a word processing package. We cannot teach advanced forms design techniques using the current forms design software, and this creates a weakness in our two-year office information systems curriculum.

The department's software selection committee reviewed trade literature and software comparison articles prior to a hands-on evaluation of three packages. After careful evaluation, we request that the department purchase the most recent version of Delrina PerForm forms design and fill software and install it on the lab computers in room 205 prior to the beginning of the fall semester. Price information can be found on the Delrina web page <http://www.Delrina.com>; we may also be able to negotiate an educational site license if we contact the sales department.

Celeste Powers

Celeste Powers, Assistant Professor

FIGURE 12-2
Internal justification report in modern memorandum format

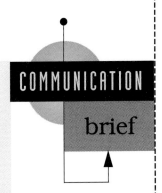

American corporations depend heavily on research in their decision-making process. The extent of this dependence can be seen in the approximately twenty billion dollars spent each year on research and development. Research and development can be seen as the engine which makes the American economy run. Whether it is a feasibility study that precedes construction of new facilities or a marketing survey that projects the success or failure of a new product, research-generated information is the basis for most business decisions.

Thomas J. Farrell and Charlotte Donabedian, *Writing the Business Research Paper: A Complete Guide* (Durham, NC: Carolina Academic Press, 1991), 6.

FORM REPORTS

Form reports may be completed by filling in data on a preprinted, standardized form. Status reports that focus on predominantly numeric data, such as statements for the Internal Revenue Service, the Equal Employment Opportunity Commission, or the Securities and Exchange Commission, may need little narrative. Submitting the information as a form report helps speed preparation and aids the reader in comprehending the information. If the form report can be submitted and processed electronically, those using the form gain additional efficiency benefits.

FORMAL AND INFORMAL REPORTS

Purpose and readership determine the degree of formality a report writer should use. The words *formal* and *informal* are relative as they describe reports; there is no exact and distinct dividing line. Reports that are not definitely and conclusively formal are best described as *informal*, a description that fits most business and professional writing and speech. In written messages, the words *formal* and *informal* are used to describe format, writing style, or both.

FORMAT AND CONTENTS

A completely formal written report includes preliminary and supplementary parts omitted from more informal arrangements, as shown in Chapter 15. Some of these preliminary parts are *letter of transmittal, letter of acceptance, table of contents, list of tables,* and *synopsis*. Supplementary parts include a *bibliography, appendix sections,* and perhaps an *index*.

Informal reports may be presented in letter or memorandum format or in various other short-form arrangements such as preprinted form reports. The reports in Figure 12-1 and 12-2 are both examples of informal reports in memorandum format.

The long = formal and short = informal rules do not always apply in report writing. A fairly short report—six or seven pages, for example—may appropriately include preliminary and supplementary parts if these parts are necessary or helpful to the reader.

▶ WORDING AND WRITING STYLE

Formal writing, as explained in Chapter 4, includes no contractions, expressions that could be considered slang, or abbreviated sentences or sentence fragments. An informal writing style may include contractions and casual, conversational phrases or modes of expression. While most reports are written more formally than routine memorandums, all business and professional writing should be interesting, natural, and easy to read; writing should be grammatically correct and worded with the reader in mind. A more complete presentation of formal and informal style is addressed in Chapter 4; you may wish to review this material prior to writing any report your instructor may assign.

The *impersonal writing style*, also discussed in Chapter 4, is more formal than the personal writing style. The impersonal style is ordinarily used when a report is considered formal in format and wording. Written material can convey formality even with the use of first- and second-person pronouns. *Formal writing style and impersonal tone are not synonymous, although they are often used together in the same report.*

The *impersonal writing style*, also referred to as the *third-person objective writing style,* includes no *I*'s, *we*'s, *you*'s, or other first- or second-person pronouns. Some researchers prefer the impersonal style because it appears more objective and nonbiased. In addition, more emphasis is given to the facts and analyses being presented. While most business letters and memorandums are written in the *personal writing style*, the report writer must always assess whether the personal tone is appropriate for the report's audience.

Many traditionally minded readers of reports will judge a report written in the impersonal tone to be more professional, more objective, more scientific, and more carefully prepared than one written in the personal tone. If you are likely to encounter this reaction, you are decreasing the likelihood of the acceptance of your ideas by using the personal tone. The use of *I*'s, *we*'s, and other first- and second-person pronouns may be a form of noise, distracting the reader's mind from whatever it is that you are trying to say.

A report that is formal in format and wording is likely to be written in the impersonal writing style. An informal report such as a memorandum report is more likely to be written in the personal writing style.

INFORMATIONAL AND ANALYTICAL (PROBLEM-SOLVING) REPORTS

Informational reports simply present information, with no attempt to analyze or interpret the meaning of the data or to make recommendations for action.

Analytical reports also provide information and in addition include analysis and interpretation. Those that include recommendations are also referred to as *recommendation* or *problem-solving reports.*

Informational reports tend to be shorter than analytical ones, but this distinction is not applicable to all. Informational reports can be of any length, depending on the amount of information to convey. Conversely, an analytical report can be short. (*Long* and *short* are relative terms, in reports as well as in everything else.) We do, however, often hear the term l*ong analytical report* or *complete analytical report.* Complete may mean that the report contains various preliminary and supplementary parts, as discussed and illustrated in Chapter 15. The word may also be used to signify that the report and the investigation that precede the report are broad in scope.

The distinction between informational and analytical reports will be important as you consider a proposed project. One of your first steps, especially if you are a new employee, will be to find out exactly what is expected in a report.

REPORTS IN THE DIRECT (DEDUCTIVE) AND INDIRECT (INDUCTIVE) ARRANGEMENTS

Like all other forms of written communication, reports can be arranged in the direct (deductive) order or in the indirect (inductive) order, as described in Chapter 6. In addition, they can be arranged in chronological order, but this arrangement usually does not give proper emphasis to whatever should be emphasized.

The indirect arrangement, as applied to reports, begins with an introduction, presents findings and their interpretation, and ends with conclusions and recommendations. This arrangement is also described as the *logical order*—an inexact and nondescriptive term in that a well-organized report arranged in the direct order is also logical if it makes sense.

Many analytical reports, especially short ones, present *conclusions* as the first section of the report. (Conclusions may be only recommendations, or they may present the writer's most important interpretations and also include recommendations, either stated or implied.) This "gist of the message" is followed by purpose, methods, or other necessary explanatory material, followed by supporting facts and interpretations on which the conclusions and recommendations are based.

Compare the indirect and the direct arrangements:

Indirect arrangement	Direct arrangement
Purpose, methods, other introductory material	Conclusions (includes recommendations)
Findings	Purpose, methods, or other explanatory material
Conclusions (includes recommendations)	Findings

Even if a report is presented in the inductive (indirect) order, the use of a synopsis combines the features of both the direct and indirect arrangements in the overall *report package*, which consists of the preliminaries, the report itself, and the supplementary parts. (See Chapter 15.)

The *synopsis* (also called an *abstract*) is a greatly condensed version of the complete report and includes summations of the *introduction, findings, conclusions,* and *recommendations*. Because of the placement of the synopsis before the actual report, the report package is arranged in the direct order because the gist of the entire report is presented before supporting details and information.

A PROBLEM-SOLVING SITUATION

Research, like the even broader term *communication*, applies to almost everything we do. As we attempt to solve ever-occurring problems, large and small, we engage in a form of research. Suppose, for example, that your department is expanding and you have hired an additional person. You must now select a computer system for the individual and have it in place for the new employee's first day.

What should you do? Should you order the same system two other employees use (purchased 11 months ago)? Or should you order a different system? If you order something different, what system is best? While you may not put the problem statement into written form, you need to define the problem, choose a method or methods of finding information, collect and organize data, evaluate and interpret their meaning, and arrive at a solution to the problem.

What kind of research could you conduct to determine the best computer system to select? You could check purchase orders to determine the specifications of the existing computers in use in your department. Or you could ask another department manager what specific system she ordered four months ago. Perhaps you should ask employees in your department to identify various hardware and software needs for their job tasks. Another research option might involve reading various software and hardware comparison articles in trade journals. You could use any combination of methods of finding information.

In the problem-solving situation, you would collect all this information, analyze it for its validity and applicability, and arrive at a conclusion on which you would make your recommendation of the type of computer system to purchase.

Your conclusion has been based partly on assumptions, or *inferences*. An inference is an assumption, or "an educated guess," based on known facts. If you have not heard any complaints about inadequacy of existing computer systems in your department, you may be assuming that the systems your employees are using are indeed adequate. Reasonable inferences supported by sufficient facts may serve as a basis for recommendations, although at times these recommendations will be incorrect. Your value judgments, unsupported by facts, should not be used as a basis for recommendations.

As you may have realized by now, much of successful business research and report writing is the application of mere common sense. But then common sense cannot be exactly described as "mere."

IDENTIFYING AND DEFINING THE PROBLEM

A *problem* exactly stated is a problem well on the way to being solved. Determining that a problem exists is not difficult from the standpoint of knowing that something is wrong or needs improvement. Yet stating in specific terms exactly what you wish to determine in a particular research study *is* often difficult.

Perhaps several studies of a problem within an organization will be necessary before a major issue is resolved, and perhaps your particular report is planned to cover only one part of a major question. Or your study may be a comprehensive one with several contributing parts; if this is the case, you are in effect investigating a number of questions and combining the answers into a solution of the larger problem.

If the research project has been assigned to you, as ordinarily it will be, make sure that you and the person who authorized the report are in complete agreement about the purpose of your particular report, including limitations and boundaries of the study. *(You need to know exactly what you are and are not attempting to find out.)* You also need to discuss cost considerations.

Other items of information that you must have before proceeding with the research process are these:

► What has been done in the past on this problem? Have previous reports been prepared? If so, where are they? Were recommendations, if any, put into effect? If so, were they successful? If not, why not? If they were not put into effect, why not?

► What other information is available from sources within the employing organization?

► What use is to be made of this report? How the report will be used is not contained in your stated purpose; the purpose, or problem, is the question you are trying to answer by finding relevant information and interpreting that information. The report may be filed away; it may be presented to a committee for further consideration; or its recommended changes may be put into effect.

► Who is likely to have more information on this particular subject?

► What limitations apply as to time, money, and facilities?

► When is the report needed?

► What are the exact terms of the contract or assignment? If the study is a part of your regular employment responsibilities, the agreement is not likely to be referred to as a contract. A letter of authorization, followed by the researcher's letter of acceptance, serves as a written agreement about what is to be done. If you are working as a consultant for a firm other than your own, you should have a written contract. Written specifications should be complete and exact. (Often instructions are given only through oral communication, but written authorizations can save time and misunderstanding.)

Review "A Problem-Solving situation" concerning the purchase of a computer system for a new employee. While various research options were identified in that section, many of the questions presented in the bulleted list above would also have to be answered before proceeding with the research.

► **INFORMATIONAL REPORTS: STATEMENTS OF PURPOSE**

The following statement, worded as an infinitive phrase, applies to an informational report:

> *To present a summary of academic computing resources at Nicholls State University during the 1997–1998 school year.*

The wording of the statement of purpose for any report can be presented in slightly different forms, as

> *The purpose of this report is to present a summary of academic computing resources at Nicholls State University during the 1997–1998 school year.*

or

> *This report will summarize academic computing resources at Nicholls State University during the 1997–1998 school year.*

Notice that *this report will summarize* is appropriate for a proposal, or report plan, prepared at the beginning of the report process. In the final report, the sentence should read: *This report summarizes.*

Subtopics are necessary for comprehensive informational reports as for analytical reports. For example, a breakdown of the preceding statement of purpose might be:

► Open computer labs

► Restricted computer labs

► Faculty computers

► Academic computing support personnel

► Academic computing usage statistics

► Academic computing repair statistics

► Software seminar and training offerings

Statements of purpose are useful for other kinds of informational reports, including those that present results of historical research and descriptive research. *Historical* research, as the term indicates, presents information about the past; *descriptive* research ordinarily depicts present conditions, situations, activities, facilities, or circumstances.

PROBLEM-SOLVING REPORTS: HYPOTHESES

A *hypothesis* is a statement to be proved or disproved by research. An *affirmative hypothesis* states that a relationship exists between stated variables. A *null hypothesis* states that no relationship exists between stated variables. The use of a null hypothesis is sometimes considered more scientific than the positive because a positive statement supposedly indicates that the researcher has already decided on what the results will be. A hypothesis is a possible solution that may be proved correct and in agreement with evidence gathered by research, or it may be proved wrong. Bias can occur regardless of the wording of a hypothesis.

AN AFFIRMATIVE HYPOTHESIS

Employee morale will increase and absenteeism decrease if the company provides career apparel.

A NULL HYPOTHESIS

No significant difference in employee morale or absenteeism will occur if the company provides career apparel.

You may wish to reword a hypothesis and present it as a problem and purpose statement within your written report. Thus:

The purpose of this study is to determine whether employee morale will increase and absenteeism decrease if the company provides career apparel.

Not all research can be exactly formulated in terms of hypotheses. In the illustration of a hypothesis given above, judging employee morale is a task difficult to prove or disprove. This business problem can be solved, however, to the extent that the person or persons responsible for putting the research results into effect are reasonably sure that the recommended course of action is advisable.

The first step in the report writing process is to understand exactly what is expected. Here, the man who has assigned a research project talks with two people who will collaborate on a project.

▶ **OTHER PROBLEM STATEMENTS: ANALYTICAL REPORTS**

The statement of purpose may be in the form of a question; for example, "Why were the sales of Xtra-Ezy lawn mowers 56 percent less in District I than in District II in 1997?" Statements of purpose often include "to determine" or "to analyze."

LIMITING THE PROBLEM

The boundaries of a research problem are referred to as the *scope. Delimitations*, another term used instead of *scope*, describe specifically excluded factors that might have been expected in the report. The term *limitations* is used to refer to situations or handicaps, such as the lack of time or money, that prevented a complete research study or a thorough presentation.

However these terms are used as headings of a report, the scope of a report problem must be limited by exact and definite boundaries. You consider the scope in order to state the problem in definite and specific wording, as well as to plan research procedures.

Look at some of the preceding problem statements. Notice that these statements also include boundaries. For example, the problem statement about Xtra-Ezy lawn mowers indicates several boundaries. Answering such questions as *what, where, why, when,* and *who* can help you limit the problem.

What: Xtra-Ezy lawn mower sales (no other products)
Where: Districts I and II (no other districts)
Why: To determine how sales can be increased in the slow district
When: 1997 time span
Who: Employees in Districts I and II or perhaps general management

We are concerned only with sales, not with other factors of the two districts, unless these other factors influence sales in some way, as they may. Only the one product, Xtra-Ezy lawn mowers, is to be considered. Only one year, 1997, is to be considered. The problem is not clearly stated until the scope is definitely and specifically defined. As a researcher, you are responsible for including any material that could be reasonably expected unless you have specifically excluded such material.

Do not confuse the terms *limitations* and *delimitations*. An example of limitations, as applied to Xtra-Ezy lawn mowers, could be that statistics for competing products in District I and District II are not available. Delimitations—or *scope*, as used in this book—are the boundaries set by the researcher before the investigation is begun.

A TENTATIVE REPORT PLAN

Before beginning research to find the answer to a business problem, consider preparing a report plan, even though it must be a tentative one. Even though the plan may change during the research process, having one is a more efficient approach than no plan at all. An example of a report plan is shown in Figure 12-3.

DEVELOPING AN OUTLINE

Preparing a tentative outline or table of contents at the beginning of the study helps the final process of arranging ideas and prevents the investigation from going astray. During your final process of putting the report into written form, you are likely to see needed changes in the preliminary plan. An example outline for the report plan previously illustrated is shown in Figure 12-4.

A logical sequence of topics for the complete report is essential whether the plan of arrangement is the direct (deductive) or the indirect (inductive) order. If you are using the traditional and formal report arrangement arranged in the inductive order, you begin with the introduction, follow with findings and analyses, and end with conclusions and recommendations. Even though you already have this arrangement in mind, you must decide on the arrangement of topics in the middle section of the report, as well as the arrangement of information in the introductory and concluding sections.

Planning reports to be arranged in the direct order requires the same careful attention to an orderly sequence of ideas. In the direct order, as you remember, you place recommendations at the beginning of the report, as well as any necessary explanatory conclusions, and follow with supporting information.

FORMAT OF HEADINGS

The format and arrangement of *headings* will depend on the complexity of the material and the need for breakdown into various divisions. For example, if a report outline includes headings to correspond to I, II, III, IV, and V (main headings); A, B, C, and D; 1, 2, 3, and 4; and a, b, c, and d; the text of the report must include four levels of headings in addition to the title. With one level of division, only one form of heading is necessary in addition to the title. Unless you are following a specified format or are directed otherwise by a required guidebook, any form of heading—for example, side heads

Plan of Proposed Report

WHAT SHOULD T. L. GOEKEN LUMBER COMPANY DO TO INCREASE
CUSTOMER SATISFACTION AND INCREASE COMPETITIVENESS?

by

Gary Crawford, Assistant Manager

Statement of Purpose: The purpose of this report is to determine the overall customer satisfaction and awareness of T. L. Goeken Lumber Company as perceived by customers. The study is necessary because of increased competition in the hardware and lumber industry in the surrounding area. In addition to competition from lumber/hardware companies, Home Depot and Wal-Mart also compete directly in some product areas. The findings will provide management insight on maintaining and improving customer loyalty, store traffic, and profitability.

Scope: This study will focus on overall customer satisfaction and gather suggestions from customers on ways to improve the store's services. Information will be gathered from credit customers on such issues as company reputation on price and value, employees' product knowledge and courtesy, customers' awareness of monthly sales and promotions, and customers' awareness of services such as estimates, house plans, and fast delivery services. Since credit customers represent the larger portion of sales, they will serve as the study population. No cash-only customers will be surveyed. The level of total satisfaction with T. L. Goeken Lumber Company will also be measured. Zip codes will also be used to measure whether different perceptions exist in different communities.

Limitations: Cost constraints require that the survey be developed in-house. Constraints also prohibit mailing questionnaires to all 1,613 credit customers; a probability sampling will be used.

Readers: John D. Goeken, President, and Matt Gresham, Manager

Sources and Methods of Collecting Data: Secondary sources relating to improving customer satisfaction for competitive advantage will be reviewed prior to gathering primary data. Primary data will be gathered through a direct-mail questionnaire. Interviews will be conducted with the president and the store manager prior to developing the instrument. A probability sample of 400 of the 1,613 credit customers will be conducted; names will be chosen by selecting every fourth name on the credit accounting listing. The questionnaire will be reviewed and pretested by management. Descriptive analysis will be reported for each variable; several cross-sectional analyses will also be completed.

Attachments:

Tentative Table of Contents of Report: See attached outline

FIGURE 12-3
Example of a tentative report plan. Adapted from a marketing research class
project, M. Boudreaux and J. Donadieu, Nicholls State University.

Tentative General Outline

I. Purpose, Scope, and Methods of Research

    A. Purpose

    B. Scope

    C. Limitations

    D. Methodology

II. Data Analysis

    A. Zip Code

    B. Shopping Rates

    C. Customer Attitudes

    D. Service Awareness

    E. Main Reason for Shopping

    F. Awareness of Best Buys and Sales

    G. Overall Satisfaction

    H. Suggestions

III. Cross-sectional Analysis

    A. Advertising Effectiveness

    B. Satisfaction by Usage

    C. Product Line and Price

    D. Main Reason for Shopping by Usage

IV. Conclusions and Recommendations

FIGURE 12-4

Example of a tentative general outline

in all capitals or centered headings, either in all capitals or in capitals and lowercase—may be used. *Headings should be consistent and indicate the order of importance, or "weight," of each section. Placement and capitalization indicate the relationship of each heading to all the rest.*

The traditional outline arrangement has headings preceded by roman and arabic numerals and by letters in capitals and lowercase.

FIRST-DEGREE HEADING (TITLE)
  I. Second-Degree Heading
      A. Third-Degree Heading
      B. Third-Degree Heading
          1. Fourth-Degree Heading
          2. Fourth-Degree Heading
              a. Fifth-Degree Heading
              b. Fifth-Degree Heading
  II. Second-Degree Heading

The divisions of the report outline, which are also shown on the table of contents, may be used in a report according to the method illustrated in Figure 12-5. Note how the arrangement assists the reader in distinguishing between levels.

Ordinarily you will not need all five degrees of heading divisions illustrated in Figure 12-5, even for long reports. Although the wise use of exactly worded headings increases readability, an overly complicated system with unnecessary divisions may be confusing.

When you need fewer divisions than those shown in Figure 12-5, you need not follow the exact order of arrangement unless a variation would depart from instructions in the handbook you are using as a guide. For example, if your report requires only two levels of division and thus two levels of heading (in addition to the title), you might choose two levels of side headings; second-degree headings could be displayed in ALL CAPITALS, and third-degree headings could be shown *in Capitals and Lowercase, Underlined.*

WORDING OF HEADINGS

Headings, which are also referred to as *captions*, are useful in reports of any length, even letters, memorandums, and one-page manuscript reports. The longer the written message, the more essential headings become. Regardless of the length of the communication in which they are used, exactly worded and arranged headings show immediately the organization of the complete report and the relationship of each heading to all other headings.

Word headings carefully, not only for readability and organization but also for directing the flow of thought and the exact progression of ideas. Word headings so that they inform rather than just indicate the kind of information below them. (See Figure 12-6.)

FIRST-DEGREE HEADING

The first-degree heading (title) is centered and typed in all capitals. When the title consists of more than one line, usually these lines are double spaced; the first line is longer than the second, and the second is longer than the third. (Titles should be as short as possible, but they should also be exact and descriptive.)

Second-Degree Headings

Second-degree headings, using the arrangement shown here, are centered and underlined. They describe the major sections of the report and correspond to the headings preceded by Roman numerals, as shown in the report outline.

Third-Degree Headings

Third-degree headings correspond to A, B, C, and following letters, as shown in the report outline. In this plan of arrangement, they are placed at the left margin, typed in capitals and lowercase, and underscored.

Fourth-degree headings. Placement at the paragraph indention on the same line with the text distinguishes fourth-degree headings from third-degree headings. The period separates the heading from the remainder of the paragraph.

Fifth-degree headings are placed at the paragraph indention, on the same line as the text. These headings, however, are integral parts of beginning sentences.

FIGURE 12-5
Report heading formats

PHRASE AND SENTENCE HEADINGS

You may use noun phrases, infinitive phrases, or question headings in your reports. Some report writers prefer to use sentence headings in reports written in the direct order (conclusions and recommendations, followed by purpose and methods and ending with findings). The sentence headings often provide greater clarity for the reader. Note the sentence headings that could replace section II headings in Figure 12-6.

Company-Wide Policies Provide a Broad Perspective

Situational Examples Provide a Specific Focus

Leadership by Example Shapes Corporate Behavior

Whistle Blowing Identifies Problem Areas

PARALLEL GRAMMATICAL STRUCTURE

Headings should be grammatically parallel within each category, as illustrated in Figure 12-6. For example, the main headings (I, II, III, and IV) illustrated in Figure 12-6 are expressed as noun phrases. The A-B-C-D head-

I.   Introduction

    A.   Purpose

    B.   Scope

    C.   Methodology

II.   Techniques Used to Foster Ethical Decision-Making

    A.   Broad, Company-Wide Policies (Ethics Codes)

    B.   Situational Examples (Detailed Guidelines)

    C.   Leadership by Example

    D.   Whistle Blowing

III.   Beliefs and Opinions Identified by Future Managers

    A.   What Are the Preferred Assistance Techniques?

    B.   What Are the Preferred Deterrents?

    C.   What Are the Most Unethical Workplace Actions?

IV.   Conclusions and Recommendations

FIGURE 12-6
Portion of a table of contents or an outline

ings of Part II are noun phrases. The A-B-C headings of part III are complete
questions. As you will note, the writer has taken care to use parallel grammatical structures within parallel categories.

These headings are from a report focusing on what should be included in
a company ethics program to effectively influence employees. The arrangement of headings shown here is an *acceptable* one, not an example of the
only correct plan for all outlines or tables of contents. Do not think that you
must vary the grammatical construction of headings in the same report. For
example, the complete system of headings could be worded as noun phrases.

*Headings in the table of contents of a report must be worded in exactly the
same way as those in the text of the report itself. No single subheadings or
subdivisions should appear in your outline. You always need a minimum of
two subdivisions in any given section.* For example, do not use an "A" heading without a "B" heading, or a heading "1" without a "2." If you have only
one subdivision, either add a second, or simply incorporate the single subdivision into the larger division above.

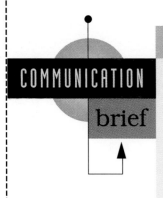

TECHNOLOGY TIPS

Use the outline feature of your word processing software as you key in your outline. This will help ensure consistency of style. In the event you later want to prepare a computer slide show to accompany an oral presentation related to your report, an outline prepared with a word processor often imports easily into a presentation graphics file. This can help reduce the amount of rekeying necessary.

You can automate the design of the report's final table of contents by using built-in heading styles available in your word processing software. As you key your report, apply the heading styles to the headings you want in your table of contents. Once your report is completed, follow the specific procedures of your software to generate the table of contents in the particular style of your choice. You will not have to worry about leaving out any headings as long as you have applied headings styles to each heading throughout the document. This approach makes generating a table of contents a simple task rather than a frustrating one.

DEVELOPING A PROPOSAL

Report plans, such as the one illustrated in Figure 12-3, are proposals for research projects. The terms *proposal*, *research proposal*, and *proposal report*, however, are used to denote a longer and more formal written presentation than what is ordinarily described as a *report plan*, particularly a plan for a class report or a short, informal business report.

The parts of a report plan discussed and illustrated earlier in this chapter are also parts of a research proposal (using the term in its more formal sense), but the proposal usually requires further information in addition to that shown in Figure 12-3. The word *proposal* is used not only as an offer to supply services as a researcher but also as an offer of other services, such as a consultation or a bid on a contract.

A statement of purpose and a description of proposal methodology are essential in the written presentation of any report project. Other categories of information often necessary for complete research proposals include an estimate of costs, perhaps with a long, detailed budget; qualifications of researchers and other personnel involved in the work; necessary equipment and facilities; a summary of previous research in the area to be studied, including a bibliography and perhaps a summary of all previous investigation; a detailed work schedule, including a date when the project is to be finished; provision for evaluation of the entire project; and suggestions for continuing research.

The physical appearance of many proposals is somewhere between the simple report plan illustrated in Figure 12-3 and a complete formal report il-

Students use university-provided computers to complete research or key assignments.

lustrated in Chapter 15. Proposals may be presented in letter, memorandum, or manuscript format, as illustrated by the short reports shown in Chapter 15. A long proposal should begin with an *abstract*, which is similar to the synopsis discussed in Chapter 15 and shown with a formal report. Like a *synopsis* (sometimes the terms are used interchangeably), an abstract summarizes the main idea of the report or proposal, with emphasis on the overall purpose and expected results. An abstract provides an immediate answer as to what the longer proposal is about and thus increases readability.

SOLICITED AND UNSOLICITED PROPOSALS

Proposals are *solicited or unsolicited. Solicited proposals* are submitted in response to requests for such proposals, which are often in the form of printed announcements. *Unsolicited proposals* are originated by the person or persons who submit them.

Requests for proposals come from government agencies, educational institutions, foundations, business and professional organizations, and many other groups and individuals. Announcements that request proposals may include detailed, specific instructions as to how the proposals are to be submitted, arranged, and written. These instructions should be followed exactly. Proposal reviewers are quick to reject those proposals that do not meet format guidelines or omit specified sections.

Unsolicited proposals differ little from solicited ones, although they may be more difficult to prepare because of the lack of guidelines. If no information is provided, the proposal should be prepared in the most easily read format and in the one that seems most likely to obtain the desired results because of the proper use of emphasis.

All the attributes of effective writing apply to the preparation of proposals of any kind. Organization, conciseness, and readability are of particular importance. As in all communication, your ideas are most likely to be accepted if your readers are convinced that what you propose will meet their needs and desires.

SUGGESTED CONTENTS OF A RESEARCH PROPOSAL

The sequence of information shown in Figure 12-3 could be adapted and expanded to serve as a research proposal. A research proposal might contain the following areas of content:

1. A cover sheet showing the title of the proposal; the name of the person, with position and organization, to whom the proposal is submitted; any necessary identifying numbers or phrasing to show that the proposal is in response to a particular announcement or set of specifications; the name, position, employing organization, address, and telephone number of the person or persons submitting the proposal; and the date the report is submitted.

2. An abstract that summarizes the entire proposal.

3. A table of contents, if the proposal is long enough for a table of contents to be helpful.

4. An introductory or background section, provided such information is necessary before going directly to the statement of purpose.

5. A specifically worded statement of purpose with necessary subcategories.

6. A summary of related research.

7. Procedures, which may be described as *methodology* or *sources of data*.

8. Personnel to be involved in the project, with a summary of their background and qualifications.

9. Facilities and equipment to be used in the project.

October 15, 19——

Sallye Starks
Vice President of Administration

PROPOSAL FOR SOFTWARE TRAINING WORKSHOPS

Many of our support staff, professionals, and managers have received upgrades in computer hardware and software within the past three months. The hardware upgrades arrived with new operating systems and new software already loaded. Many employees are currently struggling to teach themselves the new operating systems and software in between job tasks. Because we are already operating with a very streamlined staff, this is not a practical approach. Our office receives dozens of calls daily, all related to how to do a particular format, how to find a file they seem to have lost, and the like, with the new software. These calls come in after the employee has often already wasted a minimum of twenty minutes or more trying to figure out how to accomplish something and not succeeding.

The company's existing educational assistance program is no longer the solution. Employees do not necessarily need an entire semester of instruction, and evening or Saturday workshops are often unavailable.

With the cooperation of Central State University's College of Business Administration, and using two of our own people, Claire Berger and Jon Olivier, we can provide our own specialized training. Central State will make one of its computer teaching labs available to us during the weeks between regular semesters. Claire and Jon have focused on becoming power users of various software packages and have attended workshops related to training end users.

Supervisors in all departments will be asked to identify persons who need or desire training. Trainees will be grouped by software knowledge levels; if participant numbers allow, support staff will be grouped separately from management and professional staff. Both beginning and advanced workshops will be offered. Participants will complete evaluation sheets at the end of each workshop to allow us to assess the effectiveness of the activities and our trainers.

Four-hour workshops will be planned for each of four different software packages used by the majority of our employees. All training sessions will be limited to 15 persons and provide many hands-on activities. A training cycle of introduce/learn, practice, learn, practice will be incorporated. Training booklets will be used during the workshops; since many good materials are already on the market, these materials will be purchased rather than developed in-house.

Our status as a business internship partner of Central State University's College of Business will qualify us for a computer lab rental rate of $75 per half day or $150 a day. Training materials will cost an additional $500 to $700, depending on the final selections.

FIGURE 12-7
Example of a proposal in memo format

Sallye Starks

October 15, 19——

page 2

The time line for conducting software training workshops is outlined below.

- November 1   Memo to departments requesting names of individuals who need and/or want training

- November 10   Software questionnaires distributed to training participants to identify existing software knowledge and desired skills and knowledge levels

- November 22   Questionnaires analyzed and training dates established; specific workshop dates confirmed with Central State University College of Business

- December/January   Training sessions scheduled during the University's semester break; exact number of sessions dependent upon employee needs and number of employees involved

- Early March   Advanced sessions offered during the University's spring break

Workshop participants will be surveyed approximately six weeks following the workshops they attend to assess the extent to which they are using skills and concepts learned. Supervisors will also be asked to report on employee software performance.

This type of software training will help improve our overall productivity. Please call me at extension 4191 so that we may discuss implementation of the training workshops.

Jan Tomasetti

Jan Tomasetti

FIGURE 12-7
continued

10   Cost estimate, which may necessitate a long, detailed budget and a firm contractual maximum.

11   Provision for reporting results.

12   Provision for evaluation of research.

13   Provision for putting results into effect.

14   Suggestions for probable further research.

An internal proposal in memo format is shown in Figure 12-7.

PREPARING A WORK PLAN FOR THE PROJECT

You may outline a schedule of dates for conducting and completing various portions of your project as part of a formal proposal. If the written proposal does not require it, you will still want to complete a calendar of activities for your own reference. A short study that you will complete individually may have a very informal schedule. Larger studies typically require very specific schedules of start and completion dates for the many tasks. Collaborative projects also require schedules of when tasks will be completed so that all persons involved can meet deadlines and not slow the report progress.

At the beginning of a collaborative writing project, all team members need to understand the purpose and scope of the problems being addressed.

Collaborative Writing with the Aid of Technology

In today's business environment, proposal and report writing in many instances is a collaborative effort. When you are part of a team of people developing a proposal or any part of a report, use technology to enhance the group's productivity.

Even if you do not have access to true groupware software such as Lotus Notes, you can use word processing software to enter editorial comments and ideas on an electronic document. If all group members provide comments on a single electronic document, the project leader or a designated team member can make changes as appropriate. No longer will someone need to struggle with several hard copies containing handwritten comments, suggestions, and changes. When team members use strike-out features of the software, they can even note text suggested for deletion, without actually removing it from permanent view. Since comments from several team members can be viewed at the same time, revisions should be completed more efficiently and more effectively.

Groupware such as Lotus Notes is installed on a computer network server and offers group members the opportunity of reading and editing documents, either at their own individual time preference or during simultaneous electronic conversations and meetings. Groupware provides writing team members the capability of posing questions in real time, whether they are in the office or telecommuting. Those members who are shy and who may not contribute significantly in an oral communication situation may also feel more comfortable communicating electronically.

When reviewing a file, the author's name and time notation are attached to each comment, providing a "history" of the document's development. Members of the writing team are able to determine if and when something has been revised. Since activities of members may also be tracked, documentation of amount of contributions and/or work generated is also available.

When using groupware, the number and length of face-to-face meetings may be reduced; this can contribute to shortening the overall time frame required to generate the final document or report. A higher-quality final product may be generated as well.

S U M M A R Y

A report is a written or oral message planned to convey information or to present a solution. Although the basic qualities of effective reports are the same, for the most part, as those of all effective communication, in report writing we must give special attention to planned organization for coherence and readability and to an objective tone and nonbiased approach.

A report writer should assess how the report will be used. Is it for an internal or external audience? Is it a periodic or one-time report? Is the report informational or analytical? Assessing how a report will be used and by whom will help guide the choice of format and writing style.

The following classifications of reports are often used together:

► Formal format and writing style; impersonal tone; inductive (indirect, logical) arrangement

► Informal in format; formal or informal writing style; personal tone; direct or indirect arrangement, depending upon type of information

The basis of a report is a problem. The first and most important step in the report process is determining what the problem is and stating it exactly, with necessary and helpful subcategories.

The report writer should think through the complete problem-solving process before beginning the research project, even though the plans will be somewhat tentative. As a guide to further steps, a written report plan and an outline save time and keep the researcher on track.

A proposal is similar to a report plan, although often longer and more detailed. Some proposals must be long and detailed in order to present all necessary information. Others are shorter and are often presented as letters or memorandums.

Carefully consider the organization of the report into appropriate divisions. Headings should describe the material that comes under them. Headings in the text of the report should agree exactly with those in the table of contents.

Give particular attention to an objective presentation of data. Because the impersonal tone (writing style) emphasizes information, not the writer or reader, it seems to be more objective.

TEST YOURSELF
chapter content

1 Discuss at least four reasons reports are produced.
2 Briefly describe the difference between *informational* and *analytical* reports.
3 Distinguish between *internal* and *external* reports; *periodic* and *one-time* reports; *form* and *narrative* reports.
4 Briefly describe the difference between *personal* and *impersonal* (third-person objective) writing styles.
5 Briefly describe the difference between *direct* and *indirect* report arrangements as the terms apply to reports.
6 What is the first and most important step in the report process?
7 Briefly explain what is meant by the term *scope*.
8 Explain how a report writer can benefit from preparing a report plan and an outline or table of contents at the beginning of the report writing process.
9 Name and discuss five items that may be included in an effective proposal.
10 Distinguish between *formal* and *informal* as the terms apply to report formats.

TEST YOURSELF
correct usage

Rewrite the following sentences or insert punctuation so that the sentences are correct. Watch for nonparallel sentence construction.

1 One of your first steps will be to find out what is wanted. Especially if you are a new employee.
2 The impersonal writing style which is also described as the third person objective writing style only contains third person pronouns.
3 Employers want people to write and speak well and who can also think read and listen.
4 Preparing reports, presenting them, and to keep accurate records are important employment responsibilities.
5 Doing research is more enjoyable to some people than to write a report.
6 Reports should be objective clear and they should be well organized.
7 Keep sentences relatively short, and they should be concise.
8 Charts are introduced and the report writer points out the highlights.
9 It is dangerous to generalize from insufficient information we are all guilty of this occasionally.
10 Some recommendations must be based on inferences we sometimes cannot have all the necessary facts.

PROBLEMS

Note: Additional cases follow Chapter 15.

1 Determine which of the following classifications are likely to apply to the following reports:
  Informational or analytical
  Formal or informal format
  Formal or informal writing style
  Personal or impersonal tone
  Internal or external report
  Periodic or one-time report
  Direct or indirect arrangement

a. A teacher reports students' absences to the Veterans Administration by circling the names of students with poor attendance. He prepares a memorandum about unusual situations.

b. An engineering consulting firm studies the buildings on a college campus and makes recommendations about the con-servation of energy. The report is 80 pages long and includes various preliminary and supplementary parts. The last section of the report includes recommendations.

c. A vice-president of a business organization interviews applicants for the position of sales manager and chooses the three who seem to be best qualified. She describes the three applicants in a memorandum to the president of the organization, with her recommendation.

d. At the end of each month, the manager of an apartment complex submits a letter that includes information about expenditures and occurrences throughout the month and a short analysis of the progress and profitability of the complex. The monthly reports are prepared from daily listings of expenditures and activities. These listings, along with the monthly report, are submitted to the owner of the complex.

2 For each of the following problem situations, state the problem (purpose) either in the form of a question or as an infinitive phrase. For example, a report planned to study the advisability of providing career apparel can be stated as:

> Should the Countrywide Insurance Company provide career apparel for its women employees? *(Question)*
>
> Purpose: To determine whether the Countrywide Insurance Company should provide career apparel for its women employees. *(Infinitive phrase)*

Be specific, but omit subcategories of the problem.

Assume necessary and reasonable details, including names.

a. A restaurant manager wants to know how to improve crowded conditions at the midday meal.

b. A restaurant manager wants to know how to increase profits on the midday meal.

c. A restaurant manager wants to know the choices most often made from the luncheon menu.

d. A college professor is trying to decide whether to authorize monthly deductions from her paycheck for deposit in a tax-sheltered annuity fund.

e. The professor had decided to invest in a tax-sheltered annuity fund, but she does not know which one to choose. She has narrowed her choices to three.

f. The information center manager of a large corporation wants to determine what types of software training are needed by the managers, professionals, and staff in the corporate office building.

g. A business education teacher must choose computers for a classroom to be used for several business education classes including keyboarding, accounting, administrative support procedures, and cooperative office education.

h. A Chamber of Commerce wants to know what local citizens think of the Chamber's services and purposes.

i. A dean of a college of business administration wants to determine the business course or courses that former students believe to have been most beneficial to them.

j. An accounting student needs to enroll in one of three CPA review courses offered within reasonable driving distance of her home.

k. A large construction company is considering adopting a pension plan.

l. The Park Commission is thinking of installing Muzak in all offices.

m. A manufacturer needs to know how to market a new product, a compact refrigerator-icemaker.

3 Assume that each of the following paragraphs is the first one of a report planned to determine how T. L. Goeken Lumber Company can increase customer satisfaction and company competitiveness. Assume that all examples are taken from the first part of the report body, not from the preliminary or supplementary parts.

> **Example A:** The purpose of this study is to determine the overall customer satisfaction and awareness of T. L. Goeken Lumber Company's service offerings in the minds of the individuals surveyed.
>
> **Example B:** I have conducted a direct-mail survey of T. L. Goeken's credit customers. Although developing and perfecting the questionnaire was time-consuming and the cost of the preparing and mailing the survey was over $400 and not all respondents answered every question, you'll find my recommendations at the end of this report.
>
> **Example C:** More advertising will help T. L. Goeken Lumber Company hold its market share against increasing competition. Store hours should be extended to 6 P.M. Monday through Friday and until 3 P.M. on Saturday.

Example D: I recommend that T. L. Goeken Lumber Company increase its advertising to help counteract increasing competition. Also, I recommend the store stay open until 6 P.M. Monday through Friday and until 3 P.M. on Saturday.

(1) Which example(s) indicate(s) that the report is arranged in the direct order? The indirect order?

(2) Which example(s) indicate(s) that the report is written in the personal tone? In the impersonal (third-person objective) tone?

(3) Which example(s) indicate(s) that the report is written in the informal writing style?

(4) Which example(s) is (are) most likely to be taken from a complete and formal analytical report?

(5) Each of the four examples was taken from an analytical report. How can you tell?

4 Assume that each of the following paragraphs is the first paragraph of a report planned to determine a suitable location for an addition to a chain of restaurants named Country Vittles. Consider all examples to be taken from the first paragraph of the report body, not from the preliminary or supplementary parts.

Example A: A Country Vittles restaurant should be built on Highway 20 West in Galena, Illinois.

Example B: I recommend that a Country Vittles restaurant be built on Highway 20 West in Galena, Illinois.

Example C: The purpose of this study is to determine possible locations for a Country Vittles restaurant and to determine which site should be chosen for the next addition to the Country Vittles chain.

Example D: I've completed the study of possible locations for Country Vittles. Because everybody likes country cooking, I'm convinced that we need to build restaurants all over the world. But because we don't have the bread (cornbread or otherwise) for all these, I've picked out the best bet for our next restaurant. You'll find my recommenda-

tion at the end of this report. Everybody is going to be surprised.

(1) Which example(s) indicate(s) that the report is arranged in direct order? indirect order?

(2) Which example(s) indicate(s) that the report is written in the personal tone? In the impersonal (third-person objective) tone?

(3) Which example(s) indicate(s) that the report is written in the informal writing style?

(4) Which example(s) is (are) most likely to be taken from a complete and formal analytical report?

(5) Each of the four examples was taken from an analytical report. How can you tell?

(6) Of the four passages, Example D is likely to be the most undesirable. Why?

5 Choose a question that you wish to investigate in order to report the results in a formal business report. Prepare a tentative report plan, as shown in this chapter. Include a tentative title, statement of purpose, scope (or scope and limitations), readers, and sources and methods of collecting data.

6 Prepare a tentative table of contents and a tentative bibliography for the research you planned in Problem 5.

7 Rewrite the following section from the introductory section of an analytical report. Use the impersonal tone instead of the personal tone in which it is now expressed.

We completed this study for the following reasons:

a. We determined what techniques employees ranked as most helpful in assisting them in making ethical decisions. We also determined what deterrents employees preferred and which actions they viewed as most unethical. We also compared answers of male and female employees.

b. We identified the ethical decision-making assistance techniques most preferred by employees.

c. We analyzed and interpreted the results of the study in relation to what a company can do to encourage employees to make ethical decisions.

COLLABORATIVE WRITING AND
WORKING IN GROUPS AND THINK-
IT-THROUGH ASSIGNMENTS

8 After you have prepared a tentative report plan, tentative table of contents, and tentative bibliography, as instructed in Problems 5 and 6, meet with two or three other students to discuss the material that each one in the group has previously prepared. (Your instructor may wish to specify the number in each group and the students who will be assigned to each group. If several students are working on similar topics, perhaps these students should be assigned to the same group throughout the report-writing section of the course.)

An alternative is to work on a group project, as suggested in problems concerning intercultural communications, Cases 33 through 36 in the Cases section following Chapter 15.

Regardless of the topic chosen by the members of your group, each person's complete assignment (report plan, table of contents, and bibliography) should be analyzed and discussed by each member of the group. Analyze the materials in relation to each of the points below:

a. Does the plan contain a specific, exactly worded statement of purpose?

b. Does the scope clearly indicate the boundaries the writer has placed on the project?

c. Does the wording and arrangement of headings in the table of contents follow the instructions given in Chapter 12?

d. Does the table of contents seem to cover what is indicated in the statement of purpose? Does the table of contents seem to include subjects that are *not* stated or implied by the statement of purpose? If so, reword or omit.

e. Evaluate the tentative table of contents for organization, completeness, and all other applicable criteria.

f. Look ahead to the "Evaluation Sheet: Contents and Writing Style, Formal and Informal Reports" following Chapter 15. Although this evaluation sheet applies to a completed report, some of the questions apply to this preliminary assignment.

g. Check the tentative bibliography for appropriateness. Notice the dates of the publications listed. Are they still current? Even if they contain information that is still valid, the bibliography should contain recent sources as well. Some topics—for example, rapidly changing technology—should be based only on recent sources. In some fields material more than two years old is obsolete.

h. Compare the format of entries in the bibliography with the format shown in Chapter 13.

Gathering and Reporting Information

CHAPTER

13

OBJECTIVES

Chapter Thirteen will help you:

1 Identify appropriate secondary sources of business data.

2 Evaluate the quality of secondary sources and data.

3 Select an appropriate method of primary research (observations, experimentation, or surveys) for solving a problem.

4 Construct effective questionnaires.

5 Discuss effective interview techniques.

6 Use appropriate citation and reference formats for sources.

The preceding chapter emphasized the first steps of the report process: determine the problem, define it in specific terms, and decide on the methods of finding a solution to the problem. This chapter moves to what is ordinarily the next step in the report process: gathering the information on which we can base a decision.

GATHERING INFORMATION

Sources of data are described as *secondary* or *primary*. *Secondary* is used to mean that data have already been gathered and recorded by someone else. *Primary* describes data that have not already been gathered and recorded by someone else. Primary data are obtained through *observation*, *experimentation*, and *surveys*, which may include *questionnaires* and formal or informal *interviews*. Interviewing may be completed in person or by telephone. *Primary data is your original research.* Any data gathered in any way by someone else is *secondary* data.

Secondary research should ordinarily be the starting point in the data-gathering process. Whatever problem you are trying to solve, similar ones are likely to have occurred in other organizations or with other individuals. The solutions to these problems may be reported in business periodicals or elsewhere. Although these problems will be at least slightly different from your own, your knowledge of what other individuals and organizations have concluded in similar situations can help to answer your own questions.

Conducting Secondary Research

In addition to the general guides to information described in the following sections, many other reference sources that are not listed here because of limited space may be helpful to you in your particular research project. On the job, you can check with colleagues for suggestions about additional internal sources or useful online sources. When visiting a library, check for brochures and other printed material to guide you to additional sources, or talk with a librarian.

INTERNAL AND EXTERNAL SOURCES

Business professionals often have numerous data sources within the organization. Both computerized company data and noncomputerized files and documents may provide needed information for a person preparing a report. The internal data may be useful in preparing a historical overview, assessing alternatives, and justifying recommendations. In addition, researchers often need to gather external secondary information available through libraries or online.

LIBRARY SOURCES

There are a number of ways to approach locating secondary sources for a research project. *Business Information: How to Find It, How to Use It,* 2nd edition, 1992, by Michael R. Lavin, is a helpful source for anyone looking for suggestions in locating business research materials. A general guide to the literature, such as *The Encyclopedia of Business Information Sources,* 1995–1996, 10th edition, published by Gale Research, Inc., offers a bibliographic guide of more than 26,000 citations covering over 1,100 subjects of interest to business professionals. For each subject, the guide cites appropriate abstracting and indexing services, almanacs and yearbooks, bibliographies, CD-ROM databases, directories, encyclopedias and dictionaries, handbooks, online databases, periodicals, statistical sources, and other sources of information.

While some libraries offer their patrons physical card catalogs of holdings, many libraries today have fully automated catalogs. Information that was shown on cards is now displayed on the screens of computer terminals. Catalogs or lists of books displayed by computers provide, in effect, bibliographies of material on almost any topic you might choose to research; numerous titles are likely to be available. You may find that your library's computerized catalog also offers information on holdings in other libraries if your library is a member of some type of consortium.

Computer files, like card catalogs, may be accessed by author, title, and subject. The guide, *Library of Congress Subject Headings*, is useful in narrowing your topic to be researched.

For many research projects, needed data will appear only in journal articles, pamphlets, newspapers, or government documents, all of which are indexed elsewhere than in a card catalog or comparable computer files. Books, however, still provide information that cannot be found elsewhere, in a convenient and readily available form.

BOOKS

A major guide to books, whether or not they are in your particular library, is *Cumulative Book Index*, published by H. W. Wilson Company. The *Cumulative Book Index* includes books published in the English language all over the world, recorded by author, title, and subject. In addition to being available in hard copy, WILSONDISC offers the index on CD-ROM, updated quarterly. For more frequent updates, an online version with twice weekly updates is available through WILSONLINE. Ask your librarian which version is available.

Other guides to books on a particular topic are *Books in Print* and *Subject Guide to Books in Print*. They include books "in print" and currently available for purchase in the United States. *Books in Print Plus* is a CD-ROM version updated bimonthly. *Canadian Books in Print* lists books available from Canadian publishers.

Research that would have been impossible before computers is now quickly accomplished.

► ## ENCYCLOPEDIAS, DICTIONARIES, AND HANDBOOKS

Comprehensive encyclopedias are useful in all types of research, especially as a starting place and for general background information. They may also include a list of supplementary reading materials for your particular topic. In addition to general encyclopedias, a number of specialized ones are available for coverage of specific areas of knowledge. Today various encyclopedias are available on CD-ROM, as well as in hard copy.

Dictionaries remain an important library source. In addition to general dictionaries, there are many specialized ones, just as there are specialized encyclopedias.

Handbooks are similar to specialized encyclopedias and dictionaries. They tend to be more complete, usually more so than a book described as a dictionary. A business handbook presents a condensed picture of an entire field of business. These handbooks are frequently revised in order to include only accurate and relevant information.

► ## YEARBOOKS AND ALMANACS

Yearbooks, in addition to those that supplement encyclopedias, include publications of various countries, trades, and professions, as well as the *Statistical Abstract of the United States*. The CD-ROM version of the *Statistical Abstract of the United States* presents information in spreadsheet file format; this allows the researcher to use graphics software to convert tabular information into appropriate charts and graphs.

Almanacs, such as the widely available *World Almanac and Book of Facts*, contain a wealth of information on many and varied subjects. Similar information, particularly about Canadian topics, is given in *Canadian Yearbook* and *Corpus Almanac of Canada*.

If you have access to an up-to-date computer, you may have access to a CD-ROM library such as Microsoft Bookshelf that provides CD-ROM access to a group of reference sources that may include a dictionary, a thesaurus, an encyclopedia, an atlas, an almanac, and a book of quotations. You may search each reference book separately for a given topic, or you may choose to search all of the books at once for available information on the topic. Caution must be used; while the thesaurus and dictionary information may be current, other information from the atlas or almanac may be incorrect or out of date; it may be necessary to visit the local library for a current almanac and/or atlas.

► ## BIOGRAPHICAL DIRECTORIES AND BUSINESS SERVICES

Biographical directories such as *Who's Who in America* provide information about well-known persons, living or dead. Specialized directories such as *Who's Who in Finance and Industry* provide similar information about persons in a particular field. Other directories are specialized according to geographic area.

As a researcher, you must use caution; you may find conflicting information in different sources since the information in directories is often solicited from companies or individuals by the publisher. You should verify information in more than one source whenever possible.

Business services provide business information of many kinds. *Moody's Manuals* summarize data for all major companies. These manuals are issued annually in bound volumes and include the history of each company, a description of products or services, locations of home office and most important plants, a list of officers and directors, and financial data. *Standard and Poor's Register of Corporations, Executives, and Industries*, published annually, is available in hard copy, in a CD-ROM version updated every two months, or online through DIALOG and LEXIS/NEXIS. Another well-known service organization is Predicasts, Inc., which provides various services in addition to forecasts and market data classified by company, product, and service. Predicasts information is available in hard copy and online.

▶ **GUIDES TO PERIODICALS AND PAMPHLETS**

Periodicals, that is, magazines, journals, or serials, are often more helpful than books for use in business research. Various indexes serve as a guide to the contents of general and specialized periodicals.

The *Business Periodicals Index* and the *Canadian Business Periodicals Index* are guides to articles in business, industrial, and trade magazines. The *Business* Index, available on microfilm, CD-ROM, or online, covers even more business publications than the two indexes listed above. The *Applied Science and Technology Index* is a guide to articles in about 200 English language publications on scientific and technological subjects.

The *Public Affairs Information Service Bulletin*, referred to as PAIS, classifies periodicals, government publications, and pamphlets by subject, especially in the areas of economics and social conditions, public administration, and international affairs. Print, CD-ROM, and online versions are available.

The *F&S Index (United States)* by Predicasts covers company, product, and industry information from more than 750 financial publications, business-oriented newspapers, trade magazines, and special reports. The *F&S International Index* includes information about Canada and the rest of the world outside the United States, including operations abroad of U.S. companies.

▶ **COMPUTERIZED DATABASES**

Thousands of computerized databases provide a comprehensive, time-saving method of research. Consult either *CD-ROMs in Print* or *Directory of On-line Databases* for complete listings. Many of the sources described in this chapter are now available in both printed and electronic database form. Online computerized databases can be accessed through the use of telephone lines and modem-equipped computers; costs of the search are based on computer time used and downloading or mailing costs. Your library may have policies requiring a librarian to assist in a direct online search, depending on type of access offered.

An alternative to the cost of online searches is the use of databases on CD-ROM; while these CD-ROM versions do not offer the immediate updates available through full online services, many are updated either weekly, monthly, or quarterly. Your library may have some of these such as ABI/ Inform or InfoTrac; the use of these CD-ROM databases is typically free to library patrons.

Comprehensive database services are also available that provide access to numerous databases. The Dow Jones News/Retrieval Service provides full-text news from *The Wall Street Journal* and other Dow Jones sources. LEXIS/NEXIS offers enormous amounts of full-text articles and also includes such things as corporate annual reports. VISTA offers access to over 8 million full-text documents; millions of other citations are also indexed. DIALOG Information Services, Inc., and BRS Search Service are also well-known database services.

An example of a database that pertains particularly to business is ABI/Inform. Available either on CD-ROM or online through services such as

DRAWING BOARD

DIALOG, BRS, and LEXIS/NEXIS, ABI/Inform has no print counterpart. It offers information similar to but more comprehensive than the *Business Periodicals Index*. ABI/Inform provides citations and abstracts up to 250 words in length. (An abstract is a summary of a document.) Full-text electronic versions of many of the indexed articles can be accessed through LEXIS/NEXIS.

EDGAR (Electronic Data Gathering, Analysis, and Retrieval) is a numerical database system providing U.S. Securities and Exchange Commission filings information online directly through the Internet or through a service such as CompuServe or America Online. Another useful statistical database, CENDATA, is available online from the Bureau of the Census.

Effective computer database searches require careful planning of search terms, whether you are using a CD-ROM version of a particular index, using a service such as LEXIS/NEXIS or DIALOG online, or using some of the various Internet search engines such as Infoseek, Yahoo, or Savvy. Ask a librarian for assistance if you have difficulty narrowing your search.

While abstracts provided through a bibliographic database are extremely useful because they quickly let the researcher know whether or not to obtain the complete article or other work, you should not rely on an abstract alone, especially if you mean to cite the work in your own writing. Reading a number of abstracts on the same topic, however, can provide you with an overview of the topic you are researching. Today's databases typically offer provisions for either printing copies or downloading abstract files to computer disks.

No matter how you search for secondary sources, if the full text is not available online, check your library to determine if the material is available on the shelf or in some type of microform or electronic format. If the source is not available at your library, you may wish to order the materials through interlibrary loan. Check with a librarian to determine the possibility, time frame, and costs.

Evaluating Secondary Sources and Data

As you can see by now, your library and other sources such as the Internet contain an immense number of secondary-research sources. Obviously, many of these will not fit your particular research needs. Naturally, your basic criterion should be relevance: use only materials that are related to your topic. In addition, however, carefully consider each of the following points as you select secondary sources.

► *Question the materials you find.* Consider your problem statement and any outline you have prepared. Be sure to stay within the content areas you have planned.

► *Use material that you can understand.* Select only materials that you can understand: You will find it quite hard to summarize and integrate materials that you do not understand, such as complicated statistical analyses with which you are not familiar or detailed materials written for an expert on the subject.

► *Select publications with credibility.* Not all publications enjoy the same level of respectability. Well-written articles in professional journals such as *The Journal of Marketing Research* and respected trade journals often provide more depth of coverage and more credibility than certain other popular publications.

► *Select materials prepared by credible authors.* Likewise, look for authors with credibility. Certain authors focus on specific research areas for years and have established reputations. When using trade journals, look for footnotes that provide some basic information about the writer as a confirmation of credibility.

► *Select current materials.* Provide current references to support your research. While you may draw upon earlier materials if a historical perspective is needed, make sure that your sources reflect current issues, concerns, approaches, and findings.

Finally, remember that reading original materials helps guard against misrepresentation by an intermediary source. You should quote statistics with particular care.

Carefully evaluate the information you locate when using the Internet. When accessing a Web page, for instance, examine the header, body, and footer to determine the author and source. Check on-line directory sources for affiliations and biographical information. Check and compare the material against other sources. Remember: Information on Web pages has not received the same review or professional evaluation as articles in trade magazines and scholarly journals. Moreover, some materials—such as those available through governmental agency gopher sites or Web pages or on-line versions of legitimate scholarly and trade journals—are more credible than others. Always try to use more than one Internet search engine; not surprisingly, some produce more and higher-quality information than others.

CONDUCTING PRIMARY RESEARCH

Primary research describes collection of data by all methods except reading the words of other writers. Primary research goes beyond secondary research. In turn, primary research by one individual (or a group) becomes secondary research for future researchers. Many reports should not be based only on secondary data, or on primary data, but should include both, although not necessarily in equal amounts.

▶ OBSERVATION

Observation, as the term describes a method of research, means the examination of phenomena under real, presently existing conditions. Observation under controlled or manipulated conditions is referred to as *experimentation*. Observation as a method of research is often casual and informal; it may also be carefully planned, with observed actions or occurrences recorded and tabulated. Observation may be an effective method of tracking the types of customers patronizing a store, merchandise examined, helpfulness of sales associates, dress of office staff, and so forth. Observation may also be used to describe a search through company records. Many accounting and auditing reports are based on an examination and analysis of financial records. Hence, the method of data collection is observation, although such reports are not usually described as such.

The results of information obtained through observation, like that obtained in any other way, can be reliable or not, depending on the care and judgment of the researcher as well as on many other contributing factors. Comprehensive, carefully planned observational research is more likely to provide dependable results than casual and informal notice of conditions and occurrences, although the latter form of observation should not be overlooked. As in all other forms of research, accurate and complete records should be kept as data are collected. Then the data should be carefully and accurately organized, analyzed, and interpreted.

▶ EXPERIMENTATION

Scientific experimentation is reliable and accurate if it is carefully planned and conducted. But even experimentation is subject to error. In addition, many business problems are not of the type that lend themselves to experimental research. In business, as in other areas, the purpose of experimental research is to determine the effect of change under a given set of conditions. The conditions must be carefully constructed so that only one variable is tested at a time. For example, an experiment to determine the effect of career apparel upon employee morale would be difficult to conduct in a completely scientific manner because of the element of human behavior.

▶ SURVEYS (QUESTIONNAIRES)

Surveys are widely used in obtaining business information. They are conducted through personal and telephone interviews and through questionnaires. Questionnaires may be sent through hard-copy mail or electronic mail. They may also be made available through the Internet via gopher sites or Web sites, although the researcher will gather responses only from those who both access the site and choose to respond.

As you consider using a survey as a means of gathering primary data, you need to consider some inherent weaknesses of surveys. (All other methods of research also have weaknesses.) The survey is open to criticism because it depends completely on verbal responses, and words are inexact. When filling out a questionnaire or talking with a researcher in a personal interview or on the telephone, the respondent may provide untrue, incomplete, or inaccurate and misleading information. Even when respondents wish to provide complete and accurate answers, they often do not do so because of inaccurate memories, lack of knowledge and detailed information, a tendency to give the expected response, and any number of other reasons.

Influences of all kinds enter into results of interviews and questionnaires, as into all other areas of oral and written communication. People who answer an interviewer's questions are affected by their perceptions of the interviewer, of the situation, and of themselves. Their mood of the moment influences their responses and whether a questionnaire sent through the mail is returned.

Regardless of the interviewer, questionnaire, or topic being investigated, respondents tend to exaggerate income, education, social status, and other important aspects of their experiences. Respondents tend to minimize unfavorable aspects. These inaccuracies occur even when there is *no* possibility that a particular respondent's questionnaire can be identified later.

Questionnaire design, which is extremely important in achieving accurate information, is often approached casually and haphazardly. A poor questionnaire or poorly structured interview is almost certain to result in incomplete or incorrect data. Questionnaire construction requires much thought and time. Ideally, a questionnaire is tested with a small group (often referred to as a pilot test) before it is used on a large scale.

Questionnaires and interviews are so widely used, often with poorly designed survey instruments, that respondents do not consider their answers important or do not answer at all. Another drawback is that the researcher has no way of being sure that respondents who return questionnaires are representative of the entire population being surveyed. Distributing a company survey related to e-mail through the company e-mail system will likely result in responses from frequent e-mail users. Infrequent users may not respond; those with no e-mail access have no opportunity to respond.

If you survey alumni of a school and ask questions about jobs and salaries, those who feel successful are much more likely to return questionnaires, even if their names are not used, than those who feel otherwise. The researcher who attempts to obtain the mean or median salary of such a group would report an average salary higher than the typical salary of all class members.

The survey method is the only practical way to obtain many kinds of information, despite its inherent weaknesses. It is difficult to determine what people think, know, or believe without asking them. We cannot know their likes and dislikes, their desires, or their intended actions. We cannot gain the benefit of their recommendations without asking for them. In addition, events that have already occurred cannot be observed. They must be described by others in written or spoken words.

Constructing Questionnaires

When you plan a questionnaire, your goals are to secure a satisfactory rate of return and complete, objective answers. Another consideration is to design an instrument that allows you to easily and accurately tabulate and analyze responses.

Include a convincing explanatory letter, usually on a separate sheet but sometimes at the top of the printed questionnaire. The most effective way to convince readers to respond is to show them benefits to themselves. Even if there is no immediate benefit, many people will cooperate if you carefully and convincingly explain the purpose of the study and why you need their opinions. An ethical researcher also typically guarantees respondent anonymity, assuring respondents that their answers will not be treated separately. Do everything possible to make response easy; for example, make the questionnaire as short as possible, ask for check marks instead of long written replies, and enclose a stamped, addressed envelope.

► QUESTION DESIGN

How you construct the questionnaire will influence the percentage of returns and the value of the answers. Specific principles of question construction are listed below.

1   *Phrase questions so they are easy to understand and concerned with one topic only.* Avoid ambiguous wording. For example, the question "Why did you buy your last television?" could lead to the response of liking the stereo sound, the price, or the extra features and programming capabilities. Another respondent might answer that he bought the television because he wanted a larger viewing screen, or because the old television needed major, costly repairs. Avoid broad, relative terms such as *often, a long time,* and *seldom,* unless these terms are specifically defined.

2   *Make the questionnaire easy to answer.* Providing closed-end questions with answer blanks to be checked facilitates response as well as the researcher's tabulation of the answers.

3   *Provide for all likely answers.* Although some questions can be answered by a *yes* or a *no,* many are somewhere in between. Provide for categories such as *I don't know,* or *no opinion.* For some questions, allowing for

shadings of opinions such as *strongly agree, agree, no opinion, disagree,* or *strongly disagree* permits more descriptive responses.

4   *Ask only for information that the respondent is likely to remember.*

5   *Keep the questionnaire as short as possible by asking only for needed information.*

6   *Avoid questions that touch on pride or personal bias, or those that give the effect of prying.* Such areas include age, income, education, morals, and personal habits. While information about age, income status, or education may be necessary in order to accomplish the particular purpose of the report, such as marketing research, you will ordinarily not need the exact age, the exact income, or the exact number of years the person has been in school. Instead, provide ranges from which the respondent may choose to show age and income. For example, you can show age brackets *under 21, 21 to 25,* and so on, and set up income brackets in the same way. Providing ranges will encourage responses as well as facilitate evaluation of answers.

7   *Arrange questions in a logical order.* Hopping back and forth between question topics can confuse respondents.

8   *Avoid leading questions*—those that by their wording suggest an answer. For example, "Don't you agree that business majors earn the highest beginning salaries," leads the respondent to answer *yes.*

9   *Provide specialized instructions where appropriate.* If respondents should select only one answer, rank items, or skip to a certain question based on their answer to the current question, special directions must be provided to direct respondents correctly.

10   *Provide for the respondent's additional comments,* if any, by using open-ended questions that allow for comments in the respondent's own words. Although these answers are more difficult to tabulate than those that are shown by a check mark, the comments may be the most helpful answers of all. In addition, open-ended questions may encourage respondents to speak freely.

Figure 13-1 is an illustration of a questionnaire sent to customers of a lumber company to gather information related to customer satisfaction and customer awareness of services. A cover letter on company letterhead, signed by an official of the company, was included with the questionnaire.

▶ LAYOUT AND DESIGN CONSIDERATIONS

Arrange questions in an appropriate sequence. The sequence of questions can influence cooperation, interest, and the final results of a questionnaire. Use special care with beginning questions. As in other forms of communication, opening statements are emphatic by virtue of their position. If personal questions even slightly threatening to the ego must be included in the survey instrument, they should not be asked first. And, as in instructional material, questions should move from the simple to the complex. (As much as possible, keep all questions simple.)

Early questions should build reader interest and provide motivation for completing the questionnaire. In some survey situations, questions should proceed from the general to the specific.

If the questionnaire is mailed, enclose a stamped and addressed envelope. Include a response deadline date in a prominent location on the page in order to decrease procrastination.

Use white space, bolds, italics, and different type point sizes effectively. Questionnaires that appear too crowded or unattractive may not be completed. While white paper is always acceptable, you may want to consider printing the questionnaire on off-white, very light gray, beige, or cream paper to help call attention to your questionnaire. Bright, garish colors often have a negative effect; yellow, blue, and pink may not be viewed as professional.[1] Always use a sharp, clear, clean print.

Paper should be 20-pound weight or heavier; if questions are printed on the back of the page, they will not show through the paper.

When designing a survey instrument, you may elect to use response codes, often a very tiny number to the left of each response box. This type of coding assists during the data file keying. Format codes (often in the far right of the questionnaire) identify where data will be keyed to the computer record. Consulting a publication such as *The Survey Research Handbook*, 2nd ed., by Alreck and Settle, will provide more extensive information on how to set up response and format codes.

Designing a questionnaire so that respondent answers can be scanned and entered into a computer data file in one step can speed analysis and improve accuracy. This eliminates the necessity of someone keying in responses.

If appropriate, researchers may use electronic mail to survey members of a company, an Internet discussion group, and so forth. Many e-mail systems allow a respondent to simply mark answers and return the original message and completed survey to the researcher by e-mail. Verification of

T. L. Goeken Lumber Company
Customer Service Survey

1. What is your zip code? _____

2. Which of the following **most closely describes how often you shop** at T. L. Goeken? (**Please check one**)

   ___ two to three times a week   ___ once a month   ___ other (list) _____
   ___ once a week   ___ once or twice a year

3. What type of product do you **buy most often** at T. L. Goeken?

   ___ hardware   ___ lumber   ___ paint   ___ gardening supplies   ___ other (list) _____

4. Please put an **X** in the following blanks that best represent your opinion on the following items concerning T. L. Goeken Lumber Company. The middle box (4) represents a neutral opinion.

   1   2   3   4   5   6   7

   | | |
   courteous service   ___ : ___ : ___ : ___ : ___ : ___ : ___   discourteous service

   low price   ___ : ___ : ___ : ___ : ___ : ___ : ___   high price

   helpful employees   ___ : ___ : ___ : ___ : ___ : ___ : ___   unhelpful employees

   employees with
   product knowledge   ___ : ___ : ___ : ___ : ___ : ___ : ___   employees without
   product knowledge

   good delivery service   ___ : ___ : ___ : ___ : ___ : ___ : ___   bad delivery service

5. Does T. L. Goeken offer any of the following services?
   quick delivery   ___ yes   ___ no   ___ don't know
   customized paint colors   ___ yes   ___ no   ___ don't know
   house estimates   ___ yes   ___ no   ___ don't know
   special orders   ___ yes   ___ no   ___ don't know
   lock rekeying   ___ yes   ___ no   ___ don't know

6. Please **rank your top 3 reasons** for shopping at T. L. Goeken. (1 = **top reason; 2 = 2nd; 3 = 3rd**)
   ___ price   ___ wide selection of products   ___ store hours
   ___ convenience   ___ employee service   ___ location
   ___ good value   ___ delivery services   ___ other (please specify) _____
   ___ credit   ___ family loyalty

7. Are you aware of T. L. Goeken's monthly sales and best buys? ___ yes ___ no

   IF YES, How do you know? (**Please check one**)

   ___ word of mouth   ___ in-store advertising   ___ sales paper   ___ other (please specify) _____

FIGURE 13-1

Questionnaire sent to customers to gather information related to customer satisfaction and awareness of services. Adapted from a marketing research class project, M. Boudreaux and J. Donadieu, Nicholls State University.

8. How satisfied are you with T. L. Goeken Lumber Company? The middle box (4) represents a neutral opinion.

                          1   2   3   4   5   6   7

satisfied   __ : __ : __ : __ : __ : __ : __   dissatisfied

9. What suggestions would you recommend to improve your shopping experience at T. L. Goeken Lumber Company? (Please use the back side if you need additional space.)

THANK YOU!

FIGURE 13-1
continued

e-mail addresses can assist the researcher in eliminating duplicate responses. Designing forms for Web pages also allows a researcher to set up questionnaires for Web users. While Web page forms may encourage responses, the researcher typically has *no* assurance of surveying a representative sample.

Besides mailing questionnaires, you may do a survey by personal interviews, either face to face or by telephone. When you conduct a survey through face to face or telephone interviews, you should draw up a form of questionnaire as a guide. Present questions to all respondents in a uniform way, and, as in written questionnaires, make your wording objective and specific. Include necessary information about why you are questioning the reader and how the answers will be used. If you can find a reasonable reader benefit, subtly point it out.

Figure 13-2 is a questionnaire planned to determine what criteria customers use in choosing a bank to handle their checking accounts. Note the design and layout of this one-page survey; also note the question design and order.

Conducting Interviews

Interviews provide another way to gather information in instances when a questionnaire is not possible or not desirable. Face-to-face interviews also provide the interviewer an opportunity to observe an interviewee's nonverbal communication. The interviewer can provide additional clarification if the interviewee doesn't understand a question. This is not possible when a questionnaire has been mailed.

SURVEY OF CHECKING ACCOUNT CUSTOMERS

The following survey is designed for people who maintain a checking account with a bank. Please answer these questions in regard to the checking account you use most for your personal needs. While it is desirable that you answer all questions, you may refuse to answer any individual question. Your responses will be treated confidentially.

1. Sex   ___ male   ___ female

2. Do you do most of the banking in your household?

    ___ yes   ___ no

3. What bank do you presently use? _____

4. How long have you had your checking account with your current bank?

    ___ less than 1 year   ___ 1 to 3 years   ___ more than 3 years

5. How many miles is it from your home to the closest branch of the bank in which you have a checking account?

    ___ less than 1 mile   ___ 1 to 5 miles   ___ more than 5 miles

6. How many branches of the bank you have a checking account with do you visit at least once a month?

    ___ 1   ___ 2   ___ 3   ___ 4   ___ 5 or more

7. How much does your bank charge you per month for the use of a checking account? (Average service charge plus average transaction fees; not the actual checks you write.)

    ___ $0   ___ $.01 to $2   ___ $2.01 to $5   ___ $5.01 to $10   ___ over $10

8. Please **rank the top 3 reasons** you currently have a checking account with your bank. (1 = most important reason, 2 = second most important reason, 3 = third most important reason)

    ___ convenience   ___ proximity to home

    ___ pricing   ___ hours open

    ___ service   ___ bank personnel

    ___ reputation   ___ number of locations

9. How likely are you to change banks in the next year? (circle answer)

1	2	3	4	5
No chance	Not likely	Neutral	Possible	Probable

THANK YOU VERY MUCH FOR PARTICIPATING

FIGURE 13-2
Questionnaire to determine what criteria customers use in choosing a bank to handle their checking accounts. Adapted from a graduate business research project, B. Borne, D. Martin, and L. Bland, Nicholls State University.

Personal interviewing must be limited to a relatively small geographical area unless cost is of no consideration, an unlikely occurrence. Telephone interviewing, although it has other disadvantages, is less expensive and time-consuming.

▶ **PERSONAL INTERVIEWS**

Interviewing is not precise. All types of interviews must be carefully planned and conducted, and responses must be recorded carefully and completely. Although there are no magic rules to memorize that will ensure successful interviews, if you observe the five key points that follow and use good judgment, you can make interviews an effective information-gathering tool.

1   *Plan the interview.* Review the purpose of your research. Research your topic prior to the interview to clarify your own thinking; plan the questions you will ask and write them down. While some questions may be closed-end questions as in surveys, others may be open-ended questions inviting the interviewees to explain or justify their initial answers. Review the questions and organize them in a logical manner. Contact the interviewee ahead of time and arrange a meeting time. Provide an estimate of time needed.

2   *Project a professional image during the interview.* Provide a proper introduction to the interview. If the person's time is limited, get to the purpose of your interview quickly and begin asking the questions you need answered. Ask the questions in the same sequence and in exactly the same words to all interviewees.

3   *Be a good listener.* Use your eyes and your ears while the interview is in progress. In addition to listening to words, observe nonverbal communication. Guide the interview to keep it on the chosen topic.

4   *Record your interviewee's responses.* Use good judgment as to how you will accomplish this. If the interview is very short, you may simply jot down some short notes once you have ended the interview. For more lengthy interviews, it may be necessary to take notes during the interview. Don't take such detailed notes that you lose eye contact with the interviewee. If you wish to record every detail about an interview, you may elect to tape it; an ethical researcher, however, always asks for and obtains permission from the interviewee before starting the tape. People hesitate to record interviews if they are concerned that their answers may be taken out of context or presented in a negative way.

5   *Close the interview effectively.* Watch for nonverbal communication that conveys that the interviewee is ready to end the meeting. After all the questions on your list are addressed, allow the interviewee to provide any last comments.

Research is not limited to words on paper or electronic databases. Athletic coaches study films of games to determine how a team can win future games.

TELEPHONE INTERVIEWS

Interviewing by telephone is quicker and less expensive than interviewing in person. Random sampling can be used in selecting respondents to be called, provided the population is limited to individuals with listed telephone numbers. Because of the number of people with no available numbers and because some listed numbers are never reached, the selection is not truly random.

Some people consider all telephone calls (except for reasons that are of some benefit to themselves) as an intrusion on their time and an invasion of their privacy. Because of these attitudes, they refuse to cooperate, or, if they do so, are likely to give inaccurate or incomplete answers.

Telephone interviewing, in spite of its weaknesses, may be desirable in some instances. If so, the interviewer should use the same care and courtesy as in personal interviewing. As in all surveys, explanation of the purpose and benefits of the survey will help to obtain respondent cooperation.

The more practice you have conducting face-to-face or telephone interviews, the more at ease you should feel. Although you cannot control interviewees' attitudes toward the subject or their willingness to answer questions honestly and completely, your own professional approach to the interview situation should assist you in getting the most information possible from each interview you conduct.

Documenting Secondary and Primary Sources: Legal and Ethical Considerations

When you use material other than your own, whether in the direct words of the author or in paraphrased form, give credit to the originator of the material. Documenting such material helps you achieve credibility and validity and provides readers with additional related information sources. Documenting borrowed or paraphrased materials protects you against plagiarism and helps make certain you do not violate copyright laws.

Give complete information about the source of the borrowed words. If you are not completely sure that material you find in secondary sources is considered common knowledge, give credit in the usual way. Even when an item is considered common knowledge, you may choose to document in order to add authority to the statement.

Even when you give credit by documentation, you may be violating copyright law when you use material written by others without obtaining permission. You must not use others' work in any way that would unfairly prevent them from benefiting from their efforts. For example, you could not make copies of audio or video cassettes to sell as your own or photocopy large sections of books instead of buying the books.

"Fair use" laws permit a limited amount of exact quotes or paraphrased material. Although an exact number has never been specified by the courts, a general guide used by many publishers is 300 to 500 words (carefully documented). Permission should be obtained for the use of only one line from a song or a poem.

All materials published by the government are in the public domain and may be used without explicit written permission. Nevertheless, a careful and ethical researcher still provides documentation for each source used. Other materials not protected by copyright are news items from newspapers more than three months old (but not columns or other individually copyrighted work) and all material published before 1907.

Style Manuals

If you are requested to use a particular style manual as a guide, or if you are asked to use the format previously chosen for your organization, make sure that you follow the suggested methods exactly. A variation may distract or annoy your reader to the extent that it interferes with the reception of your intended message. In addition, ability and willingness to follow instructions are a necessary part of communication within organizations.

Four widely used style manuals are listed below:

► American Psychological Association. (1994). *Publication Manual of the American Psychological Association.* (4th ed.) Washington, DC: Author.

► Gibaldi, J. (1995). *MLA Handbook for Writers of Research Papers,* (4th ed.). New York: Modern Language Association.

► University of Chicago Press. (1993). *The Chicago Manual of Style.* (14th ed.). Chicago: Author.

► Slade, C., Campbell, W. G., & Ballou, S. V. (1994). *Form and Style: Research Papers, Reports, and Theses.* (9th ed.). Boston: Houghton Mifflin.

While the social sciences and many scholarly journals use the American Psychological Association (APA) style, the humanities frequently use the MLA style.

Citations [Documentation]

Both the APA and MLA style manuals use an internal text method of providing references to cited materials. *The Chicago Manual of Style* also presents internal citations as one of two major documentation methods. While footnotes or endnotes may still be used (this text, for example, uses endnotes following each chapter), the method of documentation in many of today's research papers and journal articles is the internal citation method. Both APA and MLA internal citation methods are described in the paragraphs below. Use the style required by your instructor or by your organization. If the choice of styles if left up to you, select one and use it with consistency throughout your report.

The APA style recommends an *Author-date* system. For example, (Kleen, Maxwell, and Hubert, 1996) refers to the authors and the date of publication. Several illustrations of APA style internal citations are provided in Figure 13-3. Note the slight variations required for different situations such as one or more authors, authors named or not named in the text, no author provided, and more than one source documenting the same idea. Providing correct citations of each of these situations is an important part of documentation.

The MLA style uses an *Author-page* system that includes the author's last name and a page number, with no comma separating the two. For example, (Kleen, Maxwell, and Hubert 82) refers to the authors and the page number containing the quote or idea. Several illustrations of MLA style internal citations are provided in Figure 13-4; note the slight variations required for different author and wording situations.

The *MLA Handbook* also presents a *number system* for parenthetical citations. This system is sometimes used in the social sciences literature and often in the physical sciences. A parenthetical citation such as (4, p. 112)

Internal Citations Prepared in the APA Style

Single author not named in text
CompuServe is the bulletin board system that the American Institute of Certified Public Accountants plans to use to distribute information online (Trimm, 1995).

More than one author— not named in text
The Supreme Court acknowledged that economic loss is not necessary to prevail in a claim of sexual harassment (Lee & Greenlaw, 1995).

More than one source
The move toward informal office attire is strictly an American phenomenon (McConville, 1994; Longo, 1995).

Author(s) referenced in text
Caillouet and Lapeyre (1995) believe that the strategic management process is only as strong as an organization's accounting information system.

No named author
Today's technology can help a company reduce its paper format records by up to 90 percent ("Why Your Company Should," 1994.)

More than one source, same authors
Kleen & Shell (1992, 1995) found that using writing across the curriculum activities strengthened student understanding.

More than one work by an author—same year
Fitzgerald (1996,b) noted psychological damages that may be incurred by those who experience sexual harassment.

Direct quotations
McMurdy (1995) noted, "Common wisdom decreed that 'dressing down' actually improved employee morale and productivity and encouraged the rank to mix with the file" (p. 40).

FIGURE 13-3
APA style internal citations

Internal Citations Prepared in the MLA Style

Single author not named in text	CompuServe is the bulletin board system that the American Institute of Certified Public Accountants plans to use to distribute information online (Trimm 20).
More than one author—not named in text	The Supreme Court acknowledged that economic loss is not necessary to prevail in a claim of sexual harassment (Lee & Greenlaw 359).
More than one source	The move toward informal office attire is strictly an American phenomenon (McConville 12; Longo 15).
Author(s) referenced in text	Caillouet and Lapeyre believe that the strategic management process is only as strong as an organization's accounting information system (24).
No named author	Today's technology can help a company reduce its paper format records by up to 90 percent ("Why Your Company Should" 122).
More than one source, same authors	Kleen & Shell ("Enhancing Critical Thinking Skills" 385), ("Writing Across the Curriculum" 29) found that using writing across the curriculum activities strengthened student understanding.
More than one work by an author—same year	Fitzgerald ("Sexual Harassment: Violence Against" 1071) noted psychological damages that may be incurred by those who experience sexual harassment.
Direct quotations	McMurdy noted, "Common wisdom decreed that 'dressing down' actually improved employee morale and productivity and encouraged the rank to mix with the file" (40).

FIGURE 13-4
MLA style internal citations

denotes the number of the entry in the works cited pages and the page number. The entry number only (4) is all that is needed when referring to the book as a whole.

Some researchers prefer to use footnotes or endnotes instead of the internal citation method of documentation. If used, footnotes appear at the bottom of the page and correspond to superscript numbers or asterisks in the text. When endnotes are used, superscripts within the text indicate materials with documentation; the endnotes themselves appear at the end of the entire manuscript or after chapters or sections (as in this textbook). Notes are numbered consecutively through each chapter or article and are labeled as notes or endnotes. Reports that contain endnotes may or may not include a separate bibliography.

Regardless of placement—internal citations, footnotes, or endnotes— reference notes accomplish the same purposes—that of documenting a particular printed source or of adding explanatory material. Consult a complete style manual for more details concerning footnotes and/or endnotes.

Numerous footnotes or parenthetical citations are distracting no matter where they are placed, but they must be used when they are necessary for proper credit to the original author. If you find that you are using an excessive number, to the extent that much of your report or other work consists of bits and pieces of others' works, perhaps you are doing too much citing and not enough analysis and interpretation of your own.

REFERENCES (WORKS CITED)

The APA style incorporates a *References* page that includes only cited sources, listed in alphabetical order. The MLA style typically uses a *Works Cited* page; a variation of this is a *Works Consulted* section, which includes background sources not specifically cited. The MLA style also provides for inclusion of sources such as speeches or personal interviews in the works cited.

Regardless of the title of the reference section (often referred to in general terms as a bibliography), it must include all sources used as documentation and presented in internal citations or other forms of documentation.

The *References* page illustrated in Figure 13-5 is arranged in the APA style. The *Works Cited* page illustrated in Figure 13-6 is arranged in the MLA style.

More complete information concerning citation and reference formats for numerous types of electronic sources is available in *Electronic Styles: A Handbook for Citing Electronic Information (revised edition)*, by Li and Crane, 1996. The authors include illustrations of both MLA and APA embellished styles.

The references or work cited information is considered as a supplement to a formal report. It may come before or after appendices, depending on the material included as appendices. Page numbering is often simplified by placing the references or works cited first. The arabic numerals used in the report proper continue in sequence throughout the supplementary parts.

APA Style, 4th edition, presents references in a double-spaced format. Entries are shown here single spaced for illustration purposes only. When keying in references, indent first line of each source the same as paragraphs within the text. Begin the references on a new page. Arrange references in alphabetical order by author.

References

Book—two or more authors	Chaney, L. H., & Martin, J. S. (1995). <u>Intercultural business communication</u>. Upper Saddle River, NJ: Prentice-Hall, Inc.
Book—edited	Groneman, N.J. (Ed.). (1995). <u>Technology in the classroom</u>. National Business Education Yearbook. (Vol. 33). Reston, VA: National Business Education Association.
Book—corporate author and edition	American Psychological Association. (1994). <u>Publication manual of the American psychological association</u> (4th ed.). Washington, D.C.: Author.
Chapter in a book	Wyatt, A. L. (1995). Cruising the Internet. In A. L. Wyatt, <u>Success with Internet</u> (161–190). Danvers, MA: Boyd & Fraser.
Pamphlet or report—private organization	Gateway 2000, Inc. (1995). <u>Your Gateway 2000 computer & Windows 95 users's guide supplement</u>. N. Sioux City, SD: Author.
Periodical article—paginated by issue	Kleen, B. A., & Shell, L. W. (1996). Multimedia resources: Their presence, use, and management in AACSB colleges of business. <u>Journal of Computer Information Systems, 36</u>(3), 30–36.
Periodical article—no listed author	St. Patrick teacher, students share ideas via electronic whiteboard. (1996). <u>T.H.E. Journal, 23</u>(11), 28.
Periodical—online source	Inada, K. (1995). A Buddhist response to the nature of human rights. <u>Journal of Buddhist Ethics</u> [Online serial.] Available HTTP: http://www.cac.psu.edu/jbe/twocont.html (Specify available protocol, site, path, and file; omit final punctuation)
Article—online source—not a journal publication	Shell, L. W. (1996, November 25). Designing effective internal Web pages for your company. [online]. Available HTTP: http://www.nich-nsu.edu/~li/design/html [1997, March 5] Note: Specify available protocol, site, path, and file; omit final punctuation after http addresses.
Newspaper article	Hughlett, M. (1996, June 16). Builders of the N.O. superhighway. <u>The Times Picayune [New Orleans]</u>, pp. F1–2.

FIGURE 13-5
References prepared in the APA 4th edition style

Government publication— through U.S. Government Printing Office	Bureau of the Census. (1993). <u>Twentieth census of the United States, 1990, neighborhood statistics program</u>. Washington, D.C.: U.S. Government Printing Office.
Government publication—not available through GPO	National Center for Education Statistics. (1996). <u>Enrollment in higher education: Fall 1986 through Fall 1994</u>. Washington, D.C.: Author.
CD-ROM	Louisiana Department of Education, Office of Research and Development. (1996). <u>1994–1995 Louisiana progress profiles district composite reports</u>. CD-ROM. Baton Rouge: Louisiana Department of Education.
Software	<u>Jasc Paint Shop Pro Version 3</u>. (1995). [Computer software]. Minnetonka, MN: JASC, Inc.
Interviews, letters, and e-mail	Not included on references pages. Instead, cite in text as (personal communication, month, day, year).

FIGURE 13-5
continued

Using Quoted Passages

As you include information from secondary sources, you may choose to use it verbatim; that is, in the exact words of the writer you are quoting. Paraphrased material is expressed in your own words, although you have taken the information from another source. Passages that you quote verbatim must be clearly distinguished from the rest of the text. Paraphrased passages are not set off, but your parenthetical citations or other method of documentation should make clear what portion of the text you are documenting.

According to the *MLA Handbook*, 4th edition,[2] quotations requiring no more than four lines should be incorporated into the text and placed within double quotation marks. If the quoted material is longer than four typewritten lines, it should be set off from the text by indenting all the quoted material one inch from the left margin; while the material should remain double-spaced, no quotation marks are used.

The *APA Manual*, 4th edition,[3] directs a writer to incorporate quotations of fewer than 40 words into the text and enclose the material in double quotation marks. When using the APA style, longer quotations are indented five to seven spaces from the left margin (same as a standard paragraph indent) and double-spaced. All additional lines are typed flush with the indent. No quotation marks are used.

MLA Style, 4th edition, presents references in a double-spaced format. Entries are shown here single spaced for illustration purposes only. When keying in works cited, begin each entry flush with the left margin; subsequent lines are indented one-half inch from the left margin. Begin the works cited on a new page. Arrange works cited in alphabetcial order by author.

Works Cited

Book—two or more authors	Chaney, Lillian H., and Jeanette S. Martin. Intercultural Business Communication. Englewood Cliffs, NJ: Prentice-Hall, Inc., 1995.
Book—edited	Groneman, Nancy J., ed. Technology in the Classroom. National Business Education Yearbook. 33. Reston, VA: National Business Education Association, 1995.
Book—corporate author and edition	American Psychological Association. Publication Manual of the American Psychological Association. 4th ed. Washington, D.C.: American Psychological Association, 1994.
Chapter in a book	Wyatt, Allen L. "Cruising the Internet." Success with Internet. Danvers, MA: Boyd & Fraser, 1995.
Pamphlet or report—private organization	Your Gateway 2000 Computer & Windows 95 User's Guide Supplement. N. Sioux City, SD: Gateway 2000, Inc., 1995.
Periodical article— paginated by issue	Kleen, Betty A., & L. Wayne Shell. "Multimedia Resources: Their Presence, Use, and Management in AACSB Colleges of Business." Journal of Computer Information Systems 36.3, (1996): 30–36.
Periodical article— no listed author	"St. Patrick Teacher, Students Share Ideas via Electronic Whiteboard." T.H.E. Journal 23.11 (1996): 28.
Periodical—online source	Inada, Kenneth. "A Buddhist Response to the Nature of Human Rights." Journal of Buddhist Ethics 2 (1995): 9pars. Online. Available HTTP: http://www.cac.psu.edu/jbe/twocont.html
	Specify available protocol, site, path, and file; omit final punctuation on http addresses
Article—online source—not a journal publication	Shell, L. Wayne. "Designing Effective Internal Web Pages for Your Company." (November 25, 1996) Online. Available HTTP: http://www.nich-nsu.edu/~li/design/html 5 March 1997.
	Note: Final date is date of access by researcher
Newspaper article	Hughlett, Mike. "Builders of the N.O. Superhighway." The Times Picayune [New Orleans] 16 June 1996: F1–2

FIGURE 13-6
References prepared in the MLA 4th edition style

Government publication— through U.S. Government Printing Office	United States. Bureau of the Census. <u>Twentieth Census of the United States, 1990, Neighborhood Statistics Program.</u> Washington, D.C.: GPO, 1993.
Government publication—not available through GPO	United States. National Center for Education Statistics. <u>Enrollment in Higher Education: Fall 1986 Through Fall 1994</u>. Washington, D.C.: National Center for Education Statistics.
CD-ROM	Louisiana. Department of Education. Office of Research and Development. <u>1994–1995 Louisiana Progress Profiles District Composite Reports</u>. CD-ROM. Baton Rouge: Louisiana Department of Education, 1996.
Software	<u>Jasc Paint Shop Pro Version 3</u>. Computer Software. Jasc, Inc., 1995.
Interviews	Fry, Elaine. Personal Interview. 12 September 1996.
Letters	Zachry, Benny. Letter to the author. 8 September 1996.
Electronic mail	Powers, C. E-mail to the author. 15 September 1996.

FIGURE 13-6
continued

The ellipsis is a series of three periods, in addition to a period at the end of a sentence, if necessary, typed with intervening spaces. A writer uses ellipses to note omitted material from a direct quote, as in the following example:

"Text color is important for readability too. . . . It should contrast with the background color, and the greatest contrast should be between the title and the background color."[4]

The ellipsis in the quoted material displayed above indicates that some of the exact words of the original source have been omitted. Because omissions can distort meaning, conventional usage is to insert an ellipsis to indicate that a portion of the original passage is not included. You must take care to ensure that omissions, even when so indicated, do not change the writer's overall intent and overall meaning. Omission of a paragraph or more is sometimes shown by a complete line of spaced periods.

Use care and judgment in citing secondary information. When you include a statement or opinion of someone else, you imply that you agree with the cited material unless you state otherwise. The material must be relevant to your overall approach and content. It must carry forward the flow of thought and amplify and strengthen your own discussion.

SUMMARY

Methods of obtaining information include primary and secondary research. Secondary research involves obtaining information that has already been gathered and recorded by someone else. Primary research involves finding original data that have not been found and recorded by someone other than yourself.

The *Business Periodicals Index* is a basic guide to articles that have appeared in specialized business magazines. Various other indexes serve as guides to specialized and general-interest periodicals. Many libraries today provide access to CD-ROM versions of various indexes; in some instances the CD-ROMs provided by various services are more comprehensive than a single index and offer many more search terms for the researcher. Online databases offer the most up-to-date coverage of materials and often provide both abstracts and full text of indexed material.

Methods of primary research include observation, experimentation, and surveys. Experimentation, scientifically and objectively done, is reliable and accurate, but even experimentation is subject to human error. Surveys employ the use of mailed questionnaires and formal and informal interviews and are widely used in research of many kinds. Some interviews are conducted by the use of written questionnaires or a preplanned series of questions asked by the researcher. Surveys also are conducted by telephone and person to person. Questionnaires must be constructed with care in order to encourage response, to obtain the needed information, and to facilitate tabulation of results.

All methods of research are subject to the many kinds of human error that are inevitable in communication.

To avoid plagiarism and give credibility to research, researchers must document ideas and/or direct quotes not their own. Whether internal parenthetical citations, footnotes, or endnotes are used, researchers must carefully include a complete listing of sources cited. Leading style manuals are the *MLA Handbook for Writers of Research Papers*, *Publication Manual of the American Psychological Association*, *The Chicago Manual of Style*, and *Form and Style: Research Papers, Reports, and Theses*.

TEST YOURSELF

chapter content

1   Describe the difference between primary and secondary data.
2   Name one guide to books.
3   Name two kinds of information that can be found in *Moody's Manuals*.
4   What is the name of a well-known guide to articles in business, industrial, and trade magazines?
5   If you had the option of a hard-copy, CD-ROM, or online version of an index such as the Public Affairs Information Service Bulletin, which would you choose and why?
6   Name three advantages of using a CD-ROM database as compared to printed indexes.
7   Name three methods of primary research.
8   What are two weaknesses of surveys?
9   Give five suggestions for questionnaire construction.
10   Give three suggestions for conducting effective personal or telephone interviews.
11   Name three leading style manuals.

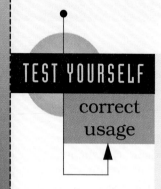

TEST YOURSELF

correct usage

(Related to material in Chapter 13 and principles of correct usage.) The content of the following sentences is correct, but ONE in each pair is incorrect in some way. Look for errors in punctuation, including use of the hyphen and the apostrophe, spelling, sentence structure; grammar; and word usage. (Refer to Appendix D.)

1 **a.** Statistical data and other information obtained from surveys is often presented in tables and charts.
   b. From gathered data a reporter draws conclusions upon which to make recommendations.

2 **a.** Many surveys consist of questionaires sent by mail.
   b. Researching topics in books, newspapers, magazines, journals, government documents, and reference works can result in a comprehensive and accurate presentation.

3 **a.** Because much information in published form is available in libraries secondary research is sometimes referred to as library research.
   b. Not all secondary research, however, is obtained from published sources in libraries.

4 **a.** We must build on the experience of other people because there is no time to do otherwise.
   b. Secondary research should ordinarily be the starting point in the data gathering process.

5 **a.** What are the leading professional journals in your field of study?
   b. Does your library have open stacks, if not how are books examined?

6 **a.** Information of many kinds, especially statistical information is collected and published by the federal government.
   b. The first Census of Population was taken in 1790, and it has been repeated at 10-year intervals since that time.

7 **a.** Not all research ends with definate results.
   b. At times, specific recommendations are undesirable.

8 **a.** A research assignment should be regarded as a priviledge that could lead to increased responsibility.
   b. Many reports are similar in arrangement and approach.

9 **a.** Some research is planned for the purpose of determining whether a planned course of action is feasable.
   b. Libraries can be both fascinating and frustrating.

10 **a.** The survey method of research has many weaknesses, but a careful researcher can decrease these weaknesses.
   b. A competent researcher must be familier with library sources.

11 **a.** After a proposal is accepted, the researcher is free to procede with his research.
   b. Research can be extremely time-consuming work.

Directions: Choose the correct word.

12 The supervisor asked Bob and (I, me) to prepare the report.

13 Jim and I met with the client (who, whom) was interested in our report on convertible bonds.

14 It was Mary and (I, me) who received the award for last (years, year's) work.

15 Hank (compliments, complements) his workers when they produce effective proposals before the deadline.

16 The personal writing style, which may include first- and second-person pronouns, is (alright, all right) for some reports but not for all.

PROBLEMS AND CASES

Note: Additional cases follow Chapter 15.

1 Prepare a tentative reference list of at least five recent sources that seem to apply to the problem for which you prepared a report plan. Use one of the reference styles (APA or MLA) shown in the chapter or another specified by your instructor.

2 Prepare a reference list of five or more recent journal articles on one of these topics or on your formal report topic.

   a. Communication as applied to one of these fields:
   - accounting
   - human resource management
   - management of a small business
   - marketing
   - office management
   - computer information systems
   - finance
   - business education
   - your major field of study, if not listed above

   b. New developments in one of these fields:
   - accounting
   - human resource management
   - management of a small business
   - marketing
   - office management
   - computer information systems
   - finance
   - business education
   - your major field of study, if not listed above

3 Prepare a list of periodicals that apply especially to your major field of study.

4 Prepare a list of gopher and/or Web sites that apply especially to your major field of study or a particular topic within your discipline.

5 Use *Moody's Manuals* or *Standard and Poor's Corporation Records* to find information about a large national corporation. Write a short memorandum to your instructor in which you describe the kinds of information available in the reference source.

6 Use the Internet (Web pages) to find information about a large national corporation. You may want to check the corporation's Web page, the Securities and Exchange Commission's Web page, and others you think appropriate. You can also use the Internet search engines to find additional sites that may provide information.

7 Can you think of a question that needs to be answered in your employing organization or in your school or university? Which method

or methods of research should be used in finding the answer to this question? Explain.

8 Explain how the following questions (not from the same questionnaire) violate the principles of effective questionnaire construction.

- Don't you feel that you earn more interest at United Bank?
- How much do you earn each month?

- How much have your grocery bills increased since 1993?
- How do you manage when your weekly check won't cover your expenses?
- Do you approve of Bill Number 213 now being considered in the Senate?
  Yes _____   No_____
- Do you leave work early?
  Always _____   Occasionally _____
  Sometimes_____   Never _____

COLLABORATIVE WRITING AND WORKING IN GROUPS

9 You are the executive assistant to the president of M & D Builders. With the addition of the Quick & Hot Cafeteria, next door to your office, many employees are completing their lunch in 30 minutes instead of the hour now allotted for lunch. Three women have requested a 30-minute lunch break with a half hour later arrival time, 8:30 instead of 8:00. Then they could take their children to school.

Other workers would like to continue to arrive at 8:00 and leave at 4:00 instead of 4:30. A few mentioned that they prefer present hours, 8:00 to 4:30, with an hour for lunch.

Although it would be more convenient for you and the office manager if everyone came and left at the same time, with staggered lunch breaks, you want to do all you can to provide convenient schedules for everyone.

The president, Harriet Glover, asked you to write a memorandum for her signature. Ask employees to state their preference according to the alternatives listed above. Ms. Glover and the office manager, Bert Lance, will make the final determination after evaluating their responses. Design a simple questionnaire for employees to complete. **Note: Additional cases that are especially appropriate for group work follow Chapter 15.**

THINK-IT-THROUGH ASSIGNMENT

10 Find a questionnaire that was sent through the mail or administered during an interview. Analyze this questionnaire according to the points listed below. (Refer also to the section of this chapter entitled "Question Design.") As your instructor directs, present your analysis in a memorandum addressed to your instructor, making appropriate notations on the questionnaire itself. If your in-

structor prefers, be prepared to show the questionnaire to the class and to comment on its construction.

a. Is each question easy to understand and concerned with one topic only?

b. Is specific language used—both in the questions themselves and in the answer choices?

c. Are the majority of questions closed-end

questions? Are there any open-ended questions you could change into effective closed-end questions?

d. Has the designer provided for all likely answers for each of the questions? If not, what should be added?

e. Is the respondent likely to remember all the information requested in the instrument?

f. Are any unnecessary questions included?

g. Are answers for necessary demographic questions such as age and income pre-sented as ranges? If not, can you re-design the questions?

h. Are any of the questions leading questions? If so, reword to remove the re-searcher bias.

i. Are specialized instructions provided where appropriate? If you identify questions where extra instructions are needed, compose the instructions.

j. Are the questions arranged in a logical order? If not, suggest an appropriate order.

ENDNOTES

1 Pamela L. Alreck and Robert B. Settle, *The Survey Research Handbook*, 2nd ed. (Chicago: Irwin, 1995).

2 Joseph Gibaldi, *MLA Handbook for Writers of Research Papers*, 4th ed. (New York: Modern Language Association of America, 1995).

3 *Publication Manual of the American Psychological Association*, 4th ed. (Washington, DC: American Psychological Association, 1994).

4 Marie E. Flatley, "Using Color in Presentations," *Business Communication Quarterly*, 59, no. 1 (March 1996): 91.

Interpreting Data with Statistics, Graphic Aids, and Logical Thought

CHAPTER

14

OBJECTIVES

Chapter Fourteen will help you:

1 Determine when using a visual aid is appropriate.

2 Prepare visual aids that are appropriate for the data being presented.

3 Produce visual aids that project a professional appearance.

4 Apply ethical, accurate, and complete analysis to data.

5 Discuss effective placement, identification, and discussion of visual aids.

6 Write a report in which conclusions are based on findings and recommendations are based on conclusions.

After data have been collected, they are evaluated and organized for presentation in the most appropriate form. A systematic method of collecting and recording information simplifies the remaining steps of the research process.

Processes of evaluating and organizing, as well as other steps in research and report writing, do not fall into discrete divisions. We do not abruptly begin evaluating material only after the collection process is completed. Ideally, data are evaluated and organized as much as possible as they are collected. Unless we use judgment in the collection process, we will find that we have gathered great quantities of meaningless or irrelevant material.

At some point we must stop formally adding to the collection of data and begin finishing the research process. However, if additional information or opinions come to light, we cannot afford to ignore them merely to end the search, although at times we may be tempted to do so.

This chapter focuses on the interpretation of data, whether the writer uses statistics, graphic aids, text, or a combination of the three.

Determining the Meaning of Data

In report preparation and presentation, we must be extremely careful to be completely and thoroughly objective. *Objectivity* is conveyed by phrasing and word choice, but true objectivity consists of far more than nonemotional writing; it is an attitude that must be kept constantly in mind throughout the entire report writing process. Objectivity, or the lack of it, influences the complete and nonbiased search for information and the organizing, evaluating, and reporting portions of the overall project.

Because we are human, predetermined beliefs or desires tend to affect everything we do, including research and reporting duties. As report writers, we must consciously work toward honest and objective interpretations.

CONCLUSIONS BASED ON FINDINGS; RECOMMENDATIONS BASED ON CONCLUSIONS

Valid conclusions are based on complete and relevant data interpreted objectively in light of the problem to be solved. Recommendations are based on conclusions about what the data mean.

Ordinarily, the conclusions and recommendation section is the last section of a formal, analytical report arranged in the inductive order. Conclusions and recommendations are sometimes presented in two separate sections. In some long and comprehensive reports, each major section is treated as a separate report; the writer arrives at conclusions based on findings presented in each section. The entire report concludes with a summarizing section.

To repeat and emphasize: Report evidence, interpret this evidence, and make recommendations. Your conclusions, usually in a report section with recommendations, are based on clearly stated evidence.

COMMUNICATION

brief

As a cub reporter, Mark Twain was told never to state as fact anything that he could not personally verify. Following this instruction to the letter, he wrote the following account of a gala social event: "A woman giving the name of Mrs. James Jones, who is reported to be one of the society leaders of the city, is said to have given what purported to be a party yesterday to a number of alleged ladies. The hostess claims to be the wife of a reputed attorney."

Clifton Fadiman, ed., *The Little, Brown Book of Anecdotes* (Boston: Little, Brown, 1985), 554.

INTERPRETING WITH STATISTICS

Simple statistical terms include the following:

▶ *Mean:* The arithmetic average obtained by totaling the figures and dividing by the number of cases.

▶ *Median:* The midpoint, or middle value, in a series of values arranged in the order of magnitude.

▶ *Mode:* The most frequently occurring value. (The mean, median, and mode are all measures of a central tendency.)

▶ *Range:* The spread between the lowest and the highest values in a series.

▶ *Standard deviation:* A measure of dispersion in a frequency distribution—that is, a measure of the spread of the normal distribution.

This book cannot cover the study of statistics in detail. You need a basic knowledge of statistics, however, for analyzing and interpreting your research findings.

The term *average* can mean almost anything or nothing, depending on how it is used. In other words, the *mean* may be meaningless. For example, a statement can be literally true that the average income of a college graduating class of a particular year is $102,850 a year, but it is very unlikely that this figure is the typical income. A few extremely high figures distort the mean. Suppose that the graduating class consisted of only ten members. Each of nine of these persons is now earning about $21,500 annually, and the tenth one earns $835,000, making the arithmetic mean $102,850. To describe this figure as the average or mean without further explanation would result in a misrepresentation of data.

COMMUNICATION brief

Averages and relationships and trends and graphs are not always what they seem. There may be more in them than meets the eye, and there may be a good deal less.

The secret language of statistics, so appealing in a fact-minded culture, is employed to sensationalize, inflate, confuse, and oversimplify. Statistical methods and statistical terms are necessary in reporting the mass data of social and economic trends, business conditions, "opinion" polls, the census. But without writers who use the words with honesty and understanding and readers who know what they mean, the result can only be semantic nonsense.

Darrell Huff, *How to Lie with Statistics* (New York: W. W. Norton, 1954), 8.

INTERPRETING WITH GRAPHIC AIDS

Graphic aids are helpful in both written and oral reports to emphasize and interpret written material. They are also used to convey supplementary information not included in the written report. Graphic aids should be considered as supplements to words, not as substitutes for them. They are especially helpful when used to emphasize important points and to show trends and relationships.

The terms *chart* and *graph* are often used interchangeably. In this chapter, *chart* refers to any form of graphic illustration other than a table.

Graphic aids, if wisely planned and attractively presented, bring out relationships that could be easily overlooked. A well-planned chart can sometimes present an analysis of important points that would require many pages to explain and discuss in text format alone.

MATCHING DATA WITH APPROPRIATE GRAPHIC AIDS

Tables, not charts, should be chosen for the presentation of numerous figures, particularly if the reader is interested in exact amounts. Approximations, trends, and relationships are best shown on a chart of some kind. A chart can be considered a pictorial representation of data.

Some kinds of information should be shown in more than one way in the same report. For example, the reader may need exact numbers shown in a table in addition to approximate figures used to show trends on accompanying charts. A detailed table may serve as the basis for several charts that each concentrate on a particular aspect of the table's information.

Graphic aids should have a definite purpose. Never use graphics only to add color or to entertain your reader. Graphic aids should explain and enhance the meaning of the text.

Not all graphics explain data equally well. Carefully assess the data you wish to illustrate and select an appropriate graphic aid. For instance, selecting a pie chart to illustrate the annual sales of each of the 78 stores in a large shopping mall would not work. How will your reader be able to grasp anything meaningful from a circle split into 78 pieces?

The four most common graphic aids used by report writers include *tables*, *bar charts* (with numerous variations), *line charts*, and *pie charts*. As Figure 14-1 illustrates, each of the four may be a "best" choice depending on the type of data to be illustrated.

Various types of graphics are discussed in the sections that follow.

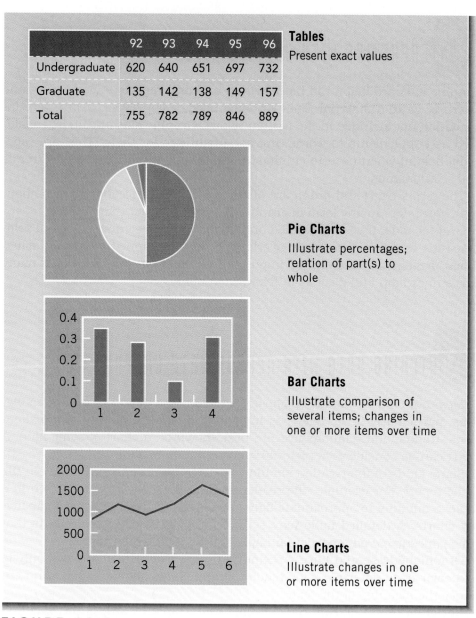

	92	93	94	95	96
Undergraduate	620	640	651	697	732
Graduate	135	142	138	149	157
Total	755	782	789	846	889

Tables
Present exact values

Pie Charts
Illustrate percentages; relation of part(s) to whole

Bar Charts
Illustrate comparison of several items; changes in one or more items over time

Line Charts
Illustrate changes in one or more items over time

FIGURE 14-1
Most frequently used graphics and key functions

TABLES

Tables are necessary for presentation of exact, detailed information. Writers often elect to use tables to report the summarized information they have gathered from surveys. In addition, tables may serve as a basis for addi-

Researchers analyze data presented in words and through pie charts.

tional visual aids, often charts of various kinds that illustrate specific groups of data that are part of the total data in the table.

A simple table is shown in Figure 14-2. Figure 14-3 illustrates responses that have been cross tabulated. By using a cross tabulation, the writer can analyze two (or sometimes more) variables together. Note that by breaking down the survey data into male and female responses, the writer gives em-

TABLE 1	MANAGEMENT STYLES OF RESPONDENTS	
Management Style	Number	Percent
Authoritative	81	34.9
Democratic	116	50.0
Other	35	15.1
Total	232	100.0

FIGURE 14-2
Example of a simple table

TABLE 2	MANAGEMENT STYLES OF MALE AND FEMALE RESPONDENTS					
	Males		Females		Total	
Management Style	Number	Percent	Number	Percent	Number	Percent
Authoritative	55	45.1	26	23.6	81	34.9
Democratic	39	32.0	77	70.0	116	50.0
Other	28	22.9	7	6.4	35	15.1
Total	122	100.0	110	100.0	232	100.0

FIGURE 14-3
Table containing cross-tabulated data

phasis to the different responses of males and females. These findings are not evident in the first table.

CHARTS

A basic consideration in the construction of charts of all kinds is that they be kept simple. Several simple charts that clearly show limited quantities of data are preferable to one complicated, hard-to-read visual aid.

The types of charts most frequently used are the *bar, line,* and *pie charts,* with numerous variations of the bar and line. Vertical bar charts are also referred to as *column charts,* and pie charts are also referred to as *circle,* or *segment,* charts.

► **BAR CHARTS**

Bar charts, both horizontal and vertical, compare quantities. The length or height of the bars indicates quantity. All bars should be the same width. Vertical bar charts include the independent variable (such as time or cause) at the bottom (*x*-axis), and the dependent variable on the vertical axis (*y*-axis).

Bar charts effectively show changes in one item over time. They can also be used effectively to show the composition of several items over time.

Charts of all kinds, but particularly bar charts, can be varied in numerous ways. In designing them, choose the arrangement that will vividly, yet simply, compare the relationships you wish to emphasize. Figure 14-4 is an example of a vertical bar chart. Figure 14-5 illustrates a horizontal bar chart.

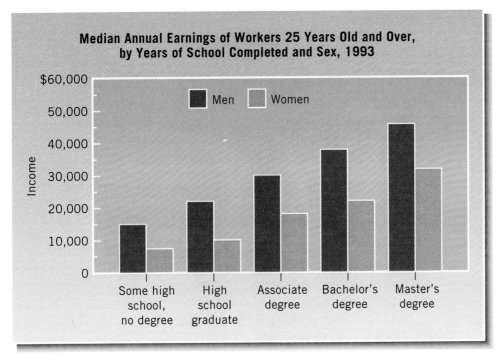

FIGURE 14-4

Vertical bar chart

Source: U.S. Department of Commerce, Bureau of the Census, *Current Population Reports*, Series P-60, Money Income of Households, Families, and Persons in the United States: 1993.

http://www.ed.gov/NCES/pubs/D95/dgif025.gif

BILATERAL BAR CHARTS

A *bilateral bar chart* shows increases and decreases from a central point of reference. Bilateral bar charts may be used for any series of data containing negative quantities. They are often used to show changes in percentages. Figure 14-6 is an example of a bilateral bar chart.

SUBDIVIDED BAR AND MULTIPLE BAR CHARTS

Variations of the simple bar chart, in addition to bilateral bar charts, include *subdivided bar* and *multiple bar* charts, with variations and combinations of each.

A subdivided bar chart is shown in Figure 14-7. This particular chart shows relative size of components of the whole. Percentages shown on bars are not usually included, but they provide more specific information.

Another kind of bar chart is the *100-percent subdivided bar*. These charts may consist of either vertical or horizontal bars. They differ from ordinary bar charts in that all bars are the same length or height, with each bar

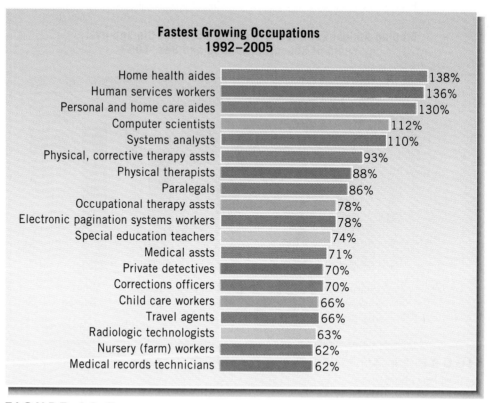

FIGURE 14-5

Horizontal bar chart

Source: U.S. Department of Commerce, Bureau of the Census, *Current Population Reports, 1993.*

http://www.census.gov/stat_abstract/img/occ.gif.

representing 100 percent. These 100-percent bar charts serve the same purpose as pie charts (discussed later in this chapter) because they show divisions of the whole. They are far more useful than pie charts when a number of 100-percent items are to be compared. For example, Figure 14-8 presents management style preferences of a total group of survey respondents, in addition to female respondents and male respondents. Thus, one bar chart can be used instead of three separate pie charts.

▶ LINE CHARTS

A *line chart* is used to show changes over a period of time, as illustrated in Figure 14-9. A line chart is often used to show rises and falls of the stock market, as well as for many other purposes. The independent variable (time, cause) is always shown at the bottom (*x*-axis) of a line chart; the dependent variable (effect) is shown on the vertical axis (*y*-axis).

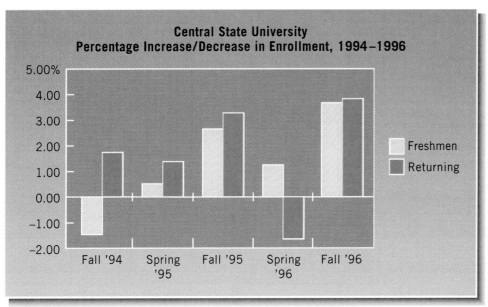

FIGURE 14-6
Bilateral bar chart
Source: Primary

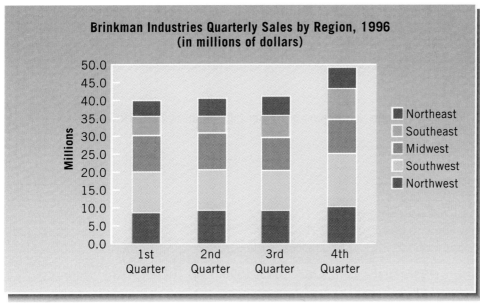

FIGURE 14-7
Subdivided bar chart
Source: Primary

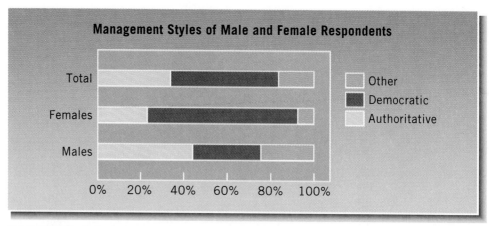

FIGURE 14-8
100-percent subdivided bar chart
Source: Primary

▶ PIE CHARTS

A *pie chart*, also described as a **circle chart** (or pie graph or circle graph), shows the component parts of a whole and serves the same function as a 100-percent subdivided bar. Exact quantities or percentages should be shown; frequently, both quantities and percentages are shown. A simple pie chart is illustrated in Figure 14-10.

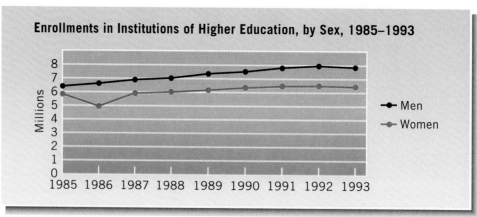

FIGURE 14-9
Line chart
Source: U.S. Department of Education, National Center for Education Statistics, "Women: Education and Outcomes," *Statistical Analysis Report*, September 1996, Table 2.

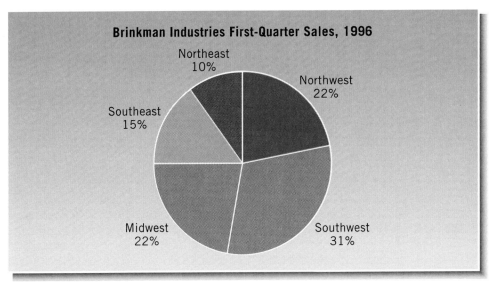

FIGURE 14-10
Simple pie chart
Source: Primary

PICTORIAL CHARTS

Pictorial charts, also referred to as *pictograms*, use pictorial images to represent statistical data. While the basic design may be that of a bar chart, symbols are used instead of bars to represent data. When using this type of chart, the writer no longer provides exact particulars to the reader; instead, the reader is presented with an eye-catching general overview of the data.

OTHER VISUALS

Although tables, bar charts, line charts, and pie charts are the most commonly used graphic aids, other visuals may sometimes be more appropriate.

Quantitative data that is presented in a geographic breakdown may be effectively illustrated by using a map. As illustrated in Figure 14-11, contrasting colors or other identifying techniques help distinguish differences.

If the writer needs to illustrate the structure of an organization or part of an organization, an organizational chart becomes an effective graphic, as shown in Figure 14-12.

Still other visuals may be appropriate. Photos, diagrams, flowcharts, and clip art are only a few of the other graphic aids you can add to your report to enhance reader understanding. As discussed in Chapter 13, however, provide appropriate citations and obtain written permission when using materials that may be copyrighted.

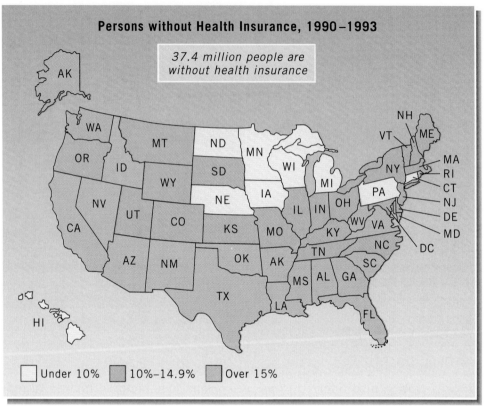

FIGURE 14-11

Map

Source: Statistical Abstract of the United States (Washington, D.C.: U.S. Bureau of the Census, 1994). http://www.census.gov/stat_abstract/img/health.gif

COMPUTER-GENERATED GRAPHIC AIDS

Today's report writer has a wealth of software available to support the construction of graphic aids of almost any type quickly and easily. All word processing packages can aid in the production of converting raw data into attractive table format. Some of the more sophisticated word processors, in conjunction with graphics software, can also generate pie, bar, line, and some other types of charts, based on data in tables already created in the word processing document.

If the data you have collected have been processed using a statistical package or entered into a spreadsheet, charts can be prepared using a spreadsheet package such as Lotus, Excel, or Quattro. After designing a chart and making certain all necessary labeling is present, the chart can be printed or imported into a word processing document. Sizing and positioning can be adjusted as appropriate. Graphical interfaces and today's soft-

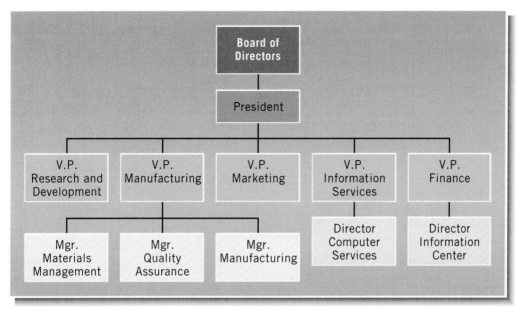

FIGURE 14-12
Partial organization chart

ware are making it easier and easier for a computer user to provide en-hancements such as color and three-dimensional charts.

Graphic aids can also be created using presentation graphics software such as Harvard Graphics, Freelance, and PowerPoint. Charts created with these software packages can also be imported into word processing docu-ments. Software suites such as LotusSmartSuite, Microsoft Office, and Corel Office offer a report writer both word processing and graphics capabil-ities in a graphical environment.

When the report writer is to make an oral presentation using graphic aids, the same charts designed and included in the printed report can be entered into a computerized slide show created with PowerPoint, Freelance, and other presentation graphics packages without the need to rekey the data or re-create the graphic.

The availability of computerized graphics brings new challenges to you as a report writer. Select the most appropriate chart or graph to display the data. All the "whistles and bells" available through computerized graphics are very tempting, but remember that the key reason for using graphics is to enhance *textual* materials. The written materials in your document must be well organized and include content appropriate for the purpose of the com-munication. Your knowledge of the principles of graphic aids presented in this chapter will continue to be important, no matter how the computer speeds the preparation of the graphics. You will find that it is important to make correct choices and give exact instructions.

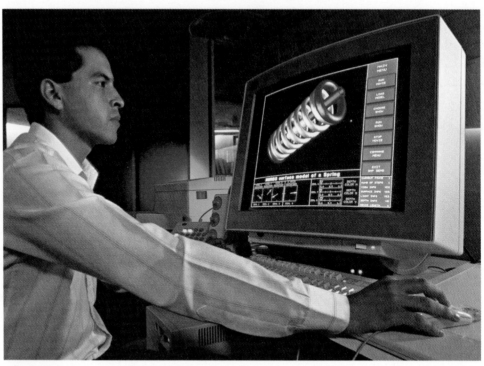

Computer-made graphic aids are widely used for small or large meetings. At times they are overused.

Placing Graphic Aids Within the Report

Ordinarily, you should place a chart, table, or other graphic aid within the text of a report as near as possible to the portion of text that it is used to illustrate or explain. If the graphic aid is not closely related to the material being discussed, place it in an appendix. Tables and charts, like other supplementary material, should go into an appendix if they cannot be considered an essential part of the report itself.

Extremely long tables or other kinds of material should be placed as appendices even if they cannot be considered supplemental. Your reader is referred to these appendices as relevant material is discussed.

Long tables placed in appendices may have short summary tables placed within the text of the report. They are woven into the discussion, as illustrated in the following list:

During 1997 the following increases and decreases, shown in percentages of dollar sales for 1996, occurred for each of the three products in each of the three districts:

Eastern	*Product A, +12*	*Product B, +5*	*Product C, −10*
Western	*Product A, −20*	*Product B, −10*	*Product C, +15*
Southern	*Product A, +15*	*Product B, −25*	*Product C, +40*

This simple arrangement, like a listing of other kinds of information or questions, adds emphasis and aids immediate comprehension of the displayed data. This table is in effect part of the discussion. Tables as short and simple as the one shown need not be labeled and numbered unless the omission would result in confusion or inconsistency with other illustrations throughout the report.

Short summary tables may be used even when other tables and charts are also included in the text of the report. Although often longer and more formal than the preceding table, all graphic aids should be part of the discussion in that they directly relate to the point being discussed. Anything that stops the reader's flow of thought, such as an unrelated illustration or inconvenient placement, is distracting and undesirable.

At times the discussion of a chart or other graphic aid may extend through several pages. When this occurs, the illustration should appear near the beginning of the discussion.

DISCUSSING GRAPHIC AIDS WITHIN THE REPORT TEXT

Introduce a graphic aid before presenting it, and, preferably, follow it with a few lines of discussion. In introductory remarks to the graphic aid, point out highlights of its information. By identifying items of major importance as shown on the table or chart, you are able to refer subordinately to the illustration, as shown below:

> *The greatest increase in sales occurred in District 1 (72 percent) and the smallest in District 7 (17 percent), as shown in Table 3.*

Although you should refer to the table, do not build introductory sentences around the fact that certain tables or charts follow and that the reader should look at them. Instead, emphasize important elements of information that are shown in following tables or charts, which are referred to subordinately.

IDENTIFYING GRAPHIC AIDS TO ENHANCE READER UNDERSTANDING

Use identifying titles and numbers on all illustrations throughout the report with the exception of minor tables or listings that can be considered a part of the text itself.

▶ LABELING AND NUMBERING

Traditionally, tables are not grouped with other forms of illustrations but are numbered separately throughout the report. This traditional method of numbering is being replaced by some writers and organizations with the word *Figure*, which may be used to refer to all kinds of illustrations, numbered consecutively throughout the report. (The method of labeling figures in this chapter is based on *The Chicago Manual of Style*.) The word processing package you use will typically allow you to provide a caption of either "Table" or "Figure" as your style manual requires.

▶ COMPOSING APPROPRIATE TITLES

Like subheadings in a report and titles of all works, titles of tables and other graphic aids should concisely but accurately describe the data presented in the illustration. Titles of tables are usually placed above the table, in larger type than material in the table itself. In typewritten work, use solid capitals with no underscore. Titles of charts or figures are some-

Visual aids can be three dimensional, as shown by this model building, which was no doubt designed with the aid of a computer.

times placed at the bottom of the illustration, shown in regular type. Titles of charts and other illustrations may also be placed at the top. When using computer software to generate tables and charts, check carefully, since software may automatically generate titles in different locations. Whichever location your style manual specifies, be sure to follow it consistently throughout the report.

▷ CITING SOURCES

Credit must be given for material taken from another source; for example,

> *Source: Business Week*, December 9, 1996, 28.

These source notes are usually placed one double space below a chart or table, but at times they may be placed underneath the title.

Ethical Considerations: Accurate and Honest Presentation of Data in Charts

The purpose of graphic aids is to show trends and relationships quickly, clearly, and accurately. Poorly constructed graphics do the opposite. Some of the ways these distortions of quantities, trends, and relationships occur have already been mentioned as the various types of graphic aids were discussed. In summary, distortions are likely to be caused by one or more of the following:

1   *An inappropriately chosen grid.* (A grid is the network of horizontal and vertical lines on which the chart is plotted.)

2   *Inappropriate plotting on the grid*; for example, not keeping the time schedule uniform.

3   *Beginning the quantitative axis somewhere other than zero* without making the omission immediately clear to the reader. This omission results in cutting off the bottom of a line or bar chart. Use all such charts with extreme caution. Even when readers are warned by broken lines that the scale has been broken, they are more likely to notice the overall effect of the chart than the broken lines.

4   *Varying more than one dimension in bar charts or pictograms.* For example, if you are illustrating computer sales, use three computers of identical size to indicate that a company sold three million in 1997 as compared to 1996, when one million were sold, shown by a computer of identical size. Do not attempt to make one computer three times larger to show the increase in number for 1997.

In order to prevent misinterpretation, in addition to distortion caused by the design of the graphic aid, observe the following guidelines:

▶ Interpret the information shown in the chart to the extent that you are sure your reader will understand its meaning. (The charts shown in this chapter are used to illustrate the different kinds of graphic aids, not to present the information itself. Thus, discussion of the information presented on the charts is less than would be required if the charts were used in a business or technical report.)

▶ Give credit where credit is due, as when using verbal passages other than your own.

▶ Make sure that titles, legends, and explanatory notes adequately describe the purpose and content of each chart.

ETHICAL, ACCURATE, AND COMPLETE ANALYSIS OF DATA; CAUSES OF ERROR

In order to interpret data correctly and impartially and to evaluate it for accuracy, the researcher must keep in mind the several ways in which communication errors can occur. These errors of evaluation and interpretation are similar to those that occur in the overall process of communication.

▶ MISINTERPRETATION THROUGH INFERENCES AND VALUE JUDGMENTS

Report conclusions are often, if not usually, based on inferences about the meaning of data. They must be. But the inferences must be based on facts.

A basic cause of error is twisting the facts—or what seem to be the facts—to obtain definite and specific conclusions, especially preconceived and desirable ones. Researchers also present inferences and value judgments as facts, omitting evidence that would raise questions about the wisdom of their conclusions. Although we should not hedge with an abundance of indefinite terms such as *it seems, possibly,* and *perhaps,* conclusions or recommendations based on inferences should not be presented as proved facts.

▶ TRYING TO VALIDATE A POINT OF VIEW

A true report does not present evidence to support a particular point of view; rather, it presents all relevant and obtainable evidence on both sides of a question and interprets the meaning of these findings. Although some so-called reports are planned to present "a case" for a decision or an emotional appeal to action, this kind of writing is not a real report as discussed here.

As you arrange information into report form, remember that most courses of action have disadvantages as well as advantages. Your work will be unconvincing if it lists only advantages—unless you have encountered a rare situation in which disadvantages are so minor that they are not worth mentioning.

FAILURE TO DISCRIMINATE

We tend to interpret two events as if they were identical or to think in terms of stereotypes. We see similarities instead of differences. We communicate and react in terms of categories, generalizations, and stereotypes when we should be looking for uniqueness. Although we do and should see similarities and use them for generalizing, categorizing, and arriving at conclusions (and recommendations), we should keep in mind the dangers of overgeneralizing and stereotyping.

ARGUING IN CIRCLES

An example of arguing in circles is given below:

Fortune teller to client: "You'll be famous if you live long enough."

Client: "What will I be famous for?"

Fortune teller: "For having lived so long."[1]

In this type of reasoning, also described as "begging the question," what is stated as a conclusion is only a restatement of the original assumption.

SELF-EVIDENT TRUTHS

If the truths really were self-evident, you wouldn't need to write a report or make an argument. Arguing through a self-evident truth is similar to arguing in circles except that the writer or speaker doesn't bother to reach the conclusion that was originally the assumption or self-evident truth. Arguing through self-evident truths is taking for granted that there is no disagreement, and it uses intimation to keep people from disagreeing, as in "all thinking people agree."

Other phrases that indicate the use of self-evident truths are these:

► It is common knowledge . . .

► As everybody knows . . .

► You can't deny that . . .

► It goes without saying . . .

► Any child knows . . .

► As known to every schoolboy . . .

► As every intelligent person knows . . .

▶ BLACK-OR-WHITE THINKING

We tend to try to fit all answers into definite categories of black or white, yes or no, right or wrong. Such arrangements simplify thought processes (or dispense with them entirely), but they are not always accurate. Not all situations or ideas can be neatly categorized into such opposing divisions. Some areas must remain in varying shades of gray.

▶ BASING CONCLUSIONS ON INSUFFICIENT OR NONCOMPARABLE DATA

Basing conclusions on insufficient evidence is an example of overgeneralization. Although we will never be able to find absolutely complete information about anything, the cliché "jumping to conclusions" applies to errors in judgment and communication of all kinds.

Not all data can be accurately compared to other sets of data. In many situations other factors must be taken into consideration. This interpretation and communication error is expressed in the well-known phrase "comparing apples to oranges."

Conclusions should be drawn after a presentation of facts. While one or more conclusions may be drawn, each conclusion must relate to specific facts presented earlier in the text. Recommendations should then develop logically from conclusions.

Graphic aids are often used to enhance oral presentations. Notice that the speaker is looking at the audience, not at the chart.

▶ **BASING DECISIONS ON PERSONALITIES INSTEAD OF FACTS**

Even nationally known "authorities" in a field can be wrong, although they are more likely to be correct than people outside the field. Communication error that results from an unquestioning belief in the opinions of other people, especially of well-known people, is described as "wise men can't be wrong." (Wise men and women know that they can be wrong.)

OBJECTIVE WORDING AND WRITING STYLE

Word all reports specifically, objectively, and exactly. Emphasize facts. Support with concrete, convincing details. When preparing an analytical report, analyze the data in order to reach conclusions and recommendations. These conclusions and recommendations must be supported by evidence instead of being based merely on beliefs, assumptions, and desires. Although at times you must state what you believe about a situation, or what the data seem to indicate, make sure that your reader understands that such a statement is an opinion. On the other hand, avoid an appearance of hedging and timidity. The conclusions and recommendations, like all other parts of the report, should be stated in specific, concrete terms, not in general, vague, abstract wording.

Avoid using a great number of adjectives and adverbs in report writing or, for the most part, in writing of any kind. Modifiers, or qualifiers, are far less direct and forceful than well-chosen, exact, and vivid nouns and verbs. The wise choice of nouns decreases the need for adjectives; the wise choice of verbs decreases the need for adverbs. Too many adjectives and adverbs slow the flow of writing. They also tend to sound effusive and exaggerated.

SUMMARY

In the evaluation of data, as well as in the presentation of a report, do everything possible to be completely and thoroughly objective. Use nonbiased evaluation and interpretation in order to present findings in a matter-of-fact way and to show how these findings lead to the stated conclusions and recommendations.

Errors in data interpretation are the same as those that occur in all forms of communication; they include inaccurate perception, the confusion of facts with inferences and value judgments, hasty generalizations, and the basing of decisions on predetermined beliefs.

Statistical measures are useful in the interpretation of data, although statistics can be used in confusing and misleading ways.

Use charts, tables, and other illustrations to express meaning quickly and clearly, but do not use them solely to impress.

Choose the appropriate type of chart, table, or other graphic aid to best convey the desired meaning or comparison. Some information should be shown in more than one way in the same report. For example, the reader may need exact figures instead of trends and relationships; if so, present these figures in tabular form.

Place a graphic aid within the text of the report, as near as possible to the portion of the text that is used to illustrate or explain. If it is not closely related to the material being discussed, it should be either omitted or placed in the appendix section of the report. Tables and charts, like other information, belong in the appendix section if they can be considered supplementary to the report itself.

Introduce the graphic device before presenting it and, preferably, include a few words of discussion after the device has been presented. Point out the highlights of the graphic aid.

Make sure that graphic aids are constructed so that relationships are not distorted. Use reasonable proportion. Start at zero or show by broken lines that, because of space limitations, it was impractical to start at zero.

Carefully label each graphic device. Provide a descriptive key (also called a legend) if it will be helpful to the reader.

Keep all tables and charts simple. Do not try to show too much information on one chart.

TEST YOURSELF

chapter content

1   Define *mean*, *median*, and *mode*.
2   Explain how the word *average* may be used in a misleading way.
3   Unless tables and charts are clearly supplemental, where should they ordinarily be placed?
4   In addition to bar charts, what are the two most frequently used charts?
5   What is an advantage of a 100-percent bar chart?
6   What kind of information is displayed on a line chart?
7   What kind of information is displayed on a bilateral bar chart?
8   What type of information should be placed on the bottom axis (*x*-axis) of a vertical bar chart? On the vertical axis (*y*-axis)?
9   Name two ways in which charts are sometimes distorted so that misrepresentation occurs.
10 What placement rules should a report writer follow when including graphics within the body of the report?
11 In addition to improperly constructed graphics, name and briefly describe five or more causes of error in the analysis of data.
12 Conclusions should be based on _____.
13 Recommendations should be based on _____.
14 Give an example of objective and nonobjective wording.

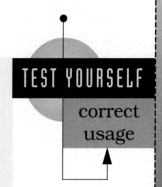

Punctuate correctly or remove incorrect punctuation. One sentence is correct as it is. (Review Appendix D.)

1 Tables not charts should be chosen for the presentation of numerous figures.
2 If you have the proper equipment and software you can construct various kinds of charts by using a personal computer.
3 Once you have calculated the mean of a group of numbers you may find that it is not always the best number upon which to base your decision.
4 Constructing charts with computers or other electronic equipment is faster than drawing them with a pen or pencil.
5 Carefully label each chart and provide a descriptive key which is called a legend.
6 All the techniques of effective graphics will effect the finished report.
7 Bilateral bar charts are also described as positive, and negative, bar charts.
8 Bar charts include the following kinds bilateral bar multiple bar and 100-percent bar.
9 The purpose of graphic aids is to show trends and relationships quickly clearly and accurately.
10 Conclusions presented in the report should be based on facts included in the body of the text not writer biases.

PROBLEMS

Note: Additional cases follow Chapter 15.

1 Which chart would you construct to illustrate the following types of information? As your instructor directs, construct these charts using assumed quantities. Use computer software to generate your charts wherever possible. If you can think of more than one kind of chart for one or more of the sets of data, describe the trends or relationships that each kind best conveys.
  a. Comparison of sales of the Local Corporation by product line (four major classifications of products):
  for the past year
  for the past 5 years
  for the past 25 years
  b. The Dow-Jones average, by year, for the past 20 years.

  c. Comparison (by either percentage or number) of freshmen, sophomore, junior, and senior students enrolled at your university for each of the past 10 semesters.
  d. Breakdown, in percentages, of how the federal government budget was spent last year.
  e. Breakdown, in percentages, of how the federal government budget was spent each year for the past five years.
  f. Comparison of 10 major companies to show increases and decreases in net profits from 1996 to 1997.
  g. Total production of automobiles in the United States by years, from 1985 through 1997, and production by General Motors, Ford, Chrysler, and "other" manufacturers.

2 Write an introductory paragraph or paragraphs for each of the following graphics illustrated within the chapter: Figure 14-2, Figure 14-3, Figure 14-4, Figure 14-6, and Figure 14-9.

3 Look at one issue each of *Fortune*, *The Wall Street Journal*, *USA Today*, and *U.S. News and World Report*. Write a memorandum to your classmates describing your findings, including a photocopy of one or more charts. Include in or with the memorandum at least one graphic aid of your own to convey in easy-to-read format your findings about the number and kinds of graphic aids you found in the four publications.

4 Decide which types of charts could be used for each of the following sets of data. Construct at least one for each set, preferably with the aid of computerized graphics software, and write an introductory paragraph.

a. Age groups of people who shop by mail: 18–24, 11%; 25–34, 26%; 35–44, 25%; 45–54, 16%; 55–64, 11%; 65 and older, 11%. (*Source: USA Today*, October 28, 1992, D1.)

b. Of the 2.2 billion acres in the United States, the government owns 30%, mostly national parks, forests, and wilderness areas. States with the most government-owned land are these: Nevada, 79%; Idaho, 61%; Utah, 60%; and Oregon, 52%. (*Source:* U.S. Department of the Interior.)

c. Total undergraduate enrollment in institutions of higher education in 50 states and the District of Columbia in the fall semester of 1994 included 72.6% White, non-Hispanic; 10.7% Black, non-Hispanic; 8.0% Hispanic; 5.5% Asian or Pacific Islander; 1.0% American Indian or Alaskan Native; and 2.2% Nonresident Aliens. (*Source:* U.S. Department of Education.)

d. Market share by product segment in the information technology industry in 1985 included data communication 8%, desktops 10%, large-scale computers 17%, peripherals 27%, servers 11%, services 17%, software 8%, and other 2%. In 1995 the product segment breakdown included data communication 7%, desktops 22%, large-scale computers 6%, peripherals 19%, servers 8%, services 27%, and software 11%. (*Source: Datamation*, June 15, 1996, 35.)

5 You learn that the average family income of your hometown, which has a population of 1,500 people, is $62,000. You know that many of the residents are eligible for food stamps. If you accept both of these descriptions as correct, explain the apparent incongruity.

6 From the following examination scores of 21 students, compute the mean, median, and mode. What is the range?
98, 97, 96, 96, 96, 92, 90, 87, 83, 80, 79, 79, 79, 79, 75, 71, 69, 68, 61, 59, 58.

7 Improve the following sentences, taken from reports, from the standpoint of objective, specific wording. For example, instead of saying that costs have increased by the enormous figure of 45.2 percent, say that they have increased 45.2 percent and be specific about particular costs and time periods.

a. The XYZ computer is shamefully overpriced. In comparison, competing models sell at bargain basement prices. (Assume amounts.)

b. The tremendous increase in stupid paperwork in our oddball office proves that it is foolish to tolerate the old copier another day.

c. The oppressive income tax awards sluggards and incompetents and penalizes those who are competent and hardworking.

d. I can't believe that we have fallen so disgracefully behind last year's quota. (Assume amounts.)

e. This amazing increase in profits—72 percent—is unquestionably due to the superb and creative leadership of our outstanding management team.

f. Enormous difficulties in production contributed to a startling date of completion, which was extremely late.

g. The unbelievable increase in defects—27 percent—is undoubtedly the result of a whopping amount of lax supervision.

COLLABORATIVE WRITING AND WORKING IN GROUPS

8 Bring to class a photocopy of a graphic presentation in a magazine, newspaper, or textbook. Work in small groups as directed by your instructor. Designate both a recorder and a group spokesperson for reporting findings to the class. As a group, review each graphic presentation to determine (a) whether the graphic used is the most appropriate one for the particular data and the desired comparison of relationships; and (b) whether the graphic is correctly and accurately made. Summarize the group's findings during a class discussion.

9 As a group, present the information requested in Problem 9 in a memorandum attached to the illustrated charts or other graphic aids. If possible, gather around a computer and compose an electronic draft. Each group member could compose the paragraph related to his or her graphic. Together, compose appropriate introductory and closing paragraphs for the memo. Work together to edit the entire memorandum.

10 Questionable research findings. Assume that you are the Director of the Bureau of Educational Research at Central College. You have been away from your office for two months because of illness, but you are now assuming full responsibility again.

You find that during your absence your assistant, Harry Siskin, has completed the following research studies:

a. He has surveyed the alumni of the college class with which you graduated. He received a 30-percent response to his mailed questionnaire. He found that the mean and median earnings of the class far exceed the national average of college graduates of the same year. He has written a news release about his findings in which he strongly indicates that graduates of this particular college are better prepared to move ahead because they re-

ceive better instruction, as proved by the survey. You have told him that the news release is not to be published.

b. He has studied the drop policy of the same college by checking student grade records before and after the policy was liberalized to the extent that students can now drop a course at any time before final examinations. After the change in policy, the grade point average increased. He believes that the results of his study show that the increase can be attributed to the fact that because students now have a less stressful semester, they are able to relax and make better grades.

c. While completing the previous survey, he also learned that more freshmen than seniors drop out of college. He concludes that freshmen courses are more difficult than senior courses.

He has written an article for a prestigious journal explaining the results of studies b and c above. He wants to list you as the co-author because of your recognized name. You would not dream of having your name appear on the article, even though you are sure it would not be accepted.

You have talked with Harry and tried to point out, as tactfully as possible, the weaknesses of his research. He insists that you put it all in writing. He says that he wants a copy to be put into his personnel file because his work during your absence has not been appropriately recognized.

Write a memorandum to Harry. Decide upon what should be included in the memo. Write it clearly but diplomatically.

11 Continue work on the report project begun with Chapter 12. Compare your charts and tables with those of others in your group. If one or more of the group members has access to a computer with chart-making soft-

ware, ask this person or persons to prepare charts for the other members of the group, after the originator has sketched them to show data and relationships. Analyze the sketches of each member to make sure that the most appropriate chart has been chosen and that the charts are objective and not misleading in any way.

THINK-IT-THROUGH ASSIGNMENTS

12 Discuss possible errors in interpretation in the following situations:

a. Finding that engineering graduates of a particular university start at higher salaries than liberal arts graduates do, a researcher concludes that the engineering school is more efficient than liberal arts departments are.

b. A study shows that the writing ability of today's average college student is inferior to the writing ability of the average college student of 1915.

c. A senator reports that the majority of letters he has received support his bill to increase the salary of postal workers.

d. You find that early-stage collection letters bring in more payments, on the average, than late-stage letters. You reason that people who have already received three or four collection letters are tired of them and that you should wait at least three months before sending any letters at all. (Besides, it would save a lot of trouble.)

e. You report that a statement is unquestionably true because Dr. Brown, who is an M.D. and a Ph.D., agrees with you.

13 Distinguishing among facts, conclusions, and recommendations. Each of the items below represents possible results of a research study you conducted concerning three computer labs on your campus. For each item, indicate whether something is a *fact*, *conclusion*, or *recommendation*. If you label an item a conclusion or recommendation, identify the specific statement(s) on which the conclusion or recommendation is based. If a statement represents a conclusion or recommendation not based on facts presented, label it as an unsubstantiated conclusion and/or recommendation.

a. Computers in Lab I and Lab II provide access to the campus academic network.

b. Workstations in Lab II have limited desk space.

c. Lab II and Lab III have their own window air conditioners. Lab I does not. A sign posted in Lab I reminds students that the university does not run central air conditioning on weekends to hold down utilities costs.

d. Lab I contains 36 workstations; Lab II contains 26 workstations; Lab III contains 24 workstations.

e. More students can access the academic network in Lab I than in Lab III.

f. Larger working spaces should be provided in Lab II.

g. Chairs in Labs I and II are secretarial style with no arms. Lab III has wood chairs.

h. Better lighting should be installed in Lab I.

i. The chairs in Lab III are less comfortable than the chairs in Labs I and II.

j. Lab I should not be used on weekends during the summer months.

ENDNOTE

1 Stuart Chase, *Guides to Straight Thinking* (New York: Harper & Row, 1956), 37–38.

Writing Short and Long Reports

CHAPTER

15

OBJECTIVES

Chapter Fifteen will help you:

1   Distinguish between short and long reports.

2   Explain the advantages and disadvantages of letter, memo, and form reports.

3   Compare and contrast characteristics of formal and informal reports.

4   Prepare all the necessary preliminary, body, and supplemental parts of a formal report.

5   Prepare a report with a professional appearance.

This chapter combines the discussion of reports that are often described as *short and informal* and *long and formal.* An important consideration, however, is that such terms are relative, particularly in regard to reports prepared in manuscript form. A short report is not necessarily informal, and an informal report is not necessarily short.

 HORT REPORTS

A *short informal report*, as considered in this chapter, is any reporting or analysis or information *not* presented in the complete, formal arrangement that includes preliminary and supplementary parts. A report decreases in formality as preliminary and supplementary parts are omitted.

Short reports may be prepared in *letter, memorandum, form,* or *manuscript* formats, depending on the reader's needs. Letter reports are often used when the report will be sent to outsiders. Memorandum reports are typically used when the report will be distributed within the writer's employing organization. In some instances the writer may desire a more formal presentation, even for a short report, and choose to present it in a manuscript format. Form reports are often used to report routine, quantifiable (numeric) information. To help decide what format to use for a short report, ask yourself the following questions:

► Why is the report being prepared? Is the report informational or analytical?

► Are the report contents largely numerical data or narrative?

While appearance is an important nonverbal component of a written report, it does not substitute for quality content, good organization, and sound reasoning.

▶ Where is the report being sent? Are the report readers employed within your organization or will outsiders be reading the report?

▶ Was the report assigned to you or is it one that you prepared based on your own motivation?

LETTER REPORTS

Figure 15-1 illustrates a report presented in a letter form. The writer is mailing the report to someone outside the company. In addition to the letter, two attachments are enclosed: a Summary of Evidence and the questionnaire that was used to find the requested information. "Summary of Evidence" is not the only acceptable heading. Another would be "What T. L. Goeken Lumber Company Should Do to Increase Sales and Customer Satisfaction." This lengthy title is unnecessary, however, in this informal report, because the purpose of the report is given in the letter.

The questionnaire mentioned as being enclosed as an attachment here is shown in Chapter 13, Figure 13-1. The letter with attachments shown in Figure 15-1 is an analytical report because the writer analyzes the reported information and makes a recommendation. The letter, like all letter reports, is correctly written in the personal tone, which includes *I*'s, *you*'s, and other forms of the first- and second-person pronouns. Because the recommendation comes at the beginning of the letter, the order of arrangement is direct. The report is informal in format. The writing style could not be classified as formal, but it is not excessively informal.

The information shown in Figure 15-1 *could* have been presented as a short manuscript or perhaps even a memorandum. Because the information and analysis to be presented is not lengthy, a one-page letter, with supporting material, is concise, emphatic, and easy to read.

■ K & M BUSINESS CONSULTANTS ■

200 West State Street   Phone: (309) 244-1212
Macomb, Illinois 61554   Fax: (309) 244-2020
                                          http://www.k&mconsult.com

November 15, 19—
T. L. Goeken Lumber Company
200 West Fourth Street
Delavan, IL 61734

Dear Mr. Goeken:

Recommendations are that you increase your advertising to increase your customer awareness levels and create more store traffic. Newspaper, in-store, and outdoor advertising should all be increased. We also recommend that you increase your store hours to retain customers and better compete with the longer store hours of competitors.

An analysis of the 193 usable questionnaires returned by your credit customers is attached. A copy of the questionnaire is also attached for your reference.

Sixty-nine percent of those responding shop at your store at least once a week; another 19 percent shop at least once a month. Based on the scale designed to measure customer opinions concerning service, pricing, and delivery service, courteous service obtained the highest average. Responses related to pricing show the company has good competitive prices. Customers are also highly satisfied with delivery service. Convenience, location, and delivery service were the three top reasons respondents reported shopping at your store. *No* respondents reported store hours as one of the top three reasons.

Only 49 percent of respondents were aware of best buys and monthly sales. Of those aware of best buys, only 2 percent reported "word of mouth" advertising; only 23 percent reported in-store advertising.

The recommendations we have made are based on the survey results. The satisfaction and awareness level of your customers is above average, but the competition of the new Handy Henry store with more store hours cannot be ignored. This increased competition calls for a strong advertising campaign and additional store hours to keep your customer base and increase store traffic.

Please call me at the number shown above if you wish to discuss this survey or if I can help in any other way.

Sincerely,

Adam Maxwell

Adam Maxwell, Consultant

Attachments

FIGURE 15-1
Report in letter format, with attachments

(Adapted from a marketing research project, M. Boudreaux and J. Donadieu, Nicholls State University.)

SUMMARY OF EVIDENCE

The recommendations to increase advertising and store hours are based on the 193 usable responses of the 400 that were mailed to credit customers.

Forty-nine percent of respondents reported being aware of "best buys" and monthly sales. As shown in Figure 1, when cross tabbed with frequency of store visits, no level of customer frequency reflects a strong awareness of in-store advertising. While the sales paper was more often the means by which customers learned of "best buys" and monthly sales, less than a fourth of each group reported this knowledge being provided by the sales paper.

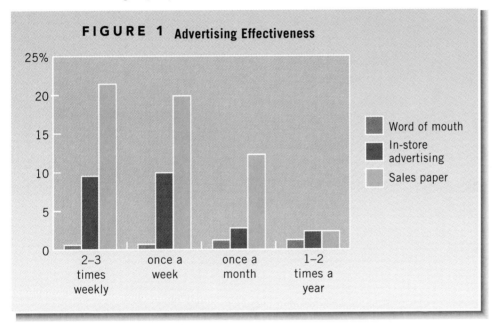

FIGURE 1 Advertising Effectiveness

Customers are not all aware of the various services offered by T. L. Goeken Lumber Company, as shown in Table 1. This further supports the need for increased advertising.

TABLE 1 SERVICE AWARENESS	
Service	**% of Respondents**
Quick delivery	78
Customized paint colors	69
House estimates	64
Special orders	85
Lock rekeying	61

FIGURE 15-1
continued

As shown in Figure 2 when respondents were asked to identify the three major reasons for shopping at T. L. Goeken Lumber Company, store hours received NO votes.

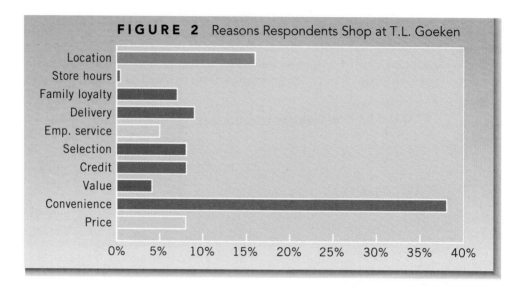

FIGURE 2   Reasons Respondents Shop at T.L. Goeken

An analysis of respondents' opinions of key service factors revealed that customers are satisfied overall. A breakdown of the responses to the semantic differential scale used to evaluate responses to these questions is shown in Table 2.

TABLE 2   RESPONDENTS' VIEWS RELATED TO KEY CUSTOMER SERVICE FACTORS

	Satisfied			Dissatisfied				
Courteous service	61%	27%	5%	2%	2%			Discourteous service
Low prices	13%	20%	20%	25%	12%	2%	8%	High prices
Helpful employees	51%	24%	5%	14%	2%	4%		Unhelpful employees
Employees with product knowledge	39%	31%	10%	7%	3%	4%	6%	Employees without product knowledge
Good delivery service	48%	30%	10%	12%				Bad delivery service

FIGURE 15-1
continued

Hardware and lumber are the most frequent purchases; these two categories encompass a large number of products, and higher purchase percentages in these two areas were expected. A breakdown of most frequent customer purchases is illustrated in Figure 3.

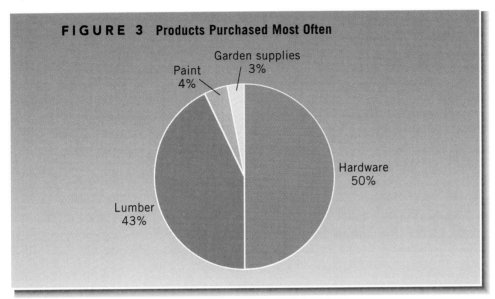

FIGURE 3 Products Purchased Most Often

As shown in Table 3, respondents reported overall satisfaction with T. L. Goeken Lumber Company when responding to a question with a 7-point semantic differential scale.

TABLE 3	OVERALL CUSTOMER SATISFACTION					
Satisfied			Dissatisfied			
39%	38%	14%	5%	2%		2%

FIGURE 15-1
continued

MEMORANDUM REPORTS

Memorandum reports, as the name implies, are simply reports prepared in memorandum format, regardless of purpose or contents. Like all other memorandums, they are arranged in the direct or the indirect order, depending on the message and the intended readers. Many of the thousands of memorandums that flow through business organizations each day are reports of one kind or another, using the general but accurate description that a business report is a relaying of business information.

Figure 15-2, which is described as a progress report, is also correctly described as a memorandum report.

DATE: June 20, 19—
TO: Board of Directors, Playhouse on the Square
FROM: Karen Robins, Manager

SUBJECT: PROGRESS OF STUDY TO DETERMINE NEEDED IMPROVEMENTS IN
            SOUND-SYSTEM EQUIPMENT

Since you authorized my research study on May 7, I have taken the following steps:

1. Interviewed all the permanent and visiting staff of Playhouse on the Square in
   order to determine their opinions about needed improvements in our sound system equipment. These people are quite knowledgeable on the subject because of
   their experience in other theaters in the city and elsewhere.

2. Talked with the architect, J. B. Herring, who designed our new building. He suggested possible changes in our present sound system.

3. Searched all local libraries and the Internet for published information pertaining
   to sound systems for theaters similar to Playhouse on the Square.

4. Discussed our needs with two representatives of Audio Communications Consultants, the firm that installed our present system.

The following actions will be completed within the next six weeks:

1. Visit theaters similar to the Playhouse in St. Louis, Louisville, Dallas, and San
   Diego, as authorized at our last meeting.

2. Talk with possible suppliers of sound equipment, some of whom are in the cities
   mentioned in Item 1.

3. Organize and evaluate all gathered information and prepare report in written
   form for presentation at September meeting of Board of Directors.

I will send you additional progress reports as I move toward a solution to improving
our sound equipment. Thank you for authorizing me to research this problem.

FIGURE 15-2
A progress report presented in memorandum format

PROGRESS REPORTS

Progress reports, as the term indicates, relate progress on a project of some kind, including research studies. The term *progress report* refers to subject matter, not to format or special arrangement. You may arrange such reports in any of the formats used for other reports in this chapter or in other arrangements not shown here. Figure 15-2 illustrates a progress report in the form of a memorandum.

FORM REPORTS

Form reports are a popular way to submit information. The author of the report presents the information requested in the specific blanks or areas provided on the form. This allows the writer to focus on specific information without including extra narrative, although there may be places on the form where narrative information can be included if necessary. As discussed in Chapter 12, presenting quantifiable information in a form report may increase the report reader's efficiency.

Figure 15-3 is a partial example of a form report used by a university faculty member to report her teaching, research, and service activities for the annual review process.

OTHER SHORT REPORTS

As noted earlier, short reports can be presented in various formats other than letters, memorandums, and form reports. An example of a short report arranged as a manuscript is shown in Figure 15-4. The writer of this report selected a manuscript format to give more formality and/or credibility to the recommendations being presented to a superior. The format is also attractive if the reader chooses to distribute the report to other readers.

Whatever the chosen format, length, and formality of a report, its readers are influenced by neatness and an attractive appearance. Keep in mind that formal reports are sometimes expected to be arranged in a conventional, expected format, perhaps in exact conformance with a particular style manual.

ANNUAL EVALUATION REPORT   Faculty:__Julie Heffelfinger__
TEACHING: Academic year:___1997_____

Spring Semester				Fall Semester			
Course	Contact Hrs.	Credit Hrs.	No. of Students	Course	Contact Hrs.	Credit Hrs.	No. of Students
BA 315 2T	3	3	25	BA 315 2T	3	3	24
BA 315 6M	3	3	31	BA 315 6M	3	3	34
CIS 221 3M	3	3	33	CIS 460	3	3	28
CIS 221 EM	3	3	38				

ATTACH ADDITIONAL SHEETS WHERE NECESSARY

Teaching Self-improvement Activities:
Attended Association for Business Communication, Washington, D.C., November.
Attended Decision Sciences national meeting, San Francisco, November
Attended Southwest Federation of Academic Disciplines, New Orleans, March
Attended International Association for Computer Information Systems, St. Louis, October
Attended teaching conference sponsored by Prentice Hall, New Orleans, September

Non-classroom Teaching Activities (Supervision of internships; clinicals, etc.):
None claimed for 1997 calendar year

Research:

Articles in Print (or accepted for publication):
Heffelfinger, J. (1997). "Impact of Technology on Instructional Delivery," Journal of Computer Information Systems, vol. 37, no. 2, 28–33. (copy attached)
Heffelfinger, J., & Zachry, B. (1997). "Accountants Communicating with Non-accountants: Developing an Effective Strategy," New Accountant, vol. 10, no. 1, 16–19. (copy attached)

Presentations:
"Improve Your Business Communication Teaching by Developing a Teaching Portfolio," Presented at the Association for Business Communication national convention, Washington, D.C., November. (program and paper attached)
"Impact of the Use of Technology in the Information Systems Classroom," Presented at southwest region of Decision Sciences, New Orleans, March. (program and paper attached)

Research Grants:
Contributing author to a FIPSE grant proposal funded in the amount of $78,000 for the first year. (Grant proposal attached)

FIGURE 15-3
Sample of a portion of a form report used for evaluations
(Adapted from a form used by Nicholls State University.)

RECOMMENDATIONS FOR IMPLEMENTING A VOICE MAIL SYSTEM

Prepared for

Linda E. Peters
Corporate Administrative Director

Johnson-Williams Investment Services

by

Milea S. Maxwell
Office Systems Manager

Corporate Headquarters

November 15, 19——

FIGURE 15-4
Short recommendation report presented in manuscript format (supporting
documents appended to the report are not shown here)

RECOMMENDATIONS FOR IMPLEMENTING A VOICE MAIL SYSTEM

<u>Recommendations</u>

I recommend that a voice mail system be purchased and installed at the home office and at all branch offices.

<u>Purpose and Scope of the Study</u>

The purpose of this study is to determine whether the existing telephone system should be upgraded to include a voice mail system. Factors considered are time and money saved after installation, satisfaction of those persons placing calls, and initial costs. The current study will not make a recommendation for purchase of a specific voice mail system nor recommend specific training needs and costs.

<u>Findings</u>

1. One branch office currently uses voice mail. The home office and all other branches have not installed voice mail systems. Seven percent of the employees at the home office and various branches have installed answering machines on their lines.

2. The home office currently has 284 separate extensions. The smallest branch has 12 extensions, and the largest branch has 61 extensions.

3. Only 2 percent of the management and professional employees have a one-to-one ratio of support staff. A typical support staff employee answers the phone for 4 to 8 lines.

4. Fifty percent of the home office employees were surveyed last month regarding telephone usage. Results show that 75 percent of the time our personnel do not reach the other company employees they are calling. The resulting telephone tag slows down the process of gathering information and making decisions; telephone tag also adds stress to the job. The employees surveyed also report an average of 9 "while you were out" phone messages being recorded by the support staff for each manager or professional staff employee each day. Detailed information is typically not recorded in the handwritten phone messages, necessitating a return call that frequently results in additional telephone tag. The sales staff noted that telephone tag has caused the company to lose sales in several instances within the last month alone.

5. Home office switchboard operators logged all incoming calls during the past month. Seventy-nine percent of the calls placed to the company's main switchboard number were transferred to either sales, customer services, or accounting.

FIGURE 15-4
continued

6. The purchasing department estimates that 50 percent of our vendors are using voice mail. The sales department estimates that one third of our major customers also have voice mail systems. A study recently conducted in New Orleans reflects that businesspeople have an overall positive reaction to using voice mail in a business environment because it increases productivity and enhances efficiency. Installing our own voice mail system will help us project an up-to-date image.

7. By installing a voice mail system, our sales representatives and any other employees away from the office can call in at any hour of the day or night from any location and obtain their voice mail messages. Likewise, they can leave voice messages 24 hours a day.

8. Sophisticated voice mail systems allow individuals to personalize messages they leave for callers to reflect being out of the office on a certain day or being unable to return calls until a certain time of day.

FIGURE 15-4
continued

LONG REPORTS

The basic principles of report writing apply to all kinds of reports, whether of a minor, limited nature or of extensive coverage.

The researcher must understand the problem and be able to state it exactly. The next steps are to find the necessary information, to evaluate and interpret this information, and to organize it in the most readable and appropriate form. This procedure remains the same although the finished report may be presented in one of several forms: the complete, formal arrangement, a more informal report arrangement (in that some or all of the preliminary and supplementary parts are omitted); a letter with attachments; or a memorandum with attachments.

COMPARING FORMAL REPORTS WITH INFORMAL REPORTS

For reports arranged as manuscripts, such as Figure 15-4, there is no exact dividing line between "short" and "long" or between "formal" and "informal" format. The overall length and the inclusion of preliminary and supplementary parts are the most obvious differences.

Some similarities of formal and informal reports are these:

1 The purpose of the report and the method of investigation should be clearly stated in both formal and informal reports.

2 Objectivity and a nonbiased approach are essential, regardless of the format and arrangement of the finished report.

3 Conclusions and recommendations, if included, must be clearly based on reported findings.

4 Internal citations or another method of documentation must be used as needed to establish credibility and to give credit where credit is due.

The most important consideration in choosing format and arrangement is the nature and purpose of the report, along with the needs and expectations of the readers.

Using a laser printer results in a crisp clear copy.

Preliminaries	Body	Supplements
Cover	Introduction	Appendix
Title fly	Text (divided into sections)	Bibliography
Title page	Conclusions and recommendations	Index
Letter of authorization		
Letter of acceptance		
Letter of transmittal		
Table of contents		
List of charts and tables		
Synopsis/abstract		

FIGURE 15-5
Parts of a long report package

THE LONG, FORMAL REPORT PACKAGE

Complete formal reports are comprised of three major divisions: *preliminaries*, the *report body* (or report proper), and *supplementary parts*. These three major divisions make up the report package. A list of items included in each of the three major divisions is presented in Figure 15-5.

PRELIMINARIES

The *cover*, *title page*, *letter of transmittal*, *table of contents*, and *synopsis* are the most commonly used preliminaries. Few reports need all the preliminaries discussed in the following paragraphs, and preliminary parts not included in this section are desirable for some reports.

COVER

Use a *cover* to protect and to hold the report together, as well as to add to its attractive appearance. A cover shows that you are careful enough about your report to present it in a neat manner. Don't force your reader to open the cover to find the title and author; this information should appear on the cover itself or through a cutout section.

▶ TITLE FLY

The *title fly* is a full page that shows only the title. As this page serves no useful purpose, you may omit it unless the particular handbook you are following tells you to include it.

▶ TITLE PAGE

The *title page* includes the title of the report, the person to whom the report is submitted, the complete identification of the report writer, and the date.

Work for a concise but descriptive title. Although some titles are unnecessarily wordy, short ones are likely to be vague, nondescriptive, and overly broad, promising more than the report includes. A specific title indicates the nature, purpose, and limits of the research. The title is the major heading of the entire written work. Like all other headings, it must describe the contents that come under it.

▶ LETTER OF AUTHORIZATION

The *letter of authorization*, as the name indicates, is written by the person who authorizes the report. It may not be a letter at all, but a memorandum. Some authorizations are given orally.

When you receive a written authorization, either a letter or a memorandum, include it in the finished report. This authorization serves as a reminder that you prepared and presented the report according to specific instructions.

▶ LETTER OF ACCEPTANCE

The *letter of acceptance* is written by the researcher near the beginning of the report process as an acknowledgment of the letter of authorization. It makes clear that the report writer understands the problem and any specific instructions given orally or in the written authorization. Like the letter of authorization and the letter of transmittal, this message may also be in memorandum form. The letter arrangement has the advantage of being slightly more personal, yet more formal, as this important situation merits.

▶ LETTER OF TRANSMITTAL

The *letter of transmittal*, as the name indicates, transmits the finished report. It may be used for helpful and informative comments about the research process, particularly those that do not seem to fit into the report itself. It should include some reference to the authorization and to the purpose of the study.

Other information that may be included in the letter or memorandum of transmittal are suggestions for follow-up studies or other side issues of the problem. The transmittal may mention special limitations or difficulties encountered in the research or in the report-writing process, as well as the highlights or other details of the research process. *Do not include in the letter of transmittal a synopsis or statement that sums up the findings and recommendations if you also prepare a separate synopsis.*

TABLE OF CONTENTS

The *table of contents* is the report outline with the addition of page numbers. A table of contents is helpful in many reports that would not be described as formal in arrangement or format. It indicates the topics covered in the report, the sequence of that coverage, and the relative importance of the divisions and subdivisions.

All headings and subheadings of the table of contents must agree exactly with the headings and subheadings in the report itself.

LIST OF CHARTS AND TABLES

A list of charts may also be headed by such terms as *Illustrations*, *List of Illustrations*, *Charts and Illustrations*, or *List of Figures*. If numerous charts and tables are included within the body of the report, the report may also include separate lists, as a *List of Tables* and a *List of Charts*. This part of the report should be headed by the term that best describes the illustrations used. The List of Charts or the List of Tables can be a continuation of the overall table of contents or shown on a separate page.

SYNOPSIS/ABSTRACT

A *synopsis*, sometimes referred to as an *abstract* or *summary*, is a much condensed overview of the entire report, including the introduction and the conclusions and recommendations. In order to stress results, the synopsis is often arranged in the direct order, presenting conclusions, results, or recommendations first, even if the report itself is presented in the indirect order. Usually two thirds to three fourths of the synopsis should be devoted to the final results. The remaining portion of the synopsis contains a very brief statement of the purpose, scope, methods, and, perhaps, the background and need for the study.

The synopsis should be brief, no more than one tenth of the length of the entire report. For a very long report, the proportional length of the synopsis is even shorter. *At its longest*, the synopsis should fill no more than two single-spaced, printed pages. The synopsis may be used by a busy decision maker to gain an overview of the entire report. If appropriate, it may even be distributed to others to provide a quick summary.

Laptop computers enable writers to continue a report as they travel.

▶ OTHER PRELIMINARY PARTS

Acknowledgments are another preliminary report part. You may include them in the letter of transmittal unless they are so numerous that the letter would be longer than one page. Another preliminary part useful in some reports is a *list of definitions of specialized terms* used in the report. Definitions may also be placed in the introduction, if the list is fairly short (no more than half a page). Another choice of placement is in the supplementary section of a report, where such a list is usually described as a *glossary*.

BODY OF THE REPORT

The body of the report, or the "report proper," begins with the introduction and continues through the conclusions and recommendations, if the report is arranged in the indirect order. A report arranged in the direct order, which is less likely to have preliminary parts, begins with the gist of the message, which is ordinarily termed the *recommendations section*.

INTRODUCTION

The *introduction* may include these sections:

1 *Authorization.* (Not necessary if you use a letter of authorization.)

2 *Purpose.* (Essential)

3 *Scope.* (Essential if it is not obvious from the title and statement of purpose. Scope may be combined with limitations.)

4 *Limitations.* (Use only as needed—and with caution. Limitations often appear to be excuses for a poor report.)

5 *Historical background.* (Also described as *background, background conditions, history,* or in other terms.) This section should be included in the introduction only if it can be kept brief. In some reports this information deserves a complete division, often as Part II of the report body.

6 *Sources and methods of collecting data.* (Essential) In a few long reports for which detailed and complicated methods of collection and analysis are used, these methods can be reported in Part II of the body of the report.

FINDINGS (TEXT)

The *findings* section of the report, also referred to as the *text*, consists of divisions that come after the introduction and before the conclusions and recommendations section (or before the summary in an informational report).

Although this middle section of the report is described by the terms *findings* and *text*, divisions of the report should *NOT* be titled with these words but with more descriptive captions, as illustrated in various tables of contents throughout this book. Ordinarily the text of the report, or the findings section, should be divided into several major divisions, each of which is headed by a caption that specifically describes the contents below it. Major divisions are in turn divided into subcategories, each of which is specifically described by a subheading.

As the term indicates, the findings section presents the data you have collected in your research study. This is the important section of the report on which you base your conclusions and recommendations in an analytical report. *For the most part, specific findings, stated in objective terms, provide the only kind of information you place in the findings section of the report.*

CONCLUSIONS AND RECOMMENDATIONS

Conclusions and *recommendations* are based on the findings presented in the middle section of the report. *Do not bring new information into these concluding sections or into the summary of an informational report.*

You may present conclusions and recommendations in a combined section or, occasionally, as two separate parts of the report. *Another word for conclusions, used in this sense, is interpretations; you interpret your collected findings for the reader. Informational reports, as discussed previously, merely present information; they do not include an analysis. Thus, the ending section of an informational report is usually referred to as a summary.*

Even though the conclusions are your own, do not switch from an impersonal tone (third-person writing style) used earlier in the report to the use of *I*. You can present your personal interpretations without the use of *I*. Avoid the awkward term *the writer*. Because you have collected and analyzed the data, obviously the conclusions are yours unless you state otherwise.

Be as objective and impartial as possible in presenting the conclusions and recommendations.

To repeat and emphasize: Base conclusions and recommendations only on the findings presented in earlier sections of the report, not upon your unsupported beliefs.

SUPPLEMENTS

Supplementary report parts typically include *appendices* and *bibliographies*. An *index* may also be included if it provides value to the reader of a very long manuscript report.

APPENDICES

The *appendix* section is used for supplementary material. (*Appendixes*, as well as the Latin *appendices*, is now correctly used as a plural form of *appendix*.)

If you used a questionnaire to gather information, you *must* include a complete copy as an appendix; otherwise the readers cannot judge the validity of the reported information. The covering letter or letters that accompanied the questionnaire should also be included as an appendix. Sometimes statistical formulas or computations are appended, as are computer printouts. Extensive tables, large maps, diagrams, or other long materials are placed in the appendix section if they are too bulky for inclusion in the report itself.

The main consideration, however, as to whether materials should go in the report itself or in the appendix section is whether the material relates directly to the text of the report or can be considered as additional and supplementary.

BIBLIOGRAPHY (REFERENCES)

The *bibliography* pages list secondary sources used in gathering data and in writing the report. A list of interviews or similar materials may also be included with the secondary sources. Reference sources include both secondary and primary research.

As discussed in Chapter 13, the APA (American Psychological Association) style manual uses the term *References* when listing only those materials actually cited in the paper, or *Bibliography* if the writer wishes to include works consulted in addition to those cited. The MLA (Modern Language Association) style manual uses the term *Works Cited* or *Works Consulted*, as appropriate.

INDEX

An *index* is unnecessary in almost all business reports; it is used only for very long, extensive ones. A well-made table of contents makes an index unnecessary and even undesirable, except in book-length manuscripts. If you do use an index, make sure that you use extreme care in its preparation. An incomplete index is worse than none at all.

If an index is needed, the writer should investigate the capabilities of the word processing package being used. Numerous packages available make generating an index a relatively easy task once the terms to be included have been selected in the text.

Report writer seems to be happy because he has successfully completed his report.

Example of a formal report

A formal report is shown in Figure 15-6, using the APA method of internal citation. Variations of this method are illustrated in the *MLA Handbook*, *The Chicago Manual of Style*, and other style manuals. An overview of both the APA and MLA citation styles is provided in Chapter 13.

For your own reports, try to determine the citation preference of your reader or readers. If you cannot determine a preference, follow one of the handbooks, choosing one of the accepted methods shown in your chosen manual. *Most important, be consistent in your placement, arrangement, and format.*

When you write a report, you should take care to revise and edit to ensure that you are presenting appropriate and readable content in the most effective manner. The evaluation sheet for report contents and writing style presented later in this chapter includes a key list of questions you should answer about your report. If your answer to any of the questions is "no," revise or edit until you can answer "yes."

Report appearance

Work for an attractive appearance. Your readers are favorably or unfavorably impressed by the overall appearance of the report.

▶ MARGINS

If the manuscript is to remain unbound, use a six-inch line, which provides slightly more than one-inch side margins. For manuscripts to be bound, move side margins an additional one-half inch to the right.

On the first page of a report manuscript, leave a two-inch top margin. On the following pages, leave a top margin of approximately one inch. On all pages, leave a bottom margin of one to one and one-half inches.

▶ SPACING

Formal reports are traditionally double spaced, but many organizations are now preparing all typewritten work in single-spaced form to economize. Your choice will depend on organizational policy, purpose, readership of the report, and cost considerations.

▶ HEADINGS

Be consistent in the use of headings. Use the same format for headings of the same weight. *Use no single subheadings.*

CREATING ETHICAL DECISION-MAKING ENVIRONMENTS
FOR FUTURE MANAGERS

Prepared for

Business Administration 310

Nicholls State University

Dr. Betty Kleen

Prepared by

Guy E. Courrege
and
Diane C. Dugas

July 19—

FIGURE 15-6
Example of a long, formal report

July 15, 19—

Dr. Betty Kleen
College of Business Administration
Nicholls State University
Thibodaux, LA 70310

Dear Dr. Kleen:

Here is the report you requested about ethical decision making environments for future managers. A copy of the questionnaire used to gather opinions of college business students is included as an appendix of the report.

We believe our findings can be of benefit to companies that are searching for effective ways to provide an appropriate internal environment for ethical decision making. The information can be useful to organizations of all types.

If you would like to discuss the findings or recommendations of this report with Diane Dugas and me, please call me at 504-555-1212.

Sincerely,

Guy Courrege

Guy Courrege

ii

FIGURE 15-6
continued

Table of Contents

iii

FIGURE 15-6
continued

SYNOPSIS

Recommendations are that broad, company-wide policies, situational examples or detailed guidelines, leadership by example, and whistle blowing can all help an organization create a foundation for ethical decision making. Any technique, when used by itself, however, will fall short of accomplishing a complete ethical environment.

Organizations that place heavy emphasis on situational guidelines and leadership by example can help influence newly hired college graduates in making ethical decisions. Codes of ethics can also provide a written outline of the organization's commitment to ethical actions.

Male and female respondents expressed similar views concerning the preferred assistance techniques and preferred deterrents. Ninety-eight percent of respondents considered unethical actions to be a threat to the reputation and profitability of a firm.

iv

FIGURE 15-6
continued

CREATING ETHICAL DECISION-MAKING ENVIRONMENTS
FOR FUTURE MANAGERS

INTRODUCTION

In the 1990s, ethical behavior can be essential to the very life of an organization because customers and suppliers are becoming increasingly aware of the need to do business with respectable firms. According to Richardson (1991), the making of unethical decisions by management and employees can severely harm the reputation and sales of an organization. In addition, Campbell (1993) states that, " . . . the absence of ethics carries a price which is often severe and is paid in both financial and personal terms" (p. 28). Therefore, it is to the advantage of all organizations to use the techniques necessary in creating an ethical decision-making environment in the workplace.

Purpose

The purpose of this report is to determine which ethics-improving techniques are most likely to positively influence the decision making of today's business graduates. This report is intended to help tri-parish area businesses in developing ethics programs that will appeal to and effectively influence future employees.

Scope

This report will consider the likely effectiveness of alternative techniques for guiding future managers in ethical decision making. It does not consider, in depth, the effectiveness of those techniques on current employees, nor does it consider the cost of the procedures necessary to implement those techniques.

Methodology

Secondary information for this report was obtained from journal articles, anthologies, and books. In addition, a survey of 100 business majors at Nicholls State University was conducted to gather information regarding preferred techniques for encouraging ethical decision making.

Plan of Presentation

Initially, this report will discuss four of the various ethics-improving techniques available to businesses: broad, company-wide ethics codes, situational examples, leadership by example, and whistle blowing. After each technique is discussed, survey findings will be presented. Finally, the report will offer conclusions and recommendations as to the techniques most likely to influence future managers.

TECHNIQUES USED TO FOSTER ETHICAL DECISION MAKING

There are several techniques available to organizations that enable the creation of an environment conducive to ethical decision making. This section discusses broad, company-wide policies, situational examples, leadership by example, and whistle blowing. As each technique is discussed, some advantages and disadvantages of each will be reported.

FIGURE 15-6
continued

Broad, Company-Wide Policies (Ethics Codes)

Broad ethics policies are usually formal statements outlining an organization's general commitment to ethical behavior (Daft, 1991). A formal code of ethics announces an organization's intention toward ethical decision-making and can make employees aware of the need for ethics.

Although ethics codes alert employees to the organization's commitment to ethics, vagueness in ethical codes may make them impractical for day-to-day use (Hyman, Skipper, & Tansey, 1990). Therefore, employees of an organization may rarely even refer to that company's code of ethics when performing daily tasks. Siers (1990) calls this situation, " . . . the difficulty some have in relating an established code of conduct to complex circumstances" (p. 17). One way to enhance the effect of a code of ethics is to supplement it with more detailed, situational examples.

Situational Examples (Detailed Guidelines)

Situational examples are detailed guidelines that clarify the procedures an employee should follow when faced with an ethical dilemma. These examples elaborate on the proper procedures for tending bids, accepting gifts from vendors, treating fellow employees, obtaining competitor information, and a host of other job-related activities. In addition, guidelines can set forth corporate fines, demotions, or other punishments for breaking the firm's ethics guidelines. In fact, managers may even have a moral responsibility to provide detailed guidelines. Campbell (1993) suggests that managers are partly responsible for ethical mishaps when they assume that employees can relate ethical behavior to their own job tasks.

There are drawbacks, however, to the use of detailed, situational examples. Employees may look upon a penalty-oriented system as either not applying to upper management, too dictatorial, a way for a firm to cosmetically comply to accepted norms, or simply punitive (Paine, 1994). Another drawback is that employees may use the absence of a rule as an excuse to knowingly engage in unethical actions (Hyman, Skipper, & Tansey, 1990). Therefore, the presence of rules or guidelines may not change the behavior of individuals predisposed to unethical actions, especially if others are engaging in unethical behavior on the job.

Leadership by Example

Another technique used by organizations to create environments conducive to ethical decision making is leadership by example (Daft, 1991). This technique is best carried out by immediate supervisors and upper management. In fact, Werner (1990) states that, "Organization leaders . . . play an important role in shaping the opinion and behavior of their followers" (p. 64).

Regardless of how detailed a code of ethics is or how ethically employees are inclined to behave, the unethical actions of managers and supervisors can foster or even encourage unethical behavior on the part of employees. Therefore, it is essential that codes of ethics and situational examples be supplemented by a managerial commitment to ethical business practices. Siers (1990) states that, "The tone and behavior at the top are the most important ingredients in reinforcing ethical behavior" (p. 17).

FIGURE 15-6
continued

Managers can lead by example simply by conducting their business affairs in an ethical manner. Employees look to their immediate and upper level supervisors for both direct advice and indirect signals to help them shape their own actions.

Whistle Blowing

Whistle blowing occurs when an employee of an organization alerts top company officials or public officials to unethical or unlawful actions within the firm. Encouragement of whistle blowing has both beneficial and harmful effects.

A firm may benefit from supporting whistle blowers simply because communication channels are more open. Employees may feel more comfortable discussing work-related problems with their supervisor. Supporting whistle blowers may also lead to higher profits if product or public relations snafus are brought to light and corrected.

Too much whistle blowing, however, can have harmful effects. James (1983) explains that when whistle blowing is overly encouraged or rewarded actions such as revenge-seeking or profit-seeking by individuals could increase unnecessary whistle blowing occurrences or encourage false whistle blowing.

ANALYSIS OF OPINIONS OF UNIVERSITY BUSINESS STUDENTS

To provide primary evidence for this report, 100 students enrolled in the Nicholls State University College of Business were surveyed to determine which techniques they thought would be most and least valuable in influencing their decision-making behavior. First, some demographic information on the students is provided. Then rankings regarding techniques most likely to assist and deter students are given. Afterward, survey results regarding student opinions on each specific technique will be discussed.

Demographic information gathered on respondents consisted of age, gender, and management experience. Of the 100 respondents, 59% were between 18 and 23 years old, 23% were between 24 and 30 years old, and 18% were 31 years or older. The number of male and female respondents was almost equal—52% were male and 48% were female. In addition, 33% of the students reported some type of work experience in which they had supervised one or more people.

Preferred Assistance Techniques

Survey respondents were asked to rank a listing of techniques, from most likely (1) to least likely (5), they thought would assist them in making ethical decisions. Rankings were determined by calculating an average ranking for each of the techniques. In total, respondents thought situational examples would be most helpful; advice from co-workers, least helpful. While males and females ranked the techniques in the same order, female responses were more extreme. As Table 1 shows, when ranking assistance techniques, female respondents thought more highly of situational examples and less highly of co-worker advice and supervisor behavior than did male respondents.

FIGURE 15-6
continued

TABLE 1 AVERAGE RANKINGS OF PREFERRED ASSISTANCE TECHNIQUES	Females *n*=48	Males *n*=52	Total *n*=100
Assistance Technique			
Detailed guidelines and/or situational examples	2.00	2.25	2.13
Broad, company-wide ethical policies	2.52	2.50	2.51
Ethical behavior of immediate supervisor	2.94	2.62	2.77
Advice from immediate supervisor	3.31	3.44	3.38
Advice from co-workers	4.31	4.19	4.25

Preferred Deterrents

Survey respondents were asked also to rank a listing of deterrents that they thought, in order from most likely (1) to least likely (5), would deter them from making unethical decisions. As in the previous section, rankings were determined by calculating an average ranking for each deterrent. In total, students thought that loss of jobs, promotions, or future pay raises would be most likely to deter them from making an unethical decision.

As shown in Table 2, males and females ranked deterrents somewhat differently. Females ranked supervisor examples second and internal fines third; males ranked fines levied by the firm second and examples set by immediate supervisors third. Given the closeness of the average rankings, the fact that rankings by males matched the total could be caused by the fact that more males were surveyed. In addition, the relatively high ranking of examples set by immediate supervisors emphasized the importance of leadership by example.

TABLE 2 AVERAGE RANKINGS OF PREFERRED DETERRENTS	Females *n*=48	Males *n*=52	Total *n*=100
Deterrent			
Loss of job, promotions, or future raises	2.06	2.11	2.09
Fines levied by the firm	3.06	2.94	3.00
Examples set by immediate supervisor	2.98	3.10	3.04
Poor job performance evaluations	3.19	3.23	3.21
Presence of whistle blowers	3.69	3.37	3.52

FIGURE 15-6
continued

Respondents were also asked about their thoughts on each area separately so that the prospective effectiveness of each technique could be evaluated.

Responses to Individual Techniques

Broad, company-wide policies. In total, 76% of the respondents said they were more likely to work for an employer that emphasized ethics regularly, while 2% were less likely to work for a similar employer. Additionally, 22% were equally as likely to work for an employer that does not emphasize ethics regularly as they are for one that does. Therefore, a general code of ethics may help an organization attract capable, ethical future managers. Seventy-eight percent of respondents indicated they would be more conscious of ethics if a general code existed.

Situational examples. In total, 90% of the students thought ethical gray areas would be somewhat eliminated by the use of situational examples. In addition, 74% of the respondents indicated that the guidelines would not overly restrict them in performing their job tasks. Of the remaining, 15% would feel overly restricted and 11% were not sure. Apparently detailed guidelines would clarify and help solve many ethical dilemmas for future managers without overly restricting job performance.

Leadership by example. Ninety-one percent of the respondents thought that they would be more positively influenced by a supervisor who acted ethically as opposed to one who did not act ethically. To underscore the importance of leadership by example, 36% of the respondents said they would be more likely to bend the rules if the company emphasized profits over ethical decision making, 30% said they would not, and 34% were not sure whether they would follow the company's lead into unethical behavior. Judging from the above responses, leadership by example will be crucial in steering future managers in the right direction.

Whistle blowing. A total of 55% of the respondents said they would inform on an unethical co-worker, 9% said they would not, and 36% were not sure. However, the presence of whistle blowers would positively influence the decision making of 77% of the respondents. Only 22% of the respondents said that their overall job performance would be negatively affected by the presence of whistle blowers; 59% said it would have no negative effect, and 19% were not sure. It seems that while whistle blowing may be somewhat effective, 45% of future managers may never consider its use and 41% may experience negative effects on their job performance.

Workplace ethics were very important to the respondents. Of those surveyed, 98% said that they considered unethical practices to be a threat to the reputation and profitability of an organization.

CONCLUSIONS AND RECOMMENDATIONS

This report has discussed four techniques that can help create a workplace environment that is conducive to ethical decision making. As mentioned earlier, those four techniques are company-wide ethics codes, situational examples, leadership by example, and whistle blowing. In addition, survey results were presented outlining the opinions of 100 business students at Nicholls State University.

FIGURE 15-6
continued

Conclusions

In summary, secondary research shows that each specific technique has its uses and drawbacks. Broad, company-wide policies convey the firm's commitment to ethics but may provide little guidance in daily job tasks. Situational examples or detailed guidelines provide guidance in daily tasks but, in solitary, may appear dictatorial or create resentment between employees and upper management. Leadership by example is the catalyst that welds the first two techniques together. By providing visible examples of accepted behavior and following their own rules, upper managers can make employees aware of the need for ethics and limit resentment toward detailed guidelines. In addition, whistle blowing can open lines of upward communication in the organization. However, if rewarded, whistle blowing may become chronic or false accusations may occur.

Almost all of the students surveyed thought that ethical decision making is important to the profitability of any organization. The students most preferred situational examples to assist them in making ethical decisions. Furthermore, the influence of job loss or internal corporate fines on the employees indicates that detailed examples should contain more provision for fines or job loss if ethical codes are violated. The least favored or influential technique among the students was whistle blowing.

Recommendations

Each of the techniques discussed in the report can help an organization create a foundation for ethical decision making. However, if used by itself, any technique will fall short of accomplishing the creation of an entire ethical environment. In addition, if any technique is overemphasized, negative effects may occur. Therefore, the key is to use a combination of techniques.

To influence newly-hired college graduates, an organization should place heavy emphasis on situational guidelines and leadership by example. A code of ethics should also be used to outline the firm's commitment to ethical actions.

Whistle blowing, however, should be used sparingly to avoid creating a negative workplace atmosphere. Specifically, an organization should support but not reward whistle blowers.

REFERENCES CITED

Campbell, M. (1993). Making your company ethical. Canadian Manager, 18(3), 14–17, 28.

Daft, R. L. (1991). Management (2nd ed.). Orlando: The Dryden Press.

Hyman, M. R., Skipper, R., & Tansey, R. (1990, March–April). Ethical codes are not enough. Business Horizons, 33, 15–22.

James, G. G. (1983, March–April). Whistle blowing: Its nature and justification. In M. Snoeyenbos, R. Almeder, and J. Humber (Eds.). Business ethics (287–302). Buffalo: Prometheus Books.

FIGURE 15-6
continued

Paine, L. (1994, March–April). Managing for organization integrity. <u>Harvard Business Review, 72</u>(2), 106–117.

Richardson, H. L. (1991, April). Improve corporate performance with ethics. <u>Transportation & Distribution, 33</u>(4), 40–42.

Siers, H. L. (1990, May). Reinforcing ethical behavior. <u>Management Accounting, 51</u>(11), 17.

Werner, S. B. (1992). The movement for reforming American business ethics: A twenty–year perspective. <u>Journal of Business Ethics, 11</u>(1), 61–69.

NOTE: An appendix (copy of survey form) is not shown here because of space limitations. For an actual report, the form should be included.

FIGURE 15-6
continued

▶ PAGINATION

The first page of the report itself (the "report proper") is considered as page 1. This page number is centered about one inch from the bottom of the page or omitted. Page numbers of following pages are placed in the upper right-hand corner, on line 5 to 7 from the top. Thus the "approximately one-inch" top margin refers to the "white space" above the page number. Leave at least one blank line after the page number before beginning the first line of text. (Some word processors number pages only at the bottom. This method is acceptable.)

▶ ADDITIONAL GUIDES TO REPORT APPEARANCE

1 Use sturdy, good-quality paper, preferably 20-pound weight.

2 Use standard-size paper, 8½ by 11 inches.

3 Use word processing and computer charting and/or graphing software to prepare your report.

4 Use a laser or ink-jet printer, or a good, clear ribbon on a printer of another type.

5 Leave at least two lines of a paragraph at the bottom of each page and carry over at least two lines of a paragraph to the next page. Thus, three-line paragraphs cannot be divided.

6 Follow a subheading (caption) near the bottom of a page with at least two lines of type, preferably more. A wider-than-average bottom margin is preferable to a subheading with insufficient following material.

7 Indent paragraphs in all double-spaced material. Paragraphs are usually indented a half inch, but some style manuals require a slightly different indention. Paragraphs of single-spaced material may be indented or blocked. Leave a blank space between all paragraphs.

8 Arrangement and spacing of headings should be consistent. Check the style manual you are required to use, or refer to the acceptable style illustrated in Chapter 12.

Take care to check your report for necessary preliminary and supplementary materials. Also check the physical appearance carefully. Use the evaluation sheet provided at the end of the chapter to review your report. If you can answer "yes" to all the questions, the format and appearance of your report should favorably impress your reader(s).

SUMMARY

The term *short, informal report*, although relative and inexact, ordinarily means all summary reports that are not prepared in a *complete, formal arrangement*. Many informal reports are presented in letter, memorandum, or form format. Others are arranged as manuscripts. Informal reports are often, but not necessarily, arranged in the direct order, with recommendations given first.

Complete formal reports are comprised of preliminary parts, the report body or text, and supplementary parts. The complete report, including preliminary parts, report body, and supplementary parts, is known as the *report package*.

Even when reports are correctly described as "complete formal reports," their content and arrangement often differ. Many variations occur; for example, recommendations and conclusions may be given first (although not so often as in informal reports), and various preliminary parts other than the ones discussed in this chapter may be used.

Some similarities of formal and informal reports are these:

1 The purpose of the report and the method of investigation should be clearly stated in both formal and informal reports.

2 Objectivity and a nonbiased approach are essential, regardless of the format and arrangement of the finished report.

3 Conclusions and recommendations, if included, must be clearly based on reported findings.

4 Internal citations or another method of documentation must be used as needed to establish credibility and to give credit where credit is due.

The most important consideration in choosing format and arrangement is the nature and purpose of the report, along with the needs and expectations of the readers.

TEST YOURSELF
chapter content

1 What is a good definition for the term *short, informal report*?
2 What is a letter report?
3 What is an analytical report? (This term was also discussed in previous chapters.)
4 When a report is presented in a formal format, is the personal or impersonal tone (writing style) more likely to be used?
5 In a letter report, which writing style, personal or impersonal, is more appropriate?
6 For a report presented as a memorandum, is the personal or impersonal tone (writing style) more likely to be used?
7 For a report presented as a memorandum, is a direct or indirect order of arrangement more likely to be used, provided the report is primarily informational?
8 For a form report, how much narrative information should be included?
9 Classify each of the following report parts by a *P* (for preliminary); an *R* (for the report itself, or the body of the report); or an *S* (for supplementary part).

appendices	letter of transmittal
references cited	list of charts and tables
conclusions	recommendations
cover	synopsis
index	table of contents
introduction	text of report
letter of acceptance	title fly
letter of authorization	title page

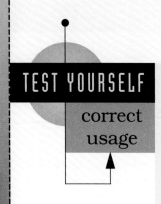

TEST YOURSELF

correct usage

(Related to Chapter 15 and information presented in Appendix D.) All content in each pair of sentences below is correct, but one of the two sentences contains one or more errors in word usage, spelling, or capitalization. Find the correct sentence.

1 **a.** Logical organization and appropriate headings in the text of a report are similiar to a road map.
   b. Reports are a fact of life; nevertheless, some are prepared unnecessarily.

2 **a.** Items in the table of contents must agree exactly with the headings in the text of the report.
   b. The reports purpose must be made clear near the beginning of the report.

3 **a.** The appearance of a report will affect all your reader's evaluations, for you often have more than one reader.
   b. The synopsis has been called "the report in miniature."

4 **a.** *The Elements Of Style* is the title of a small book on English usage.
   b. Reports must be specific, but not all come to definite conclusions.

5 **a.** The letter of transmittal should not include a synopsis if a separate synopsis is included.
   b. As you might expect, Accounting reports contain many figures, but words are also important.

6 **a.** Undergraduates reports are sometimes truly professional.
   b. Leave plenty of "white space" so that your writing is not crowded.

7 **a.** You are to be congradulated if you proofread perfectly.
   b. Uncorrected errors are embarrassing, but prevalent.

8 **a.** When reports are based on the results of a questionaire, the questionaire should be attached or included as an appendix.
   b. The preceding advice is not routinely followed.

9 **a.** The recipient of a survey instrument does not always respond.
   b. A principle reason that people do not respond to surveys is that to do so takes too much time.

10 **a.** An effective outlining procedure is to write tenative headings on note cards and to arrange the note cards.
    b. Headings in each group should be parallel in sentence structure.

EVALUATION SHEET: CONTENTS AND WRITING STYLE, FORMAL AND INFORMAL REPORTS

__ Yes __ No **1** Is the title completely, specifically, and clearly worded?

__ Yes __ No **2** Do major headings adequately describe and include the minor headings placed under them?

__ Yes __ No **3** Do major headings adequately describe the contents of the report as stated in the title?

__ Yes __ No **4** Are headings of each group parallel in wording and form?

__ Yes __ No **5** If the report is expected to be in the third-person writing style (impersonal tone), is this style maintained consistently throughout the report, including the concluding section? (This style also omits all implied you's.)

__ Yes __ No **6** Does the introduction include a specifically worded statement of purpose?

__ Yes __ No **7** Does the introduction include the scope (if not exactly stated in the purpose) and the methods of research?

__ Yes __ No **8** Are all unusual technical words or other unfamiliar terms defined as they are used, in the introduction, or in a separate glossary?

__ Yes __ No **9** If necessary for understanding, does the introduction include a brief description of the historical background of the problem?

(If this section is long, it should be placed in a separate section of the report.)

__ Yes __ No **10** Is the entire report written in an interesting style, with most verbs in the active voice and few expletives ("It is," "There are," and so on)?

__ Yes __ No **11** Are sentences fairly short, although varied in length and type?

__ Yes __ No **12** Does thought flow logically from the beginning of the report until the end?

__ Yes __ No **13** Is the report written throughout in an objective style, with no personal opinions or judgmental words?

__ Yes __ No **14** Does the report present both sides of the question being investigated?

__ Yes __ No **15** Are all major points substantiated with concrete, convincing evidence?

__ Yes __ No **16** Is the present tense used in all instances where it makes sense?

__ Yes __ No **17** Although subheadings are used, as they should be, does the text read coherently without the headings?

__ Yes __ No **18** Is the report easily readable throughout?

__ Yes __ No **19** Are techniques used to display with proper emphasis the points that should be emphasized?

___ Yes ___ No 20 Are all paragraphs fairly short?

___ Yes ___ No 21 Are topic sentences used to make paragraphs clear?

___ Yes ___ No 22 Are words simple, but exact?

___ Yes ___ No 23 Is the report concise?

EVALUATION SHEET: FORMAT FOR FORMAL ANALYTICAL REPORTS

___ Yes ___ No 1 Does the report include a cover?

___ Yes ___ No 2 If a cover is used, are the title and the author's name shown on the cover or through a "window"? (Other information may also be visible.)

___ Yes ___ No 3 Does the title sheet contain at least the title, name of the reader, name of the writer, and the date?

___ Yes ___ No 4 Is the information on the title sheet attractively arranged?

___ Yes ___ No 5 Does the report contain a letter of transmittal?

___ Yes ___ No 6 If the report contains a letter of transmittal, is it presented in a complete letter arrangement?

___ Yes ___ No 7 Does the report include a table of contents?

___ Yes ___ No 8 Do all headings on the table of contents match exactly the headings in the report itself?

___ Yes ___ No 9 Does the report include a synopsis?

___ Yes ___ No 10 If a synopsis is included, does it summarize the complete report, including pur-pose and other introductory material, findings, and conclusions and recommendations?

___ Yes ___ No 11 Is the synopsis no longer than two single-spaced pages? (A synopsis can also be double spaced.)

___ Yes ___ No 12 Is the report double spaced? (Some manuscript reports are correctly single spaced.)

___ Yes ___ No 13 Are subheadings arranged in order to indicate immediately the importance of each section?

___ Yes ___ No 14 Are paragraphs divided between pages so that at least two lines of a paragraph are left at the bottom of the page and two lines are carried to the top of the next page? (Two- and three-line paragraphs cannot be divided.)

___ Yes ___ No 15 Are at least two lines (preferably more) left after subheadings near the bottom of a page?

___ Yes ___ No 16 Are pages numbered properly? (Ordinarily, the first page is not numbered, or, if so, the number is centered about one inch from the

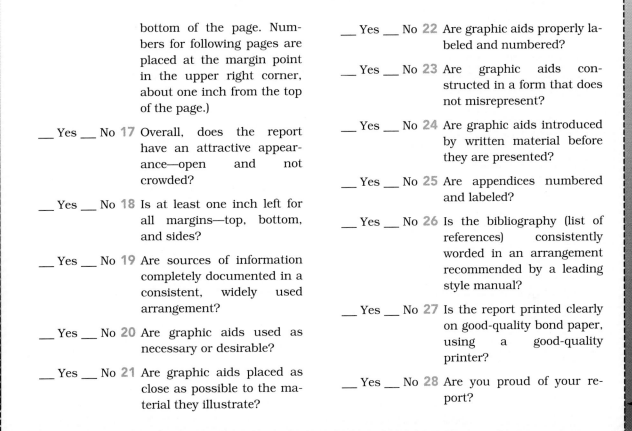

bottom of the page. Numbers for following pages are placed at the margin point in the upper right corner, about one inch from the top of the page.)

__ Yes __ No **17** Overall, does the report have an attractive appearance—open and not crowded?

__ Yes __ No **18** Is at least one inch left for all margins—top, bottom, and sides?

__ Yes __ No **19** Are sources of information completely documented in a consistent, widely used arrangement?

__ Yes __ No **20** Are graphic aids used as necessary or desirable?

__ Yes __ No **21** Are graphic aids placed as close as possible to the material they illustrate?

__ Yes __ No **22** Are graphic aids properly labeled and numbered?

__ Yes __ No **23** Are graphic aids constructed in a form that does not misrepresent?

__ Yes __ No **24** Are graphic aids introduced by written material before they are presented?

__ Yes __ No **25** Are appendices numbered and labeled?

__ Yes __ No **26** Is the bibliography (list of references) consistently worded in an arrangement recommended by a leading style manual?

__ Yes __ No **27** Is the report printed clearly on good-quality bond paper, using a good-quality printer?

__ Yes __ No **28** Are you proud of your report?

CASES FOR PART V, CHAPTERS 12 THROUGH 15

INSTRUCTIONS

In some of the following cases, necessary information is given, although additional research may be used. You are free to make reasonable assumptions and to add minor details. Retain the overall content and meaning of the problem to be solved, and do not change facts and instructions given with each case.

The names of individuals and organizations are fictitious. Addresses given are not actual ones. If real names of individuals or organizations are used, the use is completely coincidental.

Do not lift phrases, sentences, or paragraphs from the cases and insert them into your own reports. The wording given is for the most part inappropriate for use in your "solutions" to the cases.

Any case in this section may be completed as an individual assignment or as a collaborative assignment, as your instructor directs. Cases 26 through 30 are specifically designed for collaborative work.

Unless you are given specific instructions in the case itself, use the format and arrangement you consider best for the particular information and situation. For all cases, more than one format and order of arrangement is acceptable and appropriate. As in all writing, work for simplicity, clarity, and reader interest.

You should use appropriate available technology to generate your reports. Take advantage of word processors, spell checkers, grammar checkers, and computerized charting and graphing software. If possible, use collaborative writing tools such as Lotus Notes for any report assigned as a team project. If requested by your instructor, submit memo reports via electronic mail, either as regular electronic memos or as attachments to brief electronic cover memos.

CASES THAT REQUIRE NO FURTHER RESEARCH

1 Macon Industries

(Used by permission of Dr. Ruth C. Batchelor, Associate Professor Emeritus of Business Communication, New York University.) As director of the Transportation Department of Macon Industries, a large corporation with a fleet of 5,000 vehicles, you have been asked to look into what the president feels is an excessive number of accidents involving company vehicles.

From your records you find there were 2,319 accidents during the past 24 months. The causes of 1,725 of these accidents were charged to the employee operating the vehicle. Of these accidents, 401 involved 157 employees who had had two or more accidents in the 24-month period, but 53 of these 157 have left the company.

The remaining 104 employees were given a series of tests:

a. Eye test by company doctors to check vision

b. The standardized Porter Reaction Test

c. Road test (in a vehicle similar to the one(s) in which the accident(s) had occurred) to determine driver habits, driver attitudes, operating proficiency, and knowledge of vehicular equipment. The road tests were conducted by driver-training experts supplied by the National Safety Council.

The results of these tests, along with other employee information (age, sex, date of initial employment with company, previous job, position or positions held in company, accident record, etc.), were placed in individual employee portfolios.

An examination of the 104 portfolios reveals that of these 104 accident repeaters:

- 98 are in 19–27 age group
- 63 have eye deficiencies
- 89 have bad driving habits
- 94 have fewer than 5 years with the company
- all 104 are male
- 88 are on their first job
- 21 have very poor reaction time
- 91 do not have adequate knowledge of equipment
- 61 have received no formal company training
- 72 have poor driving attitudes

Write a memorandum report to the president clearly defining the problem, presenting your data, interpreting the data, and making suitable recommendations.

2 Survey of Checking Account Customers

Refer to Figure 13-2 in Chapter 13. The following data are the assumed results of the questionnaire. Assume that you have surveyed 225 people at a local shopping mall. Report the results of your study in an appropriate and readable format.

- Question 1: male, 110; female, 115
- Question 2: yes, 145; no, 80
- Question 3: First National, 64; Commerce, 55; Interstate Trust, 40; Pacific National, 27; United Northern, 19; various other banks, 20
- Question 4: less than 1 year, 37; 1 to 3 years, 95; more than 3 years, 93.
- Question 5: less than 1 mile, 67; 1 to 5 miles, 119; more than 5 miles, 39
- Question 6: one, 77; two, 83; three, 43; four, 19; five or more, 3
- Question 7: $0, 69; $.01 to $2, 25; $2.01 to $5, 56; $5.01 to $10, 49; over $10, 26.
- Question 8:

FACTOR	Rank 1	Rank 2	Rank 3
Convenience	84	38	25
Pricing	3	20	17
Service	82	54	26
Reputation	4	17	19
Proximity to home	25	34	30
Hours open	15	17	10
Bank personnel	2	18	33
Number of locations	10	18	56

- Question 9: no chance, 72; not likely, 90; neutral, 30; possible, 23; probable, 10

3 **Electronic Mail and Its Impact on Business Communication**

(Based on a study completed in 1995 by Suzanne B. Durocher and K. Renee Troxler, Nicholls State University, and used here with permission of the authors.)

The authors surveyed 100 persons in the Thibodaux, Louisiana, area who used e-mail in the course of their jobs. Results of a portion of their study are shown in Tables 1 through 6.

a. Write a synopsis/abstract summarizing the results of this study.
b. Write an introductory passage to precede each of the six tables.
c. Write a recommendations section of a report based on the data shown in the six tables.
d. Chart some of the various tables as bar or pie charts as appropriate. Rewrite the related introductory passages from step b above.

TABLE 1

HOW RESPONDENTS' EMPLOYING COMPANIES USE E-MAIL

Company Use	% of Respondents
Internal messages only	49
External messages only	4
Internal and external messages	47

TABLE 2

PERCENTAGE OF E-MAIL DIRECTLY RELATED TO RESPONDENTS' JOB TASKS

Amount of Job-related E-mail	% of Respondents
Less than 25%	46
26 to 50%	18
51 to 75%	9
76 to 90%	14
More than 90%	13

TABLE 3

FREQUENCY OF E-MAIL READING BY RESPONDENTS

Frequency	% of Respondents
Once a week	11
2 to 4 times a week	8
1 time a day	34
2 to 4 times a day	28
more than 4 times a day	19

TABLE 4

RESPONDENTS' OPINIONS CONCERNING E-MAIL EFFICIENCY AND SECURITY

	Agree	Disagree	Don't Know
E-mail increases operational efficiency	73%	8%	19%
E-mail is more private and secure than a telephone call	34%	46%	20%

T A B L E 5	RESPONDENTS' PERCEPTIONS OF E-MAIL FEATURES			
E-mail Feature	**Advantage**	**Disadvantage**	**Both**	**No Opinion**
Speed	86%	1%	9%	4%
Cost	58%	4%	5%	33%
Privacy/Security	40%	26%	11%	23%
Reliability	74%	4%	12%	10%
Ease of use	75%	7%	13%	5%
Accuracy	79%	2%	9%	10%
No face-to-face communication	27%	31%	30%	12%
Amount of information	70%	4%	18%	8%
Anytime use (convenience)	85%	2%	9%	4%
Communication efficiency	78%	2%	11%	9%

T A B L E 6 RESPONDENTS' OVERALL PERCEPTION OF E-MAIL	
Perception	**% of Respondents**
More advantages than disadvantages	93
More disadvantages than advantages	6
No opinion	1

4 **Writing a Position Paper to Disagree with Management's Current Policy of Accounting**

You have recently joined the staff of a large public organization that raises money for charity. In your position as director of ad- ministrative services, you are responsible for purchasing and control of all support staff, including word processing, reprographics services, and maintenance. One of your prime directives from the executive director was to cut the internal operating costs and increase efficiency.

Probably the greatest task ahead of you is the control of inventory and disbursement of supplies to the various departments within the organization. The current process is so complicated that one must requisition a requisition to receive supplies. That policy, you are told, was the brainchild of the director of accounting, who believes in charging each department for every item its employees use. The accounting clerks must spend a great deal of time each month processing the many forms being used and charging each department.

After taking a look at the process, you have decided that the organization is small enough (only 35 employees) that it does not need such an elaborate system. Further, you have determined through analysis that each department uses an average percentage of supplies and duplicating time which has held constant over the last several years. Your analysis shows the following figures for each of the departments:

Department	Supplies	Printing
Administration	35%	30%
Budgeting	20%	23%
Campaign	25%	40%
Community Service	20%	7%

You did notice that the charges would vary from month to month, affected mostly by the timing of the campaign to raise funds. Yet, over the past three years, these percentages have been accurate.

You have now decided to write a memorandum to the executive director, Mr. Harry Goodsen, to whom you report. He is a man who requires details, presented in a personal tone. He will usually go along with his subordinates' recommendations if they are supported by a thorough analysis. You propose that the nitpicky accounting system be dropped for a percentage system, a plan that will save many hours of labor for both employees as well as those in accounting.

5 Recommending Action

You are the supervisor of the inventory control department at First Line Tire, Inc. Your department consists of three women clerks. (They do not belong to a union.) You report to the controller of the company. The entire accounting department consists of 5 department supervisors and 15 clerks.

The personnel problem arose on a Thursday when the inventory control department was very busy. You were told by the controller that a major price change was to be effective the following Monday. So that prices could be changed in the computer, overtime for Friday and Saturday was scheduled and was considered mandatory for all accounting employees.

When you notified your employees, Carol Ruff, your senior employee, refused to work overtime for either of those days or in the future. Her reasoning was that since she was divorced and was raising her two small girls by herself, she could not leave them alone more than her normal working hours. As her supervisor, you know her feelings toward her job: She enjoys the work, but financially she is under no great burden. Carol had a strong will and an outgoing personality. Usually these would be assets to your department, but in this case, instead of the company, she was setting the parameters of her employment.

What will you recommend to the controller, Ruth Jones? Or do you wish to report the facts and ask to meet with her and Carol? Do you think the requirements of the department should be changed? Why or why not? If requirements should be changed, in your opinion, in what way? Write a memorandum or any other form of communication to support your decision.

CASES THAT REQUIRE FURTHER RESEARCH

6 Your Own Subject, Your Own Report

Ideally, this problem is an actual one you have encountered in your business or profession. You can solve a real problem and complete a class assignment at the same time. With your instructor's approval, prepare a report based on real problems or questions in your business or profession.

7 Recommending Hardware and/or Software

Assume that your office has need for one of the following items:

a. A desktop personal computer
b. A laptop computer
c. A fax machine
d. A photocopier
e. A high-quality color printer
f. Accounting software

g. Software suite containing word processing, spreadsheet, database, and presentation graphics software

h. Web browser software

i. Project management software

j. Local area network management software
Investigate the products available and recommend your choice, considering the particular needs of your organization.

8 **Local Census Information**
Find the volume of the *Census of Population and Housing,* (latest edition) that reports data for the town or city in which your college is located. Determine the number of the census tract in which your college is located. (A map showing census tracts of your city will ordinarily be available for your use in the Government Documents Room of your library.)

a. Write a memorandum or other report to your instructor describing the kinds of information available about your neighborhood as listed in the *Census of Population and Housing* (latest edition).

b. Include the following information in this memorandum, or write a separate one.

1. What is the median income of households in the census tract in which your college is located?

2. What is the mean income of these households?

3. What is the total number of persons 65 years of age or older in this census tract?

4. How do the greatest number of people in the census tract earn their living? Use the name of the category as it is listed in the census report.

9 **Letters to the Editor**
Examine the "Letters to the Editor" section of your local daily newspaper for the past three weeks. (As an alternative, use the number of weeks specified by your instructor.) Determine the most important topics of discussion, the number of writers "pro" or "con" on one or more controversial questions, and the effectiveness or lack of effectiveness of the let-

ters. Although this report could be presented in any of the formats and arrangements illustrated in Chapter 15, a simple method would be to use a summarizing letter or memorandum followed by a collection of tables or charts, with explanatory discussions.

10 **Casual Dress Day**
Your study should determine whether your organization or one with which you are familiar should allow employees to come to work in casual attire (dressing down) one day a week. Include information based on library research, the opinions of management and nonmanagement employees concerning productivity, morale, communication, and professional image, and information concerning appropriate casual day attire. Make recommendations to company management.

11 **A Report of Three Cities**
Your company is preparing for labor negotiations. The manager of industrial relations wants figures to compare living costs in Chicago, where the company has headquarters, with two other cities in which branches are located, Boston and Dallas. Find the latest figures published by the U.S. Bureau of Labor Statistics or find the figures in another recent and reputable source. Write a report to Miss Roberta Hardin, manager of industrial relations. You are her assistant.

12 **Flextime Options**
Investigate the advantages and disadvantages of various employee flextime options being used in business. In addition to library research, interview management and nonmanagement personnel to gather their opinions on the pros and cons of flextime in general and of the variations you discover during your library research. Recommend the action your organization, or one with which you are familiar, should take.

13 **Acquisition Research for Houser Corporation**
You work for Houser Corporation, a prominent heating and air conditioning manufacturing company. You have been asked to in-

vestigate three companies that are possible considerations for acquisition. (For the purposes of this assignment, choose the three companies or study those suggested by your instructor.) No negotiations have yet been made with any of these companies, and you do not want your research publicized. You cannot go to these companies for information but must confine your investigation to their annual reports and other published sources. Find all the published information you can about these companies. Present a summary of your findings in a report to the president of Houser Corporation. Include possible problems and advantages likely to occur with the acquisition of each company.

Modify this problem as your instructor directs. Perhaps you will wish to consider only one company or to prepare the report for your own organization. You have not been asked to make specific recommendations about any of the companies because much further research would be necessary.

14 Investigating Employment Opportunities
Investigate two organizations for which you would like to work. Study their annual reports, recruiting brochures, and other secondary sources published by some individual or organization other than the organizations you are investigating. Talk with at least one present employee of each company. Also try to find past employees, who may be able to tell you more than present employees. Try to find people who are or were in jobs similar to the one you seek.

Consider all aspects that are important to you on the job, including whether or not relocation is likely and whether there are opportunities for promotion. In the concluding section, summarize the reasons you have chosen one company over the other.

15 Resume Style and Content
Gather information published in the last two years (hard-copy sources and Internet sources) concerning resumes. Write a memorandum report about the differing opinions you find in the information you gather. De-

sign a questionnaire you could distribute to executives in your geographic area to gather opinions on desired resume styles, content categories, main heading formats, inclusion of job objectives, and inclusion of references.

16 The Concerned Citizen
Look into legislation that you consider unfair to you or to some segment of the population. For example, you may wish to research a topic such as welfare versus workfare, balancing the federal budget, Social Security legislation, or gaming/gambling. Write a report about this law, or these laws, and make recommendations for change, with reasons. Remember that you are most convincing when you give specific, definite evidence. Although your mind is made up before you start (you could decide that you are wrong), use an objective approach and wording. Be considerate of your reader. Make photocopies of your report and send it to your senators and representatives.

17 Sales and Marketing
Assume that you are the new sales manager of a company that sells a product that you know well or one about which you can find complete information. Compare this product with its leading competitors. Write a report in which you compare your product with the others. Include strengths and weaknesses. Summarize with recommendations for features to be stressed in sales campaigns. Also include recommendations for improvement of your product.

18 Opening a Small Business
You have decided to open a small retail business in your town or city. For the purpose of this research, assume you have the necessary capital. Decide on the kind of business according to your real interests and present knowledge. For example, if you like to play tennis, investigate the possibility of starting a tennis shop. If you love computers, consider a computer hardware and software store, and so on.

The purpose of this report is to determine the location in your town or city to establish your store. Use information from the Bureau of the Census about particular areas in your city. Also consider the location of competing businesses.

A variation of this report is to assume that you are a consultant preparing this preliminary study for some other person.

Prepare the report in the form and arrangement recommended by your instructor.

19 Recommending Whether to Lease or Buy an Automobile

Your aunt has asked you to investigate whether she should lease an automobile for a two-year time period or whether she should buy a new automobile. Your aunt drives approximately 15,000 miles a year, and in the past she has traded automobiles every four or five years, since she never wants to own a car that has been driven more than 75,000 miles. She wants a comfortable four-door model, with a sporty appearance and room for herself and at least three friends. What is your recommendation? Write a letter to your aunt, carefully explaining the reasoning behind your recommendation. Do not rely on brochures available from automotive dealers alone; use other sources to determine the attributes of leasing versus purchasing.

20 Telecommuting

Investigate the advantages and disadvantages of telecommuting as an employment option. Gather information from library and Internet sources, as well as by interviewing several persons who telecommute and managers who supervise telecommuters. Specifically address issues such as stress, flexibility, family care, promotional opportunities, getting away from work, financial opportunities, and so forth. Write an analytical report for management in which you recommend what types of jobs and what types of employee attributes are good matches for telecommuting.

21 Security Issues Related to the Internet

Your company (a retail organization selling various products ranging in price from $15

to $500) has decided that it must establish a Web site and market its products via the Internet. Management wants to provide full electronic purchase options for customers who shop using the Web.

You have been asked to investigate the security issues related to shopping via the Internet and make recommendations about what your company can do to protect itself and its customers from electronic fraud. Gather information from the library, the Internet, and from interviews with persons knowledgeable about Internet security provisions and present your recommendations in a memorandum report format.

22 Comparing Web Pages

Compare Web pages of a dozen (or a number designated by your instructor) major corporations.
  a. What are the similarities and differences? Overall, which of the Web pages is the most effective? The least effective?
  b. Write a memorandum report in which you recommend improvements for the Web page you consider the least effective. Write the report to the Web master (person who maintains the organization's Web site).

23 Investment Counseling

Assume that you are an investment counselor. Your friend, Ann Moore, asks your advice about what to do with $75,000 cash that she inherited. She is 42, single, with no dependents. She owns a large townhouse that she bought 15 years ago for $60,000. She earns $42,000 a year and has no debts except for mortgage payments of $490 a month. She is happy with her residence and does not plan to move. She has been employed by the federal government for 17 years. She is interested in investing the $75,000 for long-term growth. What do you recommend? She must be given specific reasons supported by adequate background information. Present your findings in a letter to Ann.

24 Write a Report on a Selected Subject

The use of secondary sources is likely to form an important part of your investigation. According to the directions of your instructor, you may wish to add primary sources by interviewing people who, because of their background, education, or work experience, have firsthand knowledge of the subject you are investigating.

a. What a business executive should know in order to communicate effectively with businesspeople in Japan. (Or choose Saudi Arabia, Russia, Mexico, or any other country or part of the world with culture and customs different from those in the United States and Canada.)

b. How (name of real or imaginary product) should be promoted in (name of country or part of the world in which culture and customs differ from those in the United States and Canada).

c. Communicating through the use of color.

d. The use and misuse of statistics.

e. The impact the Americans with Disabilities Act has on small and large businesses.

f. Laws that apply to honest advertising.

g. Careers in the field of business communication.

h. How an understanding of kinesics (body language) relates to effective communication for business and the professions.

i. How an understanding of proxemics (communication through the use of personal space) relates to effective communication for business and the professions.

j. Planning meetings and conferences.

k. Effective listening.

l. Increased job satisfaction through communication.

m. Pay incentives.

n. Interviewing (to obtain a job).

o. Interviewing (to select employees).

p. Parliamentary procedure.

q. Continuous quality improvement.

r. Teleconferencing and videoconferencing.

s. Special telephone services.

t. Electronic mail.

u. Overcoming job-related stress.

v. Writing sales messages.

w. How to dress for success (men) or how to dress for success (women). Use only recent sources.

x. A comparison of software available for computerized multimedia presentations.

y. Different programming languages available for software development.

z. An overview of software packages for word processing.

aa. An overview of software packages for financial analysis.

bb. Differences in word usage and spelling: England and the United States.

cc. Techniques for effective television appearances.

dd. Regional language and usage (expressions peculiar to one or more sections of the United States).

ee. Designing questionnaires.

ff. Positive versus negative words. (Include examples, and add other elements of persuasive and diplomatic words and phrases.)

gg. Optical scanning methods of computer input.

hh. Voice recognition as a method of computer input.

ii. Legal considerations that affect written and oral communication within and from a business organization.

jj. Designing effective Web pages.

25 Combine Three or More Related Topics Listed in Case 24

For example, Parts bb, dd, and ff are concerned with language usage. You could combine these related topics into one report. Other similar groups can be chosen, or you can combine similar topics of your own with one or more of those shown.

COLLABORATIVE WRITING AND WORKING IN GROUPS

26 **Combining Your Efforts**

With your instructor's permission and assistance, investigate some problem in your school or community. This research can be planned as a class project with individual class members investigating some phase of the problem and preparing individual reports. The total findings can then be combined for an overall report on the situation. Or the class can be divided into committees, with each to assume special responsibilities in researching and reporting a portion of the situation. If your topic has been investigated previously, try to obtain the results of these investigations. Test these results, or use the information to form the basis for further investigation of the problem. Present the results of your study in the form suggested by your instructor.

27 **Report Assignment on Intercultural Communication**

Note: Students should read Chapters 1, 16, and 17 before beginning Case 27 or the following variations of Case 27.

This assignment is partially a group report and partially an individual report. It provides experience and knowledge in these important areas of communication: primary research, secondary research, report writing, evaluating and editing the written work of other students, oral presentations, interpersonal communication, communication within groups, supervision (by chairperson of each group), and intercultural communication.

Much time will be saved in gathering material because members of each group share information. Furthermore, in organizations several people are likely to work together on long reports.

Because of varying class sizes and other factors, specific directions for this case must be provided by your instructor. Depending upon the approval of your instructor and any necessary modifications, follow the suggestions given below:

a. Fill out a questionnaire (to be prepared by the class members or by the instructor) to determine the country or area of the world in which each student is most interested. The questionnaire should also request information about the reason for each student's choice of country or group of countries; for example, some students are particularly interested in Germany or another country because their parents, grandparents, or other ancestors came from there. As another example, some students will want to study Japan because they now work or hope to work for a Japanese firm in the United States. In addition, the questionnaire should be designed to determine whether students have visited their chosen countries or worked with persons from these countries.

b. Divide into groups of four to six. As much as possible, groups should be formed to allow students to study the country of their choice.

c. Elect (or ask the instructor to appoint) a chairperson for each group.

d. Decide on the particular topic of intercultural communication each group member is to research. As an example, a group studying Japan (or any other country) might divide research and writing responsibilities into these areas, some of which may overlap:

- Government and economic conditions
- Probable attitudes toward people from the United States (or toward people from Canada or your particular native country)
- Social and religious customs and holidays

- Nonverbal communication, particularly the use of space and time
- Business etiquette
- Cost of living, methods of travel, housing, and other necessary information for a person planning to make a business trip to Japan.

e. Write, as a group, an introduction that will be used for the combined report.

f. Cooperate with other group members by giving and receiving information applicable to particular subtopics. For example, if you are preparing a section of the combined report that relates to nonverbal communication, share with the student preparing a section on government and economic conditions any important information about his or her topic that you find in your own research.

g. Write your section of the report after completing the methods and extent of research specified by your instructor.

h. Depending on the technology tools available, supply every other member of your group with a photocopy, e-mail attachment, or file accessible via collaborative writing software of your section of the completed report.

i. Decide, as a group, the order in which the various report sections should be arranged. Write a table of contents for the entire report. (This table of contents is to be used by all group members.)

j. Edit, in a group meeting, the report sections previously prepared by all group members. If collaborative writing tools such as Lotus Notes are available, ask each member to individually read and edit the report sections electronically prior to meeting as a group for final editing decision.

k. Write, as a group, a concluding section that includes recommendations.

l. Write a letter of transmittal to your instructor (individually or as a group). Along with other information, specify the author of each section of the report. (Your instructor will perhaps base much of

your individual grade on the portion of the report for which you were directly responsible.)

m. Write, as a group, a synopsis of the entire report. Photocopy this synopsis for the entire class.

n. Prepare and deliver oral presentations to the entire group. These presentations may be done individually or as a panel, but all reports on each country should be given on the same day.

o. Distribute copies of your synopsis to all class members after you have given your oral report.

p. Plan a visit to the country on which you are now an expert.

28 **Report Assignment on Nonverbal Communication and Intercultural Communication (a Variation of Case 27)**
Follow the instructions given in Case 27 with the following modifications:

a. The overall topic of your report is nonverbal communication, with an emphasis on nonverbal communication in various cultures.

b. Each group studies nonverbal communication in a particular country or area; for example, Saudi Arabia, Japan, China, England, Germany, Russia, France, Australia.

c. Individuals in each group choose or are assigned some particular element of nonverbal communication; for example, kinesics; proxemics; use of and attitudes toward time; business dress and appearance; attitudes toward women in business and the professions. Thus, as in Case 27, each student reports on an individual topic; for example, how people in Saudi Arabia use personal space (proxemics).

29 **Report Assignment on Written and Oral Communication in Various Countries (Variation of Cases 27 and 28)**
Each group is assigned a particular country. Subcategories might include the use of the telephone or face-to-face communication versus written communication; style and

formality of letters; word usage (especially applicable to the study of England); meetings and conferences; courtesy; formality.

30 **Report Assignment on Nonverbal and Intercultural Communication (Variation of Cases 27, 28, and 29).**

Each group is assigned a certain aspect of communication to be investigated; for example, nonverbal communication (which can be divided into separate factors), business etiquette, living conditions, social customs and taboos, written and oral communication. As with Cases 27, 28, and 29, each student in the class has an individual topic, although it is related to all other topics and closely related to the topics of class members in the same group. Students in each group research a particular area of communication as it applies to a particular country. Thus, the subject of one student's investigation might be nonverbal communication in Japan. Another student, a member of another group, might investigate living conditions in Japan or in any other chosen country.

Speaking to Groups

CHAPTER

16

OBJECTIVES

Chapter Sixteen will help you:

1 Build self-confidence in public speaking by being thoroughly prepared.

2 Analyze your audience.

3 Select and use visual aids.

4 Consider the importance of appearance and other nonverbal communication.

5 Deliver speeches and oral presentations with confidence, interest, and conciseness.

More and more people are speaking in public. Almost everyone in business offices may be called upon to speak to small or sometimes large groups. Members of professional organizations, neighborhood associations, and church groups find that speaking to groups is not only desirable but necessary. As you are promoted to more responsible positions in your workplace, public speaking becomes even more important, even if it is not included in your job description.

Nothing will add to your self-confidence more than becoming or continuing to be a good speaker. Few situations are more satisfying than seeing in the faces of your audience that they are interested in what you are saying and they admire you for doing a great job.

B UILD SELF-CONFIDENCE

As the saying goes, the brain starts working the moment you are born and never stops until you stand up to speak in public. But this adage is not true. If you are thoroughly prepared for your talk, your brain will be working at a high rate of energy. The stress of the situation will be good stress, the kind that causes you to function with an extra amount of stimulation and results in high performance.

Speakers of long experience state that they continue to have stage fright before they actually begin speaking but that it disappears as they address the audience. Some people believe that this stage fright is beneficial as long as it is not so severe as to be paralyzing. They say that when they are not nervous at all they know that they are too complacent—and consequently will not give an enthusiastic presentation.

The following passage was published in *Investor's Business Daily*, September 17, 1996:

> But overcoming the fear of public speaking is a step toward self-mastery. If you can't effectively communicate your winning strategies, management techniques, or leadership ideas, you might hurt the progress of your firm. Your ideas will, literally, die with you.
>
> How do you master presentation panic? When your stomach begins to churn, your palms begin to sweat, your hands shake, and your voice cracks—how do you lift yourself above the panic and deliver a calm, collected, and poignant speech?
>
> The first step is to understand the reason for the fear. . . . So many people prepare their presentations based on themselves and not on their audience. . . . By reversing this focus, you get out from under your own "internal microscope."[1]

Suggestions for building confidence are these:

1   Try not to be afraid in advance. Worrying or being afraid won't change anything for the better, but only make matters worse. Use the time you would spend in being afraid in preparing your talk.

2   Be completely and thoroughly prepared. After all that preparation, you'll be an expert on the subject. And why should an expert be nervous?

3   Finish the preparation of your notes and your rehearsals a day or two before your scheduled appearance. Look over your notes occasionally during the intervening time.

4   Unless you are positive that your listeners are actually hostile (an unlikely situation), assume that they are friendly and supportive. This assumption is likely to be correct whether they are friends, acquaintances, or strangers.

5   Plan to speak to your audience as you would to one friend or a small group of friends, or to explain something to your family.

6   Use positive imaging. Picture yourself walking confidently to the podium, looking great in your well-chosen clothing, composed, smiling, and looking out over the people in the audience, who smile back at you. Notice their air of expectancy and admiration. Listen to your ringing words of the speech you have so thoroughly prepared, one that you know so thoroughly that you barely glance at your notes. Best of all, listen to the thundering applause after you finish—or perhaps even while you are speaking. (You might as well go on and receive a standing ovation.)

7   Get plenty of rest on the night before your talk.

8   To relax before your speech, breathe in through your nose and out through your mouth.

9   Have some water at the lectern in the event your mouth or throat becomes dry.

10 You are likely to make a few mistakes, as all the other experts do. Go on from there.

Choose Method of Delivery

Speakers—ministers, teachers, politicians, and professional speakers—use four basic methods of delivering their material, or sometimes a combination of methods. These types of delivery are *written*, *memorized*, *impromptu*, and *extemporaneous*. Almost always your best choice will be *extemporaneous*, as the term is used in this chapter and as will be explained later.

For years, textbooks on public speaking have included these four categories as being discrete; now the difference between *impromptu* and *extem-*

Speaker at a conference emphasizes spoken words with natural-appearing gesture, probably unplanned.

poraneous is blurred, and the word *extemporaneous* is often used in the same way as *impromptu*. Toastmasters International (a well-known organization planned to help public speakers) seems to use the terms interchangeably to describe presentations for which no advance preparation is allowed.

The Random House Dictionary, 2d edition, defines *extemporaneous* in this way:

> 1. Done, spoken, performed, etc. without special advance preparation; impromptu, an extemporaneous speech; 2. Previously planned but delivered with the help of a few or no notes; extemporaneous lectures.[2]

The Random House definition No. 2 is used in this textbook as the meaning of *extemporaneous*.

▶ WRITTEN

Professional speakers often read from a manuscript written in full, either on paper or, more often, on a monitor that supposedly is inconspicuous to the listening audience. Truly professional speakers can read material and still maintain eye contact, or what appears to be eye contact. For less experienced speakers, maintaining a conversational approach while reading from a manuscript is most difficult. They tend to "read" the words instead of "speaking" them, resulting in a monotonous and boring tone.

For complicated scientific information, or for manuscripts that are to be printed exactly as read (an unlikely occurrence), reading may be the most practical approach. For most oral presentations of any kind, prefer *not* to read the material; speak it.

Even for presentations that are to be read, consider the writing style in relation to spoken words. Applbaum and Anatol state:

> If you're going to use a manuscript, be prepared to write the speech in a style that's appropriate for an *oral* presentation. . . . Written manuscripts tend to be more formal in style. When you write a speech, however, you need to use shorter, simpler, more direct sentences to maintain listener attention and understanding. The speech must be written for the ears, and not the eyes.[3]

Applbaum and Anatol might have added that manuscripts written only for the eyes would often benefit from the use of shorter, simpler, more direct sentences. It has been said that if writing sounds like writing, rewrite.

One advantage of writing an entire speech, however, is to use it in preparation for a talk that is to be given extemporaneously, as discussed later in this chapter.

▶ MEMORIZED

Unless you are an actor preparing for a play or movie, do not attempt to memorize your entire talk. Possible exceptions are short material such as toasts, poems, jokes, radio commercials, and so on. Key points of longer talks can be advantageously memorized, even though you have them on note cards.

Memorizing a talk of 20 minutes or so is time-consuming, but regardless of how long you rehearse, you may forget part of what you meant to say. (Most people do.) Even worse, your delivery is likely to sound mechanical, or "canned." Remember, you are conversing with an audience, not reading to them or lecturing to them. Neither are you performing. Keep the emphasis upon the audience, not upon yourself. (Yes, we're back to the familiar you-attitude once more.)

Pleasant surroundings encourage participation and ensure that all attendees can see and hear the speakers.

▶ IMPROMPTU

Impromptu speaking means "on the spur of the moment," or unplanned. When you're asked at a meeting for your opinion on a subject, you may or may not have had the forethought to formulate an answer in your mind. If before the meeting you have been wise enough to think through your response, even though you are using no notes, then your talk is not completely impromptu, although it is usually thought of as such. But you are not likely to be asked to comment on a subject that you know nothing about; your knowledge, confidence, and overall ability to communicate is ordinarily preparation enough.

Another term for *impromptu* is *ad lib.* Mark Twain once said that it takes three weeks to prepare a good ad lib speech.

▶ EXTEMPORANEOUS

Extemporaneous is used here to refer to a researched and planned talk, yet one that is delivered spontaneously. You do not rely on a manuscript; you have not memorized; neither are you "winging" it.

You will probably want to use a set of note cards to provide the sequence of key points and the order of presentation. You should know your topic thoroughly and have planned and rehearsed what you are going to say.

UNDERSTAND THE IMPORTANCE OF NONVERBAL COMMUNICATION

Nonverbal communication occurs constantly, whether in speaking to groups or conversing. It is impossible not to communicate with other people around you, even when you do not speak.

Nonverbal communication includes gestures and other bodily movements, facial expressions, posture, clothing, overall appearance, use of time and space, and various other methods of expressing meaning. You communicate by tone of voice, rate of speech, the "oh's" and "ah's" that you insert into speech, pauses, hesitations, and silence. You also communicate through what you omit from your spoken words.

Like all other forms of communication, nonverbal messages should be sincere and natural. Planned gestures and body movements usually appear to be just that—faked. Use gestures naturally to reinforce the meaning you are expressing through words. Too much hand movement is distracting and annoying, but gestures that you use naturally can add to the presentation. For example, if for some unlikely reason you wish to describe in a business speech a fish that you caught, can you imagine trying to describe only in words the length of the fish?

Videotape equipment is helpful in determining whether your gestures and other forms of nonverbal communication are appropriate and effective. If such equipment is not available, ask friends to evaluate your speech from all aspects, especially the use of gestures, posture, and overall movement. It may be dangerous to try to "spice up" your talk by adding gestures, even if you are now using none. In case you are using too many hand movements, make an effort to avoid these distracting movements.

You communicate more through your nonverbal messages than with words. Much of nonverbal communication is unplanned; thus, it is a sincere form of communication. Your nonverbal messages are influenced by your feelings about your listeners, your subject, and yourself. Nevertheless, some nonverbal communication is unlike your real feelings. For example, if you frown because you are tense or afraid, the frown may be mistaken for dislike of your listeners. Even if the frown is correctly interpreted, it results in a negative impression and a form of distraction.

Suggestions for effective nonverbal communication are these:

1   Like your audience. (If you don't yet like them, at least pretend that you do.)

2   Know your subject thoroughly in order to appear (and to be) confident.

3   Be well dressed, but not overdressed.

4   Look your listeners in the eye (but not too long at any one person) and talk with them.

5   Avoid excessive, meaningless gestures and movements.

6   Keep calm.

7   Remain objective. Do not let your anger show, no matter what the provocation.

8   Speak clearly and pleasantly. Make sure that you can be easily heard throughout the room, but don't shout.

9   Smile, but not continuously.

10   Relax. (You can't if you're unsure of yourself. That's why the nine preceding suggestions are important.)

Use your knowledge of nonverbal communication to analyze the feedback you receive from your audience. Nothing is more satisfying to a speaker than to notice a look of intense interest on the faces of the listening audience. You will recognize sincere approval and agreement. If your listeners are only pretending to be interested in your remarks, you will learn to recognize simulated approval and agreement. If your listeners are sitting straight in their chairs and looking you in the eyes, steadily and directly, beware. This is a pose of faked attention. Watch for listeners leaning toward you,

NONVERBAL COMMUNICATION

A horse that could solve mathematical problems caused quite a stir in Germany at the turn of the century. When asked to subtract—for example, six from nine—Clever Hans would tap three times with his hooves. And he could even do it when his owner, retired schoolteacher Wilhelm Van Osten, wasn't in the room.

Eventually it was discovered that Clever Hans understood human psychology better than math: The horse kept tapping until the amazed faces of his audience showed he had reached the right number. People were unaware that they were communicating with the horse nonverbally.

Like Clever Hans, we have the ability to detect and understand subtle clues in people's faces. Nonverbal communication is just one of the skills that human beings have perfected over the centuries, primarily to cope with the enormous complexity of dealing with other human beings.

"Talk to me: Audience-driven speeches." Reprinted from an article appearing in CMA Magazine by Julia Moulden, September 1995 issue, with permission of the Society of Management Accountants of Canada.

even when you are sure they are having no difficulty in hearing. This attitude is a sign of sincere attention.

Notice in your audience such telltale signs of boredom as fidgeting, random glances around the room, and looking at watches. If they are pretending to be interested in your remarks, they will not look at their watches. Frequent checkers of time are honestly telling you to move on. When listeners start shaking their watches to see if they are still running, sit down as soon as possible.

You can tell by facial expressions, to a great extent, whether or not your audience agrees with you. You can tell when they do not understand or when they are disappointed or annoyed. You can always tell when your audience is pleasantly surprised (perhaps astonished) that you are doing such a good job.

We communicate far more nonverbally than with words. Before you make your next speech, review the section on nonverbal communication in Chapter 1. The subject is also discussed further later in this chapter.

ANALYZE YOUR AUDIENCE

Audience analysis is an essential preparation for communication of any kind, and one of the most difficult. As when planning a direct-mail sales campaign, a television series, or a business letter or memorandum, predicting the reactions and acceptance of your message is essential to success.

Some audiences are easier to evaluate than others. When you plan a classroom presentation, you already have the advantage of your previous association with your listeners throughout the term or the semester. You and they are likely to have somewhat similar interests, goals, and experiences because of your educational backgrounds and the fact that you are working for a college degree. Although you may differ in age and nationality, your class members are far more homogeneous than many other groups.

In the workplace, you also have an advantage, on many occasions, of being acquainted with your listeners. On other occasions, the audience will consist of many listeners you have never seen before.

Before agreeing to speak anywhere, at any time, ask for an overall estimate of the makeup of your audience. Some speakers believe that because of their ability to adapt at a moment's notice, their planned presentations will be enthusiastically received by any group. (These speakers need help.) You cannot always determine the characteristics of your audience or hope that they will act or think alike. (You wouldn't want such an audience). Nevertheless, intelligent guessing about your listener's interests and previous knowledge of the subject will result in a better presentation than would otherwise occur.

UNDERSTAND YOUR LISTENERS AS INDIVIDUALS

James N. Holm describes audience analysis in this way:

> What present desires or hopes may you be able to help fulfill? What do they lack at the moment? What problems, difficulties, fears, or discouragements exist that can be related to your message? The answers to some of these questions will provide you with the key which opens the way to their attention, their interest, and their motives.[4]

In addition to these things, you must also try to estimate the possible attitudes of your audience. What attitudes toward you as a person will they likely possess? Will they be hostile toward or suspicious of you? Will their attitude be positive and friendly, disposing them to an open mind? Or will they more likely be neutral or passive in attitude? And what attitudes may govern their reception of your subject? Are they concerned with it, indifferent to it, or averse to hearing about it? Further, what of their attitudes toward your purpose? Will their predisposition to respond be negative, positive, or neutral? Each listener will have a complex of attitudes toward you, your subject, and your purpose.

Estimate the knowledge and background of your listeners according to the subject of the report. Everything you say will be influenced by the past experiences of the audience, especially as these experiences pertain to the content and approach of the report.

UNDERSTAND THE AUDIENCE AS A GROUP

Consider your audience as a group, as well as a collection of individuals who make up that group. What characteristics do the listeners have in common? Do the members of your audience think of themselves as part of the group, subject to group values, goals, and standards of behavior? Do the members of the group have a common motive or goal? Do they like and accept one another?

Some groups contain individuals whom other members recognize as leaders. If you can identify these leaders, perhaps you should direct a portion of your message directly to them, although this approach must be used with extreme caution and should not be noticeable to the rest of the audience.

According to Thomas K. Mira, author of *Speak Now or Forever Fall to Pieces*, it's important to find out the group's interests, background, and even such details as race, age, and income level. As reported by L.M. Sixel in *The Houston Chronicle*:

> Mira still gets red-faced when he remembers speaking to a retirement home about nuclear power. He was a young buck then working for the public relations office of Southern California Edison.
>
> Mira didn't prepare a bit and started out his talk describing the company's boiling water reactor. He didn't get very far, because an elderly man corrected him, telling Mira it was a pressurized water reactor.

Applause makes planning and work worthwhile. It indicates that you have done a good job.

Mira insisted he was correct. The man, growing angry, told Mira: "I know you think I'm old and stupid but before I retired five years ago I was vice president of engineering (for Southern California Edison) and I built it. . . ."

If he had prepared better, Mira said he would have realized the reactor was a pressurized vessel. And if he had asked his hosts about the group, he would have realized they had a former company official living there.

Then, Mira said, he could have introduced the man and won the audience to his side because of the respect he had shown.

It's also important to know the audience's age background so you refer to examples that have meaning to them, Mira said. For example, a speaker shouldn't assume anyone in a nursing home would have heard of the Smashing Pumpkins rock group.[5]

► UNDERSTAND THE OCCASION AND THE ENVIRONMENT

Communication of all kinds is affected by the environment in which it occurs. As a speaker you can do much to control that environment or to adapt the presentation to the setting and the situation. The acceptance of your remarks, of your ideas, and of yourself will be influenced by the setting in which they are presented. As you plan your report or other oral presentation, be sure that you have the answer to these questions:

1 Why is the meeting being held? Is it a regularly scheduled meeting or one called for a special purpose?

2 What is the relationship of your report to the presentation of other speakers?

3 What is the sequence of oral presentations?

4 How will listeners be affected by the time your report is presented?

5 How much time do you have available for your presentation, and can you expect to have your listeners' undivided attention for this period of time?

6 Where is the meeting to be held?

7 Is the room small or large, and will listeners be crowded together or scattered over a too-large area?

8 Will you need and have available a public-address system?

9 Is a speaker's stand available?

10 Is equipment available for the use of transparencies or other graphic aids?

11 Will there be enough light for you to read your notes without hesitation?

12   Will the room be heated or cooled to a comfortable temperature?

13   Will the room be free from outside noises?

14   Will your listeners be comfortable in all other respects of environment?

15   Is the room of a size and arrangement that all members of the audience can hear your words and look at you? Can you see all members of the audience?

If possible, examine the room and equipment well in advance of your talk. If that is not possible, at least arrive early on the day of your presentation and consider the environment in relation to your talk. An early examination of the setting may result in a modification of your planned presentation; for example, if you have planned to use transparencies and find that they cannot be easily seen by every person in the room, you are wise to omit them altogether or to enlarge them.

Even the most thorough preparation and planning cannot prevent all distractions or disturbing elements. Although you should do everything possible to arrange for the environment most conducive to the acceptance of your talk, an outstanding, interesting, convincing presentation will do much to atone for unfavorable aspects of the setting. And the most pleasant room will not compensate for a mediocre presentation.

ANALYZE YOUR SUBJECT TO DECIDE WHAT TO INCLUDE

Expressing your central idea in a few words enables you to see the subject in its entirety and to understand the relationship of each part of the report to the central idea. Only when you look at your topic in this way can you decide on the best way to present it.

LIST KEY IDEAS IN ORDER OF PRESENTATION

Write a specific statement of purpose for your presentation. (What do you hope to accomplish?) Then make a list of your key ideas. Decide on the essential information and explanation to be included; then resolve how to present it in the available time. Always work for simplicity. Be interesting and clear. At times you must also be convincing. A multitude of details is not simple, interesting, clear, or convincing.

After you have stated specifically the purpose you hope to accomplish and your central idea, estimated your listeners' reactions, considered the occasion and the environment, and analyzed the subject in terms of what must be included, you are ready to prepare an outline of how you will express and expand on the central idea. This planning process is similar to preparing a tentative table of contents for a written report.

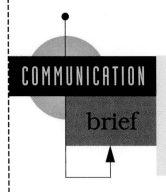

COMMUNICATION brief

As you consider the length of your talk, remember that the shortest inaugural address, 135 words, was delivered by George Washington. The longest, 9,000 words, was delivered in 1841 by William Henry Harrison, who spoke for two hours in a freezing wind. He became sick with a cold the next day and died of pneumonia a month later. History does not provide details about the mood or fate of his listeners.

The skeleton of your entire speech, an outline contains your main ideas in the sequence you will present them. Other helpful, interesting, or perhaps amusing details will be added as you progress in the planning of your talk.

▶ CONSIDER TIME LIMITATIONS

It is absolutely essential to plan oral presentations to fit the material into the allotted time. The best way to plan your time exactly is to practice your speech with the aid of a tape recorder. Even this timing will not be exact because of intentional or unintentional departures from the planned sequence of topics.

You should work to make the report or other oral communication no longer than it needs to be to convey the desired information and to achieve the desired results. As with written communication, however, too much concern with brevity may result in your audience's lack of understanding, acceptance, and conviction.

Stop before your listeners begin to squirm. About 20 minutes is ideal. One hour is the limit for interest and comfort. Question periods can effectively extend the total time.

> Chester Gibson, a professor of speech at West Georgia College and an ex-officio advisor to House Speaker Newt Gingrich, has this generic advice for the long-winded: Hire a trusted person to stand in the audience and give the finger across the Adam's apple, the universal sign for "cut" at the first sign that the audience is turning somnolent. . . .
>
> Not that brevity is always a panacea. Short speeches delivered in a rush or without proper preparation meet disaster, too.[6]

In addition to avoiding too-long speeches, do not make them much shorter than the expected length. For example, if you are scheduled for a 30-minute time slot in a conference, ending in half that time would give the impression that you don't know much about the subject or that you had so little interest you did not prepare a complete presentation. Besides, your listeners may be forced to wander up and down the halls while waiting for the next session.

You should decide how much time should be allotted to each of the key ideas you listed on your previously prepared outline. A presenter at a professional meeting talked so long while giving his introduction that time was called—after the previously announced and published time limit of 20 minutes. The presenter's remark was "But I haven't finished my introduction!" (Something was seriously wrong in the preparation stage.)

Apart from the overall length of your talk, your speaking rate will have a positive or negative effect on the reception of your message. Many speakers talk too fast.

Doug Malouf, author of *How to Create and Deliver a Dynamic Presentation*, makes these statements:

> Delivering an effective speech is like driving a car. You need to speed up and slow up now and then, but mostly you move along at a steady pace.
>
> Moving along at a steady pace does not mean you should be boring. Use variations in pace for effect, and remember, a pause to focus people's attention on you is a more effective way of getting them to listen than a rapid-fire delivery.
>
> Remember: the pace of your delivery should reinforce your message.[7]

Linda Kundell, vice president of a public relations firm and an instructor of public speaking at the 92nd Street Y (a New York city cultural landmark) is also concerned with the speed of delivery:

> The cardinal rule of public speaking is that an audience needs time to process information. "We have become used to speaking so fast that we almost gulp the words down," continued Kundell.
>
> By altering the pace and speed of a speech, the speaker can hook a crowd. "Slow down to emphasize a phrase or sentence and don't be afraid to pause before or after an important point," she said.

COMMUNICATION

brief

Never forget that no matter how brilliant and well constructed your formal address is, even the most attentive listener is not going to absorb your entire message. This is a tragedy, but like all tragedies it must be faced, not denied.

Our concentrated attention wanders, literally every few seconds, when we are attempting to overcome such a natural failing. You can prove this very simply by saying a sentence equivalent in length to two or three lines of printed type, then asking your listener to repeat what has just been said. Not once in a hundred times will you hear the sentence repeated exactly as you spoke it.

Steve Allen, *How to Make a Speech* (New York: McGraw-Hill, 1986), 39.

A good pause gives the listener an opportunity to digest what you have to communicate and underscores the importance of the point.[8]

▶ CONSIDER THE USE OF VISUAL AIDS

Visual aids can add to the clarity and interest of an oral presentation. They can also weaken the oral presentation by detracting from the spoken words. Use illustrations only if they are needed to supplement your talk. Do not assume that your most important goal is to comment on the information presented by graphic aids but that the illustrated material supplements your spoken words.

Graphic illustrations such as bar or line charts express relationships much more quickly and accurately than spoken words do. The same advantages that graphics bring to written reports are brought to oral reports; in many instances, graphic aids are even more necessary for oral reports.

An overhead projector can be used to project written or pictorial material. Many photocopy machines can make a transparency from the original copy in a few seconds.

Computer slide shows have become very popular visual aids to supplement oral presentations in the 1990s. It is important to note, however, that unless a computer slide show is designed carefully, you run the risk of letting your slide show become the presentation (instead of having the audience focus on you) or of turning off your audience because of ineffective slide design. Use the following list of design tips for computerized presentations and slide shows.

▶ Plan a slide show that will enhance, not echo, the oral presentation.

▶ Select slide *templates* carefully. (Templates are preformatted layouts into which data is inserted. Templates are included with various software packages, such as Harvard Graphics.)

▶ Select color schemes with distinct contrasts between background and text. Blue backgrounds and yellow text work especially well.

▶ Plan a format and use it consistently.

▶ Include one key concept per slide.

▶ Use upper and lower case letters in the wording.

▶ Select appropriate fonts and point sizes.

▶ Limit slides to 5 or 7 bullets, with no more than 7 words per line ($7 \times 7 = 49$). Even better is the $5 \times 5 = 25$ rule.

▶ Avoid clutter, which causes confusion.

▶ Use bolds and italics to emphasize, but use sparingly.

▶ Limit font and style variations on a slide.

- ▸ Use a consistent transition format from slide to slide.

- ▸ Use meaningful and relevant clip art, photos, or videos.

- ▸ Provide source notes for any copyrighted materials.

- ▸ Run a spell check; proofread carefully for context errors.

- ▸ Obtain a copy of speaker notes or a printed outline to accompany your slides; print audience handouts if appropriate.

- ▸ Practice running the slide show before presenting it to your audience.

Duplicated handouts also serve as a visual aid. Some speakers believe, though, that the use of such material distracts from the immediate proceedings. Avoid distributing several pages at one time, some of which do not apply to what is being discussed at the moment. Members of the audience, instead of looking at the speaker or participating in discussion, may spend their time reading the handouts. Also consider the use of videocassettes, flip charts, posters, and props.

Be careful not to become so involved in presenting the illustrations that you lose your audience. Talk with the audience, not to the illustrations. The illustrations are not telling the story, you are.

Avoid using too many graphic aids. Some presentations consist only of a series of transparencies, with a few remarks from the speaker about each

COMMUNICATION
brief

At the Coca-Cola Company, internal auditors are borrowing techniques from actors to improve their oral communication skills. "PowerTalk," a course introduced by the Bergerac Company, a Dallas-based consulting firm, teaches internal auditors to use acting techniques to enhance oral communication. . . .

Niki Flacks, chairman of Bergerac, contends that too many business presenters rely on overheads, slides, and visuals, forgetting their audience. "Communication," she writes in material distributed to students, "has become dehumanized, and audiences are drowning in overhead projections, pointers, and charts. If business communication is stilted, constricted, or monotonic, the listener's brain tunes out." "PowerTalk" encourages auditors to inject energy and vitality into their presentation skills by doing the following:

1 Writing a thesis and a logical, concise, results-oriented outline.
2 Mastering presenting skills, such as getting the audience involved.
3 Rehearsing to review what you want to say.
4 Concentrating on being listener-driven.
5 Synthesizing all skills by creating a blueprint that can be applied to any speech.

"Improving Verbal Communication" by Gary M. Stern. This article was reprinted with permission from the August 1993 issue of *Internal Auditor*, published by The Institute of Internal Auditors, Inc.

one. This kind of presentation is nothing but an adult "show and tell." Even if the transparencies (or other graphic aids) are attractive and colorful, they quickly become boring. If they are hard to read, the speaker should have stayed home.

▶ CONSIDER THE USE OF ANECDOTES AND HUMOR

Nothing adds more to a presentation than the effective choice and delivery of relevant anecdotes and humor. These additions to the main ideas of your talk, provided they emphasize the points you are trying to make, can be the most effective portions of your entire speech. But you must use care.

First of all, do NOT think that you must begin every speech with a joke. Even worse, do not begin a speech—or use at any other time—a completely unrelated story or joke.

Do NOT use stories that disparage any person, or any groups of people. If you must ridicule anyone, then that person should be yourself.

Do not spend a great deal of time telling any one story, or a combination of stories, unless the main purpose of your talk is to entertain.

Do not begin with words such as "Now I want to tell you a funny story." Be more subtle and original. Besides, listeners are likely to think "Prove it."

Try to find stories that most people (you think) have not heard. To do so is not easy. Even better, make up good ones of your own or relate actual personal experiences—provided they carry forward your overall message.

Tell stories and jokes well or do not tell them at all. Julia Moulden states:

> . . . they will listen with even more attention if you keep them entertained. It's too much pressure to think of your speech as a performance, but do try to make it lively. Jokes are unnecessary, unless you're good at telling them, or know of one that will help you make a point with humor. Personal stories that reveal a little about the human being behind the demi-god at the podium work much better.[9]

Anecdotes not only help people warm up to you, but they are what your listeners are likely to remember about your speech.

▶ FURTHER PREPARATION

Write a complete first draft of the manuscript on which you will base your talk. Determine necessary time, as previously discussed. Edit. Read manuscript onto tape. Try to read as if you were speaking. A tape recorder is immensely helpful in improving your tone of voice and gaining a conversational approach as well as in checking on pronunciation, logic, appropriate use of emphasis, conciseness, timing, and all other qualities of effective speech. Video equipment that records both sight and sound is even better, but it is more expensive and less convenient to use.

Use note cards, approximately 5 × 8 inches, rather than sheets of paper. They are easier to handle without shuffling, and you can turn them less obviously. Put the cards into a notebook designed especially for the size of card you are using.

Make sure your notes are large enough for you to see as the notebook lies on the speaker's stand. If you have thoroughly prepared yourself for the presentation, you will have no need for constant use of your notes, but having them available will add to your poise and confidence. Do not write your notes in great detail; they will be harder to refer to and will require more cards and thus more turning of cards than if only major ideas are listed. Do not take the risk, however, of omitting important information from your talk because you do not have it in your notes.

REMEMBER THE ESSENTIALS

Maintain eye contact.

Speak pleasantly and distinctly.

Remember the principles of emphasis.

Avoid distracting mannerisms, actions, and phrasing.

Maintain control of the meeting.

Keep within time limits.

MAINTAIN EYE CONTACT

You talk with people, not with a vague, collective mass. You are communicating with individuals, with people like yourself.

When you talk with people, look at them. In a pause just before you begin speaking, look out over the room and focus on one person—then look at the other people. Let your eyes meet theirs, briefly. Make sure that you include members of the audience at far edges of the group. This action is a form of greeting, perhaps even more important than your spoken words of greeting. This pause also prepares your audience for your opening remarks by getting their attention. Otherwise, if you rush too quickly into your spoken greeting, some of your words will be lost to some of your listeners. By your glances, you invite your audience to enter into a conversation with you.

Marjorie Brody, professional speaker, trainer, coach, and writer, made the following remarks about eye contact:

> One of the most effective tactics a speaker can use to connect with his or her audience is proper eye contact. . . . Contrary to common

This speaker is addressing executives at a boardroom meeting. Some women choose red jackets or suits for speaking engagements because they believe the color gives them confidence and gains the attention of the audience.

adages, effective eye contact is not delivered by looking over the tops of your listeners' heads. . . . With a small audience, select one person to look at first. Once you have made the connection, move on to someone else. Reach "everyone" in your audience by tracing a random zig-zag around the room. If you approach people row by row you'll lose others in your audience.

Hold your eye contact approximately three to five seconds. Finish a brief thought, phrase or idea with one person before moving onto the second.

With a larger audience, begin your eye contact with people in the back corners of the room, which tend to be neglected. Hold your contact longer, perhaps to 25 seconds. Everyone in the general area will think you're looking at them.

Avoid staring.[10]

The audience's part of the conversation, when you are speaking without verbal responses from your listeners, is communicated through facial expressions, nods or frowns, posture, and actions. Your listeners provide vivid, instant feedback without saying a word.

▶ SPEAK PLEASANTLY AND DISTINCTLY

An opening scan of the audience (do not extend it too long) relaxes you because it takes your mind away from yourself, so that you can concentrate on your audience. When you have prepared your listeners and yourself, start talking with them. Speak rather slowly at first until your listeners have had time to become accustomed to your voice. Every person has unique voice qualities and speaking characteristics. After a few sentences, speak at

COMMUNICATION
brief

INTERCULTURAL

The major differences in American and English pronunciation are intonation and voice timbre. . . . Our voice timbre seems harsh or tinny to the English, theirs gurgling or throaty to us. English conclusion: Americans speak shrilly, monotonously, and like a schoolboy reciting. American conclusion: the English speak too low, theatrically, and swallow their syllables.

Stuart Berg Fletcher, *Listening to America* (New York: Simon & Schuster, 1982), 210–211.

your natural rate, making sure that each word is distinct. (If you have not listened to your recorded voice, preferably as a rehearsal of the particular talk you are preparing, you are not yet ready to give that talk.)

Make absolutely sure that everyone in the room can hear you. If you are not sure, ask. If necessary, adjust the public address system or project your voice. Speak conversationally, not as an orator.

Try to arrange for a clip-on microphone instead of one on the lectern. You need to be able to move around without losing amplification. If you must use a stationary microphone, avoid moving away from it, as speakers often do. Some of your words will not be picked up. Standing close to the microphone, although not ideal, is better than permitting some of your words to become inaudible.

REMEMBER THE PRINCIPLES OF EMPHASIS

The principles of achieving emphasis and subordination, as discussed in Chapter 5, apply to oral communications as well as to written ones. You learned that opening and closing positions are particularly important; thus, make sure that the opening and the closing of your talk are interesting, informational, and forceful. Listeners should know from the beginning what you are going to talk about; at the end they should know, perhaps because you reminded them, what you have said.

Repetition, used judiciously, is also an effective method of emphasis, as is summarizing.

If the purpose of your talk is persuasion, end with an action close, as you learned to do when writing letters. If your talk was merely informational, reiterate or illustrate with an anecdote your most important points.

Short words and sentences are emphatic in addition to being understandable. Julia Moulden, author and speaker, agrees with this advice in these words:

> Finally, for the audience's sake, remember that the best things
> come in small packages. Keep your sentences short. A listener
> can't re-read a paragraph. Short sentences full of short, simple

words are even better. In the famous Thousand Points of Light speech she crafted for George Bush, speechwriter Peggy Noonan used the words "kinder, gentler," not "more benign, more clement." And brief is always best.[11]

▶ AVOID DISTRACTING MANNERISMS, ACTIONS, AND PHRASES

In addition to taking your listeners' attention away from your spoken words, distracting actions and mannerisms indicate a lack of confidence. They result in a rather negative approach, not a cheerful, positive one.

Do NOT apologize or say that you are unaccustomed to public speaking. Do NOT say that you are nervous. Such remarks are extremely negative and self-defeating.

Do not write your notes on sheets of paper; use note cards instead. Notes on paper are almost impossible to refer to without time-consuming shuffling that often causes noise picked up by a microphone. The sound may be greatly amplified.

Also avoid moving the microphone unless it is necessary to achieve a desired volume of sound. Many speakers move the microphone unnecessarily, resulting in distracting noise.

Another distraction is frequent glances at your watch or at a clock in the room. Although you must keep close track of time, you should do it inconspicuously. A solution that you may find helpful is to tape a wristwatch with an easy-to-read dial to the inside cover of the notebook containing your note cards. If you are standing with the notebook placed on a speaker's stand, you can look at the watch so unobtrusively that your viewers will never guess it is there.

Think of all the gestures and actions that have annoyed you as you listened to other speakers. Do they include any of these?

▶ Frequently removing and replacing eyeglasses.

▶ Pushing eyeglasses up or down. (Have glasses adjusted before you speak.)

▶ Constant pacing.

▶ Frequent use of "ah's, "um's" and so on.

▶ Frequent use of phrases such as "if you will," "frankly," "I'll be honest with you," "It goes without saying," and many more.

▶ Clearing of throat.

▶ Jingling coins in pocket.

▶ Leaning on lectern.

► Constant frowning or smiling.

► Mumbling.

► Talking too loudly.

► Hands in pockets.

► Movement of foot back and forth.

► Playing with pencil.

You can no doubt think of others. Refrain from adding new ones of your own.

► **MAINTAIN CONTROL OF THE MEETING**

Sometimes the chairperson of a meeting loses control of the audience. Distractions occur that are not the fault of the speaker. Various kinds of interference (noise, physical or otherwise) hinder the transmission of communication from the sender to the receiver.

When external noise occurs, pause momentarily in order to bring your listeners' attention back to you.

Sometimes members of the audience are distracting. What would you do if the group you were addressing included the following people? (Let's hope they are not all in the same audience.)

1   A latecomer who arrives 10 minutes late. Pause briefly until he or she can be seated. Briefly summarize important points the person has missed and offer to provide more information after the meeting. Don't waste a great deal of time.

2   People who engage in side conversations. Don't frown or scold, although you would like to. Instead, pause. (If they do not stop talking after your pause, other group members will frown and scold.)

3   A sleeper. Accent a point by raising your voice in enthusiasm. He or she will awake.

4   Squirmers, daydreamers, and doodlers. Are you sure this is not your own fault? Be more interesting. Or perhaps it is time for a break or for the meeting to end. If not, try the pause again.

Besides the distractions previously discussed, various other actions and mannerisms hinder the understanding and acceptance of your intended message. Although you cannot eliminate all distractions, careful planning will do much to prevent them. Perhaps a more concise presentation should have been planned.

▶ **KEEP WITHIN TIME LIMITS**

No matter how brilliant your presentation, it becomes less so after too much time has elapsed. Thorough preparation, including rehearsals, will enable you to complete your talk, without haste, in the allotted time.

ANSWER QUESTIONS CLEARLY AND DIPLOMATICALLY

Leave time after a presentation to answer questions. The question-and-answer period is crucial to your success as a speaker.

1 Anticipate the questions you are likely to receive and be prepared to answer them. (Politicians are rehearsed on likely questions, particularly controversial ones.)

2 When you don't know an answer, say so. In some cases you should volunteer to find the requested information and send it to the questioner and to anyone else who wishes it. Ask for their names and addresses.

3 Control the amount of time a questioner consumes. Some wish to become another speaker. Politely interrupt, answer the question briefly, and move on to another questioner.

4 Avoid overreacting to hostile questions. Under no circumstances should you show anger or resentment.

5 Address your responses to the entire audience.

6 When you have a limited amount of time for questions, provide this information in advance in order not to appear abrupt.

7 If possible to do so, offer to talk with individuals to answer their questions after the session is over.

8 Be open with your audience. Do not be evasive.

TAKE CREDIT

After the presentation, when you are complimented, say "Thank you," "I'm glad you liked it," or something else that indicates you also think you did a good job. Never say, "Oh, that was terrible," "I forgot and left out some of it," or "I was absolutely scared to death."

Your excellent presentation will remain an enjoyable memory.

S U M M A R Y

Principles of effective communication to be used in written messages also apply to effective oral presentations.

Predicting the probable response of your listeners will enable you to communicate more persuasively and diplomatically. The environment, as well as the speaker and other members of a group, influences listener response.

Careful planning of all phases of an oral presentation is necessary for success. It involves analyzing which items of information must be included, how to present the pertinent information in a specified time, the sequence of presentation, and control of the environment.

Principles of emphasis that apply to written communications also apply to oral presentations.

TEST YOURSELF
chapter content

1   What are two advantages of outlining a presentation?
2   What is an advantage of oral communication over written communication?
3   Give three suggestions for estimating audience reactions.
4   Name five questions about the physical environment of your oral presentation that you should try to determine in advance.
5   Give nine suggestions for effective nonverbal communication as you make an oral presentation.

TEST YOURSELF
correct usage

Related to material in Chapter 16 and principles of correct usage, specifically the use of numbers as discussed in "Writing Numbers," Appendix D. Choose the correct usage from each pair or group, based on the "Under 10 rule."

1   (50, Fifty) people scattered throughout a large room may not be able to hear a speaker who does not use a microphone.
2   (8, Eight) people attended the committee meeting; as with most small groups, the procedure was rather informal.
3   She spoke on Monday, an unfavorable day, at (1, one) P.M.
4   For some oral presentations, even (seven, 7) minutes is too long.
5   Some speeches are not worth (5 cents, five cents.)
6   The speaker used (twenty-five, 25) transparencies, (17, seventeen) slides, and (5, five) blackboard illustrations.
7   Please refer to page (two, 2).
8   Photographs, when used as visuals, must be large enough to be seen easily; make (5, five) (16, sixteen)-by-(20, twenty) enlargements.
9   Listeners may remember less than (four, 4) (percent, %) of what you say.
10 Because you cannot predict the exact words your listeners will retain, try to begin and end with (three, 3) memorable, interesting, and important sentences or illustrations.

EVALUATION SHEET: SHORT TALKS AND OTHER ORAL PRESENTATIONS

____ Yes ____ No   **1**   The speaker has an accurate and comprehensive knowledge of the subject.

____ Yes ____ No   **2**   The speaker was poised and confident.

____ Yes ____ No   **3**   The speaker was sincere and friendly.

____ Yes ____ No   **4**   The speaker was dressed appropriately; overall appearance helped presentation.

____ Yes ____ No   **5**   The speaker's voice—tone, pitch, speed, enunciation, other—helped presentation.

____ Yes ____ No   **6**   The speaker opened and closed the presentation effectively.

____ Yes ____ No   **7**   The speaker held the attention of the audience.

____ Yes ____ No   **8**   The speaker gained the confidence of the audience.

____ Yes ____ No   **9**   The speaker used visual aids wisely and effectively or as desirable and necessary. (Some presentations do not require visual aids.)

____ Yes ____ No   **10**   The speaker spoke in a conversational tone, as if talking with the audience, not lecturing.

____ Yes ____ No   **11**   The speaker maintained appropriate eye contact with the audience, without too much reliance on notes.

____ Yes ____ No   **12**   If the speaker referred to notes at all, such use was not obvious or distracting.

____ Yes ____ No   **13**   With the exception of necessary excerpts to illustrate a portion of the talk, the speaker did not read the speech.

____ Yes ____ No   **14**   The speaker responded well to questions.

CASES

1   Give an oral report to the class based on a written report you have prepared earlier in the course. Adhere strictly to your allotted time as assigned by your instructor or as agreed on by you and your classmates. If audiovisual aids are appropriate and practical, use them to illustrate and emphasize. Allow time for questions from your audience.

2   Prepare an outline of a speech on a subject with which you are thoroughly familiar.

3   Prepare a short talk to present to your classmates. Plan the time according to your instructor's specifications of the amount of time available. Choose some subject related to communication but preferably one that is not discussed at length in this book. Suggestions include recent developments in technology that speed the process of writing; the choice of a personal computer; differences between language usage in Great Britain and America; and regional differences in pronunciation or word usage.

All these topics are broad enough for long presentations. If you attempt to cover them in a short talk, you will of necessity be giving only a broad overview. Or perhaps you can limit your topic to some particular aspect of these; for example, a few illustrations of extraordinary word usage in the Ozarks, or from any other section of the country that you know well. In addition to these suggested topics in communications, many more will occur to you.

The topics for written reports, as listed in the Cases section following Chapter 15, are appropriate and interesting as the basis for oral presentations.

THINK-IT-THROUGH ASSIGNMENTS AND WORKING IN GROUPS

4   Members of the class are to form into four- to six-person groups. Assume that the members make up a panel on a convention program. Each group is to select a topic similar to the one described in Case 3. One member of the panel is to act as both chairperson and master of ceremonies. On the day of the class presentation, each member is to be allowed a specified time, according to the total time available, in which to present a report on one aspect of the overall subject. The chairperson is to introduce the panel members to the class before they make their presentations. After all presentations have been made, allow time for the audience to ask questions, which may be directed to any member of the panel.

5   After the panel presentation, each group is to meet to write a one- or two-page summary of the most important points brought out in the presentation. (See instructions for summarizing at the end of Chapters 1 and 2. You are free, however, to arrange your summary by the method you think is best.)

ENDNOTES

1   "Getting a Grip: How You Can Get Over Stage Fright," *Investor's Business Daily*, September 17, 1996, A4.

2   *The Random House Dictionary of the English Language*, 2d ed., unabridged (New York: Random House, 1987), 683–684.

3   Ronald L. Applbaum and Karl W. E. Anatol, *Effective Oral Communication for Business and the Professions* (Chicago: SRA, 1982), 233.

4   James N. Holm, *Productive Speaking for Business and the Professions* (Boston: Allyn and Bacon, 1967), 336.

5   L. M. Sixel, "Some Pointers about No-Sweat Public Speaking," *The Houston Chronicle*, January 8, 1996, Working, 2.

6   Ron Suskind and Joann S. Lublin, "Giving Windbags the Hook," *Pittsburgh Post-Gazette*, January 27, 1995, B8.

7 Doug Malouf, Carolyn Dickson, and Paula DePasquale, "The Seven Deadly Sins of Speakers," *Training and Development*, November 1995, 13.

8 J. R. O'Dwyer, "Public Speaking Is Potent but Lost Art in Electronic PR ERA," *O'Dwyer's PR Services Report*, September 1996.

9 Julia Moulden, "Talk to Me: Audience Driven Speeches," *CMA Magazine* (Society of Management Accountants of Canada), September 1995, 8.

10 Marjorie Brody, "Delivering Your Speech Right between Their Eyes," *American Salesman*, June 1996, 14.

11 Moulden, *CMA Magazine*, 9.

Intercultural Communication

CHAPTER

17

OBJECTIVES

Chapter Seventeen will help you:

1   Explain the increasing importance of intercultural communication.

2   Work harmoniously with people of different nationalities, gender, age, and backgrounds.

3   Recognize barriers to intercultural communication, particularly ethnocentrism and stereotyping.

4   Identify language difficulties in intercultural communication.

5   Identify various nonverbal messages between people from differing cultures.

6   Realize that rules of etiquette differ from culture to culture.

Communication now must be worldwide. Within our home country, we communicate daily with people from differing backgrounds and languages, often with people who have recently left their native countries. Many of us go abroad to visit or to work. Business and professional people increasingly communicate by letter, telephone, e-mail, facsimile transmission, and personal visits to people around the world.

Ordinarily we think of *intercultural communication* as existing only between people from different countries, but it also exists between people and groups of people who have spent their entire lives in the same country, the same city, even on the same block. We are all different from every other person, in many ways, but these differences are increased when people come from unlike backgrounds, religions, and cultures.

This chapter is only a brief overview of the many factors that enter into successful intercultural communication. This chapter, however, can be a beginning of your study, which should be continued through reading, learning the language of the people with whom you attempt to communicate, and, best of all, visiting or living abroad.

[NOTE: Information about Japan, as included in this chapter, was provided or evaluated by Mr. Kimihiro Imamura, Itochu Academy, Tokyo.]

THE INCREASING IMPORTANCE OF INTERCULTURAL COMMUNICATION

The study of intercultural communication has received much interest and attention during the past decade, although intercultural communication itself is as old as civilization. Primitive men and women, in their "hunting and gathering" activities, no doubt encountered other humans whom they perceived to be vastly different from themselves. Greeks and Romans communicated interculturally with the rest of the civilized world at the time. Columbus and early settlers in North America were forced to communicate with Native Americans.

In ancient times, as now, a knowledge of one culture sharpens our ability to appreciate our own. This knowledge may also help us to examine our own culture—or even to improve it.

In recent years, international tensions, the ease of travel, the development of multinational organizations in North America and elsewhere all over the world, and the increasing number of immigrants to the United States and Canada have made us realize that we as individuals and as organizations must communicate and cooperate with people unlike ourselves in order to succeed or even to survive. In addition, we have a moral obligation and a natural human need to communicate with people of all cultures and to develop an understanding of these people as individuals, not as stereotypes.

> According to a U.S. Census report released October 22, 1996, immigrants will keep on fueling the explosive population growth in California and the rest of the West throughout the next century.
>
> "By the year 2,000, everyone in California will be a minority in the literal sense of the word," says Peter Morrison, demographer at the Rand Corporation, a think tank. "And that reflects what will happen in the rest of the country decades from now. You will see cultural pluralism emerging in Iowa as well as California."
>
> Highlights of the Census report are these:
>
> - The non-Hispanic white population, now the largest, is expected to grow at the slowest rate in the next 30 years.
>
> - The non-Hispanic black population is the second slowest growing group, except in the South.
>
> - The Asian population is the fastest growing group in all regions.[1]

The writers Farahmand and Kleiner discuss the importance of the study of intercultural communication in this way:

First, by understanding the concepts of intercultural communication, one may be able to avoid unintentional conflicts and misunderstandings.

Second, one may be able to better understand intercultural conflict when it occurs. . . . For example, when one is seeking to persuade another person that his or her way is morally or naturally right, he or she may be able to deduce that the other person may feel the same.

Third, in addition to being more aware of one's options within a conflict, one may learn more about himself by trying to perceive and comprehend alternative feelings.[2]

The number of Americans working abroad is fast increasing. Countless companies that originated in the United States are now multinational with subsidiaries all over the world. The budgets of some multinational companies are larger than the budgets of some nations.

The need for harmonious communication between people from differing countries continues to increase. A 1996 survey by the National Foreign Trade Council showed that the number of Americans working overseas grew by 30 percent in 1995; this growth is expected to continue. The percentage of women working overseas has increased substantially in the past four years, from 4 percent to 12 percent.[3]

In addition, many Americans work in the United States or abroad for foreign employers, and many people from all over the world live and work in the United States. People from the United States establish businesses in

COMMUNICATION brief

In the life of the overseas American worker, the road to cultural mishaps is paved with the best intentions.

Take, for example, what happened to an American manager in Japan.

The first day at work, the American manager called a meeting to praise a model employee who was Japanese.

The result? "The manager now wonders why that employee is looking at him in a funny sort of way," says Noel Shumsky, senior vice president and managing director of Prudential Relocation Intercultural Services in Boulder, Colorado. The reason is simple, Shumsky says: "The Japanese say if the nail sticks up you have to hammer it down."

The Japanese are oriented toward the group rather than the individual, says Jim Auer, director of the U.S. Japan Center at Vanderbilt University in Nashville, Tennessee. "A person who is singled out in front of his peers might be embarrassed by that."

Evelyn Tan Powers, "Culture Clash in the Workplace," *USA Today*, June 21, 1995, 2A.

South America and elsewhere. Professional people from practically every field spend or have spent years abroad. Overall, the need to communicate on an international level is becoming more important each year.

Even if you should never leave your home country, an unlikely occurrence, you will almost surely work with men and women from various countries. No doubt you now share classrooms with students from nations other than your own—or you may be an international student studying in America. In any event, like all people, you will benefit by cross-cultural associations and experiences as you learn to communicate.

TERMS PERTAINING TO INTERCULTURAL COMMUNICATION

As with many other areas of knowledge, several descriptive terms have come into use, including *cross-cultural communication, interethnic communication,* and *international communication.* According to *The Random House Dictionary* (unabridged), *intercultural* and *cross-cultural* are similar in meaning, but the precise use of the adjective *international* pertains to "relations between or among nations; involving two or more nations."[4]

The term *intercultural* is used in this book to refer to interpersonal communication. *Intercultural* is descriptive of communication between people living in the same country as well as in different countries. Various cultures exist side by side in the workplace and in neighborhoods. Some of these differing cultures are based on national origin, but others are based on race, religion, and ethnic, educational, and economic backgrounds. Differences may be based on the regions of the same nation where the individuals grew up.

Compare, for example, a lifelong resident of Saudi Arabia with a lifelong resident of Australia. Because of their nationalities, experiences, language, and overall backgrounds, their communication is truly intercultural.

As another example, consider a high school dropout who has always lived in poverty in an isolated village in Appalachia; compare this individual with a Harvard graduate from a wealthy family in Boston. Except for the common use of the English language (which in itself is likely to be different), cultural barriers may be as great as that of the two persons from Saudi Arabia and Australia.

As we think of the high school dropout, however, as well as of the Harvard graduate, we are in danger of stereotyping, as discussed in Chapter 1. It is possible that the mountain man, through individual study and a curious and creative mind, has amassed more knowledge and wisdom than the Harvard graduate. It is also possible that the Harvard alumnus does not fit another stereotype—that of being a snob.

DEFINITIONS OF CULTURE

The word *culture* means the total system of language, values, beliefs, customs, religions, art, education, and manners. It also includes and is affected by the economic system of the country. Culture has developed over generations and is the depository of the values listed above, as well as educational philosophy, myths, hierarchies, attitude toward time, roles of men and women, spatial relationships, concepts of the universe, attitudes toward work, family responsibilities, material possessions, and all the other ideas, customs, and guidelines upon which people build and maintain their lives.

To a certain extent the background and experiences of every individual differ from those of every other individual. Families who live on the same

Conversing by telephone with someone who uses English as a second language is more difficult than when speaking face to face.

block are often very different from one another, even when all are of the same nationality. People who grew up and have remained in the same neighborhood, however, are likely to have values, beliefs, customs, religions, and manners more like those of their neighbors than those of people who live in another part of the nation. Their culture is likely to be different from that of people who have spent their lives in other countries or have been influenced by family and friends of other nationalities.

Barriers to intercultural communication include the inability to speak and write the same language, but using a common language is no guarantee of complete understanding between people of different cultural backgrounds. Important differences arise and remain because of ways of thinking and value systems.

Vem Terpstra believes that the following elements of culture affect successful or unsuccessful intercultural business relationships:

Language (spoken, written, official, hierarchical, international, and so on)

Religion (sacred objects, philosophical systems, beliefs and norms, prayer, taboos, holidays, rituals)

Values and attitudes (toward time, achievement, work, wealth, change, scientific method, risk taking)

Education

Social organization

Technology and material culture

Politics

Law (common law, foreign law, international law, antitrust policy, regulations)[5]

An important element that Terpstra does not include is nonverbal communication—unless he meant to include it under "language."

Chaney and Martin state:

Language holds us together as groups, differentiates us into groups, and also controls the way we shape concepts, how we think, how we perceive, and how we judge others. The closest things to common languages the world has are numbers and music. Unlike mathematicians, business people must be sensitive to the nuances of a language to assure understanding when communicating with people whose first language differs from their own and even with those whose language is the same as their own. Language is only part of communication. How the language is used in relationship to nonverbal communication and the beliefs and values of the culture is very important.[6]

IMPORTANT CULTURAL DIFFERENCES TO BE CONSIDERED

Religion and traditions that go back thousands of years influence business negotiations in the last decade of the twentieth century—so does the philosophy upon which these cultural elements are based.

▶ **HIGH- AND LOW-CONTEXT CULTURES**

Edward T. Hall, author of *The Silent Language, Beyond Culture*, and other books and research studies, first used the word *contexting* to describe the sending and receiving of messages and how it differs among cultures. Any communication relies on the context in which it takes place.

Low-context cultures rely more on explicit words than do high-context cultures, which rely more on nonverbal communication, including silence. High-context cultures place higher values on close interpersonal relationships than do low-context cultures.

Low-context cultures value directness and "getting to the point." In high-context cultures, directness may be seen as abrupt or demanding. Inappropriate directness may cause people in these cultures to "lose face," a matter of supreme concern. What an American manager considers to be frankness and constructive criticism can be a devastating blow to a high-context worker, an insult to personal pride and dignity.

Low-context businesspeople prefer specific written contracts; high-context people value personal trust and prefer oral communication and agreements. Americans want to get down to business; Latin Americans and Arabs want to wait a while in order to build friendships and trust.

North America, Germany, Norway, Sweden, and Denmark are among low-context cultures. Arabic countries, Latin America, Japan, China, and other Asian countries are high-context countries.

According to Varner and Beamer,

> Members of low-context cultures put their thoughts into words. They tend to suppose that if thoughts are not in words, then the thoughts will not be understood correctly. They tend to think that when messages are in explicit words, the other side can act on them. But high-context cultures have less tendency to trust words to communicate. They rely on context to help clarify and complete the message.[7]

▶ **RELIGION**

In many countries, religion is not an area separate and apart from the business organization, as it is in the United States, but the central theme of the business organization as well as of everything else. This factor is especially applicable in countries where Islam is the dominant religion.

From a purely practical standpoint, if for no other, you need to know and respect religious holidays and customs. For example, in Muslim countries, believers are advised to pray five times a day. (As in the United States and elsewhere, tenets are not always exemplified.) Although non-Muslims are not expected to pray, they would be extremely ill-advised to try to conduct business during these times, as well as on religious holidays. Ramadan is the month-long holiday season, occurring during the ninth month of the Islam calendar, during which time Muslims fast from sunrise to sunset.

The Arab culture, like all others, must be respected. Islam, the world's largest religion except for Christianity, is based at least partly on Jewish and Christian tradition in addition to the Koran. Adherents of the Islam faith hold Judaism and Christianity in much the same relationship as New Testament Christianity holds Old Testament Judaism. Mohammed is considered the last of the prophets. Jesus is also considered to be a prophet. Both Judaism and Islam trace their beginnings to Abraham. Islam, like Christianity, is divided into sects; 90 percent of Muslims are Sunnis, who are conservative and relatively tolerant.

Alcohol in any form is strictly forbidden in Saudi Arabia. Pork is considered unclean. The worst mistake that an expatriate could make would be to serve pork and an alcoholic beverage to an invited guest. (Because the cow is considered sacred, beef should never be served to Hindus.)

A long accepted custom in some Islamic cultures is for women to keep their faces covered in public or at least to cover most of their heads, leaving space available for seeing, eating, and talking. This manner of dress is no longer the most prevalent in most Arab countries other than Saudi Arabia. Women from America or similar cultures are not expected to dress in the manner expected or required of Muslim women. Nevertheless, women visiting Muslim countries should be somewhat more conservative in their manner of dress than that which would be acceptable in their home countries. For example, shorts and sleeveless blouses should be replaced with clothing that covers more of the body. For business or social affairs, a dress or suit is preferable to pants.

In all countries outside of North America (and in some localities in North America), prefer conservative and slightly formal attire to informal. This manner of dress is desirable not only from the standpoint of religious beliefs of the country you are visiting but also because of differing opinions about the importance of formality. Many people all over the world, with varying religious beliefs or none at all, are far more formal in dress, speech, and other aspects of life than are some people from the United States.

Such advice about attire is particularly applicable when you are serving as a representative of your business or organization. Even if you travel only as a tourist, you are a representative of your home country.

Religion is more closely related to business decisions in Muslim and Hindu countries than in North America, South America, Europe, Australia, or Japan. In all countries, the influence of religious beliefs must be recognized, even in routine business transactions.

ATTITUDES TOWARD WORK AND EMPLOYING ORGANIZATIONS

Japanese attitudes toward work differ from the usual attitudes in America. An individual is said to be more loyal to the employing company, where he may stay for a lifetime, although this custom is beginning to change. (The *he* is used intentionally; career employees in Japan are still likely to be men, although the outlook toward women is becoming more liberal.) Japanese people prefer to make decisions in groups, not as individuals. Van Zandt states:

> The Japanese prefer to work as members of a group, rather than individually. This characteristic is often cited as one of the most important in explaining Japan's economic success. . . . The preference for group rather than individual action may be attributed in part to the Buddhist teaching of *shujo no on*, or feeling of obligation to the world and all living things for one's success.[8]

Related to a sentence in the preceding paragraph, "This characteristic is often cited as one of the most important in explaining Japan's economic success," Mr. Kimihiro Imamura comments:

> Up to now, yes. But the group decision is now acting as a brake to a speedy decision. Group management is delaying deregulation's processes and making the Japanese economy stagnant. Now Japan is far behind the United States in many fields, including the once dominant auto industry.[9]

Attitudes toward work, like religion, are an important part of every culture. When you work with people from other countries, either in the United States or abroad, be prepared to have your own values and customs questioned. For instance, young executives working for Sharp, a Japanese company in Memphis, were made to feel like shirkers (as the executives perceived the situation) because they left work each evening in time to reach their seven o'clock graduate classes. On the other hand, some people from the United States question the ambition of shopkeepers in numerous countries who close for an afternoon nap.

In Saudi Arabia, workers are likely to be employed by members of their own families and to remain with the organization for a lifetime. To leave would be viewed as betrayal. Like the Japanese, they consider their employing organization to be family, as it often is.

In the Persian Gulf states of Kuwait, United Arab Emirates, and Qatar, the majority of workers are expatriates, especially in the petroleum industry. Saudi Arabia and other surrounding areas also receive a great number of workers from all over the world. In these oil-rich countries, such as Kuwait, many natives do not work at all because they are generously supported by their governments.

To be successful in working with individuals and organizations from other cultures, we must avoid rigid adherence to what we have always considered as the only correct way to think and act. We can do so without compromising our own values.

UNDERSTANDING AND ACCEPTING CUSTOMS OTHER THAN OUR OWN

Successful communication with people from other countries results not only from acceptance and objectivity, but also from a number of other factors. Probably the most important are patience and a sense of humor.

ETHNOCENTRISM

The word *ethnocentrism* describes the tendency to view all other people, at times unconsciously, by using our own culture as a guide to interpret their actions, customs, values, religions, and manners. Richard E. Porter describes ethnocentrism in this way:

> We place ourselves, our racial, ethnic, or social group, at the center of the universe and rate all others accordingly. The greater their similarity to us, the nearer to us we place them; the greater the dissimilarity, the farther away they are. We place one group above another, one segment of society above another, one nation-state above another. We tend to see our own groups, our own country, our own culture as the best, the most moral. This view also demands our first loyalty and, carried to extremes, produces a "my country first—right or wrong" attitude. . . .
>
> The way we view our world is a function of our culture, and it affects our social perception. . . . As we encounter people with differing world views, our communicative behavior is hampered because we view events differently; we use frames of reference that may seem vague or obscure to others, just as theirs may seem to us. Our perceptions become clouded and our attitudes interfere with our ability to share perceptions with others.[10]

Robert Kohls, in *Survival Kit for Overseas Living*, describes ethnocentrism in these words:

> An equally key point is that every group of people, every culture, is, and has always been ethnocentric; that is, it thinks its own so-

Speaker uses hand gestures, speaks slowly, and watches
listener's face in order to note comprehension.

lutions are superior and would be recognized as superior by any
right-thinking, intelligent, logical human being. It is significant
that to each group, their own view of the world appears to be the
"common sense" or "natural" view.[11]

Porter is not advocating that we change our own customs and system of
values to agree with those of people from other cultures with whom we try
to build harmonious relationships; to do so is neither necessary nor desirable. Neither should we try to change the personal outlook of those with
whom we communicate.

▶ STEREOTYPING

Stereotyping is a communication error likely to occur as we consider people
from other cultures, who in turn see and communicate with us in light of
their stereotyped impressions. We are forced to generalize somewhat as we

study the usual customs and thought patterns of the country that we are to visit (as much as can be learned from books and other sources), but we should continue to consider individual differences. Just as no two people in Gary, Indiana, are identical, no two people from Saudi Arabia, France, or Japan are identical.

An example of stereotyping is the way in which many people categorize people from the Middle East; like people from every other region, they differ widely. In the first place, what is usually referred to as the Middle East consists of about 22 countries, including those of North Africa, which are not in the "Middle East" but closer to Europe. Another error is thinking that all Arabs, regardless of homeland, are Muslims, and that all Muslims are Arabs. Neither concept is correct.

Nothing could be more mistaken than expecting every person from any country (or any city, neighborhood, or classroom) to be like every other person there. Nevertheless, an understanding of the culture from which the person comes aids communication, both oral and written, and builds harmonious personal relationships.

As a rule, educated people in countries other than the United States know more about our nation than people in the United States know about other countries. *Reader's Digest* has an international readership of more than 100 million in 13 language editions. Motion pictures and radio and television programs are distributed throughout the world. American products are advertised and sold throughout the world.

Sometimes, however, the views of people from other countries are distorted by the same sources from which they receive their information. Because of television and other media, the United States is perceived as an extremely affluent and wasteful society. Visitors to the United States com-

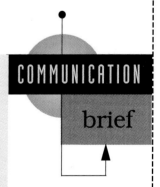

COMMUNICATION

brief

One form of ethnocentricity is seen in stereotyping. If a communicator imagines that a person from another culture will react in a particular way, he will usually convey this attitude in his speech, expectations, or behavior. A man attending an international-relations banquet was seated across from another man who possessed Asian physical characteristics. Wishing to advance international relations, he asked the Asian, "Likee foodee?" The man politely nodded his head. During the program, the Asian was introduced as an award-winning professor of economics at a prestigious university and was asked to make a few projections about world trade imbalances. After a brief discussion in perfect English, the Asian professor sat down, glanced across at his astonished neighbor, and asked, "Likee talkee?"

Rose Knotts, "Cross-cultural Management: Transformations and Adaptations," *Business Horizons*, January 1989, 29.

ment on the numerous automobiles discarded in junkyards. Most of the world has reason to envy the American standard of living, even in recession years.

People outside the United States have developed stereotypes about Americans (used here to describe people from the United States), just as Americans have done concerning people from other countries. They often do not consider differences among individuals, which occur not only from nationality to nationality, but also from family to family in the same small town and from individual to individual within each family. Americans may be judged as inaccurately and as unfairly as they have at times judged others.

Parts of Canada differ from parts of the United States, and areas of the United States differ widely from other sections. Stereotyping and other weaknesses in intercultural communication occur not only among people of different nationalities at home or abroad, but also among people from different regions of the United States. Southerners stereotype people from the North in various flattering and unflattering ways, and the opposite is also true. In addition, ethnocentrism applies to residents of the United States as they compare themselves to residents of other parts of the country.

Another problem is that societies are constantly changing, sometimes rather rapidly. If you do not believe that the ideas and perceptions of many people in the United States have changed, talk with someone who remembers the years before World War II or look at a number of old movies. It is true that change is ordinarily more rapid in the United States than it is in countries with extremely old cultures, such as China and India, but change occurs everywhere all the time. Consider the rapid progress and "modernization" that have occurred during the past few decades in Japan, which is also an old, traditional society. Because change is so constant and often rapid, research about countries we plan to visit must be based on recent sources, or at least supplemented by recent sources.

LANGUAGE DIFFERENCES AND DIFFICULTIES IN INTERCULTURAL COMMUNICATION

English is the principal language of international business. English is taught in elementary schools, high schools, and colleges (or their equivalents) throughout the world. The study of English receives far more attention abroad than the study of other languages receives in the United States.

Courses in business communication, taught in English, are common in many countries; they are particularly strong in Japan. These courses are taught under such names as commercial correspondence, commercial English, business English, business writing, foreign trade practices, business communication, and marketing communication.

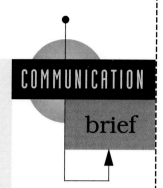

COMMUNICATION
brief

Estimates of the number of languages in the world usually fix on a figure of about 2,700, though almost certainly no one has ever made a truly definitive count. In many countries, perhaps the majority, there are at least two native languages, and in some cases—as in Cameroon and Papua New Guinea—there are hundreds. India probably leads the world, with more than 1,600 languages and dialects (it isn't always possible to say which is which).

Bill Bryson, *The Mother Tongue* (New York: William Morrow, 1990), 37.

English is likely to be spoken wherever one goes, at least by some employees in major hotels. Translators are usually available in the offices of major companies, in the United States and elsewhere. Nevertheless, Americans have a responsibility to learn the language of the people with whom they communicate. Even the best translations are not 100 percent accurate. Some English words have no equivalent in other languages; the opposite is also true.

As you have noted throughout your course in business communication, language difficulties occur even between persons whose native language is the same. Words have varying connotations, nonverbal communication intrudes into verbal messages, the language itself is not exact, and speakers and writers do not always choose words to express their intended meaning. Listeners do not listen, and readers do not or cannot read well. Even greater difficulties occur between people of different cultures.

In addition, although people from other countries may have studied English throughout their school years, textbook English is not complete preparation for conversing with Americans or putting their thoughts into natural-sounding sentences and compositions. These people are not prepared for numerous idioms and slang expressions that we take for granted. For example, how would you explain to someone who had never heard the phrase "You're pulling my leg" or "wild goose chase"?

On the other hand, foreign students may have a greater knowledge of "formal" English than many American students, including the rules of sentence structure, parts of speech, and punctuation.

How, then, do all these considerations affect the way we should speak and write to someone from another culture? First, we must be absolutely correct in our use of the English language (assuming, as is usually the case, that we are using English), avoiding colloquial expressions, regional expressions, and slang. Even disorganized conversation and poor writing usually can be understood by other Americans, at least after questioning the speaker or rereading the written material. Such communications will remain incomprehensible to foreign-born readers and listeners.

It's easy and fun to point out the differences between the American and the English vocabulary: the differences seem quaint and there are comparatively so few that we can easily spot them. Many of the differences are merely a matter of preference: we prefer *railroad* and *store* while the English prefer the synonyms *railway* and *shop*, but all four words are used in both England and America. In addition, we know or can easily guess what *braces*, *fishmonger's*, or *pram* means, just as the English know or can figure out what *innerspring mattress*, *jump rope*, and *ice water* mean.

Finally, many of the words that once separated American English from English English no longer do: our *cocktail* (1906), *skyscraper* (1833), and *supermarket* (1920's) are now heard around the world, and the English increasingly use *radio*, *run* (in a stocking), and *Santa Claus* instead of *wireless*, *ladder*, and *Father Christmas*.

Stuart Berg Flexner, *Listening to America* (New York: Simon & Schuster, 1982), 203.

All the features that increase readability and understanding of oral communication are doubly important in intercultural communication. Use simple language and short sentences and paragraphs. Be particularly careful of connotative meanings. As much as possible, use the denotative, or "dictionary," meaning of the word. Do not be overly informal. Avoid exaggerated expressions like "This coat weighs a ton" and "I'm so hungry I could eat a horse." Such expressions, weak in any communication except in the most informal conversation, seem absurd to listeners or readers who never heard them before.

Speak slowly and distinctly. Notice the expression of your listener. Does he or she understand you? If not, repeat your message in different words. Ask for feedback.

If you have learned to be a good communicator in the many ways stressed throughout your course in business communication, you will be far better prepared to communicate with persons everywhere than you would be otherwise. Even then, work for empathy and sensitivity, using the same consideration that you expect from your reader or listener. To a person from another country, you are the "foreigner."

▶ DIFFERENCES IN WRITTEN BUSINESS COMMUNICATION

Business letters reflect the culture of the country from which they come. Letters from Americans, like face-to-face interchange, are likely to seem blunt and impolite to Japanese readers and perhaps even to people in England, who are nearest to America in cultural patterns except for people in

Canada. A letter that we consider to be diplomatic—as well as clear, concise, direct, and businesslike—may convey an impression of abruptness and lack of courtesy to some readers in other countries.

In principle, letters to a company or business executive should be written in the language of the recipient. Ideally, exporters or others writing to someone in another country should find someone qualified to translate their letters into the appropriate language for their readers. According to some studies, however, businesspeople in the United States are likely to write in English, leaving the translation to the readers. Each company has different practices concerning the form of business correspondence, and these should be followed.

A study completed by Retha H. Kilpatrick in 1984 reports the opinions of representatives from 66 American and foreign companies who carry on international correspondence. According to her study, English-, Spanish-, and French-speaking countries dominate the list of countries with which American firms correspond. The vast majority of American letters sent to other countries are written in English. Foreign languages used most often in correspondence to American firms are Spanish, French, and German. An

Business cards are essential when meeting people from Japan and from many other countries outside the United States.

analysis of letters collected during the research study showed that American letters are more personal, informal, and less "flowery." Letters from other countries tend to be less personal, more formal, more courteous, and more flattering.[12]

A study by Casady and Wasson, published in 1994, provided information from administrators in 120 international companies throughout the United States. "Of the European countries, the two major correspondents are Great Britain (reported by 27% of the companies) and Germany (reported by 18% of the companies). Among the Far Eastern countries, Japan is the most popular (reported by 21% of the companies). Next in reported frequency of correspondents are Canada (24%), Australia (19%), Mexico (15%), Middle East (13%), and South America (11%)."

Major suggestions from representatives of the international companies were these: (1) Involve skills of bilingual employees or use translators or interpreters for critical or sensitive messages; (2) keep messages short and simple, with clear wording; (3) avoid slang; and (4) use the facsimile (fax) machine to transmit information. Faxed messages enable information to be exchanged quickly, while permitting equally speedy clarification of confusing or misunderstood terms before the exchange is concluded.[13]

► A COMPARISON OF AMERICAN AND JAPANESE BUSINESS LETTERS

A letter written in Japan, as quoted by Jean Johnston, begins this way:

> *Now we are in the splendid autumn season. I hope that you are enjoying the best of health and that things are going very well with you and with your association. I want to offer sincere congratulations to you.*

A paragraph within the letter is this: *"Although I myself am a man of little ability."*[14]

Japanese people, throughout their letters and in their conversation, assume an attitude that to Western minds seems to be entirely too apologetic, servile, and overly humble.

Jean Johnston lists other appropriate phrases for opening letters, all relating to the seasons. These phrases are used whether or not the writer knows the reader, much as we use "Sincerely" or other words as complimentary closes. One of the opening phrases recommended for January is "In this fierce coldness. . . ." A recommended opening for May is "In this season of fresh greenery. . . ."[15]

(Japanese people are very mindful of the seasons; for example, the traditional Japanese haiku, a poem of 17 syllables, must include a reference to a season.)

Haneda and Shima describe Japanese letters in this way: As long as you observe the rules, you are always on safe ground. No matter how difficult the situation may be, you can begin a letter with stereotyped greetings that serve as a buffer to bad news or refusal. An example of a salutation is this: "Allow us to open with all reverence to you." The closing sentence of the same letter is "We solicit your favor."[16]

Sorry and *regret* are two words often used by the Japanese. Other people well experienced in overseas life say that you should not use these words unless you are prepared to admit your mistake and pay for it. But when a Japanese writes "We are sorry" in reply to a complaint or claim, he does not necessarily mean that he would take legal responsibility but that he sympathizes with the customer who is not satisfied, whether the customer is right or wrong. So the eventual refusal is not inconsistent with apologies at the beginning in Japanese.[17]

A COMPARISON OF AMERICAN AND FRENCH BUSINESS LETTERS

Format constitutes one difference between American and French letters. Usually the French use the indented style instead of the block style. As in most other places outside the United States, the date is shown in this form: 14 November 1997, compared to the American November 14, 1997.

Some French letters are handwritten, and some companies prefer that letters of application be handwritten so that the applicant's character traits can be analyzed through handwriting. (Asking for handwritten application letters was once common in the United States, but for the reason that the employer wanted workers whose handwriting was legible—not a bad idea at the present time.)

Iris Varner concludes thus:

1 American and French letters share similarities, but there are also many differences.

2 From an American viewpoint French business letters have a more traditional and less action-oriented format. Convenience and time required for typing do not seem to play as important a role as in the United States.

3 The style of French letters is less concise. This may be a result of a greater use of the subjunctive and a more abstract writing style.

4 French openings and endings of letters are very polite and very formal. In fact, Americans might look at them as stilted and old-fashioned. When writing to French businesspeople, Americans should use a more formal writing style.

5 Generally, the French emphasize the same writing principles as the Americans, but they are not concerned about the use of the passive voice. Sentences tend to be a bit longer in French letters than in American letters.

6 The organization of letters in some cases follows different principles. The French handle collections and negative messages more directly. On the other hand, they tend to show more appreciation for orders and receipts of letters.[18]

A COMPARISON OF AMERICAN AND BRITISH BUSINESS LETTERS

American business letters differ from British letters in several respects, one of which is the difference in language itself. U.S. English is not the same as British English.

As one of many examples that could be cited, people in the United States refer to *attorneys* or *lawyers*; in Britain these professional people are described as *solicitors* or *barristers*, two terms that in themselves have different meanings.

As another example, the word *billion* may not mean the same to a British reader as it does to a U.S. writer; traditionally, the British billion is one thousand times as much, 1,000,000 million versus 1,000 million. This usage is changing, however, and the American billion is now widely used. (If you should have the opportunity to write or read about billions, make sure that the term is exactly defined.)

Variations in spelling are well known, such as *color* and *colour* and *practice* and *practise*. Minor differences exist in punctuation, including the use of fewer commas and hyphens in British writing. Another difference is that the British still distinguish between *shall* and *will*, as grammar was formerly taught in the United States. Overall, British writing in business letters is more formal; in some instances, it retains phrases that business writing textbooks describe as "stilted" or "old-fashioned." (Many letters written by people in the United States also fit this description.)

If you are unsure about spelling or word usage, you may wish to consult an unabridged dictionary, which is likely to include British usage. Even better, use a British-American dictionary, several of which exist.

A comprehensive study by Scott and Green[19] and a further study by Scott[20] indicate that British business writing practices have evolved slowly, particularly from the standpoint of organization. Until the mid-1980s, business writing textbooks and handbooks advocated only the traditional British organizational pattern.

This traditional arrangement consists of a brief beginning paragraph that refers to the purpose of the letter and, if applicable, gratitude for previous communication or business dealings. The middle portion of the letter, which consists of one or more paragraphs, conveys the main message. The content of the short closing paragraph is determined by the main message and is used to establish an atmosphere of courtesy, similar to the goodwill close that is taught in the United States. A variation of the traditional British organizational pattern is a letter that consists of only one paragraph, regardless of the length or type of message.

In bad-news letters, writers using the traditional pattern convey the bad news directly instead of using a clear implied refusal, often recommended in the United States. (As discussed in Chapter 8, business writing teachers in the United States advocate exceptions in some kinds of bad-news letters, both for an implied refusal and the indirect order of arrangement.) Of the bad-news letters that Scott and Green collected from 100 of the largest British industrial companies, more than 60 percent were written in the traditional British organizational pattern. About 25 percent were organized directly (deductively), and about 10 percent were organized indirectly (inductively), as the terms are used in the United States.

Scott and Green state:

> From the perspective of the business subculture of the U.S.A., many bad-news letters from the U.K. seem to be rather curt and blunt, with the customary apology or statement of regret further emphasizing the explicitly stated bad news. Since the British culture in general highly values courtesy, politeness, consideration, tactfulness, and diplomacy, why the British business subculture often circumvents these traits when conveying bad news is puzzling; apologizing or expressing regret for the bad news does not seem to compensate adequately for the frank manner in which the bad news is presented.[21]

Scott states that in recent years British writers about business communication have offered advice that parallels that offered by their American counterparts, including suggestions for simplicity and clarity. Because business communication receives little emphasis, however, the older pattern of organization and writing style continues in many letters.

Scott found that the format of letters in the United States and the United Kingdom are becoming increasingly similar, although format has been much slower to change in the United Kingdom. Even now, some companies use the indented style (all paragraphs, opening, and closing lines indented) that has almost completely vanished from correspondence in the United States. (The indented style wastes preparation time and thus increases cost. Its cluttered appearance decreases readability, at least to some Americans, who also consider it old-fashioned. Nevertheless, we should keep in mind that even letter arrangement is judged by individual perception. For decades the indented style was considered to be the only acceptable one in both Britain and the United States, and no doubt the entire English-speaking world.)

Scott concludes:

> Since Britons value tradition, the prudent writer of business correspondence bound for the U.K. will be knowledgeable about British standards in organization, style, mechanics, and format. By implementing culturally sanctioned ways of conveying busi-

ness messages, American business writers can avoid risking business relationships by offending British business persons, who are proud of their British commercial heritage and its mix of sometimes modern and sometimes old-fashioned ways of conducting business.[22]

Adaptation is one of the attributes that makes communication successful. Nevertheless, our adaptation should not extend to the point of being curt or blunt, a description used by Scott and Green to describe some business letters written in the United Kingdom. Neither should we place the contents of a letter into only one paragraph; to do so would decrease readability, regardless of the nationality of the reader.

As mentioned several times in this chapter and elsewhere, written, oral, and nonverbal communication with people from other countries all over the world ordinarily requires more formality than would be expected in the United States. Letters that seem breezy or brash are less desirable than conservative, traditional ones.

A further benefit of research about letters in the United Kingdom and elsewhere is that we are better able to understand and accept letters that we receive. This understanding enables and motivates us to write effective messages in return, even if we forget and spell *color* "our way" or confuse *will* and *shall*. Another consideration is that messages composed in English in other countries throughout the world are likely to be more like those from Britain than those from the United States. Students throughout the world have studied British English for centuries, not American English.

A summary of some of the differences between Japanese, French, and British letters is given in Figure 17-1.

DIFFERENCES IN LETTER CONTENTS AND STYLE

	Japanese	French	British
Openings	Usually related to seasons	Very polite and formal	Formal, refer to purpose
Body	Servile, humble, apologetic	Less concise; longer sentences; more passive voice	Direct arrangement for bad-news letters; spelling variations
Closing	Trite, stereotyped	Very polite and formal	Courtesy and goodwill

FIGURE 17-1
Variations of letters written from Japan, France, and Britain

FURTHER SUGGESTIONS FOR WRITING LETTERS TO PEOPLE
IN OTHER COUNTRIES

As you will notice, many of the following suggestions about writing to readers in other countries are the same as those that apply to readers everywhere. They are even more important when writing to people from other cultures, especially those whose native language is one other than English.

Be courteous and extremely polite.

Write simply, using rather short words, but do not give the impression of over simplifying or "writing down."

Use short sentences and paragraphs.

Be specific. Many English words have multiple meanings. Repeat in different words if necessary, but be careful not to confuse the reader with unnecessarily wordy material. As when communicating orally, avoid slang or idioms that are likely to be unfamiliar to your readers.

As much as possible, use the "textbook English" that your reader has studied. Prefer denotative ("dictionary") meanings to connotative ones.

Avoid emotional words or exaggerations.

Avoid nonobjective adjectives such as *horrible* or *fantastic*. (As in all good writing, avoid using a great number of adjectives and adverbs of any kind. Well-chosen nouns and verbs decrease the need for modifiers.)

Try to determine the communication style, both written and oral, that is preferred by the people of the particular country to which you write. In some instances, modifying the usual direct and indirect organizational pattern may be advisable. For example, Asians are less direct than most people in the United States, and Germans are even more direct. When writing to a reader in Japan, avoid an emphatic, bluntly stated "no," even though your meaning must be understood. For a German reader, the direct approach could be the better choice even for a bad-news letter. For a British reader the traditional British organizational pattern may be the best choice, especially if such is the arrangement of a letter to which you are replying.

As in oral and nonverbal communication, formality in business letters is more important in other countries than it is in the United States. Be extremely careful not to use an individual's first name unless you are sure that you are on a first-name basis with your reader. Also be sure to determine your reader's title and to express it correctly. Include your own title or position, or both, with your typewritten name. (An exception that still applies is that "Mr." is never used with the writer's own name.)

Use care in the expression of numbers. Use figures, not words. Your reader is likely to use the metric system. Do likewise—but do so correctly.

Remember that our "decimal point" is expressed in some other countries as a "decimal comma"; for example, 27200,17 instead of the U.S. 27,200.17.

Spell out months shown in dates instead of using numbers. (This method is preferred in all letters, even those sent and received in the United States.) Aside from the fact that numbers are too informal, they are also confusing.

In the United States, 8/10/98 means August 10, 1998; in most other countries it means October 8, 1998.

NONVERBAL MESSAGES IN INTERCULTURAL COMMUNICATION

As discussed in Chapter 1 (please review at this time), nonverbal communication, a constant process, is extremely important in oral messages of all kinds, often more so than words themselves. Nonverbal communication is also present in written messages. Nonverbal communication is extremely important in intercultural communication because of language barriers and differing background and perceptions.

As with verbal communication, categories of nonverbal communication overlap. Because *nonverbal* includes all meaning other than that expressed through written or spoken words, aspects of culture discussed elsewhere also consist of forms of nonverbal communication. For understanding and organization, however, the overall field of nonverbal communication is broken down here into separate topics.

People from some other cultures use hand gestures more frequently than most people in the United States.

SIGN LANGUAGE AND SYMBOLS

Sign language, also known as *emblems*, includes specific gestures that usually have a verbal equivalent or translation. For example, in the United States the index and middle fingers raised and slightly spread apart means "peace"; and the index finger held to the thumb while the other fingers are raised means "OK." In some cultures, the emblem used to signal "OK" has an obscene meaning, as can raising the thumb by itself, a gesture meaning "thumbs up" or good luck in the United States.

In Europe, Japan, and elsewhere, the wave used in the United States is a beckoning signal.

In Japan, bowing, an age-old custom, is still the rule, although handshakes are becoming more common. Traditionally a bow is an act of humbling oneself before another, an act of showing respect.

Diana Rowland states: "It would be rude not to return a bow. Be prepared for perhaps a handshake, too, but remember that for the Japanese a bow is a cultural way to greet people and to express sincerity and humility."[23]

Some other researchers and writers about Japanese customs advise Westerners not to attempt a bow. Because of the various methods of bowing (quick, deep, low, and so on), Westerners cannot be expected to "do it right."

In relation to the preceding paragraph, Mr. Kimihiro Imamura comments:

> I think this opinion goes to extremes. If we know that people are from other countries, we will take it for granted that they make odd bowing and we'll be permissive. Bowing (of any kind) or handshaking is acceptable in the business community, depending on the circumstances.[24]

Because gestures can be easily misunderstood, the best approach is to avoid them altogether if possible.

Symbols differ from country to country. For example, the Wise Corporation uses an owl as a trademark for its potato chips. If the potato chips were to be marketed in India, where the owl is a symbol of bad luck, the owl would no doubt be changed.

Our nods and shaking of the head to indicate *yes* or *no* are unknown in some countries, where opposite movements indicate *yes* or *no*. "People from certain parts of India typically move their heads in a sort of figure-eight motion when they are listening to someone talk. . . . It is likely to suggest to Americans that the Indian has a sore neck."[25]

THE USE OF COLOR (CHROMATICS)

Colors have varying meanings in different cultures. In Japan, white and black are symbols of mourning. Black, rather than white, is more prominent. In Japan, red is a symbol of celebration. In a number of Asian countries, red is the symbol of aggression, connoting Japan's Rising Sun and military aggression. Among Iranians, Peruvians, and Mexicans, yellow has negative connotations. In Armenia, yellow flowers send the message, "I miss you." Green is not an appropriate color for wrapping packages in Egypt. Purple is associated with royalty. In the time of the ancient Phoenicians, purple dye was extremely expensive; hence, it could be afforded only by royalty.

Marketing experts study color preferences and traditions in the countries where they plan to sell their products. Often packaging and advertising that are successful in the United States must be changed when the products are distributed internationally.

▶ **THE USE OF TIME (CHRONEMICS)**

Americans live by schedules, appointments, and alarm clocks. We value promptness and deplore the waste and passing of time. Natives of some other countries exemplify the idea heard but not usually practiced in the United States, "Take time to smell the roses."

Americans do not like to be kept waiting, although most do not object to a 5-minute delay. A comparable time to be late for an appointment in Latin America is likely to be 45 minutes or so. Even then, the appointment may not be with one individual alone, as several appointments are scheduled at the same time.

Even after obtaining an appointment, the American who wants to get down to business immediately is likely to be disappointed. In the American culture, discussion is a means to an end: the deal. The goal is to get to the point quickly, efficiently, and neatly; this is not the expected procedure in Latin America, the Middle East, or other places in the world, where discussion is considered part of the spice of life. What we consider as strictly business becomes a social affair.

Although people throughout the world are becoming more Westernized than they were formerly, vast differences still exist in their outlook toward time.

▶ **THE USE OF SPACE (PROXEMICS)**

Americans feel uncomfortable when crowded together and require their own personal space. People around the Mediterranean, including France, seem to enjoy closer personal contact, as can be observed in the crowded homes, trains, buses, and sidewalk cafés. (Such crowding is perhaps not always a matter of choice.) People in Latin America, the Middle East, and some other countries also crowd together. In Saudi Arabia and other countries, pushing and shoving in a public place is not considered impolite.

In our culture, physical contact is reserved for intimate moments. Such reservations do not exist in a number of other cultures.

Americans, like people in Britain and northern Europe, want their own "bubble of space" and feel violated when others intrude without a special invitation. We also maintain greater personal distances, particularly in business and formal situations.

Because people from countries such as Saudi Arabia stand and sit closer together than we do, to Americans they seem to be crowding in and being pushy and demanding. Americans, in turn, may seem cold and distant to Arabs.

The sheer availability or unavailability of space has had an effect on the culture of the Japanese as compared to that of the United States. The people of Japan are crowded together on a small island (although areas are not populated equally), whereas the United States and Canada still contain vast, sprawling areas of vacant land. Our houses and lots are far bigger, as are cars and furniture. Another aspect of the use of space is seen in Kuwait, Saudi Arabia, and other surrounding countries. Most middle- and upper-class people live in very large houses. Americans who go there to work are often pleasantly surprised at their spacious living quarters. Nevertheless, as pointed out repeatedly by Edward T. Hall and other researchers in nonverbal communication, people from the Middle East seem to require little personal space and prefer to stand close to their listeners as they converse.

Japanese families share a small space and live close to their neighbors. (Yes, so do many Americans, but not to such an extent, unless it is in an apartment in a large city.) The Japanese also work close together. David Victor states:

> Perhaps most significant for the business communicator is the difference in the way U.S. and Japanese offices are arranged. The

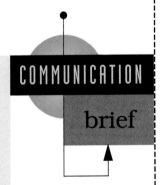

COMMUNICATION brief

In his landmark 1969 book, *The Hidden Dimension*, anthropologist Hall found that, however similar the organizational charts of global companies may appear, an office in France differs from an office in Germany, and an office in Germany differs from an office in the United States.

For example, all humans need some privacy; how much, and in what circumstances, however, is largely a function of culture. The Japanese, French, and Italians are examples of "high-context" cultures. . . . High-context personality types are accustomed to a high level of bustle, and so are not as easily distracted as Americans.

Americans, British, and Germans are members of so-called "low-context" cultures and share a tendency toward privacy and social independence. . . . Hall describes how a U.S. manager likes to be ensconced in a corner, but a French boss prefers to place his desk in the middle of the floor. English workers do not place the same premium on enclosed workspaces that Americans do; their sense of class and status derives from the larger social system rather than work. Germans are much more protective of their privacy and thus more likely to leave their office doors closed than Americans.

James Krohe, Jr., "What Makes an Office Work?" *Across the Board*, May, 1993, 16.

majority of Japanese companies employ the open-space format in their offices where people of all ranks work in large rooms without intervening walls to separate their desks. . . . Privacy and secrecy have no role in such an environment, and teamwork is reinforced by the physical layout.[26]

The office layout of China is similar to that in Japan. Privacy seems not to exist. Privacy is also lacking in Middle Eastern offices where outsiders or other office workers wander in and out in the middle of a conference, an occurrence most disturbing to American representatives who are trying to make a sale. Germans, however, are even more concerned with their privacy than Americans; every person, even secretaries who must enter an employer's office dozens of times a day, knock before each entrance.

You may appear pushy (to Germans) or distant and unfriendly (to Latin Americans, Arabs, and some of the people around the Mediterranean) because of your particular need for space. You may seem brash and impertinent to the British if you invade their "space" of wanting to be silent when you want to talk. (On the other hand, relationships are also less than perfect in the home office, are they not?)

▶ **THE SENSE OF TOUCH (HAPTICS)**

The use of touch varies from country to country. "Touching" areas include, among others, Latin America, Italy, Greece, and Middle Eastern countries. Touching is obviously tied in with greetings. In "non-touching" countries (which are said to be Japan, the United States, England, Germany, Scandinavian countries, and others), customary touching, as a greeting or on other occasions, is limited to handshakes. In Algeria and Tunisia (with their traditions of Arabic and French), anything less than a handshake plus an embrace would be considered an insult. In the Middle East, Latin America, and southern European countries, male friends exchange greetings with hugs and kisses on the cheek. In these countries, there is also more touching while carrying on casual conversations and more hand gestures and "body language."

As reported by Mary Munter:

> Anglos usually avoid touching each other very much. In a study of touching behaviors reported by Mark Knapp, researchers observed people seated in outdoor cafes, in each of four countries, and counted the number of touches during one hour of conversation. The results were San Juan, 180 touches per hour; Paris, 110 per hour; Gainesville, Florida, one per hour; and London, none per hour.[27]

(Mark Knapp is a well-known writer and researcher in nonverbal communication.)

EYE CONTACT (OCULESICS)

Eye contact differs according to the particular culture. In America speakers are taught to maintain eye contact with their listeners. Arabs maintain eye contact to the extent that Americans become uncomfortable. People from some other cultures are taught to avoid direct eye contact in order to show respect.

A FEW POINTS OF ETIQUETTE

The pointers listed here are far from sufficient for your needs when you plan to travel to a particular country. Read widely and at length. Your librarian will be of help. Also try to talk with people who presently live in the particular country or have lived there in the past. The Foreign Students Association of your local college or university can put you in touch.

JAPAN

- Do not say "no." Do not ask for a "yes or no" answer. (The Japanese believe that surface harmony must be maintained at all costs.)

- Remove shoes before stepping from the enclosed porch (genkan) into a Japanese-style home.

- Dress conservatively, even though casual Fridays are now observed in many companies.

- Always have your business cards available. (This advice applies to other countries throughout the world.) Have the cards printed on one side in English and on the other side in Japanese. Present the business card with both hands. Give your full attention to the card that is given to you.

- Expect less direct eye contact than is common in the United States.

- Say thank you for a gift. Follow up immediately with a note or telephone call. Another acknowledgment may include a personal visit. (Perhaps you will consider yourself fortunate to receive only a few gifts.)

- Do not talk loudly.

- Do not be overly familiar. In Japan, first names are seldom used, even among friends.

- Do not kiss or embrace a Japanese when you meet.

- No tip is required or expected. Most first-class hotels prohibit employees from accepting tips.

- Although it will be difficult, try to be as polite as your Japanese hosts.

► CHINA

► Dress conservatively.

► Do not embrace, kiss, or touch a Chinese person.

► Do not give a clock as a gift; it supposedly brings bad luck.

► Remember that in China the surname is given first.

► Be ready with the business cards, printed on both sides in both languages.

► Always accept the tea that you will be offered several times a day.

► Do not tip.

► Smile.

► SAUDI ARABIA AND OTHER ISLAMIC COUNTRIES

► Respect all religious practices. Do not attempt to do business during Ramadan, other holy holidays, or times of daily prayer.

► Be patient.

► Expect more direct eye contact than in the United States.

► Take the many cups of tea or black coffee that will be offered.

► Begin with small talk. Perhaps continue with small talk for a long time.

COMMUNICATION brief

"It is never too late to mend a wrong." This Japanese proverb describes a deep belief that it is never too late for people to admit that they are in error. That is why the apology plays such an important role in Japanese culture. While it is true that many Japanese apologies are ritualistic and may mean very little, an apology conveyed in a sincere manner can serve to right a wrong. For example, a Japanese involved in an auto accident who apologizes to the victim's family may not be sued. Apologies may reverse a negative decision in a business relationships.

Dr. Suzuki, who introduced the Suzuki music method, says in his book *Ability Development from Age Zero* that if you do a child wrong, you must apologize. Very few Americans realize how important the transaction of apology and forgiveness is in human relationships.

The Japan Center of Tennessee Newsletter (Winter 1991), 7.

▶ Learn and use a few Arabic words, or the entire language if possible. (This advice applies to all languages.)

▶ Do not smoke. Most important, do not bring liquor, as discussed previously.

▶ Do not inquire about a man's wife or family. To do so is considered too personal if you have not met them.

▶ Do not praise their possessions or they will feel compelled to give them to you. (It's true you may covet their beautiful Oriental rugs, but restrain yourself.)

PREPARATION FOR AN OVERSEAS ASSIGNMENT

A manager or other worker far from the home office must possess the technical skills and initiative to make decisions that would be left to superiors if he or she had remained in the United States.

Individuals working abroad must have a tolerance for ambiguity, adaptability, and flexibility. Although technical skills are essential, the idea that "If you can do a good job in New York, you can do a good job in Japan" is a myth. Expatriates must be able to work with diverse groups, including foreign governments, labor organizations, and employees of foreign subsidiaries. They must be able to understand and accept business practices and customs far different from their own.

The best way to prepare for an assignment in a foreign country is to spend a few years living and working there, becoming proficient in the language and immersing yourself in the culture itself. This ideal approach, however, is not likely to be possible when you need most to learn about a country—when you have been assigned there.

You will need to do much preparation on your own, even if you receive excellent support from your employing organization. As in all other circumstances requiring new knowledge and responsibilities, the answer is research. Find out as much as you can about the country to which you are going. Even more important, make sure that you know exactly why you are going there and what your responsibilities will be, particularly your communication responsibilities. (This step is the same as the first one in the research process when beginning a project that will result in a written report.)

Learn the language if at all possible. Short intensive courses are highly successful in giving even a beginner enough language ability to survive. In addition, people with whom you communicate appreciate your efforts to learn their language (many Americans do not do so) even if it is incomplete and broken at first.

It is not enough to learn a few or many habits of what seem to be oddities of the people of a country; for example, in Saudi Arabia women do not drive automobiles. In some countries, to show the sole of a shoe is an insult. It is not enough to know that a Japanese businessman holds a business card in two hands and bows as he presents it to you. Neither is it extremely beneficial to know that a Buddhist wedding is conducted mostly in silence. Although these are interesting customs and, because of the etiquette involved, not unimportant, you should research more important questions, such as tradition, religion, history, politics and government, past and present economic conditions, natural resources, and philosophy pertaining to work and business organizations.

Other information you will need includes the cost of living, available housing, schools, recreational facilities, and access to shopping facilities.

Another question to be researched is how you as a resident of the United States (or of Canada) will be perceived abroad. Although "the ugly American" is a cliché, the fact remains that you will be judged at least partially by stereotyping, as, even with the best intentions, you are likely to judge others.

SUMMARY

Culture means the total system of values, beliefs, customs, religions, and manners. Although cultural differences exist everywhere to a certain extent, they are more extreme between people from greatly differing countries.

The number of Americans working abroad is increasing, as is the number of people from other countries who now visit or live in the United States and Canada.

We tend to view all other people by using our own particular culture as a guide, an attitude that is described as *ethnocentrism. Stereotyping* is a frequent communication error as we consider people from other countries.

People from some other cultures, particularly Latin America and the Middle East, are much more casual about the exact use of time than are persons in the United States. Cultures also differ in their use of personal space and in various other methods of nonverbal communication.

Most international business is transacted in the English language. Even a common language, however, does not eliminate communication difficulties.

Business letters written in America tend to be more informal and personal than letters written in many other countries. Because Americans wish to be concise and direct, their letters may seem blunt in comparison to those from other countries.

For an overseas assignment, you should attempt to learn the language and to find out as much about the country as possible. Even more important, work for adaptability and sensitivity.

1   What is your understanding of the meaning of the term *intercultural communication*?
2   Name three other terms that mean approximately the same as *intercultural communication*.
3   What is your understanding of the word *culture*?
4   What is the meaning of the word *ethnocentrism*?
5   Summarize the differences in the use of time in the United States and Latin America.
6   Summarize major differences in the use of personal space in the United States and some other countries of the world.
7   What is the primary language used in international business?
8   Briefly describe the differences between business letters in the United States and Japan.

(Related to material in Chapter 17 and principles of usage and appropriate wording.) Choose the correct word and make all necessary corrections.

1   (One's ones) individual perception is (affected, effected) by (their, his or her) entire background.
2   Our culture exerts a tremendous influence on our world, it patterns our response to experiences.
3   No 2 people in Sacramento California are identical and no 2 people from Egypt Japan or Brazil are identical.
4   Some of the stereotypes by which Americans are judged are positive not negative.
5   The nail that sticks up is hit is a well known saying in Japan.
6   If management (personnel, personal) are to (suceed, succeed) in Japan they must understand (its, it's) culture.
7   Intercultural communication is not new it is as old as humanity.
8   The Japanese see decisions as a product of the (concensus, consensus) of the group not of an individual.
9   Cultural identity is a aspect of a persons (existence, existance).
10 In countries where two or more languages coexist confusion often arises.

CASES AND PROBLEMS

1 Report problems about intercultural communication follow Chapter 15. They are also referred to after Chapter 16 as topics for oral presentations. These assignments can be used in various ways, either here or with Chapter 15 or 16, or with all three chapters. (Some also apply to Chapter 18.)

2 Ask one or more persons from other countries to visit your class and to comment on one or more of the areas of information presented in this chapter. Possibly members of your class are natives of some other country. If so, they should be considered the "experts" for this particular chapter.

3 Suppose that someone who had never been to the United States asks you to describe what the people are like. What would you say? Put your remarks into a written reply of no more than one page. (This is indeed an abbreviated assignment. Libraries are filled with books about the people of the United States.)

4 Suppose this person has asked you to describe the culture of the city or town in

which you live. Follow the same instructions as for Problem 3.

5 Describe the characteristics of a foreign country you have visited or one that you have read about.

6 Do you think that the actions of people in the United States are similar to their letters—as much as actions and letters can be similar? Explain.

7 Why is translation not 100 percent accurate?

8 From your reading or from your classes in management, marketing, or other areas, give examples of how advertising policies, product names, or slogans used in the United States have been ineffective elsewhere.

9 Which features of letters widely used in the United States (and discussed in this book) serve approximately the same purpose as phrases in Japanese letters?

THINK-IT-THROUGH ASSIGNMENTS, AND WORKING IN GROUPS

10 If cases about intercultural communication, following Chapter 15 were used as the major report assignment, you may wish to give an oral report as a group to the class as a whole with the study of Chapter 17. A variation is to present information as committee reports

in a business meeting, as discussed in Chapter 18. Topics on intercultural communication are especially appropriate to be used with Chapters 15 through 18. (Your instructor will direct.)

E N D N O T E S

1 Haya El Nasser, "Immigration to Lead Population Boom in West," *USA Today*, October 23, 1996, 7A.

2 Shariar Farahmand and Brian H. Kleiner, "Helping Americans Adapt to Other Cultural Systems," *Agency Sales Magazine*, July 1994, 21.

3 Cassandra Hayes, "The Intrigue of International Assignments," *Black Enterprise*, May 1996, 98.

4 *The Random House Dictionary of the English Language*, 2d ed., unabridged (New York: Random House, 1987), 480, 993, 996.

5 Vern Terpstra, *The Cultural Environment of Business* (Cincinnati: Southwestern, 1978), xiv.

6 Lillian H. Chaney and Jeanette S. Martin, *Intercultural Business Communication* (Englewood Cliffs, NJ: Prentice Hall, 1995), 95.

7 Iris Varner and Linda Beamer, *Intercultural Communication in the Global Workplace* (Chicago: Irwin, 1995), 18.

8 Howard F. Van Zandt, "How to Negotiate in Japan," in *Intercultural Communication: A Reader*, 2d ed., ed. Larry A. Samovar and Richard E. Porter (Belmont, CA: Wadsworth, 1976), 309.

9 Kimihiro Imamura, Letter to Malra Treece, January 20, 1997.

10 Richard E. Porter, "An Overview of Intercultural Communication," in *Intercultural Communication: A Reader*, 2d ed., ed. Larry A. Samovar and Richard E. Porter (Belmont, CA: Wadsworth, 1976), 6–7.9.

11 L. Robert Kohls, *Survival Kit for Overseas Living* (Chicago: Intercultural Press, 1979), 19–20.

12 Retha H. Kilpatrick, "International Business Communication Practices," *Journal of Business Communication*, 21, no. 4 (Fall 1984): 33–44.

13 Mona Casady and Lynn Wasson, "Written Communication Skills of International Business Persons," *The Bulletin of the Association of Business Communication*, December 1994, 39.

14 Jean Johnston, "Business Communication in Japan," *Journal of Business Communication*, 17, no. 2 (Spring 1980): 66.

15 Ibid.

16 Saburo Haneda and Hirosuke Shima, "Japanese Communication Behavior as Reflected in Letter Writing," Journal of Business Communication, 19, no. I (Winter 1982).

17 Haneda and Shima, "Japanese Communication," 24, 27.

18 Iris Varner, "A Comparison of American and French Business Correspondence," *Journal of Business Communication*, 25, no. 4 (Fall 1988): 64.

19 James Calvert Scott and Diana J. Green, "British Perspectives on Organizing Bad-News Letters: Organizational Patterns Used by Major U.K. Companies," *The Bulletin of the Association for Business Communication*, LV, no. I (March 1992): 17–19.

20 James Calvert Scott, "Preparing Business Correspondence the British Way," *The Bulletin for the Association for Business Communication*, LVI, no. 2 (June 1993): 10–17.

21 Scott and Green, "British Perspectives," 19.

22 Scott, "Preparing Business Correspondence," 14.

23 Diana Rowland, *Japanese Business Etiquette* (New York: Warner, 1985), 12.

24 Kimihiro Imamura, Letter to Malra Treece, January 20, 1997.

25 Gary Althen, *American Ways* (Yarmouth, ME: Intercultural Press, 1988), 142.

26 David Victor, *International Business Communication* (New York: HarperCollins, 1992), 62.

27 Mary Munter, "Cross-Cultural Communication for Managers," *Business Horizons*, May 1993, 29.

Effective Management Through Communication

CHAPTER

18

OBJECTIVES

Chapter Eighteen will help you:

1   Explain why effective management consists largely of effective communication.

2   Emphasize quality in all organizational and employment functions.

3   Consider the importance of etiquette in business.

4   Interview employees, applicants, and other individuals or groups.

5   Plan and conduct meetings and conferences, including television appearances.

This chapter briefly discusses certain aspects of managerial communication, as does Chapter 2. Topics include (1) the search for quality throughout an organization, based on the assumption that quality in all areas is an important element of ethical management and also of a company's success; (2) business etiquette, which is related to ethics, management, and intercultural communication; (3) interviewing; (4) planning and conducting meetings and conferences, a topic related to Chapter 16, "Speaking to Groups"; (5) teleconferencing and television appearances, also related to Chapter 16; and (6) economy in communication methods.

As discussed previously and as you have no doubt observed, different methods of communication are quite similar. For example, an oral report is organized much like a written one, depending on the subject matter, the environment, the results, and the audience. Harmonious and pleasant conversation about business matters is similar to that of social and personal encounters. Speaking to groups, whether as the leader or as another participant, is basically similar in all situations, provided sufficient and correct adaptations are made according to the material, the situation, time limits, and the listeners.

QUALITY—THE ETHICAL DECISION

Management and personnel throughout an organization must be constantly concerned with the quality of products, services, and management itself. Citizens must insist on high quality throughout all government, civic, and professional organizations.

Quality is defined as "character with respect to fineness or grade of excellence; high-grade superiority; excellence" by *The Random House Dictionary of the English Language* (2d edition, 1987). A definition of *ethics*, from the same dictionary, is "a system of moral principles, as of an individual." Other definitions describe ethics as a branch of philosophy or as the ethical standards of a culture.

Compare the definitions of quality and ethics. Can we work for one without also working for the other? In an organization, efforts toward quality, in all respects, correlate with the moral principles of the people who make up that organization. This correlation is especially true of those in leadership positions, but it also extends to workers at all levels.

All successful communication is related to quality in some way, particularly the quality of interpersonal relationships and the quality of the work we produce, whether or not this work is in tangible form. Although an imperfectly worded letter, for example, is less serious than an important management decision, both the letter and the decision are affected by the dedication (a facet of ethical conduct) of the people involved.

An unidentified writer with the Royal Bank of Canada writes thus:

> Quality can be anywhere and everywhere provided enough effort goes into it. Where some have gone wrong is in lavishing more time and money on creating an impression of quality than on actually delivering it. . . . Anyone who aims for excellence should be aware that it is a moving target that keeps rising higher and higher. You create this effect yourself by continually improving your performance and setting fresh criteria.
>
> As the phrase "the honest workman" suggests, workmanship is founded in personal integrity. Those imbued with it have nothing but scorn for sloppiness, shabbiness, cheapness, sharp dealing, or false fronts. . . . In a "quality society," honesty, excellence, and the principle of giving full value for what we receive would become the rule of conduct in both business and personal relationships. What began as an effort to improve the quality of work could end in a revolutionary improvement in the overall quality of life.[1]

The prestigious Malcolm Baldrige National Quality Awards, which were created by Congress in 1987 and named for the former secretary of the Commerce Department, are awarded annually to honor companies for superior products or service. These awards, the most sought-after prize in U.S. industry, are based on leadership, information and analysis, strategic planning, employee training and development, process management, customer satisfaction, and business results such as revenues and earnings. Two awards may be given in each of three categories: manufacturing, service, and small business.

In 1996, four winners received the awards: ADAC Laboratories of Milpitas, California; Dana Commercial Credit Corporation of Toledo, Ohio; Custom Research of Minneapolis; and Trident Precision Manufacturing of Webster, New York. Among the winners of the Baldrige Award since 1988 are AT&T, Ritz-Carlton Hotels, Motorola, Xerox, IBM Rochester, and Federal Express.

All these companies stress employee involvement, a continuing quest for quality throughout the organization, and product and service excellence. Efforts are devoted not only toward a profit-making goal (although from a purely pragmatic standpoint such an approach is monetarily profitable) but also to goals of a far wider scope. Perhaps the greatest satisfaction of all is the pride and self-respect of all members involved in a continuing search for excellence, which is the ethical way of running an organization.

Total quality management (TQM) has become a basic business practice throughout the world. Total quality management techniques are designed to improve performance. As stated in the *Journal of Business Ethics*,

> Concurrently, organizations are striving to eradicate the concept that the term business ethics is an oxymoron. . . . TQM encompasses concepts and practices that are in the best organizational interest for all stakeholders. . . . One of the underlying features of total quality management is its emphasis on employee empowerment. . . . TQM focuses on the customer as the ultimate dictator of quality. . . . Customers may be external or internal. Without satisfying external customers, repeat sales will not occur; without sat-

COMMUNICATION brief

Architect David Hansen is a principal of the Chicago-based firm of Perkins & Will, which has designed headquarters complexes for several Fortune 500 companies, including the sprawling new complex housing the Sears Merchandise Group in suburban Chicago. Hansen explains that Sears staff members (especially those working in disparate departments) found it hard to communicate in their skyscraper headquarters in downtown Chicago. The only place for people to chat outside their departments was in the elevators, and people don't talk much in elevators.

For the new offices, Hansen and his colleagues designed seating areas at various "crossroads" inside the complex, and put near each one a fountain or other source of splashing water to create "white noise" sufficient to conceal conversation from prying ears of passersby. Visitors are thus greeted with that rarest of sights: people actually sitting and chatting in the places that the architects meant them to.

Hansen adds that providing a physical infrastructure for conversation is not enough. "Chance communication has to be culturally okay before people feel comfortable being seen apparently lounging during work hours. But Sears bought into this 100 percent."

James Krohe, Jr., "What Makes an Office Work?" *Across the Board*, May, 1993, 16.

isfying internal customers, products or services will never be completed. Thus, the customer is an integral component and stakeholder in the primary function of business.[2]

A General Accounting Office study concluded that the U.S. government could save taxpayers $350 billion a year by practicing total quality management.

To survive global competition, companies in the United States must promote and maintain a total quality approach. They have no other choice.

ETIQUETTE IN BUSINESS

We have considered etiquette with the study of ethics, goodwill letters, word usage, letter arrangement, and other subjects. Proper etiquette is important as it applies to written, oral, and nonverbal communication.

An authority on business and personal etiquette opens her 519-page book, *Letitia Baldrige's Complete Guide to Executive Manners*, with these words:

> This is a book about manners but also about the quality of excellence. It is a book about the importance of detail and about how details linked together can create the strong, effective executive presence that propels an individual upward in his or her career. This is, therefore, a book about success. . . .
>
>   This book is based on the theory that good manners are cost-effective because they not only increase the quality of life in the workplace, contribute to optimum employee morale, and embellish the company image, but they also play a major role in generating profit. An atmosphere in which people treat each other with consideration is obviously one in which a customer enjoys doing business. Also very important, a company with a well-mannered, high-class reputation attracts—and keeps—good people.[3]

As Baldrige emphasizes, etiquette is necessary for quality, harmonious interpersonal relationships, and even for profitability. Although she does not use the word *ethics*, the meaning is implied in "people treat each other with consideration."

Ethics is a broader term than *etiquette*, at least from its usual meaning of following the rules of proper behavior in polite society. Etiquette, however, consists of far more than knowing the exact wording (there is none) of introductions and which fork to use at a dinner party. Nevertheless, violating the usual and expected contentions of behavior, either knowingly or because of lack of knowledge, is at least inconsiderate and at most insulting and dangerous.

The "rules" of etiquette are based on consideration, first of all, but also on common sense and a recognition of the usual customs and mores of the society in which we live or work. This recognition of particular customs is particularly troublesome when we travel or work abroad.

Either at home or abroad, questions regarding etiquette include greeting visitors, making introductions, table manners, choice of clothing, the etiquette of business letters, business entertaining, proper forms of address, smoking, conversation, business relationships between men and women in the office, gift giving, planning seminars and meetings—and many, many more.

True etiquette increases the comfort, confidence, and self-esteem of other persons. Words and actions that build these qualities, however, must be sincere, as all real communication must be.

Some of many possible guidelines are listed here:

1   Listen to the words of others instead of concentrating on your own words.

2   Remember and use people's names. Spell and pronounce them correctly.

3   Make introductions promptly and correctly. Traditionally, a man is introduced to a woman (saying the woman's name first); a younger person is introduced to an older person (saying the older person's name first);

COMMUNICATION brief

PATIENCE

Behavior that is high-handed and harsh from people in control toward people economically beholden and unable to fight back is cheap.

There's a great story about passengers mobbing the reservation counter after a canceled flight. Airline personnel were doing their best to rebook passengers quickly. A demanding passenger pushed to the front of the line, pounded on the counter, and shouted repeatedly, "You have to get me on this plane!" The reservationist remained accommodating and unrattled.

The passenger's tirade became even more incensed and insulting. "Do you know who you're talking to?" he shouted. "Do you know who I am?"

The reservationist calmly took the microphone and announced over the intercom, "We have a passenger here who doesn't know who he is. Will someone who knows this passenger please come identify him?"

This caused the other passengers to erupt in applause.

Ann Chadwell Humphries, "Don't Look Down on the People Who Are Working for You," *The Florida Times-Union*, July 29, 1996, 14.

and other people are introduced to a guest (saying the guest's name first). Introduce a peer in your own company to a peer in another company, a lower-ranking person to a higher ranking person, and a person in your company to a customer or client.

4   Be careful about using new acquaintances' first names, especially if they are older than you or in higher positions. This advice is extremely important when addressing people from countries outside the United States, where businesspeople are far more formal than most people in the United States.

5   Keep your promises.

6   Give sincere compliments.

7   Do not criticize others. If you are a supervisor and must reprimand an employee, do so in private only, and then with fairness and courtesy.

8   Apologize when an apology is due, but do not apologize unnecessarily or profusely.

9   Be especially considerate of newcomers or people alone, either in an office environment or at a party.

10   Do not smoke without obtaining permission of those around you. Even better, leave the room. (Many smokers now choose to smoke only in their own homes.)

11   Use care and discretion when giving gifts. Do not embarrass a co-worker who is not expecting a gift and may feel obliged to reciprocate. Make sure that any gift is impersonal and not extravagant. Provided it is wisely chosen, a gift is appropriate as a return for past favors or on a special occasion, such as a wedding or a retirement.

12   Write personal letters of congratulations, sympathy, offers to help, appreciation, and praise.

13   Dress appropriately for all occasions. If you are not sure of appropriate dress for a party or other occasion, ask the host or hostess.

14   Be punctual at meetings, at social gatherings, and at work. Do not keep visitors waiting.

15   Return telephone calls within 24 hours.

16   Answer important letters within three days, and answer all letters within two weeks or sooner. (Try to answer all letters within three days, even with only a note to say that a longer letter will follow.)

17   Shake hands firmly, graciously, and often.

18   Remember the table manners that you were taught at home.

Ann Marie Sabath, writing for *The Washington Times*, considers the following actions to be the most fatal business faux pas committed by both men and women in business today:

▶ Assuming that business associates want to be called by their first names.

▶ Sending out sloppy business letters.

▶ Being lax about keeping appointments.

▶ Lack of telephone courtesy.

▶ Smoking in the wrong places.

▶ Failing to put thank-you's in writing.

▶ Inviting out higher-ups socially before they have taken the initiative.

▶ Giving conflicting signals about who pays for a business meal.

▶ Talking only business at a function that is both business and social.[4]

Opening doors

Whoever arrives first, whether it is a man or a woman, should hold the door for those that follow. Exceptions are that the door should be held for customers or clients and assistance should be given to the disabled or handicapped. (Be careful not to give assistance to the disabled who obviously do not want assistance; some are proud of being able to open their own doors and to take care of themselves otherwise.)

Elevators

Postpone most conversations until after you leave the elevator. At the very least, speak softly.

Copy and Facsimile Machines

People copying a few sheets should have priority over those who have a time-consuming job.

Personal Space

(See Chapter 1 and Chapter 17.) Respect the space of co-workers. Excessive noise can be an intrusion of personal space; examples are loud telephone conversations and meetings held in passageways. Perhaps the worst intrusion of all is smoking in an area where co-workers can breathe the smoke.

Constant interruptions with questions, requests, personal matters, or gossip are an intrusion of another's space and time.

Hibernia employees gather informally in a small group.

The Telephone

Use of the telephone can build or destroy the goodwill of customers and co-workers. Brandon and Kleiner state:

> It is often necessary to place callers on hold. However, a caller should be asked rather than just thrown into a musical twilight zone. Try not to keep anyone on hold for more than 20 seconds, and always give the first call priority unless the second call is from overseas or an emergency. If you cannot be reached for some reason, return your calls promptly and as politely as possible. Failure to return calls is one of the most common telephone etiquette faults. Another commonly encountered etiquette problem involves the other party eating during a telephone conversation. Similarly, talking to others around you while engaged in a phone conversation is bad manners.[5]

INTERVIEWING FOR MANAGEMENT DECISIONS

This section briefly considers effective interviewing as it applies to management through communication. Employment interviews from the standpoint of the prospective employee are discussed in Chapter 11. Interviewing in order to obtain information is discussed in Chapter 13. Listening and nonverbal communication, both important parts of interviewing of any kind, are discussed in Chapter 1.

All aspects of communication discussed earlier in regard to written messages and forms of oral communication also apply to interviews, including empathy, a positive approach, and clearness.

Interviewing is used for various purposes in organizations of all kinds. Besides employment interviews and those done in primary research, there are performance appraisal interviews, settlements of disputes and grievances, counseling interviews, and orientation interviews. Exit interviews are used to learn why employees have resigned.

▶ PLANNING THE INTERVIEW

As with most other forms of communication, preliminary planning is helpful to the successful interview. The interviewer should obtain background information applicable to the situation, such as job requirements, activities, and opportunities.

The interviewer should review the applicant's resume and other available information in order to know as much about the interviewee as possible. When interviewing present employees, the interviewer should review personnel files and determine applicable details.

The purpose of the interview should be kept firmly in mind. In employment interviews, the obvious purpose is to determine whether the applicant is the wisest choice for the available position. Another purpose is to inspire confidence in the interviewer and in the employing organization, even if the interviewee is not chosen for the particular opening.

The physical environment should be made attractive, comfortable, and conducive to pleasant, relaxed conversation. Distractions should be avoided. The interviewer should not accept other visitors or telephone calls while the interview is in progress.

▶ PROCEEDING WITH THE INTERVIEW

The visitor should be made welcome and put at ease. The atmosphere should be one of confidence and trust. A relaxed, friendly approach is far more conducive to obtaining the necessary information and arriving at wise decisions than is an overly formal one or a harsh and threatening one.

Interviews may be structured or unstructured. Structured interviews follow a predetermined sequence of questions or comments. Unstructured interviews are less formal, and discussion proceeds naturally from one subject to another. Unstructured interviews are best for putting visitors at ease, and they are often more successful in encouraging open communication. Unstructured interviews should not be allowed to be too free-flowing and informal, however, or purposes of the interview will not be achieved.

As with other forms of communication, success is achieved through knowledge, skillful techniques of communication, and goodwill.

LEGAL AND ETHICAL CONSIDERATIONS

Laws that prohibit discrimination in employment do not prohibit employers from requesting personal data on applications. These laws do, however, prohibit discrimination itself. Questions about such topics as race and religion should be completely omitted, along with all other questions that are not related to the job the applicant seeks.

Topics to be avoided include race, color, religion, sex, credit rating, financial status, home ownership, length of residence at current address, past garnishment of wages, arrest and conviction records, membership in organizations, union membership, marital status, pregnancy and future childbearing plans, child care plans, Human Immune Virus, physical or mental handicaps not affecting job performance, citizenship status, availability for work on Friday evening, Saturday, or Sunday (all of which are religious holidays for some applicants), and native language. Mary Ellen Murray writes:

> Care must be taken, therefore, when writing help-wanted advertisements, recruitment letters, and questions to be asked during employment interviews. While few employers would include a dictum such as "No Catholics Need Apply" in a recruitment notice, many business persons may not realize that phrases such as "Recent College Graduate Wanted" or "Minorities Encouraged to Apply" could be deemed discriminatory. Statements evidencing favoritism toward certain groups may be considered exclusionary by nonfavored job seekers.[6]

The Occupational Safety and Health Act (OSHA) of 1970 states that employees must be warned orally or in writing of possible hazards in the workplace. Although the act does not apply to applicants for employment, from an ethical standpoint hazards of a serious nature should be pointed out to potential employees.

Under the Americans with Disabilities Act of 1990 (the ADA), an employer may ask disability-related questions and require medical examinations of an applicant only after the applicant has been given a conditional job offer, as discussed in the following stipulations from the U.S. Equal Employment Opportunity Commission:

> In the past, some employment applications and interviews requested information about an applicant's physical and/or mental condition. This information was often used to exclude applicants with disabilities before their ability to perform the job was even evaluated. . . .
>
> Employers *may* ask about an applicant's ability to perform specific job functions. For example, an employer may state the physical requirements of a job (such as the ability to lift a certain amount of weight or the ability to climb ladders) and ask if an applicant can satisfy these requirements.[7]

Employers should be extremely careful to avoid defamation of present or past employees. (Defamation is discussed in Chapter 4, "Choosing Appropriate and Effective Words.") Because of the possibility of being sued for defamation, some organizations and individuals include only factual, verifiable information in letters about employees, colleagues, or anyone else. Some organizations have adopted policies against dissemination of employment records to third parties.

Supervisors should keep detailed employee records, especially if the employee is likely to be reprimanded or discharged. The organization should provide employees a written statement about how records are kept and make sure that employees understand that they have a right to examine their records. Written reports of interviews or meetings with employees should be documented with dates and other supporting details.

PLANNING AND CONDUCTING MEETINGS AND CONFERENCES

The principles and techniques of speaking to a group apply to business meetings and conferences of all kinds, although the role of the leader of a meeting, at least in small groups, is likely to be less formal than that of a scheduled speaker. On the other hand, some conferences, as the word is ordinarily used, are quite formal, with strict time limits allowed for each participant.

▶ WHAT KINDS OF PLANNING SHOULD BE DONE?

The ultimate success or failure of any meeting or conference rests on the extent to which it has been planned. In some cases, preliminary planning may result in the decision that the meeting is unnecessary.

John Malmo discusses meetings in this way:

> Most people in any business spend more time in meetings than any other single work activity, and there are only two kinds of business meetings: costly and productive meetings and costly and unproductive meetings.
>
> There are no cheap ones.
>
> A two-hour meeting of five $50,000-a-year people, for instance, costs your company $312.50.... Such a meeting, therefore, should produce something of at least $312.50 value to the company, or it is an unprofitable meeting. . . .
>
> Yet, more meetings are unproductive than are productive for three reasons: because a meeting was held prematurely, because a meeting was called to do something for which meetings are inef-

ficient, or, most frequently, because there was inadequate or no planning. . . .[8]

Preparation must be made in several major areas, including the choice of persons who will attend; speakers, if any; the room; sound or visual equipment; other physical facilities; and the program or agenda. Speakers should be furnished this information in time for them to plan their own presentations.

An *agenda* is a plan of the flow of business or discussion. As the one most familiar with all the concerns and issues, the leader of the group writes the agenda. The leader must make a value judgment as to the relative importance of the various items and arrange these items on the agenda from the most important to the least important. Because participants' minds are fresh at the beginning of the meeting, important items should be considered first, after routine activities such as reading the minutes and, if customary, committee or officers' reports.

Dianna Booher states:

> Set an agenda. Some people think that agendas lend too much structure to a meeting, that they prevent people from being spontaneous, and that they make the atmosphere too formal. Nonsense. That's like saying that if you plan for a vacation by packing the right clothes, arranging for transportation, and deciding on a destination, then you can't relax and be spontaneous along the way.[9]

The leader should attempt to estimate and allocate the length of time necessary for discussing each item on the agenda. If no time limit is imposed, some group members will continue talking endlessly, leaving little time for following items on the agenda.

Once the leader has prepared the agenda, it should be copied and made available to all members of the group several days before the time of the meeting. In this way, members will know the topics to be discussed and can come prepared to present ideas. Many organizations include all materials that will be covered at the meeting, such as budgets or lengthy reports, with the distribution of the agenda. This procedure provides members with time to consider the material and to make decisions.

Agendas are unnecessary for some small, informal meetings, but the leader should have planned the order of business and made notes to himself or herself to make sure that the procedure does not become disorganized. The lack of preparation by the leader is the most important reason for nonproductive meetings. Some semblance of order and formality must be maintained to avoid wasting time and to ensure that all matters that need to be discussed by the group will receive recognition.

Before the meeting, the leader should arrange for the secretary or some other person to take the minutes and to transcribe them or have them transcribed. These minutes should be copied and distributed to group members within a few days after the meeting.

A typical agenda follows:

1 Call to order.

2 Roll call. (This is often omitted, especially in large groups.)

3 Determination of a quorum. (A quorum is the number of members legally able to conduct business; it usually consists of the majority of the group. A quorum is necessary when a vote is to be taken.)

4 Reading and approval of minutes of last meeting. (A written copy of the minutes may be distributed with the agenda in order to save time and confusion.)

5 Reports of officers and committee chairpersons.

Interviewees should be made comfortable and welcome.

6   Unfinished business. (The leader should list on the agenda the items of unfinished business, with necessary details, from the most important to the least important. Supporting materials, if needed, should be distributed with the agenda. The group should also be asked whether there are additional items of unfinished business that should be considered.)

7   New business. (The leader should list on the agenda the items of new business to be discussed, and supporting materials should be included with the agenda. The items of new business should be listed in order of descending importance. Before leaving the new business section of the meeting, the leader should ask the group if they wish to bring up any additional items of new business.)

8   Announcements.

9   Adjournment.

WHEN AND WHERE SHOULD MEETINGS BE SCHEDULED?

Find the most favorable time and place possible to schedule meetings. Late afternoon is not good because workers will be tired and eager to go home. Do not plan a late-afternoon meeting that may run past closing time. Although few meetings should run longer than their allotted time, at times discussion, added information, or importance of the question being considered warrants additional time.

Mondays and Fridays are not ideal choices for meeting days. Friday afternoon is probably the worst time of all.

The meeting room should be attractive and comfortable. Conference tables are a wise choice for a small group. Round tables encourage participants to communicate with all others in the group; participants are less likely to form into subgroups, as they may do at a long, narrow table. If the group is too large to sit around a conference table, try to find a room that is an appropriate size for the group, one that is spacious enough for comfort but not an oversized one that encourages members to cluster in small groups scattered around the room. In addition, a too-large room is not ideal for eye contact or for hearing the words of the speaker or other group members.

HOW SHOULD THE MEETING BE CONDUCTED?

The leader must be prepared. The leader has the responsibility of keeping the meeting on schedule while at the same time encouraging all members to ask questions or to participate in some other way.

The person who chairs the meeting must assume control without being autocratic, even when one or more "listeners" tend to dominate the conversation or to express their opinions at the expense of others who want to comment. Although such occurrences are rare in organizations with clear, open, and honest communication systems, they do occur. In fairness to the

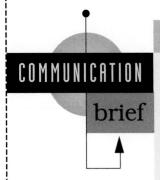

Participation will have different styles of contribution depending as much on individual personalities as on nationality. The following examples are extremely stereotypical. . . .

German style is to be well-prepared and to contribute only when they feel well-qualified to so and when they have something useful to say. They will not expect to be interrupted or immediately contradicted, and they regard their prepared positions as incontrovertible.

French contributions tend to be adversarial, dogmatic, and models of rationality.

Italian contributions tend to be innovative, complex, creative, and usually stimulating. They are embellished with definitions, caveats, analogies, allusions, and asides and are, in the opinion of the rigorously pragmatic, not always relevant.

British contributions tend to be pragmatic and realistic. . . . Their predeliction for humor may relieve tense or tedious moments, but it can also be regarded as trivializing. They are the least likely to lose interest or temper.

The Dutch have a similar approach to the British . . . using humor to defuse conflict and tedium. Their contribution will be brutally frank.

Spaniards tend not to risk embarrassment or discomfiture by saying anything that might be criticized for any reason ranging from a poor command of the language to the actual content.

John Mole, *When in Rome* (New York: Amacom, American Management Society, 1991), 191–192.

chairperson and to the other members of the group, communication must be shared. Individuals who "hog the floor" should be politely muzzled.

If the leader has proved by words and actions that he or she is knowledgeable and worthy of trust, the meeting is likely to be successful. Even so, skillfully and diplomatically following the agenda is necessary in order to make worthwhile the time that participants spend together.

Occasionally a participant may dogmatically refuse to support your point of view even when everyone else does. Thank the individual for his or her opinion and for expressing it so well and at such great length. Then move on to the next topic or item on the agenda. Do not by words or nonverbal communication show that you are annoyed. Never show anger or annoyance. (Not all business meetings are rose gardens.)

When you chair a meeting, you are the leader until the meeting is over, even if people in higher positions are in the audience. Quietly maintain this leadership without being dictatorial or autocratic.

WHAT ARE THE RESPONSIBILITIES OF ATTENDEES OF MEETINGS?

As is true for the leader, the major responsibility of group members is to be prepared. Consider the agenda and read all supporting materials that have been provided before the meeting. Review the minutes of the previous meeting. Think through the questions to be discussed and complete any needed research.

According to John Malmo, "The person who comes to the meeting with the best preparation is most likely to sway the group. There's an old adage, 'The guy with slides wins.' "[10]

During the meeting, your responsibility is to contribute when you have something to say. You will have valuable contributions if you are thoroughly prepared.

Dianna Booher offers this advice to attendees and to leaders:

> Take your seat with forethought. Choose seating arrangements as you choose your meeting site. Where you sit makes a great deal of difference in how you interact with others and how they interact with you.
>
> Studies show that people seated across the table from each other tend to communicate more than those seated to the left or right of each other. The across-the-table communication, however, may be adversarial rather than supportive.
>
> Take your body with you. Appearances and posture count, even when you're in an informal meeting, seated around a table. Yes, rolled-up sleeves, an open collar, and stocking feet may be the attire for a "working meeting," but that's not always the attitude you want to convey. Someone who's "laid back" (in other words, is sprawling in his or her chair, with loose papers scattered around, ruffled hair, and hands playing with trinkets and toys) conveys an informal look—and a disorganized mind and agenda.[11]

Jacqueline Dunckel makes these observations:

▶ If the seating is at a rectangular table, the chair sits at the end of the table farthest from the entrance to the room. The seats on either side of the chair are for senior management and honored guests.

▶ The most desirable seats are those near senior officials.

▶ The least desirable seat is opposite the chair because you will get the full attention of the chair. If you are placed there, stay alert and interested.

▶ Watch that you don't sit in segregated sexes or all one department together unless you are making a joint presentation.[12]

WHAT DO MEETINGS ACCOMPLISH?

Meetings, conferences, workshops, seminars, and even parties can increase employee morale. Meetings provide a communication medium by bringing face-to-face a group of people who have common interests and problems.

Meetings can result in wiser decisions by drawing on the combined wisdom and experience of many, thus avoiding hasty, unwise judgments. A disadvantage of a group decision is that it may result from what is known as *groupthink*, the tendency for members to go along with what seems to be the consensus of the group instead of relying on individual experience and judgment. Another obvious disadvantage is that group decisions are often slower than individually made ones.

Meetings can help to improve or modify the attitudes of participants as they gain understanding and insights by hearing the viewpoints of others. On the other hand, this accepting of others' opinions can be a form of groupthink.

Meetings can help develop a more willing acceptance of change. Participants will be even more willing to accept change if they have had a part in bringing it about.

HOW IMPORTANT IS PARLIAMENTARY PROCEDURE?

Parliamentary procedure is a set of rules used to structure and control the conduct of a meeting. The guide that is best known is *Robert's Rules of Order*, which was written near the end of the last century by General Henry M. Robert, a U.S. Army officer. It has been revised many times since and is considered the authority for parliamentary procedure in the majority of organizations throughout the United States and Canada, as well as in other parts of the world. An even earlier guide was a manual written by Thomas Jefferson when he was presiding over the United States Senate.

The purpose of guides to parliamentary procedure is to provide an orderly system for achieving the goals of a meeting and to protect the rights of all group members. Rules, whether or not they are based on *Robert's Rules of Order*, are "law" only when group members adopt them. Many organizations, however, specify in their bylaws that meetings will be conducted according to Robert's.

Some informal meetings are not conducted according to customary guidelines; to do so is unnecessary. Others would be more democratic and productive if a standard method of parliamentary procedure were followed to the letter.

Space available in this book does not permit a complete discussion of parliamentary procedure. Before you participate in formal meetings, however, read more complete guides, including *Robert's Rules of Order*. Your confidence will be greatly increased.

VIDEOCONFERENCING AND TELEVISION APPEARANCES

The high cost of travel and the need for immediate spoken communication has made videoconferencing a desirable choice for some meetings. (See Chapter 3.) In addition, many people in business and the professions are interviewed on television or participate in panel discussions on local or national programs.

Sue Potton, U.K./North American sales manager for the Queen Elizabeth II Conference in London, provides the following advice:

> Choose your clothes carefully. Bright tones and patterns will come across more intensely on the screen. Worse, the TV may not show true colors: greens can turn a sickly blue and reds often change into a garish orange. It's much better to stick with a neutral suit in navy or gray, accented by a pale blue shirt or a solid-colored silk blouse. Women should shy away from dangling jewelry; simple, bold pieces work best in this medium.
>
> Watch make-up and personal grooming. On the video screen, blush that gives a dewey glow in regular lighting can look like it was spackled on by Bozo the clown. . . .
>
> Watch expressions and nervous habits. The bored expression, the wrinkled nose, the smirk, and the stifled giggle may go unnoticed in regular meetings. On camera, they're not only magnified but often transmitted to a much wider audience. The same goes for gestures, such as chewing on a pencil or the stems of eyeglasses. . . .[13]

Although dining etiquette is not the only type of etiquette business employees should be aware of, correct table etiquette conveys a positive image about you and the company you are representing.

CUTTING THE COSTS OF COMMUNICATION

Business communications, both within and from the organization, are expensive. Their cost has been increasing for many years and is expected to continue to do so. Companies have instituted programs to study the various items of expense and have taken steps to simplify and improve their entire communication systems.

Some progress has been made toward achieving economy, largely as a result of the recognition that it is possible to reduce costs and still maintain an effective, goodwill-building system of communication. Costs have been cut by the installation of automated processes of transcription, reproduction, and mailing, voice mail, e-mail, and numerous other technological innovations, as discussed in Chapter 3. Nevertheless, as has been proved over and over, newer methods and media of communication, along with older ones, will not be cost-effective unless they are wisely planned and managed.

Because of intensive training programs in business writing, within organizations and through courses in colleges and universities, many businesspeople now write more efficiently than writers did a number of years ago. Letters have been improved from the standpoint of economy because, on the average, they are shorter than they were in previous years. This decrease in length usually is accomplished by eliminating wordy, trite phrases and unnecessary repetition, so that the letter is not only more economically worded but also more interesting and readable. The use of e-mail has also cut the cost of written communication.

When we work to achieve economy, we must not lose sight of the fact that our efforts to economize are unwise if they lower the quality of communications. A poor letter, memorandum, or e-mail message hastily written in order to save time is no bargain at all if it requires further communication to explain what should have been included in the first one, or if the message does not build or maintain the goodwill of the reader. A serious effort to improve communication will result not only in more economical methods, but also in better-quality communications.

A LOOK AHEAD

Your knowledge of the basic principles of communication—and your ability to apply this knowledge—will be a valuable asset to you throughout your career. Your career is likely to change, whatever your current specialization.

Larry D. Lauer, associate vice chancellor of Texas Christian University, sees the need for what he refers to as "integrated communicators," as reported below:

> What kind of communicator will best meet the needs of tomorrow's more aggressive and complex business environment? . . .
>
> Most academic programs today are not doing an adequate job of educating integrated communicators. Most business schools still teach marketing with little offered about advertising, less about public relations, and not enough in liberal arts and writing skills. . . . Those who aspire to communication management and leadership will need to have a different, broader view of their work.
>
> The designer and manager of integrated communication will need a solid and broad education.[14]

Workers not only change jobs and move from company to company but also change their entire professional fields. What you are learning to do in your area of specialization may be obsolete long before you are of retirement age. But wherever you go and whatever you do, nothing will be of more importance to you than relationships with other people—and these relationships are built through communication.

Continue to study communication and to build your skills in writing and speaking and in receiving the messages of other people. The more you learn of the English language, the more interesting it will become to you. In addition, because the study of communication is an interdisciplinary one, it will enable you to grow and adapt to many employment opportunities. At least one thing in this uncertain world is certain—change.

If possible, in addition to the English language, learn one or more other languages. You are almost certain to be working with people who speak English as a second language, or perhaps those who speak no English at all.

Experiment with different kinds of writing, including poetry, essays, short stories, or even novels. Write to the "Letters to the Editor" column; your opinion needs to be read.

If you are able to do so, buy a personal computer, word processing software, and a printer. Because you can compose directly at the keyboard and revise without retyping, writing will be fun, not work.

Most important of all, enjoy your creative ability as it is expressed in writing. Enjoy your pleasant relationships with other people because of your written and spoken words.

Best wishes to all of you.

S U M M A R Y

As a matter of principle and in order to survive, organizations must work for high quality in products, service, and relationships with personnel. Striving for excellence in all aspects of professional and personal life is one facet of ethics.

Etiquette in business is similar to etiquette in personal life; both are based on consideration for others. Etiquette, like striving for quality, is also related to ethics.

Management interviews should be planned. Interviews with employment applicants or with current employees must not violate laws against discrimination in hiring or in management.

Successful meetings and conferences depend on planning, including an agenda, skillful conducting of the meeting, and cooperation by the participants. Following accepted conventions of parliamentary procedure improves the democratic process and speeds the flow of the meeting.

The costs of communication can be decreased by efficient personnel, proper equipment, materials, and procedures, and an analysis of organizational needs in order to eliminate or decrease the number of communications.

TEST YOURSELF
chapter content

1 Name five purposes of interviews.
2 Describe structured and unstructured interviews.
3 What are four advantages of business meetings?
4 What are two disadvantages of business meetings?
5 What is an agenda?
6 What is the name of the best-known guide to parliamentary procedure?
7 What is defamation?
8 Name three ways of cutting the costs of communication.
9 Give three suggestions for successful television appearances.
10 Name two things that can go wrong in a meeting you are chairing.

TEST YOURSELF
correct usage

(Related to Chapter 18 and Appendix D, including word choice, commonly misused or misspelled words, and the correct forms of verbs and pronouns.) Make all necessary corrections.

1 Concern about behavior and customs are understandable when an executive is making plans for his time away from his native country.
2 Etiquette—speech and behavior that is considered polite and proper—differ according to the situation and according to the particular culture.
3 The chairperson pointed out the desirability of parliamentary procedure to my secretary and I before she and I prepared the agenda.

4   The word agenda, which comes from Latin, was originally used as a plural noun, but it's use now is singular.

5   One criteria is that participants contribute ideas.

6   The chairman inferred that Joan and me were talking too long; I thought it was alright to keep on talking as long as everybody kept their own thoughts to themselves.

7   Good communication through effective meetings improves the moral of all concerned personnel.

8   A too-long meeting can adversely effect comprehension.

9   In addition to the topics listed on the agenda, the leader should plan the procedure to follow in order to stay within time limits.

10   The president wrote a letter of congratulations to my secretary and I because of our cost cutting ideas.

PROBLEMS

1   Examine *Robert's Rules of Order* or another recognized authority on parliamentary procedure. Write a one- or two-page memorandum to your instructor, summarizing your findings.

2   Plan a short oral report to present to the class about one item you found in *Robert's Rules of Order* or another authority on parliamentary procedure.

3   Write a memorandum to your instructor and to other class members describing a meeting you have attended.

Evaluate this meeting according to recommendations for successful meetings included in this chapter.

THINK-IT-THROUGH ASSIGNMENT AND WORKING IN GROUPS

Note to students and teachers: The following problems, with modifications, are also appropriate to use with Chapter 13, which is on the subject of obtaining information for research reports. They are also applicable to Chapter 16, which applies to public speaking.

4   Meet in groups of four or five (or as directed by your instructor). Plan as a group for each

member to interview one businessperson and one professor. (No person should be interviewed by more than one student.) What do you want to find out? One possibility is to determine the approximate number and length of meetings that the interviewee conducts or attends. (Unless your instructor directs otherwise, the subject of your interview may be any aspect of communication presented in this textbook or discussed in class.)

What questions will you ask? All members of your group should plan to ask the same questions in approximately the same way; draw up a list, which should be only a guide. The interview should not be of the kind that merely asks the interviewee to answer *yes* or *no*, but basically the same information should be obtained by each member of the group.

Obtain the permission of the people you plan to interview and make appointments. Try to keep each interview to no more than 15 minutes.

5 After all interviews have been completed, meet with members of your group. Combine notes. Summarize. Prepare a memorandum to your instructor and to the entire class. Plan a panel presentation to be given to the entire class; your group should select a panel leader. Make photocopies for the entire class, to be distributed after your panel discussion.

6 Assume that your panel presentation is being televised, as discussed in this Chapter. Ask someone to videotape the session. Ask that it be played back—if you dare.

ENDNOTES

1 "The Quest for Quality," *The Royal Bank Letter*, The Royal Bank of Canada, November–December, 1988, 3–4.

2 Cecily Raiborn and Dinah Payne, "TQM: Just What the Ethicist Ordered," *Journal of Business Ethics*, September 1996, 963–972.

3 Letitia Baldrige, *Letitia Baldrige's Complete Guide to Executive Manners* (New York: Rawson Associates, 1985), 3.

4 Ann Marie Sabath, "Profit from These Tips on Conduct," *The Washington Times*, April 23, 1991, F2.

5 Neil Brandon and Brian H. Kleiner, "Etiquette for Managers," *Agency Sales Magazine*, April 1994, 36.

6 Mary Ellen Murray, "A Comparison of the Perceptions of Business Law Instructors and Business Communication Instructors Concerning the Emphasis to Be Given Selected Federal Legislation in the Undergraduate Business Communication Course." Unpublished dissertation, Memphis State University, 1990, 28.

7 "ADA Enforcement Guidance: Pre-employment Disability-Related Questions and Medical Examinations," U.S. Equal Employment Opportunity Commission, Washington, DC (no date)

8 John Malmo, "Before Calling a Meeting, Plan; Then Invite Only Essential People," *The Commercial Appeal [Memphis]*, June 9, 1996, C4.

9 Dianna Booher, "Holding Your Own in Meetings," *Training and Development*, August 1994, 54.

10 Malmo, "Before Calling a Meeting," C4.

11 Booher, "Holding Your Own," 54.

12 Jacqueline Dunckel, *Business Etiquette* (North Vancouver, British Columbia: Self-Counsel Press, 1992), 30.

13 Sue Potton, "Videoconferencing Etiquette," *Meetings & Conventions*, November 1995.

14 Larry D. Lauer, "Integrated Communication? Business Communication," *Communication World*, August 1995, 26.

Appendix A

The Appearance and Format of Business Letters

The overall appearance of a letter, memorandum, or report affects the reception of the intended message. If a reader's attention is drawn to obvious corrections, poor centering, or an unusual arrangement rather than to the words themselves, the intended meaning is delayed, distorted, or incomplete.

An even greater disadvantage of an unattractive communication is that of discourtesy to the reader, as if the writer does not care enough to make sure that the message is sent out in perfect form, with clear, crisp type, on high-quality stationery in a matching envelope.

CHOOSING ATTRACTIVE, APPROPRIATE STATIONERY

Stationery is important to the image of the organization and the writer from which a letter comes. Buying less than the best quality, as is true with many other purchases, is not economical. Less expensive paper may be costly from the standpoint of the image that you and your company project to your readers.

The most frequently used size of sheets of business stationery is $8\frac{1}{2}$ by 11 inches. Choose this size for general use throughout the organization. A size described as Monarch, $7\frac{1}{4}$ by $10\frac{1}{2}$ inches, is used by some executives. Monarch is also appropriate for personal stationery, whether or not it is personalized with the writer's name and address.

In addition to size, paper is classified by weight. For most business writing, prefer 20-pound weight; never use a lighter weight than 16-pound. Paper also comes in 24-pound weight, which is sometimes used by executives, perhaps in the Monarch size. Paper heavier than 20-pound is not the best choice for general use because it increases postage costs. It is hard to fold and more expensive to buy.

Look for a watermark on stationery that you buy for your organization or for personal use. Although a watermark does not guarantee top-quality paper, its absence is an indication that the paper is not intended for correspondence.

A further classification of paper is by cotton content, which is frequently 25 percent. Paper with no cotton content is likely to be unsuitable for letterhead stationery, although it has other uses, including photocopying. (Photocopies can be and often are run on bond paper, but at additional cost.)

White remains the most widely used color of business stationery, although light pastels—such as ivory, cream, or buff—may also be used. The choice of color, like the design of a letterhead, depends a great deal on the particular kind of organization. A company that wishes to be considered conservative and traditional would most likely choose white or off-white stationery. A florist might use a pastel, even pink or yellow, with pictures of flowers on the letterhead.

CHOOSING THE MOST APPROPRIATE AND EFFICIENT LETTER STYLE

The choice of letter style is important from the standpoints of appearance and efficiency. Letter styles convey different impressions of the company or of the writer.

Companies wishing to project a conservative image ordinarily prefer either the full block or the modified block. Other considerations that apply to choosing a letter style are described in the letters used to illustrate the various styles. The full-block style is the one most frequently used in the United States.

WRITING PERSONAL BUSINESS LETTERS

Personal business letters are letters from an individual about personal business matters, not letters from a representative of an organization. Personal business letters are written on personal stationery or plain paper.

Never write personal business letters on printed letterhead stationery of the employing organization. Doing so implies that you represent the organization by whatever you say in the letter.

The application letters and other letters about employment illustrated in Chapter 11 are examples of personal business letters. An example of a personal business letter is shown in Figure A-7.

The letter shown in Figure A-7 is arranged in the modified-block style, but personal business letters may be correctly arranged in any other of the styles shown in this appendix, Figures A-1 through A-6. The return address, if not printed on personalized stationery, is typewritten immediately above the date, as shown below:

5290 Sonata Court
Oklahoma City, OK 73130
June 27, 1998

■ **THE UNIVERSITY OF MEMPHIS** ■

THE FOGELMAN COLLEGE OF BUSINESS AND ECONOMICS
Memphis, Tennessee 38152

December 18, 19—

Mr. Joe Galloway, Office Manager
Countrywide Insurance Company
5983 Maplewood Cove
Memphis, TN 38117-6714

Dear Mr. Galloway:

As you requested, I am sending you a group of letters that illustrate various letter styles. I am glad to help you in this way in the preparation of your new correspondence handbook. You are wise to pick one particular arrangement to be used by all offices and departments.

This letter illustrates the semiblock style. This arrangement is also called the modified block with indented paragraphs.

When referring to letter styles, remember that terminoloy differs, but the basic formats are standard.

This old and rather conservative arrangement would be appropriate for use at your insurance company, but I do not enthusiastically recommend it. Although the paragraph indentions effectively separate the paragraphs, they are not really necessary, for there is always a blank line space between paragraphs. This letter is less efficient than one with no indentions.

Sincerely,

Binford H. Peeples

Binford H. Peeples
Professor

ns

FIGURE A-1
The semiblock style (also described as the modified block with indented paragraphs)

■ THE UNIVERSITY OF MEMPHIS ■

THE FOGELMAN COLLEGE OF BUSINESS AND ECONOMICS
Memphis, Tennessee 38152

December 18, 19——

Mr. Joe Galloway, Office Manager
Countrywide Insurance Company
5983 Maplewood Cove
Memphis, TN 38117-6714

Dear Mr. Galloway:

This letter illustrates the modified-block letter, which is also described as the modified block with blocked paragraphs. In addition, it is described simply as the block, or the blocked.

If you should decide to adopt this style, or the semiblock shown in the preceding letter, I believe that you should recommend that the date and the closing lines begin at the center—that they not be backspaced from the margin point. Although they often are placed by the backspace method, beginning them at the center or near the center is quicker and just as correct and attractive.

In all the letters shown so far, "standard" punctuation has been used. This term refers only to the colon after the salutation and the comma after the complimentary close. The "open" style will be shown in the next letter, the full block. In open punctuation the colon and the comma are omitted. Either style of punctuation can be correctly used with any letter style.

As you may have decided by now, there is no exact answer as to the best letter style for every office and every situation.

Sincerely,

Binford H. Peeples

Binford H. Peeples
Professor

ns

FIGURE A-2
The modified-block style

■ THE UNIVERSITY OF MEMPHIS ■

THE FOGELMAN COLLEGE OF BUSINESS AND ECONOMICS
Memphis, Tennessee 38152

December 18, 19———

Mr. Joe Galloway, Office Manager
Countrywide Insurance Company
5983 Maplewood Cove
Memphis, TN 38117-6714

Dear Mr. Galloway

This letter illustrates the use of the full-block style. Because of the efficiency with which this letter can be keyboarded, its use is growing in popularity.

Some persons object to this arrangement because everything is at the left; they believe that the date and the closing lines should be centered or backspaced from the right margin in order to give balance to the letter. Other persons prefer the crisp, businesslike appearance of the full-block style.

Notice that the open style of punctuation is used in this letter. Although open punctuation (no punctuation after the salutation or complimentary close) is not an essential characteristic of the full-block arrangement, the two styles are often used together.

You will notice that the simplified letter, shown next in this series, is a modification of the full-block style.

Another modification is simply to omit the salutation and the complimentary close; this arrangement is especially appropriate when writing to a company or organization when you do not have the name of the reader.

Sincerely

Binford H. Peeples

Binford H. Peeples, Professor

ns

FIGURE A-3

The full-block style with open punctuation. The full-block style does not require open punctuation; standard punctuation may be used

■ **THE UNIVERSITY OF MEMPHIS** ■

THE FOGELMAN COLLEGE OF BUSINESS AND ECONOMICS
Memphis, Tennessee 38152

December 18, 19——

Mr. Joe Galloway, Office Manager
Countrywide Insurance Company
5983 Maplewood Cove
Memphis, TN 38117-6714

THE SIMPLIFIED LETTER

Mr. Galloway, do you like this letter style? It has several advantages, but possibly some disadvantages, too.

It is the easiest letter to set up and type. In addition, it has a businesslike, no-nonsense look about it. A subject line, which can be used in any letter style, is always included in the simplified style.

Some readers feel that this letter arrangement is unfriendly and impersonal because the customary salutation and complimentary close are omitted. These lines are unnecessary, though, for if the letter is written as it should be, the reader will believe and understand that it is "sincere," "cordial," and "very truly yours."

Perhaps you will choose this letter to be the standard one for your office. If not, I think full-block would be a good choice. Either the semiblock or the modified block could be your standard arrangement, if you prefer their appearance—but your secretaries will lose some time in setting them up.

Binford H. Peeples

BINFORD H. PEEPLES, PROFESSOR

ns

FIGURE A-4
The simplified style

■ SCHRODER MUSIC COMPANY ■

2027 Parker Street, Berkeley, California 94704
Telephone: 415-843-2365

June 4, 19——

Business Forms, Inc.
1212 Union Avenue
Los Angeles, CA 90032

Please rush more forms to replace those that were delivered yesterday to the address shown above. A copy of your invoice No. 13705 is enclosed.

At the time of delivery, it was not possible to tell that the forms were improperly printed. When they were tested in a trial run on the computer, however, it was evident that the forms varied considerably.

Changes that should be made are shown on the enclosed sheet of specifications, which is a copy of the sheet sent with the original order.

I am aware that errors like this will happen in spite of precautions, and I am confident that you will take care of the exchange with your usual efficiency.

Because we need the forms by the end of next week in order to print lengthy reports, please have the replacement shipment here by that time. In addition, please let me know what I should do with the improperly printed forms.

John Cotton

John Cotton

rt

Enclosures: copy of invoice
                specification sheet

FIGURE A-5
Functional style

■ SCHRODER MUSIC COMPANY ■

2027 Parker Street, Berkeley, California 94704
Telephone 415-843-2365

June 4, 19——

Business Forms, Inc.
1212 Union Avenue
Los Angeles, CA 90032

REQUEST FOR REPLACEMENT SHIPMENT OF FORMS, INVOICE NO. 13705

Please rush more forms to replace those that were delivered yesterday to the address shown above. A copy of your invoice No. 13705 is enclosed.

At the time of delivery, it was not possible to tell that the forms were improperly printed. When they were tested in a trial run on the computer, however, it was evident that the forms varied considerably.

Changes that should be made are shown on the enclosed sheet of specifications, which is a copy of the sheet sent with the original order.

I am aware that errors like this will happen in spite of precautions, and I am confident that you will take care of the exchange with your usual efficiency.

Because we need the forms by the end of next week in order to print lengthy reports, please have the replacement here by that time. In addition, please let me know what I should do with the improperly printed forms.

John Cotton

John Cotton

rt

Enclosures: copy of invoice
            specification sheet

FIGURE A-6
Functional style with subject line

2580 Canyon Street
San Diego, CA 92064
October 16, 19——

Mr. Robert Kothenbeutel
Director of Human Resources Management
State Department of Education
Andrew Jackson State Office Building
Nashville, TN 37423

Dear Mr. Kothenbeutel:

Will you help me find a lost friend who once worked in your department?

Her name when she worked there was Sandra Bryant Lee. I have heard that since that time, which was approximately 1987 to 1989, she has remarried. I do not know whether she has changed her name, or if so, what her name is now.

I realize that you may have policy restrictions that prevent you from providing information about past employees, but can you send me her present address or her telephone number? If you wish, you may contact her and ask her to get in touch with me at the address shown above or by telephone at 619-000-0000.

She and I once made a recording of a song that she wrote. This recording was never released, but now I have found a publisher and need her approval.

I will appreciate any help that you can provide. You can reach me at the number shown above any morning before eleven. Please call collect.

Sincerely,

Alison Gray

Alison Gray

FIGURE A-7
Personal business letter arranged in the modified-block style

ARRANGING THE USUAL AND SPECIAL PARTS OF THE LETTER

With the exception of the simplified style and the functional style, business letters will almost always contain (besides the body of the letter) the following parts:

- letterhead
- date
- inside address
- salutation
- complimentary closing
- signer's name and title
- typist's initials, referred to as reference initials

Other lines used on many letters, as desirable or required, are the following:

- attention line
- subject line
- typewritten company name preceding name of writer
- enclosure notation
- copy notation, formerly referred to as the carbon copy notation
- postscript

The simplified and functional styles omit the salutation and complimentary close, as illustrated in Figures A-4 and A-5.

LETTERHEAD

Letters coming from a business office, written by a company representative about matters concerning the company, should be typewritten on printed letterhead stationery. The choice of letterhead is important to the overall appearance of company correspondence. It should include all needed information, including the company name, address, and telephone number. If the company name does not specifically indicate the type of business, this information should be made clear by additional descriptive lines.

The complete letterhead should fit within the top two inches (12 vertical lines) of the sheet. A deeper letterhead will leave too little space for the letter itself, causing a crowded appearance for long letters or increasing the number of two-page letters.

Ordinarily the left side of letterhead stationery should be left blank. Like a too-deep letterhead, printing at the side decreases the amount of space available for letters and may result in unattractive centering.

DATE

The date is ordinarily set up in this way: November 18, 1998. Do not abbreviate the month. Do not use an abbreviated form, such as 11-18-98. Another form that is increasing in use is this: 18 November 1998. All letters, like all other written messages, should be dated. The date is ordinarily placed on about line 14 or 15 from the top, a position that is about two spaces below a two-inch letterhead.

INSIDE ADDRESS

The name, title, and complete mailing address make up the part of the letter described as the inside address. The individual's name should be preceded by a courtesy title except in the rare instances when the writer cannot determine whether the addressee is male or female.

Examples of inside addresses are shown here:

Ms. Ruth Billings
Apartment 17-B
1187 Oak Lane
Yonkers, NY 10028-7980

Mr. Bill Bond, CPA
95 State Street
Camden, NJ 08108-2211

Lee Brown, M.D.
1068 Cresthaven
Provo, UT 84604

Inside addresses should be single spaced, like the rest of the letter.

SALUTATION

Salutations for the preceding inside addresses are these:

Dear Ms. Billings:
Dear Mr. Bond:
Dear Dr. Brown: (or Dear Doctor Brown:)

If you use the reader's first name in conversation, your salutation should also do so, as shown below:

Dear Ruth:
Dear Bill:
Dear Lee:

Be extremely cautious with the use of the reader's first name. Do not use it to address a person you do not know or one who could possibly be offended by such familiarity. Readers in Europe, more so than in the United States, are likely to be offended.

The salutation is followed by a colon, not a comma. *Omit the colon only if you also omit the comma after the complimentary close.* This style is referred to as open punctuation; its use is infrequent.

COMPLIMENTARY CLOSING (OR COMPLIMENTARY CLOSE)

Always use a complimentary closing when you use a salutation; omit it when you omit a salutation, as illustrated in Figures A-4 and A-5.

Frequently used complimentary closings are these:

Sincerely,
Sincerely yours,
Cordially,
Cordially yours,
Yours truly, Very truly yours,   [Often considered old-fashioned]

SIGNER'S NAME AND TITLE

The writer's name and title may be placed on the same line or on separate lines. For example:

Mary Holt, President

or

Mary Holt
President

A man should *never* use the courtesy title of *Mr.* with his name (writer's identification) or with his signature. A woman, however, may precede her printed name (not her signature) with a courtesy title in order to let the reader know how to address her in a responding letter. (In a letter addressed to a woman, use *Ms.* as the courtesy title if you do not know her preferred courtesy title.)

TYPIST'S INITIALS (REFERENCE INITIALS)

The reference initials are usually placed at the left margin two lines (a double space) below the last line of the signature block. Ordinarily only the initials of the typist are listed. An illustration:

Cordially yours,

Wayne Johnson

Wayne Johnson, President

en

No reference initials are shown on letters composed and keyed by the signer of the letter.

ENCLOSURE NOTATION

The enclosure notation is used on each letter with which something is enclosed. Sometimes the word *attachment* is used instead to indicate an attachment, not an enclosure. The enclosure notation is placed one or two spaces below the reference initials.

COPY NOTATION

The copy notation is placed a double space below the enclosure notation unless the letter is running low on the sheet; if this is the case, the copy notation may be placed a single space below.

The copy notation may be arranged in one of the following ways or in other variations. The notation "cc" refers to carbon copies, which are now almost always replaced by photocopies or copies from a computer printer. Prefer to use *copy* or *copies.*

Copy to Mrs. Harriet Jenkins
Copies to Jenkins and Harris
Copies: Harriet Jenkins and Walter
         Harris

POSTSCRIPT

If you use a postscript, it should be the last item on the letter. The purpose of the postscript is to emphasize, not to include material that has been mistakenly omitted from the letter.

COMPANY NAME PRECEDING NAME OF WRITER

The company name, if used in the signature block, appears like this:

Sincerely yours,

SMITH MANUFACTURING COMPANY

Mary Duncan

Mary Duncan, Treasurer

Many organizations do not use the company name in the signature block. If the company name is included, it should be shown in all-capitals.

At least three blank lines should be left for the penwritten signature.

ATTENTION LINE

The attention line, when used, is usually placed a double space after the last line of the inside address and a double space before the salutation. It may also follow the company name.

Smith Manufacturing Company
2081 Hickory Ridge Road
Macon, GA 30567

Attention Sales Manager

Ladies and Gentlemen:

OR

Smith Manufacturing Company
Attention Sales Manager
2081 Hickory Ridge Road
Macon, GA 30567

Ladies and Gentlemen:

The use of the attention line is less desirable than addressing a letter to the sales manager, by name, if the name can be determined, as shown here:

Ms. Ann Barnes, Sales Manager
Smith Manufacturing Company
2081 Hickory Ridge Road
Macon, GA 30567

Dear Ms. Barnes:

When addressing a letter to an organization, as in the first example above, you may omit the salutation, along with the complimentary close, resulting in the functional letter style if all lines begin at the left margin.

SUBJECT LINE

The subject line, an expected part of the simplified letter style and all memorandums, may also be used in any other letter arrangement. Word a subject line with care so that it will describe specifically the most important contents of the letter. A subject line is not always desirable, especially when the letter involves bad news or another unpleasant subject.

The subject line is usually placed a double space below the salutation. If no salutation is used, the subject line is spaced a triple space below the last line of the inside address.

HEADING OF A MULTIPLE-PAGE LETTER

The heading of the second and following pages of a letter includes the first line of the inside address, the page number, and the date. The heading may be set up in one of three ways:

Mr. John D. Rich   2   February 18, 1998

Mr. John D. Rich
February 18, 1998
page 2

Mr. John D. Rich,   February 18, 1998, page 2

TWO-LETTER ABBREVIATIONS FOR STATES AND CANADIAN PROVINCES

TWO-LETTER ABBREVIATIONS FOR STATES
(AND GUAM, PUERTO RICO, U.S. VIRGIN ISLANDS, AND DISTRICT OF COLUMBIA)

State	Abbr.	State	Abbr.
Alabama	AL	Nebraska	NE
Alaska	AK	Nevada	NV
Arizona	AZ	New	
Arkansas	AR	Hampshire	NH
California	CA	New Jersey	NJ
Colorado	CO	New Mexico	NM
Connecticut	CT	New York	NY
Delaware	DE	North	
District of		Carolina	NC
Columbia	DC	North Dakota	ND
Florida	FL	Ohio	OH
Georgia	GA	Oklahoma	OK
Guam	GU	Oregon	OR
Hawaii	HI	Pennsylvania	PA
Idaho	ID	Puerto Rico	PR
Illinois	IL	Rhode Island	RI
Indiana	IN	South	
Iowa	IA	Carolina	SC
Kansas	KS	South Dakota	SD
Kentucky	KY	Tennessee	TN
Louisiana	LA	Texas	TX
Maine	ME	Utah	UT
Maryland	MD	Vermont	VT
Massachusetts	MA	Virginia	VA
Michigan	MI	Virgin Islands	VI
Minnesota	MN	Washington	WA
Mississippi	MS	West Virginia	WV
Missouri	MO	Wisconsin	WI
Montana	MT	Wyoming	WY

TWO-LETTER ABBREVIATIONS FOR CANADIAN PROVINCES

Province	Abbr.	Province	Abbr.
Alberta	AB	Nova Scotia	NS
British		Ontario	ON
Columbia	BC	Prince Edward	
Labrador	LB	Island	PE
Manitoba	MB	Quebec	PQ
New Brunswick	NB	Yukon Territory	YT
Newfoundland	NF		
Northwest			
Territories	NW		

CHOOSING AND ADDRESSING ENVELOPES

Envelopes should match exactly the letterhead stationery in quality, weight, finish, color, and printing. Large (No. 10) envelopes are used almost exclusively in business, although the smaller size (No. $6\frac{3}{4}$) is still available.

The traditional method of addressing envelopes, which is still widely used, is exactly the same as the inside address on the letter. For example:

Ms. Thelma Michalski
4630 Cooley Lake Road
Milford, MI 48042-1201

The U.S. Post Office, however, advocates a form of address shown in all capital letters without punctuation of any kind, as shown below. (The return address is shown similarly.)

ATTN SUSAN J CRANE
ABC INTERNATIONAL
123 ANYTOWN AVE RM 31
MARKSTOWN NY 10010-5104

The Post Office version seems impersonal and like a "computerized form letter" to many users, who continue to use the traditional method. If you adopt the Post Office method, at least replace the "ATTN" with "MS." If Susan Crane is to receive the letter, be courteous enough to address it to her. (Attention lines are unnecessary when you have the name of the person concerned.)

FOLDING AND INSERTING THE LETTER

Fold a standard-size of paper ($8\frac{1}{2} \times 11$) in this way: (1) Fold into approximate thirds, with the bottom of the page turned up and the top third turned down to approximately $\frac{1}{16}$-inch of the first fold. (2) Insert into the envelope so that when the letter is removed it is in the correct position to be read. The second fold will be at the bottom of the envelope and the open side will be facing the back.

EVALUATION SHEET: LETTER FORMAT

___ Yes ___ No   **1** Is the letter attractively centered on the sheet, with the date on approximately line 15 or two spaces below the letterhead?

___ Yes ___ No   **2** Is the date shown in full, NOT abbreviated?

___ Yes ___ No   **3** Is a courtesy title (*Mr., Mrs., Ms., Dr.,* and so on) shown on BOTH the inside address and the salutation?

___ Yes ___ No   **4** Is the letter single spaced, with an extra space left between paragraphs?

___ Yes ___ No   **5** Are all abbreviations omitted everywhere, except in courtesy titles or for a few other words, such as *Incorporated,* that are routinely abbreviated?

___ Yes ___ No   **6** Do most of the paragraphs start with some word other than *I* or *we*?

___ Yes ___ No   **7** Is the letter arranged in one of the widely used letter styles, not in a mixture of styles?

___ Yes ___ No   **8** Is the two-letter state abbreviation used in the inside address? Is this abbreviation followed by one space and the ZIP code?

___ Yes ___ No   **9** Are all paragraphs fairly short?

___ Yes ___ No   **10** Is the first paragraph no more than five lines? (Even a shorter one is better.)

Appendix B

Solutions to "Test Yourself: Correct Usage," Chapters 1–18

Chapter 1

1. We never know the effect our words will have on our listeners.

2. Spoken or written communication is affected by nonverbal signals.

3. A principal reason for poor listening is lack of interest in the subject being discussed.

4. A dog communicates nonverbally by wagging its tail.

5. Although nonverbal communication is expressive, we should not consider each gesture to have a definite meaning.

6. Regardless of the communication situation, some nonverbal communication will occur.

7. The study of nonverbal communication is not altogether scientific.

8. Effective communication within a corporation requires the cooperation of all personnel.

Chapter 2

1. Much of a company's communication efforts are directed toward building goodwill with its customers and increasing employee morale.

2. Informal oral communication within an organization includes face-to-face communication, telephone calls, and voice mail.

3. The United States Postal Service, which is the nation's largest civilian employer, delivers more than 160 billion pieces of mail annually.

4. Within an organization communication flows upward, downward, or horizontally; these communications are both oral and written. (*Note:* A period could be correctly used after *horizontally*, and a comma could be correctly inserted after *organization*.)

5. Three important management issues are these: intercultural communication, changing technology, and ethical considerations.

6. Although e-mail (or *E-mail*) is faster than "snail mail," it is less personal and private.

7. During the Civil War the word *grapevine* was used to describe tangled telegraph wires that resembled grapevines.

8. Written memorandums are used less often than formerly because of e-mail.

Chapter 3

1. Since telecommuting offers numerous advantages to both employers and employees, the number of telecommuters is expected to increase dramatically in the next few years.

2. Lincoln's Gettysburg Address, when analyzed by a computerized writing style checker, was described as weak in various ways.

3. Anything sent by e-mail can conceivably become public property; employees in all organizations should consider the content of a message carefully before sending it via e-mail. (*Note:* Another correct method is to use a period and divide into two sentences.)

4. Using Internet search engines and search directories—such as Yahoo, Infoseek, Savvy, and Magellan—a computer user can search Web sites, newsgroups, and other net sites.

5. When creating a computerized multimedia slide show to accompany a formal presentation, the user must take care to plan a show that will enhance, not echo, the oral presentation.

6. Successful business writers and speakers must have meaningful messages to send forth; that is, they must know what they are talking about.

7. The term "paperless office" refers to an office where everything is recorded by electronic means, not on paper.

8. Some people believe that they receive unnecessary messages through electronic mail and voice mail.

9. Further additions to the office of the future, which could be described as the "ultimate office," include picture telephones and computers that take dictation.

10. The computer, like any other tool, can be used unwisely.

Chapter 4

1. Shall we proceed with our discussion about words?

2. How do words affect our everyday behavior?

3. Words have emotional effects.

4. Connotative meanings are based on individual experiences, attitudes, beliefs, and emotions.

5. Words are described as being synonyms for other words, but there are few real synonyms.

6. The English language is constantly changing; all other languages also change.

7. Well-chosen words are likely to be short words.

8. In past years, this street was rather quiet. (Comma may be correctly omitted.)

9. The stationery store is quite profitable although it formerly lost money every month.

10. Participants spoke continuously throughout the morning without even a small break.

11. An efficient and concerned personnel department builds employee morale.

12. This department was not apprised of the fact that the building must be appraised.

13. I advise you not to give advice.

14. I am not altogether sure that this procedure is all right for our particular purpose.

15. The City Council voted to pass the amendment.

Chapter 5

1. A letter or memorandum should be no longer than necessary to accomplish its purposes, but one of these purposes is to build or maintain goodwill.

2. If the writer is overly concerned with brevity, the letter or memorandum may lack courtesy or completeness.

3. One purpose of your letter or memorandum is to convince the reader to accept your instructions or ideas.

4. The successful business writer is adept in the use of language and altogether sure of company policies and procedures.

5. Business jargon affects a letter in several undesirable ways.

6. Short paragraphs increase readability, especially short first and last paragraphs.

7. The student cited William Faulkner's long sentences when the teacher recommended short sentences.

8. A table or chart emphasizes specific data.

9. The arrangement of charts and tables affects comprehension.

10. The first paragraph as well as the last paragraph of letters and memorandums is emphatic.

Chapter 6

1. The you-approach, a concept long taught in business communication classes, is not always understood.

2. Some writers seem to think that in order to convey a you-approach they must no longer consider themselves; this is a mistaken idea.

3. The you-approach and the positive approach are interrelated and often used together, but the two techniques are not identical.

4. A well-known adage is expressed in these words: "You can't judge a book by its cover."

5. A direct arrangement is the better choice for most letters and memorandums, but an indirect arrangement is often more persuasive when conveying bad news.

6. At one time the word "he" was used routinely to refer to either sex; this usage was taught in classes in English composition.

7. Although the indirect order of arrangement is widely recommended for bad-news letters, the writer must use his or her own judgment depending on the situation.

8. The use of the word "you" in itself does not guarantee a true you-approach.

9. Although the word "I" is often used unnecessarily and ineffectively, the word alone does not prevent a writer from achieving the you-attitude and a positive approach. *Note:* Words *he*, *you*, and *I* (sentences 6,

8, and 9) may be shown in italics instead of being enclosed in quotation marks.

10. Correctness alone is not enough; many other positive factors are necessary for good writing.

Chapter 7

1. The principles of effective letters and memorandums are similar.

2. The you-approach is as important in memorandums as in letters, perhaps more so.

3. Increasing readability in many memorandums is accomplished simply by shortening paragraphs.

4. Some people say that they receive too many memorandums.

5. Although subject lines may be used or omitted in letters, they are expected in all memorandums.

6. The secretary asked: "Was the invitation meant for my husband and me?"

7. Make sure that you correctly spell the name of the person whom you address.

8. When you write a memorandum to members of a committee, make sure you know the names of those who are expected to attend.

9. The ability to write clear memorandums will affect your credibility in an organization.

10. In memorandums one-sentence paragraphs are acceptable and often desirable.

11. The secretary asked, "Who shall I say called?"

12. When some action is desired from the reader, the requested action should be specifically stated near the end of the memorandum.

13. Most paragraphs in letters and memorandums should begin with words other than "I" or "we."

14. A long memorandum was sent to Mr. Harris, Ms. Brown, and me.

15. Slow openings, such as "I have your memorandum of July 7," should be avoided in letters and memorandums.

16. An action close should specify how, when, why, and where the requested action is to occur.

17. The action close should be definitely worded, but it should not be dictatorial.

18. A well-chosen subject line is useful in routine and favorable letters.

19. Writing is the hardest way of earning a living, with the possible exception of wrestling alligators. (Olin Miller)

20. If people cannot write well, they cannot think well. If they cannot think well, others will do their thinking for them. (George Orwell)

21. Although the apostrophe has only three basic uses, it is frequently omitted or used incorrectly.

22. Apostrophes are used to form possessives, to form a few plurals, and to indicate omissions.

23. A letter or memorandum in a direct arrangement states the most important news near the beginning, usually in the first paragraph.

24. Short paragraphs, especially first ones, are desirable in letters and memorandums.

25. It's true that a well-written paragraph, regardless of its length, is easier to read than an incoherent one.

Chapter 8

1. One or two paragraphs ordinarily make up a buffer.

2. The buffer should let the reader know what the letter is about; it won't if it is completely unrelated.

3. A subject line, if used in a letter or memorandum that contains bad news, is less specific than the subject line in a good-news letter or memorandum.

4. Although a subject line is expected in all memorandums, it is not required in most letter styles; in some letters a subject line should be omitted. (*Note:* A new sentence may begin after *styles.* A comma may follow *letters.*)

5. Resale and sales promotion can be effective when used with discretion, but they can sometimes result in an I-approach.

6. Sometimes congratulations should be expressed in a refusal letter, provided the words are sincere.

7. Words can have a favorable or unfavorable effect on the acceptance of a refusal.

8. We can never be sure how our words will affect a particular reader.

9. Although an indirect order of arrangement is recommended for most bad-news messages, we must continue to use judgment and discretion. At times this arrangement may not be the best possible choice.

10. Because a one-sentence paragraph is emphatic, do not express the bad news in a sentence standing alone.

11. The use of the indirect arrangement, beginning with a buffer, should not be considered insincere; it is only a technique for achieving diplomacy and persuasion.

12. In order to subordinate a refusal, the writer should include only necessary details.

13. A refusal letter should include only pleasant or neutral words, not negative ones.

14. Discuss only relevant information.

Chapter 9

1. You do not convince a reader to buy with vague generalities, but with specific facts.

2. Sales letters have many advantages; for example, you can present your product to a specific group of individuals.

3. Sales letters have disadvantages, one of which is that people call them "junk mail."

4. Because you can mail sales letters to specific groups, provided you have accurate mailing lists, you can vary the central selling point for each different group.

5. Some sales letters use low price as the central selling point; in such

letters the price is emphasized, not subordinated.

6. A central selling point is a principal characteristic of a letter that will achieve the desired effect.

7. We must give specific, objective details about the product we are attempting to sell.

8. In order to receive a reply, be sure that the reader or readers understand the requested action and how it is to be accomplished.

9. If an individual's name is inserted into a previously prepared letter, the name should be shown in the same type as the letter itself.

10. Buying by mail has several advantages, one of which is convenience.

Chapter 10

1. Designed window displays and wrote advertising copy. (It is not necessary to mention assistant here, although credit should always be given where credit is due. If the applicant wrote the copy, even if the assistant also did so, this solution is correct. If the assistant wrote all the copy, then the entire mention of advertising should be omitted unless the applicant supervised the project; if this is the situation, wording should specifically describe the supervision.) In addition, the statement as previously worded is not grammatically parallel. The first two phrases are active, the third is passive.

2. Possibly this statement should be omitted entirely, depending on applicant's further education and the desired position. If the statement is used, capitalize *English* because it is a proper noun, but do not capitalize *accounting* and *history*.

3. As this statement is worded, it contains a dangling modifier. *Starting* does not intentionally modify *you*.

4. Statement should be included but should be more specific, including dates of employment and the name of store—unless the time is not recent and the position is unrelated to the position sought. As statement is presently worded, *years* should be *year's* and *womens'* should be *women's*.

5. Name, kind, and date of scholarship should be designated. *Recipient* is the correct spelling.

6. Responsible to three counselors.

7. Principal responsibilities were financial ones.

8. Planned capital expenditures.

9. Earned 90 percent of college costs.

10. Sold advertising space to businesses.

11. Omit.

12. Majors in physical education and English, minor in mathematics.

Chapter 11

1. The enclosed resume describes my qualifications in more detail.

2. Omit. This is trite, inappropriate phrasing.

3. (Much too demanding.) I will arrange to come for an interview at a time convenient for you.

4. You can reach me at this number after 10 A.M.

5. Omit. This is the I-approach, not the you-approach.

6. Omit. This is the "desperate" approach.

7. Omit, for obvious reasons.

8. My present employer knows of this application and will tell you of my work in her organization.

9. Omit. Never use a company letterhead. Also notice that *stationery* is misspelled and that *company's* should include an apostrophe.

10. Omit. Negative and demanding.

11. Omit. Negative because it implies doubt.

12. Omit.

13. Omit. Negative and presumptuous.

14. Omit.

15. I can begin work on Monday, November 6, 1999, in your Los Angeles office.

Chapter 12

1. One of your first steps will be to find out what is wanted, especially if you are a new employee.

2. The impersonal writing style, which is also described as the third-person objective writing style, contains only third-person pronouns.

3. Employers want people who are proficient in thinking, speaking, writing, listening, and reading.

4. Preparing and presenting reports and keeping accurate records are important employment responsibilities.

5. Doing research is more enjoyable to some people than writing a report.

6. Reports should be objective, clear, and well organized.

7. Keep sentences concise and relatively short.

8. The report writer points out highlights in an introduction to each chart.

9. Although generalizing from insufficient information is dangerous, we all do so occasionally.

10. Because we cannot always have all necessary facts, some recommendations must be made on inferences.

Chapter 13

1. *b* is correct. (*are*, not *is* in *a*.)

2. *b* is correct. (*Questionnaires* is misspelled in *a*.)

3. *b* is correct. (Comma is omitted after *libraries* in *a*.)

4. *a* is correct. (Notice the omitted hyphen in *data-gathering process*.)

5. *a* is correct. (Comma fault in *b*.)

6. *b* is correct. (A comma is needed after *information* in *a*.)

7. *b* is correct. (*Definite* is misspelled in *a*.)

8. *b* is correct. (*Privilege* is misspelled in *a*.)

9. *b* is correct. (*Feasible* is misspelled in *a*.)

10. *a* is correct. (*Familiar* is misspelled in *b*.)

11. *b* is correct. (*Proceed* is misspelled in *a*.)

12. *me*. (Objective case; indirect object of *asked*. The infinite phrase is the direct object.)

13. *who*. (Subject of verb *was interested*.)

14. *I, year's*.

15. *compliments*.

16. *all right*. (A comma may correctly follow *reports*.)

Chapter 14

1. Tables, not charts, should be chosen for the presentation of numerous figures.

2. If you have the proper equipment and software, you can construct various kinds of charts by using a personal computer.

3. Once you have calculated the mean of a group of numbers, you may find that it is not the best number upon which to base your decision.

4. Constructing charts with computers or other electronic equipment is faster than drawing them with a pen or pencil.

5. Carefully label each chart and provide a descriptive key, which is called a legend.

6. All the techniques of effective graphics will affect the finished report.

7. Bilateral bar charts are also described as positive and negative bar charts.

8. Bar graphs include the following kinds: bilateral bar, subdivided bar, and 100-percent bar.

9. The purpose of graphic aids is to show trends and relationships quickly, clearly, and accurately.

10. Conclusions presented in the report should be based on facts included in the body of the text, not writer biases.

Chapter 15

1. *b* is correct. (*similar* is misspelled in *a*.)

2. *a* is correct. (In *b*, *reports* needs an apostrophe.)

3. *b* is correct. (In *a*, *readers'* is correct, not *reader's*.)

4. *b* is correct. (The preposition in a title should not be capitalized.)

5. *a* is correct. (*accounting*, in *b*, should not be capitalized.)

6. *b* is correct. (*undergraduates'* should be used in *a*.)

7. *b* is correct. (*congratulated* is misspelled in *a*.)

8. *b* is correct. (*questionnaire* is misspelled in *a*.)

9. *a* is correct. (*principal* is misspelled in *b*.)

10. *b* is correct. (*tentative* is misspelled in *a*.)

Chapter 16

1. Fifty people scattered throughout a large room may not be able to hear a speaker who does not use a microphone.

2. Eight people attended the committee meeting; as with most small groups, the procedure was rather informal.

3. She spoke on Monday, an unfavorable day, at 1 P.M.

4. For some oral presentations, even seven minutes is too long.

5. Some speeches are not worth 5 cents.

6. The speaker used 25 transparencies, 17 slides, and 5 blackboard illustrations.

7. Please refer to page 2.

8. Photographs, when used as visuals, must be large enough to be seen easily; make five 16-by-20 enlargements.

9. Listeners may remember less than 4 percent of what you say.

10. Because you cannot predict the exact words your listeners will retain, try to begin and end with three memorable, interesting, and important sentences or illustrations.

Chapter 17

1. One's individual perception is affected by his or her entire background.

2. Our culture exerts a tremendous influence on our world and patterns our responses to experiences.

3. No two people in Sacramento, California, are identical, and no two people from Egypt, Japan, or Brazil are identical.

4. Some of the stereotypes by which Americans are judged are positive, not negative.

5. "The nail that sticks up is hit" is a well-known saying in Japan.

6. If management personnel are to succeed in Japan, they must understand its culture.

7. Intercultural communication is not new; it is as old as humanity.

8. The Japanese see decisions as a product of the consensus of the group, not of an individual.

9. Cultural identity is an aspect of a person's existence.

10. In countries where two or more languages coexist, confusion often arises.

Chapter 18

1. Concern about behavior and customs is understandable when an executive is making plans for time away from his or her native country.

2. Etiquette—speech and behavior that are considered polite and proper—differs according to the situation and according to the particular culture.

3. The chairperson pointed out the desirability of parliamentary procedure to my secretary and me before she and I prepared the agenda.

4. The word *agenda*, which comes from Latin, was originally used as a plural noun, but its use now is singular.

5. One criterion is that participants contribute ideas.

6. The chairman implied that Joan and I were talking too long; I thought it was all right to keep on talking as long as everybody else was silent.

7. Good communication through effective meetings improves the morale of all concerned personnel.

8. A too-long meeting can adversely affect comprehension.

9. In addition to the topics listed on the agenda, the leader should plan the procedure to follow in order to stay within time limits.

10. The president wrote a letter of congratulations to my secretary and me because of our cost-cutting ideas.

Appendix C

Dictating Business Messages

Many businesspeople, including executives, keyboard their own letters, memorandums, and other material using a personal computer with a word processing package. Dictation as a method of originating material has declined in use, but it still exists.

If you are fortunate enough to have the services of a secretary or other clerical help, you may wish to originate messages through dictation, most likely by use of a tape recorder or other voice-writing machine. Even when such assistance is available, however, many writers prefer to keyboard their material, or at least the first draft, because they can more easily see needed improvements.

Nevertheless, dictation can save a great deal of time and effort, in many situations and for various kinds of material. For example, a person who travels a great deal can dictate material to be transcribed by someone in the home office before or after the traveler returns. Other uses for dictation occur in various occupations, such as a physician describing a patient's symptoms during or after an examination, or an architect dictating notes about the progress of a building while he or she walks over the site.

Another purpose of dictation that may be important in the future is dictation to computers that will transcribe from voice input. Such computers have been planned for years, but they are still not widely available.

Effective dictation requires skill and practice. Perhaps the most emphatic way to realize such need is to transcribe material that has been put on tape by a number of speakers with varying language abilities and different speaking styles.

Consider the following suggestions:

1. Plan the content of each letter or other bit of writing to be dictated. A brief outline of each letter may consist of only a few words. You may wish to make notes on the letter being answered. Consider the contents of each paragraph. Less detailed planning will suffice after you have obtained considerable experience in writing and in dictating, but some planning will always be essential.

2. Speak clearly at a fairly even pace. If you are dictating to a machine, make sure that it is adjusted properly and that you speak directly into the telephone or microphone. Be sure that no distracting noises detract from the clarity of your voice.

3. Give special instructions before you begin dictating the material to be transcribed. For example, specify the number of copies and the persons to whom the copies are to be sent. If a particular letter is to be transcribed

first, say so at the beginning of the dictation. Give any special instructions about delivery.

Perhaps for a long, complicated letter or manuscript the first copy should be in the form of a rough draft for you to revise before the final copy is printed. If so, give this instruction at the beginning of the dictation.

4. Dictate paragraph endings. As you have learned from preceding chapters, paragraph construction is part of the composing process. You change emphasis and meaning by rearranging paragraphs.

5. Dictate unusual punctuation. Punctuation is also a part of the composition itself; and, as in the construction of paragraphs, punctuation conveys a portion of the meaning. If you are sure that the person transcribing your work knows the rules for the ordinary and expected use of punctuation, to dictate each comma may indicate that you do not trust his or her ability. On the other hand, dictating all punctuation provides an advantage because your meaning as it comes through spoken words is more immediately clear, just as meaning through the written word is made more immediately clear through punctuation.

6. Spell out all proper names. Spell out all unusual technical words or phrases.

7. Even though errors are not your own, you are responsible for them. Check all work carefully and thoroughly until you are sure that your assistant is conscientious and accurate. Even when you are confident of your assistant's ability and dedication, your checking of the copy is an extra safeguard.

8. Add handwritten notes for a personal touch, but use judgment and discretion. Some organizations frown on this practice. If they are overused, or used inappropriately, they appear as an inconsiderate shortcut.

9. Play back your voice occasionally when dictating to a machine. You may be surprised!

Appendix D
A Brief Guide to English Usage

This appendix is of necessity an incomplete guide to the use of the English language. Many comprehensive handbooks on English usage are available for your use through school and public libraries. Every writer should own one or more reliable handbooks and a large, up-to-date dictionary.

ABBREVIATIONS

Ordinarily you should not abbreviate except for a few well-known exceptions, which include two-letter state abbreviations in addresses (for example, *MO* for *Missouri* and *NY* for *New York*); courtesy titles and other designations customarily abbreviated (such as *Mr.*, *Mrs.*, *Dr.*, *Jr.*, *Sr.*, *Ph.D.*, *M.D.*); abbreviations that are a part of a company name (such as *Inc.*, *Co.*, *Ltd.*); and expression of time (such as *A.M.*, *P.M.*, *CST*, *MST*, *A.D.*, and *B.C.*)

The courtesy title *Miss* (now seldom used) is not followed by a period, although *Ms.* is followed by a period. (Do not expect customary and expected conventions to be completely logical. Even so, we are usually wiser to go along with expected usage. To do otherwise creates distraction, at least momentarily, diverting the reader's attention from the meaning of our words to such things as the use or omission of periods.)

Abbreviations are frequently used in technical writing, tables, and statistical material.

An acronym, a form of abbreviation, is derived from the initial letters of the complete form (for example, *OPEC for Organization of Petroleum Exporting Countries*). In report writing, indicate the meaning of an acronym the first time it is used, such as "*OPEC (Organi-*

zation of Petroleum Exporting Countries) is responsible. . . ." The acronym may be used alone after it is once identified.

CAPITALIZATION

1. Use capitals for proper nouns and adjectives.

2. Use capitals for the first and last words of titles of books or other works; capitalize all other words except articles, prepositions, conjunctions, and the *to* in an infinitive.

3. Capitalize a compass point used as a definite region of the country, but not a compass point used as a direction; for example, *Arizona is in the Southwest* and *it is southwest of Maine.*

4. Capitalize a title that comes before a name, such as *Professor King*, but do not capitalize *professor* in this sentence: Dr. King is an economics professor.

5. Do not capitalize unless there is a definite reason to do so. Some writers capitalize unnecessarily.

Capitalize
   Cost Accounting II (name of specific course)
   I am taking a course in French. (proper adjective)
   President Carpenter (title used as part of name)
   The President (of the United States)
   West Coast (section of country)
   Mother is late. (used as name)
   Mississippi River (River is part of name)
   He said, "We shall proceed." (direct quotation)
   Summer Series of Lectures (part of title)

Do not capitalize
   major in accounting (general subject field)
   I am taking a course in history. (general subject field, not a proper adjective)
   He is president of his fraternity.
   Our company has a new president.
   He rode west into the sunset. (direction)
   My mother is late.
   Mississippi and Tennessee rivers
   He said that we would proceed. (indirect quotation)
   This summer is unusually cool. (season shown in usual way, not poetically or as a personification)

PUNCTUATION AS AN AID TO READABILITY

"Rules" are guidelines to punctuation in order to make sentences and entire messages understandable. Punctuation is an integral part of composition.

Although it is true that some rules about punctuation given here and in English handbooks are not always followed exactly, even by professional writers, exact adherence to the guidelines in Appendix D is advisable, at least in business writing. (Poetry, as well as some fiction and advertising copy, is not bound by "rules," although all writing should express meaning.) Punctuation is an important method of expressing and of making messages clear during the first reading.

THE APOSTROPHE

1. Use an apostrophe in contractions.

- won't
- it's (it is)
- couldn't
- you're (you are)

Avoid contractions in formal writing.

2. Use an apostrophe to indicate the possessive case of nouns and indefinite pronouns.

- Mary's cat
- anybody's guess
- a stone's throw
- a year's experience
- two years' experience
- women's shoes
- children's books
- the student's paper (one student)
- the students' paper (more than one student)
- Mr. Ross's automobile
- The Rosses' automobile (an automobile owned by more than one person named Ross)
- Jefferson Davis's home or Dr. Jennings' office (see note)
- Bob and Mary's house (joint ownership)
- Bob's and Mary's shoes (individual ownership)

(*Note:* If a singular noun ends in *s*, the apostrophe and *s* are usually added; but if the second *s* causes difficulty of pronunciation, the apostrophe alone may be added.)

3. Use an apostrophe in plurals of lowercase letters and abbreviations followed by periods. An apostrophe may be used in plurals of capital letters, figures, abbreviations not followed by periods, and words referred to as words.

- C's
- Ph.D's
- B's or Bs
- CPA's or CPAs
- 8's or 8s
- the 1940's or 1940s
- and's or ands
- %'s or %s

Be consistent in your use of the apostrophe. For example, use *and's* or *ands*, but do not use both in the same paper.

(*Note:* The use of the apostrophe is sometimes described as being an aspect of spelling, not of punctuation.)

One of the most frequent ways in which an apostrophe is misused results from the confusion of *its* and *it's.* Another inconsistency is the various ways in which an apostrophe is used with singular and plural names, and other nouns.

The possessive form of *it* is *its*, with no apostrophe. *It's means it is, and absolutely nothing else.*

Another error, although much less frequent, is the incorrect use of an apostrophe in theirs, in which no apostrophe is used.

Another construction in which a needed apostrophe is commonly omitted is illustrated by these phrases: *two weeks' vacation, one year's experience.* (No apostrophe is needed in the following phrases: *two weeks of vacation, one year of experience.*)

Apostrophes are often omitted or used inconsistently in family names, particularly on mailboxes. Consider the name *Johnson.*

If only one person lives in the house, his or her mailbox may be labeled *Johnson* (or Ann Johnson or Bill Johnson). If two or more people named Johnson live in the house, *The Johnsons* adequately identifies the place, but does not show possession. (We can assume that Johnson or The Johnsons have possession, at least temporarily.)

If Bill Johnson wants to show that the house is his alone, the term *Johnson's* will so indicate. If Bill and Ann share the house and mailbox, the possessive designation should be *The Johnsons'*. If Betty and Joe Box share a house and mailbox, the sign should read *The Boxes* (a simple plural) or *The Boxes'* (plural possessive).

Check your use of the apostrophe in the often-used words, *company* and *companies*. The plural of *company* is *companies*, with NO apostrophe.

CORRECT: Two new companies have been established in our town during the past year.

INCORRECT: Two new companys have been established in our town during the past year.

INCORRECT: Two new company's have been established in our town during the past year.

The singular possessive of *company* is *company's*.

CORRECT: One company's profits have increased.

INCORRECT: One companys profits have increased.

The plural possessive of *company* is *companies'*.

CORRECT: Both of the companies' profits have increased.

INCORRECT: Both of the companies profits have increased.

INCORRECT: Both of the company's profits have increased.

INCORRECT: Both of the companys profits have increased.

THE COLON

1. Use a colon to introduce a series of items.

■ The points to be considered are these: cost, speed, and simplicity.

■ Three possible areas of operation could be the source of the loss: shipping, advertising, and collections.

Within a sentence, use a colon ONLY after a complete thought. (Notice that the colons after the introductory words "CORRECT" and "INCORRECT," shown below, are NOT within a sentence.)

CORRECT: The shipment consists of four categories of equipment: computers, printers, monitors, and modems.

INCORRECT: The shipment consists of: computers, printers, monitors, and modems.

INCORRECT: The kinds of equipment are: computers, printers, monitors, and modems.

CORRECT: The kinds of equipment needed are these:

computers
printers
monitors
modems

2. Use colons before long quotations.

3. Use a colon after the salutation in a business letter. (An exception is a letter set up in the "open punctuation" arrangement in which no mark of punctuation is used after the salutation. Do not use a comma after a salutation in a business letter.)

4. Use a colon to join two independent clauses when the second clause explains or restates the first clause, as illustrated in the following passage from *Fowler's Modern English Usage*, 2d edition (Oxford University Press, 1965), 589. "... but has acquired a special function: that of delivering the goods that have been invoiced in the preceding words."

THE COMMA

1. Use a comma to set off an introductory subordinate clause from an independent statement.

■ If Johnny can't write, one of the reasons may be a conditioning based on speed rather than on respect for the creative process.

■ If you don't like the weather in New England, wait a few minutes.

■ Although the ability to use a computer is a requisite to many jobs, it remains less important than the ability to read, write, and speak the English language.

■ When in doubt, tell the truth. —Mark Twain (Introductory element with "you are" understood.)

2. Use a comma after introductory participial phrases,

■ Dreading the long, boring task, he left it until the afternoon.

■ Having received the notice of cancellation, we tried to stop shipment.

■ Elated over the news of his promotion, he kissed everyone on the third floor.

Distinguish between a participle, which is a verb form used as an adjective, and a gerund, which is a verb form used as a noun. A gerund is also referred to as a verbal noun. In the following sentences the gerund acts as the subject; it should not be followed by a comma:

■ Seeing is believing.

■ Driving along the Natchez Trace is a memorable experience.

3. Use a comma after introductory infinitive phrases.

■ To enter the stacks, go to the admission desk and present your identification card.

An infinitive, like a gerund, is not followed by a comma when it is used as the subject. In the following sentence, both clauses of the compound sentence contain an infinitive used as the subject:

■ To err is human; to blame it on someone else is even more human.

4. Use a comma after an introductory sentence element consisting of a long prepositional phrase or of two or more phrases.

■ In addition to the many books in the general library, many others are shelved in specialized collections.

5. Use a comma after introductory words and phrases.

■ Confidentially, this policy is to be changed.

■ Nevertheless, we must continue the usual procedure throughout this month.

6. Use a comma to separate words, phrases, or clauses in a series.

■ He visited Spain, Italy, and France.

- His morning consists of eating breakfast, reading the newspaper, and sitting in the sunshine.
- Go to the end of the hall, turn left, and follow the arrows on the wall.

7. Use a comma to separate coordinate clauses joined by *and, but, for, or, nor, yet.*

- All would live long, but none would be old.—Benjamin Franklin
- To be good is noble, but to teach others how to be good is nobler—and less trouble.—Mark Twain
- The show had no chronological order, nor did it have an intelligent narration.
- Short words are best, and the old ones when short are best of all. —Winston Churchill

In short sentences the comma is sometimes omitted, as in

- I came late and you left early.

8. Use a comma to set off nonrestrictive (nonessential) clauses. Do not set off restrictive clauses that come within or at the end of a sentence.

- Our salespeople, who are paid a salary plus commissions, earn from $2,500 to $5,000 a month. (nonrestrictive)
- Salespeople who attended the national meeting met our new president. (restrictive)

9. Use a comma to set off parenthetical (nonrestrictive, nonessential) or appositive words or phrases.

- He said that, in the first place, he was not interested in our product.
- The sales manager, Harvey L. Wells, is a friend of the customer's sister.
- The store first opened its doors on Monday, May 13, 1904, in St. Louis, Missouri, on the bank of the Mississippi River.

- The statement is true, perhaps, that our prices could be reduced.

Words that are at times used parenthetically are at other times used adverbially. If a word or phrase can be considered supplemental, interrupting, or explanatory, precede and follow the word or phrase with commas. In the following sentences, *perhaps, however,* and *also* are used as adverbs and, because of their placement in the sentence, should not be set off by commas:

- It is perhaps true that our prices could be reduced.
- However it happened, it was not according to customary office procedures.
- The second statement is also false.

10. Use a comma to separate adjectives of equal rank if the conjunction is omitted.

- She is an efficient, considerate sales representative.

Do not use commas between adjectives of unequal rank, as in

- The cold late autumn days are here again.

To check whether a comma is needed, try inserting the word *and.* If the expression now makes sense, use a comma.

11. Use a comma to set off contrasting expressions.

- The world is becoming warmer, not colder.

THE DASH
Use a dash to show a sudden change in the structure of a sentence or to indicate emphasis.

- Indeed, it was a long leap from the jungle home of the chimpanzee to our modern civilization—and apparently we didn't quite make it.[1]

- Several items—a stapler, two calendars, and three or more chairs—were lost by the movers.

Do not overuse the dash, especially in formal writing, as it may give a "scatterbrained" appearance.

ELLIPSES

Three periods with one space before and after each is used to indicate an omission in quoted material. If the omission occurs after the end of a sentence, four periods are used, one in its usual end-of-sentence position and three to indicate an omission.

THE HYPHEN

1. Use a hyphen to join a compound expression used as a single modifier before a noun.

- Is this an interest-bearing note?
- We need up-to-date equipment.

Omit the hyphen when the first word of the compound is an adverb ending in *ly*. Omit the hyphen when the modifier comes after the noun:

- Is this note interest bearing?

2. Use a hyphen in some compound words in which the hyphen is considered part of the accepted spelling, such as "self-control" and "sister-in-law."

Consult a dictionary to determine hyphenation of compound words.

3. Use a hyphen to divide words at the end of a line.

Do not divide words unnecessarily, as many lines ending with hyphens can be more distracting than uneven lines. ("Justified" lines can also be distracting.) When you feel you must divide to avoid extreme unevenness of lines, follow these guides:

- Divide only between syllables.

- Do not divide a word with fewer than seven letters.
- Do not separate the following syllables from the remainder of the word:
  syllable that does not contain a vowel (couldn*'t*)
  first syllable of only one letter (*e*cology)
  last syllable of one or two letters (extreme*ly*)
- Do not divide hyphenated words at any place other than at the hyphen. (*well-being*)
- Divide after a one-letter syllable within a word unless the word contains successive single-letter syllables. (*congratu-lations*)
- Try to avoid dividing proper names and numbers.
- Do not divide the last word of a paragraph or the last word on a page.

PARENTHESES

Use parentheses to set off explanatory or nonessential material.

- A choice of commas, dashes, or parentheses (used in pairs) can be used to set off parenthetical material.

You can change the meaning slightly according to your choice of punctuation. Dashes are more emphatic than commas. Parentheses indicate a more definite separation in meaning from the rest of the sentence than commas imply.

THE PERIOD

1. Place a period at the end of a sentence that is a statement.

2. Use a period at the end of an indirect question.

- The teacher asked whether we had completed registration. (indirect question that requires a period)

- The teacher asked, "Have you completed registration?" (direct question)

3. Use a period OR a question mark after what can be described as a polite request, as shown by the examples below.

- Will you please reply soon.
- Will you please reply soon?

According to Frederick Crews in *The Random House Handbook*, 5th ed. (New York: Random House, 1984), 346, the question mark displays more real courtesy.

4. Use a period after certain abbreviations.

5. Use a period (depending on chosen style manual) in bibliographic references and in footnotes.

QUOTATION MARKS

1. Use quotation marks to enclose the exact words of a writer or speaker.

2. Use quotation marks to enclose titles of songs, magazine and newspaper articles, poems, reports, and other short written works.

3. Use quotation marks to enclose slang expressions.

4. Use quotation marks to enclose words used in an unusual way.

Note: Quotation marks are placed with other marks of punctuation in this way:

- Place commas and periods inside quotation marks, always.
- Place colons and semicolons outside quotation marks, always.
- Place question and exclamation marks inside the quotation marks when they refer to the quoted material, outside when they refer to the sentence as a whole.

An example is this:

- "Amazing Grace," a well-known hymn, is one of the most requested in the South and probably in the entire nation.

The quotation marks apply to the song title, not to the rest of the sentence. Some people say that in a sentence such as this the comma inside the quotation mark does not make a great deal of sense. They are right. On the other hand, you as a writer are saved a great deal of time and indecision by the constant rule that, regardless of use or meaning, the comma and the period are always inside quotation marks and the semicolon and colon are always outside.

The usage is confusing to many writers, but it is especially confusing to those who have lived in English-speaking countries outside the United States where the usage is likely to be different—and perhaps more logical.

THE SEMICOLON

1. Use a semicolon between main clauses that are not joined by one of the coordinate conjunctions (*and, but, for, or, nor, yet*).

- Punctuation is more than little marks to be sprinkled like salt and pepper through written words; punctuation determines emphasis and meaning.

2. Use a semicolon between main clauses joined with a conjunctive adverb.

- A readable writing style is simple and direct; consequently, it requires less punctuation than a more formal, complicated style.

- Semicolons are useful for clarifying meaning through punctuation; nevertheless, a great many long compound sentences such as this one, with the main clauses joined by a semicolon and a conjunctive adverb [nevertheless], tend to suggest a rather heavy and formal writing style.

Important Note: Substituting a comma for a semicolon to separate main clauses, as in sentences constructed like the preceding ones that contain no coordinating conjunction, is considered a serious error in punctuation and sentence construction.

3. Use a semicolon to separate items in a series if they are parallel subordinate clauses, or if they are long or contain internal punctuation.

■ Those attending included Susan Smith, a college professor; Mark David, a field engineer; Diana Wallace, an executive secretary; and Leonard Brown, a credit manager.

■ We use language to talk about language; we make statements about statements; and we sing songs about songs.

4. Use a semicolon to separate complete clauses joined by a coordinate conjunction if the semicolon will increase readability when clauses are long or contain internal punctuation.

■ The semicolon, which is sometimes overused, indicates a stronger break in thought than that indicated by a comma; but it is not as strong as that indicated by a period and somewhat different in usage from a colon.

UNDERSCORES
Underscore the names of books or other works in a solid line. When words are used only as words, not as part of a title, underscore individually.

The titles of magazines, journals, newspapers, and other periodicals are usually underscored in bibliographies. In ordinary use they are more likely not to be underscored, but shown in capitals and lower case. Words underscored in type are shown in italics in published form.

AVOIDING FREQUENTLY OCCURRING GRAMMATICAL ERRORS
CHOOSE A VERB TO AGREE WITH THE SUBJECT
Verbs must agree in number with their subjects; most writers know this, but the subject "gets lost" in complicated sentences, or even sentences that are not complicated at all. For example:

The logic of good communicators seems to be . . .

Because the plural word *communicators* immediately precedes the verb, *seem* may creep into the sentence, although in a sentence no more involved than this one there is little reason for the wrong verb form. As more words intervene, the likelihood of error is more apt to occur. One principle of good writing, however, is that it be simple and direct; another guide is that the subject and verb be close together in a sentence. Sentences constructed in this way are likely to include the correct form of the verb.

In the sentence below, the verb is singular to agree with the subject *box*:

■ The box, together with the baskets, was sent to the shipping room.

The word *baskets* is not part of the subject, but because baskets immediately precedes the verb, it seems natural to use *were*. In the following sentence, *were* is the correct verb:

The box and the baskets were sent to the shipping room.

Compare the preceding sentences with the following:

Neither the box nor the basket was sent to the shipping room.
Neither the box nor the baskets were sent to the shipping room.

The following guideline applies to sentences like the immediately preceding ones: When one subject is singular and the other is plural, the verb agrees with the subject closer to the verb.

CHOOSE THE CORRECT PRONOUN

Using the wrong case of the pronoun is an error that seems to occur more in speech than in writing. It is especially common in sentences in which *I* is used incorrectly (instead of *me*) as the object of a verb or preposition. Few persons, whatever their position or educational background, say something like this:

Me and Jim are friends.

However, many persons say or write, incorrectly:

Jim and he are good friends of Mary and I.

In the preceding sentence, "Mary and me" should be used because the pronoun is the object of the preposition *of*. The *I* is just as incorrect as the *me* in "me and Jim," but for some reason the *I* seems to many persons to be more "cultured," more "elegant," more correct.

SENTENCE CONSTRUCTION

Illustrations of types of sentences are given below:

Simple sentences

- I have returned.
  —Douglas MacArthur

- Understanding is joyous.—Carl Sagan (Understanding is used here as a noun and the subject of the sentence.)

- Towering genius disdains a beaten path.—Abraham Lincoln

- England and America are two countries separated by the same language.—George Bernard Shaw

- The fog comes on little cat feet.
  —Carl Sandburg

- Play it again, Sam. (The subject is the understood *you*.) (title of film; also adaptation of line from another film, *Casablanca*)

- I hate quotations.—Ralph Waldo Emerson

Complex sentences

- When people are least sure, they are often the most dogmatic.—John Kenneth Galbraith (introductory dependent clause)

- In spite of everything I still believe that people are really good at heart.—Anne Frank (Dependent clause begins with *that*.)

- He who enters a university walks on hallowed ground.—James B. Conant (Here the dependent clause, beginning with *who*, separates the subject and verb of the main clause: *he* and *walks*.)

- The future offers very little hope for those who expect that our new mechanical slaves will offer us a world in which we may rest from think-ing.—Norbert Wiener (This sentence contains one independent clause and three dependent clauses. What are they?)

Compound sentences

■ Wit has truth in it; wisecracking is simply calisthenics with words. —Dorothy Parker

■ Life was meant to be lived, and cu-riosity must be kept alive.—Eleanor Roosevelt

■ All animals are equal, but some ani-mals are more equal than others. —George Orwell

■ Talk low, talk slow, and don't say too much.—John Wayne (three in-dependent clauses)

Compound-complex sentences

■ Read over your compositions, and wherever you meet with a passage which you think is particularly fine, strike it out.—Samuel Johnson (*You* is the understood subject of both independent clauses; *read* and *strike* are the verbs. In the depen-dent clauses, *you meet*, *which is*, and *you think* are the subjects and verbs.)

■ We can secure other people's ap-proval if we do right and try hard; but our own is worth a hundred of it, and no way has been found of securing that.—Mark Twain (three main clauses and one depen-dent clause, beginning with *if we do*)

■ And so, my fellow Americans, ask not what your country can do for you; ask what you can do for your country.—John F. Kennedy (two in-dependent clauses and two depen-dent clauses)

BASIC ERRORS IN SENTENCE CONSTRUCTION

Most conspicuous weaknesses in sen-tence construction are the following:

1. Sentence fragment (although these can at times be used effectively)

2. The comma fault, also called a comma blunder, a comma splice, and a baby comma

3. A fused sentence, also called a run-on sentence

4. Nonparallel sentences or sentences of mixed construction

5. Sentences with dangling or mis-placed modifiers

A sentence fragment, the comma fault, and the fused sentence can also be considered as errors in punctuation. These weak constructions occur be-cause the writer is not sure of what constitutes a sentence. The lack of nec-essary and wisely chosen punctuation results in these sentence weaknesses.

A *sentence fragment* is incomplete in itself; it is usually a phrase or a depen-dent clause, as in the following exam-ples:

Incorrect:
This information is presented here. Because it is necessary to the understanding of the following pages.

Improve by eliminating the period:

Correct:
This information is presented here be-cause it is necessary to the under-standing of the following pages.

The comma fault occurs when two sentences that are definitely separate have been joined together with a comma. They should be punctuated as two separate sentences, joined with a conjunction, or joined with a semicolon. The method of connection depends, to a certain extent, on the desired meaning and emphasis. If the ideas are not related enough so that they belong in the same sentence, express them in separate sentences. Avoid using a great many semicolons as they can result in a choppy effect, just as a great number of short, simple sentences can. When one idea is more important than another, use a complex sentence.

Incorrect:
English is the principal language of international business, it is taught in schools throughout the world. (Improve by starting a new sentence with it or by using a semicolon before it.)

This sentence could also be revised in the following way, although the meaning and emphasis would be slightly changed. For example:

Correct:
English, the principal language of international business, is taught in schools throughout the world.

The comma splice (or fault) occurs when two main clauses of a compound sentence are joined by a comma only, not by a comma and a coordinating conjunction or by a semicolon.

Incorrect:
The public library rents, but does not sell, videocassettes, they are interesting and also inexpensive.

The preceding sentence would be improved somewhat by replacing the comma after videocassettes with a semicolon or by inserting *and* after the presently used comma. Even with either of these changes the sentence would remain weak, although correct according to the rules of punctuation. The following modification is a simple sentence:

Correct:
The public library rents, but does not sell, interesting and inexpensive videocassettes.

The following sentence is complex.

Correct:
Although the public library does not sell the interesting videocassettes available there, it provides an economical rental plan.

The immediately preceding sentence illustrates the rule that an introductory dependent clause should be followed by a comma.

In short and closely related sentences, commas may at times be effectively used to join the clauses of compound sentences, as:

I came, I saw, I conquered.
Don't hurry, don't worry.

This construction, however, should be used with discretion and extreme caution, especially by the inexperienced writer. (See the discussion of the use of the semicolon under "Punctuation as an Aid to Readability" in this appendix.)

A fused sentence occurs when two sentences are "run-on" with no punctuation at all. The sentences should be separated by a period, a semicolon, or a comma and a conjunction.

Nonparallel sentences occur when parallel ideas are not expressed in parallel form. An orderly arrangement is necessary for the immediate recognition of relationships of ideas.

The following sentences are not parallel because of the unnecessary shifts from active to passive voice.

Incorrect:
Jane wrote the music, and the lyrics were written by Mary Hicks.
The play was well written, and the director did a capable job

Correct:
Jane wrote the music, and Mary Hicks wrote the lyrics.
The play was well written and capably directed.

The following sentence is nonparallel because similar ideas are expressed in differing ways by the infinitive and by the gerund:

Incorrect:
Taking the elevator is not so healthful as to climb the stairs. (Improve by changing *to climb* to *climbing*.)

The following sentence is nonparallel because a clause and an infinitive phrase are used to express similar ideas:

Incorrect:
We want a personnel manager who can motivate all workers and to recruit experienced sales representatives.

Correct:
We want a personnel manager who can motivate workers and who can recruit experienced sales representatives.

A more concise version is:

We want a personnel manager who can motivate workers and recruit experienced sales representatives.

The following phrases are not parallel because two gerunds and one infinitive are used in a sentence in which similar expressions should have the same form:

Incorrect:
Buying supplies, keeping the books, and to answer the telephone . . .

Correct:
Buying supplies, keeping the books, and answering the telephone . . .

The following sentence beginning is not parallel because two phrases are used with a clause:

Incorrect:
Government of the people, by the people, and that is for the people . . .

The following sentences are nonparallel because of a misplaced correlative. (Correlatives are pairs of joining words, such as *either, or; neither, nor; both, and; not only, but also.*)

Incorrect:
Either to make a living or a life is not an easy task, if it is done well.
Not only must we be concerned with the initial cost but also with the upkeep.

Correct:
To make either a living or a life is not an easy task, if it is done well.
We must be concerned not only with the initial cost but also with the upkeep.

Dangling or misplaced modifiers may consist of adjectives or adverbs; phrases, including participial, infinitive, or prepositional; and clauses. Any modifier is misplaced if it does not exactly and logically qualify (restrict, limit, describe) the word or words that it is intended to qualify.

A modifier is said to dangle when it has no reasonable or logical words to modify.

Incorrect:
Working without a coffee break, the telephone calls were completed before noon.

As this sentence is constructed, the participle working seems to modify telephone calls, when obviously it cannot. The modifier here could also be described as all the words that come before the main part of the sentence.

Correct:
Working without a coffee break, I completed the telephone calls before noon.

Dangling participles sometimes occur because the writer is too much concerned with avoiding the word *I*. *I* and *we* should be used when they are natural and necessary to the sentence, except for the few kinds of business writing that use only the impersonal tone.

Incorrect:
Being dark and winding, she could barely see the road.
Completely renovated two years ago, I was most impressed by the old building.

Avoid using a great many participial openings, even if they do not "dangle." Usually the sentence is more direct and forceful when it opens with the subject-verb combination.

Misplaced modifiers may be in sentence positions other than the beginning.

Incorrect:
The woman riding the motorcycle in a red jogging suit is my grandmother. (misplaced prepositional phrase)
In the downtown section, with sirens screaming, we saw the fire truck skid to a stop. (misplaced prepositional phrase)

On my ranch I like to ride to the top of a ridge and watch the sun set on horseback. (misplaced prepositional phrase)

The word *only* is easily misplaced. *Rarely*, *merely*, *hardly*, *just*, *even*, and other words are also often not in the best location to refer to the exact word or group of words that they modify. As a general rule, put closely related words together.

The following sentence contains a misplaced *only*, although this particular construction is often used in conversing and sometimes in writing.

Incorrect:
He only receives an entry-level salary.

In formal writing, and preferably on all occasions, the following construction should be used:

Correct:
He receives only an entry-level salary.

WRITING NUMBERS

1. According to the "rule of 10," write as words all whole numbers from one through nine and as numerals all numbers 10 and over, with certain exceptions. This method should be used when material contains many numbers. The "rule of 10," however, is not the only correct way to express numbers.

The MLA Handbook for Research Papers and *The Chicago Manual of Style* state that the general rule is to spell out all numbers through 100 and all round numbers that can be expressed in two words. *The APA Manual*, however, recommends that figures should be used to express all numbers 10 and above.

Follow your chosen style manual or the known preference of your reader. Be consistent, not only on the same page but throughout your entire manuscript.

2. Spell out numbers that represent time when they are used with *o'clock.*

3. Spell out the smaller number when two numbers come together.

■ We ordered sixteen 24-inch mirrors.

4. Spell amounts of money shown in legal documents; follow with the amount shown in figures. Do not use this method of expressing numbers in ordinary business writing.

5. Use figures, regardless of the expressed quantity, to state:

■ dates: April 15, 1978—*not* April 15th

■ money: $5, $17.20, 5 cents

■ percentages: 5 percent

■ page numbers: page 7

■ age (22 years old)

■ tables of statistics

■ abbreviated units of measurement: 6 lb., 5 oz.

■ figures containing decimals

■ all related amounts in a sentence that contains at least one numeral; for example, 107 men, 5 women, and 28 children.

6. Use words for dates in formal communication, such as wedding invitations or similar correspondence: fifth of October or October fifth.

7. Use words at the beginning of the sentence. If the number is long, recast the sentence so that the number comes elsewhere.

ENDNOTE

1   Wendell Johnson, People in Quandaries (New York: Harper & Bros., 1946), 268.

Index

Employers, desired employee traits and, 4
Employment applicants. *See also* Employment interview; Job search
  appropriate dress for, 344–346
  bad-news letter to, 228, 229
  central selling point of, 298–299
Employment interview, 341–353
  appearance preparation for, 344–347
  ending, 353
  follow through to, 354–360
  legal considerations in, 352–353
  planning and preparing for, 341–348
  proceeding with, 348–350
  questioning interviewer in, 349–350
  research prior to, 347–348
  responding to questions in, 350–352
  self-analysis in preparation for, 341–343
  truthfulness in, 352
  ways to flunk, 353
Employment market analysis, 303–305
Employment objective section, of resume, 311
Employment packet, for job search, 294
Encoding process(es)
  and noise, 10–11
  nonverbal, 8
  verbal, 8
Encyclopedia of Business Information Sources, The, 401
Encyclopedias, dictionaries, and handbooks, 403, 404
Endnotes, 419–420, 482
English language
  American English vs. English English, 554
  changing nature of, 105–106
  correct usage of, 124–125
  geographic spread of, 93
  in international business, 552–553
  as "official" language, 93
  as "second language," 93
  slang words in, 105
  Standard, 123

words derived from other countries, 105
  you and *I* usage in, 151
Entertainment purpose, of communication, 8, 9
Entry-level positions, Web sites for, 296
Envelopes, 612
  addressing, 612
  choosing, 612
  folding paper for, 612
Equal Credit Opportunity Act (1974), 237
Errors, of data evaluation and interpretation
  arguing in circles, 453
  black-or-white thinking, 454
  conclusions based on insufficient or noncomparable data, 454–455
  decisions based on personalities instead of facts, 455
  failure to discriminate, 453
  misinterpretation, 452
  self-evident truths, 453–454
  validating point of view, 452–453
E-Span, 296
Ethics. *See also* Codes of ethics; Legal considerations
  in business communication, 111–114
  criteria for ethical decision making, 44–46
  definitions of, 43–44, 577
  and etiquette, 579
  in interviewing process, 585–586
  and quality of products, services, and management, 576–577
  and secondary/primary source documentation, 417–419
  technological advances and, 81–83
  typical ethical problems, 45–46
  and unfavorable messages, 234–237
  values, and communication, 42–47
Ethics in Practice, 42
"Ethics without the Sermon," 44

Ethnocentrism. *See also* Stereotyping
  and intercultural communication, 549–550
Etiquette
  business, 579–583
  cellular phone, 74
  Chinese, 568
  Japanese, 567, 568
  Saudi Arabia and other Islamic countries, 568–569
Eubanks, R.T., 56n22
Evaluation
  of data, 433–460
  of what you hear, 18
Evidence, for report conclusions and recommendations, 435
Ex machina, AirMedia division of, 80
Experimentation, in primary research, 408
Explanation and analysis, in unfavorable messages, 218, 222–223
Expressions, overused, 136
Extemporaneous
  defined, 515
  delivery of oral presentations, 517
External communication, organization and, 41–42
External e-mail, 65
External reports, 367–368
External sources for secondary research, 401
Eye contact (oculesics)
  and different cultures, 26
  as nonverbal communication in intercultural communication, 567
  in oral presentations, 529–530
  in U.S., 25

Face-to-face communication, 19
  employee and supervisor, 36
Face-to-face selling, 260
Facsimile transmission. *See* Fax(es)
Fader, Shirley Sloan, 343
Fadiman, Clifton, 435
Fair comment, and free speech, 114
Fair Credit Billing Act (1974), 237